P9-CBL-052

Speech

ITS TECHNIQUES AND DISCIPLINES IN A FREE SOCIETY

Franklin D. Roosevelt addressing Congress on the 150th anniversary of the first Congress.

Speech

ITS TECHNIQUES AND DISCIPLINES IN A FREE SOCIETY

BY *William Norwood Brigance*
WABASH COLLEGE

APPLETON-CENTURY-CROFTS, INC.
NEW YORK

APPLETON-CENTURY-CROFTS, Inc.

542

PRINTED IN THE UNITED STATES OF AMERICA

CONTENTS

Part IV: The Speaker

Part V: Occasions and Forms

Part VI: The Influence of Speechmaking on Industrialism and Democracy

FOREWORD: *Why Speak? Who Listens?*

The title of this book, *Speech: Its Techniques and Disciplines in a Free Society*, is an attempt to indicate the assumptions on which the book is based, to fix its point of departure and its frame of reference.

These, in brief, are that *speechmaking in the beginning grew out of man's first attempts at self-government, that it is inherent in a free society, that a course in speechmaking ought to be based on this concept, and speech training in a free society ought to be recognized as being essentially at variance with that in countries where governments are sustained by thought control.* May I sketch the broad outlines of these implications in the following pages.

I

Why do we have public speaking? How did it get started? What keeps it going? In almost every generation an insistent minority has hailed it as, "The key to personal success," "The way to dominate a few persons or several thousands," and "The secret of how to overcome resistance by your magnetic personality." In almost every generation a dissenting frustrated minority has disputed the worth of public speaking altogether. "It is medieval, outworn." Or "Scientists do not settle things by speaking; they investigate." Or "Oratory is a sort of disease, for once a man has found the sound of his voice in public address, he finds himself in proximity to the American flag and a water pitcher." Of these two viewpoints, the first mistakes the purpose of public address, and the second ignores the facts of life.

If public address were wholly a private enterprise, solely and simply a means of personal power and personal success, doubtless in every country it would long since have been put under the regulation and control of a National Communications Commission which would issue licenses for speakers to operate in particular geographical areas and in specific subject-matters. If public address were medieval and outworn, replaceable by the New Science, it would have gone out just as feudalism went down before the Industrial Revolution. It has done neither. Why? Because from the beginning of man's laborious attempts at civilization it has been inherent in human society and it is imperative in a free society. Even the most primitive peoples, in their earliest stages of intellectual growth, developed a crude natural public address. Finally, after the centuries, a *theory* of public address arose. It became a discipline that could be reduced to a system and taught. That this theory arose in the early Greek world was not an accident. That it arose in the fifth century B.C. was not an accident. Both place and time had a definite cause, and were related to a free society. That cause, as we shall see later, still operates and influences the content of speech courses as they ought to be taught in American colleges.

As to place, it arose in the Greek world, rather than in the older civilizations of Egypt or Sumeria or Syria, because the latter were authoritarian. In contrast, wherever the Greek spread his culture there went the concept of individual justice wherein a wronged person had a right to be heard in his own behalf; and that when an issue had been decided by the majority, the minority was bound by the decision. Oligarchies might narrow its application and dictators at times might suspend it, but at least this principle existed as an ideal in the minds of Greeks in whatsoever distant islands they planted their culture. Out of this early concept of a free society arose the necessity for a formal and systematized public address.

As to time, a system of public address developed at that instant when the Greeks, having passed through autocracy and tyranny, threw off the rule of tyrants and established a democracy. Citizens of the city-states, now ruling themselves as free men, faced the compulsion of establishing a procedure for organized and responsible talk. Take one example: The tyrants had banished and confiscated, effaced towns and transferred people—even as the Sudeten Czechs, the inhabitants of Danzig, and the residents of East Prussia were uprooted during the 1930's and 1940's. Now the tyrants were overthrown, and displaced persons came to the new people's government with lawsuits to recover old claims and property: "I was run out. My home was taken from me and given to the tyrant's henchman." There were true claims, there were false claims, and many of the documents had been destroyed. These claims were decided, not by juries of twelve good men and true, but by juries of several hundred persons. Under these conditions a theory of speechmaking was quickly developed and systematized, until within one generation speeches were being prepared in accordance with a definite theory.

As every teacher of speech knows, the place where this system of speaking started was Syracuse (in Sicily, we may add, not New York) and the beginning year was probably about 460 B.C., although neither place nor year are primarily significant. The significant fact is that *a theory of public address grew swiftly and inevitably out of the compulsion laid upon people to govern themselves by persuasive talk.*

There are two kinds of nations and two kinds of people in the world: Those who in disagreements and crises want to *shoot* it out, and those who have learned to *talk* it out. To shoot it out is the way of the concentration camp, machine gun, and the bomb. To talk it out is the way of mediation, parliamentary discussion, and political campaigns settled by the ballot. That is what Macauley meant by his famous and sometimes misunderstood statement that "Parliamentary government is government by speaking." No free society, of course, can survive without speaking. But it cannot survive by mere speech, nor even by free speech alone. Speech is a form of power that may also be used as an instrument of *tyranny*. Speech, even free speech, may be used as an instrument of *double-talk and deception*. Speech, and especially free speech, may be used as an anesthesia for *self-complacency*. Speech is a dangerous form of power, and its danger is barely lessened when speech is free. A free society survives only when speech is used in the main as an instrument of *enlightenment*.

Hence the point of departure for this text: *That the system of speechmaking was born of man's early struggle for democracy, that it is still inherent in a free society, that it is a dangerous form of power requiring a sense of high responsibility by those who use it, and that a course in speechmaking ought to be founded on this premise and proceed from this point.*

II

Next—and this is important for students to know from the outset—*during the twenty-three centuries since that beginning, effective speeches have been prepared in accordance with a theory of public address.* Uninformed people, of course, mouth loose statements to the contrary, such as, "Most great speakers ignore rules and regulations." (I am copying from an open book on my desk written by an "authority" on the "new scientific techniques" of "modern" speaking.) Whose rules? Whose regulations? On what evidence? Research has shown that discerning people knew better as early as 392 B.C. Surely, 2350 years ought to be enough for even the slow-minded to catch on. The evidence need not be repeated here. It is available in any authoritative history of public address, and in such standard references as R. C. Jebb's *Attic Orators,* in J. W. H. Atkins' two works on literary criticism, in Thonssen and Baird's *Speech Criticism,* not to mention the uncounted volumes dealing with specific instances such as Sister Miriam Joseph's *Shakespeare's Use of the Arts of the Language.* Two examples, one ancient and one modern, will serve as illustrations:

1. In the beginning, there never was any really effective speaking until after speeches began to be prepared in accordance with a theory of public address. As Jebb stated, "It was the essence of Greek oratory . . . that its practice should be connected with a theory. Art is the application of rules . . . and the Greek conception of speaking as an art implied a Rhetoric." (*Attic Orators,* II, 370.) Furthermore, the decline several hundred years later in quality of Greek public address did not come alone from "loss of freedom" as scholars once assumed. It began before freedom was lost, and its contributing cause was a deprivation of theory taught in the schools. "The Old Oratory was an art, and was therefore based on a theory. The New Oratory was a knack, and was founded upon practice [only]." (*Attic Orators,* II, 441.) This is a fact of history before which teachers of speech should pause in sober reflection. Are we today teaching a *theory* of public address? Or merely a *knack?*

2. The ebb tide of quality in American public address came in the closing years of the nineteenth century and the opening years of the twentieth. (I am not forgetting William Jennings Bryan, either.) In those years there was less good speaking, less effective discussion of public issues, than either before or since. *Is it without significance that this is the period in which men in public life had emerged who had been trained in elocution instead of the theory of public address?* The classical curriculum had fallen apart, in which Campbell and Whately and Channing's Rhetorics had been a part, and the new departments of speech had not yet risen.

Bruce Barton back in 1937 put the case vividly, and in general accurately: "When my father went to college the art of public speaking was one of the most important subjects in the curriculum. No man was accounted worthy of a diploma unless he could think straight and talk convincingly on his feet. When an important issue came before the country, the professions and businesses were ably represented. Then the fashion changed. Colleges ceased to train men to speak; to be a good talker became not an asset in business but a cause for suspicion. With what result? Labor is vocal. Politics is vocal. Radicalism is vocal. But try to find a speaker to represent the point of view of industry, and where is he? . . . Face the situation frankly. Talkers always have ruled; they will continue to rule. The smart thing is to join them." (Editorial, *Colliers,* July 10, 1937.)

The sudden appearance of competent speakers for industry, beginning with Wendell Willkie and Eric Johnston, since Barton wrote his indictment, is not unrelated to the reappearance of speech in the college curriculum. Whether any individual speaker was himself trained in classroom speaking (as Willkie and Johnston were trained) is beside the point. *The essential thing is the existence of a theory of public address in each generation and the example in public life of a nucleus of speakers who apply that theory.*

I hardly need say that in this book there is no claim of "public speaking made easy," nor any formula for "The modern speaker of the new school." Instead it sets forth the theory of public address as developed by human experience and experiment through twenty-four centuries, fusing both the fundamental contributions of the old rhetoricians and the enormous and invaluable research of modern times. Above all, it postulates that effective speaking requires the application of a theory, exactly as effective surgery and effective airplane building require it.

III

We come now to *Who Listens?*

A loose notion, here to be challenged, is that the influence of the public speaker has declined in modern times. The lament is hoary with age. It was invented centuries ago. It was voiced conspicuously by Edward T. Channing in 1819: "We hear constantly how it [public address] has fallen from its old supremacy." In that year, particularly unhappy for such a lament, Clay was 42 years of age, Webster and Calhoun were 37, Lincoln was ten, Douglas and Beecher were six.

Only recently has the history of modern public address been carefully investigated on a wide scale, and it shows the opposite to be true.

Two centuries ago even representative governments were, in the words of Disraeli, "for the few, and the very few." Even when Thomas Jefferson in 1776 wrote that "all men are created equal," in America not more than one adult in five was eligible to vote or hold any form of political power, and Roger Sherman of Connecticut voiced the opinion of the majority of the Founding Fathers when in the Constitutional Convention of 1787 he said: "The people should have as little to do as may be about the Government. They . . . are constantly liable to be misled." But the people who had read Thomas Paine's *Rights of Man* and the Declaration of Independence intended to have those rights of men, including the right to vote; and by 1832 they had forced universal manhood suffrage in every state in the American union. The result was not instantaneous, or even quick, but in the long run the world has not been the same since. Universal manhood suffrage, followed ultimately by universal women's suffrage, both perfecting the nature of modern free society, fundamentally altered the pattern of *Who Listens?* You can see it against the skyline of history.

In the American Revolution—preceded as are all such crises by intensive speechmaking—who were the speakers, and to whom did they talk? Patrick Henry, who spoke to a jury and to a legislature. James Otis, who spoke to a colonial supreme court. John Adams and Richard Henry Lee, who spoke to the Continental Congress. Samuel Adams was one of the few who spoke to the *people.*

Three quarters of a century later came the crisis of Civil War. Who were the speakers and to whom did they talk, now that America had universal suffrage? Lincoln and Douglas, Yancey and Phillips, Beecher and Alexander H. Stephens may be taken as typical examples. Besides whatever special groups to whom they talked—Congress or the pulpit audience—all of them also spoke to the *people,* in mass meetings, on lyceums, on what might broadly be called the public platform.

So it has been ever since. Down through 1860 only one Presidential nominee ever made a really active speaking campaign. Jefferson did not. Jackson did not. Lincoln did not. Only Stephen A. Douglas did. Down to 1896, when Bryan made his famous 17,800-mile campaign, the speaking part of a Presidential campaign was tame and restricted. The politicians, it might be said, were slow in catching on to the implications of universal suffrage. But if they were slow, they were, in the end, sure. Today every Presidential nominee has his 14-car, or 17-car, special train. He travels 15,000 miles or perhaps 30,000. He speaks at whistle-stops and hamlets. His large-city addresses are broadcast to the nation. Altogether, he delivers from 150 to 350 addresses. In short, he talks to the *people,* and to the whole people.

Franklin D. Roosevelt's fireside chats were given to the *people.* Wendell Willkie's campaign for goodwill and respect toward business and industry was made to the *people.* George C. Marshall's original proposal of the Marshall Plan for European recovery was made first in a speech to the *people,* and only after that to Congress. Douglas MacArthur on his return from Japan spoke ostensibly to Congress; actually his important audience was the *people,* of whom nearly seventy millions heard him.

The coming of universal suffrage has changed fundamentally the scope of Who Listens? No longer is it merely juries or legislatures, or even the faithful congregation. It is the people, the mass of people.

Now this has fundamentally affected the nature of public address. If Aristotle could complain of the highly select Athenian audience of his day—when hardly one adult in forty voted or sat in the popular assemblies—that "There are people whom one cannot instruct," and that speakers must remember that they are talking to "persons who cannot take in at a glance a complicated argument, or follow a long chain of reasoning," then it is even more true today when every adult has the right to vote and the right to listen. Pale theorists and anemic academic intellectuals may complain of speakers who are "popular." They are misfits, born two centuries too late. In a free society the speaker's compulsion is to be "popular," if by that derogatory term it is meant to be understood by the masses. But to be "popular" does not mean to be careless in reasoning, weak in judgment, or irresponsible in talk. It means to be *understood by the people.* This is a distinction that students must be taught to recognize, and to which they should be held accountable from the beginning.

Inevitably in this expansion of *Who Listens?* from the select few to the whole people, has come an incredible increase in the amount of speaking. Two hundred years ago few speakers traveled far, and few listeners went far to listen, because of physical reasons. Land transportation had not changed since 500 B.C. It was still by the horse and the highway. Then in swift succession came the steamboat and the railway, and later the automobile and the airplane, all of which multiplied the amount of speaking beyond the dreams of man. Consider a few particulars. In 1828 there were perhaps 100 branches of the lyceum; in 1834 there were 3,000. In 1835 Emerson confined his speaking largely to his own state; in 1855 he was making annual western tours to places like Chicago and Milwaukee, and in that year at far-away Davenport, Iowa, he crossed the river ice to keep a speaking engagement. A hundred years ago there was no National Association of Manufacturers, no American Chamber of Commerce, no American Federation of Labor, no CIO, no Speech Association of America—and therefore there were no conventions held by them and no speaking before their members. A hundred years ago there were no service clubs and no women's clubs, and no speaking before groups of that sort.

The truth is that even one hundred years ago there was very little speaking compared with the per capita amount that exists today. *Who Listens?* More people listen, and they listen to more speeches.

IV

Finally, *Why Speak?*

Cynics repeatedly have said that "all the speeches ever given never changed a vote or altered an opinion." Were that true, it would not lessen the necessity for speechmaking, as we shall presently see, but it would alter the theory of speechmaking, and indeed it would alter the whole structure of free societies in Western civilization. Is it true?

One remembers the time when Dr. Gallup thought it was true, on the eve of that stunning upset-Presidential-election in 1948. Writing as a Scientific Expert, an authority on New Knowledge, he asked himself the question: "Do speeches change many votes?" and answered that the Gallup Institute "has tested political opinion just before a candidate arrives in a state for speaking and again after he has left. The difference is almost always negligible." Now Aristotle, Quintilian, St. Augustine, and Bishop Whately—masters of the theory of public address—could have told him better. As early as 450 B.C. it had been discovered that speechmaking did change votes, and it was known how it changed them. The records of other scientific polltakers would have told him better (for they are essentially accurate in spite of mishandling from time to time). For example, in the Presidential campaign way back in 1936, accurate polls showed that Franklin D. Roosevelt's popularity rose from 38% to 58% immediately following his speech in Dubuque, Iowa; and that the average gain that year in voting strength in the areas in which he spoke was 15%, and that the gain came immediately following his speeches. But Dr. Gallup chose to learn neither from the knowledge of the rhetoricians nor the evidence of his own tribe; he learned it perforce the hard and bitter way, in the November elections of that year. As Archibald M. Crossley, another disillusioned polltaker, explained in a post-election confessional, "We *assumed* that campaigns did not change many votes and we stopped polling too early."

The knowledge that people's opinions are altered and modified by speechmaking not only has been known for twenty-four centuries; it is, in fact, the foundation of all free societies, and the *one* factor whereby the Hellenic and Western civilizations rose above the other 19 civilizations that flourished for a time on this planet. Walter Bagehot posed the question and gave the answer in his monumental *Physics and Politics*, published in 1873—a book that certainly every speech teacher ought to read: "A large part, a very large part, of the world seems to be ready to advance to something good . . . , and then to have stopped, and not advanced. India, Japan, China, almost every sort of Oriental civilisation, though differing in nearly all other things, are alike in this. They look as if they had paused when there was no reason for pausing." Why? These arrested civilizations were not governed by talk. Nor were they free societies. They allowed no varieties of thought, but only fixed custom "imposed on all minds." In contrast, the civilization to which we belong "was made in states where the government was to a great and growing extent a government by discussion. . . . In this manner all the great movements of thought in ancient and modern times have been nearly connected in time with government by discussion." (*Physics and Politics*, passim 53 to 166. The whole book is devoted to this viewpoint.) Likewise, Arnold J. Toynbee's *Study of History* rests on the premise that civilizations are never created by the masses of people, but only by the "dominant minorities," and that members of the dominant minority must lead the masses always and forever by "charm" (i.e., persuasion), and never by force; and that whenever they resort to rule by force instead of by persuasion, they are destroyed by their numerical superiors, the masses. This being true, it is the business of the creative dominant minority in every free society to learn to persuade. For them it is literally as Wallace Carroll has put it, "Persuade or Perish." Like it or not, this is a law of a free society. An educational system that ignores it is betraying the people it would serve. An individual who ignores it will be broken and cast aside.

Nevertheless, even were it not possible to persuade by speech-making, and even were persuasion not the keystone of a free society, the making of speeches would still be inherent in human life. It has other functions than modifying opinions. People need continually to have their faith renewed and their courage strengthened. Again and again they need to be told that the righteous shall be saved, that truth can be made to triumph, and that democracy is the hope of the world. Continually and without ceasing, they need to be told that life has a purpose, and that they have a duty. This cannot be done wholly while people are separated as individuals. It must come to them also while they sit together elbow to elbow and are stimulated by the presence of others. They must see and hear the man who talks, take measure of him, and find his deeper meanings. "My voice goes after what my eyes cannot reach," exclaimed Walt Whitman.

Hence it is that you cannot have a church without a minister and a meeting place, nor a political party without political rallies and speakers, nor any movement, intellectual or industrial, without conventions and conferences. And correspondence-school universities have never seriously competed with those who put their students in the classroom face-to-face with the teacher.

Why Speak? To keep a free society free. To settle differences by talk instead of force. To alter and promote thought. To water and cultivate ideas, hopes, sentiments and enthusiasms in a way and to a degree that cannot be done while we are separated one from another.

This is the frame of reference. We proceed in the pages that follow to the treatment of ways and means.

N. N. B.

ACKNOWLEDGMENTS

To give full acknowledgment of my indebtedness is impossible, however much I might wish to do so, simply because the sources of ideas distilled over long periods are too often lost in the filter of time. It is exactly ten years since this book was projected, and in that decade I have travelled, by count and not estimate, 120,000 miles in visits to educational campuses and attending educational conferences—invariably returning with sheafs of notes containing knowledge and ideas gleaned alike from colleagues whose opinions I value and from those philosophers of education, happily outside the field of speech, with whose doctrines I disagree, but who forced me to active thinking and wider reading. These notes were filed for reference, and though by their nature were not usable as quotations or citations, nevertheless they did profoundly influence the selection of chapters and their modes of treatment.

Without overloading the book with footnotes, I have tried to indicate the major sources of ideas, and to refer students to other works, especially to those in allied fields of learning, where more extensive information could be found than was possible to include in a single book like this. To all who are identified in footnotes, I herewith express debt and appreciation. At the risk of overlooking others who might be entitled to equal recognition, I wish to express appreciation to the sociologists, anthropologists, political scientists, and psychologists whose names appear in footnotes for their combined contribution to the nature and operation of public opinion. I am also in debt to the many speakers who gave permission for their addresses to be cited as examples. To avoid a profusion of thanks I refrained from expressing appreciation in each footnote, but I here express thanks to each of them.

To the following persons I owe a special debt:

Armel Dyer, once a member of the Wabash College faculty and

now a Colonel in the United States Army, for the first draft of the chapter on parliamentary procedure.

Victor M. Powell, a colleague whose sound judgment and advice on knotty problems of planning was especially valuable.

Dan McCullough of television station WOR in New York and the Mutual Broadcasting System for advice and counsel on the chapter on radio and television speaking.

John W. Black of the Ohio State University, formerly director of the Voice Communication Laboratory and now supervisor of the Acoustic Laboratory, U. S. Naval School of Aviation Medicine, Pensacola, for assistance in the ways and means of overcoming bureaucracy in order to secure the articulation tests found in Chapters 17 and 18; and also for advice on which of the several tests developed by the armed services were most helpful for college students.

Andrew T. Weaver, University of Wisconsin, who read the manuscript during its last two years of writing and revision.

James A. Winans and Charles H. Woolbert whose contributions to the field of speech during its early days of renaissance became a permanent part of my professional heritage.

Two additional acknowledgments cannot be avoided:

George Campbell, onetime of Marischal College, Aberdeen, Scotland, whose *Philosophy of Rhetoric* published in 1776 contains a body of enduring substance. Especially his treatment of the four purposes of speaking seems to me superior to the traditional ends of speech used by later writers; hence they are the basis of the purposes of speech as set forth in Chapter 9 of this book.

Aristotle—court adviser to Hermias, tutor to Alexander the Great, analyst of constitutional government, and founder of the Lyceum—for his brushing aside the confusion of Plato's vision "half seen and half communicated," establishing rhetoric as a science, and demonstrating its necessity to citizens in a free society. With the general semanticists I share the protest against the extremes of Aristotelianism propagated by little men who followed after. With leading semanticists I agree that Aristotle returned among us would be a dissenter against such Aristotelianism.

N. N. B.

PICTURE CREDITS

PAGE

Frontispiece, *Underwood & Underwood*

2. *Wide World*

15. *Bettmann*

17. St. Augustine, Erasmus, *Bettmann*; George Campbell, *University of Aberdeen*

31. *Ewing Galloway*

59. *Acme*

85. *Black Star*

97. *Wide World*

97. *Inde World*

135. *Ewing Galloway*

169. *Underword & Underwood*

185. *Black Star*

PAGE

209. *Underwood & Underwood*

227. *Black Star*

243. *Wide World*

269. *Ewing Galloway*

299. *Bettmann*

321. *Wide World*

397. *Official photograph, U. S. Navy*

431. *Wide World*

441. *Black Star*

457. *National Broadcasting Company*

475. *Wide World*

501. *Wide World*

527. *Press Association*

Part I GETTING STARTED

. . . talking to living people

CHAPTER 1

The Rights of Listeners

CHAPTER 1

Prose, poetry, and public address are the three forms of communication. You have studied the first two, but presumably have studied little if anything of public address, which is the oldest of them all. What, then, is the relation of public address to prose and poetry? Prose, as T. V. Smith, statesman-philosopher, reminds us, "is good to make things clear," and "poetry is good to get things appreciated." But public address "serves to get things *done*." Speakers, of course, use both the clear thoughts of prose and the intense feelings of poetry, but they use them as a means to get things done. For example, Edmund Burke and Franklin D. Roosevelt were masters of prose, and there was not much poetry in their nature. In contrast, Abraham Lincoln and Winston Churchill were almost poets. But Burke and Roosevelt made things clear to get things done; and Lincoln and Churchill made things felt to get things done. The purpose of public address is not mere clearness or appreciation, but action.

There is another difference. Prose and poetry are canned and preserved in books and magazines, to be read in quiet and solitude. Public address presents a living speaker talking to living people. They sit before him. They are visible to him (except in radio and television where they are not physically visible, but are sharply in his mind's eye and are listening at the moment of utterance). The speaker talks *to* them. He talks *with* them. He looks *at* them. He sees their nods of understanding or expressions of misunderstanding, their direct look of attention or bored restlessness of inattention. In public address, always there are the listeners.

In a proper sense, these listeners are the most important persons involved, more important than the speaker. Public address, at least in a free society, exists to serve the listeners, not the speakers. Therefore, before discussing the speaker's problems, let us look first at the often-neglected listener.

From the listener's standpoint there is altogether too much public speaking, and much of it is trite, dull, boring, or simply worthless. Beneath the humorous complaint of the columnist Robert C. Ruark, flows a justifiable serious undercurrent: "I have noticed no plank in either GOP or Democratic platform which promises the shortening of speeches, or the prevention—painfully, if necessary—of extraneous wind from the speaker's perch. Yet that is a campaign which if faithfully executed might win a party more friends than the combined pledges of both." The editors of *Time* added the grave indictment that, "Most painful to the ordinary listener was the cumulative effect of politicos who cannot speak without orating and of well-meaning citizens who aired sincere and hollow banalities." [1]

There is no justifiable place for such speaking. There is a place only for speaking that is worth listening to; and *speaking is not worth listening to unless it delivers useful goods to the listener.* The two things, then, that every listener has a right to expect of a speaker are these:

1. *Useful* goods
2. Ability to *deliver* these goods

Let us consider these in detail and in more formal language.

From a speaker, listeners have the right to expect interesting and useful ideas

The average educated person hears approximately one hundred speeches a year. Why listen to so many? Why listen to *any?* Not because we are forced outwardly, for outwardly we are free to listen or not. We are rather driven by forces within us. We are human beings, living in a very real world. In that world we face problems which in a free society must be understood by responsible people; we are beset by choices and temptations; we are haunted by the shadows of fear. We listen to speakers because we hope they will throw light on our problems, temptations, and fears. We listen because we hope they will give us new information, new ideas, or will simply water and cultivate old ideas. We listen because we want to be given encouragement, to renew our faith, to strengthen our determination. We listen perhaps because we want to escape from reality for a time, to laugh and forget our troubles.

These are the services expected of speakers, and listeners have

[1] Courtesy of *Time*, April 23, 1945, p. 68. Copyright, Time Inc. 1945.

the right to demand that every speaker who consumes public time shall deliver the services expected. From the listener's standpoint, the following three types of speakers do not deliver the expected services; they are parasites who ought to be put out of business:

1. *The Stratosphere Speaker*—who never gets down to earth where ordinary mortals breathe and live, but speaks from the stratosphere of abstract and hazy words. He seldom cites a fact; he rarely takes the trouble to illuminate thought by an illustration; he never relieves a tired audience by humor. He stays at high altitude, where all below him is vague and hazy. Here is a verbatim quotation from such a specimen:

> We have learned in the past, and now it has been catastrophically reaffirmed, that this world is cosmos.

What did he mean? Oh, possibly that, "This is one world." One cannot be sure. The speaker probably was not too sure himself. The Stratosphere Speaker simply misses the purpose of public speaking. He thinks of it as an altitude flight, *whereas public speaking is for the purpose of watering and cultivating the listener's ideas on important subjects, and it requires plain words, plain facts, and lucid ideas.*

2. *The Witless Wit*—who believes in the salvation of man by funny stories. He is determined to set the audience in a roar, and comes armed with twenty anecdotes—but no thought. He recites with gusto his hodgepodge of jests, which illustrate no theme, and measures his success by the amount of laughter. To listeners who have previously heard part or all of the jokes, they are no longer funny.

3. *The Phonograph*—who reproduces a magazine article and thinks it makes a good speech. The Phonograph is a common species among students. He is the one who puts off preparing a speech until the night before, then evades the issue by seizing a magazine article, swallowing it undigested, and attempting to reproduce it as a speech. He does not plagiarize outright; that is, he does not recite verbatim the words of the article. But he does reproduce the outline and the contents, and he adds nothing of his own. He is a Phonograph, and his speech is a failure, because even a good article when recited is not a speech. "The voice is Jacob's voice, but the hands are the hands of Esau." The magazine article was written six months or a year ago. It was intended for a reading audience of perhaps a million people, a group with a broad and vague educational level, scattered over the

entire United States and in foreign lands. In contrast, the speech is to be given *today* to *one* particular group of thirty people who have already heard two speeches on the same general topic during the past month, and it is given by a student whose voice and manner proclaim loudly that he knows nothing about the subject except what he is reciting from the magazine. In other words, the student has failed to focus the speech on the particular audience meeting at a particular place on a particular day. Being a Phonograph speaker, he simply reproduces another person's thoughts.

Listeners also have the right to see and hear a human being who talks with the audience, and not a dull or nervous creature who talks mainly to himself

There are people who believe that "delivery" is not important. They assume that a speaker needs only to "say what he thinks" and that these thoughts will find their way into the minds of the listeners. A fair statement of this belief is, "It does not matter how you deliver a speech; the only important thing is what you say." Now this is a comfortable belief. It relieves the speaker from any responsibility beyond writing a paper. But it is naïve, unreal, and does not square with the facts of life. It assumes that you literally "deliver" a speech in the same way you deliver a loaf of bread. It assumes that when delivered, the speech, like the loaf of bread, arrives intact and cellophane-wrapped no matter how long the delivery man took, whether he arrived drunk or sober, or how many detours or breakdowns he had along the way. These are grand assumptions, but only assumptions, for *there is no such thing as delivering a speech.* The very word "delivery" is a turn of expression and not a statement of fact.

WHY NO SPEAKER CAN REALLY "DELIVER" A SPEECH

You can deliver a book, a pencil, or a loaf of bread. You carry them to their destination and give them up to another's keeping. You cannot so deliver a speech. What we call delivering a speech is actually *translating a speech through seven stages from your mind to the mind of the listener. These seven stages are as follows:*

1. You start with a *thought* in your mind.
2. This thought is coded into a series of impulses and sent through

your nervous system. These impulses are roughly like the dot-dash telegraph code, and are known as a *neurogram.*

3. This neurogram is coded further into phonetic symbols by *muscular movements* of the tongue, lips, face, diaphragm, etc.

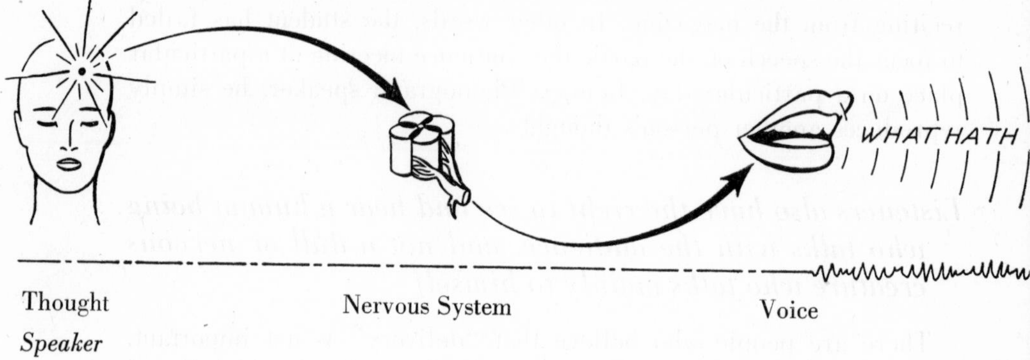

PROCESS

4. These phonetic symbols, thus produced by muscular activity, are coded still further into *sound waves* that travel invisibly through the air. When these sound waves reach the listener, the decoding process begins.

5. The sound waves *strike the listener's ear drums* and produce a mechanical action in the bones of the middle ear and in the fluid of the inner ear. In this process the sound waves are decoded again into phonetic symbols.

6. These decoded phonetic symbols are sent in the form of impulses along the nerve fibers to the brain. These impulses, as in stage 2, are roughly like the dot-dash telegraph code and compose a *neurogram.*

7. In the listener's brain this neurogram is decoded further into a *thought.* This last step is the semantic stage, wherein the various brain assemblages translate the incoming symbols into meaning. The amount of meaning in each instance will depend on: (1) on the distinctness and clarity of incoming symbols, and (2) on the variety of brain connections, built-in and temporary, that are available for use.

Thus you do not "deliver" a speech at all in the way you deliver a book, a pencil, or a loaf of bread. There is no "delivery" to it. Instead, you *use sound waves and light waves to create thought in the listener's mind.*

So far, of course, we have discussed only sound waves. This was not because light waves are not important or not inherent, but solely and simply because the complex process glibly miscalled "delivery" is more easily understood if taken one part at a time. We can now

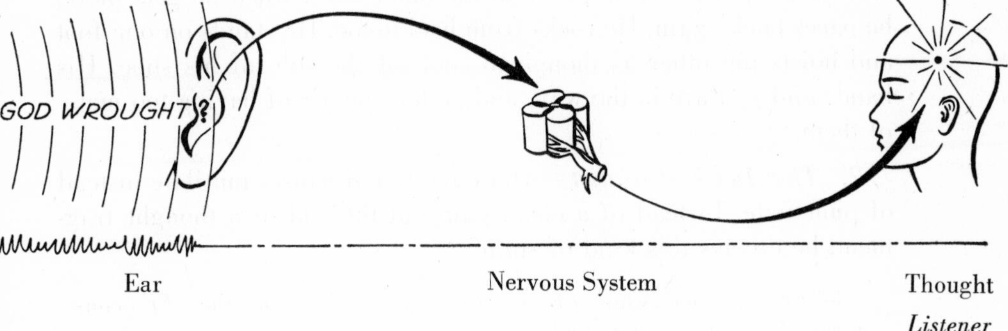

consider light waves. They follow a process parallel with that of sound waves: (1) The *thought* in the speaker's mind is coded into (2) a *neurogram* in the nervous system, then (3) further coded into *muscular movements* of posture, body, hands, face, and head. These in turn are (4) transmitted by *light waves* that are (5) received by the listener's *eyes* where it is (6) decoded into a *neurogram* via nerve impulses sent along the optic nerve to the brain. Finally, in the brain this is (7) decoded into a *thought*. Now this thought is not so refined and exact as the thought conveyed by words, but it is older in the human race, is written deeper in the human organism, and carries more basic meanings. Sound waves carry the refined, precise thought. Light waves carry the broad basic background of meaning. To the listener they say, "That speaker does not mean what he says; his actions deny his words." Or, "He is not thinking, but is only reciting." Or, "I see exactly what he means, for he both *shows* and *tells* me." The inherent part of light waves in communication will be covered more fully in Chapter 16.

WHY SPEAKERS FAIL IN "DELIVERY"

The following are common types of speakers who create barriers that prevent their arousing full thought in listeners' minds:

1. *The Fidgeter*—whose actions distract the listeners' attention. The eye is quicker than the ear. What the listener sees takes priority over what he hears. Hence the Fidgeter's actions interfere with his words. Behold the Fidgeter's behavior: If his hands are in his pockets, he takes them out; if they are out, he puts them in. If he is at one side of the platform, he paces to the other side; when he gets there, he paces back again. He rocks from heel-to-toe. He stands on one foot and hoists the other as though to cool off the sole of his shoe. His hands and feet are in the way, and he has the air of having too many of them.

2. *The And-Er-Vocalist*—whose irrational pauses mutilate instead of punctuate. Instead of a clean pause at the end of a thought fragment, he creates this kind of static:

> I—*Er*—am one who—*Er*—is—*Er*—concerned about the—*Er*—consequences of—*Er*—such action.

To Er is human; but to listeners it is infuriating, and for a speaker it is unforgivable. He needs to be forced to listen to a recording of his own voice.

3. *The Mumbler*—who can hear himself and does not care that others cannot. He looks at the ceiling, at the floor, or out the window, but not at the audience. He keeps his mouth closed "like the front room in an old-fashioned farmhouse," and opens it only to eat and yawn. His lips and tongue are on vacation. His jaw is fixed and rigid, like the much-pictured Rock of Gibraltar. His voice is flat, and his tones are weak. He believes that talk is cheap, and his talk is cheap indeed.

4. *The Listless Voice*—who talks loud enough to be heard, but who lacks vocal emphasis, inflection, and variety of tone. His words are without color, informing inflection, warmth, friendliness, or life. He simply drones in a listless voice. The result of this type of speaking was frankly stated by Edward R. Murrow in assessing ex-Prime Minister Clement R. Attlee's listless voice; his speaking was "not a success," because he managed to "discuss the whole subject as though elucidating some obscure unimportant passage in a Latin translation."

It may be self-satisfying to the speaker with a listless voice to imagine that how he talks does not matter, that what he says is the only thing that counts. But the plain truth is otherwise. Experimental evidence suggests that listeners will remember only about 40 per cent as much of what is spoken in a listless voice as compared with that spoken in a voice with lively emphasis, variety, and inflection. In other words, imagine two speakers. Both talk loud enough for every word to be heard, but one speaks with color, warmth, and informing inflection; the other speaks in a tone that does not vary in pitch, time, intensity, or quality. The audience will remember only about 40 per cent as much of what is said by the listless speaker as compared with what is said by the lively speaker.

To summarize: *In speaking, the know-how as well as the know-what is important; and audiences have the right to demand that speakers face this fact honestly and frankly, that they take an inventory of their competence and overcome the barriers of fidgeting, of articulating "and-er-r's," of mumbling, and of speaking in a listless voice.*

CONVERSING WITH THE AUDIENCE

Basically public speaking is enlarged conversation, and it should be enlarged enough to fill the room and reach that slightly hard-of-hearing listener in the eighth row who leans a little forward as you begin to talk. This requires certain mental, and perhaps moral, qualities that are well stated by James A. Winans as follows:

1. *Full realization of the content of your words as you utter them,* and
2. *A lively sense of communication.*[2]

When the first element is lacking—that of fully realizing the content of words at the instant of utterance—the delivery is *absent-minded.* When the second element is lacking—that of a lively sense of communication—the speaker seems to be *talking to himself.* A genuine enlarged conversation with the audience requires that you subordinate thoughts of yourself and think foremost of your listeners. Present your ideas to *them,* interest *them,* look for *their* response. Even better than talking to them is talking *with* them. When you talk with them you look to see that they have understood each point before you pass to the next.

Let us be frank about this. It takes courage as well as self-control to talk earnestly with an audience. "It is four-fifths will power," admitted M. W. Stryker, a college president and a speaker of great power. Somewhere along the way you have to face it. If the speaker

[2] James A. Winans, *Public Speaking* (New York, Appleton-Century-Crofts, Inc., 1915), page 31.

does not exert the will power, but weakens and backs up inside himself, he loses control of himself and naturally loses control of the audience. Hence those speakers who mumble or gaze at the floor or out the window. They lack the courage or the self-control; or having only a little of either, they speak in that well-known *half*-direct way. They are not entirely lacking in a sense of communication, but they simply do not come out of themselves, nor do they vigorously take command of their hearers' attention. Arthur Schopenhauer's statement, "Style is the physiognomy of the mind, and a safer index to character than the face," is more true of delivery than of composition. So in a round-about way we are saying that listeners have the right to demand that speakers be men of character, persons who have earned their right to speak, and who will make it worth while for others to listen.

A HIPPOCRATIC OATH FOR PUBLIC SPEAKERS

Since democracy, as Macaulay put it, is "government by speaking," a standard of responsibility ought to be demanded of its speakers. A totalitarian state can coerce, but a democracy must persuade. In it issues are aired, "talked out of existence or talked into solution." The persons who do the talking, then, ought to be held accountable for their manner of talk. We have progressed to a stage where no citizens are permitted to practice law or medicine without passing an examination to test their fitness. Examinations usually are also required of such persons as engineers, public accountants, and taxicab drivers. We might imagine a truly Ideal Republic in which a test of competence was also required before persons were allowed to speak in public. They would be required, first, to show that they were capable of producing ideas, and, further, that they were capable of refining them into a form fit for human consumption. Finally, they would be required to demonstrate a mastery of that complicated process so glibly called "delivery," of translating thought from speaker to audience.[3]

[3] As an aside it may be interesting to note that Athens at its time of greatest achievement safeguarded its citizens against irresponsible public talk through a system of "responsibility of public statement." The system was simple in administration in that all public speaking was done before one Athenian assembly, but even so its adoption testified to the high level of the Athenian democracy. One safeguard, for example, permitted any speaker "suspected of not giving the best advice to the people" to be impeached in the assembly. Nor was this a dead-letter law. In practice, speakers were impeached.

Having passed these tests of professional competence, then in the Ideal Republic would come the oath of moral responsibility, a Hippocratic oath in which each citizen certified to speak in public would make the following vow: "*I swear in the name of God and my own conscience that I will never speak in public unless I have prepared myself with substance worth saying, and unless further I have put it into form that can be comprehended. I further swear that when I appear before an audience I shall think of its welfare and not of my own pride, that I shall not mumble or fidget, or otherwise evade or shirk my task, but shall present my ideas with such sincerity, earnestness, and consideration for the audience that none can fail to hear or comprehend.*"

Such would be indeed an Ideal Republic. In the chapters that follow we shall consider how a speaker could learn to fulfill this vow.

ASSIGNMENTS

ON SPEAKERS HAVING INTERESTING AND USEFUL IDEAS

1. Report on two speakers you have recently heard, one good and one poor. A suggested analysis for each speaker:
   a. In what way was the subject worth (or not worth) listening to: a new idea? cultivated an old idea? gave stimulation or encouragement?
   b. How was it made interesting: facts and figures? illustrations? comparisons? suspense? humor, etc.?

2. Make a brief report on the most interesting speaker you have heard during the past year or two. Analyze *why* he was interesting in terms of the principles set forth in this chapter.

ON SPEAKERS WHO REALLY TALK TO LISTENERS VERSUS DULL OR NERVOUS PERSONS WHO TALK MAINLY TO THEMSELVES

3. In terms of principles found in this chapter, report on the "delivery" of each of the speakers selected in the above assignments. Why was it good? Or why was it poor? Or why merely a sad average?

ON STARTING TO BECOME A SPEAKER

4. As an ice-breaking speech, give a two-minute talk on some personal experience that you think would be interesting to other members of the class. Apply the principles of this chapter on respecting your listeners' rights.

5. Give a two-minute how-to-do it speech in which you present a simple explanation of something that would be of interest to members of the class. Apply the principles of this chapter on respecting your listeners' rights.

6. Give a two-minute reading of any prose selection that you happen to like especially well. Remember that before the printed words of this selection can reach the audience, they must go through *seven stages*. Review them, then rehearse reading the selection until you can carry the thought through all seven stages.

ON PLANNING AHEAD

7. There are two kinds of speakers: those who "have something to say," and those who "have to say something." Obviously, not much can be expected of the latter group, and you will want to plan now to keep out of it. Therefore, copy and fill out the following Speech-Subject Analysis Form. Its purpose is twofold: (1) to examine your background and locate speech subjects that others may want to hear you talk about; (2) to collect a list of subjects that you would like to hear other speakers talk about.

After the forms are turned in, the instructor, or a committee of class members, can assemble a list of subjects that one or more students would like to hear. Preferably this list should be mimeographed and given to each student. If this is not possible, then it can be posted in an available place.

SPEECH-SUBJECT ANALYSIS FORM

Name________________________ Course No.______ Section No.______
(last name) (given name)

College address________________________ Phone______ Date________

1. Where you were born, where you have lived or travelled, and what schools you have attended
2. Your special interests and hobbies
3. Your extracurricular activities in college
4. Jobs you have held in the past or now hold
5. Your probable major study in college, and why you chose it
6. Your probable minor study, and why you chose it
7. Other courses you have especially enjoyed
8. Your reading preferences, including both areas in which you have read (history, drama, or science, etc.) and particular individual books
9. Your political affiliations or sympathies
10. Your economic (labor-management, etc.) affiliations or sympathies
11. Your religious affiliations or sympathies
12. Your social affiliations or sympathies
13. Your possible or probable vocation
14. On the basis of the above analysis, list ten subjects you might use for speeches. Place a check before those you think the class would especially like to hear:
15. List ten subjects you would like to hear other class members discuss:

Quintilian (ca. 40-118 A.D.) was Rome's great teacher of public speaking. This title page from an early edition of his *Institutes of Oratory* shows Quintilian and students.

CHAPTER 2

Four Fundamentals for Speakers

CHAPTER 2

Before starting the study and practice of making speeches let us examine the four fundamentals on which this book is based. They are principles on which all good speaking is based and which all good speakers, consciously or unconsciously, use.

FIRST FUNDAMENTAL

Effective public speaking is a technique, as definitely as are the techniques of designing airplanes and removing appendixes, except that it is older and more complex than either

Centuries upon centuries have gone into developing this technique, and some of the best men who ever lived gave their lives to it.[1] Now a technique requires a method of procedure. The method is not set forth in a set of fixed rules, for as Charles Henry Woolbert repeatedly said, "There is only one rule in public speaking and that is that there are no rules." Rather, it is a method of procedure founded on understanding and judgment.[2] Especially is it important that you do not surrender to the cheap notion that you can substitute

[1] Among earlier eminent persons who made noteworthy contributions to this technique are Corax (about 470 B.C.), Aristotle (384-322 B.C.), Cicero (106-43 B.C.), Quintilian (35-100 A.D.), St. Augustine (354-430), Erasmus (1466-1536), and Francis Bacon (1561-1626). Significantly, Shakespeare, not a public speaker but a playwright, had mastered the technique of public speaking, and his mastery is seen in the scores of speeches made by the characters in his plays. The most famous example, of course, is Antony's speech at Caesar's funeral. "I come to bury Caesar, not to praise him. . . . ," which is a model of classical speech composition. George Campbell (1719-1796) should also be added. First of the famous Scotch rhetoricians, he was also the most penetrating and original. His analysis of persuasion was sustained by later research, and his classification of speech purposes surpasses that of most later writers.

[2] This explains the fallacy of the popular notion that "most great speakers ignore rules and regulations." In truth, research has shown that great speakers—Daniel Webster, Abraham Lincoln, Woodrow Wilson, Franklin D. Roosevelt, Winston Churchill, Wendell Willkie, Eric Johnston, to mention a few modern ones—were careful students of speaking techniques. The supposed "rules" they ignored were false rules set up by inept writers.

Six eminent men who contributed to the theory of speechmaking. *Reading down:* Aristotle, Cicero, St. Augustine, Francis Bacon, Erasmus, George Campbell.

bypaths, or bag-of-tricks magic for a technique that has taken centuries to develop. This has been tried before.

Nor can you be an effective speaker, as some people want to believe, by having a rich voice or a fluent tongue. These may be assets, but they have handicapped many an aspirant who tried to use them as substitutes.

Nor yet can you be an effective speaker simply because you possess untrained natural ability. Of course natural ability helps, just as it helps in music or surgery. But people do not become competent musicians or surgeons from natural ability alone. They also have training, and it takes training as well to become a competent speaker. The slogan "You Can Master It in Ten Easy Lessons," appeals to a certain type of people. It might be interesting, therefore, to know that men were seeking short cuts to effective speaking and bag-of-tricks substitutes long before Columbus sought his short route to India by going west; and, like Columbus, they never found the way. Indeed the whole idea was satirized by one Lucian of Samosata about the year A.D. 179 in the following words:

> Never let it disturb you that you have not been through the laborious preliminaries with which the ordinary system besets the path of fools; they are quite unnecessary....
>
> Bring then above all ignorance, to which add confidence, audacity, and effrontery; as for diffidence, equity, moderation, and shame, you will please leave them at home; they are not merely needless, they are encumbrances....
>
> The tongue is an unruly member; do not attempt to rule it; never care whether your firstly is logic's firstly, or your secondly and thirdly in the right order; just say what comes....
>
> People of sense, remember, are rare, and they will probably hold their tongues out of charity; or if they do comment, it will be put down to jealousy. The rest are awed by your costume, your voice, gait, motions, falsetto, shoes, and sundry; when they see how you perspire and pant, they cannot admit a moment's doubt of your being a very fine ... performer.[3]

This answer nearly 1800 years ago to the would-be speakers who wanted a short cut was the answer of a competent and celebrated speaker who knew that short cuts were a delusion. It is an answer affirmed by the centuries. Public speaking is a technique, and technique, and techniques require method of procedure for expertness. Do not look for short cuts.

[3] *The Works of Lucian of Samosata,* trans. by H.W.Fowler and F.G.Fowler (Oxford, 1905), III, 224-227.

SECOND FUNDAMENTAL

Effective speaking is also an intellectual discipline

Effective speaking is not merely a technique and nothing more. It is very much more. It is also an intellectual discipline. Now exactly what is an "intellectual discipline?" *It is developing the ability to produce and manage ideas.*

Consider first the ability to produce ideas. William Hawley Davis quotes the amusing plight of a master of technique who complained, "I can express anything, but I have nothing to express." Let us have no nonsense about the importance of ideas. To speak well, you must be able to produce ideas, to test them for soundness, to know when you are doing straight thinking or crooked. But the ability to produce is not come by easily. Whence arises the maxim, "Thinking is hard work but prejudice is a pleasure." Even when we have ideas on a subject, they are not full blown in our minds at the moment. They are dormant, they are forgotten, they are scattered about, unrelated, half-thought-out. Even worse, we may not have any ideas, or hardly any, and must go forth to find them.

This hunt for ideas is part of what we call "intellectual discipline." Really there is no discipline about it, and no orderliness. "Thinking," said Barzun, "is inwardly a haphazard, fitful, incoherent activity. If you could peer in and see thinking going on, it would not look like that trimmed and barbered result, A Thought. Thinking is messy, repetitious, silly, obtuse, subject to explosions that shatter the crucible and leave darkness behind. Then comes another flash, a new path is seen, trod, lost, broken off, and blazed anew. It leaves the thinker dizzy as well as doubtful: he does not know what he thinks until he has thought it. . . . Young scholars should believe all this if only in order to overcome their too frequent discouragement at the sight of their first thoughts. . . . Too much has been talked about 'cold reason' and 'orderly processes of mind.' The impression has got about that Euclid began with a fresh sheet of paper, wrote down 'Proposition I,' and pushed on through to the end of the book without an erasure. Even if his manuscript was neat, which I doubt, his previous fits and starts were doubtless many. The momentary glimpse that shows a relation, a truth, or a method of proof does not come at will. It is watched for like big game, and only when captured and tamed with others like it can it be shown off in orderly sequence." [4]

This is old knowledge to experienced speakers, and as early as 336 B.C. Aristotle listed twenty-eight sources of ideas that could be found within the speaker's mind. Yet each new generation must learn it anew—that ideas must be stalked with persistence and patience.

All of this is only the first step. Assume that with patience and persistence you have finally assembled the ideas. Do you now have a speech? No. You have, in fact, only finished preparing to begin. *The real steps of intellectual discipline are: (1) meditation, (2) judgment, and (3) finally the management of ideas.* In this threefold process the ideas must be sifted, sorted, and tested. Those found fit for human use must be formed in line—in marching order. In other words, the speech must be given structure and its parts be proportioned. Here are some of the problems involved:

> Where does your speech begin? Where does it end? What have beginning and end got to do with the listener?
>
> What shall be the main topics? Where and how shall each topic begin, and what are their internal relationships and how can these be made instantly clear to the listener?
>
> How shall the orientation of main topics toward one another and toward the final speech purpose be maintained?
>
> Where is the best place for this or that theme to enter, how far shall it be developed there, and where shall it re-enter?
>
> How shall vitally important shades of emphasis and subordination be effected?
>
> What is the most effective way of developing any given main topic?
>
> Can suggestion or humor sharpen or illustrate this part of the speech?
>
> How shall emotion be handled?
>
> How shall the time limit be handled? [5]

These are problems in the managing of ideas, and they constantly confront everyone who gives a speech. If at first they seem acute, remember that as H. L. Mencken said, "Thinking is something new to man and he does it very badly. We have lost the baboon's sureness of instinct and have not yet perfected sureness of reasoning."

Added to them is another problem particularly sharp and constant. Throughout, you must be reminding yourself: *My listeners will hear*

[4] Jacques Barzun, *Teacher In America* (Boston: Little, Brown and Co., 1945), pp., 306-307.

[5] Many of these questions have been presented in sharpened form by Bernard DeVoto, as they related to historical writing, in "The Easy Chair," pp. 50-55, *Harper's Magazine*, April, 1949. To him I recognize a debt in the above sequence and phrasing of questions.

this speech but once. They cannot go back and read it again. They must get it instantly as I speak, and I must at all times make it possible for them to do so. Therefore, I must present my ideas with proper labels: *firstly, secondly,* and *thirdly.* Each part I must define, or explain, or illustrate, or perhaps do all three. I must point ahead to the place where I am going, and point back to the place where I have been. For the listeners hear it but once, and that once they miss it, they miss it forever. Can I, then, enable listeners to say of my speech what was said of Hobart D. McKeehan's: "One thing I like about your speeches is that you have *handles* on them. A man can pick them up and carry them home with him."

This, then, is the problem of producing and managing ideas. It is the intellectual discipline of effective speaking.

THIRD FUNDAMENTAL

You must earn the right to give every speech

"How long did it take you to prepare that sermon?" a listener once asked that powerful preacher, Henry Ward Beecher. "Forty years," was the significant answer. A youth once approached Daniel Webster with a question on how he might learn to speak impromptu. Retorted Webster, "Young man, there is no such thing!"

Many persons, of course, possessed by the lust to speak, are not impressed with the necessity of earning the right. Emerson remarks with unusual sharpness for him on "those who prematurely boil, and who impatiently break silence before their time," and of "a small-pot-soon-hot style of eloquence," in which the speaker thinks of his own enjoyment without regard for the suffering audience.

In contrast, the characteristic note of effective speakers is thorough preparation. You may go back as far as you will, back even to that day when Quintilian thought (he was writing 95 A.D.) that "men of the earliest ages did not speak with our exactness and care," and still the characteristic note of good speakers was thorough preparation. Of *Demosthenes* (384–322 B.C.) a scoffing critic complained that his speeches "smelled of the lamp," for he was known to spend enormous hours in preparation. *Cicero* (106–43 B.C.), after listing the details of speech preparation required, a preparation that he was known to give to his own speeches, concluded, "Let us then cease to wonder at what is the cause of the scarcity of good speakers." To *Father Massillon,* eloquent French cleric of the early eighteenth century, Louis XIV said, "Father, I have heard many great orators in this chapel, and have been highly pleased with them; but for you, whenever I hear you, I go away displeased with myself, for I see more of my own character." These sermons that so touched Louis were written and rewritten many times. *Edmund Burke*, English speaker of the late eighteenth century, "more than Cicero in the senate, almost Plato in the academy," spent more labor on his speeches than any of his great contemporaries. *Patrick Henry* was once thought to have flashed his "Give me liberty or give me death" on the inspiration of the moment. He is known to have rehearsed it for months before backwoods audiences. *Daniel Webster* was notoriously slow and laborious in his preparation. He was able to make his famous Reply to Hayne on short notice because he had been studying the question for twenty years, had for months been preparing special notes on it, which Hayne "could not have better fit if he had tried." *Wendell Phillips*, that 'infernal machine set to music," labored upon even the minutest points of his speeches. After his seemingly spontaneous address on "The Scholar in a Republic," T. W. Higginson said to him, "This could not have been written out beforehand," and Phillips replied, "It is already in type at the *Advertiser* office."

Of twentieth-century speakers, *William E. Borah*, voted by newspaper men to be the most effective speaker of the Senate in his generation, was reported by an observer never to talk until he had exhausted the subject and never to make a speech that he had not gone over many times in the privacy of his office. *Franklin D. Roosevelt* was a speaker of consummate skill. Competent authorities agree that he drew freely upon a selected group of counselors of general ideas, that he wrote his own talks, and that the final draft represented the fifth to the twelfth revision. *Winston S. Churchill*, probably the most effective British speaker of the past two centuries, prepared so thoroughly, yet spoke so spontaneously, that his opponents "used to get the laugh on him" by referring "to the rumors that he had been a week or so practicing in his bedroom the brilliant impromptu with which he planned to crush an adversary."

Sir Austen Chamberlain, after a careful study of English speakers, summarized the one factor common to all: "Those who say to public men, 'Oh, speaking is no trouble to *you*,' have not seen them in the hours of preparation. Their wives and their private secretaries tell a different tale."

A good part of every college speech course is wasted by students who try to speak without earning the right. Their technique is feeble, their discipline of ideas is flaccid—the stuff is simply not there—not because they are beginners and not because they cannot learn or have no talent, but because they do not put forth the effort. Months go by, and a large part of the course is gone, and yet they have not learned one simple fundamental—that a speaker must earn the right to give every speech.

FOURTH FUNDAMENTAL

A speech is not an essay on its hind legs. It does not become a speech until you put it out to the audience by sound waves and light waves

Even though you have on paper a splendid speech plan—organized in detail and every part of it thought out—it is not yet a speech. It is still only an idea on paper, an outline, an essay, or a set of notes, but definitely not a speech. It will not become a speech until you lift the thoughts off the paper and make them come alive. As James A. Winans put it, a speech is not an "essay standing on its hind legs." In saying this Winans possibly was remembering his many students who had had difficulty turning an outline into a speech, and of the many distinguished scholars he had known—wise and learned, but innocent and inept at lifting a speech off paper.

How to turn an outline or a manuscript into a speech, this is one of the real problems of speechmaking. It is a problem that confronts students and older persons alike. A lecture bureau manager stated it in these words: "We try to book among others, a few eminent thinkers. But it often gets us in trouble. For example, we might capture a real prize, a Nobel prizewinner, a Pulitzer prizewinner, a college president famous for his ideas, or someone who has written a book or produced ideas that everybody knows about and wants to know more about. We book him for a series of lectures. Then letters and telegrams start arriving, saying he was 'disappointing,' or 'failed to satisfy,' or 'could not speak,' or was just plain 'terrible.' This sort of thing keeps us awake at night, for we never know whether anybody famous for having ideas can make a speech."

Mere ideas, then, do not make a speech. The best of plans put on paper do not make a speech. *There is no speech until you carry the thought to the listener. Nor can you "deliver" the speech as you would deliver a book or pencil. Actually there is no "delivery" to it. You must use sound waves and light waves to tell the audience what you are thinking. You have no other media.*

Other elements of so-called "delivery" will be discussed later (see pages 59-81), but the basic principle is this: *Get enthusiastic about what you have to say. If you are enthusiastic, your "delivery" will probably be earnest and moving. If you are enthusiastic, you will not bother about how you stand, gesture, breathe, or use your voice—and later through practice you can clear away faults and barriers. If you are enthusiastic, you can forget yourself into reasonably good speaking. Enthusiasm is contagious. Unless you have a good time talking, your audience will not have a good time listening. This is the basic foundation of "delivery."*

These are the four fundamentals: (1) that effective speaking is a definite technique, (2) that it is also an intellectual discipline, (3) that you must earn the right to give a speech, (4) that a speech is not an essay on its hind legs. Throughout the centuries in which speech-making has played its important part in human life they have been the fundamentals of effective speakers. Some have followed them partly by intuition. Others have learned them through the painful process of trial, error, and discouragement. But in one way or other, they have used them. A circuit rider of the last century stated his method of use in homespun words. Asked the secret of his power as a preacher, he replied: "It's simple. I read myself full. I think myself clear. I pray myself hot. And then I let go."

ASSIGNMENTS

ON EFFECTIVE SPEAKING REQUIRING A TECHNIQUE

1. Make a list of speeches you have heard during the past month or so. Include the incidental speeches, such as announcements, introductions, explanations, etc. Go over the list and check speeches that were positively superior—i.e., those you could easily hear and easily understand, those that held your attention closely, and those whose content you still remember. (Obviously you won't check many! But there ought to be a few.) Now go over the *unchecked* speeches on your list, and itemize the reasons that prevented each from being as good as it ought. Finally, draw up a general list of five or six barriers that most often prevented these speeches from being their best. Make a permanent entry of the list in your notebook, and in the future note how many of them injure your speaking.

2. Prepare a short speech relating to the technique of speaking on one of the following subjects:

a. An effective teacher I know; how he uses effective techniques
b. A poor teacher I know: techniques he needs but fails to use
c. Our preacher: techniques he uses well and those he fails to use
d. Techniques used by salesmen
e. Techniques used by short-story writers
f. Any other subject fits this assignment

ON EFFECTIVE SPEAKING BEING AN INTELLECTUAL DISCIPLINE

3. Prepare a speech on one of the following subjects, using the procedure described below:

a. What a man or woman should get out of college
b. What employers expect of college men
c. My favorite author: and my reasons for thinking so
d. Poetry I like best, and why
e. Shows I like best, and why
f. The college course from which I profited most, and why
g. What I like (or dislike) about the college fraternity system
h. Campus politics: an analysis of how it is run
i. The ablest man in Congress: an analysis of his ability
j. Things about the race problem on this campus that disturb me
k. What religion means to me
l. Any other subject that fits this assignment

Pick this subject ten days or two weeks before your next speech and develop by the following procedure:

a. Without doing *any* reading or conversing on the subject, make an outline of what you already know (if you don't know how to make an outline, turn to the next chapter, pages 44-49).
b. The next day make a *second* outline and note whether time, and perhaps unconscious meditation, has added to your stock of ideas.
c. Now do some reading on the subject, or talk it over with other persons. Then after three or four days make a third outline. Obviously this should be a more mature outline than either of those preceding. In it your best judgment will be used in testing, sifting, and arranging ideas.
d. After a few days more, expand this third outline into the final one to be used for the speech, and on the day you speak hand it to the instructor.

ON EARNING THE RIGHT TO SPEAK

4. Prepare a report on how one particular speaker, or a group of speakers, prepared speeches. The following useful bibliography can be expanded by library research:

Blanks, Anthony F., *Essay Backgrounds for Writing and Speaking* (New York, 1929). Contains reprints of Chamberlain and Brigance articles listed below.

Brandenburg, Earnest, "Preparation of Franklin D. Roosevelt's Speeches," *Quarterly Journal of Speech,* XXV (April, 1949), 214-221.

Brigance, W. N., "In the Workshop of Great Speakers," (Theodore Roosevelt, Jane Addams, Fosdick, Bryan, Wilson, etc.), *American Speech,* August, 1926.

Chamberlain, Austen, "How Great Speakers Prepare Their Speeches," (Pitt, Gladstone, Disraeli Macaulay, John Bright, etc.) *Living Age,* January 3, 1925.

Hatch, Alden, "Men Around Dewey," *Harper's Magazine,* October, 1948, pp. 38-46. Pages 44-45 contain account of Thomas E. Dewey's methods of speech preparation.

Time, November 22, 1943, p. 24; and October 14, 1946, p. 33 (Winston Churchill).

Time, November 4, 1940, p. 12 (Wendell Willkie).

Time, October 2, 1944, p. 22 (Thomas E. Dewey).

Time, May 22, 1950, p. 20 (Harry S. Truman).

5. Prepare a four-minute speech on one of the subjects you listed in the Speech-Subject Analysis Form in Chapter 1 (see page 13). Use the following general method:

a. Read yourself full
b. Think yourself clear
c. Sift, sort, and test your materials
d. Arrange the materials into a simple, easy-to-follow outline
e. Remember that your listeners will hear the speech only once, and therefore help them get each separate part. Present the parts with proper labels: *first, second,* etc. Forecast where you are going. Summarize what you have said.
f. Rehearse the speech five or six times over a period of several days.

6. Make a Time Table of your speech preparation. In it record both the total time spent and the distribution of time, to wit:

September 25—35 minutes
September 26—0 minutes
September 27—2 hours, 15 minutes

a. Hand a copy of this Time Table to the instructor along with the outline when you deliver the speech.
b. Make a permanent record of this Time Table in your notebook, and do the same with the following speeches. In this way, throughout the course you can compare each speech grade, and your over-all general progress, with the *total* time and with the *distribution* of time spent in earning the right to speak.

ON A SPEECH NOT BEING AN ESSAY

7. Prepare one of the following selections to read before the class, using the following general procedure:

a. Make sure you know that the selection as a *whole* is trying to say.
b. Get the author's structural parts.

c. Look up unknown words. Absorb the full meaning of sentences. Note how each one is related to the sentence before and the sentence after.
d. Now practice reading it aloud until you can—by means of mind, imagination, voice, and action—lift the black marks off paper and turn them into a living thought:

HAMLET'S ADVICE TO THE PLAYERS

Speak the speech, I pray you, as I pronounced it to you, trippingly on the tongue: but if you mouth it, as many of your players do, I had as lief the town crier spoke my lines. Nor do not saw the air too much with your hand, thus, but use all gently; for in the very torrent, tempest, and, as I may say, whirlwind of your passion, you must acquire and beget a temperance that may give it smoothness. O, it offends me to the soul to hear a robustious periwig-pated fellow tear a passion to tatters, to very rags, to split the ears of the groundlings, who for the most part are capable of nothing but inexplicable dumb-shows and noise: I would have such a fellow whipped for o'er-doing Termagant; it out-Herods Herod: pray you, avoid it.

Be not too tame, neither, but let your own discretion be your tutor: suit the action to the word, the word to the action; with this special observance, that you o'erstep not the modesty of nature: for anything so overdone is from the purpose of playing, whose end, both at the first and now, was and is, to hold, as 'twere, the mirror up to nature; to show virtue her own feature, scorn her own image, and the very age and body of the time his form and pressure. Now this overdone or come tardy off, though it make the unskillful laugh, cannot but make the judicious grieve; the censure of the which one must in your allowance o'erweigh a whole theatre of others. O, there be players that I have seen play, and others praise, and that highly, not to speak it profanely, that, neither having the accent of Christians nor the gait of Christian, pagan, nor man, have so strutted and bellowed that I have though some of nature's journeymen had made men and not made them well, they imitated humanity so abominably.

SHAKESPEARE

THE GREEN PASTURES

NOAH. Yes, suh, dis seems to be complete. Now 'bout the animals, Lawd, you say you want everythin'?
GOD. Two of everythin'.
NOAH. That would include jayraffes an' hippopotamusses?
GOD. Everythin' dat is.
NOAH. Dey was a circus in town las' week. I guess I kin fin' dem. Co'se I kin git all de rabbits an' possums an' wil' turkeys easy. I'll sen' de boys out. Hum, I'm jest wonderin'—
GOD. 'Bout what?

NOAH. 'Bout snakes. Think you'd like snakes, too?

GOD. Certainly. I want snakes.

NOAH. Oh, I kin git snakes, lots of 'em. Co'se some of 'em's a little dangerous. Maybe I better take a kag of likker, too?

GOD. You kin take a kag of likker.

NOAH. (Musingly.) Yes, suh, dey's a awful lot of differ'nt kin's of snakes, come to think about it. Dey's water moccasins, cotton-moufs, rattlers—mus' be a hund'ed kin's of other snakes down in de swamps. Maybe I better take two kags of likker.

GOD. (Mildly.) I think de one kag's enough.

NOAH. No. I better take two kags. Besides I kin put one on each side of de boat, and balance de ship wid dem as well as havin' dem fo' medicinal use.

GOD. You kin put one kag in de middle of de ship.

NOAH. (Buoyantly.) Jest as east to take two kags, Lawd.

GOD. I think one kag's enough.

NOAH. Yes, Lawd, but you see forty days—an' forty nights—(*There's a distant roll of thunder.*)

GOD. (Firmly.) One kag, Noah.

NOAH. Yes Lawd, one kag.

MARC CONNELLY [6]

A LETTER TO THE CORINTHIANS

If I speak with the tongues of men and of angels, but have not love, I am a noisy gong or a clanging cymbal. And if I have prophetic powers, and understand all mysteries and all knowledge, and if I have all faith, so as to remove mountains, but have not love, I am nothing. If I give away all I have, and if I deliver my body to be burned, but have not love, I gain nothing.

Love is patient and kind; love is not jealous or boastful; it is not arrogant or rude. Love does not insist on its own way; it is not irritable or resentful; it does not rejoice at wrong, but rejoices in the right. Love bears all things, believes all things, hopes all things, endures all things.

Love never ends; as for prophecy, it will pass away; as for tongues, they will cease; as for knowledge, it will pass away. For our knowledge is imperfect and our prophecy is imperfect; but when the perfect comes, the imperfect will pass away. When I was a child, I spoke like a child, I thought like a child, I reasoned like a child; when I became a man, I gave up childish ways. For now we see in a mirror dimly, but then face to face. Now I know in part; then I shall understand fully, even as I have been fully understood. So faith, hope, love abide, these three; but the greatest of these is love.

PAUL (1 Corinthians, 13; Revised Standard Version)

[6] Copyright, 1929, by Marc Connelly, and reprinted by permission of Farrar & Rinehart, Inc., publishers.

THE TWENTIETH CENTURY

We entered this terrible twentieth century with confidence. We thought that with improving transportation, nations would get to know each other better. We believed that as they got to know each other better, they would like each other more, and that national rivalries would fade in a growing international consciousness. We took it almost for granted that science would confer continual boons and blessings upon us, and would give us better meals, better garments and better dwellings for less trouble, and thus steadily shorten the hours of labor and leave more time for play, and culture. In the name of ordered but unceasing progress, we saluted the Age of Democracy, democracy ever expressing itself more widely through parliaments freely and fairly elected on a broad or universal franchise. We saw no reason why men and women should not shape their own home life and careers without being cramped by the growing complexity of the state, which was to be their servant and the protector of their rights. You had the famous American maxim, "Governments derive their just powers from the consent of the governed," and we both noticed that the world was divided into peoples that owned the governments and governments that owned the peoples. At least I heard all this around that time, and liked some of it very much.

WINSTON CHURCHILL, at the Massachusetts Institute of Technology, March 31, 1949.

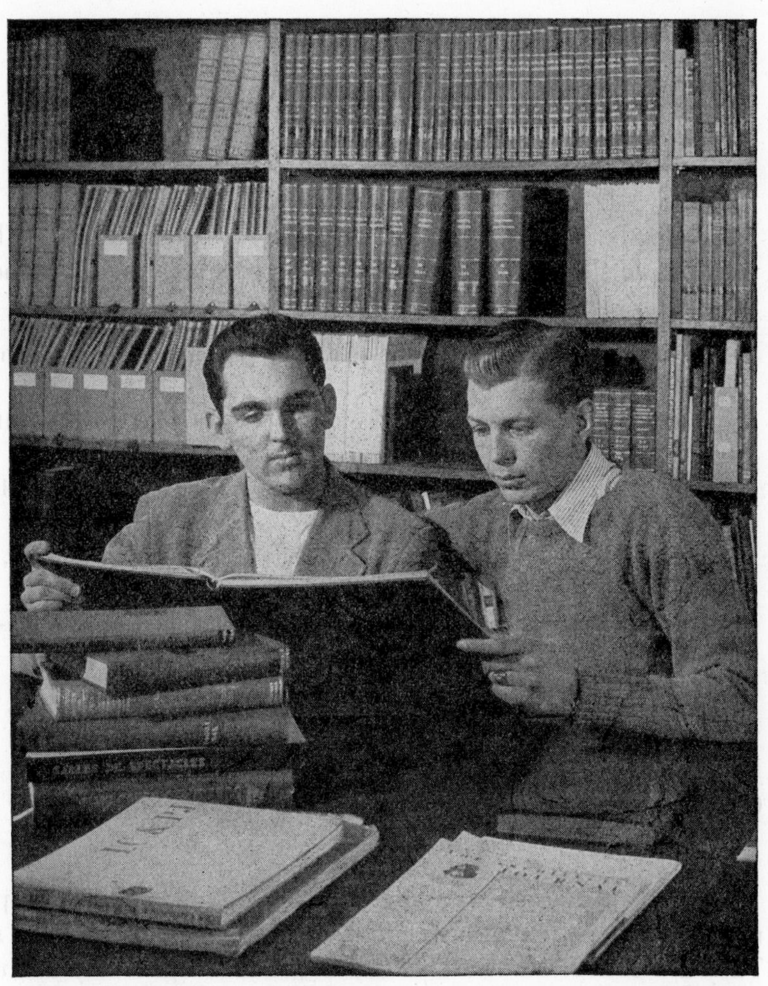

"I have made it a fixed rule to spend one hour in preparation for every minute I am to speak—five minutes, five hours," said William DeWitt Hyde.

CHAPTER 3

First Steps in Managing Ideas

CHAPTER 3

You cannot wait to study all the speech principles before making your first speech, therefore we shall start with simple speeches and elementary procedures. These are the steps to be followed in making the first speeches:[1]

1. Choose a subject of interest to you, and one that can be made interesting to the audience.
2. Do not try to cover the whole subject, but select one specific part for your central idea.
3. Phrase the central idea into a Purpose-Sentence so you will know where you are going.
4. Make a list of two or three main points of your central idea, or not more than four at the most.
5. Obtain specific and interesting material to support each of these main points.
6. Organize the speech into an outline.
7. Practice delivering the speech until you have it well in mind.

Choose a subject of interest to you, and one that can be made interesting to the audience

Where can one find an interesting subject? you ask. If you please, not so fast. Look first at the audience to whom you are going to speak. They are college students, mostly about your age. They are not industrialists or business executives or labor leaders, or anything of that sort, and you cannot talk to them as such. Nor are they high-school students; and so you cannot work off on them that speech you prepared back in high school. Better forget it entirely and get a new subject. These college students have a wide range of interests. Some might be called scholars; they are interested in books and ideas. Some are

[1] Notice please that these steps are only an abbreviation to help you during the first few weeks of the course. They are not complete and they are adequate only for first speeches. As you advance through the textbook the full process will be developed step by step.

athletes; they spend several hours a day in athletic practice, and it is a subject very much on their mind. Some are especially interested in the sciences, and much of their time is spent in a laboratory. Some are interested in the humanities; for them literature and languages are life's deepest currents. Some are interested in economics and business. Some are going to become engineers, teachers, lawyers, physicians, what-have-you.

You may ask how anyone can find a subject to fit people so widely separated in interests. Finding a subject, of course, is never easy, yet it is easier to find subjects for college audiences than for most other types of audiences, because their range of interest is wider. Here are guides:

1. Choose a subject you know something about already, and about which you can find out more.

2. Choose a subject the audience may know a little about, but wants to know more.

Are you a science major? Then explain to the class what antibiotics are, and why they are important to everybody. Or what sonic speed is, and why it was once a hazard to airplanes. Or how DDT was discovered, and how it works. Or what Galileo did. Or how Einstein's concept have changed the world of Isaac Newton.

Are you majoring in literature? Tell the class who the newest writers are, and what they are trying to do. Or how Shakespeare's stage differed from the stage today. Or what is free verse. Or who was Omar Khayyam, or Homer, or Plutarch.

Are you majoring in economics or business? A wealth of subjects is yours: prices, labor, wages, taxes, unemployment compensation, old age pensions, government interference in business, wages and prices, the small business man, the consumer....

Are you an athlete? Then increase your hearers' understanding of the game and pleasure in watching it. If it is football, explain the type of offense used by the team this year so your listeners may watch games more profitably; or explain the general plan of defense, or the special defense against forward passes. If it is basketball, track, swimming, baseball, tennis, wrestling, golf—explain what spectators should look for and how they can get greater enjoyment from witnessing these sports.

Thus a wide range of subjects can be made interesting to college audiences, for under stimulation people have eternally questing minds. Yet, even in college, most students' time is too much taken with one field of study. Already they are specializing, and most of them have an uneasy feeling that outside their field of study are many things they ought to know about. Terence, the Roman playwright, brought thunderous applause with the line, "I am a man and interested in all *manly* things." So are intelligent and educated people always. So are your listeners. In choosing subjects this is your opportunity.

Do not try to cover the whole subject, but select one specific part for your central idea

Young speakers at first are likely to cover the moon, the sand, and the stars in a single five-minute speech. The coverage is thin. Narrow your subject until you can cover it specifically and in reasonable detail within the time limit.

Is your subject football? Behold the coverage attempted by a student speaker before he learned better:

History of football
Some famous early players
Four types of offense used today
Methods of defense for these offenses
Some famous players of today
The value of the game

Now that may be all right for a book (if it were a big book) but you cannot cover it in a speech, in a one-hour speech, much less a short classroom speech. To narrow it down to a five-minute coverage, you might take this one central idea, which, with diagrams and explanations could be covered in five minutes:

The type of offense used by our football team this year

Is your subject labor? Here is a speech that covers too much:

History of labor unions
History of labor legislation

From this large area you might take the following single point for your central idea:

The effect of the Taft-Hartley Act on labor elections

Is your subject radio and television? Here is a speech that tries to cover too much:

How radio was invented
Development of Standard Modulation system
The short wave radio
The Frequency Modulation system
Where radar and television come in

From this large area you might choose the following central idea that would interest almost everybody:

Why television requires coaxial cables instead of regular telephone wires

Is your subject art? Behold a speech that tries to cover the whole wide range:

Greek and Roman art
Italian masters
Dutch, Flemish, and French painters
English and American painters
Oriental types of art
The Moderns: Realism, Surrealism, etc.
Why we have art

For a classroom speech you might settle for a fractional part of the last topic, "Why we have art," and use the following for a central idea:

How lines and colors can improve your looks

A good speech is not unlike a good photograph. It is in focus. It centers on one specific thing, a central idea. And a good close-up is worth a dozen hazy distant shots.

Phrase the central idea into a Purpose-Sentence so you will know where you are going

As this is stated you may not at first see what it means, or why you should do it. Yet it is important, and if you don't do it you can later run into trouble. It is important because a speech, unlike a private conversation needs a definite purpose. A private conversation may be aimless, but a good public speech moves definitely toward a predetermined goal. The speaker is going somewhere. He is aiming at a target. He wants the audience to *know* something, to *understand* something, to *believe* something, to *do* something. Therefore, in order to keep in mind where your speech is supposed to go, put it down in writing.

You are going to talk on football, let us assume, and have selected the following central idea:

The type of offense used by our team this year

With such a central idea you may have any one of several purposes, as indicated by the following purpose-sentences:

I want to increase your enjoyment in watching football this year by explaining the type of offense being used by our team [i.e. *information*], or

The type of football offense being used by the team this year is superior to the one used last year [i.e. *argument*], or

The type of football offense used by the team this year is superior to all other types [i.e. *argument*], or

The type of football offense used by the team this year is not as good as that used by our major opponents [i.e. *argument*].

Now any one of these four could be a good speech purpose, but do not try to wander across two or three of them in a single speech. Choose *one*, write it out in a clear cut Purpose-Sentence, and stay by it as you plan the speech.

AVOID ARGUMENT AND CONTROVERSY IN FIRST SPEECHES

A final suggestion: For these first speeches, better avoid subjects involving argument and controversy. At its best, argument is an explosive and you have to know how to handle it. "*Win an argument and you lose a soul*," said Bishop Fulton J. Sheen. There will be plenty of time later for speeches on controversial subjects, but right now avoid them. Start with the fundamentals—and the most fundamental thing in speaking is to be able to *explain something clearly and interestingly to your listeners*. It is the basis of all other kinds of speaking, so make your first speeches clear-cut interesting speeches of information.

Make a list of two or three main points of your central idea, or not more than four at the most

These main points should cover the whole central idea. Later (see pages 213-217) we shall take up the various formal methods of arranging main topics, but for the present rely on common sense plus your general knowledge of composition. Make these main points simple and obvious. Especially, do not have too many of them, for listeners cannot remember too many. (Furthermore, you do not need them.) Generally speaking, five main points are too many. Other things being equal, three main points are better than four, and two are better than three. Keep them few in number.

For example your first draft might have five main points like this:

PURPOSE-SENTENCE: You can improve your looks by the proper use of lines and colors.

Main Points:
I. People should know how to look their best.
II. Stout people can be helped by artistic lines.
III. Thin people can also be helped.
IV. One set of colors enhances dark eyes and hair.
V. Another set of colors enhances blue eyes and light hair.

Not only are there too many main points, but they are spread out too thin (and this is often true when a speech is divided into too many main points). A better arrangement would be to reduce them to two main points, as follows:

PURPOSE-SENTENCE: You can improve your looks by the proper use of lines and colors.

Main Points:
I. If you are either fat or thin, skillful use of *lines* can improve your looks.
II. If you are either blond or brunette, you can be helped by knowing which *colors* to wear.

Note the improvement: First, there are only two main points instead of five. Second, these points are easy for the listeners—who will hear the speaker's words only once—to remember, for one deals with *lines* and the other with *colors*.

Obtain specific and interesting material to support each of these main points

In these main points you state an idea or a principle. Technically they are known as *Assertions*. The Assertion does not elaborate, explain, or prove. It only asserts. But in speechmaking Assertion is not enough, for no idea or principle can hang in the air unsupported. To assert that "older people have an unfair advantage over youth because they have lived longer," or that "John Steinbeck is a great writer," hangs unsupported in the air. It does not by itself increase our knowledge or change our belief. Standing alone, it is "as broad and general as the casing air." Its content is too large for us to comprehend in a single statement. Or if we did comprehend, sheer inertia would prevent our thinking from being altered by an isolated assertion. Finally, and most important, we will seldom remember unsupported Assertions. We hear the speaker's words but once. Unlike a reader, we cannot pause to think back, to weigh and judge, or to consult a dictionary. We must go right on, keeping pace with the speaker's words at a continuous and unbroken rate. Of the hundred speeches a year (which an average educated person hears), how much do we remember? By and large, certainly not many of the unsupported Assertions. They are like drifting clouds. They may catch our attention for a moment, but we do not remember them easily one from another.

What do we remember? We remember things that are kept vividly before our attention. We remember ideas that are supported by a succession of details, by examples, by comparisons, by illustrations. We remember ideas that are *hammered in.*

HOW TO USE SUPPORTING MATERIAL

Therefore, one of the speaker's main tasks is to support his assertions with effective materials. For the present we shall consider the following five kinds of supporting materials:

1. Facts and Figures
2. Specific Instances
3. Illustrations
4. Comparisons
5. Testimony

The manner of using these supporting materials can be seen in the following cross section of an outline:

I. ASSERTION
  A. Supporting material
  B. Supporting material
  C. Supporting material

Or the speech might be more elaborate and have two or more levels of assertions. But however many levels it has, a good speech in the end gets down to the bedrock of solid supporting materials. The following is a cross section of outline for *two* levels of assertion:

I. ASSERTION (FIRST LEVEL)
  A. *Assertion (second level)*
    1. Supporting material
    2. Supporting material
    3. Supporting material

B. *Assertion (second level)*
1. Supporting material
2. Supporting material
3. Supporting material

FACTS AND FIGURES

This is the most elementary type of supporting material, plain Facts and Figures. Yet student speeches, it ought to be inserted here, are notably weak in Facts and Figures. In general, students don't get the pertinent facts, and don't use what few facts they have. They rely too much on assertion, as if anyone cared about their unsupported assertions. Therefore, make this your basic rule: Where Facts and Figures are to be had, get them, verify them, and use them. Beware of alleged facts, synthetic facts, and rumors. Check the sources from which your facts come, and remember that a great deal of printed material today is deliberately planted for propaganda. The "facts" may be accurate (but they are not always accurate), yet their selection—and their careful omissions—make them misleading. One of the first tests of an educated person is to read carefully and read suspiciously, and know how to detect propaganda.

The following example demonstrates the use of verified facts as supporting material:

MAIN POINT (ASSERTION):	I. Shakespeare's plays do not today reach the lusty, semi-literate audience for which he wrote.
Facts and Figures	A. Even the motion pictures of *Henry V* and *Hamlet* were seen by an estimated 5 per cent of the people in cities where they were shown —including those who went because of culture-snobbery and those who went unwillingly, led by the ears.
Facts and Figures	B. Yet the forgotten picture *Mr. Blandings Builds His Dream House,* which was produced about the same time as *Hamlet,* was seen by over 20 per cent of the people in cities where it was shown.
Facts and Figures	C. *Gone With the Wind,* which holds the record for modern pictures, was seen by over 50 per cent—over ten times as many as saw either of Shakespeare's plays.
Facts and Figures	D. The average Hollywood movie hit is seen by roughly 30 per cent to 40 per cent of the people in cities where they are shown.

SPECIFIC INSTANCES

By Specific Instances is meant condensed examples. These examples are brief, even pithy, but specific. For such examples to be effective, the audience must know enough about the general subject, or the example, for it to carry an instant meaning. Suppose, for instance, the speaker said, "Early labor and management relations were marked by bitter strife [Assertion]. There was the Haymarket Riot, the Homestead Strike, and the Pullman Strike [Specific Instances]." Such Specific Instances would not carry an instant meaning to listeners, excepting only the very few who had studied labor history. Don't use that kind of Specific Instances. Sift and discard those about which listeners know little. Use only those referring to things that listeners know, or know about.

The following example shows how an assertion might be supported by effective instances:

MAIN POINT (ASSERTION): I. Great achievements have been made by men and women under 30 years of age.

Specific Instance A. At that age Elizabeth Barrett Browning had published two volumes of poems.

Specific Instance B. Margaret Mitchell had finished half of the book, *Gone With the Wind.*

Specific Instance C. Kathleen Windsor had written *Forever Amber.*

Specific Instance D. Lord Byron had written *Childe Harold* and published 14 volumes of poems.

Specific Instance E. Mozart had published over 200 of his musical compositions.

Specific Instance F. William Pitt, the Younger, had been Prime Minister of England for 6 years.

Specific Instance G. Alexander Graham Bell had invented the telephone.

Specific Instance H. Henry Ford had produced his first automobile.

Specific Instance I. Arthur H. Compton had done research on cosmic rays for which he later was awarded the Nobel Prize.

The above specific instances have an instant meaning to listeners because they know the names as well as the achievements of most of the persons cited (and this effect is deliberately attained by omitting the achievements of less widely known persons like William DeWitt Hyde, Rupert Brooke, and Ernest O. Lawrence).

ILLUSTRATIONS

An Illustration is a detailed Specific Instance. It tells the full story and does not depend on the listener's previous knowledge. At times a single Illustration may carry the weight of the whole Assertion, as in the Parable of the Good Samaritan ("And who is my neighbor?") and that of the Prodigal Son (There is joy over "one sinner that repenteth"). At times two or more illustrations are used, as in the following example:

MAIN POINT (ASSERTION): I. The racketeers went forth, a gat in one hand and the palm of the other extended saying, "Cut me in on your business or get killed."

Illustration A. Maxie Eisen walked into a fish market on Taylor Street, Chicago, owned by Abie the Fishman. When Abie awakened several hours later, eighteen stitches had closed the revolver butt wounds on his head and he found himself a member of Maxie's Retail Fish Dealers' Association. The fee for admission was $500.00.

Illustration B. But the acme of rackets was the Master Cleaners and Dyers Union. It hired George Bugs Moran at $1,800 a week to make depredations on stubborn independent cleaners. When Big Tim Murphy, who was a formidable gangster himself, attempted to muscle in, he got one of those $31,000 funerals. The union grew so rich that it maintained a $700,000 defense treasury, and law abiding people appealed in vain to the police for protection.

COMPARISONS

By Comparison is meant what earlier writers have called *analogy and antithesis, comparison and contrast,* etc. (You have met with these terms before, and may be able to recall useful information about them.) Comparisons show likeness and differences between things and ideas. Especially are Comparisons valuable supporting materials for the following purposes:

To connect something known with something unknown. As an example, if you are explaining how uranium 235 was first separated from uranium 238, you might explain how one of the first attempts was to set up a sort of cream separator and whirl the atoms about until the heavier 238 units would be thrown to the outside; then when that failed a successful attempt was made by setting up a sort of race track. (People know about cream separators and race tracks.)

To connect something meaningless with something meaningful. If you say "Last year 40,000 people were killed by automobile accidents," the statement has less meaning than if you said, "Last year exactly as many people were killed in automobile accidents as were killed in action in the Army, Navy, and Marine Corps during World War I," (But check such Comparisons to be sure they are accurate: For your information, the killed-in-action figures here cited were checked against those given in the current issue of *Information Please Almanac*, which were taken from the War Department records.)

To explain something new, about which people are suspicious, with something old which they accept. People often are suspicious of new things. They were suspicious at first of automobiles and higher education, even as they had once been suspicious of printing presses and democracy. Therefore, when you explain or advocate something really new, it can often best be done by showing that it is like this-or-that, which people already know about and believe in. Eric Johnston used such a comparison in his frank speech "A Warning to Labor—and to Management": "Gentlemen of labor. . . You are just where we of management were ten years ago. [Then] we had everything all our own way. A friendly administration in Washington. Low taxes. And a friendly public. . . . [Ten years later] you were tops. A friendly administration in Washington. All sorts of favors fed to you. . . ."

The following example shows in detail how Comparison may be used as supporting material:

Main Point (assertion): I. New York City is still a melting pot.

Comparison	A. It has more Irish (500,000) than Dublin.
Comparison	B. It has more Jews (2,000,000) than Palestine.
Comparison	C. It has almost as many Italians (1,095,000) as Rome.
Comparison	D. It has almost as many Poles (412,000) as Warsaw.
Comparison	E. It has more Negroes (500,000) than Atlanta and Birmingham combined.

TESTIMONY

This is the authority of others. In effect, the speaker says: "I am not the only one who believes this. There are two of us, or three of us, and these others are famous, or are experts, or are in a special position to know." The use of Testimony has been cheapened by modern advertisement, and intelligent people are not impressed by the testimony of Joe Speed, the dirt-track race driver, on the kind of cigarettes he smokes—or the enthusiastic words of the young plainfolks housewife on the suds that make her hands look beautiful. Nevertheless, intelligent people do live largely by authority, the right kind of authority. We accept the authority of our church, our fraternal orders, our social groups. We respect the authority of courts and judges. On questions of judgment and on complex ideas, we accept the authority of qualified experts. In reading a book we must accept, or reject, the authority of the author, and in the main we accept it.

Therefore, to present the Testimony of competent authorities is one of important methods of supporting assertions. The following example illustrates its use:

MAIN POINT (ASSERTION): I. Too much education consists of studying the past and ignoring the present.

Testimony — A. Thomas Jefferson warned against this danger a century and a quarter ago. At the age of 73, when many minds look backward instead of forward, Jefferson wrote urgently that "institutions must go hand in hand with the progress of the human mind," and "as new discoveries are made... institutions must advance, also, and keep pace with the times"; and he warned society against remaining "ever under the regimen of their ancestors."

Testimony — B. Ralph Waldo Emerson repeated the same warning a little over a hundred years ago, saying that "Each age, it is found, must write its own books."

Testimony — C. Charles Francis Adams II, when he was a member of the Harvard University Board of Overseers, protested to the university against the education he had received in college, because it had ignored the present and buried itself in the past: "No matter how long I may live, I shall never be able... to overcome some of the great disadvantages which the ... wrong theories and worse practices of my *alma mater* inflicted upon me. And not on me alone."

USING COMBINED METHODS OF SUPPORT

Not often does a speaker limit himself to one method of support for an assertion. He uses more than one kind—two or three or four. He uses every available kind in order to get the best possible support for his Assertions. The following example illustrates the use of *four kinds* of supporting materials for a single Assertion:

MAIN POINT (ASSERTION): I. New York is not merely a large city, it is complex and unique.

Facts and Figures	A. Its 157 banks and 94 insurance companies are the financial center of the world, having overthrown London's 300-year reign.
Facts and Figures	B. Its 32 legitimate theatres so dominate the American stage that to the sophisticated American "Broadway" means "stage."
Specific Instances	C. It is the world's greatest manufacturing city, the world's greatest port, the world's greatest tourist attraction.
Comparison	D. Unlike London, Berlin, Paris, Rome, Tokyo and other large cities, it is not the capital of a nation; in fact, it is not the capital of its own state.
Comparison	E. It has more Irish than Dublin, more Jews than Palestine, almost as many Italians as Rome and more Negroes than any two cities south of Mason and Dixon's line.
Testimony	F. One can sense the reverence, if not awe, of its former mayor, William O'Dwyer, when he said, "I love it. It's a hell of a town."

Organize the speech into an outline

A distinguished novelist, Martin Flavin, after serving as a judge in a writing contest said that as he read the new novels two things stood out. First, there was a lack of plan. Second, there was too much digression and repetition, too many scenes that did not advance the story but merely interrupted it until suspense and interest leaked away. These are also characteristics of beginners' speeches, and both of them are inherent in the first weakness, the lack of an outline.

Anyone can learn to make an outline. Following are the basic steps:

1. Set down the purpose-sentence so you can keep in mind what the speech is intended to accomplish. (This has already been discussed, see pages 34-36.)

2. Make a list of the two or three main points of the central idea. (This has also been discussed, see pages 36-37.)

3. Arrange these main points in the most effective order for your audience. In doing this rely for the time being on common sense.

4. Develop each of these main points with specific and interesting supporting material. (For discussion of this see above, pages 37-44.)

5. Plan an introduction that will explain the subject if necessary and will capture the attention of the listeners. Most introductions total about 10 per cent of the whole speech, but this proportion obviously varies.

6. Plan a conclusion that in some way will round out the speech. This may be a summary to enable listeners to remember the main points, or it may be other material that will leave the listeners with a lasting impression. Usually, a conclusion is even shorter than the introduction. The average is perhaps 5 per cent of the whole speech, although this also obviously varies.

The following shows a complete outline for a twenty-minute speech that has been developed through the above six steps:

THAT JAPANESE LANGUAGE [2]

PURPOSE-SENTENCE: The Japanese language in its written form is a barrier to the Japanese understanding one another and to our understanding the Japanese people.

INTRODUCTION

I. My speech is not only about the Japanese language, but also about the Japanese people.

II. The Japanese are more difficult to understand than either the Germans or Russians, so difficult that before 1941 we practically gave up trying to understand them.

  A. I want to call attention to one of their puzzling national traits.

    1. The Japanese started the Russo-Japanese War in 1904 with a sneak attack.

    2. They started the Sino-Japanese war in 1937 with a sneak attack.

    3. They started the war with the U.S. in 1941 with a sneak attack.

    4. Japan started all her modern wars with sneak attacks: Formosa in 1894, Korea in 1911, and Germany in 1915.

  B. Admiral Spruance, the brains of our Navy in the Pacific, said that the Japanese always started wars with a sneak attack because their language was so complex that whenever taken by surprise they could not think quickly, and they assumed that other people reacted the same way.

    1. After going through the Japanese Language School in the Uni-

[2] This was a speakers bureau address given by Tony J. Cefali, a college student during the late 1940's. He delivered it to about 25 audiences of business men.

versity of Pennsylvania and serving as interpreter of a sort in Japan, I know that Admiral Spruance is right.

2. One reason we don't understand such a people is their written language.

III. (Purpose-Sentence) The Japanese language in its written form is a barrier to the Japanese understanding one another and to our understanding the Japanese people.

DISCUSSION

I. The Japanese language in its written form is a barrier to the Japanese understanding one another.
   A. It is unbelievably complex.
      1. An American typewriter has 26 letters plus 10 numbers and 19 symbols, but a Japanese typewriter has 1,000 symbols.
      2. You read a newspaper that is printed in combinations of 26 letters, but a Japanese newspaper uses up to 4,500 symbols.
      3. A good college student in Japan is supposed to learn up to 10,000 symbols, and a Japanese Ph.D. would be supposed to have learned around 30,000 symbols.
      4. The problem is so acute that after the war General MacArthur asked for a commission of American educators to study the problem, and this commission found that Japanese students spent 6 hours out of 8 throughout school, even college, learning symbols—not ideas, but symbols.
   B. This has resulted in widespread ignorance among the people of Japan.
      1. After spending 6 hours out of 8 learning symbols, the average Japanese does not remember even the 4,500 symbols necessary to read everything in a newspaper.
         a. In Tokyo the average citizen can read 600 symbols.
         b. In the rural districts the average can read only 325 symbols.
      2. In other words, when the common people of Japan try to read a newspaper, which uses up to 4,500 symbols, and can read only 600 or 325 of those symbols, they can read only the headlines and the simplest parts; the rest of the paper is a mystery to them.
      3. Even that small percentage of well-educated people cannot read all the 4,500 symbols without using a dictionary.
         a. They had once learned up to 10,000 symbols, but they cannot remember them.
         b. It's the same as your studying Latin; once you may have been able to dig out the translation of Cicero or Vergil, but you cannot do it now.
   C. This language barrier is partly responsible for the lack of Japanese inventiveness.
      1. The Japanese had the world's greatest gift for borrowing ideas, but were the most backward of great nations in inventiveness.

a. I've heard they got their battleship blueprints from other nations.
b. I've heard that their famous Zero airplane was copied from the planes of three other nations.
c. And of course they got radar from Germany.

2. This lack of inventiveness did not come from lack of ability, but in part because they spent 6 hours out of 8 through school merely learning symbols, until they were weighted down with them, and did not have time or energy to do creative thinking.

II. The Japanese written language is also a barrier to our understanding them, and in a larger sense to international understanding.

A. During World War II the Army tried to find men of military age, able to pass its physical examination, who could speak fluent Japanese.
1. They found about 15, no more.
2. My instructor in the Army Language School was not an American, but a native-born Japanese and a former Japanese naval officer.

B. Our training in Japanese was equivalent theoretically to 5 years of college foreign language, but actually it was more because of the intense motivation (if we flunked out, back to the infantry for us!)
1. We ate, drank, and slept Japanese for 9 months at 40 hours a week formal study plus about 15 more that was informal.
2. We even sat together at football games and cheered for Pennsylvania in the Japanese language!

C. Compare the result with training in other foreign languages.
1. A high-school teacher of French or German is required usually to have 4 years of the language; and right after the war there were hundreds of young language teachers in college who had barely had that minimum, but got by.
2. With 4 years of French or German I could do a reasonably good job of learning it, but with the equivalent of 5 years, or more, of Japanese, I did not learn as much as I'd like to pretend.
3. We were supposed to know about 1,000 symbols (out of the 4,500 required to read fully a newspaper), but we never really learned over 500.
4. Then with my 500 symbols I sailed for Japan just as the war ended.
a. We arrived in Yokohama, where the first thing I saw was a street sign—and I could not read it!
b. On up to the assignment post we passed about 50 signs, and I could not read a single one of them!
c. I was not totally ignorant, for I could make out a word in this town and a syllable in the next one, but I could not get the full meaning of even one.

d. With 5 years of German I could have read its newspapers, magazines, and half its books, but with 5 years of Japanese I could not read a street sign.

III. There are two things that can be done to reduce this barrier.

A. The first is to throw overboard the whole system of Japanese writing and adopt the American-European alphabet.

1. At present there are three kinds of Japanese writing, and educated people must learn all three.

a. The first is Konji, the picture symbols I have been talking about.

(1). There are about 30,000 to 40,000 Konji symbols.

(2). Books are published in Konji, street signs are in Konji, and newspapers use both Konji and Katakana.

b. The second is Katakana, a syllable alphabet of 52 letters.

(1). It is the "poor man's alphabet."

(2). Newspapers use Katakana as well as the picture symbols (Konji).

c. The third is Hirakana, another syllable alphabet of 52 letters.

(1). It is the "rich man's alphabet," for the wealthy and the educated people would not stoop to use the poor man's alphabet.

(2). Letter writing is done in Hirakana.

2. The MacArthur Education Commission recommended that all three of these systems of writings be abandoned and that the American-European alphabet be introduced in Japan.

a. The drawback would be to cut off the Japanese from their past, for henceforth no child could read anything written previously in Japanese.

b. Even so, this would be the best way out, but it is the least likely.

B. A less satisfactory but less drastic compromise would be to abandon the picture writing (Konji) and the "rich man's alphabet" (Hirakana) and use only the "poor man's alphabet" (Katakana) of 52 letters.

1. Everybody in Japan already knows this alphabet, so living people would need no re-education.

2. School children henceforth could learn it within a few weeks, instead of spending 6 hours out of 8 throughout school learning picture symbols.

3. Foreigners could learn it as quickly as they learn French or German.

4. Its adoption would create only minor problems.

a. Large newspapers which now use both Katakana and Konji would simply drop the latter.

b. Rural newspapers and books could start at once using

Katakana, since most of them already have these letters in stock for special purposes.

c. Henceforth, earlier books could no longer be read by the general public, but only by scholars; yet books really cannot now be read by the general public.

5. This is less satisfactory than using the American-European alphabet but it can be done more easily.

CONCLUSION

I. A language should be a highway of understanding and not a barrier; and this is especially important to the average American business man in this day when language isolation is impossible.

A. Twenty-five years ago this city was two weeks away from any large foreign-language country outside Mexico.

B. Today it is not over 48 hours by air from any large city on earth.

C. In Europe for centuries business houses have had to handle at least three languages, and 50 years hence large American business houses will have to handle two or three languages.

D. Some of your grandchildren are going to have to learn Japanese, just as others will need to learn Spanish and Russian.

E. It is important that they don't have to learn Japanese the way I had to learn it.

This is a detailed outline for a twenty-minute speech, and it contains about 60 per cent the number of words as the full speech. Each idea, even the smallest, is set down. It thus affords a guide for a speaker who might want to pick up the outline next week or next month, refresh his mind from the outline, and give the speech again.

For your first speeches you will probably find it advisable to make outlines as complete as this one, although this is not a rule. Each speaker will develop his own particular system, yet by and large *responsible* speakers—as contrasted with loose talkers and demagogues—are characterized by having longer and more detailed preparations on paper. If a student starts early to develop glibness at the expense of thoroughness and accuracy, he puts a ceiling on his own progress.

Practice delivering the speech until you have it well in mind

Each of the previous six steps has been concerned with developing ideas in your mind and getting them down on paper. You do not yet have a speech. It is not yet even an "essay on its hind legs." It is lying flat on paper. Now comes the task of making it a living thought for those who are to listen. How can you make it live? How can you be sure, when you stand up to speak, of not forgetting, of not rambling and getting ideas misplaced? How can you avoid those long pauses when the mind is blank, and avoid filling them up with tiresome *ahs* and *er-r-s*? How can you keep within the allotted time? These are no idle questions. When you try to speak in public but the words won't come, the failure becomes very real and personal.

Many people who fail deserve to fail. This is a hard unsympathetic way of putting it, but it is true. Turning an outline into a speech requires a definite technique, which the many ignore or try to avoid by short-cuts.

First, remember that extemporaneous speaking is not impromptu speaking. To be sure many people still think so, even as they once thought the world was flat. They think that extemporaneous speaking is speaking without preparation. Of course, this is wrong. It is completely wrong. Unprepared speeches are *impromptu,* and we are not here interested in them simply because real impromptu speeches usually are not good. Other people think that extemporaneous speeches are those "given with hasty or meager preparation." Of course, this is also wrong. It is completely wrong. These are simply poorly prepared speeches, nothing more. "It was with awe as well as eagerness that I braced myself for the supreme effort," wrote Winston Churchill of his first speech in Parliament, an extemporaneous speech. "I need not recount the pains I had taken to prepare, nor the efforts I had made to hide the work of preparation."

What really is meant by extemporaneous speaking is delivering a speech that has been carefully thought out, carefully planned, and carefully outlined—but not written out and memorized. A speech haphazardly planned and outlined is not a real extemporaneous speech—and that is the trouble with many of the so-called "extemporaneous speeches."

Next, assuming that you have a good outline, how do you convert it into a good extemporaneous speech? You have taken part in a play, or at least seen one, so let's start from there. The actors start with a manuscript, a complete manuscript, with every word set down. Of course, it could be argued that there is no point in presenting a play if it is all written out. It would be cheaper and simpler for everyone merely to read the play. They could read it at leisure. They could read it at home. But the manuscript is not the play, for the play is a *living* thing. In the same way, an outline is not the speech.

How do the actors turn the manuscript into a play? (1) They study the lines to find their meaning and their mood. (2) They learn the lines. (3) They perfect their memory and develop the play by rehearsals.

In turning the outline into a speech you do not follow these same steps, but you do use the same *process*. You do not need to study the outline to find the meaning, since you made the outline, and you, above all others, know what meaning and mood each part of it is supposed to carry. Nor do you "learn the lines," as in a play, which is to say you don't memorize the speech word-for-word. (Of course you can write out the speech and memorize it if you wish. Many great speakers have done so. But it is not good business for a beginner. Unless you are close to a Franklin D. Roosevelt or a Claire Booth Luce in ability—and the odds on that are slim—your memorized speech will *sound* memorized. You will have a dead, stiff carcass on your hands. For the present, you had better avoid writing and memorizing speeches.) Individual methods vary, but in general they involve the following procedure:

MEMORIZE THE SEQUENCE OF IDEAS

That is to say, fix in mind the two or three main points, then fix in mind the proper sequence of supporting material. This does not need to be formally memorized like a poem. It does not need to be word-perfect. You need fix in mind only the thought pattern, not the words. The simplest and quickest way of doing this is to follow the approved steps which psychologists have found to be most effective:

1. First, read the outline *silently* from beginning to end. Read it slowly, feeling your way along, but do not back-track even once, for back-tracking breaks the memorizing of sequence.

2. Next, read the outline *aloud,* thoughtfully, but again without back-tracking.

3. Now put aside the outline and rehearse the speech aloud, still without back-tracking. If you forget parts of the speech, go right on. Do not look at the outline, and do not back-track. You are trying to get the whole thought pattern in mind, therefore, do not get entangled in details.

4. Study your outline again and note the places where you skipped parts of the speech or got the sequence out of order. After mentally patching up these parts, read the outline again *aloud,* slowly and thoughtfully, but still without back-tracking.

5. Put aside the outline and rehearse the speech aloud from start to finish without back-tracking.

REHEARSE THE SPEECH FORMALLY FROM FIVE TO TEN TIMES, REHEARSE ON YOUR FEET AND PREFERABLY IN A LARGE ROOM

The above rehearsals were intended to fix the outline in your mind. Now come rehearsals for the purpose of carrying the speech out to the audience. For these, you need to be on your feet, exactly as when you give the final speech, and you need to be in a room roughly the size of the classroom, and you need to be where you can rehearse without interruptions.

All of this is a large order, we know. (But for a beginner a good speech *is* a large order.) Nevertheless, out of centuries of experience man has accumulated the knowledge on how good speeches are made, and this is part of that knowledge.

Rehearse on your feet. You do not remember merely with your brain. You remember with your nerves and muscles also. This is often called "muscle memory," and it is essential to any speaker. You are going to give the speech while standing up. Therefore, rehearse the speech in the same position, where you can get the muscular set you will use in the final speech. Also (as we shall see later) you must pay attention to posture and action. These, too, are part of the rehearsal.

Rehearse in a room roughly the size of the classroom. This is not necessary for all rehearsals, although it is preferable, but certainly for a few rehearsals you need to stand up in a full-size room and get the feel of your voice as it comes back to you from the four walls. For this use one of the college classrooms in late afternoon or evening. Sometimes groups of students organize practice sessions, meet together, and practice on one another. Sometimes two students pair off, and hear and criticize each other. It needs to be done. It can be done.

Rehearse where you are free from interruptions. This is so obvious that it needs no elaboration.

Rehearse the speech formally from five to ten times. The number of needed rehearsals is not fixed, and these numbers are suggestive. A few students will need less than five. A few will need more than ten. But one thing is positive: Most students need more rehearsals than they think.[3] During the first few rehearsals you are still fixing

[3] Over a period of three years I asked students to keep a record of their number of formal speech reheasals. It was understood that this record was for the purpose of research, and that it bore no relation to grades in the course. I have every reason to think that it was reasonably accurate. In those speeches where students gave about the best they were

the speech in mind. The next few allow you to pay attention to posture and action, and especially to that essential in all good speaking, poise. The last rehearsals allow you to make sure that the fine shades of thought—and the humor and suspense and all the other elements that make up what is known as "feeling"—is projected to the entire room.

CLASSIFIED SPEECH SUBJECTS

THE STORY OF (NARRATIVE)

The calling of the Constitutional Convention
College life in colonial days
Modern jazz
Hybrid corn
The microscope
Einstein and the atom
The 1849 Gold Rush
Noah Webster's dictionary
McGuffie's readers
The fight against yellow fever
The rise of Hitler
How Stalin succeeded Lenin
Why Washington, D.C. is on the Potomac
The Panama Canal

THE CAUSE OF (ANALYSIS)

New York being the largest U.S. city
Coal strikes
Juvenile delinquency
The depression of 1929
The First World War
Detroit being the automotive center
Iowa being the corn center
Television's swift expansion after 1948
Hollywood being the moving picture center
The rise of Socialism in England
The low living standard in Spain
The Monroe Doctrine
The pleasant summer climate in Mexico City
High prices following World War II
High taxes in the U.S.

A CRITICAL EXPOSITION OF (DESCRIPTION)

A speaker I recently heard
A play or moving picture I recently saw
A course I am taking
The Madonnas of Raphael
Chain store methods
The Japanese soldier
Russian foreign policies
The Jerusalem situation
Canadian-U.S. trade relations
The curriculum of this institution
Jet plane development

---

capable of, formal rehearsals ranged from three to fourteen. There were few at either extreme, about 1%. The majority of rehearsals ranged from four to ten, the average being six to seven rehearsals. During these three years, in every instance but one where a speaker forgot during the speech and could not proceed, or got through it with repeated memory difficulty, the number of formal rehearsals had been fewer than the average. Often there had been only one formal rehearsal, or even none.

HOW IT WORKS

Radar
Television coaxial cable
Offset printing
Color photography
Focal plane shutters
The wind tunnel
Running a student paper
Pressure cookers
Proportional representation
The calculating machine
The electric clock
The photo-electric cell
The bazooka
The "numbers" racket
Grading beef
The corn picker
Rockets
A woman's mind

WHAT IT IS

Meissenware
Junior Chamber of Commerce
Mortar Board
Democracy
Socialism
Communism
Industry-wide collective bargaining
Closed shop
Check off
Featherbedding
Shop Steward
Reciprocal trade agreement
Mediterranean fruit fly
Boll weavil
Corn borer
Termites
Valve-in-head engine
Magneto
Octane rating
Synthetic rubber
Anti-freeze fluids
Antibiotics
Balanced diet
Vitamins
Hope Chest
Youth hostels
Honor system
Grade-point system
Farmer's cooperatives
Farm parity prices

HOW TO DO IT

Fencing
The grip and swing of a golf club
Handle a fly rod
Navigate
Draw a cartoon
Give first aid
Get a date
Buy a house
Buy a second-hand car
Read a book
Study
Win friends and influence people
Get elected
Choose a husband or wife
Sell life insurance
Make a speech
Apply for a job
Drive a car
Make Easter flowers bloom on Easter
Raise money for a cause
Write a good business letter
Budget study hours while in college
Organize a political campaign
Use a slide rule
Develop fine-grain prints
Take action pictures
Put on makeup for stage or television
Read with meaning

PERSONAL AND OTHERWISE

"What you would like about my town"
"Some of my habits that I don't like"
"A teacher I especially like"
"A teacher who made me study"
"Take this course"
"See this television program"
"Read this book"
"See this show"
"Listen to this symphony"
"See this art exhibit"
"Vote for this man, or party"
"Make this change in the law"
"Don't make up your mind about this yet"
"Better be a Doubting Thomas than a Gullible Guppie"
"Why I came to college"
"Why I believe in extracurricular activities"
"What I ought to learn in college"
"What I will have to unlearn when I get out of college"
"What different courses I would take if I could do it over again"
"This I do believe"

HISTORY AND BIOGRAPHY

Life at Jamestown in 1607
What happened at Lexington and Concord
The strange case of Aaron Burr
The feud between Jefferson and Marshall
The incredible Genghis Khan
Man 20,000 years ago
Churchill's England
Samuel Johnson's England
Last Days of Hitler
The Normandy landing
Florence Nightingale
Mr. Justice Holmes, the Great Dissenter
Samuel Gompers
The Incredible Eleanor Roosevelt
The San Francisco Vigilantes
The early railroads
Steamboats on the Ohio and Mississippi
What happened at Pearl Harbor

BOOKS, ART, AND MUSIC

Bach
Richard Strauss
Wagner's influence on Hitler
A defense of classical music
A defense of popular music
Modern art
"Superman" comics
Dagwood, typical American husband
Origin of the comic strips
Backstage in Hollywood
Backstage on Broadway
Pulp magazines
The detective-story magazines
Cooper's Leatherstocking Tales
Walt Whitman's slow rise to fame
Carl Sandburg, poet and biographer
The real Mark Twain
Modern Southern writers like William Faulkner and Lillian Smith
Zane Grey and the westerns
A Mississippian named Tennessee Williams
Does anybody remember Amy Lowell?

ASSIGNMENTS

ON FINDING AND PHRASING PURPOSE-SENTENCES

1. Select a subject. (For possible subjects see Classified Speech Subjects just above. See also subjects listed in your Speech-Subject Analysis Form, Chapter 1, page 13.):

   a. Select three specific phases of this subject, each of which would be suitable for a speech.

   b. Phrase each of these three specific phases into a suitable Purpose-Sentence according to the principles found in this chapter.

2. Read one of the speeches found in the Appendix and write out the Purpose-Sentence.

ON THE USE OF SUPPORTING MATERIALS

3. To study the use of Supporting Materials, prepare a one-cell section of an outline after the manner seen on pages 39-44. Set down your Assertion as a main topic, then beneath it in subhead form organize the Supporting Materials—Facts and Figures, Specific Instances, Illustrations, Comparisons, and Testimony.

4. Read one of the speeches listed in the Appendix. From various parts of the speech, outline three one-cell sections showing how the speaker used Forms of Support. Follow the general method of outlining one-cell units as shown in this chapter, pages 39-44.

ON OUTLINING

5. Make a 3- to 5-page outline of one of the speeches listed in Assignment 2 above. Include everything: Purpose-Sentence, main heads, Supporting Materials in the subheads. For the general form and arrangement, see the specimen outline on page 45.

6. From the subject you used in Assignment 1 above, or any other suitable subject, prepare an outline for a speech. Include everything a good outline should have: Purpose-Sentence, main heads, Supporting Materials in the subheads. For the general form and arrangement, see the specimen outline on page 45.

ON PUTTING THE SEVEN STEPS TOGETHER

7. Prepare a 4-minute speech, following the Seven Steps set forth in this chapter. In order not to overlook or treat casually any step, use the following procedure:

   a. Make a Time Table of your speech preparation, and hand it in with the outline. On this Time Table list the Seven Steps, and show when you *started* on each of the steps and when you *completed* it. This procedure—obviously mechanical for mature speakers—is a tested superior device for inexperienced ones, because it will show the source of trouble or failure in first speeches.

b. Make a permanent record of this Time Table in your notebook, and do the same with later speeches. You can then compare each speech grade, and the over-all general progress, with the amount and method of speech preparation.

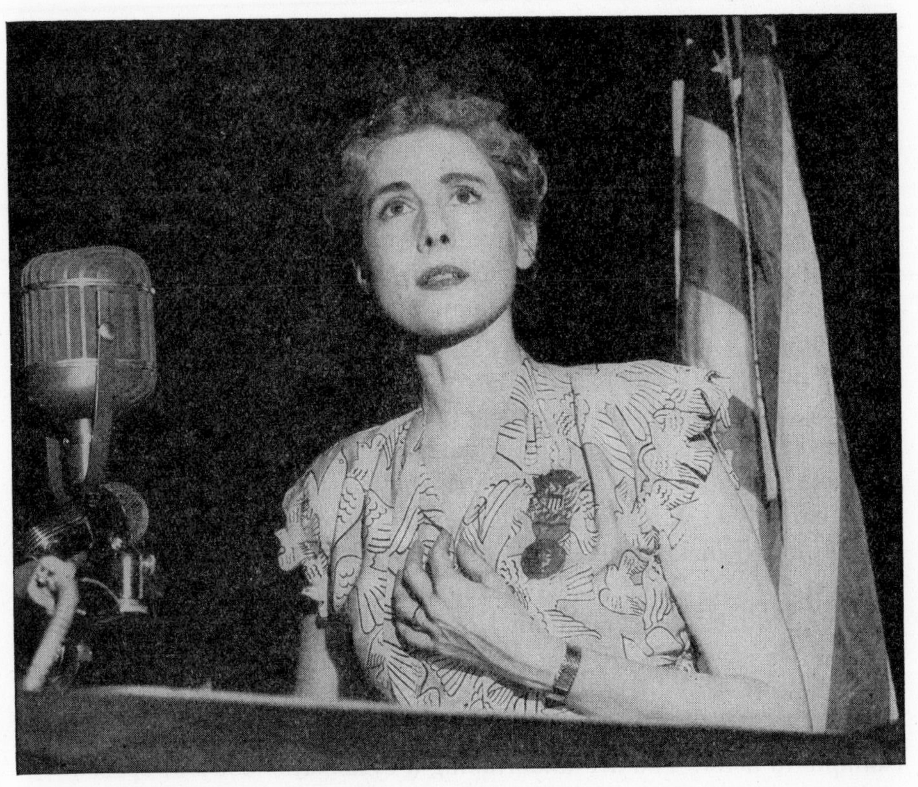

Clare Boothe Luce, playwright and former Congresswoman, addressing a political convention.

CHAPTER 4

First Steps in Managing Yourself

CHAPTER 4

The mine run of speakers that you hear from day to day have never learned to manage themselves in public. Many, of course, simply do not know that public speaking involves a technique. They believe that "anybody can talk," and that's that. Others have what Emerson tartly described as a selfish enjoyment of their sensations, "and loss of perception of the sufferings of the audience." The many speak in a half-direct manner, really talking to themselves and not to the listeners. They do not open their mouths wide enough to allow clear-cut speech. They do not use energy enough to lift their voices above the hum line of noise. Their hands and feet are out of control. They are not effective speakers. As Oliver Wendell Holmes' Autocrat of the Breakfast-Table observed roguishly, "Self-made men?—Well, yes. . . . It is a great deal better to be made in that way than not to be made at all."

Such speakers for you are not a pattern to imitate, but are an example to deter. You are undertaking a systematic study of speech-making, which includes mastering its technique. You are not to be a vaunted self-made speaker, but are to be trained in technique and discipline. From the first day of that training you face a responsibility you cannot ignore, that of managing yourself effectively in public. In this chapter we shall see how to meet this responsibility.

Stage fright

The first besetting problem is stage fright. "How can I overcome stage fright?" is perhaps the most frequently asked question about public speaking. Surprising numbers of men and women, even in middle life, approach speech instructors wanting to learn the formula by which public speakers overcome stage fright. As with all the problems of human life, there is no formula. It must be done through understanding and intelligent effort.

EXTENT OF STAGE FRIGHT

First, you ought to know that stage fright is almost universal among public performers: singers and actors as well as speakers. Some experience it in severe form and few ever escape it in its milder forms, no matter how long they appear in public. Lily Pons, after twenty-five years of concert singing, "feels faintly seasick all day long before a concert or opera performance." That grand old prima donna Madame Schumann-Heink, after nearly fifty years before the public, frankly said, "I grow nervous, . . . I become sick, almost; I want to go home." The actress Eva Le Gallienne, after she had just rounded out her one thousandth repertory performance, was asked by an interviewer if she experienced stage fright. She answered, "Yes. And it gets worse every year." Abraham Lincoln suffered from stage fright throughout his life. When he first arose to speak, he "froze in his tracks," and "he had a far away prophetic look in his eyes." When he went to Washington as a member of Congress, he wrote home that during his speeches in Congress, "I was about as badly scared, and no worse, as I am when I speak in court." Even Cicero, more than two thousand years ago, struggled with stage fright and left us a record of his feelings (he attributes the words to Crassus but is describing his own feelings): "I turn pale at the outset of a speech, and quake in every limb and in all my soul."

THE CAUSE AND NATURE OF STAGE FRIGHT

Why do people have stage fright? Eisenson explains it as follows: "When an individual's pattern of responses are *inadequate to meet a situation,*" he gets stage fright. "Stage fright is a manifestation of an emotion—probably that of *fear—arising out of difficulty in coping with a speech situation.*" [1] There is the core: Stage fright comes from feeling "inadequate to meet a situation." One of the paradoxes of human nature is that most of us *want* an audience, yet *fear* it. We possess a deep craving to be noticed by others, and are beset by a fear—sometimes a terrible fear—of being neglected or ignored. But when we get attention (as in giving a speech), or know we are going to get it, we become afraid. If we are inexperienced, we are afraid to

[1] Jon Eisenson, *The Psychology of Speech* (New York: Macmillan Company, 1938), p. 264. Eisenson is elaborating the viewpoint of Charles W. Lomas as set forth in "The Psychology of Stage Fright," *Quarterly Journal of Speech*, February, 1937, pp. 35-44.

stand alone against the audience, afraid of forgetting, afraid of being made a spectacle, afraid of failure. Even if we are speakers of experience we are afraid of not doing our best, of having it said of us, "He is slipping; he used to do better." In both cases the fear arises from our feeling "inadequate to meet a situation."

Stage fright is not merely a mental state. It is also positively physical, for now enter the mysterious endocrine glands, especially the adrenal glands and possibly also the thyroid. When the impulse is sent to these glands, at once adrenalin (and possibly also thyroxin) is shot into the blood stream. At the same moment a trigger is pulled that dumps glycogen (a special form of sugar) from the liver into the blood stream. When these powerful secretions hit your heart, it starts to thump. When they hit the respiratory center in the brain, you start to gasp. When they hit the blood vessels going to the brain, they contract and you feel woozy. These are the obvious effects. Less obvious effects are even more profound. Blood is drawn away from the internal organs and transferred to outer muscles—arms, legs, etc. —and as a result the digestive process is slowed down or stopped altogether. (Ergo, don't eat too much just before you give a speech!) The blood clots more easily. Muscles become tense all through the body, and your tense throat muscles tend to produce a harsh and constricted voice. Salivary glands stop secreting, the mouth becomes dry, and you feel thick-tongued. In contrast, the sweat glands increase secretion, until beads of perspiration stand on your forehead and skin is moist. Breathing, of course, is difficult, for the breath stream is short and jerky. All of this takes place in the body of one who is afflicted by stage fright in its extreme form. In milder forms, the body undergoes a lesser amount of the same changes, and we feel "faintly seasick," have faint disagreeable sensations, or are simply keyed up and tense.

THE PROBLEM RESTATED

However uncomfortable stage fright may be, remember that it is not unusual. Seasoned speakers are tense before they take the platform. Many of the best are like Henry W. Grady who found that "every nerve in my body was strung tight as a fiddle-string." They tremble, and their breathing is irregular. But seasoned speakers have learned how to control and use stage fright.

Your problem is not to overcome stage fright, but to reduce it, get it under control, and use it. For stage fright if properly controlled helps a speaker instead of hinders. What Amelita Galli-Curci said of singers is just as true of speakers: "The person who does not get the least bit nervous at the prospect of stepping on a stage will never move an audience to wild ecstasy." Indeed, Cicero had discovered this twenty centuries ago: "For the better the speaker, the more profoundly is he frightened of the difficulty of speaking, and of the doubtful fate of a speech, and of the anticipations of an audience." Cicero did not know *why* this was true, but modern psychologists have learned the reason. We have already given the explanation in the section just above on the cause and nature of stage fright, namely that stage fright is accompanied by chemical changes in the blood—the most important being the excessive secretion of adrenalin (and possibly of thyroxin). *But psychologists have further discovered that adrenalin is also secreted by vigorous bodily action, even in the absence of stage fright or other emotion. Finally, they have discovered that the physiological changes produced in the body by such means, if they are controlled and directed, "increase our adequacy" of performance.* In others words, a reasonable amount of stage fright, if controlled and directed, makes you a better speaker.

Restated, then, the problem is not how to overcome stage fright, but how to reduce it, control it, and give better speeches because of it.

CONTROLLING STAGE FRIGHT

There is no formula for controlling stage fright, but there are tested procedures, especially the following four:

1. *Get an interesting subject.* Ask yourself, first of all, whether you are really afraid of your audience or whether down at the bottom you are mostly afraid of your *subject.* Many students are mostly afraid of their subject, and for a good reason. They don't *know* much about it. They don't *care* much about it. But a speech is coming up, and they've *got* to have a subject, so they picked this one—a little desperately perhaps—and are going through the motions with it. Is it a wonder they have stage fright?

The first step in controlling stage fright, therefore, is to get an interesting subject. You have read about this already (pages 32-34). Possibly you have finished making that Speech-Subject Inventory (page 13), and you have a list of subjects that other class members say they would like to hear. If so, you ought to have on hand half a dozen really good subjects. Meanwhile, stay off dry and dusty subjects, and avoid talking about something simply because "it might be a good subject." Instead, get a subject that really interests you, one that fires you up when you think of it. Ask yourself: What do I mostly think about when I am not working? (There you have a *good* subject.) Or ask: Which course in college do I like most of all, and why? Which do I like least, and why? (Here are two more good subjects.)

2. *Be well prepared.* Charles W. Lomas, after some ten years of investigating causes and case histories of stage fright, stated the case in a nutshell:

"Many of these cases of severe stage fright are simply the result of inadequate preparation, sometimes without the student himself being aware of it. He may, for example, have simply memorized something that he has not made his own. The slightest distraction may destroy his set of cues, and he has not sufficient knowledge of the material to reconstruct them. Or he may have crammed his preparation into the period immediately preceding the speech class, or he may have tired himself by late hours in preparation the night before. To the student it will look as though sufficient time had been spent to insure mastery of the speech situation. But the same amount of time spread over several days would give him a far better grasp of the material and more assurance before the audience." [2]

The second step in controlling stage fright is to be well prepared. If you want to review the ways and means of thorough preparation, turn again to pages 32-53.

3. *Use physical action.* The person who has stage fright is physically tense all over. This tension is not merely the effect of fear; it is also in part the cause of fear. One is not simply tense because he is afraid; but in part he is afraid because he is tense. He is caught in a vicious circle: Because he is afraid he becomes tense, and because he becomes tense he becomes still more afraid. At some point he must break this vicious circle.

To prescribe a cure is easy. Simply relax. Use only those muscles needed to keep the body poised and erect, and relax all others. Free the tension in the arms, in the hands, and, above all, in the face. In short, get the tonus of the body back to normal, and stage fright will be reduced.

[2] Charles W. Lomas, "Stage Fright," *Quarterly Journal of Speech*, December, 1944, p. 483.

This, of course, cannot be done by merely commanding the body to relax. You need to start at the other end, and *use* those tense muscles. Put them in action, and the action will reduce the tension. Here are suggestions:

BEFORE YOU SPEAK

1. During those minutes of tension before you speak, sit upright and start breathing *deeply* and *regularly*. One of the bodily changes that accompanies stage fright is irregular breathing. Watch particularly, therefore, that your breathing is not only deep, but is regular.

2. Relax your hands. (Aren't they clinched, or your fingers fidgeting?) Press the fingertips of one hand against those of the other until the fingers when opened feel easy and relaxed.

3. Relax the muscles of your face and jaw and throat. Let your jaw "flop like an idiot's" said Woolbert. Lean the head forward as if you were almost asleep and let every muscle in the face sag. Finally, *yawn* (even in public you can hide a yawn behind a hand or a handkerchief!) A yawn is the best of all exercises for relaxing the whole region of the face and throat.

4. With the yawn still lingering and the face relaxed, think again about your breathing. Is it regular? And deep?

WHILE YOU SPEAK

5. When you stand up before the audience, *get set to speak* first of all. This "getting set" needs to be rehearsed beforehand, using the following procedure:

   a. Set both feet firmly on the floor, so they will not be tempted to shift or wander.
   b. Stand up to your *full* height, with no sagging in your chest, and no drooping of the hip or knee.
   c. Draw in a deep breath. (You need power to fill that room!)
   d. Open your mouth *wide* to give your voice a decent chance of getting out. The very sound of your voice coming out full and strong will go a long way toward getting you over the hump.

6. During the speech use communicative action. Use gestures that show listeners what you are talking about. Use gestures that explain your idea. Nod your head to emphasize a point. Lift the eyebrows when you ask a question. Throw the weight of your whole body behind emphatic words. Action like this will divert the stresses and tensions of your body to their proper use. (But action will not at first come spontaneously. You must rehearse it.)

4. *Don't think of yourself, but of your subject and audience.* Perhaps the majority of frustrated people in the world are victims of the inability to forget themselves. Among these is the speaker who thinks of himself too much, for he manufactures stage fright. Putting

your mind on "How am I getting on?" tends to make you self-conscious and muscle bound.

A centipede was happy quite
Until a frog in fun
Said, "Pray, which leg comes after which?"
This raised her mind to such a pitch,
She lay distracted in a ditch,
Considering how to run.

Develop the eager-to-share attitude, and your stage fright tends to disappear. Choose a speech subject that fills you with enthusiasm and you forget your worries in the enthusiasm of the subject. Before you speak, say to yourself, "I want the listeners to see this just as I see it. I want them to know it, to understand it, to appreciate it. I must give the speech so the listeners will be benefited."

During much of our lives we think of ourselves, but if we would speak effectively me must acquire what Ralph Dennis called "a vivid sense of the brotherhood of man, of the universality of human experience." We must lose ourselves in the welfare of those to whom we talk. Can they hear us? Can they understand us? Have we made the point clear? Are we helping them appreciate something they had not appreciated before? Are you throwing a little light on problems that have puzzled them? Are we inspiring them to look above the humdrum of daily life?

He speaks well who gives something of *himself* to the audience. He speaks not well who thinks too much *about* himself—and stage fright will not be his only affliction.

IF YOU FORGET WHILE SPEAKING

But if you do forget in spite of everything, what then? It is a fearful point.

First, be assured that if you have prepared thoroughly, and have followed the other steps set forth in this chapter, you are not likely to forget more than momentarily if at all. Indeed, even if your mind goes blank for a time and the room grows dark, you are likely to keep on talking—if you have prepared thoroughly and rehearsed the speech while standing on your feet.[3]

[3] We may properly draw a parallel between the effect on beginners of speech rehearsals and the effect on green soldiers of military drill. The effect of military drill is to fix patterns of behavior so firmly that soldiers when first under fire will follow them, even when momentarily unnerved by shock or surprise. Here is a typical testimony from a soldier

More than one beginner has had the room grow dim and his conscious mind go blank, only to regain full mental possession and find his voice going right on with the speech! But this does not happen to people who have not thoroughly prepared.

Suppose that in spite of careful preparation you forget anyhow. What then? Be assured that all is not lost, even then. There are the ways and means such as the following:

Don't go into a panic, but take a deep breath and try to remember the next point. A deep breath will tend to keep you from tightening up. Perhaps a step forward will help put your mind on the track. (But don't back away from the audience. They won't harm you, and you really are not afraid of them!) After three or four seconds if a deep breath, or a step forward, does not help, then move on to the next method, as follows:

Summarize aloud what you have already said. By summarizing you will get started down the track again, and this tends to lead you into the next idea. Or if it does not lead you into the next idea, it may lead you to some idea that follows. If so, go right ahead. You are on the track again, and if it is not exactly where you got off the track, don't worry about it. If summarizing out loud does not work, then turn to the third method, as follows:

Tell your listeners frankly that you cannot remember the next point. When you forget, everybody in the audience knows it anyway. Your freezing up is as visible as a fire wagon. Be sensible, then, and talk about it frankly. How much better it is to hear a student say, "Well, friends, for the life of me I can't remember what I was going to say next, but you know how rough public speaking is on beginners. I had been saying [here he goes back for another summary]." In other words, if you have forgot you might as well be gracious about it and bring the sympathy of the audience over to your side. By the time they chuckle and you smile back, you will feel far more comfortable than you were a few moments ago. You will be able to move about. You will have felt the warm sympathy of those people out front, who won't be monsters any longer but kind, friendly people who want to be nice

---

under fire for the first time. "I was in the midst of giving an order to a platoon some fifty yards away when a sudden shellburst threw me into a mental blackout. As my mind cleared slowly—it was a moment later but it seemed hours—I heard a voice giving my order. It was a strong voice without a tremor. I was puzzled for a moment. Who was giving my order to my platoon? Then I recognized the voice. It was *my* voice. While my mind was blacked out, my voice had kept on with the order. It was an order that I had given in drill a hundred times."

to you. By that time, you can *say something,* just as though you would speak if you met a friend on the street. After that, you can *say something about your subject.* It may not be what you had planned to say, but no matter what it is, you can follow it through like a conversation. Maybe you will get back onto your planned speech. Maybe not. But you will have the thrill of discovering that the people out front are not enemies, but are really friendly; and that if you treat them as friends they will listen earnestly, laugh with you, and applaud you. Under that uplift, you will not need to worry about forgetting.

The mental attitude for good speaking

Stage fright was discussed first because it is often a barrier in the student's mind. Actually, stage fright is part of a larger and more important problem of developing the mental attitude for good speaking. Behind much of the beginner's excessive stage fright, behind much of the mumbling and fumbling and fidgeting that one hears from self-made speakers, lies a poor mental attitude. " 'Tis hard for an empty bag to stand upright," observed Benjamin Franklin.

A SENSE OF COMMUNICATION

First and foremost, the effective speaker really loses himself in the effort to make listeners see and feel and understand. We call this the sense of communication. In some respects it is very much the same in public speaking as in conversation. In fact, the sense of communication in public speaking is simply an outgrowth of the sense of communication in conversation. A great deal has been said by some writers of the differences between public speaking and private conversation. In truth, the differences are largely superficial and the likenesses are fundamental. How is public speaking different from personal conversation anyhow? Where is the dividing line between the two? How sharp is the dividing line? Or is there a dividing line at all?

James A. Winans in his book *Public Speaking* raises the issue in a vivid way. He imagines a man who has been in a great battle or is fired with a great enthusiasm meeting a friend on the street and pausing to talk. Others gather; he lifts his voice that all may hear. Still others gather, and they wish to see as well as hear him, so he mounts a cart and goes on with his talk. Obviously, the man started with a conversation and ended with a public speech. Where, asks Winans, did the conversation become a public speech? What was the dividing line?

We might, of course, pick a given point and say that here conversation becomes public speaking. We could say that it becomes public speaking when the number of listeners reaches ten, or when it reaches fifty, or when the speaker stands on a cart or platform. But obviously these are arbitrary points, representing no fundamental distinction.

The fact is that conversation *gradually* becomes public speaking, and that public speaking is simply *enlarged* conversation. Therefore, get rid of the idea that you are "making a speech." You are not declaiming. You are not unloading an idea. You are not talking to the wall or ceiling or simply into the air. You are not even talking at the audience. You are talking to the people, and there must be no dreamy look in your face or far-away tone in your voice. You are talking *with* the people, and you must learn to observe their responses while you talk. Plainly they will say to you, "I agree, go ahead," or "I don't quite understand that; make it clearer," or "I am bored and I wish you would stop."

Enlarged conversation, however, presents certain definite problems. First, not all people are good conversationalists. Some are boring in private speech, and on the platform their speaking manner amounts to mass boredom. These present a delicate problem in class, for when the instructor comments on their tiresome tones they are likely to reply honestly and innocently, "But that's the way I naturally talk." Shall the instructor tactfully avoid the issue? Or shall he be brutally honest and say, "That's exactly the trouble. In private conversation you bore two or three. In public speech you bore thirty." Furthermore, other people speak passably well in private, but public enlargement brings out cracks and flaws. All in all, then, we should look at some of the attributes of good enlarged conversation.

EARNESTNESS

Some speakers talk as though they were spraying water over a garden with a hose. Their words are sprayed into the air, and fall on the audience like drops of water. Word-spraying is not communicative speaking.

The communicative speaker is genuinely earnest. He throws aside all pretense, all pomp and pose, and he plunges into his subject with a deep personal sincerity. Says James A. Winans, "An audience will forgive a speaker almost any lack, if he is manifestly earnest. . . . Earnestness moves our emotions, thaws our indifference, and gives us the faith which a leader must create."

It is not easy for a speaker to be earnest the first time he stands before an audience. He has not had enough experience with this sort of thing. He stands up alone, like a man before a firing squad, and the eyes of the audience gleam at him like shining gun-barrels. He wishes he were home, or in a foxhole, or anywhere else than standing here alone and unprotected from the eyes that never cease to be focussed on him. Under such circumstances, he is likely to do one of two wrong things: Either he shrinks within himself to escape those eyes and talks in a small voice that cannot be sufficiently heard, or he fights back and bellows defiantly in loud tones so as to prove he is unafraid.

Neither of these is communicative speaking; and both come from the wrong mental attitude. Uppermost in the speaker's mind—even in the first speech he ever makes—should be this concept: "I am here to tell this audience about this subject, and I want to do it in the same way I would in a very important private conversation. There are many more people, I know, than in private conversation. I must magnify and intensify my whole tone and manner. I must reach all of them, even in the back row. I must make them see this subject and feel about it as I do. To do this I must talk to them and with them. Above all, I must be earnest."

DIRECTNESS

Directness might be termed looking-the-audience-in-the-*mind*.

Did you ever observe people in earnest conversation, really observe them closely? They do not gaze out the window or at the floor or at the ceiling. They look at one another, directly in the eye. Now this eye-directness is an outward sign of an inward state of mind. Mentally these people are aware that two minds are engaged with an idea, and they want to know what progress the other is making. The person talking looks at the listener to see whether he is giving attention, whether he understands, or agrees, or disagrees. The listener looks at the speaker in order to follow him better, to learn from his face and bodily expression what his voice alone will not tell him, to take measure of him and find his deeper meanings. Thus in conversation the speaker and listener are both constantly observing the other's responses. In a sense they are continually *looking into each other's minds.*

In public speaking you have essentially the same relation. It really does not matter how large the audience, or how small. The speaker's posture, action, and manner may change to fit the size of the audience or the formality of the occasion. But the speaker and the members of the audience still look one another in the mind. In your first speeches, you may not be aware of the audience except as a mass out front that frightens you. But the audience is looking at you, looking you right in the mind and taking your measure. Its members know whether you are managing your ideas, are managing yourself, or have let yourself get out of control. Now and then, even in your first speeches, you may see the audience for a moment as group of individual people —when they laugh or respond in some manner so obvious that you cannot miss it. When that moment comes seize on it and hold it. Cultivate the feeling of looking your listeners in the mind. Later you will learn to know whether they are looking at you, or are shifting about restlessly. You will know whether their faces are alive with interest, or are dull from indifference. You can see the flash that tells whether one of your points strikes home, or can see from their immobile faces whether you have missed the mark. We hate to confess it, but you can learn almost as much from reading the minds of your listeners as from reading this textbook (but not, probably, until you have read the textbook).

PHYSICAL VITALITY

Enlarged conversation demands also what seems to the beginning speaker like an unbelievable amount of physical vitality, so much that at first they simply do not believe it. Talking to one or two persons close by requires relatively little energy. Listless conversation requires almost no energy. But when you speak to twenty people in a classroom, or a hundred in an auditorium, it requires five, ten, fifty, or a hundred times the energy of good private conversation in order for the speaker's voice to sound as loud, earnest, and direct as in good private conversation.[4]

[4] The following pertinent data is taken from Judson and Weaver, *Voice Science* (New York: Appleton-Century-Crofts, Inc., 1942), pp. 285-288:

1. Speech power:

of soft whisper	0.001	microwatts
of soft speech	0.1	microwatts
of average speech	15.0	microwatts
of loud speech	1000.0	microwatts

(*Continued on following page.*)

The speaker who talks earnestly to everyone in the audience, therefore, is a fountain of vital force. Uninhibitedly he communicates with head, body, and arms. He opens his mouth wider than he ever would dream of doing in private conversation, and he makes sure that even those farthest away can hear him easily. This is the compulsion necessitated by "enlarged" conversation.

PERSONALIZED SPEAKING AND THE RHYTHM OF TALK

Queen Victoria said of her two prime ministers that Gladstone addressed her as a public meeting, whereas Disraeli talked to her as a woman. She preferred Disraeli, because even a queen is a woman. Excepting rare instances, public speaking, like private conversation, is personalized. The good speaker, like a good conversationalist, sprinkles his speech with personal pronouns like "we," and "you," and "I." He uses the language of talk, the everyday words used by well-bred people in conversation. He avoids stilted words and forms. He does not say, "A manifestation of good speaking is the ability to approach a point without deviating." Rather he puts it in the language of genuine talk: "A good speaker comes directly to the point."

He uses also the rhythms of genuine talk, especially the contractions that are the very stuff of speech rhythm. Read aloud the sentences below and compare the stilted rhythm with the genuine speech rhythm:

STILTED RHYTHM	SPEECH RHYTHM
It is over there	*It's* over there
I *do not* think so	I *don't* think so
He *is not* here	*He's* not here, (or) He *isn't* here
I *have not* found it	*I've* not found it, (or) I *haven't* found it

In formal writing we commonly use the form shown in the left column (though not always.) But we don't talk that way except in unusual circumstances. If we try to talk that way the rhythm is stilted and we sound like a schoolboy reciting. In talk we use contractions, "*it's*" and "*don't*" rather than "*it is*" and "*do not.*" This is a basis of speech rhythm.

Thus loud speech requires 66 times the power of average speech, 10,000 times the power of soft speech, and 1,000,000 times the power of soft whisper.

2. Sound intensity and distance: The intensity of sound varies inversely as the square of the distance from the source. A speaker, let us assume, produces a sound of given intensity at a certain distance. At twice the distance this sound has one-fourth the original intensity, and at three times the distance it has only one-ninth the original intensity. (See below, p. 400, for further discussion of this.)

This is one reason (though not the only one) why most people sound artificial when they try to read. They don't use contractions, but use the formal written form, which in speech produces stilted rhythm. To compare the two, read aloud the following passage without using contractions:

> I know it is said that the rule of the majority is the rule of the stupid. I do not believe it.

Now read it again, using the contractions that permit speech rhythm:

> I know it's said that the rule of the majority is the rule of the stupid. I don't believe it.

Now read it still again, this time not only using contractions but also giving full emphasis to the important words and unstressing less important ones:

> I know it's *said* / thatth' *rule* uvth' *majority* / izth' rule uvth' *stupid* / I *don't believe* it /

Read in this way, it does not sound like a recitation but like real talk.

A SENSE OF HUMOR

At the risk of being misunderstood, we list a sense of humor as being important to a speaker's mental attitude.

First, let us see what is meant by sense of humor. The term humor is frequently used to mean the same thing as *fun.* Sometimes it is used synonymously with *wit.* As used here, however, it is to be distinguished from both fun and wit. Fun and wit have their proper places in public speaking, but neither can take the place of humor.

The *Standard Dictionary* defines *humor* as "distinguished from wit by greater sympathy, geniality and pleasantry, and less of intellectual subtlety and keen cold analysis." It defines *fun* as "that ruder or more boisterous quality . . . that excites hilarity or glee." Thus *fun* is marked by its ability to excite boisterous laughter; *wit* is characterized by intellectual subtlety and is frequently sharp and biting; *humor* is gentle and understanding, sympathetic, genial, and pleasant. But these definitions do not give a wholly accurate description of humor. To see how humor derives its peculiar nature let us look beneath the surface. On what is it based?

Real humor springs from deep insight, an insight that means more than knowledge, for it implies understanding and wisdom. Humor is not attained except by an objective view that permits one to see details in their true perspective.

Fanatics are lacking in a sense of humor because they lack perspective. Hence they become not merely serious, but solemn. They are true zealots, often unable to laugh or even smile, and, significantly, unable to see their subject in the light of fairness.

The essence of humor is the ability to see things as they are. When things are seen as they are and in their true relation to other things, hysterical tension is relieved, and we are able to appreciate how the subject stands in the great scheme of things.

Someone has listed the ten most common subjects of jokes. The list includes the most serious things in life. Death itself stands near the top. Marriage, divorce, and like subjects follow closely. Think of the jokes you have heard about these serious things, and you will realize the startling fact that we make our jokes about things that are certainly not in themselves funny. Why? We learn to see them in perspective, and they lose, at least momentarily, their solemn nature. After all, seen in proper perspective, they are of limited importance. Life is important, but countless people have thrown it away for something that they have considered more important. Death is serious enough, in all conscience, but countless people have met it with a smile.

One whose sense of humor is in good repair has a truer and saner view of his world. The speaker who has a sense of humor, who can be amused at his own stage fright, who can see the sunlight of laughter in human problems as well as the serious side, is one to whom an audience is instinctively drawn. It is his guarantee of mental balance. In him the people recognize a sane leader and in him they put more trust.

A SENSE OF LEADERSHIP AND SELF-RESPECT

In a true sense the speaker is a *leader*. He cannot escape the implications of leadership. What do they imply?

To gain the respect of others, a leader must respect himself. You wish to be believed? Then believe in yourself. But you may say: I *don't* believe in myself; I have doubts and fears about the whole business! Of course; and so does every speaker and every leader in those long years of growth; only they learned with Emerson that "Do the thing you fear and the death of fear is certain." Within reasonable limits self-respect can be cultivated, if you cultivate the foundations on which to base it. How?

First, *prepare thoroughly*. If you have not really prepared the speech, you do not deserve self-respect, and down in your own heart you know it. If you have not earned the right to speak, you have hardly earned the right to self-respect. If you have waited until the night before, and are then wondering frantically what to do, it is time to take an honest inventory of yourself. Self-respect must be earned.

Second, *get enthusiastic about your subject*. Enthusiasm is not a rare quality, but it is a precious one, without which speaking—and life itself—would lose much of its interest and meaning. We can almost say that without it speaking is futile. Certainly it cannot rise above the level of routine; and routine speaking is seldom heard with pleasure, or looked forward to with expectancy. A Midwestern Town Hall director complained to Harold Peat of the scarcity of dynamic and convincing speakers. "I can't understand," he protested, "why men who know their subjects thoroughly, and their trade equally well, leave an audience cold and unconcerned. They believe what they are saying, but they can't make anyone else believe it." The answer is, that though they believe in their subjects in a sort of way, they don't burn to make the audience believe. They lack a sense of leadership and its essential element, enthusiasm. Said Emerson, "Nothing great was ever achieved without enthusiasm." Without it, no speech is effective.

Third, *act as if you had complete self-respect and confidence*. Emotions and mental attitudes can be induced by deliberately assuming the physical positions and by going through the actions that characterizes such emotions and attitudes. Double up your fists, grit your teeth, walk up and down, frown—all the while thinking of something that would naturally lead to anger—and you can work yourself up into a fair state of anger. Or deliberately turn up the corners of your mouth and smile, relax the muscles, and think of something cheerful, and you can go a long way toward getting rid of a grouch. In the same way, stand straight, chest up and eyes to the front, and think how important it is that people believe you, and you will tend to acquire that self-respect and confidence without which there is no good speaking.

Fourth, *be careful not to overdo self-respect!* Carried too far, it can become egotism or conceit. "For I say, through the grace given unto me, to every man that is among you, not to think of himself more highly than he ought to think; but to think soberly." The speaker must somehow achieve a full respect, tempered with proper modesty. He must not, on the one hand, go about with a metaphorical "please kick me" sign pinned to his coattail, or act, on the other hand, as if he had, with some assistance from God created the universe!

Physical appearance and activity

A speaker is like a fish in a glass bowl. The things we ordinary mortals do consciously and unconsciously are magnified the moment we step on the platform. We cannot escape the staring eyes. Even our smallest movement in under scrutiny by eyes—eyes that never let us go. We cannot resolve to "act natural," for there is no such thing as "acting natural," and furthermore we are not in a "natural" situation. To "act natural" would be to act nervous, awkward, and ill at ease. How do we go about the business of behaving under the spotlight of eyes?

A significant illustration was given by Margaret Lee Runbeck in telling about her growing terror as her turn came to speak at her high-school graduation. She confessed her stage fright to the commencement speaker seated at her side. "I'm scared too," he said. "I've got a speech written down, but I don't think it's much good, and besides. . . ."

"But *you* don't have to be afraid," she protested.

"Neither do you," he replied. "I'll tell you a secret; then you'll never need be frightened again. Everyone on earth is shy, self-conscious, and unsure of himself. Everybody is timid about meeting strangers. So if you will just spend the first minute you are in the presence of a stranger trying to help *him* feel comfortable, you will never suffer from self-consciousness." The speaker was a young man in his early thirties, and the program told her who he was: "Commencement Address by the Honorable Franklin D. Roosevelt, Assistant Secretary of the Navy."

This is the opening wedge: Think of helping the audience, and not of your own self-consciousness. Next, remember that good physical action is never conspicuous, never calls attention to itself, never distracts attention from the thought. Indeed the listeners are seldom aware that the speaker is using action, because words *and* action, combined, stand for the thought. Many a listener has said of an effective speaker, "He never gestures," when in fact the speaker gestures constantly. What the listener meant was, "His gestures never call attention to themselves." This is the highest art. It is art that conceals art.

DRESS AND PERSONAL APPEARANCE

Dress *carefully,* but not conspicuously, and let your clothes be in harmony with the occasion. Generally speaking, a man ought to wear a coat and necktie, and a woman should be correspondingly correct. Overdone dress is as bad as underdone. Flashy dress calls attention to itself, and therefore distracts attention from the speech.

Likewise, personal appearance ought to be above criticism. Uncombed hair and general personal slovenliness simply affronts an audience and handicaps a speaker. It is true that there have been speakers of great power who manifested little care about personal appearance, but it is also true that their power did not spring from their carelessness. Some speakers—a very few—are effective in spite of unfortunate personal appearance. They could have been more effective had their appearance been less distracting.

If this seems to be the elaboration of the obvious, the answer is that it is not obvious to all speakers including students. Unkempt personal appearance, rolled-up sleeves, and slacks are handicaps that a student in a short speech cannot expect to overcome.

GETTING TO THE PLATFORM

It is a long walk from your seat to the platform, and the eyes of everyone in the audience are on you. You are talking all the way, not in words but with action. Do not slink, or shuffle, or tiptoe, or walk like Shakespeare's schoolboy ". . . creeping like snail, Unwillingly to school." Do not stride belligerently, or walk with a show of pomposity. Simply walk as though you were alert and interested, going forward to meet a friend.

When you get to the platform, do not stop over at one side. Go to the center. If there is a speaker's table or stand, get behind it or at one side of it, but do not hover around the corner as though you could not make up your mind.

When you are in position there comes a critical moment. The temptation is to start speaking before you are mentally or physically set. Don't do it! Pause a moment and get set. Make sure of your posture. Take a deep breath, or two of them, until your breathing is easy. Then look at your audience as though you would look at friends.

Smile if you can. (You would smile if you met them off the platform, you know.) Wait a few moments until they are all looking at you, ready to hear your first words. Then begin your speech, *and be sure that your first words reach even those in the last row.*

POSTURE

There is no single posture that is best for everyone, although there are some postures that are definitely bad for everyone. From the standpoint of the audience, a good posture should not call attention to itself. From the standpoint of the speaker, a good posture should allow freedom of bodily movement, ease of breathing, and a projection of voice to fill the room.

For developing a good speaking posture suppose we start with a good military posture. Understand that a military posture is *not* a good speaking posture. It is too stiff and formal. But we can modify a good military posture into a good speaking posture:

1. Heels together on the same line (or, for speaking, heels fairly close together).
2. Feet turned out and forming an angle of about 45 degrees.
3. Knees straight without stiffness.
4. Hips level and drawn back slightly; body erect and resting equally on hips; chest lifted; shoulders square but not lifted.
5. Arms and hands hanging naturally at the sides.
6. Head erect, chin drawn in so that the axis of the head and neck is vertical, eyes to the front and not on the ceiling or floor.
7. Weight of the body sustained partly on the balls of the feet, heels resting on the floor.
8. The entire posture to appear natural and graceful, to be without rigidness or exaggeration, and to be one from which action is possible without first relaxing muscles that have been constrained in an effort to maintain the posture.

From this fairly rigid military posture, you can develop a speaking posture that fits your individual personality and mode of speaking. Probably the one essential of a good posture is to *"stand tall." To stand tall, reach up with the top of your head. Reach up with your spinal column. Reach up with your chest and abdomen.* And with your legs reach *down* to the floor. Rehearse this posture day after day. Practice even how to *sit tall* and to *walk tall.* Make this a part of your speech behavior, and you will be saved from the afflictions of the sagging chest, drooping hip, and bent knee.

Three universally bad postures should be especially avoided:

The Fence-Straddle Posture. In the fence-straddle posture the feet are spread wide apart, and the speaker resembles an inverted Y. The weight is distributed equally and constantly on both feet. In fact, the speaker cannot change posture or shift weight without a tremendous visible effort. He is battened down for the duration of the speech. This posture is bad because it looks grotesque. It is bad because it prevents easy bodily movement.

The One-Legged Sag. In this posture the speaker stands on one foot and lets the other foot go for a free ride. At its extreme, one whole side of the body sags. One shoulder sags, one hip sags, one knee sags. Usually the neglected foot is restless, and it wanders, seeking a comfortable place of rest and never finding it. This posture is bad because it is inert. Primarily, only one side of the body is used. Breathing is perforce shallow, the voice tends to be weak and dull. The eyes of listeners tend to look at the conspicuous knee and follow the wandering foot instead of following the speech.

The Rigor Mortis Posture. In the rigor mortis posture, the body is tense and rigid. The speaker fixes himself into what might have been a good posture, but freezes it and is incapable of moving. It is bad because it permits no bodily action. It is bad because it tends to tire the audience by making them also tense. A good posture must allow freedom of movement.

USING THE BODY TO COMMUNICATE THOUGHT

The earnest speaker uses his body all over. Of the two hundred muscles in the body he uses them all. Some will say, "Gestures are not natural to me." What do they mean by "natural"? It is "natural" for people to think of themselves first and last. It is "natural" to be selfish and ill-mannered. In a "natural" state, people are without education, government, hospitals, or churches. All education, indeed civilization itself, is a long, hard process of substituting higher values for the primitive "natural" state of man.

In conversation, normal people are not inert. They are animated. They use sight waves as well as sound waves to tell others what they think and how they feel. They talk with their bodies as well as their hands.

On the platform we do not feel "natural." We are the center of all eyes. We cannot escape. Therefore, we "naturally" think of ourselves instead of our speech, and thereby freeze up until it seems "unnatural" to use action. But that is the wrong way out. Gestures talk. Lack of gestures talk. Gestures tell the listeners what you mean and how you feel. They reinforce words. They give them added meaning. Lack of gestures tell the audience that you are inhibited, tense, ill at ease, do not know your way about. *You can't escape talking with your body. You can only decide whether you will talk badly or well.*

Bodily action, of course, is not confined to the hands. We talk also with the eyes, the face, the mouth, the eyebrows. We carry meanings with a shrug of the shoulders, with step forward or backward. In a later chapter (see pages 322-341) we shall discuss action in detail. For the first speeches, rely on your experience in conversation, observe others, and give attention to the ways and means that normal people use in communicating thought by bodily action.

USING A TABLE OR SPEAKER'S STAND

Be careful of the table or speaker's stand. Treat it with respect. The thing is not as harmless as it looks. It can do you damage. The purpose of this article of furniture is to make the platform look less bare and to serve as a convenient resting place for a water pitcher, a vase of flowers, or the speaker's manuscript or notes. Too often the speaker appropriates it as a crutch, or as a pedestal over which he drapes his weary frame. For the beginner, probably it would be better if he had no such dangerous contraption around. He has enough to think about anyhow. Yet sooner or later he must learn to master tables and speaker's stands, or be mastered by them.

It is permissible to stand behind it, and rest one or both hands on it if you feel more at home that way. *But don't put your weight on it!* Don't hook your elbows on its edge, or slump over it. Don't pull it, push it, kick it, or fiddle with it. These mannerisms distract the audience, until tomorrow they are likely not to remember your speech, but only that you wrestled with the table and lost.

GETTING OFF THE PLATFORM

The following are common errors of getting off the platform:

The I-Thank-You Exit. To say "I thank you," at the close of a speech is a habit that is meaningless and hackneyed. What is the speaker thanking the audience for? If the speech is a good one they will want to thank him. If it is not good, they may also want to thank him—for sitting down. In truth, the phrase "I thank you," is a cover-up for the speaker who wants to get off the platform and does not quite know how. It leaves a bad flavor. Don't use it.

The Talk-While-I-Walk Exit. In this exit the speaker beats a retreat as he nears the end of his speech. Of course the surprised audience pays no attention to what he is saying. Their amused interest is centered on his hasty quitting the scene of action. Better stay put until you finish the speech.

The Change-of-Character Exit. This is an exit peculiar to certain types of students, and is not found among mature students or older speakers. It is an exit where the student changes character as he leaves the platform, and by his manner plainly says, "I really didn't mean what I said; I was only giving a speech." Do we need comment further?

How, then, does a speaker best get off the platform when he has finished? Simply pause a moment, as you would in leaving a friend's house; and then, without confusion or any I-thank-you cover up, walk off—without haste or without lagging.

ASSIGNMENTS

ON UNDERSTANDING STAGE FRIGHT

1. Prepare a report on stage fright. For further information consult the footnote references on the subject in this chapter, other speech texts, biographies of speakers or other public performers, or works on psychology. The psychologies probably will not offer a discussion of stage fright per se, but will include it under social stimulation, fears, inhibitions, frustrations, etc. Therefore, consult these topics in the indexes.

2. Give a two-minute talk on muscle tensions during stage fright, and in the speech *use movement* to demonstrate its use in relieving stage fright.

3. Give a four-minute talk, and after finishing it fill out the following chart:

a. I felt the following aspects of stage fright (write 0 if you felt none, 1 if you felt it mildly, 2 if reasonably strong, and 3 if extremely so):
(1). Rapid heart beat ___
(2). Dry mouth ___
(3). Perspiring body or forehead ___
(4). Felt cold or chilly ___
(5). Trembling body ___
(6). Weak knees ___
(7). Muscles tense or partially paralyzed ___
(8). Felt dizzy ___
(9). Felt clumsy ___
(10). Felt I was not doing my best ___
(11). Weak voice ___
(12). Voice sounded distant or unnatural ___
(13). Felt like running away ___
(14). Felt like apologizing ___
(15). Could not think clearly ___

b. I chose the subject for the following reasons:
(1). Suggested by a magazine article ___
(2). My own experience ___
(3). A college bullsession or other discussion ___
(4). Reading ___
(5). One of my courses ___
(6). A student or friend ___
(7). A faculty member ___

c. My quality of preparation was as follows:
(1). Started the speech last night, spent little time on it ___
(2). Started the speech yesterday, and worked hard on it ___
(3). Started it 2 to 4 days ago, but did little work on it ___
(4). Worked hard on it for 2 to 4 days ___
(5). Worked hard on it for over 4 days ___
(6). (Other) ___

d. My speech material came from the following sources:
(1). Personal experience ___
(2). Discussion, conversation, listening ___
(3). Observation ___
(4). Reading ___
(5). Combination of above ___

4. Check the above chart against the suggestions given in this chapter on controlling stage fright, then write out a diagnosis on where you were weak in preparing your last speech and a prescription on what you ought to do in preparing the next one. If necessary, talk with your instructor, but not until *after* you have written your prescription and the diagnosis for the next speech.

TO DEVELOP A SENSE OF PERSONALIZED SPEAKING AND RHYTHM OF TALK

5. Hear a speaker and write a brief report on his earnestness, vitality, directness, and rhythm of talk. Before hearing this speaker, better make a brief outline of the suggestions contained in that part of this chapter. Then you can check the speaker against these items.

6. Listen to a good radio or television speaker or announcer, and evaluate his sense of communication. (Avoid announcers who have acquired the *patternized* radio-announcer tone. This is recognized by a forced enthusiasm which tries not to say, "I know this advertising script is ridiculous, but I've got to read it for a living and make the sponsor believe I think it is wonderful.") Before starting the assignment, make a brief outline of the suggestions contained in this chapter on how to develop an effective mental attitude, and note especially the matter of stilted rhythm compared with genuine speech rhythm.

7. Read aloud the following passage. In preparing to read it, change the stilted-rhythm form into genuine speech rhythm, and mark the changes on your copy. Then rehearse and read it so that it sounds exactly like superior earnest talk:

> "What is democracy? It is not a form government. It is not easy to define. Indeed we might say of it as Lincoln said of Liberty, 'The world has never had a good definition, and the American people, just now, are much in want of one.' But the inner spirit of democracy is respect for human dignity. It is a rule of the majority with protection of the rights of the minority."

8. Prepare a short story and tell it to the class in your own words. Remember that not all short stories are adaptable to telling. Some move too slowly. Others are too complex in detail, or are too subtle in atmosphere for any but a skilled and experienced story teller. The best type for your purpose is a story with a simple plot, a minimum of character analysis, and a maximum of action and of vivid description—like the stories of O'Henry and Kipling.

Since your time is limited and you cannot tell *all* the story, cut unnecessary scenes and even characters. In general this is done easiest by cutting from the earlier part of the story (summarizing it like the magazine summary of a serial), then treating the climax in detail.

The following procedure will help you prepare the story:

a. Read the story through silently to get the atmosphere, setting, characters, plot, etc., using your imagination and entering into the spirit of the story.
b. Familiarize yourself with the plot by writing down the incidents in order, noting how one leads to the next and how all lead to the climax.
c. After looking over this chain of incidents, decide which parts can be omitted without losing the dramatic effect.
d. If you desire, plan to read certain parts of the story directly from the book. But know the danger of this, for most people read poorly, flattening their tones, speeding up the rate of utterance, and losing the meaning

and feeling of the words. Blend your reading and speaking so smoothly that a person with his eyes shut could not tell one from the other.

e. Rehearse the story 5 to 8 times. If that is not enough (and for some it is not enough), then rehearse it still more. Give the class a finished product, not a midpoint rehearsal.

TO DEVELOP AWARENESS OF PHYSICAL APPEARANCE AND ACTION

9. Study the physical appearance, muscular tone, and bodily action of a speaker who is notably ineffective. Select a fellow student, a teacher, a minister —any speaker who is invariably dull.

a. Observe his posture. Is it inert, sagging, or stiff?
b. Observe the over-all muscular tone. Is it listless, inert, or merely awkward?
c. Observe the changes of posture. Are they related to changes of thought, do they distract from what he is saying, or do they seem unrelated to anything he is saying?
d. Observe the specific action of his head, arms, and hands. Are they listless? Are they awkward? Does he merely fidget? Does it make you uncomfortable to look at them?
e. Assess the speaker's mental attitude behind all of this. Does he seem to be also mentally inert? Is he seemingly ill at ease? Does he show a desire to communicate his ideas to others?

10. Attend a moving picture or television play, and report on the amount and type of action used by the actors. To simplify this, do not attempt to study all of the actors, but concentrate on two or three:

a. How were special attitudes carried by posture, and by changes of posture?
b. Study facial expressions. How did they reinforce the actor's words? List some of the special meanings carried by facial expression.
c. What conventional head gestures were especially used? How were they timed with the actor's words?
d. How was action used to hold attention?

Listening to a speech is a more complex process than the short-spurt listening in private conversation. It involves (1) attitude, (2) attention, (3) retention, and (4) evaluation. Here are students listening to a lecture on celestial navigation.

CHAPTER 5

Efficient Listening

CHAPTER 5

In the preceding four chapters we have laid the groundwork for getting the speaker started. Now we want to look at getting the listener started. No matter how often you speak, you listen more than you talk. In this class alone you will listen to fifteen, twenty, or thirty times as many speeches as you give. What does a listener do, if anything, beyond sitting politely and not annoying the speaker? We can give the obvious answer: The listener listens. Indeed unless the audience listens systematically, analytically, and precisely there is not much point in making the speech. The speaker is responsible for producing, processing, and delivering useful material. It is a high responsibility, but that is as far as he can go. For the speech to be profitable the audience must listen intelligently and intently.

You have been listening all your life, but most of it is the short-spurt listening done in private conversation. It is a single-thought, hook-and-eye sort of listening that is easy to handle. Listening to a speech is something else. It takes a longer spread, weaving together hundreds of single-thought, hook-and-eye units into a larger pattern. As every college teacher sadly learns on examination day, many students who can listen reasonably well in private conversation emerge from class lectures with only a mass of half-heard, half-understood, tangled-up matter. In short, there is a great difference between mere hearing and alert listening, and the difference is magnified in listening to a sustained sequence of thought like a speech.[1]

[1] The listening ability of college freshmen is suggested by the research of Ralph G. Nichols. Ten-minute excerpts were taken from full-period lectures given college freshmen in literature, economics, biology, sociology, psychology, and chemistry. These were presented to two hundred freshmen, under controlled room conditions and with precautions to insure complete audibility. Following each of the short readings listeners were given twenty multiple-choice questions, slightly easier than would be given in an ideal examination. The results were reported by Nichols as follows: "On the average the listeners comprehended but 68 per cent of the material tested after each ten-minute presentation. This seems to suggest a need for either improvement in lecturing methods, or a refinement of the listening habits and abilities of college students, or a combination of both measures." Furthermore, there was a "tendency of poor listeners to over-rate their own conscientiousness, the merit of their study practices, and the responsibility of the speaker when listening

Listening and literacy

Let us look, then, at the emerging importance of efficient listening. Listening is the counterpart of reading. For four hundred years since the invention of the printing press our educational system has given primacy to the reading-writing process. Now after these four centuries of increasing print-mindedness, of measuring literacy in terms of writing, and reading, within the twentieth century the radio, television, and moving pictures have re-established the importance of the speaking-listening process. Henceforth to be literate one must also be able to speak as well as write, be able to listen efficiently as well as read efficiently. Even a quarter century ago the most conservative investigations revealed that of the total time devoted to communications by adults, 45 per cent was spent in listening, 30 per cent in speaking, 16 per cent in reading, and 9 per cent in writing.[2] In the quarter century since, the growth of radio and the appearance of television have obviously increased the percentage of time given to listening.

The reason for this growth is not merely the appearance of radio and television. To be sure these have given the opportunity, but more fundamental is the fact that a larger percentage of people are ear-minded rather than print-minded. The primacy of the printing press for four centuries favored the print-minded. Now radio and television have opened to the ear-minded opportunities of learning that were denied them during the centuries of domination by print. At first we assumed that these were golden opportunities and required no training. Anybody could listen; efficient listening was determined by hearing acuity and intelligence; schools could do little about either. These were the assumptions. Research found them to be wrong. We have long known that efficient reading does not depend solely on eyesight and intelligence, and that efficient speaking does not depend solely on articulateness and intelligence. They require also training in techniques. So with listening. Even ear-minded people do not listen at highest efficiency without training. Furthermore in a world where mass communication is carried on by print and by radio-television (as well as an increasing amount of person-to-person speak-

---

performances are poor. . . ." "Factors in Listening Comprehension," *Speech Monographs,* XV (1948), No. 2, pp. 154-163.

[2] Paul T. Rankin, "Listening Ability," *Proceedings of the Ohio State Educational Conference, 1929* (Columbus: Ohio State University, 1929), pp. 172-183.

ing), every literate person—whether ear-minded or print-minded—needs an adequate mastery of the techniques both of reading and listening. You belong to the generation that presumably has been taught to read. You were born too soon for the educational system to have caught up with the world and to have set up a curriculum that would teach you to listen. You now have the chance to make up for that deficiency.

In a speech class you are in a favored position. You will hear a hundred or more speeches, each of them offering opportunity for applying the techniques of systematic listening. As you hear these speeches there are *two* kinds of listening you ought to do. First, is the creative listening, the active listening, that everyone who hears a speech or keeps up with the world through radio and television needs to develop. That is the listening for the purpose of getting meanings.

Second, you ought to listen for the purpose of evaluating speech techniques. Most of you will take only this one speech course before going into a world where your usefulness to society—and your personal success—will depend in a large measure on your ability to communicate ideas orally. What you get out of this one speech course will do more to determine how effectively you live, and how successfully in a material sense, than what you get out of almost any other course you take in college; for in a large measure it will determine how effectively you *use* what you learn in other courses. As one business man put it: "One semester or one term of superficial training in speech is not enough. He needs more than a superficial orientation. The entire field of speech, logical thinking, discussion, debate, conducting meetings must be incorporated into and made a vital part of the total education which he receives. His technical training cannot be of maximum effectiveness until he has been provided with a means of communicating it to other people." [3] You can read this textbook, take a series of examinations, and find out how much you have learned about speaking techniques. You can give five or ten speeches attempting to put those techniques into operation, look over the instructor's grades and comments, and see where you have succeeded and where you have failed. You can thereby make progress. But if you would make the maximum progress, you will listen critically to every speech given by every other student in the class, and will evaluate critically

[3] W. E. Bennett, Coordinator of Training, The Cities Service Refining Corporation, "Speech in a Technological Society," *Journal of Communication* I (May, 1951), No. 1, p. 19.

his use of speaking techniques. Instead of five or ten opportunities for learning techniques, you will have a hundred or more.

Your role while others speak, then, is not to fade into a coma and be merely aware that there is a noise. It is not to be half conscious, dully skim what is said, and rouse yourself when there is a pause, change of pace, an especially emphatic word, or an interesting tidbit. If you listen in these ways, opportunity once gone cannot be recaptured. Rather, when others speak you are in position to say, "Here is the chance to learn without making mistakes, or having to pay for them." As each speech is given, you do those *two* kinds of listening.

First, you want the answer to "*What* did the speaker say?" That is, you listen to get the idea and determine its worth: What is the speaker talking about? What is his proposition? What is his skeleton of supporting ideas? Are his facts accurate? Can his judgment be trusted? Can the speaker himself be trusted? Or is he a concealed propagandist?

Second, you want the answer to "*How* did the speaker say it?" That is, you listen to discern and evaluate his speaking techniques: What kind of introduction was that? Was he too slow getting to the point? Did he make the proposition clear? Did he state it too soon, or too late? Should he have used a summary of that topic? Would not an illustration or comparison have made that point clearer? If he talked louder would listeners have got more? If he had used action in explaining that would it have been clearer? He made that point perfectly clear in two minutes; I wonder if I can use that method in my next speech? He certainly knows how to use examples; ought I to look into how to use them better? Note how he drove that topic home with a climax; that's where I fell down on my last speech.

Levels of Listening

There are at least five levels of listening. Literate listeners at different times use each of them. Semi-literate listeners use only the three lowest. In ascending order of difficulty these five levels are:

1. *Listening for entertainment.* This is listening merely for enjoyment to funny stories and interesting talk. It is the kind of listening we do to variety shows on radio and television. It is the kind of listening we do at popular moving picture shows.

2. *Listening for escape or sublimation.* Men like to listen to sportcasts. Women like soap operas. They let us escape from the humdrum

and responsibilities of daily life. They epitomize our wishes and ambitions in the stories of other people. For a moment in the imagination we can become Superman or Cinderella, and can live in an unreal world. Listening for escape allows a release for our wishful thinking.

3. *Listening for inspiration.* We listen also for a renewing of faith, an uplift of spirit, an inspiration to be better and do more. Sermons and religious music, inspiring drama, patriotic themes, all are founded on the human quest for inspiration.

4. *Listening for information and ideas.* Sometimes we listen for information only. This generally is the type of listening done, or at least attempted, in classroom lectures, explanations of technical subjects and new discoveries, and newscasts. We want to know what is to be known, to keep up with the world. At other times we want to have the meaning of facts explained to us. At still others we want ideas on problems that face us. In short, this type of listening is a search for facts and a quest for ideas.

5. *Listening to evaluate and form opinions.* Most listening on controversial subjects is done with a closed mind. We listen, not for facts or ideas or to form opinions, but simply to ratify old beliefs. Nevertheless, some people can listen critically, to weigh and judge and modify old opinions. Not all want to do it, or can do it. They prefer to listen only for entertainment, or for escape into a dream world, or to gain pleasure from hearing what they already believe. Some try to listen critically, but get tired after a few minutes and give up. They have never been trained to listen literately, and they go through life listening only at lower levels. Critical listening is not learned in a day. It is cultivated by slow degrees.

Obviously the kinds of listening with which we are henceforth concerned are the last two levels: listening for information and ideas, and listening to evaluate and form opinions. The third level, listening for inspiration, is useful indeed; but you can learn it easily once you have acquired efficiency in the final two.

The listening process

Before considering specific listening techniques we should examine the nature and limitations of listening.

Listening is instantaneous. In reading you can stop and ponder. You can reread. In listening there is no backtracking. A skillful speaker will help you by repetitions and summaries, but no full rehearing is possible. Therefore, you get it straight the first time, or you don't get it straight at all. So it is that an active intelligent mind that gets meanings instantly will have about the same efficiency in listening as in reading. But if the mental activity is lowered, a reader can compensate by rereading, whereas the listener is passed by and left behind. In some degree, then, a listener is like Longfellow's daughter:

When she's good, she's very, very good;
When she's bad, she's horrid.

In listening you can get meanings from voice and action that cannot be given you by print. Assuming a competent speaker, a listener can get meanings that no reader can get out of print. These come from the speaker's color of voice, informing inflection, pause, emphasis, and by action that points, describes, divides, discriminates. Talk is older than print. Man has evolved a code of meaning by action, a sign language, that is understood over all the world. He has also evolved an exact and subtle code of meaning by voice inflection and pattern which is far older than any words of the English language. Print is a new-comer. It offers mere black on white. It cannot carry as full meanings as effective talk.

On the other hand, the mine run speaker has not mastered the techniques. The listener may be borne toward a state of coma, or even hypnotic drowsiness, by the dripping of a dull unchanging voice. He may have the flow of thought broken by *ahs* and *ers*, and by action that distracts or misleads. Yet under motivation, listeners, in reasonable measure, can compensate for poor delivery, and make a poorly-delivered speech more effective than might be supposed. But it takes a strong and constant motivation.[4]

Efficient listening depends on (1) attitude, (2) attention, (3) retention, and (4) evaluation. Here we are summarizing the complicated process that goes on in a listener's mind. Consider first the effect of *attitude.* Research shows that strongly opinionated listeners learn less than others. Those who tend strongly to disagree or agree also fail more than others to get the speaker's central ideas and to form valid inferences. Apparently such people spend their listening time in

[4] For a summary of research on this, see James I. Brown, "The Objective Measurement of Listening Ability," *Journal of Communication,* I (May, 1951), No. 1, p. 45.

rationalizing their own fixed views rather than in opening their minds to the opinions of the speaker. In a sense they are not listeners. Those who strongly disagree tend to become disputers, and those who strongly agree tend to become nonthinking applauders.[5]

Attention means that you take an active part. Note the word "active." Many people think of listening as merely receiving communication from someone who is giving it. This is partly right, but then they make the error of assuming that communication is like receiving a gift or a judgment from the court. Not so. Listening is not passive, but active. It is a different kind of activity from speaking, but it is an activity. It is more like the activity of catching a baseball. You don't wait for the ball to hit you. You reach out and gather it in. If you don't do this actively, the ball bounces off or goes on past. Listening is like catching a ball in still another way. It requires a skill, a technique of knowing how. Listening is unlike catching a ball in one respect, however. You either catch the whole ball or miss it, whereas in listening you can catch merely a piece of the thought. Nevertheless, the analogy is a good one. Listening is like catching a ball. You get set for it, watch the windup, follow the throw. This calls for attention. You watch the speaker, watch his face and gesture, get each point as he delivers it, and relate the point to the material he delivers in support of it.

Next, there is *retention.* Listening is not efficient unless you remember the main lines of thought. To continue the baseball analogy, you keep track of the innings, the number of strikes, balls, outs and the total score.

Finally, there is *evaluation.* Here the baseball analogy no longer holds, for in baseball an out is an out, a score is a score, and the umpire's decision is final. Not so with listening. In a way you make up your own score, and it may be a different score from those made up by other listeners. It depends on your intelligence, understanding of the subject, previous attitude toward it, and listening ability. Before evaluating, you first must be able to say with reasonable certainty, "I *understand.*" Until you do understand, evaluation is folly. But once you do understand, you then talk back—silently, of course. You say, "I understand, and agree." Or "I understand, and agree with reservations or modifications." Or "I understand, and suspend judg-

[5] For a summary of research on this, see also James I. Brown, *op. cit.*, p. 46.

ment until I can think further." Or "I understand, and disagree, for your analysis was unsound, . . . or your reasoning was illogical, . . . or your evidence was rigged." In this way you sift, measure, and judge. You place one fact against another, one judgment against another, and emerge with a concept that is a fusion of material already in your mind plus new ones delivered by the speaker.

Evaluation is the highest of listening skills. Some listeners fail in the essential first step; they do not *understand* what the speaker says, hence their evaluation is worth little. Another type of listener is efficient on pure reception of details, but has trouble combining these details into a thought pattern, or in judging their relevancy. Finally there are those undisciplined minds found in every class who are propelled almost entirely by prejudices. Often mentally rude, and as often insensitive to the responses of others, their prejudices to them are the Voice of God, and rational judgment is the Whisper of the Serpent. Such persons cannot evaluate. They can only dispute.

How to listen effectively

From this background we can set down six steps in the technique of efficient listening.

1. *Get ready to listen.* Have you observed how many people sit at the back of the room, or near an exit where outside noises mask the speaker's voice? Have you seen a student enter a classroom, and slouch down in a seat, feet out and head back? Seldom do these people listen efficiently; in fact, many do not come to listen efficiently. In getting ready to listen, seat yourself where you can see and hear, take a comfortable but alert posture, focus your eyes on the speaker and your mind on what he is about to say.

2. *Switch off emotional attitudes.* We already know what research has found about attitudes. People with strong emotional attitudes don't listen well. Not only do they fail to make relevant judgments, but they even fail to get the speaker's central idea. You cannot listen efficiently when strong emotions are chasing themselves through your mind, when you are saying mentally, "Of course he's right; any fool could see that," or "There's nothing to be said on his side of the question," or "I wish I were not stuck with this assignment." You cannot yield to emotional attitudes and at the same time listen efficiently. The emotions win, and listening comes in a poor second. Therefore, switch off emotional attitudes.

3. *Start listening on the first sentence.* You can reread printed matter, but you hear a speaker's words only once. If you don't get them straight the first time, you don't get them at all. Good speakers often state the central idea in the first minute or so, or even the first few seconds. If you miss the central idea, you will have trouble throughout the speech getting the thought pattern. Start listening, then, on the first sentence. If it is mere windup, let it pass, but keep set for the statement of the central idea, or for definitions, ground clearing, or orientation of any sort. The first minute or so is critical. After that listening becomes a little easier.

4. *Get the central idea.* Every speech worth listening to has a unity and an organization of parts. Find, first, the unity, the central idea. If the speaker does not put it into exact words, do so yourself. If when the speech is over, you can't state briefly what the theme was, you have not listened efficiently. You may have a lot of interesting details, but the speech will be what William James said the world is to a baby: "a big, buzzing, blooming confusion."

5. *Get the chief supporting ideas in their relation to the whole.* A speech, like a human being, has a skeleton that holds it erect. This skeleton, like the human skeleton, is covered up with muscles and dressed up in clothes. Your job is to X-ray through clothes and muscles to find the skeleton. Then you can see what kind of creature the speech is, how it hangs together, and how its parts are articulated. In other words, a speech is a *complex* unity. You have not grasped its complex unity if you know only its central idea. You must know also its major parts, how they are organized into a whole, and how they are organically related.

To borrow an analogy from Mortimer Adler,[6] a good speech is like a good house. It is under one roof, but has different rooms on different levels, and the rooms are used for different purposes. In a degree each room is independent, each having its own structure and interior design. Yet no room is totally independent and separate; they are connected by corridors, stairways, arches, and doors; and the special use of each room contributes to the total usefulness of the house. A speech, like a house, has an orderly design of parts. Each major part has a degree of independence, each has its own interior structure and design. Yet no part is totally independent and separate from the

[6] *How to Read a Book* (New York: Simon and Schuster, 1940), p. 164.

others. Each is connected by passageways called transitions; and the special contribution of each part contributes to the total usefulness of the speech.

You may say this looks as if it were a rule of speaking instead of listening. So it is. Speaking and listening are reciprocal. If speakers do not organize their ideas, if they fail to present a central idea and an orderly skeleton of parts, there would be no point in the listener's search for unity and for uncovering structure. For that matter, there would not be much point in speaking, or in listening.

A skillful speaker helps you get the major parts, their relation to each other, and their relation to the whole. Watch for the cue phrases as "First," or "At the beginning." They tell you that here comes the first major part. Then watch for cue phrases like "Another consideration," or "Second," which tell you that the speaker now is coming to the second major part. If you have trouble at first in carrying these parts in your mind, write them down. A little practice in writing down the major parts will help soon to carry them in your head.

Watch also the cues the speaker gives you at the end of a major part. He may wrap it up, round it out, or even summarize it: "What I have been saying, then, amounts to this," or "To put it another way," or "In summary."

Especially watch the summary that often comes at the end of the speech. Here you have a chance to get a bird's-eye view of all the speaker has said, and to pick up points and relationships you missed the first time.

6. *Weigh and consider*. So far we have been talking about *reception*, getting clearly what the speaker says, so with reasonable certainty you can say "I understand." ". . . And with all thy getting get understanding." Now comes the final end of listening: evaluating what you understand. You can pronounce any sort of judgment—biased, bickering, undisciplined; or reflective, relevant, mature. You can make no effort to evaluate, but simply forget it. You can damn with faint praise, then put it aside. You can reject without judgment. But assuming an ability for critical judgment, or a willingness to develop it, you can undertake the final step of criticism, judgment, and evaluation. Criticism, of course, is not disagreement. It is not listening to doubt or to scorn. It is evaluating under the terms so well stated in Francis Bacon's recommendation to readers: "Read not to contradict or confute; not to believe and take for granted; nor to find talk and discourse; but to weigh and consider."

ASSIGNMENTS

1. Test first your ability to listen for information. Your instructor will read 5-minute article from *Time*, *Newsweek*, or other similar source. Take no notes during the reading, but immediately afterward write a brief summary stressing only important items.

2. Listen to a public speech (a radio or television speech if you prefer) and write a report as follows: (a) the speaker's central idea, (b) the chief supporting ideas, (c) your evaluation of these ideas.

3. Listen to an argumentative speech on a controversial issue, and write a report as follows: (a) the speaker's central idea, (b) the chief supporting ideas, (c) the main lines of evidence used in support of those ideas, (d) your evaluation of the speaker's assumptions, facts, and inferences.

4. In listening to the next round of class speeches, evaluate the speaking techniques of each speaker. Which were well used? Which were poorly used? Which were ignored?

5. Draw up a list of the factors that make it difficult for you to listen efficiently. Prepare your next speech with these factors in mind, taking special care to organize, word, and deliver the speech so these missing cues are given your listeners. Attach your list of factors to the outline. On the left margin of the outline explain the methods you plan to use for giving special aids to listeners.

Part II THE AUDIENCE

Harry S. Truman speaking in 1948 at Wendover, Wyoming. Supposedly not a good speaker, Truman understood the voting masses better than both his advisers and his critics, and turned a seemingly certain defeat into victory.

CHAPTER 6

The People to Whom You Talk

CHAPTER 6

You have now studied certain elementary aspects of speechmaking, have had some experience with simple types of speeches, and are ready to approach the more comprehensive techniques.[1] In doing so, we shall again consider first the audience, the people to whom you talk.

The people to whom you talk are not inert. They are not a mere mass. They are not all alike. Each listener is a tiny world winging through space. He is a human asteroid propelled by motives, desires, wants, ambitions, cravings, aspirations—common to all of his kind. He has been cultivated and changed on the surface by the culture of his particular group, until he is surprisingly—and sometimes embarrassingly—like others of his group. Unlike celestial asteroids, however, he can guide his course within reasonable limits; and his instruments of navigation are his intelligence and education and immediate interests. Further, unlike asteroids, no man moves alone on a solitary orbit. Each is member of a group, of many groups: his nation, state, city; his church, political party, social stratum, clubs.

Now there are only two means by which these groups are controlled: forceful domination, or the peaceful persuasion of men's minds. Forceful domination is the totalitarian method, persuasion is the

[1] But remember that even the so-called comprehensive techniques in a basic text are still elementary. Regretfully but deliberately we must exclude the broad sweep of rhetoric—its concern with urgent public affairs, its mode of influence on thought and democratic institutions, its relationship to the function of leadership and especially the conditions under which a speaker can change public opinion compared with the conditions under which he must follow it and wait for the opportune time to effect change. Even the constituents of style and the inquiry into human wants and culture patterns are touched on lightly. This word of caution is added so none will think he can learn to speak by formula, or learn it in a single college course. Daniel Webster, at the age of forty-six, read Richard Whately's *Elements of Rhetoric* then just off the press, and commented that he had "found in it twenty things which I have thought of often, and been convinced of long, but never before saw in print." Henry Ward Beecher in later years said he did not preach his first sermon until after he had been speaking some ten years in college and in the pulpit; he had preached *at* a good many sermons before, but this was "the first real one." Franklin D. Roosevelt reached maturity as a speaker in 1932 at the age of fifty, preceded by what might be termed twenty years of apprentice speaking after he became Assistant Secretary of the Navy.

democratic. The democratic view rests literally on the belief of man's right to life, liberty, and the pursuit of happiness, and on governments deriving their just powers from the consent of the governed. The democratic view, therefore, rests on man's right to make decisions —be they rational or not—and to do so without either sanction or supervision of an all-wise elite. Democracy thus "condemns" the mass of people to make decisions, with or without full knowledge of available facts and ideas, and to suffer the consequences thereof.

So it is that in a democracy competition for the mind of man is keen, and skillfully organized. Armies of research workers have compiled and classified up-to-date directories of our wants, our fears, our frustrations. Using these directories, special groups carry on never-ceasing campaigns to capture the public's mind. They are the advertisers, politicians, labor leaders, business leaders, religious leaders, minority racial groups, assorted pressure groups and vested interests. Of them the advertisers are the single-cell amoebas, who perform at the most elementary biological level. From them we can learn something of our primal instincts. They appeal to fear ("Even your best friends won't tell you,"; "do you have Halitosis, B.O., or Office Hips? "). They appeal to snobbery ("Men of distinction"). They offer release from frustration ("Women who use This Soap get their man").

Now persuasion of *ideas* in public address is more complex. But it is not haphazard, or even causal. Never for one moment think that mere talk will persuade, or that "giving the facts" will persuade, or that because truth and justice are on your side you will therefore win. Ponder the classic statement of Aristotle in 336 B.C., now valid by the test of twenty-three centuries: that truth and justice are stronger than falsehood and injustice, and hence when the latter win it is not the fault of depraved voters, but of inept speakers who neglected the science of persuasion. Read Machiavelli's *The Prince*, or its twentieth-century equivalent *The Autobiography of Lincoln Steffens*, for case histories on manipulating people's minds. Remember Hitler, who trained sinister men to speak well, overran an almost helpless German educational system that had neglected to train good men to speak at all, and set about a world conquest by declaration of a war of words.

The mid-twentieth century, more than ever during the past twenty-five centuries, is one of "organized persuasion." Therefore, you must learn its science— or be counted out.

The influence of reason, logic, and evidence

You don't need to be told that people are filled with all sorts of attitudes and beliefs that did not come from reason, or logic, or objective assembling of facts. Now that you are in college, of course, it would be delightful to say that education will change all that; that to be sure less educated and less intelligent folk are ruled by prejudice, but that when really intelligent people become educated, henceforth they are ruled by reason; and therefore when you talk to *them* all you need is to "know the facts," "assemble the evidence," and "give the reasons." Such would be delightful indeed—but utter nonsense. Of this myth Woodrow Wilson said, "We talk a great deal about being governed by mind, by intellect, by intelligence, in this boastful day of ours; but. . . . men, no matter what their training, are governed by their passions, and the most we can hope to accomplish is to keep the handsome passions in the majority."

Experimental psychology confirms this judgment. Maria Zillig, a German psychologist, for example, experimented with both pupils and teachers. First, she had elementary-school children select by ballot the best-liked class members and the least-liked. Keeping the results secret, and supposedly choosing persons at random, she had the five most-liked and the five least-liked stand before the class, and she then arranged them in alternate order. Privately ahead of time she had instructed the five best-liked students to do the *opposite* of whatever she commanded. Now she told all ten to raise their right hand. The five least-liked did so, but, of course, the best-liked raised their left hand. Zillig now asked the remainder of the class to list the names of pupils who did the exercise wrong. After this first trial run, she instructed the class to use utmost care in observing and listing accurately the names of all who might do it wrong. Following this, she repeated the experiment four times more—with the best-liked pupils always raising the wrong hand and the least-liked raising the correct hand. For the total experiment, then, the best-liked pupils were 100 per cent wrong and the least-liked were 100 per cent right. *But when the class scores were totalled, it was found that the best-liked pupils had been graded higher than the least-liked!* (If you are my friend, you're right. If I don't like you, you're wrong!)

Zillig next turned her attention to the teachers. From eighteen teachers she got the names of the two students they liked best and the two they liked least. Then she procured copies of a spelling test that had been graded by these teachers. On checking the test, she found that *the teachers had overlooked over 38% of the errors of the best-liked students, but only 12% of the errors of the least-liked.* (Moral: Don't get on your teacher's least-liked list.)

But lest you think teachers are especially irrational, consider the impressive research of Edward L. Thorndike. For each of 117 cities he computed a *factual*-index. Then he asked people distinctly above average in ability to give him their opinion on the quality of government, schools, morals, culture, etc. To these people he stressed that he did not want guesses, but only judgments based on facts. His list included 99 business men, 97 educators, 72 clergymen and social workers, and 31 reformers—all *leaders* in their respective fields. When their judgments were checked against the factual-index, where did they stand? Here are the correlations. They speak for themselves:

97 educators	.59
31 reformers	.51
72 clergymen and social workers	.36
99 business men	.27

All of the groups gave "far too little weight to the facts." Instead, they tended to believe what they *wanted* to believe, and the (hard-headed?) business men were the least objective of the groups. Thorndike significantly adds that these results are typical and are statistically valid, and would be altered only slightly if the number of persons interviewed had been "increased tenfold or more." [2]

A. T. Poffenberger, psychologist, summarized his experiments on the conditions of belief: "Belief is rarely the result of reasoning. . . . We tend to believe what arouses our desires, our fears, and our emotions generally." [3] F. H. Lund undertook to answer by research such questions as: (1) Is belief conditioned by emotional factors? (2) Is the *rational* an ideal among people? (3) What is the relation of

[2] Zillig's experiments are reported in William H. Burnham, *The Wholesome Personality* (New York: Appleton-Century-Crofts, Inc., 1932), pp. 92-104. Thorndike's is reported in "Facts *vs.* Opinion: An Impirical Study of 117 Cities," *Public Opinion Quarterly*, II (Jan., 1938), 85-90. All three are reported in Robert T. Oliver, *The Psychology of Persuasive Speech* (New York: Longmans, Green and Co., 1942), pp. 36-37.

[3] "The Conditions of Belief in Advertising," *Journal of Applied Psychology*, VIII (March, 1923), 4-9. See also the same author's *Psychology of Advertising* (New York: A. W. Shaw, 1926), pp. 544-545. For the viewpoint of contemporary psychologists, who use a different terminology to express the same view, see Hadley Cantril's famous "Laws" of public opinion in *Gauging Public Opinion* (Princeton: Princeton University Press, 1944), pp. 226-230, especially laws No. 6, 7, 8, and 14. See also Leonard W. Doob, "Principles of Public Opinion," in *Public Opinion and Propaganda* (New York: Henry Holt and Company, 1948), pp. 87-89.

belief to knowledge, etc.? In presenting the results, he noted that "there is a marked tendency to idealize the rational principle, and to conceive of it as the most important" factor in determining belief, whereas in truth the "non-rational factors appear to outweigh it so largely." Furthermore, he found, the college students used in this experiment tended to rate *themselves* as being more rational than other people. ("Lord, I thank Thee that I am not as other men.") Reduced to statistics, he found the following correlations:

Between belief and evidence	+.42
Between belief and knowledge	+.64
Between belief and desire	+.88 [4]

Belief and *desire*, as you see, has the highest correlation; belief and *evidence* has the lowest. Such is the nature of man.

But pause for a moment before you turn from man with disgust. Remember that he has lived on this planet for untold thousands of years. To survive during these years he has been forced to adapt himself to biological conditions and to the physical universe. Out of this survival he has acquired wants and culture patterns. These wants and culture patterns are *old*. Through them man has survived. Reason and logic, on the other hand, are *new*. If they interfere with wants, drives, urges, instincts, and culture patterns—well, since reason and logic are younger they are also the weaker, and they must go the way of the weak who wage combat. Ralph Linton, studying man from the standpoint of anthropology and sociology, remarked that "we are anthropoid apes trying to live [in social groups] like termites while lacking most of the termite equipment. One wonders whether we could not do it better with instincts." [5]

Nevertheless, as we shall see in the next chapter, logic and reason are extremely important to man's living, in spite of the low estate to which they seem to be assigned at the moment.

The influence of wants and impelling motives

WHY THEY INFLUENCE PEOPLE

To persuade others you must talk in terms of their wants. You must know their needs, their hopes, their ambitions, their fears. Know to

[4] "The Psychology of Belief," *Journal of Abnormal and Social Psychology*, April 1925, XX, 174-196.

[5] Ralph Linton, *The Cultural Background of Personality* (New York: Appleton-Century-Crofts, Inc., 1945), p. 15.

"what gods they pray and what kind of fights they love," know what songs they sing, and what sentiments they applaud.

Wrote John Ruskin: "The first and last, and closest trial question to any living creature is 'What do you like?' Tell me what you like, and I'll tell you what you are. Go out into the street, and ask the first man or woman you meet, what their 'taste' is and if they answer candidly, you know them, body and soul. 'You, my friend in rags, with the unsteady gait, what do *you* like?' 'A pipe and a quartern of gin.' I know you. 'You, good woman, with the quick step and tidy bonnet, what do you like?' 'A swept hearth and a clean tea-table and my husband opposite me, and a baby at my breast.' Good, I know you also. 'You, little girl with golden hair and the soft eyes, what do you like?' 'My canary, and a run among the wood hyacinths.' 'You, little boy with the dirty hands and the low forehead, what do you like?' 'A shy at the sparrows, and a game of pitch farthing.' Good; we know them all now. What more need we ask?" [6]

Frederick J. E. Woodbridge, psychologist, put the premise in scientific form; "We ought to stop talking about what is consciousness and what is behavior and what is sentiment and what is emotion and what is sensation and what is idea and all this, that, and the other thing, and tackle these more obvious things: what do people want? How do they go about getting it? How effective is their way of getting it? I confess it all seems to me to be as simple as that." [7]

What are the basic human wants common to all? Sir William Osler once said that natural man has only two wants: *"to get and to beget."* This obvious oversimplification can be expanded to five basic wants that are behind every human belief or act. They fall into five levels, starting with the basic and biological, and rising to levels representing higher human development. These five wants influence or determine everything people believe or do:

[6] *The Works of Ruskin: The Crown of Wild Olive* (New York: Oxford University Press, 1921), Lecture II, "Traffic," p. 267.

[7] *Minutes of the Dartmouth Psychological Conference, August 1925,* privately printed. There are many schools of psychologists, of course, including gestaltists, behaviorists, organismists, functionalists, reflexologists, hormists, and other -ists. They use different terminologies and often dissent vigorously from one another. Almost all have made significant contributions to human behavior, public opinion, and the nature of persuasion. But none holds a monopoly, and the weakness of most is their tendency to become a self-sealing system. The viewpoint here is, therefore, deliberately *selective.* It presents the major contributions of Greek thinkers, and the pertinent concepts of early psychologists. Especially also it uses the invaluable research of modern psychologists, anthropologists, and sociologists. Of the latter groups, none quite brings into focus the problem of persuasion, but they have uncovered valuable tangent material which speakers ought to have at their disposal.

1st level: Basic physiological needs, including hunger and sex.
2nd level: Safety, including self-preservation and security.
3rd level: Love, including affection, friendship, and tender emotion.
4th level: Esteem, including self-respect, pride, reputation.
5th level: Self-realization, including personal achievement and artistic tastes.

But human nature is not so elementary as this might suggest, for these motives do not operate singly or in simple form. Indeed civilization is a process of multiplying and institutionalizing human wants, of intellectualizing and socializing them. Hence civilized man has split and combined and refined his wants into many channels. He has developed institutions like governments and churches and social clubs to protect and promote them. Furthermore, opposing motives conflict with one another, and we are compelled to decide in favor of one or the other: Do I want comfort more than I want freedom? Do I want security above prestige? Do I put the welfare of my family above or below the welfare of myself? Again at different age levels, motives operate with different strength, as Aristotle bluntly observed centuries ago: "Young men have strong passions and tend to gratify them indiscriminately. . . . They are hot-tempered and quick-tempered, and apt to give way to their anger. . . . While they love honor, they love victory still more; for youth is eager for superiority over others, and victory is one form of this. . . . They would always rather do noble deeds than useful ones." As for Elderly Men, "They are not generous, because money is one of the things they must have, and at the same time their experience has taught them how hard it is to get and how easy to lose." They care "less for what is noble than for what is useful." "They live by memory rather than by hope," and "they are continually talking of the past, because they enjoy remembering it." They "are often supposed to have a self-controlled character; the fact is that their passions have slackened, and they are slaves to the love of gain. They guide their lives by reasoning more than by moral feeling; reasoning being directed to utility and moral feeling to moral goodness." [8]

Whether you agree with this provocative analysis is beside the point. It shows how one of the world's great thinkers—who for better or worse has influenced the thinking of the Western World more than any other—thought a speaker should adapt himself and compose his speech to fit the audience.

[8] *Rhetoric,* II, 12 and 13.

SPECIFIC WANTS

The following list of 20 specific wants will serve as a useful guide. Necessarily, they are incomplete and overlapping, for specific motives are indefinite in number, but they offer a useful analysis of the mainsprings that cause people to reject or accept a speaker's idea. They are the *universals* shared by all human beings everywhere: [9]

1. Security
2. Property
3. Freedom
4. Recognition, Prestige, Power
5. Reputation
6. Self-respect and Pride
7. Honor and Duty
8. Fair Play
9. Love and Friendship
10. Loyalty
11. Sex Attraction
12. Sympathy
13. Physical Enjoyment
14. Competition and Rivalry
15. Adventure
16. Conformity
17. Curiosity
18. Artistic Tastes
19. Fear
20. Reverence and Worship

SECURITY

"Give us this day our daily bread," is a universal prayer of man, not confined to Christian sects. It arises from the want for Security. To be secure from loss of job, to be secure from loss of property or income, to be secure from the uncertainties of tomorrow—even to be secure from *change* of daily habits—this desire gnaws at the vitals of mankind. For Security, people in crises have sold even their freedom and the right to rule themselves.[10] Of this desire, Mr. Justice Oliver Wendell Holmes said, "The timid and faint-hearted long for security and repose, not knowing that security is an illusion, and repose is not

[9] Psychologists generally agree that these wants or motives include urges, drives, sets, tendencies, instincts, propensities, unlearned behavior, and habits. Thus a motive may be biological, physiological, or social. Often it is all three.

[10] A segment of political essayists and speakers recently have assumed that the desire for Security is *new,* and was produced by depraved voters. This segment praises the rugged virtues of our forefathers who (say they) wanted not Security, but faced fearlessly the risks of life. Now this is mournful nonsense, and any party or pressure group that rests its persuasion on such a premise will lose in the long run. The desire for Security is not new, but is biological and was old, very old, even 25,000 years ago when it was aflame in the breast of the Palaeolithic Cro-Magnon Man. As for the early American, he was indeed rugged and had many virtues, but Forest L. Whan after long research summarized the attitude of one typical group: "They seemed to place security above comfort." (*History and Criticism of American Public Address,* p. 782.) Herbert Agar, after analyzing this factor in recent American political elections, pithily advised such politicians to "look and live as if they enjoyed democracy, and stop their . . . nonsense about the corrupted voter." (*Harper's Magazine,* April 1950, p. 35). The desire for Security is not new or depraved, but is old and biological.

the destiny of man." His maxim applies to most of the less timid and less faint-hearted.

You may challenge people to adventure, or rouse them to conflict, or impel them to take risks. These, too, are human wants. A few—the most courageous and farsighted—are willing to live by the standard of great men, that "There is no security; there is only opportunity." Little men may also be challenged momentarily by that standard. But broad and deep in human behavior is the want for Security. Show listeners that what you advocate will increase Security, or preserve it better, or at less cost—and you have premissed persuasion on a basic want.

PROPERTY

The desire for Property overlaps that for Security, but is not identical. It means the desire for lands, goods, money in all their forms: machinery and tools, a city home and a country retreat, stocks and bonds, coins and currency, wages, interest, dividends, profits. Here is the desire that drives management to create jobs for workers, that sends workers into the shops and factories, that keeps the stores open, the trains running, and the airplanes flying. It is the foundation of our industrial momentum. Remove it, or weaken the incentive, and the machinery would slacken its pace.

Show others, then, that your proposal will increase Property, and your persuasion rests thereby on a basic want.

FREEDOM

Man wants Freedom from restraint and external dominion. Take an infant even ten days old, and press his arms to his side or hold his legs tightly. He becomes angry almost instantly, for he is born with the desire to be free from restraint. In mature man the want includes both physical and mental freedom, not merely the right to come and go physically, but also the right to think as we please, to speak our minds openly, to worship at whatsoever altar we choose. Yet Freedom from external dominion is not as strong a want as certain others and it operates within definite limits. People will sacrifice it for other wants, for Security, for Prestige, for Physical Enjoyment. They will deny it to others. Indeed they fear others having too much Freedom, and limit it by law or by social pressure. Even in free societies there are limits to freedom of discussion. People will speak freely of the weather and the soil, but they do not speak as freely of powerful persons or groups in their community. Majorities everywhere tend to raise formidable barriers against complete Freedom.

Nevertheless, even though institutionalized and limited, Freedom is a fundamental want. Base your persuasion on it, and others are impelled toward accepting your view.

RECOGNITION, PRESTIGE, POWER

This is essentially a competitive want arising from the craving to assert and assure superiority over other people. Nobody wants to be the Common Man. To be noticed, to be favored as the object of attention, to be complimented and acclaimed as the Uncommon Man or Woman is a universal desire. It moves in different directions with different people, and differently in the same people at different times, but it is as ceaseless as the infinite flow of a river. It impels young people to seek athletic prowess, to be applauded on the playing field or floor, to be recognized as the wearer of an athletic letter or emblem. It impels others to seek recognition of intellectual powers ("He wears a Phi Beta Kappa key"), still others to attain political power ("They say he works for a dollar a year in Washington"), industrial power ("He organized the Associated Industries"), or social prestige ("She is a society leader"). It includes the desire to own a bigger house, drive a costlier car, or have a more expensive wedding than your neighbor.

Desire for Recognition, Prestige, Power is a motive that drives fiercely strong men, and would-be great men. But it flows, more futilely perhaps, though insistently, in the lives of little men. Show listeners how to increase Recognition, Prestige, or Power, and you have given them a motive to be persuaded.

REPUTATION

Reputation comes from the same basic desire to be superior that is found in Recognition, Prestige, and Power; but in specific form it operates differently. People find pleasure in being thought of as honest, kind, generous, noble. They find pain in being known as knavish, spiteful, stingy, contemptible. They want to feel that "eyes are turned kindly toward them and that tongues speak their praise." Reputation is a powerful motive. Rather than lose Reputation, people have been known to sacrifice life itself. To win Reputation the indolent have been driven to work harder, and the penurious to open their purse strings.

"Of course you have a reputation for fair-mindedness (or good judgment); therefore, I know you will listen to what I say without prejudice (or judge it on its merits, etc.)," says the understanding speaker. What listener wants to deny such a reputation?

SELF-RESPECT AND PRIDE

A man resigns from his job rather than take a demotion. "I have my self-respect," he says. True, and also his pride. "Let me ask the man. . ." said Lincoln, "what compensation he will accept to go to church some Sunday and sit during the sermon with his wife's bonnet upon his head?" Nothing could compensate such an act. Why? Pride and Self-respect. We don't like to be made fun of, laughed at, belittled. We aspire to a decent sense of dignity and self-respect.

Therefore, never say to listeners, "Since you don't know much about this subject I want to discuss it," or "How many of you ever stopped to realize that. . . ?" or "Please quit being prejudiced, and listen to reason." Such tactless remarks hurt the listeners' Self-respect and Pride. They hurt the speaker's chance of success. The tactful speaker reverses this. He uses Self-respect and Pride. Says he: "You remember so-and-so," or "I'm sure you would rather listen to unpleasant facts than to pleasant fancy."

HONOR AND DUTY

It is true that "a plain duty, like a plain woman, attracts few wooers," yet the sense of duty is strong. "England expects every man to do his duty," signalled Lord Nelson to his ships on the eve of the Battle of Trafalgar; and men died doing their duty. On the eve of the desperate Battle of Britain, more than a century later, Winston Churchill challenged the nation to "brace ourselves to our duties, and so bear ourselves that, if the British Empire and its Commonwealth last for a thousand years, men will still say 'This was their finest hour.' " President William Howard Taft told a story on himself that suggests the attitude of the typical man toward duty when plainly seen. Elihu Root, Secretary of War, wanted to send Taft to the Philippines as governor. Taft refused; he did not want to go. But Root put it to him squarely that he had long been enjoying a series of pleasant government jobs, and how his country needed him in this distant, more strenuous duty. Put in this way, Taft accepted the duty and went. Duty is a common thing, and men perform it in the ordinary walks of life around us all the time, and make sacrifices to perform it.

Convince a listener that what you want him to do is in keeping with the highest ideals of Honor and Duty, and he is impelled toward doing it. But use this motive sparingly, and use it with tact, for we become tired of duty when told of it too bluntly and too often. Constantly we hear banal appeals from speakers who lack understanding of human motives: "It is your *duty* to do this," or "It is *up to us* to. . . ." We wince at their banality and crudeness, and declare secretly in favor of a moral holiday. Therefore, use Honor and Duty sparingly, and do so with a nice distinction of fitness and tact.

FAIR PLAY

"Play the game," is an impelling slogan. "Fair play" is a motive to which men are ashamed not to respond. We hate to feel that we have ever been unfair or unjust. Worse, we hate to have it said about us, "He won't play according to the rules," or "He plays with loaded dice." Many a speaker has softened hostility by saying skillfully, *"I know you disagree with me, and that is your right. But I know, too, that you believe in Fair Play, and that you'll listen to those who sincerely disagree."* Many a skillful trial lawyer, while selecting a jury panel, has quickened their sense of Fair Play: *"You know the background of this case. . . . Now you wouldn't want not to be fair, would you? So will you just tell the court whether you have any opinions that would be unfair to my client."*

Fair Play is one of the highest motives that influences human behavior. Persuade a hearer that the thing you want him to do is fair, just, honest, or noble, and you have given him a lofty motive to impel action.

LOVE AND FRIENDSHIP

We crave Friendship and want to be an accepted member of groups of friends: a fraternity, club, church, social caste, or informal circle. In these groups, members largely think as we do, feel as we do, and hold the same values and ideals. They share our pleasures, and perhaps our fears. What we think is good, they think is good; and what they hold to be bad, we hold to be bad. Therefore, these people are our friends, and we feel kindly toward them. Others are our friends too. Our neighbors. Our business associates (providing they are not rivals or competitors). Those who when we need help don't ask, "Is there anything I can do?" but who come and say, "Here I am." Man *needs* Friendship, and without it he withdraws too much into himself, becomes embittered, or even frustrated.

Love is a more intensive human want, biologically older than Friendship. "Children feed on love as they do on fresh air." The casebooks of child clinics and juvenile courts reveal that children who are denied Love develop sulkiness, suspicion, lying, thievery. The emotional starvation develops poison within the organism. In adults the lack of a normal amount of Love often leads to bitterness or suspicion or despair. Love and Friendship, then, is not a mere sentimentality. It is a basic want, a need in human life.

Therefore, when a speaker says to us, "Your friends believe this," or "Your family needs that," we find it humanly hard to resist.

LOYALTY

Loyalty arises from the desire to identify ourselves with the welfare of our group. It takes many forms: family pride ("My Mother bakes the best pies in all the world"), school spirit ("It is *my* school, and it is the best in the land"), state pride ("You must admit that this is the most wonderful state in the union, though I have been in but four states myself"), patriotism ("My country, right or wrong").

For a speaker to use this motive is easy and obvious. "Will . . . [you] withhold, save in strained courtesy, the hand which straight from his soldier's heart Grant offered to Lee at Appomattox?" Henry W. Grady asked his New England audience. Their answer was "tumultuous cheering and shouts of 'No! No!' " Socrates long ago observed that "it is not difficult to praise the Athenians to an Athenian audience."

SEX ATTRACTION

In man's wanderings through the confused labyrinth of sex certain motives arise that influence persuasion. Men (the male sex) want the attention and friendship of women, and women of men. Hence whatever makes us more attractive to the opposite sex gains our support. To keep this Sex Attraction within social bounds men and women have developed a special code of behavior toward each other. In this code (as followed in Western Civilization) men belong to the "stronger sex" and women to the "weaker sex," and it does not matter at all that in cold reality women in many respects are tougher and more enduring than men. Toward women, men represent Gallantry, the Armed Knight, and Protection from Danger. Toward men, women represent Virtue, Beauty, and Helplessness. Now we know this to be make-believe, but we act it out on the human stage, and shall act it to the end. If the ultimate of disaster be ours, there surely will be heard, as Hodding Carter reminds us, "somewhere in the radioactive wilderness of the survivors" a feminine voice saying, "Honey, I've found some nice bricks for a chimney, but it'll take a strong man like you to stack them up, 'cause I'm just so helpless."

Therefore, recognize the code in public address. Whatever men do in private, gentlemen in public rise in the presence of women. They place taboos on their speech. Some things they do not talk about in public before women, and certain kinds of stories they do not tell. As for women, among us they are now emancipated, but an emancipated woman does not talk like a man. She talks like the Mother of Men, who rules the world because she has rocked the cradle, or can rock it. She talks with a woman's sense of values, a woman's concern, a woman's deep sympathy. When she speaks as Woman, she speaks impellingly; but let her speak as a man-among-men, and she can become a mere female.

SYMPATHY

We give to the Community Chest, the Red Cross, the March of Dimes, to welfare funds of many kinds. We pause to comfort a crying child, visit a sick neighbor, and send flowers to friends in hospitals. At times this Sympathy arises from our knowing that such disasters could happen to us; therefore we do to others what we would have them do to us. At other times, however, Sympathy is solely for the sake of the persons helped, a feeling of compassion for the unfortunate.

If you would arouse Sympathy, describe vividly the people who need it. (Mere facts and figures will not arouse Sympathy; don't use them for that purpose.) Make listeners *see* and *feel* and *hear* the human need—sense that "when the Devil takes the hindmost, the wrench is felt by the topmost—and felt to the very marrow of his bones."

Sympathy is used in another manner also. If you would describe the greatness of a man or woman, in a eulogy or speech of tribute, remember that his capacity for Sympathy is a quality by which you can measure greatness. Did he have Sympathy of a particular quality, or a particular magnitude? Can you demonstrate it by a story or example or comparison?

PHYSICAL ENJOYMENT

Consider the life of modern man. He eats food that comes from distant places, rides in an airplane or train or taxicab or elevator. He plays golf or tennis, goes fishing or hunting. He attends a moving picture, or listens to the radio, or watches television. In America, at least, the average man has comforts that Alexander the Great would envy and George Washington would find incredible. Behind this attainment is the motive of Physical Enjoyment. It is not merely physical *comfort* or *ease*. It is rather *enjoyment*, which may include effort and action.

Modern advertising relies heavily on Physical Enjoyment. ("Smooth power," "The key to greater ease," "Go pullman.") Persuasion rests heavily on it also, for man will act fiercely to prevent the lessening of Physical Enjoyment and to increase enjoyments already possessed.

COMPETITION AND RIVALRY

We want to equal or surpass others. If they can do something (run, shoot, drive, have social ease or beauty), we want to be able to do it as well or better. If they possess something (a better house, car, clothes, reputation, or social standing), we want as much or more. Hence we have athletic contests, business competition, social rivalry, and keeping-up-with-the-Joneses. Competition and Rivalry are fierce motives. Research on fourth and fifth grade children, for example, found that those who were competing increased both speech and accuracy in arithmetic far beyond those who were not competing (.63 in speed for those not competing; but 3.93, or over six times as much, for those who were competing).[11]

Speakers, therefore, premise arguments on Competition and Rivalry, and say, "Let us not be outdone," or "Remember the victory of last year, when the odds were against us," or "Which one of you will win this award?"

ADVENTURE

"Why do you want to ascend Mt. Everest?" a reporter asked a mountain climber. *"Because it's there!"* was the reply. We want the excitation of a fast-travelling car, a high-flying airplane, or stalking big game. We want to feel the tug of a fish on the end of our line, the

[11] The study referred to here was done by E. B. Hurlock as described by A. G. Bills, *General Experimental Psychology* (New York: Longmans, Green and Co., 1937), p. 522.

roll of the deck under our feet. We want to travel to far places, see distant lands. If we cannot do these things ourselves, we can enjoy hearing and seeing others who do it.

By speakers this motive is used in many forms. One says "Here is a story of adventure." Another says, "I was there. I saw it, or took part." Still another, "We face a serious problem. I present its solution as a challenge, an adventure!"

CONFORMITY

Every society demands that each of its members conform to all. People seemingly have a universal desire to do this, and there is little impulse toward rebellion. The Pueblo Indians regard property as not being very important.Any ambitious Pueblo would thus find it easy to accumulate vast amounts of property from his unresisting fellows, but he does not. He conforms. Hindus will not drink from a Moslem well. Physically, any thirsty unseen Hindus could drink; actually, they will parch from thirst if it has been "polluted" by Moslems. It is easy to see Conformity in others, but less easy to see it in ourselves. Yet we conform in the kind of clothes we wear. Men do not wear skirts. They go shirtless on the beach, but not in stores and living rooms. Women may not go uncovered above the waist even on the beach, yet in Bali and Polynesia women wear nothing above the waist. In our society we eat three meals a day, not two or four. Men wear bow ties with dinner jackets, but four-in-hands with cutaways. We applaud whether we really like the speech or not. We accept certain ideas, not because we have thought them through ourselves, but because we conform to what others think: monogamy, private ownership of property, a nine-month school year. This is variously called the Band-Wagon tendency, or Follow-the-Crowd pull, or the Herd Instinct. It is based on the desire to conform. We say, "Everybody's doing it; I'll do it too." Or, "People have believed this for a long time; I'll believe it too."

Use of this motive has obvious virtues and obvious defects. Man is a social animal. He must conform to survive. But he is also an individual, and democratic society survives only by having an adequate number of people question outworn ideas and develop new ones.

CURIOSITY

In the town lived 10,000 people, but 12,000 gathered at the railway station when the President of the United States stopped for a ten-minute speech from the rear of his train. They did not exactly come to hear what he said; they could have heard a better speech from him over the radio that night. They certainly did not come to applaud him; most of them voted against him. The impelling motive that brought most was Curiosity. From Curiosity a boy tears down a clock to see why it ticks. From Curiosity adults go to see celebrities-in-person, in a sense to see why they tick. From Curiosity psychologists experiment on the behavior of man, to see why man ticks. From Curiosity physicists experiment on dynamics, to see why the universe ticks. Civilized man is insatiably curious, and we are debtors to generations of curious men who lived before us.

A speaker says, "As I crossed the street I saw two boys. . . ." (Curiosity: who were they? what were they doing? why is the speaker telling about them?) Or, "What caused people to think they saw flying saucers? Three reasons have been given. . . ." (Curiosity: "I know only one. What were the other two?")

ARTISTIC TASTES

These are the esthetic wants. They are old and deeply embedded. The Cro-Magnon man mixed his pigments and drew colored pictures of reindeer on the walls of his caves some 25,000 years ago. Thousands of years later man developed a word-skill, and at once he used this new-found skill to produce poetry and drama. So it has been with every skill that man developed. He makes it not only useful, but *beautiful.* Our Artistic Tastes include appreciation of nature, architecture, sculpture, painting, music, poetry, and drama. They include also appreciation of harmonious color and form in clothes, furniture, pictures, silverware and dishes, kitchen utilities—and such unsuspected things as washtubs, fishing rods and reels, football uniforms, and the makeup and type of this book you are now reading.

In using Artistic Tastes, a speaker must know the artistic *level* of his audience. Educated and cultured people probably do not have stronger Artistic Tastes than the less educated and less cultured, but certainly theirs are *different.* Educated people may appreciate classical music, others prefer hillbilly music or bebop. The educated may prefer the literary novel, others likely prefer the escape literature of pulp magazines. Make clear to the person of culture that your course of action will enable him to hear drama of highest type, or own pottery of exquisite design. Demonstrate to woman that these particular lines and colors fit best her individual personality. Persuade any group that here is something to please their particular level of Artistic Tastes. To all, you have given a motive for action.

FEAR

Not only are we impelled by things we like. We are held back from doing things, not alone by inertia or dislike, but also from fear of unpleasant consequences. The truth is that man lives much under the dominion of fear. First, there are social fears. We are afraid of what people will think if we do not belong to the right clubs and societies, use the right fork, or wear the right clothes. We are afraid of public disapproval if we stray from the accustomed path. Also, there are more primitive fears. The mother is afraid for her children. The worker is afraid for his job. The owner is afraid for his business. The man who has gained property and power under the status quo is mortally afraid of *change*—of new forms of taxes, new regulations, new laws, New Deals. Finally, there is the modern universal anxiety, a form of fear, over the state of the world and of our place in it. It was this kind of fear that Franklin D. Roosevelt was combating in his famous statement, "The only thing we have to fear is fear itself."

A speaker may drive fear from the listener's mind by presenting confidently the pleasure, profit, or honor of his course of action. He may warn them of other dangers, greater than the one they fear. He may show them how to avoid those they fear most.

REVERENCE AND WORSHIP

Man wants to reach out and up to something beyond himself. A common level of this desire is found in *hero worship*. It may be the star on the varsity team, the Sultan of Swat in baseball, a national hero—a Washington or Lincoln, Edison, or Eisenhower. We reverence also *tradition*. Among reverenced traditions are Home, Mother, Flag, Democracy, Freedom, Free Enterprise, Science, and the Scientific Method. Such traditions, we tend to think, are infallible and above criticism.[12] Finally, there is *reverence for Deity*. "If there were no God," said the agnostic Voltaire, "it would be necessary to invent one." True, indeed. You may travel across all the face of the earth—

[12] People of education tend to feel superior to the patrioteer societies that "watch o'er the ramparts" in defense of the Constitution. That is not because they reverence tradition less, but reverence a different set of traditions. Even in science, which is relatively objective, this is so. When an eminent chemist, Anthony Standen, wrote *Science is a Sacred Cow*, in which he criticized the sacredness of science, many fellow scientists came as near to shocked resentment as the learned and scientific could ever get. Biologically older than scientific objectivity is the motive of Reverence and Worship.

from the high plateaus of Tibet, through the valleys of civilizations, into the jungles that are the last retreat of primitive man—and everywhere you will find worshipping men. What they worship may differ. Whether they worship is never a question.

Speak, then, with respect of things that men reverence and worship. Show men that this thing, or these causes, which they reverence will be held in still deeper respect, or will be preserved from harm, and they will be disposed to accept your view. If, on the other hand, you must disagree with tradition, or must question the greatness of accepted heroes—do so with extreme tact, and with reverence for other traditions or heroes not in question. Walk softly and speak gently, "for thou goest among snares and walkest upon the battlements of the city."

The influence of culture patterns

At birth you landed in a society having definite customs and ways of thinking, and from that moment you have been conditioned to accept them. A Chinese reared in America by Americans will be an American. An American reared in China by Chinese will be a Chinese. Any new-born baby can be brought up to be German, Turk, Eskimo, or American. By the time you could talk, you already were a little creature of your culture. Before you were grown its beliefs were your beliefs, and its habits your habits. As Ruth Benedict points out, every child that is born into your group will share these things with you, and no child born into one on the opposite side of the world "can ever achieve a thousandth part." No problem is more important to a speaker than to know the role of culture, its laws and varieties, its influence and limitations.

Whence came these patterns of culture? (1) Some came from *6,000 years of civilization* and are common to all civilized peoples in the world. Among these are writing, architecture, and a system of taxation. (2) Some were developed in our particular *Western Civilization,* and these make us different from peoples of the Orient and Near East. Among the patterns of Western Civilization are the Christian religion, nationalism, and the scientific method. (3) Third, a narrower and sharper set of patterns came from *Anglo-Saxon culture*—the English language, the right to vote, *habeas corpus,* the Bill of Rights, political democracy, a strong sense of superiority over foreigners. (4) Fourth, came the patterns from *English-speaking North America.* These include a sublime belief in education, radio and television habits, acceptance of mass production, love of baseball, and for the varieties of jazz music. (5) Finally, comes the culture patterns of our *immediate locale*—New England, Lower South, Middle West, Far West, etc.—which shall not be considered here. (But see Locale, below, p. 127.)

We are not slaves to these culture patterns. Instead they are useful garments that come to us, as Ralph Linton points out, like suits of ready-made clothes. We do not wear them just as they are, but alter them to fit us—take them in at one place, let them out at another. Naturally there are limits on how much they can be altered, but the limits are wide enough to accommodate most people. Yet in spite of these minor variations in different people, and in the same people at different times, most people in a given culture will respond to a situation in much the same way.

We shall consider, therefore, a selected list—very selected indeed —of culture patterns that influence the American people:

1. Political Democracy
2. Private Property and Enterprise
3. Marriage and Divorce
4. Race
5. Religion
6. War and Force

POLITICAL DEMOCRACY

The American people believe in democracy as a way of life. This includes belief in the Declaration of Independence, the Constitution, the Bill of Rights, *habeas corpus,* trial by jury. We believe in the principles, and often in the sacredness, of these documents, even though we may not quite know what is in them. (In a poll, 79% of adult Americans did not know what the Bill of Rights was.) Yet our belief in democracy stems not from mere belief in its charters and documents. Instead, it comes from the universal feeling that this is a way of life we want. Political Democracy gives us freedom speech, the first and foremost freedom that lifts us above animal existence. It lets us work off frustration without too much restraint. To be sure, no one is wholly free, in a democracy or elsewhere. All must conform to certain patterns. Yet in a democracy we feel that we are free to *be* free, if we *want* to be free, and we do not have to avoid trouble by being inconspicuous, as people who survive under totalitarianism have learned to do so well.

Belief in political democracy includes belief in universal suffrage and in the right of majority rule. But it includes also belief in protecting the rights of minorities. Thus in English-speaking North America (and in parts of Europe) no defeated candidate is compelled to flee, nor even to refrain from speaking out in public against those in office. Bear in mind that this is not true of defeated candidates in all so-called democracies. In some cultures they simply do not understand our doing it, and charge it to the insincerity of opposing political parties who must secretly be conspiring together. Speaking in the British Parliament, shortly after his defeat in 1945, Winston Churchill dryly observed the bewilderment of people in the Balkans: "A friend of mine, an officer, was in Zagreb, when the results of the late General Election came in. An old lady said to him, 'Poor Mr. Churchill! I suppose he will be shot.' My friend was able to reassure her. He said the sentence might be mitigated to one of the various forms of hard labor which are always open to His Majesty's subjects." To us this is humor. To people of certain other cultures, it would simply be confusing.

PRIVATE PROPERTY AND ENTERPRISE

The culture patterns on private property and enterprise are intricate and even conflicting. A survey would lead us into a labyrinth of economic history and practice. Hence here we can offer only a snapshot hastily exposed and hastily developed, in the effort to call attention to the subject.

Americans believe definitely and positively in private ownership of property, and not in communal ownership. Even mineral rights, and hunting and fishing rights, belong to the owner—and not to the government, as in Latin-American and other cultures.

We say we believe also in private enterprise, and often call it "free private enterprise." Actually we believe in it with certain modifications. At the beginning of government under the Constitution we set up a tariff, which amended the free enterprise concept. Later we needed railroads, and gave grants of public lands to persuade private companies to build them. Then big business became too powerful, so we passed an antitrust law. These were the preliminaries. Now came the speedup. The proverbially wicked English had invented the Industrial Revolution, and the proverbially practical Americans now jet-propelled it by inventing mass production. Thereupon our culture patterns on "free private enterprise" began to undergo marked alterations. World War I brought the government into the fabric of family life through the draft, and into almost every business through economic controls. Then came the Great Depression of 1929 and "people began to say that if a man could be taken from his home by federal law and sent to die, the same power should be invoked when his house threatened to fall and he had no food." World War II, with its rationing, price controls, and total economic regulation, very nearly made permanent a new culture pattern. Americans no longer have the old sharp fear of the encroaching state. For better or worse, they have come to accept government aid and regulation as a general principle, and to believe in it. Whether this is good or bad is here beside the point. We are simply defining the culture pattern for use of public speakers.

Now it is not easy to apply this change of pattern to public address without becoming a tempting and vulnerable target, tempting because it is likely to arouse political animosity and vulnerable because the animosity will be based on emotional grounds and thus not be subject to a rational answer. But with so vital a change in this culture pattern the risk must be assumed. Applied to political speaking, this change means simply that *whereas a generation ago it was effective to demonstrate that a proposed reform meant increasing federal control, this is no longer true.* Intelligent minorities, to be sure, are more fearful of the dangers of federal control than ever before (Chambers of Commerce, National Association of Manufacturers, etc.), but not the mass of people. Therefore, those who oppose further extension of federal aid and control had best seek other premises of argument (increasing debt, higher taxes, etc.).

In this day when the study of man has become a science, and persuasion is one aspect of that science, political and economic groups who bid for public support will do it scientifically, or be defeated before they start. Applied to this particular culture pattern, this means that such groups ought to get competent experts on public opinion to work out what is known as "trend curves," in order to find out at what places they have a fighting chance. (The polltakers can do that; it is their business.) These experts can find out where the public might be persuaded to hold the line, and where resistence is futile. Equipped with such trend curves, experts in persuasion can then work out which wants and impelling motives will be the most effective for any group of people. This procedure will not prevent change that comes from events (like wars and depressions), but it will give skillful leaders a chance to direct and alter the change.

MARRIAGE AND DIVORCE

In many parts of the world marriage is arranged by the families involved, and not by the persons. The reasons are not pertinent here, but involve social class and transfer of wealth. Not so in our culture. With us the only proper basis for marriage is romantic love. This is the recurring theme of literature, from Romeo and Juliet to Edward Streeter's father-of-the-bride who yields to his daughter's announcement of love by saying "Okay, puss, if that's the way you feel about it, I love him already."

As for divorces, we recognize them, but we do *not* approve them as ideal. A growing divorce rate is cause for concern. Hollywood actors may get divorces in private life, but not on the screen. Everywhere the ideal marriage is for keeps.

Though marriage is a legal act, regulated by law, it also has a religious side. Actually, we look upon marriage as a religious sacrament. The home and family is not only a patriotic theme but also a religious theme.

Not everybody follows the code. (If you think so, read the *Kinsey Report.*) But there is a strong and constant pressure on those who don't. Young intellectuals are sometimes slow in finding this out. In class speeches they advocate free love, or regulated prostitution, or what-have-you, as the way to solve certain pressing problems of youth; then they are shocked at the backfire of their audience, and blame it on stupid listeners, forgetting that the lowest form of stupidity, as John Morley said, is to criticise the stupidity of others. These inexperienced young speakers simply do not know that they drive their arguments point-blank against the culture patterns of our society, and thus defeat themselves. You cannot attack a culture pattern head-on, but must go about it obliquely.

RACE

Race prejudice is not an instinct, but is a culture pattern. You are not born with it; you learn it. In half the world it does not exist at all; they have never learned it. It is fairly recent in Western culture, but very strong. It is not confined to America, or to the South. It is found all over the Anglo-Saxon world. Let us look at it in this country only. A *Fortune* survey in 1939 showed that majorities of Americans, up to 76 per cent, believed that Negroes were born intellectually inferior. (White population of the South totalled only 27 per cent of the whole United States population, so obviously this opinion was not confined to the South.)

For reasons beyond the scope of this book, the Anglo-Saxon culture has developed a pattern of race prejudice. It has become a caste system, not unlike the religious caste system of India. It varies in form and intensity from one part of the Anglo-Saxon world to another, but it exists in the United States, in both the North and South, and among Anglo-Saxons in Great Britain, India, and South Africa.

In the United States, for example, Emery S. Bogardus measured the feeling of "social difference" felt by 1,725 native born Americans. They lived in every part of the country: East, South, Middle West, and Far West. They were chosen from both sexes, different occupations, different religions. But all had a high-school or college education, and spoke for the more thoughtful and forward-looking segment rather than for the narrow-minded and backward. Of this group only 9 per cent were willing to admit a Negro to his club as a personal chum, only 12 per cent to admit one to his street as a neighbor, and only 39 per cent to admit one to employment in his occupation. (There was also a prejudice against Jews. Of the best-liked Jews, the German Jews, 22 per cent of these Americans would admit to their club, 25 per cent would admit them to their street as a neighbor, and 40 per cent would admit them to employment in their occupation.) [13]

Now to discuss this culture pattern in terms of speechmaking is even more dangerous than discussing the explosive culture pattern of private enterprise. Again, we shall assume the risk, for the inescapable reason that race relations is a subject that will be discussed whether or not. Hence it ought to be discussed effectively.

If your purpose is to intensify race feeling—and that is the admitted purpose of some speechmaking that we all hear—it requires only moderate skill. There is downhill momentum all the way, because you have the Anglo-Saxon culture pattern for a tailwind.

If your purpose is to lessen race prejudice, recognize frankly that such a culture pattern (or *any* culture pattern) is not susceptible to frontal attack, and is "not to be reasoned about except within narrow limits." Therefore any head-on argument against race prejudice, or any demand for immediate and total equality, will fail. More, it will backfire. Therefore, take it piecemeal. Do not attack race prejudice, but work on race *discrimination*. This is a specific, material thing.

[13] "The Measurement of Social Distance," Theodore M. Newcomb and Eugene L. Hartley, *Readings in Social Psychology* (New York: Henry Holt and Co., 1947), p. 504.

Remember that Anglo-Saxon culture patterns include also a strong democratic tradition and the heritage of the Christian religion, and so one culture pattern can be pitted against another. For example, you might select a specific discrimination, and handle that one only. Indeed, you might be interested in knowing that this is being done today with marked success by leaders in the South as well as in the North. Thus little by little race discrimination can be reduced, and as it is reduced there comes a reduction in race prejudice. But the do-gooders who attack head-on the existing race culture pattern, and seek to abolish race feeling in a single speech, will not improve race relations. This is a job for the masters of persuasion.

RELIGION

The culture pattern of religion has undergone one important change in Western Civilization during the past three hundred years. For centuries prior to three hundred years ago nations waged religious wars, and communities engaged in witchhunts. No government granted religious tolerance, and the hangings, beheadings, and burnings make unpleasant reading today. We have got over the more violent aspects of this. There are no more religious wars; and most Western nations grant freedom of worship. This does not mean that we have developed full religious tolerance. We really have not. We are sensitive about religious differences, and as a rule refrain from open and friendly public discussion of religious differences. Indeed, religious differences is one of the least discussed subjects in modern life, less so than social, economic, and political differences. But people of different religious faiths do live peaceably together, and the religious rights of minorities are protected by law. In this sense, our culture pattern of religion includes religious tolerance.

As for the intensity of religious faith today, compared with earlier centuries, it is difficult to speak with certainty. (Every generation, of course, has its semi-educated fringe which believes that in the good old days people were more patriotic, loyal, brave, moral, and religious than today. One can trace this refrain back to at least 2800 B.C. We are not here concerned with what such people imagine, but with the actual change in culture patterns.) Two centuries ago, at the beginning of modern education and scientific progress, a group of intellectuals proclaimed the arrival of the "Age of Reason," in which religion was out-of-date and churches were no longer necessary, and "my own mind is my own church." As the tempo of modern education and scientific discoveries increased, this has been a recurrent theme with many intellectual leaders. Indeed, churchmen themselves have constantly feared that modern scientific thought would weaken the spirit of worship. Actually, what has happened is that church membership has slowly but steadily *increased.* (In the United States, for example, church membership was 40 per cent of the total population in 1900, but had risen to 54 per cent in 1950.) Of these members, seemingly about the same percentage attend church today as a century ago.

Religion is universal. No people ever lived without it, whether prehistoric primitive man or modern civilized man. It is not confined to church attendants or to church members. It has been altered, but not weakened, by modern scientific thought. And today, as centuries ago, *it is less strong in young people than among middle-aged and older people.* There are many individual exceptions, but the basic pattern is that increasing religious faith comes with increasing experience and age.

Young people who are impatient with religious ceremony had best remember that they are not the first to feel that way, nor will they be the last. In discussing religion, remember that most people hold it in respect; hence topics based on respect for religion are likely to be listened to with respect. Remember also that most people are sensitive even to mild criticism of religious practice; you cannot attack religion head-on, and even the mildest criticism must be handled with tact. Witness the tact of the man who filed a court petition to compel radio stations to grant him the right to criticise certain religious practices: "I do not throw stones at church windows. I do not mock at people kneeling in prayer. . . . But I abhor and denounce those who seek to prevent others from expressing contrary views."

WAR AND FORCE

War is not an instinct. Certain peoples, like the Eskimos and Mission Indians of California, never learned it. To them the idea of a whole village going to war against another village is simply not understandable. To them, killing is killing, and they have no separate categories whereby if one man kills another it is murder, but if the people of one village kill the people of another village, it is not murder but war. To them it is still murder.

In Western Civilization, however, public opinion has been conditioned to accept cycles of war and peace, "much as mankind accepts the coming and going of the season." As Homer Lea, a military writer, points out from the fifteenth century B.C. until the present time, a cycle of over 3,400 years, there have been less than 234 years of peace. The history of Western Civilization and of its predecessors is a history of wars.

Concurrent with this, but newer in origin, is our culture pattern as a peace-loving people. It is a matter of national pride that we do not wage wars of aggression, that we ourselves fight to resist aggression and to attain "enduring peace, world democracy, and the rights of oppressed peoples." We are living, therefore, between two culture patterns. One is for settling all world differences by peaceful methods, so long as we do not have to surrender national sovereignty. The other is a willingness to wage war rather than submit to foreign aggression.

Topics based on both of these patterns are effective. On one hand, you can say, "Do this, and it will lessen the chance for war, or will promote world peace," and the argument will tend to be effective. On the other hand, you can say, "Do that, and we can make ourselves strong in case we are attacked," and that, too, tends to be effective.

Other influences

We have studied the influence of reason, wants, and culture patterns. These are broad and basic, common to all. But assemble people in small and carefully designated groups, and still other influences appear. These will be considered under five headings:

1. Age
2. Sex
3. Locale
4. Education and Economic Status
5. Activity Level

AGE

Youth is more prone than older people to romance and adventure. In romance, especially they find an outlet in hero worship—the radio and television and screen star, the star of the gridiron. (Frank Sinatra at his peak had 40,000,000 fans, with around 2,000 "Sinatra Clubs," averaging 200 each in membership. His fan mail averaged 5,000 letters a week.) They crave excitement, and find it harder than older people to listen to serious ideas. Hence they prefer thriller pictures and action stories.

Also, in America at least, younger people are definitely less interested than older people in public affairs. Older people think they have a bigger stake in politics. Younger people have not yet paid taxes or suffered from bad government. For example, in an intensive study of a typical United States county during a presidential campaign, the investigators found that on each educational level the older people were more interested in the election than the younger ones. "This is a result which should not be passed by lightly. . . . The difference between American and European experience in this regard is clear; in pre-war Europe political movements on the part of youth were very active."[14]

Young intellectuals, it should be added, tend to be radical. They are likely to be impetuous reformists, impatient at delay, eager for quick changes. As they grow older, their impatience lessens, and their ardor cools. They are more content with the world as it is. As they grow still older, they tend to oppose change, especially changes advocated by young, impatient reformists, and to wonder why youth nowadays has such dangerous ideas.

Finally, young people have not lived so long as older ones, they have had a narrower range of experiences, and they accumulated less knowledge. Therefore, they tend to accept what they are told less critically than do older persons.

In speaking to young people, therefore, topics based on Adventure, Competition, Pride, Loyalty, and Hero Worship are stronger than such topics would be with older persons. In speaking to older peole, topics based on Security, Property, Reputation, Conformity, and Worship of Tradition or Worship of Deity are stronger than they would be with young persons. In speaking to older people, remember that they will weigh and judge more suspiciously, and that they will tend to resist accepting new ideas, more than do young people.

SEX

Women, by almost universal nature, are more passive, receptive, long-suffering, and enduring of pain than men. As a compensation, they have developed an especially strong inner bulwark of self-respect and pride, which finds expression in the desire for beauty and charm, and in simply "being a woman." Hence women need to

[14] P. F. Lazarsfeld, B. Berelson, and H. Gaudet, *The People's Choice* (New York, Duell, Sloan and Pearce, 1944), pp. 44-45.

be admired and loved, and will pay great attention to clothes, cosmetics, and beautifiers.

Men are more aggressive than women. They rely more on *doing*, and women rely more on *being*. Hence it is still unusual to have a woman legislator, a policewoman, or a woman who manages a business involving risk of investment. Most women prefer to be homemakers, to preserve and protect rather than to create.

For this reason perhaps women are less concerned than men with politics and political affairs. The successful functioning of a home is more compelling to them than the successful functioning of a democracy. In studying a presidential election, for example, the investigators found that only 26% of women wanted to hear evening radio political talks or discussion about public issues—far below the men. They ran into such remarks as "I don't care to vote. Voting is for the men." "I think men should do the voting and the women should stay home and take care of their work." The workers concluded that not only did women feel no compulsion to vote, but some "actually consider aloofness a virtue."

Men are prone to say that women are more emotional than men. This is not quite true, since men are about as emotional as human beings can be and yet survive. Yet the adage points vaguely toward a difference between men and women, a difference that can be stated in more precisely these terms: *Women care more about what other people think than about following a set of abstract laws or regulations.* Thus boys adapt themselves more readily to rules, whereas girls are more sensitive to the wishes of others. So it is that laws are made by men, and observance of law is upheld by men. It is a man who would send his daughter from the home if she had broken the code, not a woman. It is a woman who would plead for a son to be excused from the penalty of reckless driving; only a man would let the boy take his medicine and learn his lesson.

Women probably have stronger artistic tastes than men, or at least they are more refined. They have a greater appreciation of good music and art, even though this taste is strong also in men. They are more sensitive than men to beautiful housefurnishings, tableware, and clothes. (The sterling silver industry could never survive on men's desire.) "The thing that sells a house more than anything else," explained a man who had loaned tens of millions on homes, "is a beautiful kitchen, and it is usually the women who decide which house they want."

Women, finally, have a stronger sense of worship and reverence for deity. With men the sense of worship comes in a measure from allegiance to the moral law, or to the sense of order in the universe. With women it tends to be reverence for a very personal God who has a personal concern for their personal welfare.

These are the major lines of difference between men and women as they concern a speaker.[15] With women, any topic will be especially strong that rests on worship and reverence, artistic tastes, home, family, or inner privation. Do not expect too many women to be interested in the welfare of government (though some will be), or the preservation of abstract principles; instead rest your topic on the welfare of home and family and friends, for these are the stronger motives.

LOCALE

People of different regions tend toward specific differences in outlook. In the Middle West isolationism lingers in many disguises. Maine votes Republican. Texas votes Democratic. Wisconsin is "progressive." Pennsylvania is "conservative." The South is "solid." These are gross differences. There are infinite finer ones. Upstate New York does not vote the same as New York City; for that matter even their speech is different. Downstate Illinois votes differently from Chicago. In the Old South, the piedmont is different in outlook from the older tidewater. In the Far West, Southern California already has developed different characteristics from those in the region of San Francisco Bay.

There is also a difference between those who live in city and country. They follow different occupations, and live in different tempos and rhythms. They enjoy different pastimes.

Many types of books and magazines are published primarily for people of different locale. Still more so must a speaker recognize the influence of locale on his immediate audience.

EDUCATION AND ECONOMIC STATUS

Because of the frontier, the expanding free-enterprise system, and opportunity for free public education, America has had less class consciousness than Europe. The ladder of opportunity was available

[15] For those interested in further inquiry into sex differences the following are especially recommended: Helene Deutsch, *The Psychology of Women* (New York: Grune & Stratton, Inc., 1944); and Lazarsfeld *et al., op. cit.*

for all to climb, and most of those at the top have not been there long enough to feel aloof from those below. The chief class difference in America, therefore, is based, not on social distinction, but on education and economic status. Unfortunately, the amount of money we possess and the extent of higher education we get tend to coincide, albeit with many individual exceptions. Hence the two forces operate largely as one.

Consider first the sources of ideas of people having different education and economic status. The educated and higher income groups read books and magazines, and listen to the more serious radio programs. They belong to civic organizations and clubs. They hear from one hundred to three hundred speeches a year. But they tend almost exclusively to read the books and magazines, and hear radio programs and speeches that repeat what they already believe in. Thus, much of what they read and hear simply reinforces old attitudes. Now this gives them an uplift, to be sure, but provides no new ideas, and fails to challenge their thinking. As George V. Denny, Jr., Director of America's Town Meeting of the Air, said: "Here's a man who . . . even with the radio right there in his room and a chance to hear what the other side has to say for itself, . . . deliberately closes his mind. And, if he is like the rest of us, he reads the newspapers he approves and doesn't read the others; he listens to friends who believe as he does and doesn't listen to others. Talk about dangers to democracy—*there's* the real danger."

What of the poorer and less educated? (Many of the less educated, of course, are less *educatable.*) They read fewer books and magazines, rely less on newspapers, and hear fewer speeches. They listen *more* to the radio than do the educated but listen *less* to radio's more serious programs. As for news, only 39% of college-educated persons rely on radio for their main source of news, but 62% of those who have had only a grammar-school education do so.

The poorer and less educated, therefore, are influenced more by radio and television than are the better educated and people of greater means. For that reason since 1930, when radio began to be common in American homes, there has been a shift in the media of political influence. Henceforth politicians might almost say, "Give me the radio and television, and you can have all the great books and little books, the magazines and newspapers."

Finally, the educated and well-to-do tend to oppose political or economic changes in the status quo. This they do for compelling reasons.

Under the status quo they have attained income and property. They have attained a comfortable way of life. They have attained a reasonable sense of security. Therefore, they dislike change. More, they are afraid of change.

For students of public address this fear of change by men of property and education is one of the most significant forces in political history. Plato, wealthy philosopher, opposed the coming of democracy in Athens. French nobility before 1789 resisted change, until they were marched to the guillotine in the Revolution. White Russians before 1917 resisted change, until they were destroyed by the Red Russians. In America, most (though conspicuously not all) of the men of property opposed the American Revolution of 1776, the Jeffersonian revolution of 1800, the Jacksonian democracy of the 1830's, and the Roosevelt New Deal of the 1930's. These oppositions to change were natural enough, arising from a group that had attained income, reasonable security, and a desirable way of life. But in resisting change, the privileged and educated and men of property ignored too much the bitter need of the underprivileged and less educated and those without property. By refusing to allow a little change, or enough change, they created delayed pressure that led to the violence of upheaval, and to their own disastrous defeat. In future crises, can the educated and privileged be persuaded to change enough, or must they always be overpowered by force?

The answer partly depends on their future education—which seemingly needs to be altered from the education given them in the past. Also it depends partly on the training and skill of those who undertake to persuade them. Here enters a dangerous new factor. In the past—down until the twentieth century—men of property and education controlled governments except during special moments of history. They could be overthrown only by revolution. Therefore (excepting only the new American West in the nineteenth century) persuasion was directed largely toward people of education and property. In America this is no longer true. For better or worse, a larger percentage of voting is done today than ever before by the poorer and less educated, and the less intelligent. The radio and television have done that. Consider what this means in terms of public opinion and persuasion. First, it means that the voting power of the country is no longer in the hands of men of property and higher intelligence and greater education. Second—and this follows from the first—it means that henceforth leaders must develop greater skill than ever before in persuading the less educated and the less intelligent to a wise course of action. It is, as Wallace Carroll has phrased it, "persuade or perish." If men of good will disdain to learn this, rest assured that demagogues will not disdain it, and we shall henceforth be ruled increasingly by men who make slight distinction between "what sounds good" and "what is good and sound."

AUDIENCE ACTIVITY LEVEL

The last item to be considered is the activity level of each particular audience. For convenience we can divide these into three levels: excited, normal, and depressed.

At the *excited activity level* the listeners are under tension. It may be extreme tension, as when they are deeply involved, aroused, or excited—like a cocked gun waiting for a finger to pull the trigger. It may be a milder tension, as with partisans or enthusiasts who are deeply interested in a subject or a speaker or an occasion. Examples of excited-level listeners are students at a football rally, partisans at a political convention, persons at a religious revival, or any group pre-aroused by the nature of the meeting such as a labor union local discussing whether to strike, or a Congress in the final discussion of a critical bill.

You will not meet the excited activity level in the classroom. But when you do meet it, you had better be prepared for its demands: (1) Waste no time on tedious details, but get to the heart of the subject at once. (2) If listeners are in an unreasoning mood, don't try to reason, for they won't listen. You can state impellingly, and in terms of their wants, the *results* of reasoning; but do so with the process left out. (3) If it is an audience concerned with finding the answer to an acute need (Shall we strike? Can we win the election with this man, or that one?), reduce the problem to its simplest terms, and keep repeating it in simplified form. (4) Speak like a man who *can* and *will* lead. Whosoever speaks in dull accents and limpid manner will not satisfy the needs of listeners at the excited activity level. They need to hear the voice of Authority, and to see behind it a man.

The *normal activity level* is one where the audience has little tension, excitement, or special interests involved. Its members are entirely willing perhaps to listen—but only if the speaker delivers the stuff. Most audiences are at the normal activity level, and the procedures of this book center on speaking to them at this level.

The *depressed activity level* you will meet often in classroom speaking. It's a Monday morning, and your class has not yet recovered from the weekend. It's any morning at eight o'clock, and they are not yet fully awake. It's the day after a heavy date, a great night, or a big social event; they are awake, but responses are slow. Or it's just another day, and they've heard seventy speeches in the course already. Ho hum, now comes the seventy-first! All of this is good training for you, because outside of class you will also meet audiences at the depressed activity level. Perhaps the program has been too long, and the hour is late. Or the preceding speaker was an *And-Er-r-*Vocalist, or was perhaps a dealer in hollow banalities. He depressed the audience, and now they are yours. Again, it may be a program that follows a meal, the audience is relaxing on a full stomach, and the demands of digestion have left them drowsy. No matter what the cause. You will meet audiences at the depressed activity level. You must learn now to deal with them. The methods are thoroughly covered throughout the remainder of this book, starting with the next chapter, but basic suggestions are inserted here: (1) Wake yourself up and use vigorous mental and physical action. Said a disgruntled drowsy listener, "I wanted to go to sleep, but that confounded speaker talked so loud he kept me awake, and I had to listen." Be that kind of speaker if the audience is at the depressed-activity level. (2) Use human interest stories and humor. Make them laugh, and they are no longer half asleep. Get their interest, and you have a chance to keep it.

ASSIGNMENTS

ON UNDERSTANDING THE INFLUENCE OF REASON, WANTS AND IMPELLING MOTIVES, AND CULTURE PATTERNS ON HUMAN ATTITUDES AND BEHAVIOR

1. From a popular magazine take a sampling of advertisements (i.e. not an assortment that you happen to like, but a stratified sampling, such as all the full-page advertisements in an entire issue, or all the advertisements in a given number of pages, etc.)
   a. Classify them into four groups: Those that appeal primarily to (1) reason and logic, (2) wants and impelling motives, (3) culture patterns, and (4) reason plus wants, or reason plus culture patterns.
   b. Classify the strongest motive appeals of groups (2), (3), and (4) above in terms of the 20 wants and 6 culture patterns discussed in this chapter.

2. Write an analysis of your attitudes and beliefs on one of the following topics. Include the influence of reason and evidence, of wants and impelling

motives, and of culture patterns. Remember that your instructor will be aware of the tendency discovered by Poffenberger of people (see above, page 102) to idealize and magnify the influence of reason in their own conduct:

a. Why I like dates
b. Why I like athletics
c. Why I came to this college
d. Why I joined my fraternity, sorority, or other society
e. Why I started smoking
f. Why I am a Republican (or Democrat)
g. Why I belong to my church
h. My attitude toward some other racial or religious groups: Catholics, Protestants, Jews, Negroes

3. Read some influential speech given at a critical moment in history. Especially recommended are Patrick Henry, "Appeal to Arms," Abraham Lincoln, "Gettysburg Address," (both found in standard references), or Winston Churchill, "Blood, Toil, Tears, and Sweat" (found in his collection of speeches, *Blood, Sweat, and Tears,* pp. 275-276):

a. Select its strongest motive appeal and classify it in terms of this chapter.
b. Explain how the appeal was made, whether through reason and evidence, vivid description only, irrational play on emotions, or some other.

4. Read a speech found in this volume, in *Vital Speeches,* or in A. C. Baird's annual volumes on *Representative American Speeches:*

a. On what wants, impelling motives, or culture patterns does the speaker base the speech?
b. Do you think the speaker chose the most effective ones? If you were speaking to this audience on such a subject, what other wants, impelling motives, or culture patterns would you use?

5. On what wants, impelling motives, and culture patterns would you base speeches on the following topics:

a. Revising the college curriculum
b. Why students should study the fine arts
c. Why they should study foreign language
d. Why they should study science
e. Why people should give money to the Red Cross
f. Why the U.S. should (or should not) have socialized medicine
g. Why the U.S. should (or should not) re-elect the President
h. Why the U.S. should prefer democracy to communism

ON USING REASON, WANTS, AND CULTURE PATTERNS IN SPEAKING

6. Prepare a 2-minute speech based on *one* want or culture pattern. Use as many different techniques as possible for making this speech effective, especially reason, evidence, and vivid description, but under no circumstances resort to illogical emotional appeal.

7. Choose a speech subject for a longer speech, one in which you intend to cultivate a change of attitude:

a. Determine as accurately as you can the wants or culture patterns of the class members that would cause them to resist changing attitude.

b. After studying your subject, select the strongest available *other* wants or culture patterns for which you have supporting material. For example, if the chief obstacle to change of attitude is desire for Security, you may be able to use against this the desire for Freedom or Property. Concentrate on the strongest motives, and reject weak or doubtful ones even though you have supporting material for them. Having thus chosen the strongest wants or culture patterns, you will now proceed to reinforce them with all the best available reason and supporting materials that can be used within the time limit.

8. Prepare a speech to win specific action from an apathetic audience, such as "study harder," "don't take snap courses," "attend the college lecture series," or "vote on election day." Choose the strongest possible want (or wants) on which to base the speech, and use as many techniques as possible to make the want effective.

9. Give a speech on how you think the principles studied in this chapter could be used in some particular field, such as (1) dormitory management, (2) student-and-teacher relations, (3) personnel work, (4) labor relations, (5) law enforcement, (6) salesmanship, (7) politics, (8) religion.

Dwight D. Eisenhower addressing students at Columbia University illustrates the most common purpose of speechmaking, not to win votes or induce a definite decision, but simply to cultivate attitudes.

CHAPTER 7

Persuasion and Public Opinion

CHAPTER 7

An experimental psychologist observed that on the basis of modern research, "Lecturing may lead to a high degree of interest. It may affect the motivation of the listener. But it seldom brings about a definite decision on the part of the listener to take a certain action at a specific time. A lecture is not often conducive to decision."[1] Of this statement the following observations may be made: First, it is true. Second, it has been known for twenty-three centuries. Third, it misses the essential purpose of speechmaking.

There are, of course, restricted conditions under which a single speech or a concentrated group of speeches may help listeners make a decision. An example is a committee, a court, or a jury. Such a group is *already committed to action,* but is undecided on what course of action is best. It is influenced by speaking of many kinds: testimony, statements of opinion, discussion, argument.[2] Also there are "times of decision," and when such a time approaches, people may be immediately influenced by speechmaking. A well-known "time of decision" is a political election. As an election approaches, a large portion of voters—somewhat over one-half in a typical American presidential election—will listen to the intense concentration of speeches. Another portion (and this was of unsuspected importance until recently) will be influenced by private conversation in which other persons have taken their cue from public speaking they have recently heard. By election day a moderate percentage of voters will have changed their minds as a result of the total campaign influence, and a larger percentage will go to the polls than otherwise would have gone except for the interest aroused by the campaign.[3] Thus under limited condi-

[1] Kurt Lewin, "Group Decision and Social Change" in Theodore M. Newcomb and Eugene L. Hartley, *Readings in Social Psychology* (New York: Henry Holt and Company, 1947), p. 336.

[2] Chief Justice John Marshall once reversed a former decision of the U. S. Supreme Court and apologized for its error by saying that the case "had not been argued by counsel." See *Congressional Record,* 44th Congress, 1st Session, Part 7, pp. 320-321.

[3] See Paul F. Lazarsfeld, Bernard Berelson, and Hazel Gaudet, *The People's Choice* (New York: Duell, Sloan and Pearce, 1944) for a thorough analysis of the percentage of

tions a given speech, or a group of speeches may have important influence on immediate action.

But such conditions are limited. Ordinarily nobody hears a speech today and changes his mind before the sun goes down. If man behaved that way, today he could be persuaded by one speech to the virtues of Buddhist monasticism, tomorrow by another to the blessings of Moslem polygamy, and the day after to the beneficence of Western monogamy. Today we would believe that college education is the best guarantee of success and happiness, and believe tomorrow that college is a waste of time. Human life would be erratic—and short. To produce such shifting opinions is not, and never has been, the purpose of speechmaking.

Consider, therefore, its real purpose. At a relentless pace, time moves on; and no human hand can stay its pace. In the inner recesses of mind we may cry:

> Backward, turn backward, O Time in thy flight;
> Make me a child again, just for tonight.

But the flow of time is never backward. It pushes man and the events of mankind onward at a rate that never slackens and never falters. As we are thus thrust into the future, we are thrust also into new problems, new needs, new duties, and new challenges. Constantly we are compelled to refocus our thoughts, reshape our opinions, alter our direction of life. Life and the world about us are constantly changing. Not one of us today can think the same as we did yesterday about youth, art, leisure, literature, sports, amusements, clothes, education, taxes, wages, prices, or profits. Today is a new day. We can live and be masters only as we learn to match the infinite diversity of change by an increasing delicacy of response.

Our ability to do this depends in a large measure on how adequately our ideas are watered and cultivated by others—by writers and speakers. "No man," said John Donne, "is an Iland, intire of it selfe; every man is a peece of the Continent, a part of the maine." The ef-

---

changes and the reasons for change of a sampling of voters in Erie County, Ohio, during the 1940 Presidential Campaign. See W. N. Brigance, "The Effectiveness of the Public Platform," *Annals of the American Academy of Political and Social Science*, March, 1947, Vol. 250, pp. 71-72, for a report on the influence of certain speeches in the 1936 Presidential Campaign as measured by public opinion polls. See Norman C. Meier and Harold W. Saunders, *The Polls and Public Opinion* (New York: Henry Holt and Co., 1949), for Archibald M. Crossley's report on the polltakers fiasco in foretelling the 1948 Presidential Election: "We have taken our medicine.... We assumed campaigns do not change many votes and stopped polling too soon." (Pp. 160-164.)

fects of mass communication was described by Wilbur Schramm as "being like drops of calcarious water falling from the roof of a cave upon an ancient stalagmite. Sometimes an especially big drop leaves an especially large deposit, in such a position that it can be seen and actually appears to change the shape of the stalagmite. Usually the residue of each new drop simply merges with the other deposits, and the structure grows, almost imperceptibly, in the direction of the source of supply." [4]

Not many techniques of persuasion are peculiar to the twentieth century. The basic ones are described by Aristotle, Cicero, Quintilian, and the medieval and Reformation rhetoricians. But during the past fifty years scientific research has proved that the best of early thinkers were right, and have contributed vastly to the understanding of details and methods. This research has come from workers in separate fields: from anthropologists, psychologists, sociologists, political scientists, and advertisers, as well as experts in speech itself. Their research can be summarized as follows:

1. The cumulative effects of mass communication are powerful. The communications blend into and form a large part of people's environment. They contribute to attitudes and opinions which remain after the facts are forgotten.

2. The radio is more effective than the newspaper, and face-to-face speaking is more effective than radio. Repeated experimental findings demonstrate that "the human voice is more persuasive, more friendly, more compelling than the written word," and that "the physical presence of a speaker establishes a more normal and satisfying social relationship than does the mere sound of his voice."

3. The amount of learning from mass communications, other things being equal, is proportional to the degree of attention, and therefore to the motivation which compels the attention.

4. It is not enough to say a thing once. Effectiveness is increased by repetition. Thus repetition with variations increases both factual and attitude learning. Repetition via different channels—magazine, radio, face-to-face—increases both factual and attitude learning.[5]

[4] "The Effects of Mass Communications," *Journalism Quarterly*, XXVI (December, 1949), No. 4, 397.

[5] One hesitates to quote the late unlamented Dr. Joseph Goebbels, Nazi Minister of Propaganda. But his lack of public morals should not lead us to ignore his ability to influence public opinion. On January 29, 1942, Goebbels wrote in his diary: "Propaganda

5. Persuasion is more effective, other things being equal, when related to people's wants. "Men think critically and precisely only under specific conditions of motivation, and then only in response to the particular pressing problem." [6]

With this background we proceed to methods of influencing public opinion that are available to the speaker. Primarily there are five:

1. Get the listener's attention and keep it
2. Rest reason and evidence on deep-seated wants and cultural patterns
3. Use indirect methods as well as direct
4. For long-run cultivation of attitudes, remember that organized information usually is more effective than attempts at immediate persuasion
5. To reaffirm old attitudes, vitalize human hopes, ideals, desires, and values

Get the listener's attention and keep it

People in an audience assuredly don't have to listen simply because they sit and you talk. They can sit and day-dream, mind-wander, or doze. They can think about what they are going to do tonight, or did yesterday. They will give you sustained attention only when you *interest* them. This, then, is the basic step in persuasion—to get listeners' interest (and thereby their attention), and to keep it.

KINDS OF ATTENTION

There are three kinds of attention. *The first is voluntary attention,* which comes from the listener's determined effort, such as a sense of duty or knowing that he must pass an examination on a professor's lecture. Ordinarily a speaker cannot rely on listeners making such a

---

must therefore always be essentially simple and repetitious. In the long run only he will achieve basic results in influencing public opinion who is able to reduce problems to simplest terms and who has the courage to keep forever repeating them in this simplified form despite the objections of the intellectuals."

[6] The following works contain useful information on recent research on public opinion: Lyman D. Bryson, *Communication of Ideas* (New York: Harper and Brothers, 1948); Leonard W. Doob, *Public Opinion and Propaganda* (New York: Henry Holt and Co., 1948); Hadley Cantril, *Gauging Public Opinion* (Princeton: Princeton University Press, 1945); C. I. Hovland, A. A. Lumsdaine, and F. D. Sheffield, *Experiments on Mass Communication* (Princeton: Princeton University Press, 1949); Joseph T. Klapper, *The Effects of Mass Media* (New York: Bureau of Applied Social Research, Columbia University, 1949); Wilbur Schramm, *Mass Communications* (Urbana: University of Illinois Press, 1949).

sustained determined effort. They simply won't. Therefore, strike off voluntary attention as being available to speakers.

The second is involuntary attention. This comes from a stimulus that slaps the listener in the eye, ear, or other sense organs. It requires no effort. Thus a passing fire engine gets involuntary attention. Speakers use involuntary attention by delivery—by being so earnest and enthusiastic that these qualities arrest the listener's eye and ear, by sheer energy of voice, by intensely personal tone and informing inflections, by gestures that catch and hold the eye. Speakers can get by without using involuntary attention, but no speaker can reach his highest potential level without using it.

The third is habitual attention. This comes from making the subject interesting—from what you talk about and how you talk about it. Choose a subject of deep interest to the listener, and you have his habitual interest even though you may not speak well. Relate your subject to something the listener is interested in, or knows about, and you capture his habitual interest. Effective speaking requires habitual attention and cannot be effective without it. Consider the illustration given below of John Tyler Caldwell's speech on "The New Birth." Talking on the goals of education at his inauguration as a college president, he gained habitual attention by (1) referring to the well-advertised recent birth of his daughter, and (2) relating his theme to one of the best-known books in the world:

> I have chosen as a subject for my remarks: "The New Birth, or Alice in Wonderland." Any resemblance of the subject to recent events or newly arrived persons to this campus is entirely deliberate and premeditated on my part. If the recent arrival objects to having her name used here, she may sue her father when she comes of age in October, 1966, A.D.
>
> All of us here recall Lewis Carroll's sprightly and gentle classics, *Alice in Wonderland* and *Through the Looking Glass.* Alice, a little blonde-headed child, grown drowsy from picking daisies, was not greatly surprised to see a Rabbit walk by, nor hear him speak plain English. But when the Rabbit pulled a watch from his waistcoat pocket, Alice, burning with curiosity (natural for women) just had to follow him to his hole.
>
> At this point, as one who so recently has accepted a college presidency, I find myself sympathizing with Alice. For the story records, "In another moment went Alice after it (the rabbit), never once considering how in the world she was to get out again." President Draughon, President Galilee and President Norton (and our wives, God bless them) are among the more recent sympathizers who surely join me in a fellow feeling for Alice's venture down the hole. . . .
>
> Goals are important; Alice found it so when she was confused and asked the

Cheshire cat, "Would you tell me please, which way I ought to go from here?"
"That depends a good deal on where you want to get to," said the cat. . . .
Since education must take its goals from society which it serves, let's have a look at our American society's goals. Or do they exist? And who established them? [7]

NATURE OF ATTENTION

What is the nature of attention? How long does a single span of attention last? How long, for example, can a listener "attend" to what a speaker is saying? First, note that *attention comes in spurts and lasts for only a few moments at a time.* Even when you give attention to such simple things as a dot on a paper, or the noise of a buzzer, it is not possible to fix attention for longer than from one to three seconds. Complex stimuli will allow longer periods of attention, but not much longer. When you face an audience, therefore, remember that you are never more than a few seconds away from losing the attention of any person who sits before you! You cannot "get attention" at the beginning of a speech and expect it to remain fixed to the end. You must recapture that attention every few seconds, or else it is soon lost and gone.

There are obvious and common-sense ways of holding attention, ways also established by experimental psychology. Some of them we have already discussed under Forms of Support (pages 38-44). They include the use of *facts and figures, specific instances, illustrations, comparisons, and testimony.* Another method of holding attention, already discussed, is of unsuspected importance: namely *arranging ideas into a simple, obvious, and meaningful pattern.* Listeners can then see the whole thought arrangement, know where the speaker has been, know where he is, and forecast where he is likely to go. In this sense, *careful outlining,* then, is a means of holding attention.

Consider the following two examples. In the first, the speaker has not one single specific instance, illustration, comparison, or testimony. Nor has he humor, suspense, or juice of any kind. His is simply a dehydrated idea:

Internal weakness is invariably the prime cause of breakdown. All history warns against short-cuts to progress. Where the uncreative majority follows the leadership of a creative minority by a species of drill, a mechanical and superficial imitation of the inspired original, the invariable danger is that

[7] Inaugural address as president of Alabama College, December 11, 1948. A. Craig Baird, *Representative American Speeches: 1948-1949* (New York: H. W. Wilson Co., 1949), pp. 197-199.

the leaders become infected by the mechanicalness of their followers. The result is an arrested civilization in which the leaders substitute the whip of compulsion for persuasion.

If that won't put you to sleep, you've got insomnia. Yet a large part speaking is made up of that sort of stuff, even though it cannot pass the first gateway to persuasion—of getting and keeping the listener's attention. Contrast the above with the devices of attention used by Carl A. Gray, a manufacturing president, in talking to fellow industrialists:

A year ago, Governor Bowles of Connecticut asked me to serve on a state commission to make a study of education in that state. I have three children and I'm interested in schools, so I accepted. . . . The next time I saw a few of my business friends, after accepting the appointment, I could sense a little coldness in the atmosphere.

One fellow literally said to me, "What's the idea of accepting an appointment with that man Bowles?"

That man Bowles! How familiar was the sound of that lament. I started to explain, but then thought better of it. He wouldn't understand. I said, "See you later." And it's later than he thinks.

I could have told him that if I had not accepted, there wouldn't have been any representative, perhaps, of business on that commission. Labor leaders had accepted appointment to the commission, headed by Norman Cousins, Editor of the *Saturday Review of Literature.* Was it better, I ask you, to let the issue go by default and then scream bloody murder if a report is finally filed that might be distasteful to some business people, rather than associate with "That man Bowles"? [8]

You will listen to a speech like that. Indeed, you can hardly keep from listening, for the speaker has used half a dozen methods all at once of holding attention: Repetition ("that man Bowles"), specific instances (Bowles, Norman Cousins), illustration ("one fellow literally said to me"), direct quotation ("See you later"), and the whole thought flowing in narrative form.

If you can get *favorable* attention and keep it, you are ready to use the next four principles of persuasion. But if you don't yet sense, deep in your chromosomes, the vital importance of attention, then it is scarcely worth while to read further. William Trufant Foster, after nearly fifty years of public speaking, testified both to the importance and to the typical slowness of young speakers in learning such essentials: "Unhappily I was slow to learn them. The first lesson was

[8] Carl A. Gray, President of the Grenby Manufacturing Corporation, to the Economic Club of Detroit. *Vital Speeches,* XVI (June 1, 1950), No. 16, 510.

that knowledge and righteousness on a man's side are not enough; in addition, he must know how to speak. Over and over again I found that out. . . . Uncle Joe Cannon, Speaker of the House of Representatives . . . giving a campaign speech declared that the United States is a great nation; great largely because of the Republican Party. Then he said it all over again with violent waving of his arms. It was the first time I had heard 'the eagle scream.' I [also campaigning for the Republicans] was disgusted; and when the audience applauded lustily, I felt still worse. My own speech was based on research and analysis. I marshalled evidence—accurate, documented, logically devastating. To my dismay the audience did not care a campaign button for what I said. . . . I began to realize that in place of half the heavy substance of my speeches, I should have substituted lightness of touch: concrete examples, humor, anecdotes, color, and adaptation to each audience. No audience can attend to serious discourse for more than a few moments at a time. I was stupidly slow in learning that. Last month I spoke to a club in Winter Park, Florida, the University Club, which takes pride in the large proportion of its members who are listed in *Who's Who in America,* who are members of Phi Beta Kappa and who have doctor's degrees. Even a highbrow audience can not stand much. If a speaker does not provide relief from abstract seriousness, his hearers will provide it for themselves, at the speaker's expense." [9]

Rest reason and evidence on deep-seated wants and cultural patterns

Man "thinks" and "reasons" under definite limitations (see page 139 for previous discussion of this), but it would be dangerously wrong to assume that thinking and reasoning are therefore of only slight importance in influencing human action. They influence a great deal of action, especially critical and important action, but do so under restricted conditions. We now come to these conditions and limitations.

The findings of psychological research in this particular are well summarized by Daniel Katz: "Analytic thinking occurs not as a prevalent mode of human response but as a limited reaction under conditions of block or need. Men think critically and precisely only under specific conditions of motivation, and then only in reference to the

[9] "Random Notes on Public Speaking," *Quarterly Journal of Speech,* XXXIII (April, 1947), No. 2, 141-142.

particular pressing problem. Ordinarily they respond according to the law of least effort."[10] In other words, when people get in a jam, they think. Or least they *try* to think, if they can think. In placid times, people drift along without using Reason, but when they face a real problem and want to know the way out—they are likely to use Reason, or turn to someone who can use it. Reason, then, is the instrument by which people solve pressing problems and get out of a jam. The use of Reason consequently will always be related to human needs or wants. It is used to show people how to solve a problem they need to have solved, how to satisfy a want, how to reach a goal, how to move toward an ideal.

Note how this operates in the objective field of science. A scientist, let us assume, *wants* to study the nature of cosmic rays. His reason for wanting to, when elaborated, can always be reduced to other wants, so we might say facetiously that "he wants to because he wants to." The *want* is the propelling force, the driving power. To satisfy this Want, the objective scientist patiently performs experiments, collects data, checks them, assembles them, and *reasons* his way to certain conclusions.

Observe the premising of Reason on Wants as it might operate in the minds of a Committee of Congress drafting a new tax law. In one sense, of course, nobody wants a new tax law, for nobody likes taxes. But since the chaos of having no taxes and hence no government is far worse, these members of the committee "want" to draft a new tax law. This Want involves the following sub-wants: (1) Each member *wants* a tax law that will "serve the greatest good of the greatest number." (2) They also *want* a tax law that will raise "enough" taxes, which may mean either taxes enough to balance the budget or leave a deficit not large enough to frighten the majority of voters. (3) They *want* a tax law that will not antagonize: (a) the housewives, (b) the farmers, (c) the laborers, (d) low-income groups. They might prefer also to please: (e) the corporations and (f) the people with high incomes, but since corporations don't vote and people of high income form only a small percentage of the voters, these latter considerations are secondary. (4) In the last analysis, each committee member *wants* a tax law that will: (a) help him get re-elected, or (b) at least not help to defeat him. On these deep-seated Wants, the committee members proceed to hold hearings, gather evidence and use their highest indi-

[10] "Psychological Barriers to Communication," in Wilbur Schramm, *Mass Communication* (Urbana: University of Illinois Press, 1949), p. 277.

vidual and collective powers of *Reason* to draft a tax law that will be acceptable to themselves and to their masters, the American people.

Consider a business man's premissings of Wants on Reason. (1) He *wants* to make a profit, for without profit he cannot keep the business going. (2) He *wants* to keep workers employed, for if there is unemployment he faces other critical problems. (3) He *wants* to sell a product of which he can be proud, one that is both durable and beautiful. Therefore, he uses all the imagination, skill, and planning —all the Reason—of which he is capable to attain these Wants.

Consider the operation of Wants and Reason in what we call "men and women of good will." (1) They *want* the "best things of life" for all people. (2) Therefore, they *want* people to be educated to these values of life. (3) They *want* freedom of the human will and self-determination of man. (4) They *want* man to be considered more important than machines. (5) They *want* right to triumph over power. To attain these ends, the best minds of the ages have used the best Reason of which they were capable.

Now a speaker follows the same process. He asks: What do my listeners *want?* What problems do they face? On what issues are they disturbed or uncertain? What impulses do they need quickened? What knowledge do they need given them? First establish the premise on a *want,* then you are ready to use all the Reason of which you are capable, and more.

Observe, for example, how Walter Lippman based his speech on the listeners' deep-seated wants and cultural patterns—in this case the *Want* for Western Civilization to survive. Later, he used Reason to assemble the evidence and argument, but first he stated the Want:

> The thesis which I venture to submit to you is as follows:
>
> That during the past forty or fifty years those who are responsible for education have progressively removed from the curriculum of studies the Western Culture, which produced the modern democratic state;
>
> That the schools and colleges have, therefore, been sending out into the world men who no longer understand the creative principle of the society in which they must live;
>
> That, deprived of their cultural tradition, the newly-educated Western Men no longer possess in the form and substance of their own minds and spirits the ideas, the premises, the rationale, the logic, the method, the values, or the deposited wisdom which are the genius of the development of Western Civilization;
>
> That the prevailing education is destined, if it continues, to destroy Western Civilization, and is in fact destroying it: ....
>
> And that, therefore, what is now required in the modern educational system

is not the expansion of its facilities or the specific reform of its curriculum and administration, but a thorough reconsideration of its underlying assumptions and of its purposes.[11]

In attempting to persuade listeners that they have been mistaken and ought to change their ways—which is always difficult—James Burnham did so by establishing evidence on the following premise: "By doing these things that you *don't want* to do, you will gain something you *want still more*." He was speaking to business executives:

All of you, or almost all of you, I imagine, regard yourself as strongly anti-Communist.... Nevertheless, the record of the business community in the fight against Communism, the inescapable fight, is not impressive....

Some of you who are here today are executives of General Motors. Do you remember the strike in 1947? Do you remember that you tried to cut the ground from under Walter Reuther's feet by settling behind his back with the Electrical Workers? Did you understand then, do you understand now, that by doing so you were playing into the hands of the Communist leadership of the Electrical Workers, and sabotaging Reuther's brilliant and bitter struggle to throw Communism out of his union and out of the labor movement?

Many of you doubtless are members of the National Association of Manufacturers. Do you recall that a few years ago you put up some tens or even hundreds of thousands of dollars to finance an inquiry into social science textbooks used by our schools and colleges—an inquiry to determine among other things, whether Communist propaganda was being disseminated through the textbooks. To take part in that inquiry, you hired a professor ... named Vladimir Kazakevich. Did any of you, or any of your friends or associates, who put up this money and sponsored the inquiry, bother to investigate Kazakevich? Evidently not. Evidently you did not discover and perhaps do not even know now that Kazakevich is a Communist agent, and has recently returned to his home base in Russia....

Since the split in the Electrical Workers' Union which took place at the last CIO Convention, the Communist-led section has been locked in an all-out battle against the new union led by the anti-Communist James Carey. How many of you have protested against the actions of your friends in the management of General Electric and Westinghouse, whose maneuvers in blocking new union elections are playing into the hands of the Communists? ...

Business must seek profits, and in that there is nothing necessarily wrong, but what is wrong and may prove fatal is to seek profits, and short-term profits at that, at the expense of everything else....

The business men should ponder a little more carefully on the fate of their business colleagues in Poland, Czechoslovakia, and Eastern Germany. Slave labor camps, revolver shots in the back of the head, and mass rape seem very unreal in Grosse Pointe [suburb where many listeners live]. But there were

[11] Address before the American Association for the Advancement of Science, December 12, 1940.

also lovely houses and lawns and happy and prosperous families in Berlin's Zehlendorf, and in the suburbs of Prague.[12]

Reason's basic use, then, is to show men how to fulfill their needs, how to solve their problems. Most men do indeed use Reason badly, and some hardly use it at all. Yet by no other means can man solve tough problems. If Reason be man's newest and weakest intellectual achievement, it is also the extremely important one by which he climbed slowly, painfully, and with many backslidings, from savagery to civilization. Let there be no misunderstanding of its importance. Without the effective use of Reason, at least by a creative and dominant minority, no free society can maintain itself.

Use indirect methods as well as direct

There are two methods of persuasion, the Direct and the Indirect. The Direct Method attacks the issue head-on. The Indirect Method takes the roundabout approach. Thus the Direct Method would show the need for old-age pensions; and the Indirect—without arguing need—tells the story of a typical aged couple who need relief. The Direct Method would present the proposition: "The Irish are a noble people." The Indirect Method would say: "Let us see the Irish at work and play, hear the songs they sing and the deeds they do."

The Indirect Method is generally more effective than the Direct. The reason is fairly obvious. If a listener does not like the speaker's viewpoint, with the Direct Method he assumes a mental set against it. ("I don't like the Irish; in my city they win the elections and hold the city jobs.") Now when a person has said "No," all his pride of self-respect demands that he stand by it. Even when he later feels that he was wrong, he yields slowly and reluctantly, for pride is a precious motive. Thus pride and the mental set may prevent persuasion. But the Indirect approach avoids this. The listener's preconceptions are not on guard, and the speaker's viewpoint gets a fair hearing.

James A. Winans' story of the farmer's hog shows the use of the Indirect Method at its best:

> Dr. Wiley tells a story of a member of a certain Middle West legislature who sought an appropriation of $100,000 for the protection of public health; but could secure only $5,000. One morning he put upon the desk of each legislator before the opening of the session, a fable which ran something like

[12] Address to the Economic Club of Detroit on "How Communism Will Be Defeated," February 20, 1950. *Vital Speeches*, XVI (June 15, 1950), No. 17, 519.

this: A sick mother with a baby is told by a physician that she has tuberculosis and that she should seek a higher altitude. Lack of means prevents her going. She applies to the government and is told that not a dollar is available to save the mother and her child from death. At the same time a farmer observes that one of his hogs has cholera symptoms. He sends a telegram, collect, to the government. An inspector comes next day, treats the hog with serum and cures it. Moral: Be a hog!

The $100,000 appropriation was promptly granted.[13]

The Indirect Method, however, has definite limitations. In the first place, the speaker who overuses it can get the reputation of deliberately looking in one direction while walking toward another. ("That man won't look you in the eye with an argument; he sneaks up on you.") In the next place, the Indirect Method cannot treat a subject *comprehensively*—that is, explore all phases and answer questions that thinking people will need answered. At best, it is either a quick hit-and-run strike (as in the "Be a hog" argument), or is a longer treatment that hovers near the proposition but never comes to grips with it. (Telling the story of an aged couple who need relief would be an example. Such a story would present vividly the need, but would not explain where the money is to come from, or how to prevent malingering, etc.)

Students should be warned not to confuse the Indirect Method with that inept one, common among beginners, known to the trade as the Barbed-Wire-Entanglement method. The Barbed-Wire-Entanglement method consists of crawling painfully through several subjects that the speaker is *not* going to discuss before coming to the true one. Here is an example:

Barbed wire; first row In 1787 our forefathers framed the Constitution which set up the government under which we live. Under this Constitution a federal government was created and the American people were guaranteed freedom of speech, press, and religious worship.

Barbed wire; second row Under this Constitution the American people have survived many crises. The first crisis was external. Would nations of the old world—Spain, France, England—hem us down on the Atlantic seaboard, or would we be free to expand westward to the Pacific? That crisis was settled during the first half of the nineteenth century. The second crisis was internal. Would the U. S. become one nation or two? That crisis was settled in 1865, during the second half of the nineteenth century.

[13] James A. Winans, *Public Speaking* (New York: Appleton-Century-Crofts, Inc., 1915), p. 209.

The break-through! This is the real subject. But none of these are problems that I want to discuss today. I want instead to talk with you about another American problem, the problem of American art. What tastes in art have the American people developed since the founding of this government? What have been the crises in art faced by people of artistic tastes?

Of the two methods, Direct and Indirect, the Direct is the normal to-be-expected method. The Indirect has definite limitations, yet within these limitations it is generally more effective than the other. A skillful speaker will learn to use both.

For long-run cultivation of attitudes, remember that organized information usually is more effective than attempts at immediate persuasion

A speech is not an act of hypnotism that suddenly mesmerises and changes people. Only seldom is it a shot-in-the-arm that infuses them with sudden belief. It is a long-range process, more like watering and cultivating soil. *In this long-range process, presenting organized information is generally more effective than attempts at quick persuasion. Give listeners the facts and in time the facts will produce attitudes.*

Nobody is quite sure why this is true, but there are plausible reasons. First, we are suspicious of many speakers—members of an opposing political party, a competing business or labor group, a rival social group—and we assume a mental set against such speaker's ideas. Our attitude is, "I don't quite trust you; therefore, I don't trust your ideas." Now what happens when such a speaker does not present "ideas" per se? What happens when instead he presents *carefully organized information,* tested information with facts-as-they-really-are instead of half-facts or selected-facts-with-omissions that are palpably intended to mislead? The listener, of course, is still hostile, but the facts hit him in the mind anyhow. Weeks later, the facts have sunk in, are buried and forgotten. But in the sinking they have done their work.

Next, when a listener is given trustworthy and pertinent information, it has much the same effect as water on a plant. It sinks in and is lost from sight. It mingles with the water that fell last week. It will mingle with the water that is to fall next week. In the case of a speech, the information makes up part of the total experience of the listener.

The next facts blend with the old, and the sum of the whole influences beliefs and attitudes.

Finally, after the facts sink in and disappear, often long after, comes the harvest. *New attitudes and opinions, based on these and other forgotten facts, tend to emerge. These are known as "generalizations beyond the evidence," and they are profoundly important in determining what people think.*[14]

A large amount of persuasive speaking, then, does not come from persuasion per se, but from speeches of information that influence the listener's attitudes and beliefs during the weeks and months after the information has sunk in and been forgotten. This may have been suspected by early writers on rhetoric, but they underrated its importance. Its importance is really a discovery of modern research. Slowly as the strands of evidence have been uncovered during the past forty years, though much of it is still indirect, the influence of information on changing human attitudes becomes increasingly obvious. John Morley, an acute observer of human behavior, observed its effect over half a century ago. In assessing the effect of Richard Cobden's speaking, he observed that, "He produced that singular and profound effect which is perceived . . . when a speaker leaves party recriminations, abstract argument, and commonplaces of sentiment, in order to inform his hearers of telling facts." [15] Recent measurements of public opinion confirm the "singular and profound effect . . . of telling facts" to a degree that even Morley did not suspect. Indeed William A. Lydgate, editor of the Gallup Poll, after a careful re-examination of the first fifteen years of polltaking, reached the conclusion that the average voter's mistakes as judged by time stem generally from lack of information rather than from lack of intelligence or judgment, that whenever the public has the information it moves on to form the right decisions and does so *two years ahead of Congress.* This confirms the axiom of Raymond Clapper: "Never overestimate the people's knowledge, nor underestimate their intelligence." [16] The sum of the whole is that a lot of groups now trying to influence people need to change

[14] For those further interested in the effect of information on persuasion, see F. C. Bartlett, *Remembering: A Study in Experimental and Social Psychology* (Cambridge: Cambridge University Press, 1932), especially pages 224-226 and 311-314. See also C. I. Hovland, A. A. Lumsdaine, and F. D. Sheffield, *Experiments on Mass Communication* (Princeton: Princeton University Press, 1949), especially pages 192-200. The latter volume presents the effects on soldiers of facts and attitudes after five-day and nine-week intervals.

[15] *Life of Richard Cobden* (Boston: Roberts Brothers, 1881), p. 119.

[16] *What Our People Think* (New York: Thomas Y. Crowell Co., 1944), especially Chapter 1 on "The People, Yes."

their method sharply and radically, and to attempt persuasion by giving information instead of by injecting ready-made doctrine.

To reaffirm old attitudes, vitalize human hopes, ideals, desires, and values

So far we have been discussing, too largely perhaps, speechmaking that changes belief and action. Yet a large proportion of speechmaking is not for this purpose at all. Its purpose is to *reaffirm old attitudes*. There are times when human beings, being human, need be told to "Do your duty." At other times they need to hear the call to "Renew your faith," or "Strengthen your determination." And still again they need to be inspired to "Rededicate yourselves," or simply to hear the voice of a leader who can say, "Come unto me, ye who are weary and heavy laden, and I will give you rest."

In times of crisis, when people are driven to defend themselves by force, they must be told (though they believe it already) that their cause is just, and that right increases their might, "for who will defend our cause if we have no faith in it ourselves?" In placid times, they need to be aroused from lethargy, lest their virtues decay and the spirit that made them great be lost.

Never underestimate the power of mere ideas or sentiment, or their importance in human life. At Gettysburg in 1863 a tall gaunt man spoke 266 words beginning with, "Four score and seven years ago. . . ." Lincoln's words are now part of the nation's heritage. So long as the English language lives, its users will be reminded that Winston Churchill said: "I have nothing to offer but blood, toil, tears, and sweat.— Never in the field of human conflict was so much owed by so many to so few.— We shall fight on the beaches, we shall fight in the fields and in the streets, we shall fight in the hills; we shall never surrender." At a critical moment his words became one of the resources of the British Empire, along with her ships and tanks, guns and planes.

Of Emerson, whose words often roused contented intellectuals, James Russell Lowell testified that: "There was a kind of undertow in that rich baritone of his that sweeps our minds from their foothold into deeper waters with a drift that we cannot and would not resist. . . . Behind each word we divine the force of a noble character, the weight of a large capital of thinking and being. We do not go to hear what Emerson says so much as to hear Emerson. . . . If asked what was left?

what we carried home? . . . . we might have asked in return what one brought away from a symphony of Beethoven?"

Arnold J. Toynbee, greatest historical philosopher of the twentieth century, assesses a people's spirit as perhaps the greatest single force in sustaining civilization. Indeed, he warns readers that civilizations have declined at the exact moment people were improving techniques, and that civilizations have ascended during times when techniques remained static. The vitality of a civilization, he concludes, is closely related to the spirit and morale of its people, and not to its command over its physical environment.[17] So it is that one of the constant purposes of public address is to revitalize convictions, hopes, sentiments, and enthusiasms—to give them fresh meaning and renewed force.

Now in such speaking, you do not use certain forms of support. First, you do not use mere facts, figures, and formal proof; for a people's faith is not renewed, nor their hopes uplifted, by syllogisms, logarithms, and binomial equations.

Further, you cannot rely on argument; for how would you *prove* that patriotism is noble, and if you did, whose pulse would be quickened? Said Oliver Wendell Holmes, Jr., in one of his characteristically brilliant addresses: "I cannot argue a man into a desire. If he says to me, Why should I wish to know the secrets of philosophy? Why seek to decipher the hidden laws of creation that are graven upon the tablets of the rocks, or to unravel the history of civilization. . . ? I cannot answer him; or at least my answer is as little worth making for any effect it will have. . . . You must begin by wanting to. But although desire cannot be imparted by argument, it can be by contagion. Feeling begets feeling, and great feeling begets great feeling." [18]

The methods to be used, generally speaking, are these:

1. *Revive the common history and memory of the past.* Tell old things over again, preferably in a new way. This is the method of Edwin P. Morrow in his address, "The Cost of Heritage":

> If we would know . . . the cost of the Heritage . . . . We must remember the pathfinders, the moccasined feet of our heroes, who broke the path for those who sought new homes and new opportunities. We must remember the early days, "when the crack of the pioneer's rifle, the ringing blow of the woodman's axe, the savage cry of the Red Skin and the crooning love song of a mother

[17] *A Study of History* (New York: Oxford University Press, 1947), pp. 254, 255-267, 290, 555-557.

[18] Address to the G.A.R. of Keene, N.H., 1884. W. N. Brigance, *Classified Speech Models* (New York: Appleton-Century-Crofts, Inc., 1928), p. 337.

as she rocked her baby on the puncheon floor, all mingled into the music of the forests; the epic of the American woods." We must behold Lewis and Clark as starting from the Missouri, guided by the pointing finger of an Indian girl, they crossed the Great Divide, found the mouth of the great river at the sea, that there might be held for us the Empire of the great far Northwest.[19]

2. *Reaffirm your faith, hope, and determination in such a way that listeners will want to share them.* This uses the method of indirect persuasion. Instead of saying "Renew your faith." it says, "This I do believe, and in this faith will I live." David E. Lilienthal uses it in an address on "The Spirit of Democracy":

I wish to speak to you this afternoon about this country we love so deeply, about the sources of her strength. And the theme of what I shall say to you is simply this: that it is in the spirit of the American people that our great strength is found, that the foundation of the Republic is in the moral sense of her people, a sense of what is right and what is wrong, in short, that the faiths we hold are the chief armament of our democracy. . . .

We are a people with faith in each other, and when we lose that faith we are weak, however heavily armed. We are a people with faith in reason, and the unending pursuit of new knowledge; and when we lose that faith we are insecure, however heavily armed. We are a people with faith in God, with a deep sense of stewardship to our Creator, the Father of us all; and when that is no longer strong within us we are weak and we are lost, however heavily armed with weapons—even atomic weapons—we may be.[20]

3. *Make your lines of thought vivid by illustration, specific instance, comparison, suspense, etc.* As we have seen, you cannot use formal "evidence" or "argument" or "proof," in this type of speaking, for they deal largely in material values and not with hopes and sentiments. Nor can you rely on *assertion* only, for assertion cannot long hold attention. Therefore, you must find vivid forms of support outside these areas. This leads us straight to those forms always required for vividness and inspiration: illustration, specific instance, comparison, suspense, and their related forms. Harry Emerson Fosdick, for example, used four illustrations in support of his topic that "Great people live greatly in times of crisis," and increased the vividness of these illustrations by quoting one poem, using five direct questions, and citing 15 specific names of persons and places:

In a commencement address delivered by Douglas Freeman, author of the great life of Robert E. Lee, he described what some people had done amid the

[19] Address to the New York Southern Society, December 13, 1922.

[20] Address at the University of Rochester, January 16, 1949. A. Craig Baird, *Representative American Speeches: 1948-1949* (New York: H. W. Wilson Co., 1949), pp. 65-67.

horror of their days to keep the light of beauty and of goodness burning for the souls of men to return to. When did Wordsworth write some of his greatest poetry? When Napoleon was collecting at Boulogne the armada for his planned assault on the English coast at Dover. When did Beethoven write the *Fifth Symphony?* The first year of the Peninsular War, with Napoleon's shadow dark over Europe. When did Beethoven finish that glorious *Seventh Symphony?* When Napoleon was assembling his army on the line of the Niemen River for his assault on Russia. Everybody knows John Keats' immortal sonnet, "On First Looking Into Chapman's Homer";

> Then felt I like some watcher of the skies
> When a new planet swims into his ken.

When did Keats write that? The summer that Waterloo was fought.

What am I pleading for—an ivory tower to escape from the appalling facts? No! Such souls as these never found in this life an ivory tower of escape, but tension—terrific tension—between the brutal and the beautiful, the evil and the good, the actual and the possible, the temporal and the eternal; and they refused to escape that tension by surrendering the higher realm.[21]

ASSIGNMENTS

ON THE USE AND INFLUENCE OF MASS COMMUNICATION

1. Make a report on the amount, nature, and seeming effect of attempts to influence public opinion by some particular group or organization:
    a. Start with the 5-step summary of research given in this chapter (page 138). Consult also, if you wish, any other studies on mass communication and public opinion including those listed in footnotes 3, 4, and 6.
    b. Using this knowledge as a basis, analyze the attempts to influence public opinion you find used by the newspaper you habitually read, by some leading popular magazine, or by the Democratic Party, the Republican Party, the National Association of Manufacturers, the American Chamber of Commerce, CIO, American Federation of Labor, Farm Bureau, National Education Association, Red Cross, or any other.
    c. Explain the various channels through which the organization operates, and its leading methods of persuasion. Rate the general effectiveness of its efforts, and consider how you think they might be improved. Consider also the ethical level of these methods.

ON GETTING AND HOLDING ATTENTION

2. Bring to class ten advertisements from a leading popular magazine (*Time, Life, American Magazine, Saturday Evening Post,* etc.). List the means of attention used by each.

[21] *Living Under Tension* (New York: Harper & Brothers, 1941), pp. 4-5.

3. From *Vital Speeches* or other sources study the introduction to six speeches. Imagine yourself sitting in each audience, and decide whether the introduction would really get your attention if effectively spoken. Don't be discouraged if most, or even all, of these introductions seem to fail. Remember that most speeches today (though conspicuously not all) are given by people who may be experts on their subject, but who have never learned either the technique or the discipline of speaking.

4. Explain the methods used to get and hold attention found in one of the speeches printed in the back of this book.

5. Rework your last speech, using new supporting material that better holds attention, and by making the speech more vivid throughout.

ON RESTING REASON AND EVIDENCE ON WANTS AND CULTURE PATTERNS

6. Read one of the following historically important speeches, and determine the extent to which it rests reason and evidence on basic wants and culture patterns. That is, (1) outline its main lines of thought and decide whether basically they are supported by reason and evidence, (2) determine what problem the speaker was trying to solve, and which basic wants or culture patterns would be satisfied by accepting the speaker's solution. Each of these speeches, of course, may be found in many library sources, and one source is listed for each speech:

   a. Franklin D. Roosevelt, "We Have Nothing to Fear But Fear," (First Inaugural) *Public Papers & Addresses of F. D. Roosevelt,* II, 11-16.
   b. Woodrow Wilson, "For Declaration of War Against Germany," *Selected Literary and Political Papers of Woodrow Wilson,* II, 234-247.
   c. Booker T. Washington, "At the Atlanta Exposition," Booker T. Washington, *Up From Slavery,* Chapter 14.
   d. Henry W. Grady, "The New South," W. N. Brigance, *Classified Speech Models,* pp. 287-297.
   e. Henry Ward Beecher, "Liverpool Address," W. N. Brigance, *Classified Speech Models,* pp. 40-65.
   f. Abraham Lincoln, "Cooper Institute Address," J. M .O'Neill *Models of Speech Composition,* pp. 341-357.

7. Prepare and deliver a persuasive speech in which you make the most effective possible use of the principles of persuasion. First, choose the subject and gather the speech material, then proceed as follows:

   a. Draft the purpose-sentence carefully so that it is impelling, i.e., rests on the strongest available wants or culture patterns.
   b. Choose main heads that not only will develop the purpose-sentence logically, but will also appeal directly to the impelling want or culture pattern on which the purpose-sentence rests. Phrase these heads so they are quickly understood, and use as few as possible. Other things being equal, three are better than four, and two are better than three.

c. Develop these heads with the best possible reason, evidence, and supporting materials.

ON USING THE INDIRECT METHOD OF PERSUASION

8. Prepare and deliver a 1-minute speech using the *indirect* ("be a hog") method of persuasion.

ON THE EFFECT OF INFORMATION FOR LONG-RUN CULTIVATION OF ATTITUDES

9. Write down the basic changes of *attitude,* as well as you can now recall them, that you have experienced during the past one or two years toward one of the following subjects *as a result of learning new information about it in a college course:* Modern art, literature, the U.S. foreign policy, industrial management, labor problems, physical science, psychology, any other. Discuss the implications of this for mass communication and persuasion.

10. Read the "Story Behind the Atomic Bomb," by Reuben G. Gustavson, found on pages 563-574: (1) What portion of this speech is given to pure information? (2) What portion is given to persuasion per se? (3) What is the net effect of the speech on your *attitude* on atomic energy control? (4) What is your attitude, after reading the speech, toward the speaker himself? (5) What is your resulting judgment of the influence of trustworthy information on persuasion?

11. Prepare and deliver a speech of information, which, *because* of the information, will influence the listeners' attitude toward the subject. You must, of course, know enough about the subject to speak with adequate authority.

ON REAFFIRMING OLD ATTITUDES

12. Report on the most inspiring speech you ever heard. Explain both *what* the speaker said that made it inspiring, and *how* he said it.

13. Prepare and deliver a speech to reaffirm old attitudes, in which you use the principles set forth in this chapter. Possible subjects for such a speech would be:

This is a great university
College people are favored people
American democracy is a special heritage

The Seven Lamps of architecture. . . .
The Seven Lamps of planning a speech. . . .

CHAPTER 8

The Seven Lamps of Planning a Speech to Persuade

CHAPTER 8

We have looked at "The People To Whom You Talk." We have examined the foundations of "Persuasion and Public Opinion." We now come to a practical chapter on "how to go about it."

The aim here is boldly at teaching you how to put together a speech that really counts. So, following John Ruskin's seven lamps of architecture and Goldwin Smith's seven lamps of fiction, we are here lighting seven lamps of speechmaking to guide those who would speak to influence public opinion. These seven lamps each lights one step of the stairway leading to the finished speech. They include the gist of this whole book, chapters that have gone before and chapters that are to come after. They are lighted here (now that we have come far enough to understand them) for you to see them all in one view. *They are set forth in a system of preparing every speech.*

Would you follow these steps intelligently? Then examine them often, and *use them in preparing every speech.* By so using them, the steps will become your habitual pathway of speech-building.

Lamp One: *Focus on a definite response that you can win from your audience*

There are really two parts to this step. The first is "focus on a definite response," which already has been discussed briefly (pages 34-37) and will be further discussed in detail (pages 178-182). This means focusing your speech so as to know *exactly* what response you want from the audience instead of attempting a fixed focus on the universe.

The second part belongs to a higher order: focus on a response "*that you can win from your audience.*" Don't attempt the impossible. First, ask yourself: Why have they not already taken the course I urge? Habit? Inertia? Lack of information? Lack of interest? Lack of need? Conflicting wants or culture patterns? Then ask: *How far can I lead them in my direction?* In one speech you can lead only so far, and no further. If you attempt too much, it will boomerang.

The following list of check questions will serve as a guide:

1. *Am I attempting a response that runs headlong into the audience's wants or culture patterns?* (You can't win it. You can only discredit yourself as having ill-considered judgment. A culture pattern or a really basic want must be approached obliquely and with finesse, not head-on.)
2. *Am I asking for too much?* (College students can't be persuaded to "Heat your home by radiation," but can be persuaded to take a favorable attitude toward the idea. Elderly people will not become foreign missionaries, but can be persuaded to give liberally to support them. Labor groups will not be persuaded to turn pro-management, but can be persuaded that cooperation is more profitable than fighting.)
3. *Am I trying to use the audience for a cat's-paw to get something I want, but they don't particularly need?* (You can't win a response unless it meets the audience's need, not yours.)
4. *Am I asking for a response that the audience "ought to give if they would only be reasonable about it"?* (There is no such thing. People are not primarily reasoning beings, but neither are they unreasonable. You simply have not discovered the wants and culture patterns on which their attitudes are based. Read Chapter 5 again, and reanalyze why they believe as they do.)

Lamp Two: *Phrase this response into an impelling proposition*

What makes a proposition impelling? From Chapter 5 we know that a proposition is impelling if it *satisfies a want, or reinforces a culture pattern.* (Wants, of course, include needs, hopes, aspirations, ideals.) You cannot argue a man into a desire. Remember that, please, for so many students forget it—or never learn it. But you can do many things about the multiple desires that man has: (1) You can quicken them and make them stronger. (2) You can show how to attain them, i.e., solve a problem, get out of a difficulty, or make progress toward it. (3) You can replace one want by another want. Thus people who want Security might be challenged to Adventure (a difficult thing, but possible within limits). People who want Property can be persuaded to give it away because of other wants: Reputation, Sympathy, Competition and Rivalry, Conformity, Fear, Reverence and Worship.

Therefore, set down the following as a convenient working definition of persuasion:

1. *If the purpose is to stimulate, to inspire, to create morale, or*

to intensify ideals—persuasion is attained by vitalizing old desires, ideals, or culture patterns.

2. *If the purpose is to secure acceptance of new beliefs, development of new attitudes, or adoption of new courses of action—persuasion is attained by substituting new desires, ideals, or culture patterns in place of old ones.*

Whether men shall pursue an immediate want or a remote one, whether they accept satisfaction of a high idealistic desire or a low material one, depends, and always will depend, in a large measure on how impellingly these alternatives are presented to them by leaders, thinkers, writers, and speakers.

The proposition of a speech, therefore, ought to be stated so as to impel acceptance by the audience. The propositions listed below illustrate both the good and the poor:

UNIMPELLING	IMPELLING
1. It is up to you to find out how to use art to improve your looks. ["Up to you" is a trite form of resting the proposition on Duty, an overworked want.]	1. Artistic clothes of certain lines and certain colors will make you look taller or shorter, fatter or thinner, warmer or cooler, more poised or less poised. [The proposition now rests on Self-respect and Pride, Physical Enjoyment, Competition and Rivalry, and Artistic Tastes.]
2. I want to tell you about football. [*You* want to, eh? Where do I, the listener, come in?]	2. If you know about the systems of football offense and defense our team is using this year, you may enjoy the games more. [Of course I want to enjoy the games: Competition and Rivalry, Physical Enjoyment, Adventure.]
3. It is up to us to do our duty and save ourselves from socialism. [(a) "Save ourselves from socialism," is like the cry of "wolf! wolf!"; too many no longer take it seriously, and hence it reaches no want. (b) Duty is an overworked want; use it skillfully, or don't try to use it at all. (c) Watch the phrase "up to us"; it is trite, and hence not impelling. (d) Beware of the conjunction "and" in a proposition; it usually is the sign of a two-headed monstrosity, whereas you want *one single* response, not two.]	3. Compulsory health insurance would make it impossible for doctors to give patients individual treatment of high quality. [People *want* individual treatment of high quality.]

Lamp Three: *Support this proposition with main heads that touch off the "springs of response" in the audience*

Main heads are the pillars to support the proposition. Main heads there must be in every speech. We are here concerned with their *choice* and *wording*. Are they trite, commonplace, vague, and indefinite? Or are they vital, impelling us (if accepted) to respond? In other words, can you find supporting main heads that will make the audience *want* to accept the proposition? Consider the main heads given below, one group that meets the test and one that fails:

POOR

I

I. Use of the lie-detector in criminal trials is practical.
II. It is sound in principle
[The "practical . . . sound-in-principle" main heads fail to meet the test. They touch off no springs of response.]

GOOD

I

I. Under present court procedure many guilty persons escape to commit crimes again, and a few innocent people are convicted of crimes they never committed.
II. The lie-detector, though not perfect, will convict more of the guilty and acquit more of the innocent than is done by present methods.
[We *want* to convict the guilty and free the innocent.]

POOR

II

I. Poe's mastery of literature.
II. Opposition to his personal life.
III. Influence of early life.
[These are not main heads, but are mere incomplete phrases. They might serve the speaker who *knew* what his main heads were, but would confuse the one who had not thought himself clear.]

GOOD

II

I. Poe was a master of three fields of literature; short story, poetry, and criticism.
II. Yet during his lifetime his literary genius was overshadowed by public criticism of his private life.
III. His early life had played an important part in developing both his literary genius and his unhappy mode of personal life.
[If I am interested in the enigma of Poe, these heads explain what I want to have explained.]

III

I. There are certain important aspects to study.
II. We should take care of the first of these before we start.
III. We should also take care of other aspects.

[From these main heads you can't learn *anything* about the speech. The speaker's mind is in a fog, and until the fog clears there can be no traffic in ideas.]

III

I. I propose to show that studying, thinking, and remembering all go hand in hand, so that the absence of one leads to the loss of all three.
II. When we study, our problem is to keep the repeated spurts of attention right on the subject—and to do this we must first attend to the physical aspects of study.
III. Finally, we should attend to the mental aspects of study.

[Each main head is *clear*, touches off a spring of response, and leads the way to next head.]

Lamp Four: *Arrange these main heads in the order that is most effective for your audience*

A speech must fit its audience, and each audience is a special-sentiment group alive and warm with desires, interests, prejudices, habits, and culture patterns. Ergo, where do you start? Which way do you go? The following are questions that will help to determine the answer:

1. Will your audience *accept* your proposition if it is stated at the outset? Then any normal order of arranging main heads will satisfy.

2. Are they *doubtful* about it, or generally uncertain? Then arrange your heads so as to follow their steps of doubt or uncertainty. "Why did you arrange that brief in such a funny order?" one lawyer asked another. "Because Judge So-and-So's mind works that way," was the reply.

3. Will the audience *oppose* your proposition at first hearing? Then don't state it early in the speech, but start with a main that presents as much common ground of agreement as possible.

For a detailed discussion on arranging main heads, see pages 212-219.

Lamp Five: *Develop each main head according to the audience's attitude toward it*

For convenience, we shall recognize four levels of attitudes:

1. *Is the audience actively favorable?* Then develop the topic by the IMPRESSIVE OR DYNAMIC METHOD. This consists of telling people in a new way of what they already know. A large amount of speaking consists of this. College graduates are drawn back to the campus after many years. Societies meet to renew old memories. Nations have holidays for the historic use of symbols in society:

> O how I long to travel back,
> And tread again that ancient track! . . .
> Some men a forward motion love,
> But I by backward steps would move.

Before the actively favorable audience you do not try to *prove* what listeners already actively believe. Instead, you review it, vitalize it, give it richer meaning, and surcharge it perhaps with a drive for action.

The following are modes of support that will be especially effective:

Illustrations	Direct Quotation
Specific Instances	Suspense and Climax
Comparisons	Concrete Language

2. *Is the audience indifferent?* Then use the MOTIVATIVE METHOD to show why the subject is important. Is it a problem dimly seen that will soon become acute? Is it a neglected problem about to boomerang? Is it a once-settled problem that now returns to life? Is it a perennial and unpleasant problem that we want to forget and Let George Do It?

Suggested modes of development are these:

Motivate it by showing the involved wants, needs, hopes, and ideals. Possible forms of support for this are:

Facts and Figures	Explanation
Testimony	Restatement

Vitalize it by making the ideas vivid. For this the following are especially effective:

Illustrations	Direct Quotation
Specific Instances	Suspense and Climax
Comparisons	Concrete Language

3. *Is the audience doubtful or uninformed?* Then develop the topic by the INSTRUCTIVE METHOD. Here the speaker says in effect, "This is the nature of the problem," or "What are the facts on this question?" He sifts and tests the information. He makes it as free from bias as his character and intelligence permit. He presents it in carefully organized form.

Especially useful are the following:

Defining your terms	Facts and Figures
Explanation	Illustrations
Restatement and Repetition	Specific Instances
Testimony	Comparisons
	Concrete Language

4. *Is the audience opposed?* Then develop the topic by CONCILIATION PLUS IMPELLING ARGUMENT. The steps in this process are relatively simple to set down in print, but exceedingly difficult to follow in practice. Basically there are four steps:

a. *Don't provoke argument.* An opposed listener is like a cocked gun—it takes only one little pull of the trigger to let go the full blast. Especially, therefore, watch name-calling and hate-provoking words like "*Radical* labor leaders," "*Communist-front* organizations," "*Selfish* business interests," "*Economic royalists,*" "*Campus snobs.*" Students find it difficult to avoid name-calling before an opposed audience. They hold in until they are about to explode, then relieve the pressure by one hefty name-calling term which they hope won't do any harm. But one is enough. Like Mercutio's wound, it may not be as wide as a church door nor as deep as a well, but it will do the business in the end. Face it frankly. Name-calling is an index of character. People without restraint of character will naturally name-call. Before favorable audiences it is effective. Before opposed audiences it is near-fatal.

b. *Seek first to get a Yes-Response.* Says one speaker, "Politics on this campus are rotten, and every campus office holder got there by secret bargaining." Listeners who voted for the winning candidates thereupon, in their own mind, say "No! I don't believe that!" This "No" is far more than merely uttering a silent word. It sets the whole pride of the listener's personality against the speaker. No matter if later the listener feels that his "No" was ill-advised. To save his face he will stand by it. But another speaker says, "How many of us are sorry we came to this institution? How many of us wish we had gone elsewhere?" Everybody is *with* the speaker. Then he continues, "I want to talk about campus politics. We must have campus politics, of course, for we can't have offices without candidates, nor candidates without supporting groups." To this all the listeners say "Yes," and the speaker continues, "Now what about the last campus election? A faculty-student committee has investigated it, and it gives the following summary. . . ." So far, not a listener has had much chance to say "No." The first speech committed suicide in the opening sentence. The second speech will go far.

c. *But beware of being ingratiating.* Listeners are not to be fooled, and they will not be mocked. They will see through insincerity as though it were cellophane. Therefore, the two-faced speaker is soon found out. Call two-facedness what you will: apple-polishing, soft-soaping, laying-it-on, or other names less printable that students all know—it all comes to the same end. To seek for common ground and a Yes-Response is a way of honestly trying to settle differences by talk, a way of learning to live with other people. To talk out of the other side of your mouth is quite something else. It does not require intelligence to distinguish between them, though it may require character to separate them in practice.

d. *Follow up by developing the subject so that the hearers either (1) forget their objections or (2) have them removed by logical processes.* It is a curious commentary on human nature, but true one, that some people can be persuaded simply by causing them to *forget* their objections. Thus vivid description, moving illustration, sustained attention of any sort, may serve to persuade. But frankly this is not the best method. The other and more effective method is to follow up by impelling argument (not to be confused with "provoking an argument"). The method of impelling argument is not so much argument as it is carefully organized *information.* As such it is discussed under Lamp Five just above.

Lamp Six: *Remember that listeners think in images; be therefore specific, pictorial, and vivid*

"With words we govern men," said Disraeli. "Give me the right word and the right accent, and I will move the world," said Joseph Conrad. These are exaggerations, but they point in the right direction. Catchwords and seductive slogans do not influence public opinion as much as formerly supposed. "But truth and force are Siamese twins." A speaker's task is to overcome mental laziness and find the exact words with which to speak the truth about what he thinks.

"Logicians may reason about abstractions; but the great mass of men must have images," said Macaulay. Therefore, beware of dullness! Never lose sight of the purpose of speech—to give people images, the right image, a bright image. Use words with verve and dash, and even audacity. Says the dull-minded bore: "It is necessary that all citizens should participate in election of public officials in order to have a government that fulfills the essential functions of a democratic society." Nonsense! Say, "If you want good government, vote on election day."

Be specific. Rather than say vaguely, "There were several things they could do," come to the point, and say, "They could do three things: Pay the fine, appeal the case, or go to jail."

Know what effect you want to get—polished, elegant, learned, vigorous, gentle, shocking—then use the words that will get it.

Finally, sustain and develop the picture with vivid illustrations, comparisons, and direct quotation.

Lamp Seven: *Keep the speech marching toward a goal*

"The moving finger writes and having writ, moves on." It is the *movement* that holds attention, and a speech that fails to have movement—fails.

But movement alone is not enough; it must be movement *toward something,* and the audience must sense this movement toward a goal. A good speech keeps it fixed in view through a "recurrence of emphasis on the central idea."

The ideal movement, of course, is toward a goal that is half-revealed and half-concealed—revealed enough to follow the thought, and concealed enough to create suspense in the final end.

These are your Seven Lamps. Use them for light and guidance in preparing each speech.

ASSIGNMENTS

ON APPLYING THESE PRINCIPLES TO SPEECHMAKING

1. Use these Seven Lamps to prepare a persuasive speech that will really *influence* the opinion of the class:
   a. Choose a subject about which you are concerned, and on which you have thought for a long time. Consider especially the subjects listed in your Speech-Subject Analysis Form in Assignment 7, Chapter 1.
   b. Reinforce your own ideas and experiences with material gathered from the library. Talk with others. Be alert to materials that always come to the speaker who is on the lookout.
   c. Follow the Seven Lamps of this chapter.
   d. Do not try to be an authority on government, politics, or world affairs. If you need authority, get it, and tell when and where your authority testified.
   e. Do not use this speech as an excuse for airing thinly-veiled prejudices. Do not damn or praise indiscriminately the military, the

President, Russia, Germany, capital, labor, democracy, communism, art, literature, nor anything else.

f. Instead, if you choose to discuss a controversial issue, get your facts, assemble your ideas, rest them on impelling wants, and present your views. Hit as hard as you want with the facts, but do not call names or sing a hymn of hate. No question is too controversial to *discuss,* but name-calling and card-stacking are beneath the ethics allowed responsible speakers.

g. Do not pretend to have proved more than you have proved. In short, do not give hearers a chance to call you a falsifier or exaggerator. Present your case in such a way that even those who disagree will respect your position and say willingly, "He was honest and fair."

Part III THE SPEECH

There are two kinds of speakers, those who "have something to say" and those who "have to say something." Is there any doubt on which kind this speaker is?

CHAPTER 9

Selecting the Subject and Purpose

CHAPTER 9

There are two kinds of speakers, those who "have something to say," and those who "have to say something." The difference between them is the difference between the lightning and the lightning bug. This is a chapter about that difference.

Selecting the subject

Finding a subject is hardly ever easy. In class you are one of a group. Your name and the date is announced, or posted. You will be one of five, or ten, who will speak that day. You will be one of fifteen, or thirty, who will speak during that round. Your first question, like everyone else's is: What shall I talk about? Your first reaction, like theirs, probably is: If only I had something really worth while to say!

This is not a problem confined to speech classes. It is a common problem, everywhere. Theoretically, one might think that, outside of class, speeches are given only when the speaker has something burning within him that wants out. Actually, spontaneous combustion in nature is rare. Energy is ordinarily released only after mining, drilling, hauling, piping, weighing, and measuring. So with speeches, and in much the same way. There are times when a speaker, because of his position, is supposed to say something appropriate. What shall it be? At other times an audience faces a problem that needs discussion. Does the speaker know enough to discuss it, and if not, can he take the risk of learning enough? Still other times audiences are willing to hear any of a score of topics discussed, and hope to have their thinking stimulated on many topics at their regular and stated meetings. Which one of these problems can the speaker discuss most profitably? Lord Balfour, British statesman, voiced the difficulty of selecting a worthwhile subject in words that apply to most speakers on most occasions: "I will confess to you at the outset that I have been much embarrassed in the selection of a subject. [My address], so I was informed, might be about anything. But this 'anything' is too apt, upon further investigation, to resolve itself into nothing. Some topics are too dull. Some are too controversial. Some interest only the few. Some are too great a strain upon the speaker who has to prepare them. Some too severely tax the patience of the audience which has to listen to them. And I confess to have been much perplexed in my search for a topic on which I could say something to which you would have patience to listen, or on which I might find it profitable to speak."

Fortunately, out of the experience of others a helpful procedure has been developed for finding and testing subjects. It can be classified into four steps:

1. The audience
2. The subject
3. The occasion
4. Special problems

THE AUDIENCE

Good subjects are often found by considering the audience. What are their particular problems, needs, tastes, or interests? *Choose a subject about which the audience may know something, but wants to know more.* For example:

Does the age or sex of the audience suggest a subject? Young people are especially interested in subjects like these:

Factors that make a successful marriage
How to live within a modest income
How to attain true happiness
Opportunities in certain professions and business fields
What qualities successful business people have that others don't have

Women, by comparison with men, are more actively interested in subjects like the following:

The home
The family
Their children's school
Special problems of women in business and professions
Music and other fine arts
Literature
How to escape from worry or fear

Do the social, economic, political, or religious beliefs of the audience suggest a subject? Club women are interested in hearing a discussion of the status of women in Latin America or the Orient. Factory workers are interested in the stabilizing of wages and prices. Business men are concerned with how to improve labor relations.

Democrats always will listen to speeches on the traditions of Jefferson or Jackson or Franklin D. Roosevelt. Republicans want to remember Lincoln or Theodore Roosevelt, or to hear about less government in business. Religious groups want to hear of their achievement and progress, and to hear their tenets restated and reaffirmed.

Does the local background of the audience suggest a subject? The local background of college students is rich in appropriate subjects:

Social life
Leisure time, especially what to do on weekends
Recreational facilities
Honesty on examinations
Snap courses and tough ones
Required courses and electives
Good teachers and poor ones
Fraternities and sororities
The value of education
Weakness in present education

Most other audiences likewise have a local background from which subjects can be drawn:

The early history of this city
How the first factory got started here
The coming of early railroads
Paving the first streets
Early juries and court trials
Passing of the old General Merchandise Store
When livery stables went out and the garages came in
How the library got started, and what books people read seventy years ago
Women's societies fifty years ago

THE SUBJECT

Good topics are also found by looking directly at the subject matter itself. A safe rule is this: *Choose a subject about which you know something, and can find out more.* For example:

Do you have any first-hand or special knowledge from which a subject can be taken? Everyone has had first-hand experiences in some field or other, and is to some degree an expert in that field. About such things you can speak in the manner of one who says, "All of this I saw, and a part of it I was." Perhaps you have stapled the wires inside a radio day after day on a factory assembly line; you know the worker's sense of insecurity and his emotional need for recognition. You may have lived among the Navajoes; and you know how their culture patterns and judgment of values are different from our own. You may have lived on a farm that employed migratory workers for harvesting; you have observed how they work and play, and perhaps why they prefer to be migrants rather than stay-at-home workers. You may have been a cowpuncher on a Western ranch, an employee at a tourist resort, an office girl, or a baby sitter; you have seen things from a different viewpoint than those who look at the occupations from the outside. . . . In addition to first-hand experiences there is also special knowledge of another sort. You are an engineering student; you know something—and can find out more—about road-building, or dynamos, or airplanes. You have studied banking; you know something—and can learn more—about how the stock market serves the public, or how banks came into existence, or what their current problems are. You are majoring in literature; you can discuss why people read literature, or what kinds of literature there are.

Students often try to avoid subjects on which they have first-hand or special knowledge. They are afraid it will be "too personal," or protest that "I really don't know enough about it to give a speech." Well, speaking *is* personal. Every speech is from the speaker's *experience.* He has had the experience in the flesh mayhap, or mayhap in the spirit or the imagination through books. But he must have *been* there.

Have you recently read a book, heard a speech, or had a conversation that suggests a subject? It may be an old book—Homer's *Iliad,* Plato's *Republic,* or Jane Austen's *Pride and Prejudice*—or the latest selection of the Book-of-the-Month Club. It may be as well known as *Gone With The Wind,* or as forgotten as Aldous Huxley's *Point Counter Point.* It is not the book, but what the book has done to you. Has it made you think? Aroused impulses? Created resentment? Has it caused you to feel that here is something that ought to be more widely known—or steadfastly refuted? A speech or a conversation might affect you the same way. Again, it is not the ideas it gave you so much as the prodding, the spurring-on, it did. You disagree with what was said; and your mind won't forget it. You thought it missed the real point; and you keep going over it again to see where it got off the track. These represent the birth of a thought—and a thought, by careful nurture, can become a speech.

Is a subject to be found in some topic before the public eye? It may be a new discovery, invention, or process. It may be an industrial crisis, like a strike or antitrust suit. It may be an economic crisis, like unemployment or a change in the cost of living. It may be a political topic before the public eye, an election, a controversial candidate, a new tax proposal, a new subsidy. Listeners know about these topics. They are concerned about them. Your job is to do what newspapers do not, and cannot do—analyze the question, show which way it is moving and why, present essential information so listeners can better understand the day-to-day headlines.

Do you want to support or criticise some cause or subject of persistent controversy? Always there are plenty of them, typical of which are the current controversies concerning following perennial topics:

- "Irresponsible youth"
- Present-day education
- Recent fiction
- Modern art
- Music since the age of jazz
- Racial minorities
- Law enforcement
- Organized gambling
- The automobile and the highways
- Labor practices
- Regulating big business
- The welfare state

There are also campus questions of persistent controversy, like these:

- Student marriages
- The grading system
- Class attendance
- Examinations
- The lecture system, the seminar method, and the laboratory
- Graduation requirements
- Fraternities and sororities: pledging, scholarship, etc.
- Subsidized athletics

Do you want to change some present custom, established law, or tradition?

Some people contend that when time has outmoded a law or custom it ought to be abolished. Others hold that laws and customs ought to be left alone unless they become actively dangerous, because stability is a form of self-preservation. The first group says that this cultural lag stagnates a people. The others reply that the wayfaring citizen is incapable of accepting quick changes, no matter how much he may desire to, because people live mainly by habit, "acting as they have been taught to act without stopping first to think." Ergo, we have scores of political legacies, social legacies, educational legacies that are hang-overs from the past. The perennial question is: Ought these legacies to be scrapped or kept? They make good speech topics. The following list suggests their nature:

The 21-year-old age limit for voting
The poll tax
The township school unit
The study of Latin and Greek
The study of Great Books
The failure to require three or four years of science in this age of science
The failure to require anthropology or sociology as being necessary to the proper understanding of man
The failure to require a reasonable skill in speaking as being necessary in this age of radio, television, industrial problem of public relations
The presidential electoral college
The four-year presidential term

THE OCCASION

Good subjects may also be found by considering the occasion. For example:

Does the occasion itself suggest a subject? Henry W. Grady, a Southerner, spoke to the New England Society of New York on the rewards to be gained from cooperation instead of antagonism between North and South. Henry Watterson, another Southerner, spoke before the same society on "The Puritan and the Cavalier." John W. Davis, American, spoke at the festival of Shakespeare's birth, at Stratford in England, on the proposition that "all men of English speech share in the legacy of Shakespeare." John A. Brett, himself a lawyer, addressed a state bar association on the subject, "Who Is a Good Lawyer?" Humble occasions may also suggest subjects: An alumni banquet, a fraternity annual meeting, a founders' day meeting.

Does the occasion suggest a related idea? You have a speech on the eve of final examinations; an idea related to the occasion would be "How to Study for Final Exams." (There is a lot of published research on how to study to be found in your library.) You have a speech on the eve of preregistration for next semester; a related idea would be, "Here Is a Course You Will Want to Take Next Semester." It is National Music Week; and you speak on a great composer, on modern music, or on the influence of radio on musical taste. It is

Constitutional Week; and you speak on "The Constitutional Convention of 1787," or "*The Federalist*, a Little Known but Important Political Document," or "How the First Law Was Declared Unconstitutional." Every occasion is rich in related ideas.

SPECIAL PROBLEMS

There are a few special problems to be considered, mostly by way of warning on testing a subject for suitability:

1. *Don't choose a subject above or below the intellectual level of the audience.* You cannot discuss the psychology of music with people who don't know the diatonic scale. You cannot discuss the implications of the quantum theory with persons who knows nothing at all of physics. Conversely, college students will not listen patiently to a discussion on the values of being a boy scout, or to a talk on high-school ways of life. What is one man's meat is another man's poison, and a speaker must know whose meat, and whose poison.

2. *Don't use a subject too difficult for oral presentation.* Some kinds of subjects are simply not adaptable to a speech, and it is worse than mere waste of time to talk on them. There is danger of a boomerang effect. The following illustrate such types:

Complicated processes requiring mental visualizing and accurate memorizing of a series of steps by the listener—such as how a rotary press operates, how to tie a knot, how to fly an airplane.

Technical subjects requiring the audience to possess a specialized vocabulary and thought-concepts, and to follow the speaker's close reasoning without the opportunity to review it and keep it fastened in the mind—such as "An Experimental Analysis of Dynamic and Static Equilibrium," or "The J-Curve Hypothesis of Conforming Behavior." These are better fitted to the printed page, not the ear.

Complex subjects requiring the listener to carry in mind a long chain of reason, master large quantities of statistics, etc.—such as "The Postulates of Symbolic Logic," or "Deviations in Actuarial Statistics."

Intimate subjects about which people might read alone without embarrassment, but which would embarrass them or make them ill at ease to listen to in a group.

3. *Don't try to cover too much in a single speech.* It takes student speakers a long time to learn this. They want to talk about the whole subject of "Labor," when in truth they cannot cover one single labor union, one particular labor law, or even the whole of one current

labor strike, in a short speech. Therefore, they had best discuss, "This One Aspect of the Current Labor Strike." Or they want to speak on "India," when all they can hope to cover in a single short speech is "How Moslems and Hindus Get Along Together in India." Or they would speak on "Public School Education During the Past Hundred Years," which for a five-minute speech would require a coverage of twenty years per minute.

A speech must be specific. To be specific, it must say "more and more" about "less and less." Ergo, choose a subject that covers "less and less" in order that you can say "more and more" about it. Let's apply this, and see how a speaker narrows a subject down to the size of a speech. Our subject is "Postwar Problems," and we divide into the folowing parts:

A. Postwar problems in England
B. Postwar problems in France
C. Postwar problems in Italy
D. Postwar problems in Germany
E. Postwar problems in Latin America
F. Postwar problems in the Far East
G. Postwar problems in the United States

Obviously this is too big, so we cut it to 1/7 and take "Postwar Problems in the United States." Again we divide it into the proper parts:

A. Problems in education
B. Problems in industry
C. Problems in labor
D. Problems in domestic political affairs
E. Problems in international affairs

Still this is too big, so we cut again—this time to 1/5—and take the following: "U.S. Postwar Problems in Education." Please note that we have now narrowed the subject to 1/35 its original size. Again we divide it into the proper parts:

A. Problems in public education
B. Problems in higher education

Now we are getting close! Yet it is still too big, for we cannot cover both halves in a really good specific speech. Therefore, we take half of the above, and get: "Postwar Problems in Higher Education." We have now cut to 1/70 of the original subject. Dividing this into the proper parts we get:

A. State supported institutions
B. Privately financed institutions

We have about arrived, but not quite. Actually, we cannot usually cover both of these topics in a single short speech. (Most long speeches given on the subject recently touch on both parts, but concentrate on one or the other.) So we choose one or the other, according to the listener's particular interest. We have now narrowed the subject to 1/140 of its beginning size, but we are not necessarily done even yet, for we might find ourselves talking to students, alumni, or supporters of one particular institution,—and consequently might choose to speak with special reference to that institution only. Since there are a total of 1800 institutions of higher learning in this country, including those of all sizes and hues, it could be said loosely that we had now narrowed our subject to 1/12,600 its original size. The fraction is unimportant and possibly even misleading, but the narrowing is obvious. The subject is now one that a speaker can discuss with profit to the listeners.

Selecting the purpose

You have a subject. Where are you going with it? What are you going to do when you get there? These are matters you want to plan in advance. Like any traveler, you also want to find out what detours and what blocked roads, if any, there are along the way. Then when the speech is finished, no one in the audience will be asking, "What was he driving at?" They will know.

This may seem like unnecessary advice, but experience warns otherwise. Many people make speeches without object or aim, and you have heard them. Their speeches might as well be left unsaid. They start nowhere, and go nowhere. They aim at nothing—and succeed perfectly in hitting nothing. Therefore, we say find out first of all where you are going, and keep on the road.

What possible purposes may a speaker have? Fundamentally, there is but one basic purpose in all speaking. The speaker wants his audience *to respond, to act, to react to his speech.* In plain words, he wants them to *do something about what he says.*

Not all responses are equally easy to attain. Some are easier, some are more difficult. They are here divided into four groups, known as General Purposes, and are arranged according to increasing difficulty:

TO INTEREST THE AUDIENCE

What shall it profit a speaker if, no matter how good the speech, the audience is uninterested and pays no attention? Obviously the stream of interest must run through *all* speaking. The "polite attention" which courteous members of the audience may give for a little while will not last, nor will it be very close attention, for the more energy spent by the hearer in "giving attention" to the speech, the less energy will be left to understand and consider the subject matter. Interest, then, is the common denominator of all successful speaking.

There are times however, when interest is not the means, but the end itself. At such times the speaker has no desire to inform, to stimulate, or to convince the audience. He desires only to interest them. He deals in wit, repartee, and dramatic movement. He tells stories, and relaxes the listeners and takes their thoughts from the tension of everyday cares.

Such is the purpose of most private conversation, of a toastmaster's introductions, of "filling-in" speeches at meetings or organizations, of much after-dinner speaking, of story-hour talks for children, and of many sustaining radio programs.

TO INFORM THE AUDIENCE

Next is the speech of information, such as reports, group instruction to workers, classroom lectures, and lectures given by specialists to the lay public.

The purpose of such speeches is to tell people something they don't already know. This is a more difficult speech than the speech to interest, for the information needs presenting so that listeners can grasp, understand, and use it. It is never enough that the speaker merely passes out the information. He must see that the listeners get it in usable shape. The following points are to be borne in mind:

Arrange the information under two or three topics, not more than four at the most. A speech cannot be strung out like the links of a long chain. Listeners simply cannot remember such scattered information. Take all your facts and group them under a few main topics. If possible, two topics are best perhaps. Three are all right. But, if you have more than three, be careful. Listeners are likely to forget them.

In giving the speech, fasten these topics in the listeners' minds. When you come to the first topic, say so. Tell listeners, for example,

"The first step in this problem is ...." When you get through with that topic, tell them you are through, and summarize it so they will remember. Then, as you take up the second topic, let them know that it is the second one: *"We now come to the second problem...."*

Always make your information specific, never abstract. This does not mean for you to clutter the speech with needless facts and figures or confusing decimals, but it does mean for you to be specific, to give details, to illustrate and compare. For example, you would not say, "The distance was 201 miles and 2,173 feet," for the listener might remember the 73 feet—which is unimportant—and forget the 201 miles, which is the essential figure. Better say, "The distance was slightly over two hundred miles," and so fix the essential figure in the listeners' minds.

Use charts, graphs, and diagrams if the material is technical or complex. The eye sees proportions easier than the ear can follow explanations about them. A tabulation of assets and liabilities makes their explanation simple; the design of a building can be quickly shown by a sketch; the operation of a machine can be better explained by a diagram. Arrange your material so listeners can see as they hear, and complex information is made easier to explain.

Make your information interesting. Remember that people who listen are just plain human beings. They can take in so much, and no more. After that, all facts begin to look the same to them. So use anecdotes and illustrations along the way. Make interesting comparisons. Add humor to give your facts flavor.

TO STIMULATE THE AUDIENCE

We come now to the more difficult levels of response that are found in persuasive speaking.

What is persuasion? We know already that it consists of vitalizing a proposition so as to make it a dynamic force in the thinking and action of other people. But people have many levels of beliefs. Some beliefs are shallow, temporary, or subject to easy change. Some are deep-rooted and hard to change. The listeners' level of belief determines the speaker's mode of approach. For convenience we here divide them in two levels. First are beliefs we hold in a mild form. Second are those we hold vigorously and sometimes obstinately.

Speeches to stimulate are concerned only with the first kind, where belief is held only in a mild form, or where lip service is given to the proposition but where the listener fails to practice it in the actual conduct of life.[1]

We may, for example, believe that we ought to study our lessons, get eight hours of sleep each night, obey traffic laws, and take an active interest in public affairs—yet our belief in these propositions may be too mild to impel vigorous conduct. Similarly, we have many other near beliefs that influence our behavior very little or not at all.

Most public speaking aims at vitalizing these accepted beliefs. Among speeches with this objective are many sermons, most political addresses, commencement addresses, inaugural addresses, eulogies, pep talks in college, inspirational talks to businessmen, and addresses at reunions, anniversaries, and other celebrations. The speaker's object is to stimulate the hearers into an active, dynamic acceptance of some mildly accepted belief, or to stimulate them to action on propositions to which they agree, give lip service, but fail to do anything about.

Such a purpose is still harder to achieve than either to interest or to inform. Interest it must have, and information also, but it must have more. It must also consider the wants of the hearers. It must set up what has aptly been called "an adequate system of rewards" for those who accept the speaker's proposition. It must *motivate* the proposition—integrate it with the hearers' ambitions, wants, reputations—until it becomes a vitalized factor in their mode of conduct.

TO CONVINCE THE AUDIENCE

The speaker here is dealing with propositions that are not accepted by the audience, or are outright disputed by them. He is asking for an about-face, for the hearer to change his mind, to buy, to pay, to vote, to join, to go, to give, to do! He may either be asking listeners to "believe this thing earnestly," or to "do this thing actively." The first is action of the mind. The second is action of the body. Both are action.

To convince is the aim of the insurance salesman who would sell a

[1] Let us be sure that our meaning of *stimulate* is not misunderstood. We are using it in the literal sense given by *Webster's New International Dictionary*, second edition: "to excite, rouse, or animate, to action *or more vigorous exertion* by some pungent motive or by persuasion." Other writers have used the word *impress* to designate this purpose, but, literally, *impress* means to stamp or imprint something, and so implies that the speaker merely stamps or imprints an idea on the inert minds of listeners. In contrast, this view is that the audience never merely *receives* an idea but *participates* by giving an active response. This response, I think, is best suggested by the word *stimulation.*

policy, of the lawyer who defends a client, of the legislator who argues for a bill, and of the military spokesman who presents the need for more ships or a different kind of defense against atomic war.

Here is the hardest of all speech purposes to achieve, because it commonly includes all the other three. There must ordinarily be interest, information, and stimulation, but also something more. There is usually added the burden arising from dealing with propositions that must be *proved true,* with proof acceptable to the knowledge, prejudices, and desires of the hearer. Ordinarily only *after* this proof is acceptable to the hearer can the speaker vitalize the subject, make it dynamic, and motivate it to operate on the behavior of the hearer.

Let us summarize this view of speech purposes. (1) All speeches have the one fundamental purpose of gaining a response. (2) But some responses are harder to win than others; therefore they are divided into four groups, known as General Purposes, and are arranged according to increasing difficulty:

1. To Interest +
2. To Inform ++
3. To Stimulate +++
4. To Convince ++++

ASSIGNMENTS

ON FINDING SPEECH SUBJECTS

1. Write a criticism on the subjects used for class speeches. Classify them into those which you regard as: (1) highly satisfactory, (2) relatively less satisfactory, (3) unsatisfactory. State briefly your reasons for the classification.

2. Consult again the Speech-Subject Analysis Form you prepared in Assignment 7, Chapter 1 (page 13). You may now want to revise and add to it.

3. Consult the Classified Speech Subjects at the end of Chapter 3 (pages 53-55), and from it select five to ten subjects that would be suitable for your speeches.

4. Read two or three recent issues of *Time* or *Newsweek,* and note what news the editors regard as currently important. Do you find additional possible subjects for your speeches?

5. Read the table of contents of several recent magazines such as *Atlantic, Harpers, U.S. News and World Report, Commonweal,* and *Christian Century.* These will give you an idea of subjects which these editors think are important at the moment.

ON SELECTING THE SPEECH PURPOSE

6. Go to hear some speaker. Determine the subject, general purpose (i.e. to Interest, Inform, Stimulate, or Convince). Note how the speaker narrowed the subject to the limits imposed by time and audience.

7. Read three speeches in *Vital Speeches, Representative American Speeches,* or any other collection. Determine the general purpose, the specific purpose-sentence, and note how the speaker narrowed the subject to the limits imposed by time and audience.

8. List four speeches that you have heard during the past year, each having a different general purpose.

9. Select one of the subjects which you have listed in Assignments 2, 3, 4, or 5. Before you prepare the speech, select the specific response you want to get, and carefully phrase that response into a purpose-sentence. Decide whether you want: (1) merely to Interest the audience, (2) to present Information, (3) to Stimulate them to a more vigorous attitude or effort, or (4) Convince them to change their minds, vote, join, give, or do. Select the supporting materials best adapted to your purpose, and if you do not have enough, go forth and get more. Outline the speech, rehearse it, and give it to the class.

Giving a good speech is the equivalent of testifying that, "Here is a subject I have thought about, and have investigated."

CHAPTER 10

Earning the Right to Speak: Thinking, Finding Speech Material, Assimilating

CHAPTER 10

When you want a suit of clothes or a dress, you buy it and it becomes yours. Not so with a speech. A speech is a highly personalized affair, a *part* of you, and not something you put on and wear for a little while. Every time you talk your mind is on parade, and giving a good speech is the equivalent of testifying that, "Here is a subject I have thought about, and have investigated." Whoever fails to do this must testify to something else: "I haven't thought about this myself, but am only reciting what somebody else said"; or, "I am not exactly honest about this; I am really a propagandist for my special group"; or, "I am not prepared and have nothing to say; but my character is such that I don't mind doing this to other people"; or, "I like to hear my voice; it is sweet music to my ears; roll on, thou rich and vibrant overtones—roll on!"

In this chapter we shall consider how to develop a speech that is *yours*. It is a tested method by which any mind can reach its highest potential. It involves four successive steps:

1. Starting in time
2. Thinking on the subject
3. Gathering speech material
4. Processing the material

Starting in time

Speeches grow. You don't prepare them the way you study fifty pages of history or do an experiment in psychology. They grow and ripen, and all things that ripen take time. "I will tell you my rule," said the Autocrat of the Breakfast Table. "Talk about those subjects you have had long in your mind, and listen to what others say about subjects you have studied but recently. Knowledge and timber shouldn't be much used till they are seasoned. . . . Put an idea into your intelligence and leave it there an hour, a day, a year, without ever having occasion to refer to it. When, at last, you return to it, you do not find it as it was when acquired. It has domiciliated itself, so to speak,—become at home,—entered into relations with your other thoughts, and integrated itself with the whole fabric of the mind." [1]

By starting on time you are able to gather useful material without work. You are reading a newspaper or magazine, and an item dealing with your speech leaps out to meet your eye. You are studying a lesson in biology, economics, soil mechanics, textiles, Victorian drama, or nutrition—and an illustration is met with, ready and waiting. You enter the library, and a book on the shelves stares at you. You walk along the street, and ideas flash through your mind. Start the speech on time, and it grows and matures partly of its own accord and without work on your part.

Furthermore, by starting on time you are able to verify and mature those first hasty conclusions about the subject. An idea that today seems splendid, may next week seem insipid or immature. An outline that today seems perfect, may prove after a little time to be incomplete. Or you reach a roadblock and simply can't get any farther (people who *think* run into roadblocks right along). So you go on your way and forget the speech for a day—when suddenly tomorrow you find you have moved around the roadblock, without quite knowing how. Everyone who speaks, or does any sort of sustained thinking, knows that is takes *time* to get around these mental roadblocks. John Dryden said of one of his best plays, *The Rival Ladies* (1664), ". . . long before it was a play . . . it was a confused mass of thoughts, tumbling over one another in the dark: . . . the fancy was yet in its first work, moving the sleeping images of things toward the light, there to be distinguished, and then either chosen or rejected by the judgment."

Thinking on the subject

In answer to an examination question given to over five hundred students, "How do you prepare your speeches?" a majority of them replied that, after selecting a subject, they next went to the library to find speech material. Here is a fundamental mistake of most beginners. Their method makes them editor of somebody else's thoughts, poor mumblers of somebody else's lines, but *not* speakers in their own right. In the end they must stand up and say, in tones that are plain to every discerning listener, "The voice is my voice, but the thoughts

[1] Oliver Wendell Holmes, *The Autocrat of the Breakfast Table* (Boston: Houghton, Mifflin and Co., 1858), p. 134.

are the thoughts of *The Reader's Digest* (or this book, or that article)." After choosing a subject and starting on time, the next step is to *think before you gather speech material.*

Stated in this blunt form, to be sure, this is not very helpful advice, because in operating practice we seldom have a full-stored mind that joyfully empties itself into an orderly outlined speech. Worse, almost nobody really knows the technique of thinking, for thinking is indeed the toughest task known to man. No one can practice it consistently, or for long at a time. In fact, we know little about how thinking is done. Yet there is a technique of thinking, and now is the time we must set about using it.

Frankly, this is a critical point in every young person's life, for there is altogether too much truth in Isaiah Berlin's recent assessment of young people in colleges and universities. Said this British reporter on American thinking and doing: "Many of these excellent young people could not . . . either read or write, as these activities are understood in our best universities. That is to say, their thoughts came higgledy-piggledy out of the big, buzzing, booming confusion of their minds, too many pouring out chaotically in the same instant. . . . Somewhere in their early education there was a failure to order, to connect, and to discriminate. . . . They tended [therefore] to look to their professors to tell them not merely what books to read but sometimes what chapters and what pages; on being told, the more serious among them would throw themselves upon the recommended pabulum and would try to absorb it in a very frenzied fashion. They read rapidly, desperately, and far too much. And because they tended to believe that all facts (and only facts) were important, and, what is more, equally important, the result was often a fearful intellectual congestion from which many of them will probably suffer the rest of their lives."

Now we have faith that such young people will survive, and indeed that this critic has overstated the case. Nevertheless, this is a good moment to pause and take stock of your own habits. Are you one of the frenzied readers? Are you one who believes that only facts are important? Do you believe that all facts are equally important? Such intellectual log-jams are, in a reasonable part, the result of *reading without prior thinking*.

Perhaps a more immediate and compelling criticism than Berlin's, given above, is that in giving speeches too many students don't really tell the truth. To be sure, they don't willfully deceive or deliberately falsify. We are not speaking of that kind of truth. But they are seldom wholly sincere. *They don't trust themselves, but echo what other people think and say. They speak what they think other people want to hear or "what the best minds are thinking this year."*

Wrote Emerson, out of the fullness of experience, "Know your fact; hug your fact. . . . Speak what you know and believe; and are personally in it; and are answerable for every word." This is a pointed way of saying, Do your own thinking, stand on your own judgments. This you cannot do by rushing first to the library to look up the ready-made thoughts of others.

At this point you may say, "But I am not sure that I know how to think, or where to begin." Very well, this is the time to start learning. We shall look at how-to-think. As the first step, *take stock of what you know already*. Again you may protest, "But I don't know anything about the subject." Actually, this is not quite true. Rather you mean that you lack specific information or matured ideas. Agreed, but let's look at what little you do know—and "think" about it. Look at it with X-ray eyes. Try to find its skeleton. Ask yourself questions like these:

PRELIMINARY

1. Why did I choose this subject?
2. What do I know about it first-hand?
3. What does the audience know about it?
4. What do they want to know?

DIAGNOSIS

1. What is the problem, or point in question?
2. What are its symptoms?
3. What have been its effects?
   Visible effects?
   Less visible effects?
4. What is its present status?
5. What caused problem, or point in question, to arise?

HYPOTHESES ON WHAT TO DO

1. What are the motives of persons who have been talking or writing on this subject?
2. How far can I trust their facts and ideas?
3. Must I discard them as untrustworthy, or can I correct for a standard deviation—and then use the corrected materials?
4. What do they think ought to be done?
5. After discarding or correcting because of their bias, where do their recommendations seem to be inadequate, and where adequate?
6. What do I think (tentatively) might be done (i.e. several things)?

7. What are the advantages and disadvantages of each?
8. Which seems (tentatively) to be the final best way?

FURTHER VERIFICATION

1. What further knowledge do I need to help verify my tentative diagnosis?
2. What knowledge do I need to help verify my tentative hypothesis on what to do?

When you X-ray a subject by this process you are *thinking*. You are also *calling up ideas from the subconscious mind*, for though you may not know it, you rarely, perhaps never fully, forget any experience or idea you ever had. They lie below the surface, hidden but not entirely forgotten. Many can be brought to light by systematic self-questioning. "It was then that I made the great discovery," said Mark Twain, "that when the tank runs dry you've only to leave it alone and it will fill up again in time, while you are asleep—also while you are at work at other things and are quite unaware that this unconscious and profitable cerebration is going on."

After you have done this sort of thinking *assemble your ideas into a skeleton outline*. Part of the outline will contain the facts and ideas you dug out of your mind. Part of it will be simply unanswered questions. But shadowy though it is—it is *yours*. As you progress, you may tear it up and make another outline, or several more. Certainly you will discard much of this first version. But the skeleton outline is time-saving rather than time-wasting, because it enables you to compare new material with old, new outline with old, weighing both and taking the better.

Now you are ready—but were not before—to gather speech material and expand the subject.

Gathering speech material

"People talk too much about what they don't know," said Briton Hadden, co-founder of *Time*. Nowhere does this frailty appear more often than among students on the platform. The plain truth is that without specific ideas and facts a speaker has nothing to say. But specific facts and ideas won't come for the wanting. You must go forth and find them, especially from three sources:

1. Conversing and listening
2. Investigating
3. Reading

CONVERSING AND LISTENING

If you are speaking on a campus question, talk to people who might supply you with ideas. There is a lot of waste in this sort of talk, to be sure, but it takes no extra time—for man is a talking animal and all you need do is to talk to a point when you meet others. Talk with them on the campus, in dormitories, at meal times—and listen to what they think, and learn whether they think. You may find significant trends, for example, in what the freshmen think, or the seniors, or the science majors. You may find that they are not interested in the question, or not informed, or have strong prejudices. All of this is useful information. "I never met a man," exclaimed Henry Ward Beecher, "from whom I did not get an idea for a sermon."

You may also interview people who are authorities. What does the athletic department think about the new penalty rule, or eligibility requirement? What do members of the art department think about Pablo Picasso? What background can a chemist give you on that newest antibiotic? What do the political scientists think of that new book on political theory?

Conversing not only brings in new information and ideas; it especially enables you to *test* your ideas. You are planning a speech on examination methods, the honor system, fraternity pledging, or the vacation schedule. You have certain ideas about the subject. These you can test in advance by talking with others. You may find unexpected objections to your plan, or find that you did not explain it clearly the first time, or discover that your line of approach antagonized listeners. All this is useful preparation. Even Winston Churchill, noted the reporters of one of his British political addresses, "after hours of discussion" with party leaders, did a last-minute revision by "dictating a new and more soothing speech in 500-word blocks to two secretaries in relays." Experienced speakers generally talk about their ideas with others more than do students. They have learned it from experience, sometimes painful.

INVESTIGATING

Wherever possible, go and see for yourself or write and find out first-hand. A student gave a speech on diseases of trees; he dug it out of books (a commendable thing), but never thought to supplement his knowledge by looking at campus trees or to note that the tree outside the class windows was afflicted with one of the diseases he discussed. A student spoke on the city manager plan of government, citing his information from distant cities; but a visit to the city hall would have refuted the biased and out-of-date figures he got from a propaganda article. Students give speeches on chain stores without ever going downtown to compare, on their own, chain-store with independent-store prices. They will criticize postal service without talking with anyone in the post office to get their side of the problem. They will advocate new methods of purifying milk (swallowed from a *Reader's Digest* article!) without knowing first-hand what method and what equipment is used at local dairies. Make it a cardinal rule, therefore, to investigate whenever possible and to see for yourself.

If you need specific information that others have first-hand, often you can get it by writing a letter. (But you can do this only if you start a speech on *time!*) For best results: (1) Make the letter brief. (2) State why you want the information. (3) State exactly what information you want. (4) Verify the initials and spelling of the name of the person you address. (5) Enclose a stamped and self-addressed envelope for reply.

READING

Reading, of course, is the most abundant source of speech material. But random reading can waste time, and leave you still with spotted knowledge. Better make the reading systematic, and start with a bibliography.

HOW TO COMPILE A BIBLIOGRAPHY

You don't want a "complete" bibliography. Indeed a complete bibliography might fill fifty pages and take a month to compile. You want a *selected* bibliography containing perhaps four or five times as many references as you will be able to read. A selected bibliography, of course, is not a hit-and-miss affair made up from the first list of references that meets the eye. It is compiled by a systematic process of selection and rejection according to date, source, author, and availability. The obvious sources of bibliography are the library Card Catalogue and *Readers' Guide*, but all the following sources are useful and ought to be considered:

COMMON SOURCES OF BIBLIOGRAPHIES

Library Card Catalogue

Readers' Guide to Periodical Literature. Cumulative monthly index of articles appearing in more than one hundred magazines. Published since 1900.

Poole's Index. Predecessor of *Readers' Guide.* Covers the years 1802-1906.

International Index to Periodicals. Similar to *Readers' Guide,* but indexes articles appearing in learned journals.

New York Times Index. A newspaper index from which can be located the dates on which similar stories appeared in other papers.

Public Affairs Information Services. Index on public affairs subjects of magazine articles, books, pamphlets, and government documents that are published in English-speaking countries.

Vertical File Catalogue. A monthly publication that lists pamphlet material published by various organizations.

United States Government Publications Monthly Catalog. Lists publications of the largest single publisher in the U.S., the federal government. Supersedes in part the former *Document Catalog.*

Bibliographic Index. A cumulative bibliography of bibliographies.

Winchell, Constance M., *Guide to Reference Books.* Based on Isadore G. Mudge's work of the same title. Presumably, like Mudge's work, it will be revised infrequently and will issue supplements.

In addition to the above, there are also special indexes that are restricted in scope. Among them are: *Agricultural Index, Art Index, Education Index, Engineering Index,* and *Industrial Arts Index.* Consult your library for additional ones.

There are three tests of a good bibliography:

Is it accurate? There are about five items on each listing where an error can occur: (1) Spelling of names, (2) wording of titles, (3) name of magazine (or publisher), (4) date of issue, (5) pages. With only a 10-item bibliography, there are fifty chances for error. Better proofread carefully, and save time.

Is it complete? Consider the dewy-eyed innocent person who lists "Smith, Standards of Practice." Which Smith? Adam Smith was an economist, Joseph Smith was a religious leader, Al Smith was a governor, MacDonald Smith was a golfer. *Who's Who in America* lists 415 Smiths, and one typical city directory lists 14 pages. Beware even of "H. A. Smith"; for *Who's Who in America* lists five. Get the full name as listed: Howard A. Smith. Next, where is the item found? Is it a book—and if so, when published and where published? Is it an article—and if so, in what magazine and in what issue and on what pages? Is it a pamphlet or document—and if so, when issued and by whom? A complete bibliographical reference would be as follows:

Drucker, Peter F., "Care and Feeding of Small Business," *Harper's Magazine*, CCI (August, 1950), 74-79.

Baird, A. Craig, *Representative American Speeches: 1949-1950* (New York: H. W. Wilson Co., 1950), p. 7.

Is it consistent? There are variant forms of listings, but a standard form is to list items in the following order:

BOOKS

1. Author's name, last name first
2. Title of book, underlined (also underline pamphlet titles, etc.)
3. Place of publication
4. Name of publisher
5. Date of publication
6. Pages (not merely the beginning page)

MAGAZINES

1. Author's name, last name first
2. Title of article, set in quotation marks
3. Title of magazine, underlined
4. Volume number, usually in Roman numerals
5. Month and year of issue
6. Pages (not merely the beginning page)

HOW TO READ

A word of how to read, for there are many kinds of reading. Some people read for entertainment. Some read for escape. Others read for inspiration and renewing of faith. Still others read to have their ideas confirmed. Only a few read critically, to weigh and consider. But that is the kind of reading you are now called on to do. Critical reading differs from other kinds in one important respect. It is an *active* process, requiring action like that for catching a ball. It demands especially three kinds of action on your part:

First, read behind the book or article. Find out what *kind* of book or article it is. Loosely, there are two kinds, theoretical and practical. Theoretical ones tell you "*that* something *is*." Practical ones teach you "*how* to do something you think you *ought* to do," or the author thinks you ought to do. Find out which kind you are reading. Then you know by which standard you must judge it. . . . Next, find out something about the author. What are his basic beliefs and assumptions? For what purpose is he presenting his explanation or argument? What philosophy or interest-group does he represent? Often he will tell you by his line of approach, by his choice of facts and examples, by the testimony he uses—or too often by his name-calling adjectives. Most authors, like most speakers, are reasonably transparent to people who look for the signs. But don't hesitate to check the author in one of the several biographical sources (see just below), or check on other things he has written.

Second, read to get the content. This is not so simple as it sounds. First, you X-ray it as you read, and locate the proposition. You X-ray further, and find the main supporting parts (i.e. main heads). In other words, you get the structural whole and the related parts—the entire framework of thought beneath the words. You don't have to read a whole book, or even the whole of a long article, to do this. In a book the preface and table of contents will often serve. In an article the opening paragraphs plus a quick skimming of its contents will do it. Now you can examine the forms of support—the facts, figures, illustrations, specific instances, comparisons, and testimony—which sustain the various parts. You know about these things, because you have studied them in this book. Now you turn them around and apply them to the authors you read.

Third, read for critical evaluation. Of all the possible things in the world, the three easiest for your mind are to (1) believe everything, (2) believe nothing, (3) believe what you want to believe. None requires judgment. But in critical reading you must *judge.* You must decide whether you agree or disagree, and this decision cannot be either a snap-judgment or a want-judgment. Therefore, you don't judge until after you have finished reading for the content. In other words, you don't say "I agree," or "I disagree," or "I suspend judgment," until you first can say, "I understand." This means that you must know and respect the difference between knowledge and *opinion.* There are specific standards for agreement or disagreement:

1. *Is the author uninformed?* (Don't take it for granted that everyone who gets in print is informed.)
2. *Is he misinformed?* (A United States Senator wrote an article for a magazine with the largest circulation in the world; he was in error on certain figures by 200,000%.)
3. *Is his analysis complete?* (Your X-ray reading will show this.)
4. *Is he illogical?*
5. *Does his evidence sustain his assertions?*

HOW TO CHECK UP AND FILL IN

When you have done critical reading there will be facts and ideas that you want to check, and open spots you want to fill in. The following are obvious sources:

GENERAL ENCYCLOPEDIAS

Encyclopedia Americana
Encyclopaedia Britannica
Collier's Encyclopedia
New International Encyclopedia
Columbia Encyclopedia (one volume)

SPECIAL ENCYCLOPEDIAS

Encyclopaedia of the Social Sciences
Catholic Encyclopedia
Jewish Encyclopedia
Cyclopedia of American Government
New Schaff-Herzog Encyclopedia of Religious Knowledge
Monroe, *Cyclopedia of Education*
Hastings, *Encyclopaedia of Religion and Ethics*
Baldwin, *Dictionary of Philosophy and Psychology*
Palgrave, *Dictionary of Political Economy*

BIOGRAPHIES

Eminent Persons of the Past

Appleton's Cyclopedia of American Biography. Long sketches of selected names.
Century Cyclopedia of Names. Many names, short sketches.
Dictionary of American Biography. Selected names, long sketches.
Dictionary of National Biography. British, similar to American Dictionary.
Lippincott's Universal Pronouncing Dictionary of Biography and Mythology. Includes men and women of all nationalities including the ancient. Some long and some short sketches.
Webster's Biographical Dictionary. Many names, very short sketches.
Who Was Who in America. Sketches of deceased persons who while living were listed in *Who's Who in America*. Since 1897.
Who Was Who. British, similar to the American. Also since 1897.

Living Persons

Who's Who in America. Includes living persons subject to inquiry or discussion.
Various regional volumes issued by the same publisher of the above volume, including *Who's Who in the East*, *Who's Who in the Midwest*, etc.

Who's Who in Commerce and Industry
Who Knows—and What. A cross-indexed dictionary of living authorities, experts, and especially informed persons.
Biographical Directory of American Scholars. Learned writers and scholars, largely confined to colleges and universities.
Biographical Directory of Leaders in Education. Includes both administrators and scholars.
American Men of Science
Who's Who. British, similar to American.
Monthly Supplement of Who's Who in America
Current Biography. Monthly publication of biographies of persons recently prominent. Cumulative index.

(The biographical volumes listed above on living persons are generally reliable. They list only persons who meet certain standards and accept no money from any person listed. Many other Who's Whos are less reliable. Some, like *Who's Who in the Western Hemisphere,* have been suspended by the Federal Trade Commission. Others, which libel laws prohibit naming here, include almost anyone who will pay to have his name included. Still others, like *Who's Who in American Education,* have required standards of admission but do not include biographies unless the biographee buys a copy of the volume, or pays for the cost of having it printed, etc. For this reason, this volume is irregular and does not include biographies of educators who decline to make payment or buy a copy of the volume.)

STATISTICAL INFORMATION AND CURRENT HISTORY

Statistical Abstract of the United States. The most authoritative and comprehensive yearbook on U.S. business, commerce, and related affairs.
World Almanac. A yearbook of facts. Vast miscellaneous information.
Information Please Almanac. Similar but not identical in coverage with the *World Almanac.*
American Year Book. A record of the events of the year.
Statesman's Yearbook. More on world affairs, less on U.S.
Americana Annual. An encyclopedia of the events of the year.
Britannica Book of the Year. A record of the events of the year, similar to the Americana.
New International Year Book. A compendium of history of the year, similar to the above two volumes.

HOW TO TAKE NOTES

You cannot carry in mind all you read. It fades out, becomes a disordered mass, or is incorrectly remembered. Therefore, take notes. But the popular hit-and-miss note taking leads to hit-and-miss results. Therefore, take systematic notes. The following is a tested method:

1. Use reasonably *large* cards (4×6 or 5×7 inches), or a *looseleaf* notebook.

2. Write on *one* side only.

3. Record each idea on a separate page.

4. Remember that direct quotations are usually, though not always, more useful than abstract summaries. Record such quotations exactly and enclose in quotation marks.

5. Use an ellipsis (three spaced dots, thus: . . .) to indicate omissions in a quotation; and use brackets [ ], and *not* parentheses, to indicate insertions of your own words, as in this example:

> "We, the People of the United States [note that it is not 'We the States'], in order to form a more perfect Union, . . . do ordain and establish this Constitution for the United States of America."

6. Check facts, figures, and quotations and do this immediately to be sure of accuracy.

7. Record the source immediately, including the exact pages, and do this for each card or sheet. You may need to consult the source again without wasting time.

8. Use a heading on each card or sheet that accurately labels the material recorded. (This heading is commonly put at the upper left.)

9. Note the classification of the material according to where it fits into your first tentative outline. (This is commonly put at the upper right, and written in light pencil so you can erase and change as you revise the outline.)

NOTE-TAKING SPECIMEN

(HEADING)
How to design a pilot
First stages of learning

(CLASSIFICATION)
Effects of first experiments

"In 1941, President Roosevelt called for 60,000 planes. . . . He got 300,000 planes before the shooting was over. Who was going to fly them? . . .

"Scientists were put to work designing planes, and social scientists were put to work designing pilots."

[They devised test batteries in which] one controlled group of 1,000 pilot candidates came up with these results:

	Eliminated in field training
No screen at all	75 percent
Prewar Army screening	61
Battery, 1944 model (three upper stanines)	36

Stuart Chase, *The Proper Study of Mankind* (Harper, 1948), pp. 25-28.

HOW TO CLASSIFY SPEECH MATERIAL

When the notes really begin to pile up you may get confused, because your mind cannot carry so large an array of *unassorted* material—not even with it on cards before the eye. Hence at some point along the way, before the notes become too numerous, you will want to classify them. There are many methods, of which the following are typical:

Time order. Here the notes are arranged according to the years, months, days, or hours.

Place order. Notes in place order are arranged according to nation, state, city, up-and-down, north-and-south, in-and-out, etc.

Topic classification. Such classifications might be (1) educational, (2) military, (3) religious, (4) political, (5) physical, (6) economic, (7) social, (8) sex, (9) age, etc.

Cause-effect. First will be grouped notes on causes or alleged causes. Next will come the notes on effects or alleged effects. Or you may reverse the order, and put the effects first and the causes second.

Problem-solution. Grouped in one set are notes on the problem—definition of, cause of, visible effects of, etc. Grouped in another set are notes relating to proposed solutions.

Processing the material

METHODS OF PROCESSING

Of course you don't wait for all the speech material to be gathered before processing it. This, from the first, is a continuous process in which the following steps are helpful:

1. Begin on time. (We've talked about that.)

2. Make a tentative outline before you start gathering speech material. (We've talked about that also.)

3. Classify your notes as you go along. (That, too, we have talked about.)

4. As soon as you start preparing the speech, *start also copying down ideas, information, examples, and exact phrases that come to mind. Do this at once, or you will be disturbed at finding that a per-*

fectly clear thought has vanished an hour hence. This means to keep at hand pen or pencil, and paper or cards, both ready to use on the spot.

5. At reasonable intervals reclassify your notes. This is merely another way of revising your tentative outline—which, in turn, is another way of *rethinking* the subject.

6. When you are ready to start on the final outline, lay out your notes in rows on a table. (Remember that you have only *one* idea on a sheet or card, and that you have written on *one* side of the paper only. Here is where the method pays off.) Now you can arrange and rearrange the main heads. You can lay out the subheads and sub-subheads under your eye. You can insert illustrations, comparisons, testimony—even humor and spice—exactly where you anticipate they will be needed. And if you don't like the first outline, you don't have to do any erasing or rewriting. You simply pick up your notes and start rearranging them. This is the time-saving—the pay-off—for what you may have thought was "extra work" involved in systematic note taking.

INTEGRITY OF IDEAS

The question of integrity is inherently involved in all handling of ideas. Especially is this so of speechmaking in a free society, where there are no "approved" thoughts, or even approved methods, to which all speakers must adhere. Inevitably, therefore, in a democracy there are crackpots, emptyheads, and propagandists who mouth opinions without reference to truth. There are also at times disloyal persons in the pay of foreign governments who use freedom of speech in the attempt to destroy freedom of speech. In the classroom there are students who use the platform to speak hollow banalities, to work off thinly-veiled prejudices—sometimes very thinly veiled—or even to misrepresent deliberately. They learn in class to improve their speaking skill, but not their ethics, and go out of class with a skilled ability to discuss a *part* in the solemn pretense that it is the *whole*. In a free society, we have always had this kind of speaking, and seemingly always will. There is no way of purging it without purging freedom itself. But in a free society, people do have the right to decide which *kind of speakers they will trust and follow;* and in colleges and universities—that presumably are taught for the preservation if not uplift of human society—the instructor has the right to decide whether there shall be a standard of integrity. Toward these ends three assumptions are offered:

KNOW A FACT FROM AN OPINION

"Every man has a right to his opinion, but no man has a right to be wrong in his facts," said Bernard Baruch. There are various ways of being wrong with facts. First, there are speakers with "a 155 mm. mouth and a .22 caliber brain," who can never learn to know fact from opinion. In a speech class probably nothing can be done to change either the mouth or brain caliber. Let them stand as exhibits of pots marred in the making. Next, there are others who have yet to *learn* the difference between facts and opinions. Typical of them are students who, early in the course, listed the following opinions as *facts:*

Stalin is a Caucasian bandit.
Labor leaders are conspiring to overthrow the government.
John L. Lewis is the greatest American since Lincoln.
The New Deal was put over by propaganda of unprincipled men.
The Republicans have always wrecked the country when they came to power and the Democrats have had to save it.
Modern art is vile and debasing.

Now these *opinions* are certainly held by particular groups of people, but in their nature they are not *facts.* What, therefore, are facts, and what are opinions? They belong to different categories, like color and size, and ought to be kept separate in the mind.

Facts are "what has really happened"—the physical or mental event. They are often hard to locate, but somewhere down beneath are the facts.

Sound opinions are thought-out conclusions derived from a sound analysis of facts. Loose opinions, of course, are those colored by feeling, sentiment, and bias. On them facts have little influence.

KNOW SOUND OPINION FROM LOOSE OPINION

Make no mistake about it, this is rough going, for man is not a thinking animal except under certain limited conditions. Nevertheless the procedure is known. In simplified form it involves four steps:

1. Do you have an adequate and reliably established body of facts?
2. Do you proceed from assumptions that are neither biased nor unwarranted by circumstances?

3. Do you substitute part for the whole—by overlooking facts that disprove what you want to believe, and using only the facts that prove what you want proved?

4. Do you attempt to use emotional excitation *in place of* facts and ideas?

CHOOSE DELIBERATELY ON WHAT ETHICAL PLANE YOU PROPOSE TO SPEAK

In *Mein Kampf* Adolf Hitler advised readers never to tell a little lie, for it would be doubted; but a big lie, he observed, would be believed because it would seem incredible to the people that a speaker would tell so incredible a thing if it were not so. This, and his other views on speaking, are significant because of the Nazis' astonishing success in taking over Germany by spoken propaganda before they were able to entrench themselves by the firing squad. Therefore, consider certain others of Hitler's views: (1) A demagogue is better suited to be a leader than a theorist because he is a better agitator. (2) Objectivity was "part of a Jewish plot to confuse the world," whereas the propaganda which Hitler used was "not to search unto truth," but a means of getting what he wanted. (3) Listeners will judge what a speaker says "not according to logical and philosophical principles, but they will judge acording to emotion. . . ."

Now all of this is nothing new. It has been in operating practice for 2300 years. Hitler's uniqueness was that he had at the peak "approximately 9800" certified party speakers unloosed on Germany, whereas the German educational system had never trained its people to speak, did not know how to train them, thought it was not important to train them—and hence was helpless against this core of sinister and skillful speakers. Probably we always will have such speakers. Always they steal the vocabulary of patriotism; they pervert the word "democracy"; they use double-talk, calling freedom slavery and slavery freedom. This they do now, have done for centuries, and will do centuries hence. In some fields, like education, their success is automatically limited. In others, like politics, such methods seem to enhance success; and men in the United States have been elected as governors and Congressmen because they have been successful at this sort of speaking. We would not here say that this kind of speaking cannot be "successful," even though the answer obviously must depend on how one defines "success."

But we do point out that the so-called "success" of such speaking is self-limiting and at times self-destroying. Hitler's case was the most notable ever occurring in Western society; he destroyed himself, and the Germany he knew, within twenty-five years. Wallace Carroll, after examining several hundred thousand enemy and allied propaganda broadcasts during World War II, reached a conclusion that should have made Quintilian rest easier in his grave after 1800 years —the same Quintilian who defined an orator as "a good man skilled in speaking." Said Carroll: The organized and successful propaganda efforts in the war "demonstrate the fallacy in the widespread belief that the propagandist's choice is between truth and falsehood.... False propaganda almost invariably boomerangs." And that "a clear and truthful picture of the situation," even when the truth is unpleasant, had more effect than deception and distortion.[2]

A working axiom in a democracy, then, is Lincoln's "you can fool some of the people all of the time, and all of the people some of the time, but you can't fool all of the people all of the time." And it works that way. Therefore, every speaker must choose—cannot evade choosing—on what ethical plane he proposes to speak. In choosing he might well remember John Milton: "Let [Truth] and Falsehood grapple; who ever knew Truth put to worse, in a free and open encounter."

ACKNOWLEDGING THE SOURCE OF IDEAS

When Wendell Phillips gave his classic eulogy on Daniel O'Connell he quoted the words or cited the opinions of other writers twenty-nine times. When Winston Churchill, himself an authority, gave one of his typical famous American addresses he quoted the words or cited the opinions of others ten times. Students on the other hand, sometimes feel that they must hide their sources of speech material. Rare is the speech class that does not hear a student talk, let us say, on our foreign policy—about which he knows nothing first hand—and present facts without revealing the source, or propose courses of action without revealing who originally thought them out—all as though he had access to the files of the State Department and advice of its staff of advisers. The same is true with speeches on military defence, labor and management, and subjects of all sorts on which the speakers are not of themselves authorities.

This has two unhappy results. First, it lowers the persuasive value

[2] Wallace Carroll, *Persuade or Perish* (Boston: Houghton Mifflin Co., 1948), pp. 237-238, 366.

of the speech, for the obvious reason that listeners know the speaker is using second-hand material but have no way of judging its value. Second, it raises a question of ethics and propriety on concealing the sources of ideas. Both injurious results are unnecessary, and usually unintended. The student simply does not know how to reveal his source of ideas. He has not the experience or the skill.

Revealing the sources in a smooth effective manner requires planning in advance. You don't want to do it awkwardly like this:

> Wallace Carroll in his book *Persuade or Perish,* published in 1948, says on page 238, second paragraph—and I quote—"False propaganda almost invariably boomerangs."

This is not only awkward, but distracts attention from the thought to the extraneous matter of dates, pages, and paragraphs. Better smooth it out in this manner:

> Wallace Carroll in his book *Persuade or Perish* says that "False propaganda almost invariably boomerangs."

Or if you want to build up the author as an authority, tell how he knows and give weight to his authority, you might state it this way:

> Wallace Carroll, who was a director of the United States Overseas Office of War Information, came to a significant conclusion as a result of analyzing several hundred thousand enemy and allied broadcasts. He says that, "False propaganda almost invariably boomerangs." He further cites examples of this. For example. . . .

Observe how experienced speakers go about the business. Said Winston Churchill:

> I rejoice in Tennyson's celebrated lines:
>
> "Men, my brothers, men; the workers ever reaping
> something new;
> That which they have done but earnest of the things
> that they shall do."

And Robert I. Gannon:

> William James was right when he wrote, "Sadness lies at the heart of every natural philosophy."

And Harold W. Dodds:

> One hundred and fifty years ago, Fisher Ames contrasted personal government with republican government in a caustic figure of speech which has been widely quoted in recent years. "A Monarchy," he said (he would have

called it dictatorship today), "is like a merchantman. You go on board in comfort and elation, but by and by you strike a reef and go down. But Democracy is like a raft. You never sink, but damn it, your feet are always in the water."

And Dwight D. Eisenhower:

To describe the attitudes of many of us toward the current international scene, I give you the following quotation:

"It is a gloomy moment in history. Not for many years, not in the lifetime of most men who read this paper, has there been so much grave and deep apprehension; never has the future seemed so incalculable as at this time. In France the political cauldron seethes and bubbles with uncertainty; Russia hangs as usual a cloud, dark and silent upon the horizon of Europe. . . ."

That, ladies and gentlemen, though so vividly descriptive of today, appeared in *Harpers Weekly*, Saturday, October 10, 1857.

And Dorothy Thompson:

It is a truism to say that we live in a time of crisis, or what the great British historian, Arnold Toynbee, calls a "time of trouble."

And, finally, Henry van Dyke:

"Know thyself," was Solon's motto, inscribed on the Delphian Shrine.

ASSIGNMENTS

ON FINDING SPEECH MATERIAL

1. Locate and write down where each of the following references is found in your library. Note whether any are not there, and list other seemingly useful references that are not included below:

   a. The ten common sources of bibliography listed in this chapter
   b. The fourteen general and special encyclopedias
   c. The seventeen biographical references
   d. The eight references on statistical information and current history

2. List the library sources for material on the following: (1) Television, (2) the atom bomb, (3) honor system in college examinations, (4) history of women's rights movement in the U.S., (5) Macedonian phalanx, (6) American folk music.

3. List the reference containing the best biographical material for each of the following: (1) Cornelia Otis Skinner, (2) Albert Einstein, (3) Walt Whitman, (4) Thomas Aquinas, (5) Wilhelm Wundt.

4. Hand in notes, properly documented, giving the following information:
   a. Circulation of the four leading U.S. magazines
   b. Total number of students in U.S. colleges last year
   c. Salary of an army first sergeant
   d. Area and population of your home state
   e. Scores in the postseason bowl games in football five years ago

5. Find the date of newspaper articles on each of the following: (1) Dropping the atom bomb (1945). (2) First allied Peace Conference of World War II (1946). (3) U.S. Coal strike of 1949. (4) Communist attack in Korea (1950). (5) President Truman's opening address to the 82nd Congress (1951).

6. List the indexes in which you will find references to each of the following periodicals: (1) *Harper's Magazine,* (2) *Annals of the American Academy of Political and Social Science,* (3) *Printers' Ink,* (4) *Scientific Monthly,* (5) *American Banker.*

7. State the method you would use in finding material on each of the following:
   a. Alaskan statehood
   b. Religions of the Near East
   c. Life on this campus 50 years ago
   d. How to study
   e. The origin of jazz music

ON THINKING, FINDING SPEECH MATERIAL, AND ASSIMILATING IDEAS INTO A SPEECH

8. Select a subject from the speech lists you have prepared previously (see Assignments 2-5, Chapter 9, page 182): (1) Think on it, using the X-ray, how-to-think process described in this chapter. (2) Make a preliminary outline.

9. *Without studying or reading on the subject,* see what information and ideas you can gather during the next week. Do this by listening, conversing, and being generally on the alert.

10. Prepare a selective bibliography of perhaps 10-30 titles on your subject: (1) Do not rely only on the library card catalogue and *Readers' Guide,* but consult also the other common sources given in this chapter. (2) Do not take merely the first items you find, but sort carefully from the whole available bibliography those that seem best to fit your speech purpose. (3) Make sure that your items are accurate, complete, and consistent.

11. Use this bibliography for gathering speech material. Remember to read cautiously, not gullibly, and always with an eye for critical evaluation. Take notes, not by a hit-and-miss method, but by using a tested method such as described in this chapter. Be prepared, if the instructor calls for them, to hand in your notes with the final outline.

12. Classify your notes, process your material, and revise your first tentative outline. *For at least this one time use the loose-leaf method of outlining as described in this chapter, and rearrange your notes several times until you get them in best order.* Perhaps you will want to revise this outline still again before you copy it in final form. Now you are ready to rehearse the speech for delivery.

Delegates, representing twenty Pan American countries, assembled in the Hall of the Americas in Washington.

CHAPTER 11

Organizing the Speech into Orderly Form

CHAPTER 11

A well-organized speech presents the ideas "as organized platoons—in marching order." How to organize ideas into platoons and how to make them march—these are problems we shall now consider.

The test of a well-organized speech is that it be (1) *simple, and* (2) *instantly intelligible to listeners.* As Jean Claude, an almost forgotten French writer of three centuries ago, warned the clergy of his day, "it ought to be remembered that the greatest part of the hearers are simple people and it is impossible to edify them unless you be *very clear;* and even the learned have fatigue enough without increasing it at church."

Lyman Abbott in his famous Open Letter on speechmaking recommends five successive steps for organizing speeches that supply a helpful preview:

> 1. What is the object of this speech? What end is it to serve? What verdict is it to win? What result is it to accomplish?
>
> 2. Central thought. What thought lodged in the mind of an auditor will best accomplish the desired result?
>
> 3. Analysis of this central thought into three or four propositions [main heads], the enforcement and illustration of which will serve to fasten in the minds of the hearers the central thought, and so to secure the desired result.
>
> 4. Some illustrations or concrete statements of each one of these separate propositions [main heads].
>
> 5. These four points firmly fixed in the mind; then an endeavour on these lines of thought to win this result with this audience, exactly as one would endeavour to win assent from an individual.[1]

Examining the so-called one-point speech

In approaching the study of vertebrate zoology a useful method is to start with the one-cell amoeba. So with speeches. Imagine a one-cell

[1] In Brander Matthews, *Notes on Speech-making* (New York: Longmans, Green, and Co., 1901), p. 90.

speech, an amoeba. This single cell would consist of two kinds of subcells:

1. A single assertion
2. Supporting material (facts, figures, specific instances, illustrations, comparisons, testimony, etc.)

In outline form it would appear something like this:

ASSERTION:	I. Having a baby is a real crisis.
Specific instance	A. You hold the new baby in your arms and say, "So this is my baby"; and now you know what the phrase means, "It's your baby."
Specific instance	B. You ask, "What will I do with it?" for you can't start it, stop it, and steer it like an automobile; it has no steering wheel.
Specific instance	C. It wakes up when it wants to, cries when it wants to, and if it decides to have you walk the floor at 2:00 A.M., you walk the floor—in undress parade.
Specific instance	D. You say, "I'm stuck; I have this baby on my hands 24 hours out of every day, with no double pay for overtime. How long does this last?" It lasts until the baby grows up and goes to college.

Or like this:

ASSERTION:	I. A good speech is like a good photograph.
Comparison	A. It must be in focus.
Comparison	B. It should center on one object, not on two or three unrelated ones.
Comparison	C. One good closeup is worth a dozen distant shots.

There are occasions on which speakers actually use a one-cell speech like these, but usually these occasions are limited to where *a speaker is himself giving only part of a whole speech,* and where the other parts are given by other persons on the program. Among such occasions are the one-point speeches given in discussion groups, in a series of short reports or explanations, in committee meetings, in business conferences.

The one-point speech, then, like the amoeba, is a single-cell animal. Also like the amoeba, it is not too often seen in everyday life. Its use is chiefly as a specimen to illustrate the structure of real speeches. But it has a supplementary use for speakers who have a one-point spot on a program alongside other speakers.

Dividing the speech into well-chosen main heads

If you examine closely the structure of well-organized speeches, you will find that the central theme is supported, or in some way developed, by a very few main heads or topics. In other words, the speaker, instead of attempting to carry the speech to the audience in one large lump, breaks it up into several smaller and compactly handled parts.

If you read a hundred, or a thousand, well-organized speeches, you might be surprised to find that the long speeches had no more main heads than the short ones. The chief difference between the long and short speeches would be not in the number of main heads, but in the extent to which each main head was developed. The longer speech would have more explanations, illustrations, specific instances, and other forms of support.

To be specific, in both long and short speeches there would be found usually *two or three main heads, occasionally four or five, almost never more than five.* So uniformly would these numbers appear in speech after speech that we should soon wonder if there was not an underlying reason. We would be right; there is a reason, or, rather, there are several reasons.

For obvious mechanical reasons there would never be less than two main heads in a speech, excepting only in the rare so-called one-point speeches discussed just previously in this chapter. Every speech has, as we know, one and only one proposition (or purpose-sentence), and *by definition,* main heads are those several divisions of the speech which elaborate, develop, or support the proposition.

There are two reasons why speeches usually have only two or three main heads and almost never have more than five: (1) A speech with too many main heads is usually arranged illogically. Any idea, if carefully analyzed, can be resolved into a very few (i.e. from two to five) *basic* parts. Not only are more parts not necessary, but in fact they usually impair the symmetry, coherence, or logic of treatment. When a speech has too many main heads, the subject matter has been analyzed, not into its *basic* parts, but into *incidental* or *subordinate* units.

(2) The audience cannot remember too many main topics. If a speech has two or three well-chosen and well-supported main heads, the average listener can remember them and carry them away with him; but if a speech has eight or ten, he is hopelessly confused and carries away only fragments and disarranged impressions.

Therefore, arrange material in an *obvious* thought pattern with *few* main heads.

THOUGHT PATTERNS

Among the common thought patterns for arranging speeches are the following:

1. *Time Order.* You begin at a given date or period of history and move forward (or backward) with time. The divisions are marked by the clock or calendar. For example:

DEVELOPING ATOMIC ENERGY

I. The earlier "billiard-ball conception" before 1890 was that matter could not be destroyed.
II. The recent "solar-system conception" after 1896 was that the atom contained a nucleus, or sun, with moving planets called electrons.
III. Working on this theory the scientists between 1942 and 1945 developed a chain reaction that released the energy of the uranium atom.

2. *Space Order.* You arrange material acording to any pattern of space—east-to-west, far-to-near, top-to-bottom, inside-to-outside. Especially is this pattern useful for description or simple exposition. Witness Victor Hugo's famous description of the battle of Waterloo:

PROPOSITION: To form a clear idea of the battle of Waterloo, imagine a capital "A" laid on the ground.
I. The left stroke of the "A" is the Nivelles road.
  A. The left-hand lower point is Hougomont.
  B. Reille is there with Jerome Bonaparte.
II. The right stroke of the "A" is the Genappe road.
  A. The right-hand lower point is la Belle Alliànce.
  B. Napoleon is there.
III. The cross of the "A" is Mont Saint Jean; Wellington is there.

3. *Classification Order.* You classify somewhat like a scientist by identifying related forms and activities. There are many forms of classification, of which the following are typical:

1. *Classification according to fields of inquiry:*

Economic
Political
Social
Educational
Religious
Physical

2. *Classification according to the parties involved:*

Producers and consumers
Labor and management
Farm voters and city voters
Men and women
Young and old
College and noncollege
Northern and Southern

3. *Classification according to cause, as:*

a. The primary cause was....
b. The contributing causes were....
c. The precipitating causes were....

Other miscellaneous forms of classification include the following:

4. Plants and animals
5. Function and structure
6. Inherited and learned
7. Experimentation and investigation
8. Public and private
9. Prose and poetry

4. *Cause-and-Effect Order.* You arrange material according to the causes and results of a condition or situation. You seek to determine causes by asking, "What events, factors, or circumstances caused—or partly caused—this result?" You seek to determine the kinds of causes by asking, "Which of these causes were primary? Which were contributing causes? Which were immediate causes?" You also seek to forecast results by asking, "What events, factors, or circumstances will result (or have resulted) from this given situation?"

Beware of False Causes. To mistake that which precedes for that which causes is an old error, for which the Romans had a name: *Post hoc, ergo propter hoc.* "After this, therefore on account of this." It is also as new as this morning's bread, for the naive and gullible still say glibly, "This happened first, and that happened next; therefore, this caused that." Beware of it. Find out which are really causes and which are mere accidents of time.

The Cause-and-Effect order is not always (1) cause and (2) effect. Often it is reversed and becomes (1) effect and (2) cause. Indeed the latter form is the more commonly used by skillful speakers. The following is an outline of an Effect-Cause order in which the speaker seeks to establish real cause instead of mere time sequence:

WAR CAUSES INFLATION

EFFECT: I. Inflation has accompanied every major war in U.S. history.
- A. The U.S. Department of Labor has compiled a wholesale index of prices, which shows that during the American Revolution prices jumped from 60 to 180.
- B. During the War of 1812 it jumped from 100 to 150.
- C. During the Civil War it jumped from 62 to 136.
- D. During World War I it jumped from 70 to 156.
- E. During and after World War II it jumped from 80 to 170.
- F. At no other times in the past 200 years have prices jumped so sharply except during and immediately following war.

CAUSE: II. The cause goes back to Adam Smith's law of supply and demand.
- A. War sets up a demand for military supplies.
  1. In the American Revolution our government spent $75 millions.
  2. In the Civil War the Federal and Confederate governments, between them, spent $6½ billions.
  3. In World War I our government spent $26 billions.
  4. In World War II it spent $330 billions.
- B. These war expenditures created a sudden intense demand which the prewar industrial machinery could not supply; and the sudden demand inflated prices.
- C. In addition, in recent wars it has been necessary to open new factories and shipyards in new locations, give bonuses to workers to move there, pay more bonuses for overtime work, and boost farm prices to farmers so they would grow more crops even though their sons and workers were in the armed forces.

5. *Problem-Solution Order.* In everyday life problems arise; we seek to analyze their nature and to find effective solutions. Problem-solving is likewise one of the important functions of speechmaking. When issues arise, when a crisis impends, men not only grope with these problems in their own minds and discuss them with their fellows, but also gather to hear leaders and near-leaders, prophets and false prophets, discuss them in public.

Speakers who undertake to solve problems assume the most difficult burden, intellectually at least, of all speaking. To reach a valid conclusion they must carry an audience through the successive steps of logical thinking. Straight is the gate and narrow is the way through which these steps lead, and many are the byways that can take one astray. Primarily, four master questions arise, each with its species of subquestions. These questions set for the *proof requirements* of the problem-solution order:

1. Is there a "felt difficulty," that makes a change necessary or desirable?
2. Would the change which I advocate remedy the conditions?
3. Might it not bring on new evils worse than the present ones?
4. Would not some other solution be more satisfactory?

Or, as Raymond F. Howes has aptly pointed out, one might for sake of vividness ask:

1. Is the man sick?
2. Will our medicine cure him?
3. Will it harm him?
4. Will any other medicine be more effective?

You will not automatically turn each of these steps into a main head. Certainly, your final heads will not turn out to be: I. Problem; II. Solution; III Refuting the dangers of new and worse evils; IV. Refuting other solutions. These are rather your *steps of inquiry*, in which you seek (1) to analyze the nature of the problem, (2) test the various avenues of solution or escape, (3) and present the description and endorsement of the chosen way. The following is an example of a Problem-Solution pattern that presents a three-step solution:

PROBLEM: I. The railroads face a critical situation that concerns us, the public.
- A. There are three major causes.
  1. They are over-regulated by the Interstate Commerce Commission.
  2. They are forced to compete with airlines that are subsidized by the government, and with trucks and buses that use the public highways.
  3. They are compelled to pay too much for featherbedding among workers.
- B. This concerns us directly and immediately.
  1. The railroads are backbone of national defense; and any poor maintenance or lack of up-to-date equipment can become critical in a national emergency.
  2. If you attend a college with an endowment, or own an insurance policy, or expect to own one—you are part owner in the railroads; for endowments and insurance money are heavily invested in the railroads.

SOLUTION: II. The railroads need a new deal.

A. The Federal government should ease the restrictions laid on them when they were a monopoly instead of a competitor.

B. Airlines should not be subsidized—unless the railroads are subsidized; and trucks and buses ought to pay the full costs of using public highways.

C. As for featherbedding, in the interests of national defense the Federal government should set up a special commission to determine where it exists, and the full power of the Federal government should be used to clean it out.

When you endorse a solution, test your thinking on it, and be temperate in your claims for its infallibility. Student speeches are too much filled with patent-medicine remedies to which listeners could reply:

By the pricking of my thumbs,
Something wicked this way comes.

Remember that we really "solve" few problems in life. Through the centuries, we have never "solved" the problems of marriage, divorce, crime, taxes, war, tolerance, and equal justice under the law. Instead, we *keep at* solving them. In real life, sometimes the only solutions open to us are to "Watch this problem carefully," or "Act with courage," or "Be tolerant," or "Make these few adjustments." There are times when even the President and the Congress and the Courts can advise us only of the general direction we should go in solving pressing political questions. It comes with ill grace, at such times, for a college student to point the way out in a five-minute speech with a patent-medicine remedy. It brings to mind Winston Churchill's apt retort to free-lance advisers: "It is easy to give advice if you have not got to carry it out."

PRINCIPLES OF SELECTING AND ARRANGING HEADS

For easy reference let us draw together the basic principles, most of which already have been stated or implied:

1. *Arrange the speech according to one consistent pattern.* Observe the confusion caused by two overlapping patterns in the following outline:

A NICARAGUAN CANAL

CAUSAL PATTERN: I. The Panama Canal cannot long handle future traffic.
II. It is also too vulnerable to air attack or sabotage.
TIME ORDER: III. Negotiations for a Nicaraguan Canal were begun in 1826.
IV. Early investigations were held on feasibility in 1876.
V. Later investigations were again held in 1929-1931.

The trouble arises in part from the speaker having *two* speeches. He needs to make up his mind which he will use, cut off the unused one, and arrange the final speech according to one consistent pattern.

2. *Divide the speech so different heads don't overlap.* The following overlapping heads would confuse the listener simply because the speaker himself is still confused:

I. In going down into the Grand Canyon one passes through climatic zones similar to those from Canada to southern Mexico.
II. This is an unusual phenomenon that is obvious to any discerning visitor.
III. Naturally, one wonders why; and it is easy to find out.
IV. The reasons are....

We try again, and seek for heads that do not overlap. We ask about the subject: *What?* and *Why?* (Useful questions always.) We get the following clearcut heads that do not overlap:

EFFECT: I. In descending the Grand Canyon you pass through climatic zones like those from Canada to southern Mexico.
CAUSE: II. This is caused chiefly by sharp differences of altitude and rainfall.

3. *Compose the parts so nothing essential is left out.* Please note the word "essential." Nothing is so dull as the speech that tries to cover the earth, the moon, and the stars—for it can only be dehydrated and tasteless, without the juice that makes a real speech. If you have tried to cover too much, narrow it down. But once the proposition is settled on, cover the essential parts. Look carefully at the following main heads:

PROBLEM: I. Too many Americans cannot pay for adequate medical care.
SOLUTION: II. National health insurance would give medical service to this neglected group.

Note the essential parts left out: (1) How much will national health insurance cost? (2) How would chronic malingerers be prevented from breaking down the system? (3) How would political infiltration be prevented? (4) What would be the effect of "socializing" the physicians on the quality of future doctors? (5) Could private health insurance give as good service? (6) Would it be cheaper or more expensive? Obviously the speaker has not considered either the "new and worse evils," or the "are other solutions more satisfactory?" that are inherent in testing solutions (see page 216).

4. *In general, beware of fewer than two, or more than four or five main heads.* This has already been discussed (pages 212-213), but it will bear repeating. Other things being equal, four heads are better than five, and three are better than four. The fewer the number, the easier for the listeners to remember them.

Phrasing the main heads effectively

The bulk of your speech is made up of facts, illustrations, explanations, and argument, but these are *tied together by the framework of main heads.* Therefore, phrase them carefully, and, if possible, impellingly. Consider the following poorly-phrased heads:

I. The history of television is the basis of its development.
II. Television is here.
III. The future of television can be predicted by the analysis of several general questions.

(No, these main heads were not thought up to serve as atrocities. They really are copied from the outline of a class speech!) Such heads make no sense because there is no analysis behind them. Better toss them out and start over.

At a higher level, but still not acceptable, is the speaker who substitutes *transitions* for main heads, like this:

I. What were the causes?
II. What were the effects?

Now these are excellent transitions. They lead right into the idea. But transitions are *not* main heads—not any more than a sign saying, "To the zoo" *is* the zoo. Transitions say "To the main head." They are *not* themselves main heads. Oftentimes—more often than not—the speaker will indeed start developing a main head with a transition ("What were the causes?"), will unfold it gradually, and not come to the full statement of the head until near the end. This is the inductive method, and it is very effective. But all along the speaker has each main head phrased in his own mind. He knows what its boundaries are. And when he gets through unfolding it he *tells the listeners* exactly what the main head is. These, for example, could be the real main heads of the above transitions:

CAUSE: I. The coming of universal suffrage since 1800 has changed the kind of government our Founding Fathers thought they created.
EFFECT: II. Universal suffrage was the ultimate cause of recent social legislation that reaches directly from the Federal government to the individual citizen.

The following is a useful check list for testing the effectiveness of phrasing main heads:

1. *Are they phrased concisely?* Have you used the fewest possible words? Have you used a simple declarative sentence instead of a complex one? Have you stripped off the distracting modifying clauses? The following is poor phrasing:

> First in importance are the early environmental factors which developed in George Bernard Shaw the ability to produce the type of plays that he wrote.

Strip the underbrush, turn it into a simple declarative sentence, and you get a concise head like this:

> George Bernard Shaw's plays show the influence of his early environment.

2. *Are they phrased impellingly?* Have you whenever possible stated them in terms of the listeners' immediate needs, impelling motives, or culture patterns? Review these principles of motivation discussed in Chapter 5 and Chapter 6, and put them to use. For example, take the following distinctly unimpelling head:

> The basic principles of art are of great importance in modern life.

This need not be unimpelling. Rephrased in terms of listeners' wants, you get the following impelling main head:

> You can improve your looks by means of art.

3. *Have you whenever possible helped listeners by parallel phrasing?* Main heads are the coordinate parts of your speech. They are roughly equal, and often parallel. At least they are parallel if well-chosen according to one consistent thought pattern. Very well, whenever possible phrase them so they *sound* parallel. The following heads fail to do this:

I. Knowledge is one of the qualities of an educated man.
II. Another quality of the educated man is wisdom.
III. The educated man is also tolerant.

Rephrase them in parallel form and you get:

I. The educated man has acquired knowledge.
II. The educated man has attained wisdom.
III. The educated man has learned tolerance.

Arranging the supporting material so it really supports

1. *As an operating principle don't make an assertion without backing it up with supporting material that develops, proves, or clarifies.* You know what supporting material is. You have already studied it (pages 38-44), and will study it further in more detail (pages 244-266). Observe its use in a speech of simple explanation:

WHAT MAKES A BEST SELLER?

I. ASSERTION:	I. The three best-selling American novels have been *Uncle Tom's Cabin, Ben Hur,* and *Gone With the Wind.*
A. *Supporting material*	A. *Uncle Tom's Cabin,* a tale of slavery written in the pre-Civil War turmoil, sold 3,000,000 copies.
B. *Supporting material*	B. *Ben Hur,* a tale of the Christ written in the Gilded Age of the late nineteenth century, sold 2,500,000 copies.
C. *Supporting material*	C. *Gone With the Wind,* a story of courage in the face of disaster, was written in the discouraged times of the 1930's. It sold over 4,000,000 copies.
II. ASSERTION:	II. In the books themselves no common element explains their popularity.
A. *Supporting material*	A. *Uncle Tom's Cabin* is a propaganda novel.
B. *Supporting material*	B. *Ben Hur* is a religious book.
C. *Supporting material*	C. *Gone With the Wind* fits no formula, but is the story of a woman always strong-willed and usually avaricious.

III. ASSERTION:	III. In the needs of the readers is found the answer.
A. *Supporting material*	A. Slavery was the most agitated topic of the 1850's, and *Uncle Tom's Cabin* told about it in story-pictures to the mass of people.
B. *Supporting material*	B. The Gilded Age following the Civil War was an era of boom and bust, and dollar chasing; and *Ben Hur* touched the still small voice of conscience that had been silenced by the noisy times.
C. *Supporting material*	C. *Gone With the Wind* was read by Americans at that moment they had developed an overdose of self-pity, a feeling that "These are the worst times that ever were"; but Scarlett O'Hara faced worse times than any reader ever dreamed of; she was neither noble nor virtuous, but right down to the last line of the book she was in there pitching, never whimpering, never saying "It can't be done." Such a book was blood plasma for the minds of readers in the 1930's.

The following pattern shows how supporting material would be used to develop a Cause-Effect arrangement.

I. ASSERTION:	I. Causes of the situation are....
A. *First subassertion*	A. Primary cause is....
1. *Supporting material*	1. Facts
2. *Supporting material*	2. Figures
3. *Supporting material*	3. Comparison
4. *Supporting material*	4. Illustration
5. *Supporting material*	5. Testimony
B. *Second subassertion*	B. Immediate cause is....
1. *Supporting material*	1. Illustration
2. *Supporting material*	2. Illustration
3. *Supporting material*	3. Facts
4. *Supporting material*	4. Specific instances
II. ASSERTION....	II. Effects are....

A Problem-Solution arrangement would have the supporting material arranged in a pattern something like this:

I. ASSERTION:	I. Problem is. . . .
A. *First subassertion*	A. Visible effects are. . . .
1. *Supporting material*	1. Specific instance
2. *Supporting material*	2. Facts
3. *Supporting material*	3. Illustration
4. *Supporting material*	4. Comparison
B. *Second subassertion*	B. Nature, or causes, are. . . .
1. *First subassertion*	1. First cause is. . . .
a. *Supporting material*	a. Testimony
b. *Supporting material*	b. Comparisons
c. *Supporting material*	c. Figures
d. *Supporting material*	d. Illustration
2. *Second subassertion*	2. Second cause is. . . .
a. *Supporting material*	a. Testimony
b. *Supporting material*	b. Specific instances
c. *Supporting material*	c. Figures
d. *Supporting material*	d. Comparisons
II. ASSERTION: . . .	II. Solution is. . . .

2. *Arrange supporting material in a consistent thought pattern.* You have already studied thought patterns as applied to main heads —Time Order, Space Order, Classification Order, Cause-Effect Order, and Problem-Solution Order. These thought patterns are also used for arranging supporting material. For each head choose whichever pattern seems most of effective. For example, the supporting material of Head I could be arranged in Time Order, that of Head II in Space Order, and that of Head III in Classification Order. Shift from one pattern to another as much as you please when you move from one head to another, but generally don't shift patterns within any particular head or co-ordinate series. The following is an example of three main heads arranged in Classification Order, but with the supporting material under Head III arranged in Time Order:

MODERN PRINTING

CLASSIFICATION ORDER:

I. Modern printing requires, first, a highly-trained staff of experts [typesetters, proofreaders who know languages, mathematics, etc.].

. . . .

. . . .

II. Modern printing requires also expensive and complex machinery [linotypes, teletypes, platen presses, web presses, flatbed presses, rotary presses, offset presses].

. . . .

. . . .

III. In printing the textbook you are using these experts used a four-step process.

TIME ORDER WITHIN HEAD III:

A. First, the editorial staff processed the manuscript.
   1. Following the publisher's instructions, they marked each heading, paragraph, and footnote.
   2. These markings were to tell the typesetter which of the many sizes and faces of type should be used for that particular unit.
   3. The total markings for the book ran well over one thousand.

B. Next, came the printing.
   1. Operators set the copy in linotype.
   2. They arranged it on long sheets of paper known as galleys.

C. Third, came the proofreading and correcting.
   1. Expert proofreaders read the copy, marked the errors and typesetters reset all lines containing errors.
   2. The proofreaders then read copy a second time and marked queries for the author.
   3. The proof was then sent to the publisher and author for additional proofreading and corrections.
   4. It was returned to the printer, where the corrections were made and the long galleys were rearranged into pages, each page with a number and a heading.
   5. Again it went to the publisher and author for a final letter-by-letter reading for last-minute errors.

D. Finally came the printing and binding.
   1. The printers made the last-minute corrections.
   2. They manufactured the plates.
   3. Then they printed the book, usually in 32- or 64-page units on a flatbed press.
   4. The book was then bound in cloth, and the title was stamped by metal dies on the front and the backbone.

ASSIGNMENTS

ON PRELIMINARY PRACTICE IN ORGANIZING IDEAS

1. You learn to organize ideas by *applying principles* in continued practice. Poorly applied, you will get poor organization; well applied, you will get better organization. As the first step, therefore, of using the principles of this chapter, make a one-cell, amoeba outline of any subject of your choice. Let it consist of a single assertion supported by three or four subheads of solid speech material.

2. For the next phase of applying principles to practice, read three speeches, each having a different thought pattern (cause-and-effect, problem-solution, etc.). You may find them in *Vital Speeches,* in this book, or anywhere else. For each write out the purpose sentence and main heads, and identify its thought pattern.

3. We are now ready to apply principles to practice on a more complex level. For each of the five thought patterns discussed in this chapter: (1) Select a subject for which such an arrangement would be fitting. (2) Phrase an impelling purpose sentence for it. (3) Select and arrange main heads so they form one consistent thought pattern. (4) Phrase the main heads concisely and impellingly; and if possible use parallel phrasing.

4. After the above preliminary practice you are ready to examine the full-scale organization of a speech. Make an outline of one of the speeches found at the back of this book, and especially criticize the following: (1) Adequacy of thought pattern for the main heads. (2) Consistency of thought pattern found in the supporting material (subheads, etc.). (3) Amount and quality of this supporting material.

5. Listen to a good speaker and make a rough-draft outline of his lines of thought. Study it critically: (1) Did he have a thought pattern, and was it consistent? (2) Did these lines of thought overlap, or leave out essential parts? (3) Did he state these main lines of thought so they "had handles on them," and you could remember and carry them away? (4) Were they impelling, and were they stated impellingly? (5) Was the supporting material arranged in a clear and consistent thought pattern, or did it seem to be a waste-basket arrangement? (6) If you were giving this speech how would you change the main heads, change their arrangement, change the supporting material, and rearrange the thought pattern of supporting material?

ON ARRANGING YOUR SPEECHES INTO ORDERLY FORM

6. Pair with a classmate and criticise each other's outlines for the remaining major speeches of this source. Especially be watchful whether:
   a. The main heads are arranged in a consistent thought pattern, and that it is the best thought pattern for this subject.
   b. The main heads do not overlap and do not leave out essential parts.

c. Each main head is a simple, single, complete statement, and is phrased impellingly.
d. The group of main heads, where possible, are stated in parallel form.
e. Assertions are supported by ample and adequate supporting material.
f. Supporting material, like the main heads, are arranged in a consistent thought pattern.

7. In all future class speeches use the principles of this chapter to make more effective what you have learned from previous chapters on thinking, finding materials, making ideas impelling, etc.; and cross-check them with at least one classmate as designed in Assignment 6.

In addressing Congress, April 19, 1951, Douglas MacArthur's introduction—"the issues are global"—disarmed critics who had accused him of ignoring Europe. His conclusion—"old soldiers never die"—was a climax audaciously beyond the limits of ordinary present-day public address.

CHAPTER 12

Beginning and Ending the Speech

CHAPTER 12

So far we have been considering the body and main theme of the speech. But a speech also has a beginning and ending—an entrance and exit—and whether we intend it or not, the first and last words will influence the listener's response. Look first at the opening words.

Orienting and getting attention with the introduction

Consider the speaker who starts with these dull words:

> The Constitution, with the amendments and interpretations which have made it a living and growing thing, has survived to this day as an expression of the will of the people.

Who wants to listen further, and why should they? But suppose the speaker had instead started like this:

> The Constitutional Convention of 1787 was approaching its close. A hush settled over the weary members as the aged Benjamin Franklin slowly arose, and pointing to the half-sun emblazoned on the back of Washington's chair, said. . . .

How different is the effect!

The speech introduction has two purposes: (1) to get attention and good will, (2) to orient the audience, tell what the subject is about, and supply the necessary background.

GETTING ATTENTION AND GOOD WILL

If you don't get attention and good will it doesn't matter what kind of speech you have. All the work you've done on it will be wasted so far as any living effect it produces. Therefore, plan the opening words with care, plan them deliberately so listeners will settle down and listen in a receptive mood. The following are methods of getting attention and good will:

1. *Get attention and good will by personal greeting.* A personal greeting or reference at times gets quick attention and good will, especially if the speaker is well-known either personally or by reputation. David E. Lilienthal used a personal reference in his address in New York City accepting a Freedom Award:

> One morning last June at the University of Wisconsin, I was supposed to be on hand to receive an honorary degree. But I wasn't there; I was in Washington before a congressional investigating committee. The President of the University explained my absence by saying that Mr. Lilienthal wasn't there for his degree because he was still answering examination questions. The examination questions in Washington at about that time concerned the garbage cans in the town of Oak Ridge.[1]

2. *Get attention and good will by paying the audience an honest compliment.* A visiting lecturer begins: "It gives me great pleasure to address college men and women today, for they are the most intelligent of our youth, and our youth today will become the leaders of tomorrow. . . ." No, it won't do. Those college men and women have heard that before.

A political candidate says: "I am glad to come to this splendid community with its wonderful schools, its magnificent churches, its noble people. They represent the best in America—the honest, God-fearing people who pay their debts and do good to their neighbors." No, it won't do either. People aren't that dumb. To be sure, the candidate's partisans forgive with easy tolerance ("The old boy was spreading it around, eh?"), but such methods win neither votes nor respect.

If you have a compliment to pay, do it skillfully, for audiences are speech-wise and skeptical of them. But it can be done—if you have the compliment and the know-how. Vice-President Alben W. Barkley did it before the Executives' Club of Chicago:

> Now I am very greatly complimented by the invitation to appear here for the third time to address this great Executives' Club. It indicates either your approval of my previous performances or a great patience on your part. Nevertheless, I am glad to be here because I recognize that it is one of the great representative clubs, not only of Chicago, but of the United States. And it is sometimes a relief to stand before an organization of business and professional men with the realization that nothing you say is going to arouse any rabble.[2]

[1] *Bulletin of the Atomic Scientists,* V (November, 1949), 294.
[2] *Vital Speeches,* XV (November 15, 1948), 70.

3. *Get attention and good will by reference to the occasion or surrounding.* Sometimes a speaker seizes on some small reference of interest value, and turns it to account, as the speaker who said:

> On the platform behind me you will notice, among others, a Catholic priest and a Protestant minister. They don't know it, but they are a symbol of what I am going to talk about—for my subject deals with the need for tolerance and cooperation between Catholics and Protestants in America.

At other times—like anniversaries and ceremonies—the occasion is the heart and core of the program, and the speaker is expected to recognize it. Woodrow Wilson's introduction to his address at Independence Hall in Philadelphia, July 4, 1914, remains a classic:

> We are assembled to celebrate the one hundred and thirty-eighth anniversary of the birth of the United States. I suppose that we can more vividly realize the circumstances of that birth standing on this historic spot than it would be possible to realize them anywhere else. The Declaration of Independence was written in Philadelphia; it was adopted in this historic building by which we stand. I have just had the privilege of sitting in the chair of the great man who presided over the deliberations of those who gave the declaration to the world. My hand rests at this moment upon the table upon which the declaration was signed. We can feel that we are almost in the visible and tangible presence of a great historic transaction.

4. *Get attention and good will by reference to matters of special interest to listeners.* Every special group has common knowledge, interests, and desires—college students, physicians, lawyers, retailers, executives, druggists, and all—and these can be used to capture attention and good will. Herman W. Steinkraus, President of the United States Chamber of Commerce, did this in speaking before the National Sales Executives Club of New York City:

> You know—it's quite some time since I have sat down with a group of sales managers... and I didn't realize how much enthusiasm the crowd has and also how much boastfulness. Goodness gracious, the things I've heard said [by] ... people up here about themselves and how good they are, but that is really what made American sales management so successful, the fact that you have confidence in each other.
>
> I have been very much interested in the idea that you have 13,000 sales managers in this organization. . .[3]

5. *Get attention and good will by pleasantry or humor.* Usually the prolonged funny story is a poor beginning. It may be beside the point,

[3] *Vital Speeches,* XVI (April 15, 1950), 402-403.

too long, or not very funny; and listeners will be saying to themselves, "Quit wandering and get going." An apt short funny story, of course, is good. But be sure that it is apt, is funny, and is short. Experienced speakers tend more to rely on other types of pleasantry or humor. Winston Churchill, speaking at Westminster College, Fulton, Missouri, found pleasantry in comparing Westminster of Missouri with Westminster of England:

> I am glad to come to Westminster College this afternoon and am complimented that you should give me a degree. The name "Westminster" is somehow familiar to me. I seem to have heard it before. Indeed it was at Westminster that I received a very large part of my education in politics, dialectic, rhetoric, and one or two other things.[4]

Dave Beck, labor leader, found his humor in the weather. Speaking at the Minneapolis Chamber of Commerce after a day and night of heavy snowing he began:

> I wish to voice a definite and distinct protest. I know that there must have been some objections in the membership of the Chamber of Commerce to inviting a representative of Labor to address this great organization. Yet, in all my experience in the Trade Union Movement, this is the first time they ever appealed to the Almighty to create a weather condition to keep me away!

6. *Get attention and good will by direct reference to the significance of the subject.* When the audience has an immediate interest in the subject, you can often get attention and good will by coming at once to a significant statement of your proposition or first main point. John A. Brett, lawyer, did this in speaking to the Oklahoma State Bar Association:

> Man's tongue is often his worst enemy, and when it is, a good honest lawyer is his best friend. But who is a good honest lawyer? That I propose to tell you.[5]

Likewise Senator Margaret Chase Smith opened her address before the United States Senate on the abuse of senatorial immunity by a significant statement on the importance of her subject:

> I would like to speak briefly and simply about a serious national condition. It is a national feeling of fear and frustration that could result in national suicide and the end of everything that we Americans hold dear. It

[4] A. Craig Baird, *Representative American Speeches: 1945-1946* (New York: H. W. Wilson Co., 1946), p. 21.

[5] *Oklahoma State Bar Journal,* III (April 1932), 18.

is a condition that comes from lack of effective leadership either in the legislative branch or the executive branch of our Government. . . .

I speak as briefly as possible because too much harm has already been done with irresponsible words of bitterness and selfish political opportunism. I speak as simply as possible because the issue is too great to be obscured by eloquence. I speak simply and briefly in the hope that my words will be taken to heart. Mr. President, I speak as a Republican. I speak as a woman. I speak as a United States Senator. I speak as an American.

The United States Senate has long enjoyed world-wide respect as the greatest deliberative body in the world. But recently that deliberative character has too often been debased to the level of a forum of hate and character assassination sheltered by the shield of congressional immunity.[6]

But note, please, that not all speeches can be started by a direct reference to the subject. If the audience is apathetic toward the subject, a direct reference to that subject will leave them apathetic still. If the audience is hostile toward the subject, a direct reference to it may be a slap in the face. This is an introduction you use when the listeners are already interested or concerned.

7. *Get attention and good will by an illustration, comparison, or quotation related to the subject.* An example from personal experience, or history, or literature can be used to reveal vividly the trend of the speech or its vital importance. Especially are these useful if the subject is remote from the experience of the audience. Walter Lippmann used an illustration at Freedom House, New York City, in speaking on the wars and revolutions of the twentieth century:

Many years ago while I was still a student at college, I read a book about which I have forgotten almost everything, including the name of the author, except one specific incident. The book contained the recollections of an Englishman who visited France a few years after the fall of Napoleon. One day, as I recall it, he found himself talking to an old peasant, who had been working on his farm, which was a day's journey from Paris, for more than fifty years. He had lived there under the Bourbon Kings, during the Revolution, during the Terror, and during the Napoleonic Empire and its downfall.

. . . So the Englishman tried to draw out the peasant, feeling I suppose, that when he returned he would then be able to tell the people of England what the people of France were thinking. But what was his surprise when he found that his excellent friend had somehow contrived to live near Paris for the past fifty years and yet never to have heard anything about Napoleon Bonaparte.

I remember asking one of my old teachers about the story and whether

[6] *Vital Speeches*, XVI (July 1, 1950), 552-553.

such a strange thing could really have happened, and I remember his saying, "Yes, it could have happened... it happens in every age, and what is more it happens to most of the people in any age, and it will happen to you, too, in one degree or another, to live in an age when history is made and not to know what that history is." [7]

Before the Economic Club of Detroit, Cecil B. de Mille used a *quotation* to begin a speech on communism:

"Ten years from now a divided, stunned and defeated United States may be trying to adjust itself to a communist-ruled world.—Ten years from now a weary, mangled and victorious United States may be trying to salvage what it can from the radioactive wreckage of the world.—Ten years from now a busy, peaceful United States may be helping to push forward the frontiers of freedom everywhere in the world."

These three prophecies, which I have quoted from *Time* magazine, ought to be printed on the face of every clock in America. For each hour that passes brings closer the fulfillment of one of these prophecies. And which one it will be depends on the decisions we make, as the hours pass.[8]

ORIENTING THE AUDIENCE

You may have noticed that each one of the Introductions given in the few pages previous not only gained attention and good will, but also did one additional significant thing. *Each oriented the listeners to the speaker's point of view.* That is, at the same time the speakers were getting attention and good will, they also told the audience what the subject was about, adjusted them to the speaker's viewpoint concerning it, and (when necessary) supplied them with background facts for understanding the discussion. These are two separate purposes of the Introduction: (1) to get attention and good will, (2) to orient the audience. They are not necessarily, or even usually, done in two separate parts, however. A skillful speaker can blend them into one smooth whole.

There is no formula for orienting the audience but the following are helpful procedures:

1. *Orient the audience by explaining the subject background.* Consider the follow-the-rule debater who opens his speech in this manner: "We are to discuss whether the Federal government should establish a Missouri Valley Authority similar to the Tennessee Valley Authority.

[7] A. Craig Baird, *Representative American Speeches: 1943-1944* (New York: H. W. Wilson Co., 1944), pp. 248-249.

[8] *Vital Speeches*, XIV (June 1, 1948), 495.

By the 'Federal government,' we mean that government established in 1787 under the Constitution and which now is centered in Washington, D. C. By 'establish' we mean to vote taxes to institute. . . ." No, this won't do at all. He is telling listeners what they already know. He is taking simple words and explaining them in complex words. This is not "explaining the subject background." It is muddying the issue. In explaining the subject background, you waste no words telling listeners what they already well know, for elaboration of the obvious tends to lose good will, and certainly loses attention.

But when the background facts are not known, or when they are not fresh in mind, a vivid background sketch permits the audience to see the subject in its perspective. Samuel B. Pettengill, in a radio speech on Communism, began by explaining the subject background:

> It was 101 years ago that Marx and Engels wrote the *Communist Manifesto* which began with the words, "A specter is haunting Europe, the specter of communism." This sounds like today's newspaper. That was the year gold was discovered in California, before the covered wagon began to roll across the plains. Please keep this date in mind. It is significant.
>
> A little later, Marx, in London, wrote *Das Kapital,* the bible of the Communists and Socialists. As a reporter of facts, Marx was accurate. The conditions of the workers in England a century ago, as he points out, were very grim. Women pulled canal boats along the tow-path with ropes over their shoulders. Women were harnessed, like beasts of burden, to cars pulling coal out of British mines. In the textile mills, children began to work when they were 9 or 10 years old, and worked 12 to 15 hours a day. In many cases, the beds in which they slept never got cold, as one shift took the place of the other. It was said that they were machines by day and beasts by night. Tuberculosis and other occupational diseases killed them off like flies.
>
> Conditions were terrible. Not only Marx, but other warm-hearted men, such as Charles Dickens, Ruskin, and Carlyle, poured out a literature of protest which was read around the world.
>
> On his facts, Marx can scarcely be challenged. But his diagnosis was wrong and, therefore, the remedy he prescribed was wrong also.[9]

2. *Orient the audience by stating and explaining the proposition.* Before a hostile audience the one thing you don't do is to state your proposition openly at the beginning, lest the listener's minds snap shut like a steel trap. Instead you start on common ground, take up the facts of the situation before you offer opinions, approach the proposition inductively, and state the proposition after the evidence is in. Before a hostile audience you orient the audience in the Introduction

[9] *Vital Speeches,* XV (May 1, 1949), 442-443.

by supplying the background facts, but you don't state the proposition openly.

Nonhostile audiences, however, can be oriented by making the proposition clear early in the speech, usually as soon as attention is gained. Indeed Eric Johnston—well known, wholly trusted, and deeply admired by his audience of American Trade Association Executives—once began a speech by stating the proposition at once in almost unpleasant terms:

> With all the unpleasantness at my command, I'd like to suggest that we—the private employers of America—are sweeping a serious problem under the bed.
>
> I am talking about the plight of the unemployed middle-aged worker—the man of 45 on up who's hunting for a job. He's finding the going mighty tough these days.
>
> Maybe he's been a wage-earner on a time-clock schedule. Maybe he's been a salesman who never thought of work in terms of hours. Perhaps he's always worked in overalls. Perhaps he's been a junior executive. But blue shirt or white collar—it doesn't make a bit of difference.

Carter Davidson used a more orthodox method in a commencement address at the University of Buffalo, by first getting attention through use of an illustration, then coming to an open statement of his proposition:

> When our friend, Alice, took her famous trip into Wonderland, she was more than commonly confused by the similarities joined with differences in the Tweedledums and Tweedledees of that looking-glass country. Lewis Carroll was no fool, but a learned professor of mathematics, attempting to show his readers what a vast amount of discrimination is needed to distinguish sense from nonsense. In this connection as an educator I always enjoy reading Alice's discussion with the Mock Turtle on the curriculum. He remarked that he had taken "the usual course," consisting of "Reeling, and Writhing, and Rhythmetic, in all four branches, Ambition, Distraction, Uglification, and Derision." These sounded so much like the real thing to Alice, that she was confused—and well she might be, for this was her first experience with the puzzling science of semantics, or the origins and meanings of words. . . .
>
> Americans seem particularly susceptible to these confusions of words and meanings, perhaps because they are distinctly an impatient people, endowed with what the medieval scientists would have called the "good humor" of red-blooded sanguinity, instead of the "bad humors" of melancholy, phlegm, and anger. Perhaps, therefore, Americans need to be warned about these words and ideas which look alike but have such different effects.
>
> For example, Americans often confuse Size with Importance.[10]

[10] *Vital Speeches*, XIII (August 1, 1947), 614.

3. *Orient the audience by explaining how you propose to develop the subject.* Sometimes this is done simply to make instantly clear where the speaker is going. J. T. Fields thus began his popular lecture by stating the subject in the opening words and explaining at once how he proposed to develop it:

> Ladies and Gentlemen: I am to speak to you this evening, without pre-pretense, but in all earnestness, if I may do so, a few thoughts on a subject which I shall call "The Masters of the Situation," and as example is always better than precept, and as it is much better to go and do a thing than to say how it ought to be done, I shall hope to interest you with now and then a short story illustrative of my theme, rather than by a long sermon, had I the ability to preach one.

This method is especially useful in treating a *complex* subject, for listeners are able to follow complex ideas more easily when the plan of arrangement is deliberately explained at the beginning. Thus a lecture on "Economic Theory," might begin by explaining that "There are three prominent schools of economic theory today, the Ricardian, the Marxian, and the Keynesian. I shall discuss first the disciples of Ricardo who believe that the government must keep out of practically everything, discuss next the disciples of Marx who hold that the government ought to get into practically everything, and discuss third the disciples of John Maynard Keynes who stand midway between the first two theories. Look first, if you will, at the disciples of Ricardo. . . .

Finally, this method of orienting the audience is used when the listeners have *doubts or mental reservations* toward the subject. Henry M. Wriston, President of Brown University, wanted to speak slightly unpalatable words to the New York Chamber of Commerce on why there were radical teachers in America. He began by an illustration and quotations, but came at the end to a clear statement of how he proposed to develop the topic:

> Every once in a while an event occurs which does not seem in itself to be of great magnitude, but which is a portent of something vastly significant. In 1820, when the admission of Missouri as a state raised the slavery issue, Thomas Jefferson wrote: "Like a fire bell in the night, it awakened and filled me with terror." Of the same event, a representative from Georgia said, "You have kindled a fire that all the waters of the ocean cannot put out, which seas of blood can only extinguish." Ten years afterward all the pollsters would have said that Jefferson's alarm and Cobb's prophecy looked ridiculous, but eventually both were amply vindicated. Great crises seldom

mature rapidly; those who read aright the signs of the times may well take thought when they perceive "a cloud small as a man's hand."

Teachers' strikes should be regarded as "a fire bell in the night." From a quantitative point of view they have not been important. Relative to the huge number of students in our schools and the huge American educational program, the teaching days lost, if your memories of school days have not faded, have been insignificant and the knowledge lost unnoticeable.

The teachers' economic situation urgently called for redress; public authorities were laggard in recognizing the issue, dilatory and halfhearted in attempts to meet it. A crisis in salaries was the occasion for the strikes, but it by no means supplies a complete explanation.... There is no possibility of accounting for the strikes without taking into consideration the drift of many intellectuals away from a profound conviction as to the rightness and the validity of the existing social, economic, and political situation, or at least the situation as existed day before yesterday....

My purpose today is neither to praise nor to condemn; I am essaying an analysis, seeking to make clear what caused the emotional tensions now all too obvious. At the end I hope to present some intimations as to how so dangerous a trend may be reversed.[11]

Producing a final effect with the conclusion

A conclusion has a single purpose, to leave a *lasting effect, to give a final impetus to the proposition.* A writer, whose name escapes recall, produced an essay a few years back on how to say goodbye. Some people, he said, make it a form of torture. When it is time to leave they remark, "Well, we must be going," then settle back for another fifteen minutes of conversation, after which they remark, "We really must be going," and sit bolt upright and talk an additional five minutes. Then they stand—thereby compelling their hosts to stand also—and talk another five minutes, after which they move toward the door slowly, still talking. At the door, hand on knob, they delay for two or three minutes of final talk, then open the door and start out. But not yet! Door open, they enter another round of sprightly conversation—while the winter cold or summer flies, according to the season, filter into the house. At last they leave—only to stop outside and, through the still-open door, tell you for the sixth time what a *wonderful* time they have had. When they have finally torn their reluctant spirits away, the exhausted hosts mutter, "I hope they never come again."

The speaker, without using the same techniques, faces the same hazard of closing a speech by degrees and with reluctance. "Learn

[11] *American Association of University Professors Bulletin,* XXXV (Autumn, 1949), 434-436.

the delightful art," said H. A. Overstreet, "of closing with a snap." This does not mean that a full-length speech is broken off with a sentence—although Robert G. Ingersoll did close his encomium on Voltaire with the terse summary, "This was the work of Voltaire." Rather it means that a good conclusion moves swiftly, without detours, and without passing a stop sign.

The following are typical types of conclusions:

1. *A Challenge.* This is the most frequently used method. The speaker in some ingenious way presents a short compelling challenge to *do* something, to take a definite attitude, position, or action. Henry W. Grady motivated his still-famous "The New South," delivered to a New England audience, with a challenge:

> Now, what answer has New England to this message? Will she permit the prejudice of war to remain in the hearts of the conquerors, when it has died in the hearts of the conquered? ["*No! No!*"] Will she transmit this prejudice to the next generation, that in their hearts, which never felt the generous ardor of conflict, it may perpetuate itself? ["*No! No!*"] Will she withhold, save in strained courtesy, the hand which straight from his soldier's heart Grant offered to Lee at Appomattox? Will she make the vision of a restored and happy people, which gathered above the couch of your dying captain, filling his heart with grace, touching his lips with praise, and glorifying his path to the grave; will she make this vision on which the last sigh of his expiring soul breathed a benediction, a cheat and a delusion? [*Tumultuous cheering and shouts of "No! No!"*]
>
> If she does, the South, never abject in asking for comradeship, must accept with dignity its refusal; but if she does not; if she accepts in frankness and sincerity this message of good will and friendship, then will the prophecy of Webster, delivered in this very Society forty years ago amid tremendous applause, be verified in its fullest and final sense, when he said: "Standing hand to hand and clasping hands, we should remain united as we have been for sixty years, citizens of the same country, members of the same government, united, all united now and united forever. There have been difficulties, contentions, and controversies, but I tell you that in my judgment
>
> "Those opposed eyes,
> Which like the meteors of a troubled heaven,
> All of one nature, of one substance bred,
> Did lately meet in th' intestine shock,
> Shall now, in mutual well-beseeming ranks,
> March all one way."

2. *A Quotation.* As exemplified above, the speaker reinforces the theme with apt words of someone else. Charles L. Anspach thus closed an address to college students:

Tonight we toast the future. May you be successful in claiming its promises and in establishing a firm pathway for those who follow. Tomorrow in the words of James Russell Lowell you say:

> "My golden spurs now bring to me,
> And bring to me my richest mail,
> For tomorrow I go over land and sea,
> In search of the Holy Grail."

3. *A Summary*. If the speech is complex, or if the speaker's purpose is to present information, then you had best draw together the important points in condensed and unified form. "If you can sum up your arguments," said J. H. Gardiner, so that listeners "will go off and unconsciously retail your points to their neighbors, you probably have them." Likewise, if you can sum up your information so that listeners can carry it away in condensed and unified form, they likely will remember it. Note the skillful summary by Charles W. Eliot of his address on "Five American Contributions to Civilization":

These five contributions to civilization—*peace-keeping, religious toleration, the development of manhood suffrage, the welcoming of newcomers, and the diffusion of well-being*—I hold to have been eminently characteristic of our country, and so important that, in spite of the qualifications and deductions which every candid citizen would admit with regard to every one of them, they will ever be held in the grateful remembrance of mankind. They are reasonable grounds for a steady, glowing patriotism. They have had much to do, both as causes and as effects, with the material prosperity of the United States; but they are all five essentially moral contributions, being triumphs of reason, enterprise, courage, faith, and justice, over passion, selfishness, inertness, timidity, and distrust. Beneath each one of these developments there lies a strong ethical sentiment, a strenuous moral and social purpose. It is for such work that multitudinous democracies are fit.

4. *An Appeal*. This is a classic form of conclusion, heavily used by the ancients. It is effective when well done, but trite or mawkish when it lacks substance. Henry Watterson, a Southerner speaking to New Englanders, found substance in specific instances of history:

So I appeal from the men in silken hose who danced to music made by slaves and called it freedom, from the men in bell-crowned hats who led Hester Prinne to her shame and called it religion, to that Americanism which reaches forth its arms to smite wrong with reason and truth, secure in the power of both. I appeal from the patriarchs [of old] to the poets [of new] New England; from Endicott to Lowell; from Winthrop to Longfellow; from Norton to Holmes; and I appeal in the name and by the rights of that common citizenship—of that common origin back both of the Puritan and the Cavalier, to which all of us owe our being. Let the dead past, consecrated by the blood of its martyrs, not by its savage hatreds, darkened alike by kingcraft and priestcraft—let the dead past bury its dead. Let the present and the future ring with the song of the singers.

5. *An Illustration.* An illustration is one of the easiest for beginners in that it is simple in structure and requires no skill beyond that of story-telling. But you need a story that carries the core of the proposition or of the action you want listeners to take. Merryle Stanley Rukeyser, speaking on economic problems, used a homespun illustration:

> It's like the story of the unemployed worker who stopped by a farm during the last depression and asked for some food, and the farmer said, "Yes, I'll give you some food. But you will have to work for it." This farmer was very old fashioned. After the man had been fed the farmer said, "Can you paint the fence?" The man said, "No, that's out of my line." The farmer said, "Well, can you hoe the field?" "Oh, no," the man said, "I don't know anything about farming." . . . So the farmer said, "Just what can you do?" The man said, "I'm an unemployed advertising writer." So the farmer said, "That's excellent. I want to sell this farm. Will you write a piece of copy for the Sunday newspapers?" The man sat down at the desk and he came forth with a beautiful advertisement, describing the pastoral scene at this magnificent farm, with its flowing brook and the old home in a colonial setting. The farmer looked the copy over and said, "I would be a fool to sell this farm."
>
> I will conclude on that note.[12]

6. *Visualizing the Future.* The speaker ends on the high note of looking forward into the future. He may, if his prestige is high, say "I shall in the future do this thing, and I ask men of courage and wisdom to join with me." Or he may merely express personal faith and hope. Thus Winston Churchill closed his first address before the American Congress by visualizing a personal faith in the future:

> It is not given us to peer into the mysteries of the future; still I avow my hope and faith, sure and inviolate, that in days to come the British and American peoples will for their own safety and for the good of all, walk together side by side in majesty, in justice, and in peace.

7. *Rounding Out the Thought.* With simpler speeches, sometimes even with more complex ones, a speaker may merely round it out with a few swift strokes.

Said Lincoln at the close of his first debate with Douglas:

[12] *Vital Speeches,* XV (March 15, 1949), 349.

My friends that ends the chapter. The Judge [Douglas] can take his half-hour.

Whatever kind of conclusion you use, remember that its purpose is to give a final motivated impetus. Make it short. Make it motivated.

LENGTHS OF INTRODUCTIONS AND CONCLUSIONS

How long is an Introduction? How long is a Conclusion? It may serve a useful purpose, and certainly will satisfy the curiosity of some, to supply the answer. Across the board, Introductions average about 10 per cent of the total speech, and Conclusions average about 5 per cent. These, mind you, are *averages* of wide extremes. Introductions of reasonably good speeches have been known to range from 1 per cent to 38 per cent, and Conclusions from less than 1 per cent to 15 per cent. Nor do these figures tell you what proportions a speech *ought* to have. They are merely a measurement of what other speakers in other days have done. Faced by the same conditions, you may possibly use approximately the same proportions.

ASSIGNMENTS

ON ANALYZING THE CAUSES FOR GOOD AND POOR INTRODUCTIONS AND CONCLUSIONS

1. Examine the introductions and conclusions of five printed speeches, preferably using speeches you have previously read in this course:

   a. Rank them as good, poor, or sad averages.
   b. Classify the method used in the introduction to get attention and good will (personal greeting, honest compliment, pleasantry, etc.).
   c. Classify the method used in the introduction to orient the audience (explaining the subject background, explaining the proposition, etc.).
   d. Weigh these introductions critically and decide what methods *you* would use if it were your speech.
   e. Classify the method used in the conclusion to give the final impetus (challenge, quotation, etc.).
   f. Consider these conclusions critically and decide what methods you would use if it were your speech.

2. Analyze the introductions in one round of class speeches: (1) List the two best and two poorest, and give your reasons. (2) Explain how you would improve the two poorest.

3. Do the same for conclusions in one round of class speeches.

ON LEARNING TO BEGIN AND END SPEECHES EFFECTIVELY

4. Analyze the introductions and conclusions of two or three of your own class speeches given previously. Use the principles of this chapter to recast and improve them.

5. Using one of your speeches previously given in class, draft three introductions suitable for three different audiences (women's club, high-school students, business men, etc.). Consider also whether you would use the same or different conclusions.

6. Assume that you are speaking on a controversial subject: civil liberties, conscientious objectors, a presidential candidate, labor unions, religious sects, progressive education, racial minorities, socialized medicine, etc. Draft two introductions to get attention and good will, one for an audience that favors your viewpoint and one for an audience that is hostile toward it.

7. Draft two conclusions for the above speech: (1) One intended to persuade listeners to respect your viewpoint even though they disagree, (2) One intended to arouse partisans to high enthusiasm and determination.

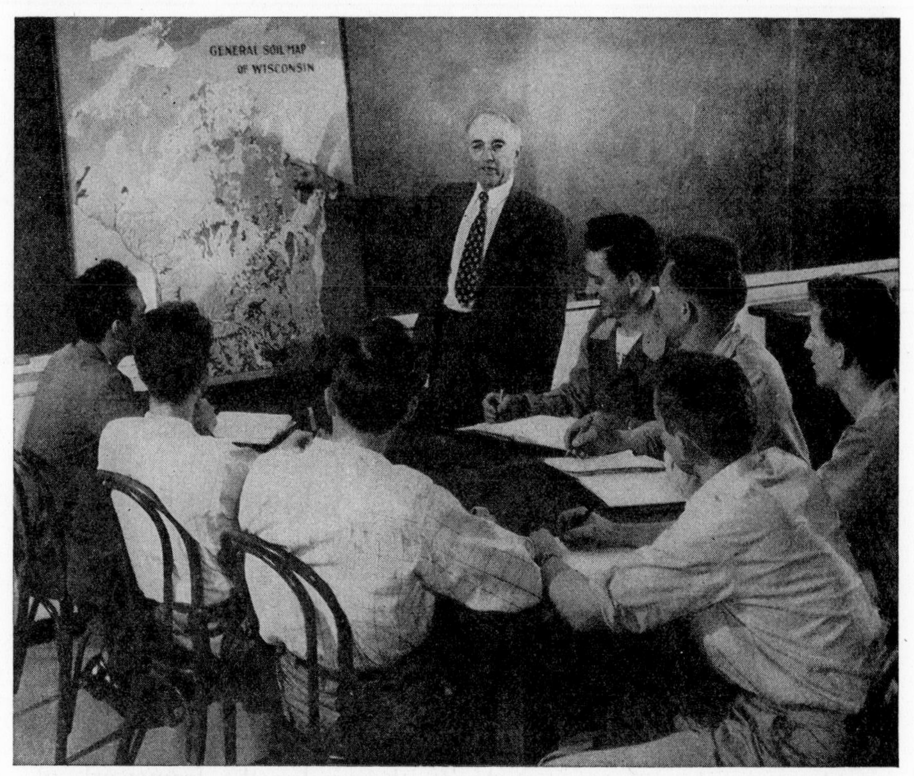

Listeners are mere human beings with a limited span of attention. Many cannot, and most others will not, listen long to abstract ideas. Ten Forms of Support are discussed in this chapter, of which one—Visual Aid Material—is demonstrated in this picture.

CHAPTER 13

Supporting the Ideas

CHAPTER 13

"The chief end of man," once wrote Justice Oliver Wendell Holmes, "is to frame general ideas—and . . . no general idea is worth a straw." So with speeches. The tendency of mine-run speakers, following this human frailty, is to fill speeches with general ideas. But general ideas at best are only abstractions, only assertions about assertions, only words about words. Listeners, on the other hand, are mere human beings with a limited span of attention. Many cannot—and most others will not—listen long to abstract ideas. What was said by Henry J. Taylor of Dwight D. Eisenhower applies to most intelligent listeners and all of the less intelligent. If the informant is vague, said Taylor, and the words beat about the bush, they "do not seem to touch Eisenhower's brain at all. . . . He simply loses interest in the obscure. Facts are his tools, and he can't work without them. But let the facts begin to flow and a sign lights up in his eyes: 'Brain at work.' "

Most listeners' minds are that way. Better minds want the tangible evidence so they can sort and sift, then judge the framework of thought. Average minds want word pictures, simply because they cannot follow abstractions. Therefore, to make an idea count, support it with concrete materials, picture it so listeners can see it as well as hear it, or create a situation of which listeners feel themselves to be a part.

The purpose of Supporting Materials, then, is to reinforce the original statement and make it live in the mind's eye of the listener. By a succession of details it directs the listener's mind again and again to the original point. It reinforces the point, heaps it up, until the listener can understand and is motivated to action. Technically, Supporting Materials can be defined as materials that (1) clarify, (2) intensify, (3) amplify, or (4) prove the original statement. Twice previously they have been discussed briefly (pages 38 and 221). Here the Forms of Support previously mentioned are amplified and additional ones are included, as follows:

1. Definition and Explanation
2. Factual Information
   a. facts
   b. figures
   c. statistics
3. Illustrations
4. Specific Instances
   (Undeveloped Illustrations)
5. Comparison and Contrast
6. Testimony
7. Repetition and Restatement
8. Description
9. Narration
10. Visual Aid Material

Often, of course, several of these Forms of Support are combined into one treatment—as in an Illustration that contains Figures, Comparisons, and Repetition—but we shall here consider them separately for purposes of explanation.

Supporting ideas by definition and explanation

Napoleon gave three instructions to the secretaries who relayed his messages: "(1) Be clear. (2) Be clear! (3) *Be Clear!*" A speaker is under the same compulsion. One of the first essentials of clarity is to *define the essential terms of your speech.* Especially are there two types of terms that will need defining:

1. The first is technical words, complex words, or strange words. They are words that listeners don't know. In this age of specialization, thousands of such words are in common use by specialized groups but are not known by the general public. Typical of a few appearing in recent student speeches are: *sublimation* (psychology), *depth of field* (photography), *tolerance* (engineering) *counterpoint* (music) *surrealism* (art and literature). When you use such words, define them, amplify your definition, illustrate what you mean.

2. Next, there are familiar words that we use frequently and loosely, but which have many meanings to different people. What, for example, do you mean by *democracy, the American way of life, the welfare state, Americanism, communism,* or *socialism?* What do you mean by such two-edged words as *fairness, justice, right, wrong,* or even *education* (is it the same as "schooling"?). To many people, these words have no real meaning. They have only emotional associations. Spoken glibly and undefined, they become trigger-happy releases for emotions, but without form and void of thought. Nevertheless, speakers often must use them, and ought to use them. Hence definition becomes essential if one is to speak with clarity and precision.

The fact that listeners know the dictionary meaning of these words does not mean that they know the real meaning as you use it, for a dictionary at best furnishes only a general scheme into which many meanings may be inserted. Real meanings, like all things human, depend on the circumstances of use; and your task is to make unmistakably clear the meaning of your essential terms. Note how Macaulay cleared up a confusion between two members of the British Parliament who were using the word "redress" in a discussion of the Repeal of the Union with Ireland:

> Redress is no doubt a very well sounding word. What can be more reasonable than to ask for redress? What more unjust than to refuse redress? But my honorable friend will perceive, on reflection, that, though he and the honorable and learned member for Dublin agree in pronouncing the word redress, they agree in nothing else. They utter the same sound; but they attach to it two diametrically opposed meanings. The honorable and learned member for Dublin means by redress simply the Repeal of the Union [with Ireland]. Now, to the Repeal of the Union my honorable friend, the member for Lincoln, is decidedly adverse. When we get at his real meaning, we find that he is just as unwilling as we are to give the redress which the honorable and learned member for Dublin demands.

Suppose, for example, you were discussing "democracy." How would you define it? Is it the same as a "republic"? Can a "monarchy" like Great Britain also be a "democracy"? Is communism really a "democracy," as the Communists claim? Note how Henry M. Wriston carefully defined the word in a speech on "Who Besides the Russians?" If you read his definition carefully you will find that he uses the following four methods of definition:

1. Definition by authority (Shaw, Lincoln, Carlyle, Declaration of Independence).
2. Definition by classification ("More than . . . an economic order").
3. Definition by negation ("Not a form of government").
4. Definition by comparison or illustration ("What Lincoln said of liberty").

Wriston's definition is as follows:

> Who besides the Russians imperils the American system? The answer can be categorical: All who directly or indirectly tarnish the ideal or retard the attainment of democracy. Maybe that seems categorical without being clear, for many have doubts that there is such a thing as democracy; at least they would agree with the cynical comment of George Bernard Shaw, "Democracy may be defined as a word that all public persons use and none of them understands."
>
> Admittedly it is difficult to define. We could say of democracy what Lincoln said of liberty: "The world has never had a good definition . . .

and the American people, just now, are much in want of one." The word has been utterly prostituted by the communists at one extreme—and many ultra-conservatives, at the other end of the spectrum, tend to feel that despair expressed by Thomas Carlyle who said, "Democracy is, by the nature of it, a self-cancelling business; and gives in the long run a net result of zero."

The difficulty arises from the fact that democracy is more than a political idea, an economic order, or a social system—it is vastly more fundamental than any of those things. Democracy is not a form of government. It exists within many forms—wherever, in fact, the consensus of mature public opinion governs public action. . . . Democracy must not be confused with ballots or any other procedural device. Instead, it is a spirit which animates political, social, and economic institutions. And the essence of that spirit is a profound respect for human dignity. . . .

Respect for individual human dignity is the inner meaning of the most striking phrase of the Declaration of Independence: "We hold these truths to be self-evident,—that all men are created equal." [1]

An idea may also be amplified by explanation, as was done by Brendan F. Brown, a lawyer, in explaining the legal foundation of the War Crimes Trials at Nurnberg and Tokyo:

Just because there was no trial by jury at Nurnberg and Tokyo does not mean that these trials were unjust. The fact that the so-called hearsay rule of evidence was not followed at these trials is no reason why they were unjust. It is obviously provincial for any lawyer in this country to assume that we shall impose upon the nations of the world our precise and particular conception of trial practice. If we do not accept the conception which the great fathers of the science of international law took, namely, that international law in substance and in procedure is a composite of law which is found in national sytems, it will be impossible for us ever to establish an international court of effective jurisdiction.[2]

But use explanation with care, lest the listeners' minds wander astray. Make it short. Make it concrete. Generally use it at the beginning of an idea, and follow up with other more concrete forms of support.

Supporting ideas with factual information

"Facts," said Owen D. Young, "are our scarcest raw material." This is conspicuously true in student speeches. Young people can less often speak with authority. They, therefore, need to have behind them the power of facts.

[1] *Vital Speeches*, XVI (June 1, 1950), 503.
[2] *Vital Speeches*, XVI (May 1, 1950), 439.

Getting and assembling the facts is not easy. In the first place, you can never get "all the facts," for "all the facts" about the simplest event—like a streetcar accident—would fill hundreds of pages: the eyewitnesses' reports, the metallurgical engineer's report, the electrical engineer's report, the optician's report, the psychiatrist's report. The simplest sort of event or idea requires a selection of pertinent facts.

In the next place, the selection of facts is not, and cannot be, "objective," or "scientific." It is done by human beings who come to the job with their own education and personal experience, and their own set of values. They must make statements about the facts, and these statements inevitably involve ideas. Therefore, there is no such thing as "impartial" facts. What every speaker should seek instead is *fairness*. You ask, What's the difference? A responsible speaker is "partial" to that interpretation of facts that seems to fit things as they really are. He is *fair* in "not twisting the facts to support his view, in not suppressing the facts that support a different view."

Once you have selected the facts, the next step is how to use them effectively; for facts, as Mark Twain noted, can be presented in such a way as to create "confusion of the mind and congestion of the ducts of thought." Generally, facts are effectively presented by arranging them in a thought pattern such as was discussed in Chapter 11 (see pages 213-217). Ernie Pyle, for example, explained the position of an artillery battery in Italy by arranging the details in Space Order:

> Our four guns are set in and around a grape arbor. On one side a ridge rises steeply 400 to 500 feet. A broad valley spreads out below us. It is very pretty where we are.
>
> The four guns form a rough square about the size of a city block, and they are so close under the brow of a hill that it's almost impossible for the German artillery to reach us. Each gun is planted in a pit about three feet deep, and the front of the pit is lined, shoulder high, with sandbags.
>
> Over the entire pit is stretched a camouflage net on poles. The net, just head high, gives you the sense of having a roof over you. . . .
>
> A few feet on one side of the gun pit is a stack of black cases about three feet long, clipped together in triple clusters. These are the powder charges. On the other side of the pit lies a double row of rust-colored shells.[3]

Figures are an effective form of explanation if used wisely and sparingly. You don't want to load a speech with too many figures. The audience won't remember, and, in fact, often won't even really

[3] Dispatch of December 17, 1943.

listen to them. On the other hand, used wisely and sparingly, they can make clear many an otherwise vague idea. You can say that, "Automobile accidents are increasing," but how can you demonstrate this without presenting figures? You can say that, "Unemployment is growing worse (or better)," but how can you know—or the audience understand—without figures of comparison with previous years? In delivering a college commencement address, Senator Albert W. Hawkes wanted to show that "young men had made great achievements." For him it was not enough merely to assert. He presented figures as follows:

> Alexander Hamilton was a lieutenant colonel at 20, a framer of the Constitution of the United States at 30, and Secretary of the Treasury at 32; Alexander Graham Bell invented the telephone at 28; George Eastman produced dry plates for photography at 26; George Westinghouse . . . invented the air brake at 22; Henry Ford produced his first motorcar at 29; Thomas Edison . . . invented the incandescent lamp at 32; the Wright brothers were 32 and 36, respectively, at the time of their first air flight; Woolworth established his first store when 24; John D. Rockefeller organized the Standard Oil Co. when 31; John Wanamaker opened his first department store at 31; Lord Byron published his first book of poems at 19; Charles Dickens published his first book of Pickwick Papers at 24; John T. Delane was editor of the *London Times* at 23; Edward W. Bok was editor of the *Ladies Home Journal* at 26; Luther Burbank produced the Burbank potato at 22; Dr. Hyde became president of Bowdoin College at 27; Mark Hopkins became president of Williams College at 34; Dr. Eliot became president of Harvard at 35; Dr. Robert Hutchins became president of Chicago University at 30. . . .
>
> This is the "march of youth" instead of the "march of time" and it indicates what is expected of you in the crisis ahead.[4]

Statistics are not the same as ordinary figures. They are groups of facts scientifically collected and classified on the basis of relative number of occurrences as the ground for induction. In short, statistics are a systematic compilation of instances for the inference of general truths. Statistics are used in reporting the mass data of economic and social trends, business conditions, and public-opinion polls. But unless statisticians present the figures with honesty, and speakers who use them know what they mean, the result can only be semantic nonsense. Therefore handle statistics with care.

First, beware of "pseudo statistics":

> Tests show that four out of five have it.

[4] *Vital Speeches,* XII (August 1, 1946), 632-633.

Who did the testing? What was the nature of the tests? How representative was the sampling tested?

Second, beware of the sample with the "built-in bias":

> The average Yaleman, Class of '24, makes $25,111 a year.

But you can prove anything by letting the sample bias itself. Was *all* the class included? Was a representative sampling used? Did the men with low incomes chuck the questionnaire in the wastebasket because they were ashamed of their income? Was this the average only of those high-income men who were willing to stand up and be counted?

Third, beware of the "well-chosen average":

> The average income of people in this neighborhood is $15,000 a year.

What do you mean by "average"? If by "average" is meant the *mean*, the arithmetic average of all the incomes of all the families, then a single family with an income of $150,000 in a neighborhood where all the other families averaged $4,000 could produce a statistical *mean* of $15,000 per family. But suppose instead you took the *median* income of this same neighborhood. It would be nowhere near $15,000, but somewhere around $4,100—for the *median* would mean that half the families has less than $4,100 and half had more. Therefore, know whether your so-called average is a *mean* or a *median.*

Fourth, beware of "unknown deviations":

> San Nicolas Island on the south coast of California has a mean temperature of 61, which is the same as some parts of the California inland desert.

True, but on the island the temperature ranges between a comfortable 47 and 87 degrees, whereas in the desert the thermometer jumps from 15 to 125. Having the same mean does not mean having the same climate.

Finally, beware of the "elusive error":

> The Gallup Poll indicates that 53% of the American people favor this law.

Does it? The Gallup Poll usually operates on a sampling that allows a 4 per cent probable error. This means that there is a *reasonable* chance that the number of Americans who favor this law lie between 49 per cent and 57 per cent. There is also a *slight* statistical chance that those favoring it are less than 49 per cent or more than 57 per cent. Don't ignore the mathematically computed probable error.

In general, handle statistics with care. Tell the audience where you got them. Don't try to cover up loose talk and transparent misuse by such phrases as:

"Records prove that . . . ."	[*Whose records?*]
"Figures establish . . . ."	[*What figures?*]
"Statistics show . . . ."	[*Many listeners will remember, at your expense the adage that there are lies, damned lies, and statistics.*]

Supporting ideas with illustrations

"They say I tell a great many stories," explained the master speaker, Abraham Lincoln. "I reckon I do, but I have found in the course of a long experience that common people—common people—take them as they run, are more easily influenced and informed by illustrations than in any other way, and as to what the hypercritical few may think, I don't care." [5] In truth, as a speaker Lincoln had two outstanding qualities, both of which every speaker could use with profit: First, he had the ability to analyze a subject so as to present it to others with complete accuracy. Second, *he learned to argue by analogy and to explain by stories.*

"Tell us a story," has been the demand of the ages, and in the long run the public speaker must comply with this demand or become "just another speaker" to whom the audience only half listens. "I have seen an audience," said Henry Ward Beecher, "time and again, follow an argument, doubtfully, laboriously, almost suspiciously, and look at one another, as much as to say, 'Is he going right?'—until the place is arrived at, where the speaker says, 'It is like—' and then they listen eagerly for what it is like; and when some apt illustration is thrown before them, there is a sense of relief, as though they said, 'Yes, he is right.' " Beecher also said—and this you must remember if you ever become a good speaker—that, "Illustrations, while they make it easier for all, are absolutely the only means by which a large part of your audience will be able to understand at all the abstruse processes of reasoning.[6]

[5] D. K. Dodge, "Abraham Lincoln: The Evolution of his Literary Style," *University of Illinois Studies,* I, No. 1 (May, 1900), 35.

[6] Henry Ward Beecher (Yale), *Lectures on Preaching* (New York: J. B. Ford and Co., 1872), pp. 157-158.

There are two kinds of illustrations. The first is *factual*. It tells of an event that actually happened. Thus when Joseph R. Farrington of Hawaii wanted to protest against the denial of American citizenship to the Polynesians of American Samoa, he used an illustration:

> The greatest center of Polynesian scientific research in the world today is the Bishop Museum in Honolulu. Its brilliant director is Dr. Peter H. Buck, son of an Irish father and a Maori mother, a member of the Polynesian race. Dr. Buck fought with distinction with the forces of New Zealand in the World War. His scholarship has won widespread recognition from universities such as Yale where he has taught. He is a man of extraordinary achievements and rare personal charm. He is a man of whom any country could be proud. But he is denied the privileges of naturalization because his mother is of the Polynesian race.[7]

The second kind of illustration is *hypothetical*. It is an illustration of what "might have been," or "could be." When Benjamin Franklin wanted to overthrow the popular notion of his day that to vote men must own property, he put the argument in the form of a hypothetical illustration that everybody could understand, even those who could not follow abstruse reasoning:

> To require property of voters leads us up to this dilemma: I own a jackass, I can vote. The jackass dies, I cannot vote. Therefore the vote represents not me but the jackass.

A Great Speaker twenty centuries ago wanted to make clear who one's neighbor was. He did not argue. He did not explain. He did not deal in exposition. He told a story, a hypothetical illustration:

> A certain man went down from Jerusalem to Jericho, and fell among thieves, which stripped him of his raiment, and wounded him, and departed leaving him half dead.
>
> And by chance there came down a certain priest that way: and when he saw him, he passed by on the other side. And likewise a Levite, when he was at the place, came and looked on him, and passed by on the other side.
>
> But a certain Samaritan, as he journeyed, came where he was: and when he saw him, he had compassion on him, And went to him, and bound up his wounds, pouring in oil and wine, and set him on his own beast, and brought him to an inn, and took care of him. And on the morrow when he departed, he took out two pence, and gave them to the host, and said unto him, Take care of him: and whatsoever thou spendest more, when I come again, I will repay thee.

[7] *Vital Speeches*, XI (August 1, 1945), 638.

For two thousand years that story has been told over and over again. On the face it is a story pure and simple. Beneath the surface it is an argument. Between the lines it is a sermon.

Supporting ideas with specific instances

A Specific Instance is a condensed illustration. It is specific, not abstract. It names the person, place, date, or event—but does not develop it by details. For that reason merely one or two Specific Instances, without any other form of support, is usually not enough to develop an idea. More likely a battery of five or ten will be used. Dorothy Thompson used seven:

> As for crime and disorder in all categories—here are the headlines from one New York newspaper, last Friday afternoon, when I was preparing this address:
>
> 4000 students stage guerrilla battle with cops.
> Stolen $250,000 vice ring bared.
> Bellevue nurses set for mass walkout.
> Knifer Slays Head of Bronx Firm.
> Factory Arsenic Perils City's Lungs.
> Rag Picker's Body Shipped in Paper Bale to Junk Yard.
> Commie-led Attempt to Blacken City Relief Spiked.[8]

Or a speaker may lead with other forms of support, such as Illustration or Comparison, then reinforce with a battery of Specific Instances. Or he may lead with a battery of Specific Instances and follow up by other kinds of support, as George W. Maxey in the illustration below who supported his idea with twelve Specific Instances overtopped by a quotation-climax from Milton:

> Industrial capitalism has been in existence less than 150 years, yet in that period civilization has made more progress than it made in all the preceding centuries. Under industrial capitalism the world has progressed from the manual shovel to the steam shovel; from the scythe to the mowing machine; from the ox to the tractor; from the rake to the reaper; from the knitting needle to the looms; from the foot courier to the telegraph, telephone and wireless; from crude drawings to moving pictures; from the horse to the automobile; from the stage coach to the express train; from sailing ships to floating palaces of sea and sky; from hand operated wooden printing presses to the printing presses which today can turn out a hundred thousand folded papers an hour; . . . from the tallow candle and the pine knot to that great

[8] *Vital Speeches*, XVI (July 1, 1950), 549.

invention of Edison's whose consequences can be appropriately described in the very language Milton used in describing creation itself. Milton wrote:

> Confusion heard His voice . . .
> At His bidding darkness fled,
> Light shone, and order from disorder sprung.[9]

Supporting ideas with comparison and contrast

Comparison measures similarities. It connects the known with the unknown, the more familiar with the less familiar. Sometimes comparisons are brief and pithy, like the traffic expert's description of safety:

> The driver is safer when the roads are dry; the roads are safer when the driver is dry.

At other times it is longer, more detailed, and literal. Observe William C. Bullitt's detailed and accurate comparison between present Communist aggression and earlier Moslem aggression:

> In our short history, we have never had to face any problem as complex as the problem of this Communist assault. The western world once did face a similar problem. The fighting faith of Mahomet overwhelmed the Christian States of the Near East and North Africa and Spain, and the Moslem forces were not stopped until they reached Tours on the Loire not very far from Paris. I do not wish to compare the Moslem religion which is a noble one, to the Communist creed which is satanic; but I do wish to point out that in the hundred years between Mahomet's death in 632 and the defeat of the Moslems by Charles Martel in 732, country after country fell before that fighting faith until it seemed that it was irresistible.
>
> The Communist attack is no more irresistible than was the Moslem attack. But to meet it successfully, we shall need the same faith and courage that the Christians had at Tours.[10]

At times a comparison makes an idea more clear, more vivid, or more interesting. At other times it establishes proof. At still others it serves as a yardstick by which to measure intangible qualities like goodness, justice, leadership, or their opposites. Wendell Phillips used it as a yardstick by which to measure the eloquence of Daniel O'Connell:

> I remember the solemnity of Webster, the grace of Everett, the rhetoric of Choate; I know the eloquence that lay hid in the iron logic of Calhoun;

[9] *Vital Speeches*, XVI (March 15, 1950), 332-333.
[10] *Vital Speeches*, XVI (July 1, 1950), 563.

I have melted beneath the magnetism of Seargent S. Prentiss of Mississippi, who wielded a power few men ever had .... But I think all of them together never surpassed, and no one of them ever equalled O'Connell.

Contrast is a measurement of opposites. We often see a thing more clearly when we see its opposite, heightened by contrast. Witness the intensified effect given by Wheeler McMillan's contrast of the buggy problem with the potato problem:

The photograph which I hold up for your view is a picture of a buggy. For those of you who do not know this object from experience I might explain that a buggy is a horse-drawn vehicle which was used for the transportation of human beings in those days of antiquity which preceded the motor age.

The market for buggies began to decline when low-priced automobiles became available to the general public. The manufacturers ... could make more buggies than the public demanded. In those medieval times there was no such thing as parity for buggies. . . .

Some of the buggy manufacturers went into the automobile business where they made a great deal of money and created a large number of new jobs. . . . Consequently, today a higher proportion of American families enjoy automobiles than ever owned buggies.

The object I now hold in my hand is a potato. The potato is agriculture's 1950 model buggy. The potato manufacturers are producing more of this model than the public demands. . . .[11]

Supporting ideas with testimony

Often listeners will not take your unsupported word, but will respect the judgment of others. If you assert that the cost-of-living index has gone up or down by 5 points, the statement will carry more weight if you refer to the United States Department of Commerce as your source of information. If you assert that modern education needs drastic revision, listeners will be far more impressed if you reinforce the assertion with testimony from Walter Lippmann, Robert M. Hutchins, or other accepted authority. Observe how Harold F. Harding skillfully builds the prestige of his authority, then presents the testimony as a climax:

Some dozen college and university administrators, under the direction of Dr. Francis J. Brown, have submitted a document [to Congress] entitled the "Effects of Certain War Activities upon Colleges and Universities" that will have far reaching effects in our educational planning for years to

[11] *Vital Speeches,* XVI (June 15, 1950), 540. Italics mine.

come. . . . I cannot summarize the document for you now. I merely wish to quote what the president of one institution wrote regarding the future: ". . . I believe most sincerely that we stand in danger of losing democracy in this country simply because we do not have enough minds that have been equipped to think broadly, deeply and clearly." [12]

Obviously you cannot use any sort of testimony that pleases your fancy. There are rigorous tests for acceptable testimony:

1. Is he an expert in the field? Does he have special training and experience in this field?

2. Is he speaking from first-hand knowledge?

3. Is he influenced by self interest? Does he represent an interest group that would profit from having people believe what he wants them to believe?

4. Is he known and acceptable to your listeners?

5. If he is not known to listeners, can he be made known by virtue of his position and achievements?

Testimony not only is used for proof; it is also used for vividness. Others have stated ideas so vividly that you can often reinforce argument, or make ideas clear, simply by quoting their lucid words. Indeed the best thoughts of the greatest minds of all ages have been preserved, and they are yours for the using. How better, for example, can you phrase the following thoughts than in the words of the persons quoted?

Wooden legs are not inherited, but wooden heads may be.

EDWIN GRANT CONKLIN

Whether there will be another war is known only to God and Drew Pearson.

FULTON J. SHEEN

Do you recall that striking story of one of the opening incidents of the Constitutional Convention related by Gouverneur Morris, an eye-witness of the scenes? "Of the delegates," he says, "some were for halfway measures, for fear of displeasing the people; others were anxious and doubting. Just before there were enough to form a quorum, Washington, standing self-collected in the midst of them, his countenance more than usually solemn, his eye seeming to look into futurity, said:—'It is too probable that no plan we propose will be adopted. Perhaps another dreadful conflict is to be

[12] A. Craig Baird, *Representative American Speeches: 1945-1946* (New York: H. W. Wilson Co., 1946), p. 230.

sustained. If, to please the people, we offer what we ourselves disapprove, how can we afterwards defend our course? Let us raise a standard to which the wise and honest can repair; the event is in the hands of God.' "

WOODROW WILSON

Supporting ideas with restatement and repetition

Study the following example of restatement:

> [1] Americans want peace. They will work for peace and they will sacrifice for peace. But they do not want peace at any price. [2] If the price of peace is injustice, they will reject peace. [3] If the price of peace is the loss or distortion of values they cherish, they will reject peace. [4] If the price of peace is spiritual denial, they will reject peace. [5] If the price of peace is living on an island surrounded by angry waters, they will reject peace. [6] If the price of peace is retreat from the rights of man, they will reject peace.
>
> NORMAN COUSINS, "Tell the Folks Back Home"

In the above specimen of restatement you will observe that the speaker presents no proof. He cites no Comparisons, Illustrations or Specific Instances. He simply says the same thing six times in different words.

This is known as restatement. Its value to the audience is plain. When an idea cannot be understood through one single statement, then restatement gives the audience time to think it over, and digest it slowly as they come to understand its full meaning. In short, a speaker uses restatement when it takes time for the original statement to soak in.

Now study the following example of *repetition:*

> We shall defend our island, whatever the cost may be. *We shall fight* on the beaches. *We shall fight* on the landing grounds. *We shall fight* in the fields and in the streets, and *we shall fight* in the hills. We shall never surrender.
>
> WINSTON CHURCHILL, After Dunkerque

Here the speaker repeated the same idea four times in the same words. This is known as repetition. Skillful repetition drives an idea home. It reinforces memory. Skillful repetition also has persuasive force. It helps establish belief. Advertisers habitually use it, so buyers will remember their goods. (LS/MFT). When better automobiles are built, Buick will build them, etc.) But as early as 44 B.C. Marc Antony was using repetition to fix the guilt of Brutus in the minds of Roman citizens. In Shakespeare's version, Antony, in a short speech, repeats *nine* times with irony that Caesar's murderers are "honorable men" —until slowly the citizens grasp the intended contrary meaning and rush forth shouting, "We'll burn . . . the traitors' houses."

Supporting ideas with description

Description tells how a thing looks, feels, tastes, smells, or how it acts. In words, it recreates places, things, and people for the listener's personal inspection. If you say, "In the Middle West summer winds blow constantly," that is explanatory fact. If you say, "Beginning with moist winds in May and continuing into dry winds in August, the summer winds are constant in the Middle West," you narrate events. But Ernie Pyle *described* those winds so you could feel them blow against your face:

> To me the summer wind in the Midwest is one of the most melancholy things in all life. It comes from so far and blows so gently and yet so relentlessly; it rustles the leaves and the branches of the maple trees in a sort of symphony of sadness, and it doesn't pass on and leave them still. It just keeps coming, like the infinite flow of Old Man River. You could—and you do—wear out your lifetime on the dusty plains with that wind of futility blowing in your face. And when you are worn out and gone, the wind—still saying nothing, still so gentle and sad and timeless—is still blowing across the prairies, and will blow in the faces of the little men who follow you, forever.[13]

The following are suggestions for effective description:

1. Determine the purpose of the description. Suppose you are to describe a storm, for example. Do you want to tell how it arose and what it did? That is factual. Do you want to demonstrate its power and malevolence? That is imaginative. Do you want to describe a physical thing? Or a mental state? Determine one purpose, and stay by it.

2. Make description brief. Few speakers have the power to hold attention long by description.

3. Strip away the cluttering adjectives that mar most amateur efforts. Let the nouns and especially the verbs do the heavy work.

4. Follow a systematic order. Describe from right to left, front to back, top to bottom.

[13] *Home Country* (New York: William Sloan Associates, Inc., 1947), p. 3.

Supporting ideas with narration

Effective speakers know the power of narration, and use it. Self-minded introverts do not use it; they are color-blind to human values. Students at first neglect it, for they have not yet discovered its power. Hence, we here pause for narrative identification.

Narrative takes many forms—among which are the illustration, story, historical incident, and anecdote. All have a common element. They do not argue or provoke controversy, but narrate what has happened to people. They are concrete, interesting, full of action. They can create suspense, or arouse laughter, or depict tragedy.

Good narrative seems so simple and natural, that anyone can do it. Unhappily, not so. It, too, has a technique, of which the essentials are these:

1. Tell the events in the order in which they occur.

2. Tell them in the form in which the listener might have seen them.

3. Organize the narration so it goes from somewhere to somewhere else—and sits down when it arrives.

All of these are illustrated in John Mason Brown's radio speech on "A Cartoonist in Words":

> When Mr. [H.L.] Mencken and Mr. [George Jean] Nathan enter Mr. Smith's apartment, they notice a stranger. He is a tall, skinny, paprika-headed fellow....
>
> The stranger approached them, much as the sea serpent approached the Laocoön group. He coiled one long arm around Mr. Mencken's neck, the other around Mr. Nathan's. Then he started talking. Nathan described it as "yelling at the top of his lungs."
>
> "So you guys are critics, are ya? Well, let me tell you something. I'm the best writer in this here blankety-blank country; and if you Georgie, and you, Hank, don't know it now, you'll know it blankety-blank soon. Say, I've finished a book that'll be published in a week or two and it's the best blankety-blank book of its kind that this blankety-blank country has had and don't you guys forget it."
>
> Three days later Mr. Nathan received a letter from Mr. Mencken, who'd returned to Baltimore.
>
> "Dear George," it said, "grab hold of the bar-rail, steady yourself and prepare for a terrible shock. I've just read the advance sheets of the book of that lump we met at Smith's and he's done the job!"
>
> The book was *Main Street;* the tall skinny stranger with the paprika hair was, of course, Sinclair Lewis.[14]

[14] *Talks*, XI (January, 1946), 40.

Supporting ideas with visual aid material

The first nine methods of supporting ideas were verbal, by use of words. There remains a tenth method—the use of visible materials such as charts, diagrams, maps, models, and pictures. A statistical curve or plan of battle are more easily demonstrated from a map or blackboard than from word-of-mouth description. An airplane design or the anatomy of a vertebrate are better understood from a drawing, a model, or a specimen. With films and slides you can bring distant scenes to the audience.

But the use of visual aid material is neither automatic nor foolproof. After listening to fumbling speakers for twenty-five years, J. R. Van Pelt summarized their abuse of visual aids "on a thousand platforms" as follows: "We have seen overcrowded slides projected by machines that could not be focused. We have watched while speakers in a large room tried to use maps or charts that could not be read beyond arm's length. We have listened in vain as able scholars talked confidentially to a blackboard while writing illegible symbols with invisible chalk. We have fidgeted, mentally if not physically, as the remarks of a renowned scientist came to a dead stop while he readjusted some ill-arranged piece of apparatus or hunted for a scientific specimen to illustrate his point. The habit of badly using bad visual aids is rampant among those who 'speak to inform.' It is an occupational disease of university professors. Severe epidemics break out at every scientific, engineering, and medical convention." [15] Let us, then, examine the techniques of using visual aids.

USING CHARTS, MAPS, AND DIAGRAMS

The rules are simple enough, but the mistakes are many and costly:

1. *Make the charts large enough to be seen.* If the design on a chart is not large enough to be seen, it will be only an annoyance. Do not guess at the proper size, or try to decide about it while standing near by. Draw an experimental chart or diagram beforehand, and go to the back of the room to see whether its outlines can be easily seen in detail. If in doubt, make it larger.

Next, make the lines of the chart or diagram heavy and broad. A light, thin line which is perfectly visible to the speaker up close

[15] "Lantern Slides and Such," *Quarterly Journal of Speech*, XXXVI (February, 1950), 45.

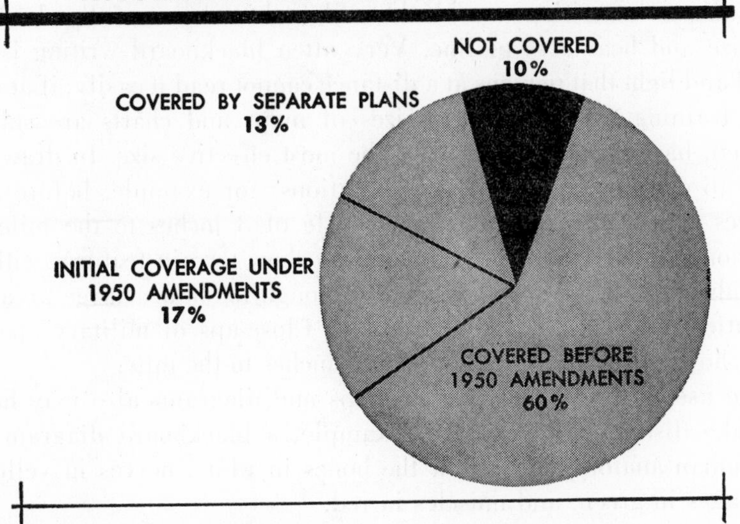
90% OF THOSE GAINFULLY EMPLOYED NOW COVERED BY SOME FORM OF GOVERNMENT INSURANCE OR RETIREMENT SYSTEM
NOT COVERED 10%
COVERED BY SEPARATE PLANS 13%
INITIAL COVERAGE UNDER 1950 AMENDMENTS 17%
COVERED BEFORE 1950 AMENDMENTS 60%

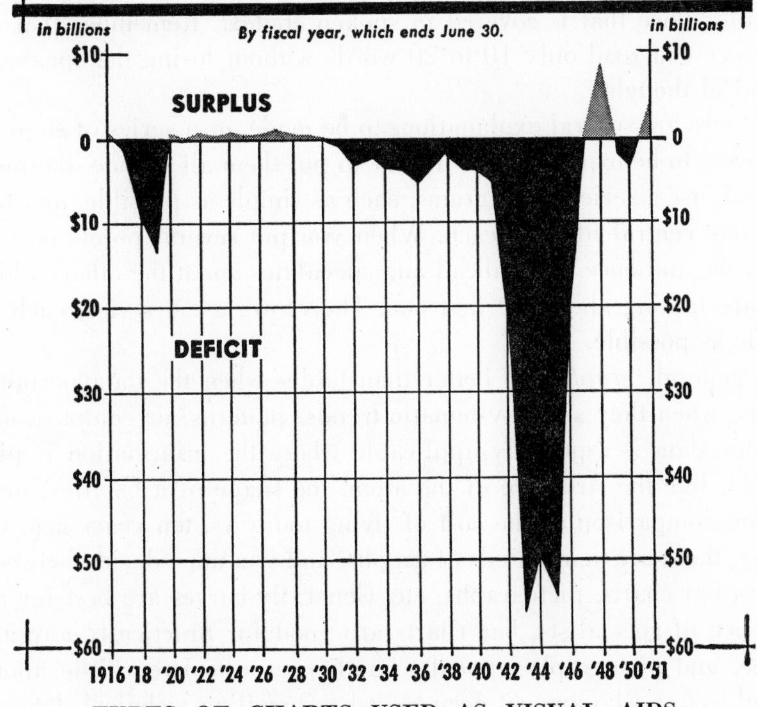
U. S. GOVERNMENT
ANNUAL SURPLUS OR DEFICIT, 1916-1951
in billions
By fiscal year, which ends June 30.
in billions
SURPLUS
DEFICIT
$10
0
$10
$20
$30
$40
$50
-$60
1916 '18 '20 '22 '24 '26 '28 '30 '32 '34 '36 '38 '40 '42 '44 '46 '48 '50 '51

TYPES OF CHARTS USED AS VISUAL AIDS

to it may be barely visible or wholly invisible from the back of the room. Even the writing on a blackboard ought to be carefully checked for size and heaviness of line. Very often blackboard writing is so small and light that persons at a distance cannot read it easily, if at all.

In training soldiers certain sizes of maps and charts are standardized, having been found to be the most effective size. In drawing maps to explain large military operations, for example, before audiences of one hundred or less, a scale of 3 inches to the mile is commonly used. This is large enough to show terrain features, cities, and other necessary items, yet small enough to show a large area of operations on one map or blackboard. Close-ups of military operations, however, are often mapped at 6 inches to the mile.

The use of different colors on maps and diagrams also may help to make distinctions clear. For example, a blackboard diagram of the human anatomy may show the bones in white, nerves in yellow, cartilages in green, and muscles in red.

2. *Do not crowd too many details into one chart.* Too many details lead to confusion. They distract attention, and provoke curiosity. Therefore, cut details and stick to bare essentials. In most charts cut the title, since that is covered in spoken context. Remember that an audience can read only 10 to 20 words without losing the speaker's thread of thought.

If there are several explanations to be made, or a series of steps in a process to be explained, do not try to put them all on one diagram. Instead, use a series of diagrams, each as simple as possible, and put only *one* central idea on each. When you put several points on one chart, the audience races ahead and speculates about the others while you are talking about the first one. Therefore, use a series, each as simple as possible.

In general, *graphs* are better than tables when the data permits; that is, when they show systematic trends, patterns, or comparisons. Graphic data is especially applicable where the information is picturable, like the structure of the atom, the shape of a bacillus, or a column comparison of the cost of living today vs. ten years ago. Of course, there are many kinds of graphs, and you must decide between curves, bar charts, pictographs, etc. Generally curves are best for an audience of specialists, bar charts are good for practically any audience, and pictographs appeal to audiences who know little about the subject or who are not accustomed to handling technical data.

3. *Talk to the audience instead of to the chart.* The young speaker finds a chart or a diagram to be a welcome refuge from the eyes of his listeners. He tends to turn away from them and to fix his gaze on the blackboard. Soon he is talking to the blackboard instead of to the audience. Of course, he feels silly talking to a blackboard in a strong and positive tone, and so he begins to mumble.

Do not look at the blackboard except when pointing to something specific on it. Even then, a glance is enough to give you the location, and you can turn again to the audience. *Learn the art of keeping a pointer properly placed on the blackboard while you are looking at the audience.*

4. *Do not stand between the audience and the chart.* The fault opposite to ignoring the audience while talking to the blackboard is that of ignoring the blackboard while talking to the audience. Remember that your chart or diagram has been put on the board because the audience needs to see it. Stand out of the way so they can see it completely. If the audience is seated close to you, this usually means that you must stand at least *three or four feet* to one side. In such situations it is best to use a pointer; this enables you to stand far enough away to keep out of the audience's line of vision.

5. *Do not let an unused chart distract attention.* If possible, charts ought to be kept out of sight until needed, and removed from sight when they are done with. The moment a chart appears, people will look at it and try to figure out what it means; so, if you put up a chart before you want to use it, *the audience will look at it instead of observing and listening to you.* Cover it up, therefore, or keep it out of sight until you are ready for it. Re-cover it, remove it, or erase it when you have finished with it.

USING PICTURES AND SLIDES

The use of pictures and slides presents certain additional problems:

1. *Use a screen that is large enough for the image to be easily seen.* It is doubtful whether the standard small screen, the 39 × 48-inch size, ought to be used where anyone in the audience is seated more than 35 feet away. At least many people without perfect eyesight even when they are wearing glasses do not easily see so small an image beyond that distance. Use a larger screen so that people, even those without perfect eyesight, can easily see.

2. *Have the room adequately dark.* For graphs and the like complete darkness is not at all necessary, and even undesirable. Better simply turn out the lights closest to the screen and get a satisfactory balance between room lighting and screen lighting. This has the advantage of the audience being able to see the speaker, which is always a distinct advantage.

The ideal room for pictures, of course, is completely dark, but pictures often must be shown in rooms that are not ideal, rooms where a certain amount of daylight filters in. How much daylight can be safely allowed depends on the quality of screen and the amount of light the projector can throw. No rule can be given. Therefore, *test* the room ahead of time. Then if necessary it can be darkened by draperies, curtains, shades, tar paper—anything at hand, even blankets and stuffing paper into cracks—until the screen image is obviously bright enough from all parts of the room.

Color pictures, be it noted, require a very much darker room and a brighter screen than black-and-white, because in color pictures the brilliancy of hue depends on the darkness of the room. Even if a small amount of outside light filters into the room, it will change the color hues. The effect is literally as though one had mixed paint to exactly the right tint for an especially attractive interior decoration, then, when the color was exactly what was wanted, one dumped into it a bucket of white paint. White light (sunlight) that filters into a room where color pictures are being shown has the same effect as white paint being poured into colored paint. The original color is faded out, and a pale, sickly cast remains.

Other details, too, demand attention—shielding corridor lights, exit lights, and especially the lectern light to avoid shining into the eyes of the audience.

3. *Use a projector that throws plenty of light.* Frankly, many projectors, made to sell inexpensively, simply do not throw enough light to show a good image. The light bulb on the inside may be strong enough (this is often stressed in selling the machine); but it is the speed of lens that determines how much of this light is thrown on the screen. In projectors having a low-speed lens not enough of the light in the bulb is thrown on the screen. Therefore, test your projector ahead of time and learn whether it really throws enough light for the size of your audience.

4. *Do not seat any members of the audience directly behind the projector.* No matter how well housed a projector may be, a certain amount of light escapes. This escaping light strikes the pupil of the eye of any person behind the projector, *causes the pupil to contract,* and so makes it difficult for the person to see the image on the screen. If your projector is set up in the room itself, and not housed in a booth, either place it behind the entire audience (this is by far the best method), or move your audience out of the V zone of light behind the projector. *(See diagram.)*

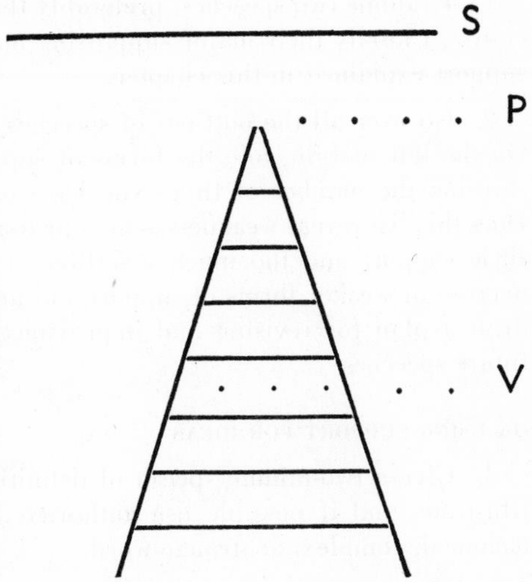

S = *Screen,* P = *Projector,* V = *Zone in which audience should not be seated.*

5. *Pay especial attention to making yourself heard and understood.* For three reasons speakers who are using moving pictures and slides tend not to make themselves adequately heard.

First, they are speaking in the dark where the audience cannot see them. The speaker's nod of the head, turn of the body, or indication of an idea with the hand are lost. The audience now must depend on the speaker's voice alone. That speaker who does not truly project his tones, who compels the audience to a partial lip reading, is now wholly ineffective.

Second, if the speaker operates his own machine (and there are obvious advantages in the speaker's doing so), he must speak from the rear of the audience or perhaps from the rear of center. The picture is in front of the audience, but the speaker's voice comes from behind. This creates a mental interference, perhaps even a physical interference, *unless the speaker uses enough energy to build up room resonance so that the direction of voice is secondary to its easy audibility.*

Third, if moving pictures are being used, the projector makes a continuous noise. This noise, although not loud, is *at a pitch that masks the intelligibility of the speaker's words.* Therefore, unless the speaker realizes this and uses adequate energy of utterance to override the projector noise, he may quite literally be *heard* but not *understood*.

ASSIGNMENTS

ON IDENTIFYING THE VARIETIES OF SUPPORTING MATERIAL

1. Examine two speeches, preferably those you have previously read in this course. Classify their major supporting materials in terms of the ten forms of support explained in this chapter.

2. Go over all the outlines of speeches you have previously given in class. On the left margin note the forms of support you have used. Draw up a list showing the number of times you have used each different form of support. Does this list reveal weaknesses in your use of supporting material, such as too little support and too much assertion? too few different kinds of support? overuse of weaker forms of support and underuse of stronger forms? Can you draft a plan for revising and improving your use of supporting material in future speeches?

ON USING SUPPORT FOR IDEAS

3. Give a two-minute speech of definition in which you classify, compare, illustrate, and if possible use authority, in making clear the meaning of a technical, complex, or strange word.

4. Give a two-minute speech of definition on some common word or phrase used loosely by different people, such as *Americanism, communism, the common man, apple-polisher, regular fellow,* etc.

5. Give a two-minute speech in which you support an idea with factual information. Identify and list your thought pattern for arranging this material.

6. Give a two-minute speech supporting an idea with valid statistics. For suggested subjects leaf through the *World Almanac, Information Please,* etc.

7. Give a two-minute speech supporting an idea with half a dozen specific instances.

8. Give a two-minute speech supporting the idea with one good illustration.

9. Give a two-minute speech in which you compare and contrast such ideas as: (1) prose and poetry, (2) East and West, (3) education and training, (4) comedy and melodrama, (5) art and science, (6) communism and democracy, (7) jazz and bebop.

10. Give a two-minute speech supporting an idea with acceptable testimony from two or more sources.

11. Give a two-minute speech supporting an idea only with restatement or repetition, or both.

12. Give a two-minute speech supporting an idea with description. Determine in advance whether you want the description to be factual, imaginative, etc.

13. Give a two-minute speech supporting an idea with a story, historical incident, or some other form of narration.

14. Give a two-minute speech supporting an idea with charts, maps, or diagrams. Each member of the class will write out and hand in a statement evaluating how well you satisfied the tests for effective visual aids as explained in this chapter.

An outline is a blueprint for the speech

CHAPTER 14

Making the Outline

CHAPTER 14

Why make an outline? Because an outline is a blueprint for the speech, a framework. Because it sets down the thought pattern in plain view, and enables you to test the analysis and the order of arrangement. Because it shows at a glance the nature and amount of your supporting materials, whether you have the right kinds and have enough. Because it enables you to spot weak points and digressions. Because it allows you to inspect the speech as a whole.

Why make an outline? Because "a speech is not an essay on its hind legs"; and it won't become a speech until you make the listeners actually think your thoughts. Because an outline is like a runway on an airfield—a runway by which thoughts-on-paper can take off and become a living speech.

The outline and the modes of delivery

The nature of the outline depends somewhat on your mode of delivery. There are four modes:

Reading the speech. Reading speeches is more common today than in any generation since Demosthenes faced the clamor of Athenian crowds. Partly, of course, this is because of the radio—where requirements of precise timing and laws of libel combine to make speakers set down their exact words in advance. Partly it is because persons in public life must guard against being misquoted. In former days, they could "say they didn't say it," but in this day when tape recorders can be attached to any radio receiver, a public official must guard against impromptu rashness. In the early days of recording, at least one United States Senator complained that an accurate quotation was unfair because "I didn't know the speech was being recorded."

Especially is reading prominent in this generation because almost all people in responsible places are compelled to make speeches, whether they would or no, yet only a few have been trained in public address (a sharp indictment indeed on twentieth-century education). They don't know how to speak. Often they are miserably poor at it. But they *can* dictate to a stenographer, for they are used to dictating letters. Or they can hire a ghost writer, which many of them do.

Most reading, of course, is miserably poor, not interesting to listeners, and not profitable to them. Indeed, live reading takes consummate skill—in some ways a higher degree of skill than live extemporaneous speaking—and the fact that a Franklin D. Roosevelt could read is only a dangerous exception. "Peter, on the day of Pentecost, did not put on his specs and read," Beecher dryly observed to aspiring ministers. In Chapter 21 on Radio and Television, suggestions for reading will be included, but for the present students will not likely use this mode of speaking.

An outline for a speech to be written and read could be short, often composed only of well-organized catch-phrases.

Memorizing the speech. This is popular with students—too popular. They feel that with the speech memorized they are "safe." Safe from what? Safe from the fear of fear, perhaps, but little else. Are they safe from forgetting? Well, they now have hundreds of words to remember instead of a simple thought pattern. The very "safety" they seek leads to danger, for a memorized speech *sounds* memorized. It is artificial, stilted, "canned." It has the sound of a hurdy-gurdy. The speaker, like the monkey, shuffles through the grave performance —and waits at the end for applause. People applaud both in much the same spirit. It was pretty good for a monkey.

Many great men have indeed memorized their speeches verbatim. But they were consummate readers of lines, came to the habit after years of experience, and were willing to expend unlimited labor to attain artistic perfection. Let's have no nonsense comparisons. Students are not consummate readers of lines. They lack the experience. They lack the time. Memorizing may now and then be used in special exercises for exercises in voice training or perfecting bodily action, but not for the main business of original speaking.

Speaking impromptu. This is speaking without preparation. More accurately it is speaking without *immediate* preparation, for the speaker does indeed use his background of experience and information. Of course most impromptu speaking is bad, because the speaker flounders physically and mentally. He has had no opportunity to make an outline, and that is the mainspring of disorder. Impromptu speaking is useful as a training exercise, but you don't depend on it when the speech is really important.

Speaking extemporaneously. You know what extemporaneous speaking is (see page 50). It is not impromptu. It is not speaking with slight preparation. It is speaking from carefully organized thoughts set down in an outline instead of a manuscript. Such an outline, of course, would be more elaborate than one used as the basis for writing a manuscript, for it is the final written form, the takeoff for the speech itself. This is the type of outline to be considered in this chapter.

Requirements for good outlines

Outlines for class speeches serve two purposes: (1) They are the construction blueprints for students learning to make speeches. (2) They are a diagnostic aid to the instructor; they tell him the kind of speech that was *planned.* From hearing the speech—and examining the outline—he can tell whether any particular problem arose from faulty planning, or from imperfect execution. Therefore, on two counts the classroom outline is not quite comparable to the outline used by experienced speakers. It will be more complete, and more attention will be paid to diagnostic details. Follow the procedure given below, except where modified or changed by your instructor:

1. *Prefix to the outline a clear and complete Purpose-Sentence.*

Wrong

This is the best solution to this problem. (What problem? What solution?)

Right

Preventing strikes by labor-management techniques is cheaper for everybody than settling strikes after they are called.

2. *Organize the outline into three parts: the beginning, the body, and the ending. Ordinarily these are known as Introduction, Discussion and Conclusion.*

Right

INTRODUCTION

I. ______________________________

DISCUSSION

I. ______________________________
II. ______________________________

CONCLUSION

I. ______

3. *Use a consistent set of symbols to indicate main heads and each descending order of subheads.* From generations of usage the symbols given below have become almost common law. To avoid being misunderstood probably you had best follow general usage:

Right

I. Roman numerals used for main heads.
  A. Capital letters used for 1st level of subheads.
    1. Arabic numbers used for 2nd level of subheads.
      a. Small letters used for 3rd level of subheads.
        (1) Arabic numbers in parentheses used for 4th level of subheads.
          (a) Small letters in parentheses used for 5th level of subheads.

4. *Number each part of the outline (Introduction, Discussion, Conclusion) as a separate unit.* The entrance and exit should not be confused with the thought pattern of the discussion. Thus if you have two parts in the Introduction, the first main head (Discussion) is numbered I, not III.

Wrong

INTRODUCTION

I. ______
II. ______

DISCUSSION

III. ______
IV. ______
V. ______

CONCLUSION

VI. ______

Right

INTRODUCTION

I. ______
II. ______

DISCUSSION

I. ______
II. ______
III. ______

CONCLUSION

I. ______

5. *Show the logical relationship of headings also by proper indentation.*

Wrong

I. Every symbol ought to stand alone in the open. easily visible to the eye; this one is partly concealed by the word underneath.

A. Likewise this subhead symbol is partly concealed by being absorbed into the line beneath.

1. This subhead symbol is partly concealed, like the two above.

Right

I. Note how this symbol stands alone and is instantly visible to the eye.

  A. Likewise this subhead symbol is instantly visible because it stands apart and to the left.

    1. Even sub-subheads like this are instantly visible when given proper identation.

6. *Use complete sentences only.* This is done for two reasons: (1) Although catch phrases are perfectly all right for experienced speakers (though relatively few good speakers use them), you are *learning*, and in learning you need to be sure to think through each idea and phrase it into exact words. (2) Your outline is also to help the instructor diagnose your individual speech problems. A catch-phrase outline is a poor diagnostic aid.

7. *Write down each main head in a simple sentence, usually with an active verb; beware of winding sentences and dangling clauses.*

Wrong

I. Problems of this generation. (Not a sentence, but only a meaningless clause.)

Poor

I. It is because of the fact that we do not know how serious were the crises that people faced in other generations and other centuries, that we underrate the relative seriousness of the crises of this generation with those of the past. (Winding and dangling!)

Good

I. Every generation faces crises, and each generation says, "My crisis is the worst ever."

8. *Check your group of main heads to insure a consistent and simple thought pattern.*

Poor; no thought pattern

I. Higher education ought to train for leadership.
II. If it does not, American democracy will face a critical future.

Good; simple thought pattern

I. The tendency to glorify the common mind, typified by the athlete and glamor girl, is a positive danger to American democracy. [Problem]
II. The challenge to higher education is to arouse latent interest in the uncommon mind. [Solution]
III. Institutions that try to meet this challenge will have rough sailing but will perform a vital service. [Solution]

9. *Check the main heads to be sure that they sustain the Purpose-Sentence.* This point is so elementary that the sight of it in print seems out of place. But in the hard school of experience it is a necessary reminder.

Poor; main heads don't sustain Purpose-Sentence

PURPOSE-SENTENCE: Public opinion polling is not an exact science, but it is accurate enough to be a useful tool for the social scientist.

Main Heads: I. The Literary Digest fiasco in 1936 led to doubt in many many people's minds about polls.
II. The polltakers' 1948 failure convinced many people that polls never could be accurate.

Good; main heads sustain Purpose-Sentence

PURPOSE-SENTENCE: Public opinion polling is not an exact science, but it is accurate enough to be a useful tool for the social scientist.

Main Heads: I. Sampling methods are now based on statistically reliable processes, like the quota-controlled sampling or the area sampling, with a known percentage of error.
II. Information thus gathered has invaluable uses, from promoting worker-management relations to aiding Congress in passing laws.

10. *Beware of trying to support any head by one subhead; use two or more.* You really can't "divide" an idea into one subhead, for "division" implies two or more parts.

Wrong

I. The tendency to glorify the common mind is a positive danger to the American democracy.
  A. It exists in many forms
    1. The movie star is aped by every schoolgirl

Right

I. The tendency to glorify the common mind is a positive danger to American democracy.
  A. It exists in many forms
    1. The movie star is aped by schoolgirls
    2. Great athletes are the focus of national attention
    3. Noisy politicians are applauded, while scientists and scholars are overlooked.
  B. But without sustained cultivation of intellectual and spiritual qualities, America cannot develop leadership needed in this disturbed age.

II. etc.

11. *See that the subheads at all levels develop the heads above them.*

Wrong

C. You don't study merely from sitting down at a desk.
  1. Let's suppose you clear your desk of *Esquire* and *Life,* and the letter from home—then sit down to study "Making the Speech Outline."
    a. Outlining, of course, is important and you ought to be interested in learning how.
    b. That is not to say that *Esquire* and *Life* are not magazines of educational value.
  2. But study is not the same as escape reading.

Right

C. You don't study merely from sitting down at a desk. (*for*)
  1. Let's suppose you clear your desk of *Esquire* and *Life,* and the letter from home—then sit down to study "Making the Speech Outline." (*but*)
  2. In the next half hour a parade of ideas marches through your head. (*for example*)
    a. You wonder about that Math assignment. (*and*)
    b. Your girl in Ohio gets on your mind again; "What's she up to now?" you wonder for the fifteenth time. (*and*)
    c. "What about next week-end?" you wonder. (*and*)
    d. "Those confounded exams, only three weeks away," you think. (*consequently*)
  3. In short, you have not been studying at all; you have been playing mental hop-skip-and-jump.

12. *Generally use personalized language, or echo the words of the actual speech.* Personalized language is wordy, but is the easiest takeoff from the outline into the speech. Less personalized language that echoes the words of the actual speech allows a shorter outline, but makes the takeoff a bit harder. Whichever you use, avoid the banal indirect phrasing, "I shall show the audience that. . . ."

Wrong

1. Here I shall tell the audience how important creating new jobs are to the workers.

Better

1. Prosperity of the workers depends on management creating jobs.
   a. In the U. S. in 1890 there were 18 million jobs; in 1950 were 62 million jobs.
   b. In 60 years, 44 million jobs had thus been created by the use of risk capital.
2. During the next 25 years 25 million more new jobs will need to be created.

Wordy, but often the best

1. Gentlemen of labor, you need something management has and without it you die, you need jobs.
   a. By 1890 management had created 18 million jobs; by 1950, 62 million.
   b. Thus in 60 years, management had created 44 million new jobs.
   c. These jobs were created by taking risks with spare capital.
      (1) By taking risks, 7 million new jobs were created in the automobile industry—that did not exist in 1890.
         (a) It cost management the bankruptcy of over 30 automobile manufacturers.
         (b) Do you remember Stutz, Marmon, Winton, Maxwell, Haynes, Franklin and Paige? They are now bankrupt.
      (2) Nearly a million new jobs were created by the airplane transport industry, which has never paid dividends equal to its losses.
      (3) Over a million have been created by radio and television.
2. Gentlemen of labor, in the next 25 years management must create 25 million new jobs—or you won't be getting $1.78 cents an hour. . . .

13. *Include the supporting materials in the outline.* An outline that contains only assertions—with no illustrations, factual information, comparison, testimony, etc.—is just about worthless. Better use the paper for doodling. For an example of an outline segment with

supporting material included, see the last two illustrations under No. 12 just above.

14. *Include also, if you wish, the transitions and signposts.* These will be not be numbered parts of the outline, of course, since they are signposts and not parts of framework of ideas. But signposts are useful, on highways and in outlines. Standard practice is to insert them, without numbers, in parentheses.

Right

I. The literary quality of American novels has dropped almost as low as their heroine's plunging necklines.

   A. I know that in every age literature is criticized by contemporaries.

   B. But I think it fairly evident that novels like *The Foxes of Harrow* and Kathleen Winsor's *Star Money* have no great merit other than a lot of broken field running around a bedroom.

      (You may say, "All of this is true, but these novels are on the best-seller lists, and therefore are what the American people want to read." But this is not strictly true.)

II. Thanks to the book clubs, not to reading taste, literary mediocrities are more profitable to write than literature.

Technical plots

Inherent weaknesses in a speech can be seen in the outline, but they are not always obvious to the inexperienced. By means of a technical plot, however, hidden weaknesses are brought to light.

To test a speech in this way, leave ample margin on the left of the outline, a margin of perhaps two or three inches. In this space set down *what you are doing in the outline.* Where you have used an illustration in the outline, write "illustration" in the left column. Where you have used a comparison, write "comparison." Where you have attempted to arouse a desire or to build a climax, write "arousing a desire for cleaning up slums," or "building a climax for overcoming resistance to a change."

When this is done you can test each part of the outline. Have you used enough facts or figures, or have you relied too much on assertion? Have you overworked explanation or testimony? Have you aroused the strongest desires connected with the subject, or have you relied only on the weaker ones? Such weaknesses can be discovered by the technical plot.

I

In the following outline, suitable for a five-minute speech, the speaker develops a speech of information on a reasonably simple subject. The main supporting materials were figures and specific instances. Each main head was developed by the *instructive method* (see page 164).

THE CENSUS OF 1950

Technical Plot	*Outline*
	PURPOSE-SENTENCE: The 1950 census enables us to understand unforeseen population problems that arise during the 1940's.
	INTRODUCTION
	I. In 1950 the U. S. took its 17th national census.
Orienting the audience	II. I want to discuss how it explains certain annoying and unforeseen problems.
THOUGHT PATTERN: CAUSE-EFFECT	DISCUSSION
	I. The American population during the 1940's took a surprising upsurge.
Figures	A. The increase in the ten years was nearly 20 millions, or over 14%.
Figures	B. It means that our population was roughly double that of 1900.
	C. This upsurge was surprising on two counts.
	1. Earlier forecasts had not anticipated it.
Figures	a. The Thompson-Whelpton projections of 1937, based on assumptions of medium *mmO*, forecast a 1950 population of only 140.6 millions, or an increase of but 6.4%.

THE CENSUS OF 1950—*Cont.*

Technical Plot	*Outline*
Comparison; figures	b. Out of a series of six such projections made in 1937-1938, each using a different *mmO* assumption, the lowest forecast for 1950 was 137.1 millions and the highest was 144.2 millions.
Figures	c. Forecasts made in 1946 and published by the Census Bureau in 1947, pointed to a population in 1950 of only 146.3 millions.
	2. This was a war decade, which heretofore has caused a sharp decline in the rate of increase.
Specific instances	a. Three earlier war decades had shown such a decline: 1810-20, 1860-70, and 1910-20.
Testimony	b. Warren Thompson, a respected student of population problems, wrote in 1944 that "even under the most favorable conditions . . . war does have a very depressing effect on population growth."
	II. This unexpected upsurge has left us with unexpected problems.
	A. In education, a flood of children are entering school for whom there are not enough schools or teachers.
Explanation	1. Experts had led us to believe that the population school ages had passed its peak in

Technical Plot	*Outline*
	1940, would remain stationary or decline thereafter.
	2. Therefore we had no long-range educational program to care for these unexpected arrivals.
	B. In farming, the forecasters and government planners have been basing government farm programs on an assumed all-time peak of around 140 millions.
Specific instance	1. Indeed O. E. Baker in 1936 set forth the peak as 139 millions.
Explanation	2. This became the unstated assumption of Congress in passing farm relief legislation.
Figures	3. Now we find an extra 10 million people to be fed, with numbers still increasing.
	C. In business, after 1945 the manufacturers mistook the buying demands of this increasing population for the temporary thirst of people who had been unable to get goods during the war.

CONCLUSION

I. Even such dry figures as the census have a bearing on the happiness and well-being of the American people.

II

In the following outline for a six-minute speech, the speaker develops a speech of information on a more complex subject than in the first outline. The main supporting materials are specific instances, testimony, illustration, and restatement. Because listeners *wanted* to know how to study, each main head was stated openly at the beginning, and each was developed by the *instructive method* (see page 164).

HOW TO STUDY

Technical Plot	*Outline*
	PURPOSE-SENTENCE: Studying, thinking and remembering go hand in hand, so that the absence of one leads to the loss of all three.
	INTRODUCTION
Getting attention and good will by pleasantry	I. In selecting a subject for this Monday morning's speech, I had to consider the heavy week-end (shall I say the "lost week-end"?) we've all had.
Orienting the audience by telling how important the proposition to them	II. I anticipated that talking to you this morning would be like talking to a wall; I also anticipated that every word I spoke this morning would vibrate my fragile head; therefore I chose a subject that would keep both you and me awake, a subject that with the coming of final examinations becomes more important to us every day; my subject is *how to study*.
Supporting the Purpose-Sentence by testimony	III. William James once said that, "The art of remembering is the art of thinking," and I propose to show that studying, thinking, and remembering all go hand in hand, so that the absence of one leads to the loss of all three.
THOUGHT PATTERN: CLASSIFICATION ORDER	DISCUSSION
Assertion	I. In order to study, you must think.
Assertion	A. The fact that we are conscious is not proof that we are thinking.
Hypothetical illustration	1. We may take a train ride and at the end of the ride say to ourselves, "I've been thinking."
	2. In truth, you probably have not thought for a single minute.

Technical Plot	*Outline*
Assertion	B. Actually you think only when you are faced with a problem.
Hypothetical illustration	1. If your train had suddenly lurched to a stop with screaming brakes, you would have started thinking, "Is there danger?" and "How can I escape it?" because you would have faced a problem that was immediate and urgent.
Restatement	2. But if you were faced with no problem on your train ride, you probably would not think.
	a. You would look at people's faces.
Mild humor	b. You would admire or deprecate their figure, form, and clothes.
Assertion	C. The process is the same with formal study.
Specific instances	1. You clear your desks of *Esquire*, *Look*, and the letter from home—then sit down to study "How to organize a speech into concise and orderly form."
Assertion	2. In the next half hour a parade of ideas marches through your head.
Specific instance	a. You wonder about that assignment in Math.
Specific instance	b. Your girl in Ohio gets on your mind again; "What's she up to now?" you wonder for the fifteenth time.
Specific instance	c. "What about next week-end?" you wonder.

HOW TO STUDY—*Cont.*

Technical Plot	*Outline*
Specific instance	d. "Those confounded exams, only three weeks away," you think.
Specific instance	3. Also, and naturally, you talked with a couple of other people who happened by.
Summary and climax that makes hearers wiggle uncomfortably	4. In short, you have not been studying at all; you have been playing mental hop-skip-and-jump.
Assertion that relieves some of the discomfort	5. This is the *normal* way the mind and body behaves; both are very restless.
Explanation	a. The human body is very restless.
Specific instance	(1) I'm restless as I give this speech.
Specific instance	(2) You're restless as you listen to it.
Specific instance	(3) Even at night you turn over from 20 to 45 times while you are asleep.
Explanation	b. The human mind is quite as restless as the body.
Explanation	(1) Attention comes in "spurts" and we can think of nothing longer than a few seconds at a time.

Technical Plot	*Outline*
Explanation	(2) What we call prolonged attention is simply repeated spurts of attention on the same subject.
Above explanations supported by testimony	(3) William James once said that the only difference between his mind and any poor mind was that he could keep his spurts of attention from getting off the subject.
Transition	(So when we study our problem is to keep our repeated spurts of attention right on the subject, and to do this we must narrow our thoughts to the point where only the problem, or point in question, is in view.)
Assertion	II. First, we should attend to the physical aspect of study.
Assertion of the first principle	A. Clean up your study area of all probable sources of interruptions.
Analysis of A, step one	1. Have a definite place to study, and at that place do nothing else but study.
Specific instance	a. Don't write letters there.
Specific instance	b. Don't play cards there.
Specific instance	c. Do nothing there but study.
Analysis of A, step two	2. Avoid disturbances.
Specific instance	a. Pictures on your desk or nearby wall can be a distraction.

HOW TO STUDY—*Cont.*

Technical Plot	*Outline*
Specific instance	b. A turned-on radio is certain to distract you; that popular notion that you can study while listening to a radio is wishful thinking.
Analysis of A, step three	3. Above all, don't get too comfortable.
Restatement	a. Over comfort is good for sleeping, but not studying.
Restatement	b. A good idea is to lean forward and put your elbows on the desk.
Assertion of the second principle	B. Follow a definite study program.
Analysis of B, step one	1. Review the previous lesson first.
Restatement	a. This will put you in the mood to study.
Restatement	b. It will also give you something to tack your new lesson to.
Analysis of B, step two	2. Look at the *whole* lesson before you begin.
Explanation	a. You can then plan your method of learning.
Explanation	b. The important points will thus come easier.
Analysis of B, step three	3. Underlining the book is a good idea, but a better one is to *write* in your own words on the margin.
Analysis of B, step four	4. Finally, recitation is a great help to learning.

Technical Plot	*Outline*
Restatement	a. Recite it to yourself a few times.
Restatement	b. The more times an idea enters your head, the better the retention.
Assertion	III. Next, we should observe the mental aspect of study.
Analysis of III, step two	A. Study with the *intent* to remember, not just to pass an examination.
Figures	1. Extensive experiments show that it is possible to remember from 20% more to 400% more simply because of the intent.
Factual information	2. These experiments showed that those who studied to pass an exam, forgot when the exam was over; those who studied to remember kept on remembering when the exam was over.
Analysis of III, step two	B. Immediately apply to life what you study.
Factual illustration	1. Harry Overstreet gives a significant example of this; he asked a philosophy student studying Spinoza to go to Coney Island and see what philosophy he could find there. a. The student stared in astonishment. b. Respectable young Ph. D. candidates did not do that sort of thing; they got philosophy out of books.
	2. This man had not learned to apply his knowledge to life.

HOW TO STUDY—*Cont.*

Technical Plot	*Outline*
Analysis of III, step three	C. Try to develop and maintain your interest in the subject.
Restatement	1. When you tire of one subject, switch to the study of another.
Restatement	2. If you have no interest in a subject, you will be less likely to remember it.
Analysis of III, step four	D. Find a good reason for studying a subject.
Restatement	1. A good reason supplies motivation for remembering it.
Factual illustration	2. Everybody knows the story of the boy who was dull in physics until he learned one day that physics explained what made a baseball curve; and this boy, who wanted to be a pitcher, had no trouble thereafter remembering physics.
	CONCLUSION
Summary	I. If you get nothing else from this speech, get these three points: 1) Clear your study area, 2) retain your interest in the subject, 3) apply your knowledge to life.
Final thrust of humor	II. Follow these rules, my lords and ladies, and I'll guarantee that you'll know and understand your freshman English by the time you leave graduate school!

III

For an eight-minute speech a student used the following outline. The listeners, of course, did *not* want to believe either of the two main heads, therefore the speaker developed them by *conciliation plus impelling argument* (see pages 164-165). *Notice that neither main head was stated at the beginning, but each was opened by a transition, followed by a step-by-step presentation of the supporting materials. Only when the evidence was presented, did he come to a full statement of each head.* The chief supporting materials are factual information, testimony, explanation, restatement, and illustration.

A COLLEGE EDUCATION IS NOT A FREE TICKET

Technical Plot	*Outline*
	PURPOSE-SENTENCES: Your college education won't have the money worth in real life that you want to believe it will.
	INTRODUCTION
Getting attention by pleasantry	I. Mayor Jimmy Walker of New York used to say that he must live down his reputation for wisecracking before anyone would take him seriously.
	A. I humbly realize that I must follow his example.
	1. For so far in this course I have placed your sense of humor above your sense of logic.
	2. And I realize that I have done you an injustice.
	B. But today I shall atone by speaking to you in a very serious mood.
Orienting the audience by explaining the Purpose-Sentence	II. I wish to explain my reasons for believing that the value of a college education is overestimated on a college campus.
	A. Of course, you will not understand me to say that it has no value; my presence here, seeking a college education under handicaps, is testimony of my belief in its worth.
	B. But, because I like this student body and love the college, I would warn against habits of thought that might be injurious to both.

A COLLEGE EDUCATION IS NOT A FREE TICKET—*Cont.*

Technical Plot	*Outline*
	C. In return, you will, I am sure, judge me sincerely as we delve into this subject together.
Transition	(May I first remind you of the claims of enthusiastic advocates of higher education?)
THOUGHT PATTERN: CAUSE-EFFECT	DISCUSSION
Main head set in brackets because it was not stated at the beginning, but was unfolded gradually.	I. [Statisticians have misled you on the cash value of college education.]
Testimony	A. I have chosen to discuss the figures of Dean E. W. Lord because they are the most extensive and the most convincing.
Figures	1. He says, in effect, that a college education is worth $72,000.
Personal testimony	2. I want to believe a statement like this as much as you do.
Restatement	3. Yet I am not always willing to accept these apparent facts; I want to dig beneath for the real reasons beneath the facts.
Assertion	B. I have reasons for believing that Dean Lord's estimate won't check with the facts out in life.
Explanation	1. I do not mean to imply that college has no advantages; I think it has advantages, and we have heard them enumerated from this platform so often that I shall not repeat them.
Specific instance	2. But, when I look around and see students sleeping through lectures, bluffing in classes,

Technical Plot	*Outline*
	never cracking a book, I wonder how much they are building for a successful future.
Figures	3. If the average student establishes a chance to earn an extra $72,000 merely by keeping residence in a college town for four years, how much could a man earn who studied hard?
Restatement	a. If I believed these statisticians, I would expect a man on the honor roll to become a millionaire in later life.
Assertion	b. Yet I know of no college whose honor-roll students have entered the millionaire class.
Assertion	4. Therefore, there must be other factors that determine to a large degree whether one is a financial success.
	C. So let us proceed to the true significance of Dean Lord's estimate.
Explanation; figures	1. He arrives at his conclusion through a survey which revealed that men who went only through grade school earned $45,000 during a lifetime, the high-school graduate earned $78,000, and the college graduate earned $150,000.
Explanation	2. I wonder if this generalization does not strike you as being another spurious case of ignoring the real cause in favor of a specious one.

A COLLEGE EDUCATION IS NOT A FREE TICKET—*Cont.*

Technical Plot	*Outline*
Restatement	a. Successful men and women are not successful solely because they have had a college education.
Restatement	b. The true statement is that these people get a college education for the same reason exactly that they later "get" success; they had "getting" brains and "getting" character.
Restatement	c. Their college education gave them no new ability; it merely improved what ability they already had—it sharpened the edge but did not improve the quality of steel in their make-up.
Explanation	3. Dean Lord's figures are really a measure of the relative natural endowments of three classes of men—those who had ability and determination only to finish elementary school, those who had it to go through high school, and those who had it to go through college.
Explanation	a. In denying that college education inherently increases one's earning of money, I am not saying that it is not worth having any more than that money is not worth having.

Technical Plot	*Outline*
Explanation	b. Both provide a richer life to the man who gets them.
Explanation	c. But rather than one causing the other, both are the effect of a common cause, namely innate capacity.
Restatement	(1) This inborn gift of brains, ambition, and character makes its possessor capable of getting an education, or success, or power, or anything within range of that gift.
Figures; Comparison	(2) Corrected, Dean Lord's figures would read somewhat as follows: On an average of every 100 men in America, 65 are inherently capable of attaining not more than a common school education, and of earning not more than a total of $45,000 by the time they are 60 years old.

A COLLEGE EDUCATION IS NOT A FREE TICKET—*Cont.*

Technical Plot	*Outline*
Explanation	(3) Not everyone who inherits ability, of course, gets a college education or a fortune; time or place or circumstances may prevent.
Restatement	(4) But no one who does not inherit it can get either a college education or a fortune.
Explanation	d. If society wants more college graduates and more successful men and women, it cannot get them by sending the misfits to college; it must rather produce more capable men and women by encouraging people of capable inheritance to have more children.
Transition	(So, without questioning the splendid facts of Dean Lord's survey, I do question the common interpretation of them. I go further; I wonder if it has not lowered the real value of education? When the college man hears that college is worth $72,000 to him what frame of mind does it put him in?)
Main Head set in brackets because it was not stated at the beginning, but was unfolded gradually.	II. [The college graduate usually injures himself by placing a false cash value on himself.]
Description	A. He takes an unbecoming attitude.

Technical Plot	*Outline*
Comparison	1. His is the attitude of a bill-collector; he wants the $72,000.
Comparison	2. He regards the world as a slot machine.
	3. I can give two interesting examples of this.
Illustration	a. A small department store in my town tried to hire a college graduate for salesman in its furniture department; but it could not get one because the college graduate wanted to start as floor manager.
Testimony	b. A road superintendent of the Pennsylvania Ry. said to my employer "I can't hire college men, for they want to start at the wages of men with five years' experience."
Summary	4. So the college man unconsciously and disastrously betrays the fact that he thinks himself a superior person.
Description	B. Now what is the reaction of the untrained man to this college-man attitude?
	1. Does he stand aside and say, "Yes, yes, Mr. College Graduate, you have a right to all the good things without working for them"?
	a. He does not.
	b. He makes the college man pay dearly for his prejudices.

A COLLEGE EDUCATION IS NOT A FREE TICKET—*Cont.*

Technical Plot	*Outline*
Illustration	2. I recall an interesting instance of this conflict; it was a college man who resented the mild initiation pranks played on him by other employers at the railroad shops; he let them know he'd been initiated into a fraternity once and that he didn't think their uneducated pranks were funny; so they kept it up for weeks, until one day he refused to clean a locomotive tender because he thought it was another prank; but it was a real order and the boss fired him.
Indirect testimony	C. Many employers, too, have drawn up an indictment against the college man. College men, they say:
	1. Are snobs.
	2. Are trouble-makers.
	3. Acquire bad habits in college, such as lack of responsibility, bluffing, looking on 60% as passing.
	CONCLUSION
Summary	I. So I am afraid that college education isn't worth quite as much as we would like to think it is. It creates no brains or initiative. It only trains them, and it trains some of them carelessly.

Using the outline

The outlines described and illustrated in this chapter construct a complete framework for the speech. They test the sequence and arrangement of the smallest subheads, all the details. Later on, you may reduce their length (though a marked distinction between really good extemporaneous speakers and the boring mediocre ones, is that the former usually have more detailed outlines). But for the present, you had better use longer outlines. They help you *plan* a good speech. They help the instructor *diagnose* your plans.

You convert the outline into a speech by steps that were described in Chapter 3 (pages 49-53). Read again those steps. Follow them. Remember that those five-to-ten formal rehearsals, for best effect, need to be distributed over several days.

ASSIGNMENTS

ON RE-EXAMINING HABITS OF OUTLINING

1. Use the following steps in outlining a magazine article:
   a. First, determine the central theme, and then phrase it into purpose-sentence.
   b. Next, study the thought movement and development until the main divisions of thought become clear; then write these out as main heads.
   c. Finally, in subhead form set down the supporting material.

2. Go to hear a speaker and make a detailed key-word outline of the speech while he is giving it. Then go home and write out the full outline, together with a critical evaluation:
   a. Did the speech have a definite purpose? If so, was it stated in plain words, or only implied? Where in the speech was this done?
   b. Did the speech have definite main heads? If so, were they stated clearly? Were they arranged in a clear thought pattern?
   c. Was there enough supporting material? Was it arranged (i.e., were the subheads) in a clear thought pattern?
   d. If *you* were giving this speech how would you change the outline?

3. Outline the class lecture of one of your instructors. A good class lecture ought to move a little more slowly than a regular public speech, and you should be able to make a full outline as the lecture proceeds.

4. For one speech round make a key-word outline of each speech as it is being delivered, and later fill out just enough details so you can remember the content. At the end of the round, submit a list of the two best-outlined and the two worst-outlined speeches. Give your reasons.

5. Take an outline of one of your earlier speeches. Check it against the 14 specifications of a good outline set forth in this chapter, revise it, and hand it in.

ON USING OUTLINES EFFECTIVELY

6. Go over your notebooks in other courses. In what form are they? Are the items, for example, numbered and are they indented? In general, does it contain only interesting knickknacks that you have picked up during the course, or does it contain an organized outline of your professor's mind? Would your notes be more valuable if you followed the principles of this chapter (slightly modified, of course, to fit a semester of lectures woven together)? Would you be willing to try using these principles for, say, one month? If so, start by adopting a consistent set of symbols, and by setting down the main topics of each lecture. Then indent the supporting materials, and label them with appropriate subhead symbols.

7. Are you willing to do the same with outside reading in other courses? By arranging notes in outline form, you can review quickly, and at a glance locate the main lines of thought and note the supporting material. The original reading and note-taking requires more time, but reviewing is cut to a fraction and the notes become useful for frequent later reference.

8. Use the following procedure in planning your next speech:
   a. While still in preliminary form, check the outline against the 14 specifications set forth in this chapter. Revise the outline, but do not yet make a full revised copy.
   b. Make a technical plot, and use it to test each part of the outline. Revise the outline again if necessary.
   c. Make a final copy of both the revised outline and the technical plot. Use the outline for rehearsing the final extempore speech.

"Not only is history written with words. It is made with words." Lincoln at Gettysburg typifies men of action who voice their words of historic simplicity: "that government of the people. . . ."

CHAPTER 15
Using Words

CHAPTER 15

Language is the greatest invention of the human race. Centuries upon centuries went into developing the technique of using language, and some of the best men who ever lived gave their lives to it. Your mastery of this technique is in a large degree the measure of your mind. Without language you cannot think, for thinking is talking to yourself, usually not out loud. Without sufficient mastery of language thinking is impaired, for ideas become actual only when you can phrase them into words. In a really advanced civilization like ours everybody has to know something of the technique of language.

You intend to design automobiles, build houses, or run a store. Your plans must first be created mentally, in words. You intend to discuss a problem or situation, like current prices or modern poetry. Your ideas are nebulous, half-existent, until they are turned into words. You think in words, plan in words, talk in words. Yet, as the semanticists properly remind us, these words in themselves have no value. They are only symbols for things and thoughts. In a sense they are like the paper and ink in a ten-dollar bill. Only by skillful techniques can they be made into a substitute for the real thing, into a currency that can be easily transferred from person to person and has a standard of value known to all.

Crude words will do the job for primitive peoples, who have only crude ideas and unarticulated emotions. Crude words may even do the job for the lower stratum in civilization, among people who don't think but only follow, and whose emotions are felt but seldom put into words. Crude words won't do the job for people who think and feel and talk about the civilized world. They must have keener tools. Public address demands the keenest tools of all; for, first, it requires thinking; and that means talking to yourself, not out loud. Next, it requires communicating your thinking to a public audience; and that demands an exact command of this word-science technique slowly perfected through the centuries.

Things that prevent a speaker being clear and accurate

What that "readability expert," Robert P. Gunning, said of newspaper editorial writers could be applied with even more force to speakers: "Most editorial writers seem to confuse dignity with pomposity. Their marathon sentences, foggy words, and abstractions put their pieces completely out of reach of all but the upper 5 or 10 per cent of their readers." Now this is not from lack of training in "English," for English is the one subject more universally required than any other—from elementary school through college. There are other reasons. Among them, to be frank, are lack of honesty, laziness, and exhibitionism.

LACK OF HONESTY

The most common lack of honesty is not deliberate falsehood—there is not a great amount of that in public speaking—but it is the use of devices such as Name-Calling or Card-Stacking to cover up and deceive. By *Name-Calling* we give a "bad name" to a person, a group, or a thing we don't like. For centuries the name "heretic" was a bad name. People were imprisoned, tortured, and put to death because they were "heretics." Today if we don't like a man we can call him a "communist" or a "capitalist." Neither word has an accurate meaning. They simply attempt to smear a man that we hate. Other common hate-words are *dictator, demagogue, Red, alien, rabble-rouser, troublemaker, economic royalist, collectivist.*

Name-Calling may also be turned around, to make you like what I like by stirring up your emotions and befogging your thinking. Instead of hate-words I use "virtue-words" such as *liberty, honor, freedom, truth, democracy, the American way, Christian ideals.* Half the pictures that come out of Hollywood are labelled *colossal* or *terrific.* These words are not intended to have a clear meaning, but only to lead the unthinking to the box office.

Card-Stacking is the plain and simple stacking of the cards against the truth. The speaker may not deliberately lie, but he does distort by discussing only part of a situation in the solemn pretense that it is the whole. He does not falsify facts, but he evades them and hopes he will not get caught.

These dishonest methods are recognized by people of even average intelligence. They hate to be thought of as gullible and they do not like the speaker who assumes that they are gullible.

Finally, there is the dishonesty of *exaggeration*. We say "many" when we really mean "a few." We say "absolutely," when it is only "probably." We insist that "everbody knows," when the truth is only that "some people believe." A dubious reward awaits such a speaker. His habit of inflation is soon recognized (people aren't *all* stupid!), and due shrinkage is allowed for. Thereafter he is distrusted.

LAZINESS

Dull speakers cling to abstract words. Why? To be frank, thinking is hard work, and abstract words cover lack of thinking. Only when our ideas are sharp and clear can we state them in exact words. So when we have not really thought, when our ideas are hazy, we cover up by using abstract words. Basically, then, the abstract word is the *lazy* word. It saves thinking. It allows one word to be used over and over again in place of using half a dozen different exact words:

> She was an awful nice girl and we had an awful nice time last night. We went to one of the awful nicest pictures I've seen all year, and coming home—that moon was awful nice to look at.

Now one may heartily enjoy the experiences of last night, but the words "awful nice" do not accurately describe any part of the enjoyment. It is merely a blurb that signifies lack of thought at that particular instant. "You aren't thinking at all," John Steinbeck has one of his characters say to a man like that, "You are just singing a kind of song."

Laziness also arises when the speaker, from sheer lack of mental energy, dodges an energy-carrying word for an inert one. Thus a clerk in the Office of Civilian Defense phrased the order for federal buildings to obtain "obscuration either by blackout construction or by termination of the illumination." President Roosevelt laughingly rewrote it: "Put something across the window, or turn out the lights."

EXHIBITIONISM

When the speaker tries to show off instead of communicate ideas he usually succeeds, for listeners are old hands at detecting showoffs. They have met them in classrooms and on playgrounds since kindergarten days. The earmarks of the exhibitionalist are plain. He uses high-sounding words to explain simple ideas. He uses agreeable words in preference to those that more accurately express what he means. Thus a *wedding* becomes "the consummation of nuptial vows"; a *birth* is "the arrival of a bundle from heaven"; and *death* is "the coming of the dark angel." The speaker intent on accuracy would say:

> The people were angry at Congress for increasing taxes.

But the exhibitionist would erupt in this manner:

> The citizenry were stirred to indignation by the recent action of its elected legislative representatives in increasing the taxation burden.

Of this tendency, Irvin S. Cobb wrote that in his youth "I had the delusion so common among beginners . . . that it was bad form to use the same noun twice in the same sentence or the same paragraph; so, if I were writing a story about a cow, I would call her a cow first, and then a female bovine, and then a ruminative quadruped—and so on."

Exhibitionism is not merely bad in itself. It leads to things worse, for the exhibitionist compromises with plain fact in order to capture a pleasant sound. Once a man has learned to love the sound of his voice above the weight of his thoughts, he tends to seek proximity to an American flag and a water pitcher, and attempts to substitute sound effects for sound ideas. He is the one who says:

> In inviting me to speak to this august assembly, you have bestowed upon me a rare privilege and a rich honor. Long have I been an ardent admirer of your magnificent organization, whose reputation reaches beyond the horizons of geography. . . .

The purpose of language is to make clear, and such language does so perfectly—in a left-handed way. It reveals a speaker whose judgment is a minor asset. Exhibitionism is a poor substitute for plain English.

Good taste in using words

There is good taste in words as well as clothes, for indeed words are garments of the mind. Most of us use everyday words that don't pass muster in intellectual company. You don't need to ban them always from your talk, for good talk is packed with salt and spirit, and slang has its use. But you do need to know their effect on listeners, and to avoid their use on wrong occasions, lest they distract from thought or put you in a bad light.

There are two tests of good taste: (1) reputable use, and (2) standard use.

REPUTABLE USE

"Disreputable" use is a term applied to a mongrel assortment that might be classified as slang, hackneyed words, improprieties, and vulgarisms.

SLANG

The Oxford Dictionary defines slang as "language of a highly colloquial type, considered as below the level of standard educated speech, and consisting either of new words or of current words employed in some special sense." The unhappy purist laments its use. Even the London *Times* complained that slang "seldom attempts to supply deficiencies in conventional language; its object is nearly always to provide a new and different way of saying what can be perfectly well said without it." The man-in-the-street disagrees. He likes slang, and uses it. It is a short cut. It substitutes picturesque speech for less colorful words. Educated people use slang, even the unhappy purist in his purest books. But the slang vocabulary of the uneducated is larger—and worked harder—than that of the educated. Much of it is also slang of a lower order.

Slang is not all alike. Some of it was sorely needed, for it was impossible to convey the ideas behind them save by clumsy circumlocutions. Some of it was a means of enriching the language; it passed into general circulation and found its way into the dictionary (for dictionaries do not decide good usage, but only *record* it). Words, once slang but now in standard colloquial use, include *nice, spurious, fireworks, joy-ride, bootlegger, crook, racketeer, O.K., pushover*. Phrases having a relatively high level of usage, yet still considered slang, include *laugh up your sleeve, high-hat, bonehead, cave in, fly off the handle*. Still other slang has never won respectability, but remained low caste, such as *talk through your hat, laugh that off, belly-laugh, attaboy, scram*. Finally there is temporary slang that comes into sudden use, flourishes vigorously a few years, and fades out. *Aber nit, skido, cartwheel* (dollar) were once on every tongue; now they are scarcely known.

Writers use slang, even formal writers. The public speaker may allow himself greater freedom in using slang than the formal writer, for he faces a live audience where familiar, informal speech is good usage. The typical audience likes slang, good slang. Pungent and pithy slang drives an idea home better than less colorful words. But the speaker should use slang with caution, perhaps extreme caution. He knows that overworked slang is not colorful, but simply follows the line of least resistance, shrinks the vocabulary, and becomes a substitute for thought. Habitual slang is not for speakers with something to say. Especially it is not for students attempting to master the centuries-old technique of using words. A good speaker masters slang; he does not let slang master him.

HACKNEYED WORDS

Certain words and phrases, once fresh and crisp, have become hackneyed from overuse. Speakers who use them are not really thinking, but are only phonographs repeating hackneyed words. The following are typical. They are far from being exhaustive:

along these lines
bated breath
busy as a bee
checkered career
conspicuous by his absence
ignorance is bliss
in close proximity to
in this glad hour
in this new day
incumbent upon me
it is of vital importance
it is up to us
method in his madness
motley crew
no effort will be spared
no sooner said than done
only too glad
our distinguished host
snare and delusion
the fair sex
the man of the hour
too numerous to mention
too funny for words
worse for wear

IMPROPRIETIES

An impropriety is the use of a good word out of its proper meaning. As the *Reader's Digest* College Department reminds students, "*Eat* is a verb; there is no such noun as *eats*. *Suspicion* is a noun; do not 'suspicion' that it is a verb." The list of improprieties heard from the lips of the half-educated is long, of which the following are typical:

He felt *badly* (bad).
He lives quite a *ways* (way) from here.
What *kind of a* (kind of) place is this?
He ran *in back* (back) of the house.
Now don't get *aggravated* (irritated).
Leave (let) me explain.
I don't know but *what* (that) I agree.
Most (almost) everybody knows him.

VULGARISMS

These are words and expressions that mark the uncouth and illiterate: *ain't, can't hardly, used to could, gent, disremember, unlax, brung.* To use them—to use even one of them—slaps listeners in the face. Even listeners who themselves occasionally lapse into vulgarisms resent them from a speaker. "Who does he think I am, somebody he can talk down to?" they think. Most listeners want to feel that the speaker is a leader, somebody who knows, somebody they can trust. They will tolerate, and appreciate, judicious slang. They will frown on improprieties. They will resent vulgarisms.

NATIONAL USE

Words ought to communicate on a clear channel, have a meaning to everybody in the audience. Words fail to do this when they are provincial words, unassimilated foreign words, or technical words.

PROVINCIAL WORDS

In this vast country, each area has developed words of restricted local usage. Inside their area they are perfectly understood. Outside it they seem uncouth, or confusing. Thus in New England you hear *I calculate* for "I think," and in the South you hear *I reckon.* New York has its *Bronx cheer,* a phrase that is known in Texas and California but is not quite accepted. Out of various regions we hear *right smart, red up, a far piece, want in.*

There are times when a speaker may use provincialisms of his own region. They lend personal flavor. They reflect a rich tradition of the soil. But use provincialisms with caution, for they suggest also a person of restricted outlook and limited experience. "He hasn't been around," or "He doesn't know the score," people are likely to say. Hence those who use provincialisms must judge well at what point the personal flavor ends, and the impression begins that they are persons who have not been around.

FOREIGN PHRASES

Once it was the style for speakers to adorn thoughts with foreign phrases. A few listeners understood them and thereby felt superior. The others did not understand them, and were supposed to be impressed by the speaker's learning. That style is gone. You don't dare today decorate a speech with foreign words and phrases just to prove you have had a course in a foreign language. If you say he was a man *sans peur et sans reproche,* few will know what you mean. If you state that he is a *chevalier d'industrie,* listeners will mark you down as an educated fool. Better concentrate on a superior command of American English.

TECHNICAL TERMINOLOGY

In this technical twentieth century there are hundreds of sets of technical languages, and no person knows them all or even a fraction. Your own technical language is familiar to you, but jargon to others. Use it with caution. What speech correctionists call the *velum* is known to the laymen as the "soft palate." What dentists call *dental caries,* to others is plain "tooth decay." The *Nieman Report's* warning to news writers applies with equal truth to speakers: "In economics they . . . drag you, without explanation, through dollar pools and over tariff walls. In science, they ignore the oaf who doesn't know the difference between atomic fission and hydrogen fusion. In labor, they blithely skip from secondary boycotts . . . into an open shop, slamming the door in the face of the uninformed." When you speak, use technical terms circumspectly, and don't use them at all if they are not generally current.

SPOKEN LANGUAGE VERSUS WRITTEN LANGUAGE

Obviously written language and spoken language are basically alike, yet there are sharp and important differences between them. One is intended for the eye, the other for the ear. The reader may absorb at leisure; the listener must take it on the wing. The reader proceeds at his own pace; the listener at the pace of the speaker. The reader may pause to reflect, and reread; the hearer must follow without slackening his pace. The basic difference between written and spoken style, then, is this: Written language must be ultimately intelligible to the reader. Spoken language must be *instantly* intelligible to the listener.

Spoken language, therefore, is more idiomatic. You say *don't, won't, isn't*—not "do not," "will not," "is not." In speech more than in writing you use the shorter, earthy, homespun words: *got* instead of "have," *pull* instead of "influence," *think* instead of "reflect."

Spoken language is more direct. A writer may say, "this writer," or skillfully avoid any direct references whatever. A speech abounds in *I, you, we, they.*

Spoken language is more repetitive. The writer may mark his main divisions of thought by numbers or subtitles. He divides his material into paragraphs. The speaker says, "This is my first point," and "I now come to the second part." He forecasts. He summarizes. He tells listeners where he now is, where he has been, where he is going.

Spoken language uses more questions. The writer says, "We have partly solved this problem." The speaker says, "Have we solved this problem, or moved toward solution?"

Spoken language uses more illustrations, comparisons, specific instances, narration—supporting materials that hold attention and make it possible for listeners to follow the thought. Written language may rely more on explanation and description.

Spoken language avoids complicated sentence structure or backward syntax. A writer might say:

> Although the Belgians have no such barrier between them and the Russians as the English Channel or the Atlantic Ocean, they are nevertheless firmly in support of United Europe.

Winston Churchill put the idea into five short, straight sentences:

> A month ago in Brussels I spoke to a meeting of thirty thousand Belgians. I could feel at once their friendship and their anxiety. They have no Atlantic Ocean, no English Channel, between them and the Russian Communist armored divisions. Yet they bravely and ardently support the cause of United Europe. I admire them.

Ways and means of making ideas clear and accurate

First of all, the audience asks a speaker, "What do you mean?" and next, "How do you know?" Language, therefore, should be so clear and accurate that you cannot be misunderstood. "Not that language *may* be understood," said that doughty old Roman, Marcus Fabius Quintilian, "*but that it cannot be misunderstand.*"

WORDS

Later we shall consider sentences. Right now we are concerned with the language techniques of the simplest unit of thought, the word.

SPECIFIC WORDS

Consider the word *building*. A building where people live is a *residence;* a modest residence is a *cottage;* a pretentious residence is a *mansion.* A building where goods are made is a *factory;* a building where they are stored is a *warehouse;* a building where they are sold is a *store;* a small store is a *shop.* A building where clerical work is done is an *office.* A building where legislators meet is a *capitol.* A building where books are stored is a *library.* A building for dramatic performances is a *theater.* A building for storing motorcars is a *garage.* A building for storing hay is a *barn.* A building for sheltering horses is a *stable.* A building for quartering soldiers is a *barrack.* A building used for worship is a *church;* a modest church or a subordinate place of worship is a *chapel;* a Scotch church is a *kirk;* a bishop's church is a *cathedral;* a pretentious church is a *temple;* a Jewish church is a *synagogue;* a Mohammedan church is a *mosque.*

A word-lazy person could use *building* for every one of these particular kinds of buildings; but whoever wants to make his thoughts clear will use twenty-two specific words, describing twenty-two specific kinds of buildings.

Suppose you say, "He *went* down the street." You tell what happened but not how. The picture is fair, but not good. Suppose, instead, you substitute a more specific word telling *how* he went down the street: "He *staggered* down the street," or *strutted, waddled, strode, slunk, sauntered, marched, raced,* or *ambled.* Each of these words describes a specific mode of going. Each carries a brighter picture than *went.*

The first technique of language, therefore, is to use specific words instead of general words.

SIMPLE WORDS

"Except as ye utter by the tongue words easy to understand, how shall it be known what is spoken? For ye shall speak into the air." St. Paul, brilliant thinker and master of persuasion, wrote these words after speaking to peoples of many nations.

Masters of language follow this principle, but little minds still want to believe that "big words" signify big ideas. With them obscurity of language is mistaken for depth of thought. "What I cannot understand must be profound," such minds seem to reason. Yet the simpler a word, the easier it can be understood. Herbert Spencer properly points out that of the several reasons for this fact the most important is early association. A child "says *I have,* not *I possess* —*I wish,* not *I desire;* he does not *reflect,* he *thinks;* he does not beg for *amusement,* but for *play;* he call things *nice* or *nasty,* not *pleasant* or *disagreeable.*" Through later years these simple words learned early in life carry a stronger meaning than words learned later.

But don't eminent speakers use big words? No. In general they use the simplest word that carries the exact shade of thought and feeling. Somebody counted and measured the printed speeches of that old firebrand, Wendell Phillips. Across the board, 71 per cent of his words were one syllable, 18 per cent were two syllables, and only 7 per cent were three syllables. Any unskillful speaker would use a larger percentage of big words. Inept speakers avoid simple words for long ones, and single words for phrases. Instead of *have,* they prefer "in possession of." They don't *ask,* but "make application for." They don't *eat,* but "consume." They don't have *homes,* but "places of residence." They don't *live,* but "are domiciled." They are not even *people,* but are "individuals." Especially they like those elephant words: "quadripartite," "unilateral," "directive." They can't just say *four-party, one-sided,* and *order.*

The simple word has a power that longer complex words can never have. "He was conveyed to his place of residence in an intoxicated condition." Of such language, Frank H. McClosky said, "Nonsense! If the man was drunk, say he was drunk. 'He was carried home drunk.' " The second technique of language, then, is to use simple words.

COLORFUL WORDS

Words not only *mean,* but *suggest.* If you say, "I ate dead hog," it means the same as "I ate roast pork," but it suggests something else. A word's *denotation* is its literal meaning. Its *connotation* is the suggestion, feeling, and associations carried by the word. *House* and *home* have almost the same denotation, but *house* is a neutral word, whereas *home* evokes sentiment and feeling. "Without hearts there is no home," said Byron.

Because of the word color you may say, "a *gang* of thieves, but not "a gang of angels," for a group of angels is a *band* or *host.* Or you may say "a *bevy* of girls," but not "a bevy of bees," for a group of bees is a *swarm.* To say "She is *skinny,*" can never have the same color as "She is *slender.*"

The color and feeling of a word gives its persuasive power. Rudyard Kipling—whose persuasive words "taught England the meaning of Empire, and the Empire the meaning of England"—said with utter candor in the last interview before his death: "You must bait your hook with gaudy words. I used to search for words in the British Museum. I read mad poets." If misunderstood to mean exhibitionist words or big words, the advice is dangerous; but if you've read Kipling you won't make that mistake.

If you would persuade others, apply yourself to the study of words. In striving for accuracy, beware of drabness. Brighten your speech with words that give it color and audacity. No rules govern the mastery of word color and feeling, but the English language offers you sharp and flexible tools. Learn to use them to get the effect you want. Using colorful words is the third technique of language.

SENTENCES

After words come sentences, a technique not too difficult but too seldom learned. For brevity and emphasis we limit the treatment to three techniques in which unskillful speakers most often fail:

USE VERBS, NOT NOUN SUBSTITUTES

The verb is a motor. It propels the sentence. If you want the sentence to have power, work the verb hard. There are inept speakers who flinch from using a live verb. They put the heavy load on nouns, and let "is," or some such colorless verb-phrase like "results in," do the work that ought to be done by a real verb. These are the "noun-users."

The inveterate noun-user would not be caught dead saying, "I *think*," for *think* is a verb with power behind it, and the noun-user is afraid of it. Instead, he substitutes the inert noun, "thought," brings in the inactive verb, "is," and says "It *is* my thought *that*. . . ." Never would the noun-user say, "A stitch in time *saves* nine." That live verb is a fearful thing, so he turns the verb into a noun and says, "The advantage of timely stitching *is* ninefold." As for "*Spare* the rod and *spoil* the child," that is a two-motor sentence, and to the noun-user is unthinkable. Out go the verbs, in come the nouns, and we get "Insufficient corporal punishment *results in* lax discipline among our youth." In the same way "Haste *makes* waste," becomes "Precipitation *entails the negation of* economy."

Are these rigged examples, you ask? Pick up any copy of *Vital Speeches,* which carries speeches of American leaders of thought. Read them and note the noun-users. Listen to Town Hall, or any such radio broadcast, and list the noun substitutes. Even Charles Luckman, the soap wizard, said that because of a food shortage the American people should practice "economy in the use of certain foods through personal restraint." It took Robert A. Taft to turn it into King's English: "Eat less."

As a corollary to using verbs instead of noun substitutes, add the following principles:

1. *Be wary of the form, "It is . . . that . . . ."* Backward syntax, generally poor in writing, is worse in speech. Instead of saying "*It is* the response of the owner *that* is the criterion," better say, "*Ask* the man who *owns* one."

2. *Prefer active to passive verbs.* Passive verbs are useful, even indispensable, or they would not exist in the language. Use them for special effects. But for regular duty use active verbs. Some day when you have the time, count the comparative number of active and passive verbs used by Shakespeare, Shaw, Dickens—or Lincoln, Wilson, Roosevelt—and compare the ratio with those found in your old freshman themes. You might be startled at the higher percentage of active verbs used by masters of language.

STRIP ADJECTIVE AND ADVERBS

Said Voltaire, a master of language, "The adjective is the enemy of the noun." He might have added that the adverb is the enemy of the verb. Before establishing a standard for determining which modifiers to omit and which to use, remember that there are two kinds:

1. *Defining* modifiers: *hot* stove, *old* man, *sharp* curve. These tell something essential. They are necessary. You don't strip them.

2. *Commenting* modifiers: These might almost be called *cluttering* modifiers. In operating practice most commenting modifiers are cluttering: *very* necessary, *most* unique. (How can a thing be "very necessary"? Isn't "necessary" the ultimate? What is "most unique"? Consult a dictionary on what "unique" means.) The plain truth is that most cluttering modifiers come from not recognizing what the modified word means. Some speakers never say *large, small, hot, cold, glad, pleased, happy, nice.* Without thinking, they say:

very large	very glad
very small	very pleased
very hot	very happy
very cold	very nice

They never say *pleasant, entertaining, uplifting, unusual, exceptional, unique,* but attach *most:*

most pleasant	most unusual
most entertaining	most exceptional
most uplifting	most unique

Believe it or not, speakers—supposedly learned speakers—have been heard to describe an event as "most unusually unique." William Allen White, who thought *very* to be the most overworked word in the English language, once told Franklin P. Adams how to eliminate it. "Instead of *very,* write the word *damn,*" he said. "The proofreader will knock out the *damn*—and there you have a right good sentence." Unfortunately, the speaker has no such censor. He must do the job himself.

On this point P. I. Prentice, publisher of *Time,* explained the editorial policy of that magazine: "We try to save space with our verbs. . . . Why say 'walked vigorously' if we can say 'strode,' 'marched,' 'tramped,' or 'stomped' and be quicker as well as more explicit?"

STRIP EMPTY WORDS

There are two kinds of words, full words and empty words. Full words include verbs, nouns, and defining adjectives. Empty words include prepositions, conjunctions, adverbs, and relative pronouns. Full words are easy to grasp. When you hear *sneered,* you see in the mind's eye the raised lip and look of disdain. But when you hear *consequently,* you have no sharp mental picture; it really means "As a result of certain things described by this speaker, certain other things, yet unknown to me, resulted; and the speaker is now about to describe them." Therefore, empty words cause trouble. A few of them you must use—but make it an operating rule not to use three where you might use two.

First, avoid what Fowler in his *Dictionary of Modern English Usage* calls "compound prepositions and conjunctions." Here is a short list:

of the character of (like)	with a view to (to)
of the nature of (like)	with reference to (about)
with regard to (about)	with the result that (so that)
in the case of (if)	for the purpose of (for)
in the event that (if)	from the point of view of (for)

Second, use the connectives of everyday speech instead of those preserved for written use. Rudolf Flesch in *The Art of Plain Talk* rightly observes that the English language really has two sets of connectives—those used in everyday speech and those used almost exclusively for print. Here is a useful working list:

SPEECH	WRITING
and, also	likewise again moreover furthermore
but	however nevertheless notwithstanding on the contrary
so, therefore	thereupon consequently accordingly wherefore for this reason thus
for example	to illustrate more specifically to take a case
besides	in addition to
in other words	that is to say

Finally, learn to handle those relative pronouns, *which* and *that*. Masters of language strip them to a minimum. The unskillful use them excessively. Note these examples where masters of language drop a *that* or *which* obviously implied, but where speakers with a lesser touch would use them:

Do you think it strange [that] they should have heard this? ARCHIBALD MACLEISH

This is the only way [that or in which] we may have peace home or abroad. ERIC JOHNSTON

We read in the Bible [that] "Jeshurun waxed fat and kicked." WINSTON CHURCHILL

Also learn the difference between these two words. *That* is used more often in speech. *Which* is the bookish form. Students in giving speeches will use *which*—because they have memorized a written outline or the written speech. But after they sit down, let the instructor ask them about such-and-such idea in the speech—and in private speech they revert at once to *that.*

Students who would really master language, therefore, face learning a dual technique: (1) learning to strip the empty words that make sentences hard to understand quickly, and (2) learning to use the speech vocabulary connectives instead of the bookish ones.

BEYOND THE SENTENCES

Certain language techniques involve groups of sentences, especially Questions, Direct Quotes, Suspense, and Climax.

QUESTIONS

Questions arouse attention. They invite an answer from the listener. A battery of questions, therefore, will project an idea vividly:

> I am a Jew. *Hath not a Jew eyes? Hath not a Jew hands? If you prick us, do we not bleed? If you tickle us, do we not laugh? If you poison us, do we not die? And, if you wrong us, shall we not revenge?*

Shylock's bitterness is thus driven home by six *rhetorical questions*—i.e. questions so phrased that the answer is inevitable and hence not stated by the speaker.

Other questions are *direct questions*—where the speaker asks a question, then answers it, as illustrated by Dorothy Thompson:

> *How about manners?* On this subject . . .
>
> *What of moral philosophy?* Under the pressure of atheists and religious groups. . . .
>
> *Who is this mass man?* Do not believe for a moment that . . . .

Direct questions may also be used in a battery to give emphasis beyond the power of a single question, as done by Emerson P. Schmidt:

> *Where are we headed? Is the country going Socialist? Is there a new virus, "Controlism," which has a high incidence among politicians? Are we in for an Over-all Planned Economy? Is it the Welfare State? The Insurance State, or what?* We're on our way. *But where to?*

DIRECT QUOTATION

Direct Quotation is not to be confused with Testimony, even though both use quotation marks. Testimony is supporting an idea by quotation of authority: "Such-and-such expert says so-and-so about this idea." Direct quotation is a technique of language that allows listeners to see and hear others speak. They listen to the imaginary conversation, see the others talk in the mind's eye. Said Wendell Phillips in his eulogy on Daniel O'Connell:

As Lord Bacon marches down the centuries, he may lay one hand on the telegraph and the other on the steam-engine, and say, *"These are mine, for I taught you how to study Nature."* In a similar sense, as shackle after shackle falls from Irish limbs, O'Connell may say, *"This victory is mine; for I taught you the method, and I gave you the arms."*

It is used in many forms, especially making illustrations effective, as seen in Woodrow Wilson's direct quotation during his speech to the Southern Society of New York:

I remember the story of a Mississippi steamboat captain who had to tie up because a fog lay low on the river. The upper decks of the boat were left above the fog. If you stood on the upper deck you could see the clear heaven above you, but all the river bottom lay shrouded in mist, and one of the passengers, impatient to get on, said: *"Captain, why don't you go ahead?"* The captain replied, *"I can't see the way." "Well,"* said the passenger, *"you can see the north star." "Yes,"* said the captain, *"but we are not going that way."*

SUSPENSE

Suspense is creating a state of uncertainty, mixed usually with anxiety or expectation. An idea that moves toward a goal half-concealed and half-revealed will carry the listeners' interest to the end. This may be illustrated by a single sentence. To say, "The piers were crowded when the ship arrived," arouses no suspense. But turn the sentence around, and say, "When the ship arrived. . ." The meaning is suspended, and interest held, until the key is supplied, ". . . the piers were crowded." This is the technique of Suspense.

It may be applied to a subhead, an entire main head, or even a whole speech, as done by Bruce Barton:

My subject today is "How Long Should a Wife Live?" . . . Some years ago there was a celebration in Boston in honor of the landing of the Pilgrim Fathers. After several very laudatory speeches had been made by men a bright and vivacious woman was called on. Said she:

"I am tired of hearing so many praises of the Pilgrim Fathers. I want to say a word about the Pilgrim Mothers. They had to endure all that the Pilgrim Fathers endured, and they had to endure the Pilgrim Fathers besides."

Do you know what happened to the Pilgrim Mothers, my friends? I will tell you. They died. They died young. . . . For ten husbands, . . . there were eighteen wives. . .

"How Long Should a Wife Live?" The answer, in the old days, was "Not very long." The homes of those days had two or three mothers, and no motors. The homes of the future will lay all of this tiresome routine burdens on the shoulders of electrical machines, freeing mothers for their real work, which is motherhood.

CLIMAX

Climax is closely allied to suspense. It consists of arranging details in the order of increasing strength or importance. Note the effect of the following: "Her heart was full of bitterness, her face was flushed, and her dress was torn." It lets you down. It won't do. Rearrange it in climactic order: "Her dress was torn, her face was flushed, and *her heart was full of bitterness.*" Climax gives the last point an added punch.

Quentin Reynolds uses climax to give primacy to religion over temporal government:

> They saw the shrines of England in ruins. They saw the scars on the House of Commons and they saw the precious stained-glass windows of Westminster Abbey lying broken in the dust. The House of Commons has always been the symbol of free speech in Britain. . . . Westminster Abbey has always been the symbol of the Christian way of life.

The language mishandlers throw details together without thought of technique. Not the masters of language. They arrange details for climactic effect.

SUMMARY

Because you have been using words, don't assume that you know the technique of language. The technique is precise. It is complex. In a sense, it is scientific. Eleven of the basic techniques, those most useful for a speaker, have been discussed in this chapter. Three techniques involve words. Four involve sentences. Four involve groups of sentences. Improve your skill in these eleven techniques, and you will have a reasonable mastery of language.

ASSIGNMENTS

ON INCREASING THE UNDERSTANDING OF LANGUAGE TECHNIQUES

1. Analyze the following passages to determine which factors prevent each from being clear or forceful:

    a. It is with very much pleasure that I address you on such an auspicious occasion.

    b. When you are asked to get behind some high-sounding social project, remember that social-projects are nothing more than cleverly concealed socialism. Do we want socialism in this country? Let these misguided "liberals" who would bring us socialism under the guise of cleverly disguised "social projects," be known for what they really are.

    c. T. S. Eliot's poems start at home as all good poems do, but they end up everywhere as only the best poems do. Partly this is because his wisdom is native to him, and partly because his education has been right. He does not parade his learning, but there it is in his poems, and it is what makes them so solid and so satisfying.

    d. "Eight and seven-tenths decades ago, the pioneer worker in this continental area implemented a new group based on an ideology of free boundaries and initial conditions of equality. Now we are actively engaged in an overall evaluation of conflicting factors. We are met in an area of maximum activity among the conflicting factors to assign permanent positions to the units which have been annihilated in the process of atttaining a steady state. This procedure represents standard practice at the administrative level." *Richard D. Fay.*

2. Study a selected passage from one of the speeches in the Appendix of this book. List which of the eleven techniques discussed in this chapter were used effectively.

3. From any issue of *Vital Speeches* determine which speech seems to you to have the most effective language skill. Then determine which speech seems to you to have the least effective language skill. List and illustrate the language techniques found in the most effective speech. List those found in the least effective speech, and write a brief analysis on why the language skill is poor, and what techniques are needed to improve it.

4. Examine one of your old outlines. Or if you have recorded a speech in this course, listen to the playback. Write a brief report estimating your skill in the use of each of the eleven language techniques.

5. Listen to a radio or television speech. Make a brief report on the speaker's use of language techniques.

6. During the next round of class speeches, assess the demonstrated skill of each student as follows: First, during the speech list the techniques used with special skill, those used with fair skill, and those used poorly. Next, check your lists against the eleven techniques discussed in this chapter, and make out a list of those not used at all. Finally, in a sentence or two, give your judgment on what is most needed to improve the use of language skills. Hand your assessment to the instructor, who in turn will deliver to each student all of the judgments submitted on him.

ON IMPROVING THE USE OF LANGUAGE TECHNIQUES

7. List the violations of language techniques found in the following passages. Then rewrite and improve them by using one or more of the techniques set forth in this chapter.

a. Special emphasis has been placed on miniaturization and ruggedization of new equipment.
b. The trip was breathtaking. We saw so many things I can't describe them. Everywhere the scenery was wonderful. Such gorgeous foliage, such colorful sunsets. I shall remember them always.
c. It is a very unique book that I have just read, a book in the nature of a biography of Thomas A. Edison. It shows how Edison, even as a boy, was most unusual. It shows how Edison as a man developed into a genius who was most exceptional.
d. The Cardinals were playing the Eagles with the advantage in favor of neither. Then the Bird's Four Horsemen lined up behind their Seven Mules, and one of them took the pigskin nearly twice as far back as usual. But there was method in his madness, for when the Eagles closed in for the kill, he whanged the pellet to a fellow Horseman, and no sooner said than done the Birds had bonged the scoreboard for 6 points. We waited with bated breath for the goal kick.

8. Revise an old speech and improve its language skill. List the techniques used in the revision.

9. In preparing your next speech, check carefully to see whether you are using language techniques with reasonable skill. In the Technical Plot, left margin of the outline, note where you are making deliberate use of these techniques.

Part IV THE SPEAKER

In Winston Churchill listeners hear the overtones of Europe's high cultural tradition, and see art used to conceal art.

CHAPTER 16

Being Seen

CHAPTER 16

In Chapter 1 we saw that no one in reality can "deliver a speech," that what we commonly call "delivering a speech" is actually a process of *using light waves and sound waves to make listeners think what you are thinking.* In this chapter we shall consider the use of light waves, what the listeners see.

Why speakers use action

A significant thing about action is that when you ask the average listener he will say it is not important. Indeed in one survey only 27% of the people in selected audiences thought "gesture" was essential to good speaking, only 46% thought "coordinated body movement" was essential, and only 54% thought that even "animation" was essential.[1] If you ask listeners whether a given speaker did, in fact, use action, they are not likely to know, unless the speaker's action was distracting. Even *Time* reported that General Douglas MacArthur, in his famous 1951 speech before Congress, spoke "without bombast or gesture," whereas television showed him instead to be speaking without bombastic gesture, yet to be using a tremendous amount of total bodily activity. So widespread is the misunderstanding of what is meant by "gesture" and "action," that we should pause for a survey of its place in thinking and in communication.

ACTION IS AN INHERENT PART OF THINKING

What do we think with? Only the brain? Hardly. The brain is like a telephone exchange. It is useless without lines running into it from the outside. It is the switchboard, but not the whole system. Its function is to receive incoming signals, make proper connections, and send

[1] W. K. Clark, "A Survey of Certain Attitudes Toward Commonly Taught Standards of Public Speaking," *Speech Monographs*, XVIII (March, 1931), No. 1, 62-69.

messages through to their destination. For efficient service the body must function as a *whole.*

In Chapter 4 we spoke of the speaker's "mental attitude." A good phrase, but where is the "mind"? Is it in the brain? Or perhaps in the nervous system? After all, can we say that the mind is in any particular *place*? It is not a thing, like a leg, or even the brain. It is an activity, a function. Aristotle, twenty-three hundred years ago, observed that *the mind was to the body what cutting was to the ax.* When the ax is not in use, there is no cutting. So with the mind. "Mind," said Charles Henry Woolbert, "is what the body is doing." We don't think merely with the brain, or even with the nervous system, but with the brain, nerves, glands, and muscles, working together as a whole. The wooden dummy speaker is simply not thinking at his fullest.

Total activity is necessary for thinking. *Total activity is also necessary for carrying thought from one person to another.* You can't stand before others with heels clamped, muscles bound, face deadpan—and arouse thought. For half a million years people have talked with head, face, hands, and body—and you cannot abolish the habits of half a million years. Note how people go about ordinary conversation. If you have never really paid attention to this, you have a surprise in store. Good conversationalists nod their heads, shake their heads, lift their eyebrows, and let change of feeling play across their faces. Their shoulders shrug. They bend, turn, swing, and droop. Their hands are still hardly more than a few seconds at a time.

Now these people are not making speeches. They are merely common folk trying to make others understand what they have in mind. They are not conscious of using action. They are mere human beings, talking the way human beings have talked for half a million years.

In short, people really think all over, and people really talk all over. A public speaker must follow the code.

VISIBLE LANGUAGE IS OLDER THAN SPOKEN LANGUAGE, AND MORE BASIC

When Columbus discovered America he found copper-skinned natives who had been separated from peoples of the Old World for some 18,000 years. They spoke approximately 100 distinctly different word-languages, none of them related to the languages of Europe or Asia, *but these newly discovered natives shook their head for "no," and nodded their head for "yes," exactly as did Columbus' crew of Mediterranean sailors and as had the Greeks, Romans, Egyptians, Mesopotamians and all the others.* These newly-discovered natives raised their right arm to greet an approaching stranger, as had the knights of Medieval Europe. They turned palms down to express disapproval, palms up to express approval, and lifted their hands in supplication—as did other people everywhere in the world. They had a universal sign language by which they could talk to members of other tribes—and this sign language was almost identical with that used in other parts of the world, as in the Philippines.

Visible, or sign language is older than the spoken code. It is more uniform. It is written deeper into our organisms, and carries more basic meanings. We use spoken words for refined thought, but for the broad, deep basic meanings we use action. We are civilized, yes; but *the eye is still quicker than the ear.*

You are about to give a speech. Before you utter a word, you begin to talk with action to all who can see. Do you stand with a timid, uncertain stance, or with poise born of confidence? Do you thrust out a jaw belligerently, or smile with winning grace? Do you gaze with a frozen face and a fishy eye, or does change of thought and feeling travel across your face? *Every speaker gives two speeches simultaneously, one with words, and one with action.* If the listener's eyes and ears bring him the same message, he listens and is disposed to believe. But when words say one thing, and action says another, the listener usually lets the words go by and gives first attention to the action. Why? Action tells him the real meaning. There he sees the sickly grin, the false smile, the evasive glances, the random grimaces of confusion. This is the real speech, and the listener knows it. The eye *is* quicker than the ear, and sign language *is* older than spoken language.

But the real use of action is to supplement and interpret words rather than to take their place. "When you call me that, smile!" said Owen Wister's character in *The Virginian* to the man who saluted him with an epithet. "Do you know what you are singing about?" Arturo Toscanini asked a soloist during a rehearsal of Beethoven's *Ninth Symphony.* "You are singing of brotherhood, but in your face you look like you hate everyone." Words and action, they are two separate forms of talk. You cannot say "I will use only words, and not action." You will use both, whether you will or no.

ACTION HOLDS ATTENTION

Did you ever lean forward, muscles tense, while watching an athletic contest? Did you ever feel your muscles pulling and pushing as if to throw a ball, make a catch, shoot a basket, or do any of the things the players are doing? Whether you know it or not, you assuredly have engaged in this sort of mimicry. It is the spectator's basis of understanding and enjoyment.

This phenomenon is known as *empathy*. It may be defined as *feeling ourselves into* whatever we perceive. All perception, in fact, involves this participation. We not only wind up with the pitcher, swing with the batter, and breast the tape with the sprinter, but also feel ourselves into static situations. When we see a painting or stand before a cathedral, our like or dislike hinges largely on whether the object evokes pleasant or unpleasant stresses and tensions in our bodies. To be sure, we are unconscious of this participation, as we are of our breathing or our heartbeat. But it nevertheless influences our behavior profoundly.

Now apply this to the audience. *Unconsciously they imitate the speaker*. The speaker has no option whatever on whether or not his gestures will affect the audience, for his gestures *must* affect them in one of three ways:

1. If he uses too little action, empathy in the audience will be weak. Because it is weak, the audience will not remain physically alert, but will relax more and more into physical (and therefore mental) inaction. But the more one relaxes, the less active the mind becomes, until in complete inactivity one goes to sleep—complete relaxation. So the speaker who uses no action puts his audience into a state too near to sleep for them to follow alertly what he is saying. They will sit and half listen; but, when he is through, they will recall little of what he has said.

2. If the speaker uses uncontrolled gestures, gestures that he never intended to use and often does not know he is using, the audience will be drawn into fitful and distracting responses. We have all seen the speaker who buttons his coat and then unbuttons it, or twists a handkerchief in his hands, or rocks up and down on his toes, or moves an object on the table before him from one place to another, then to another . . . and to another. "If he moves that watch again, I'll scream," whispered a woman after a speaker had put his watch in

twelve or fifteen places over the table. She did not scream, but neither did she listen to what he was saying. She was waiting for him to move that watch! So with all people. They are distracted by their empathetic reactions to a speaker's uncontrolled movements.

3. If the speaker uses controlled action, communicative action, listeners are roused to participate. They are lifted to alert attention. They find it easier to follow what the speaker is saying. Whenever listeners are deeply impressed, they almost always are moved to empathy. They participate, "feel in," and give the speaker sustained attention.

"Must I use gesture?" asks a timid, or diffident, or nervous student. The frank answer is that you can't say "No" to life. Action is part of the thinking process. Action is a universal sign language far older than spoken words. Action rouses attention. Action is inherent in good private conversation. Add it up yourself.

ASSIGNMENTS

1. Prepare and give a two-minute speech on empathy. To prepare this speech, attend an athletic contest, an exciting motion picture, a circus, a vaudeville performance, or any other event where you will witness alert bodily movements. (a) Observe carefully the stresses and tensions of your own body, and (b) observe the behavior of those around you. Do they "feel in" with the performer? Is this "feeling in" revealed chiefly by leaning forward with tension? Or does it break out into the open so that the spectator tenses or relaxes, moves to right or left, with the performer?

2. Practice in your room and demonstrate in class vigorous and appropriate action on the following:

   a. "Halt! Who's there? . . . Advance and be recognized!"
   b. "I mean it. I propose to stand here. Not to move, but to stand *here*."
   c. "Will you listen, please? What else could we have done? What else did we have a *right* to do?"

Making action effective

Effective action hardly seems like action at all. It appears to be natural, spontaneous, done on the impulse. Indeed, action that is conspicuous, that calls attention to itself, is bad for the obvious reason that it distracts from the speaker's thought instead of communicating it. The good speaker never seems to be gesturing at all. He is merely a person who makes you understand him, and who happens to use light waves as well as sound waves. Hence the adage, "Great art conceals art." Note the constituent parts of this art:

GESTURE WITH THE WHOLE BODY

Wrote Henry James, novelist, of the great English actress Fanny Kemble, "Mrs. Kemble is of all women in the world the most *toute d'une pièce*. If she does so little as to button her glove, she does it with her whole body." What James really said was that Fanny Kemble knew the basic secret of success in public performance: to move all-in-one-piece. Even in dumb animals the rule holds. A lively kitten is graceful; it moves all-in-one-piece, head, feet, and body. A puppy is awkward and ludicrous; it moves in several pieces at once, its body is too eager for its legs and its head is too heavy for its body. People are about equally divided between the awkward and the graceful. In the athlete we see all-in-one-piece action at its best. The sprinter does not run with legs and feet alone; he runs with his whole body. The pitcher does not throw with his arm alone; he throws with his whole body. This is the first principle of effective action: It is all-in-one-piece, made with the whole body.

If you want to be ludicrous, make gestures without this teamwork of muscles. Whether intending to be funny or not, you will be. The actor Charles P. Sale attained his first reputation in character parts by "speaking a piece" with detached gestures. His arms and hands moved like a puppet's pulled by strings. For an added punch he would throw in, now and then, a hand movement that came a shade too soon, or too late. He was never all-in-one-piece, but gave the effect of an immature person who had studied gestures as a technical thing and was following the rule without the spirit.

Now suppose we put into practical operation this principle of all-in-one-piece action. Stand before a mirror and assume a good speaking posture. Then give the following sentence with vigor and strength:

> Government *of* the *people*, *by* the *people*, and *for* the *people*, shall not perish from the earth.

The action involves every part of your physical being—hand, arm, shoulder, head, torso, leg, knee, ankle, and foot—with a gesture *built into* the whole-body action, and not "something added on." In this manner, emphasize the words *of*, *by* and *for* with any type of hand gesture—putting the body behind it all-in-one-piece. Now try it again with the head and torso perfectly still, using only the arm and hand. Note that such action is good for a funnyman in vaudeville, but not platform speaking. Finally, go back to the all-in-one-piece action, and work on it with (1) the right arm, (2) left arm, (3) both arms.

TALK TO THE AUDIENCE, NOT TO YOURSELF

In the early stages of speaking you are likely to engage in disorganized action. Typical of this is licking your lips, loosening the collar, adjusting clothes, smoothing hair, and shifting feet. Or your posture may slump, and thereby produce the notorious drooping hip and sagging knee. You may be startled to find that your hands have grown to enormous size; you cannot conceal their size from the audience, so you try to get them out of the way, behind your back, or in your pockets. These actions are symptons of inner emotions. Unwittingly, but with deadly effect, you are telling the audience that you are not in control of the situation. We have discussed this under Chapter 4 (pages 60-66), both causes and treatment.

There remains a milder form of disorganized action to be discussed here, namely *self-directed gestures. This is the tendency of speakers to gesture to themselves* instead of to the audience. It takes various forms:

1. You clamp the elbows tightly against your body and gesture toward your face.

2. You guard the stomach with your forearm, often using the hand for a weak gesture but keeping that arm-block between you and the audience.

3. Or you may reach out arms and elbows toward the audience, but still keep the palms—the real carrier of meanings—turned toward your face.

Now self-directed action is not really a problem of action at all. The real cause is your mental attitude. First, you are thinking about *yourself*, and not the audience. You have missed that "vivid sense of the brotherhood of man" in which your job is to *help* the audience. (When you start helping people you are no longer afraid of them.) Further, you are not excited, or even enthusiastic, over what you have to say. Once you get enthusiastic, once you lose yourself in the subject, you will literally "forget yourself into good speaking." The best cure that ever was for platform jitters is to put your message ahead of your ego.

Effective action talks to the audience, not to the speaker. But get first things first. *When your action fails to talk to the audience, the trouble is not with "gesturing." It is with the mental, emotional, and moral state of the speaker. You cannot talk for the sake of helping others—and at the same time gesture to yourself. You cannot be afire for people to hear you—all the people, even those on the back row—without reaching out to them with action as well as voice.*

BE DEFINITE

Effective action should point, indicate, suggest, separate, emphasize—carry some particular *definite* meaning—and should be so clean-cut that the audience can have no doubt what that meaning is.

Definite hand action involves three phases: the *approach*, the *stroke*, and the *return*.

The *approach* is the "get ready" movement. It is like raising a gun to take aim. You make this approach well ahead of time and you hold it until you are ready for the emphatic stroke. If we use the illustration, "Government of the people, by the people, and for the people, shall not perish from the earth," the best approach of the gesture should begin even before speaking the first word, "government."

The *stroke* carries the meaning. It is like pulling the trigger. Applied to the illustration, when the word *of* is spoken put your weight behind that word—carry it out to the audience with a four-to-eight-inch stroke of your hand, and time the stroke exactly with the utterance of the word. Now raise the hand to its original position and repeat the stroke on the word *by*. Raise it for a third time, and repeat again on the word *for*.

The *return* is the "as you were." After you have held the idea before the audience long enough for them to see it fully (don't hurry this and don't backlash your gestures), you simply let the hand fall to the side in its original position. Avoid bringing it back in wide curves. Just let it fall naturally.

Two kinds of indefinite gestures are habitual to beginners. Learn to recognize them and you will know why you don't want to be caught using them.

1. *The Off-Beat Gesture.* An old trick of comedians, still almost as good as fifty years ago, is to provoke a laugh by off-timing a gesture. They come in a shade late, on the off-beat, and the audience laughs. Students often do this too, in dead seriousness and without meaning to be funny, and the effect is even funnier than a comedian's because it is unintended. The student is "speaking with gestures," and the gestures say, "I don't like to do this, but the instructor says to gesture and I need a grade." The speaker, of course, looks as silly as he feels. The stroke of a gesture should fall *exactly* on (or precede by a split second) the emphatic syllable.

2. *The No-Stroke Gesture.* The "no-stroke" gesture has *two* parts instead of three—the approach and the return, but no stroke. It is not funny or silly like the off-beat gesture, but it is inadequate. The meaning of a hand gesture is carried by the stroke. The no-stroke gesture has no stroke, hence no meaning. It is only a lurch, lame and impotent.

USE VIGOR

Effective action can't be halfway or timid. It can't be flabby. It can't be held in, and let out by degrees. It can't be tentative. To have real action you must crash through inhibition and restraint, and throw weight and vigor behind it.

In beginning your training, therefore, overdo. Use abundant action. Use action with punch and power. Use it with freedom and abandon. Later on you can tone down and discipline its form, but seek first to crash through inhibition and restraint.

ADAPT ACTION TO THE NATURE AND SIZE OF THE AUDIENCE

Every speaker truly sensitive to the audience soon discovers that the amount of action needed, and even the type of action, varies with the kind of audience, the size of audience, and the occasion.

Young people are restless and energetic, unable to sit still long at a time. Young listeners demand a large amount of action, and frankly if a speaker does not deliver enough their minds wander away. Hence sedentary intellectuals generally make poor speakers for young audiences, and many a famous authority on Ovid and Browning and nuclear fission is barely endurable to college students in class room lectures. Yet they need not be, as witnessed by William James and

William Lyon Phelps whose classes overflowed. Likewise, audiences of farmers, workers, or any who engage in physical activity, require more action than sedentary workers. If they don't get enough, many will go to sleep outright. In contrast, older people, especially older sedentary people, and most especially older sedentary intellectuals, are irritated by too much action or too-vigorous action. To them it is coarse and intemperate. To an earnest speaker such people at times may seem to be afflicted by white-livered indifference and to be annoyed by earnest conviction—but it is not exactly this. To be sure, such listeners will never be persuaded to lead a crusade or vote for a new order, and many are annoyed by earnest conviction, but basically they are people who lead placid physical lives. The empathy of watching a too-active speaker wearies them.

The *size of audience* determines the expanse of action. Before a large crowd a speaker uses a wide sweep of gesture and the uplifted arm. Plutarch describes ancient speakers as "holding up their hands to Heaven" when addressing outdoor multitudes; and speakers today in addressing large crowds use the same wide sweep and the same uplifted arm. Yet before a small audience these would be out of place if not ridiculous. There a short sweep is best, as a quarter sweep of the forearm or merely a hand hinged at the wrist.

Finally, the amount of action varies also with the *occasion.* A stately, dignified occasion demands little, or at least only a moderate amount. A rally—political or athletic—demands far more. The amount of action perfectly fitted to a Sunday sermon might easily be too much for a funeral service.

ASSIGNMENTS

ON STUDYING THE EFFECT OF ACTION

1. Study the action of a flagrantly bad speaker: preacher, politician, teacher, fellow classmate, or anyone who is invariably dull.

   a. Study this speaker's muscular tone. Does his posture suggest muscular or mental alertness? Does it suggest inertness or flabbiness? Does it suggest rigidity or tension? Does he gesture with the whole body? Does he co-ordinate the ankles, knees, hips, torso, shoulders, arms, elbows, wrists, fingers, neck, and head? Which parts are used? Which are not used? Did his action "talk to the audience," or "talk to himself"? Was it definite? Was it vigorous?

b. Study the empathy of the audience. Do most of them follow the speaker with an alert eye? Do any appear to be drowsy? Do some avoid looking at the speaker? Do they respond physically to the speaker's action? Do they tend to relax into emotional and physical lassitude?

c. Write a paper on your assessment of the speaker's action and the audience's response.

2. Do the same thing with a notably good speaker.

3. Attend a social gathering and study the posture, muscular tone, and general bodily action of some person who is supposed to have social poise. Note the changes of posture. Note the kinds and amounts of action when meeting different people. If you have time, do the same with a person who is obviously ill at ease. What are your general conclusions?

4. Walk through a department store or other large retail establishment and observe the behavior of the clerks. Note their posture and muscular tone. Study the expressions on their faces. Observe their total bodily activity. What are your conclusions?

5. Study your reaction to the posture and action of fellow classmates. Do they get mentally organized before coming to the platform? Do they talk first with words or actions? What do their first actions tell you? What conclusions do you draw about your own posture and action?

ON FREEING INHIBITION AND DEVELOPING ACTION

Practice the following exercises in your room and be ready if necessary to repeat them in class. Follow these directions:

a. Use *spontaneous* action, not planned action. Pay no attention to rules, elegance, or correctness, but act on impulse.

b. Use *abundant* action; avoid timid, restrained, or half-hearted movements.

c. Use the *whole* body, all-in-one-piece.

d. First try simply to express your thought and feeling. Later repeat the exercise in front of a mirror and observe how it would look to others.

6. "He knifed through tackle and started for the goal, sixty yards away. A sure touchdown! Then out from nowhere came Hurry Up McCammon. He hit that fellow so hard the ball bounced four feet in the air, and three of our men landed on it!"

7. "I looked out the window—we were flying at only 2,000 feet—and there was New York coming slowly toward us. The Statue of Liberty passed by on our left, looking small as a ten-cent toy. Steamships below us moved like bugs that walk on the water. Ahead were the skyscrapers. But from the air they didn't scrape the sky. They were only toys made to imitate the real skyscrapers you see from the streets. In fact, from the air all New York was a toyland, and I felt like Gulliver landing in Lilliput."

8. "Hush! Here he comes! Don't let him see you! That's right, follow me. To the left. Watch that low beam. Wait a moment while I close the door and find the light. Whew! That was a close call!"

9. "They tell us, sir, that we are weak. But when shall we be stronger? Will it be the next week, or the next year? Will it be when we are totally disarmed, and when a guard shall be stationed in every house? Shall we gather strength by irresolution and inaction? Sir, we are not weak, if we make proper use of those means which the God of nature has placed in our power. Three millions of people, armed in the holy cause of liberty, and in such a country as that which we possess are invincible."

10. "How ill this taper burns! Ha! who comes here?
I think it is the weakness of my eyes
That shapes this monstrous apparition.
It comes upon me. Art thou any thing?
Art thou some god, some angel, or some devil,
That mak'st my blood cold, and my hair to stare?—
Speak to me what thou art."

ON USING DEFINITE ACTION

11. Standing before a mirror practice the three phases of hand action, counting to five as follows:

1 2 3	4	5
approach	stroke	return

12. Now change the count, make the action with a wider sweep:

1 2 3 4	5	6 7
approach	stroke	return

13. Use the action practiced just above to carry the following meanings:

a. The first thing to remember is this. . . .

b. Would you people at the back mind coming down to the front rows?

c. I'm sorry, Jim, I can't do it.

d. Here's another side to the question we haven't yet considered. . . .

e. A horse. A horse! My kingdom for a horse!

f. There is a tide in the affairs of men,
Which, taken at the flood, leads on to fortune.

g. I'll sing you a song of the world and its ways,
And the many strange people we meet—
From the rich man who rolls in his millions of wealth,
To the struggling wretch on the street.

Kinds of action

OVERT AND COVERT ACTION

Action is really of two kinds, overt and covert. Overt action is conspicuous movement like walking on the platform, nodding the head, turning the body, or lifting an arm. *Covert* action is the more subtle, but usually more significant, muscle sets and tensions that tell you the mood, state of mind, and often the character itself, of the person talking. *Covert* action tells you that this person is hesitant, uncertain, insecure—or is conceited, overconfident, flamboyant. *Covert* action tells you that this person is exultant or elated—or is dejected or despondent. *Covert* action tells you that this person is headlong, impetuous—or is cautious, wary.

Obviously, covert action is not voluntary, like nodding the head or lifting an arm. It arises from muscular and glandular systems inside the body. A child stands in front of a window filled with candy. He is standing stock still, and at first you might say "He's not doing anything," or "He's looking at the candy." But a second look will tell you that his posture and face are saying, "I want that candy," and you know that his salivary glands are overworking, his stomach is contracting and expanding, his blood pressure is up, and his endocrine glands are pumping fluids into his blood. You don't see this terrific internal activity; you do see the hungry look in the boy's face and posture. What you see is *covert* action. Rather it is the outward signs of covert action; and when you see these outward signs you infer the inner action and react to it.

Apply this to speaking. A student is reading Kipling's, "If you can . . . walk with kings—nor lose the common touch, . . . you'll be a man, my son!" His overt action is perfect. Every gesture is fitting, well-timed, well-executed. But he does not fool you at all! By his *covert* action you know that down inside he does not *feel* Kipling's majestic test of a man. He is only reciting lines with gestures.

In contrast, you see an actor or reader—it may be Desdemona in *Othello,* Nora in *A Doll's House,* or Ruth Draper in one of her superb interpretations—speak their most dramatic lines while standing perfectly still. They are without a single overt movement. But their covert action—bodily set, tilt of head, total muscular tension—tells you of their intense feeling within. You find that your body has caught the same muscle sets and tensions. Empathy, of course.

Again, you watch a student go forward to give a class speech. By his covert action as he walks, by the way he stands in that moment of pause before starting to speak, by the muscular set of his body and his face, you can tell much—very much—of his inner state of mind.

In speaking, you are not privileged to choose whether you will use overt action, or covert action, or neither, or both. You will use both, willingly or unwillingly, knowingly or unknowingly, as man has been doing for half a million years. Your only choice is whether you will bungle them, or master them.

The procedures and would-be rules set forth in this chapter largely apply to the overt action—the obvious and major movements of the head, hands, and body. *Covert* action is not easily controlled, for it springs from glandular secretions and inner muscle action. It is talk from the inside, the real person-that-you-are. How, then, do you learn to master covert action? You don't learn it. You learn rather to master yourself. The best way to seem sincere is to *be* sincere. The best way to seem earnest is to *be* earnest. Even in interpreting the lines of poetry or plays, the best way is to *revive the author's feelings in your imagination.* As Ruth Chatterton stated it, "Really good acting does not require 'technique,' but only a fine sensitiveness to situation." Constantine Stanislavsky put it even more precisely: "In order to make the public listen to the fine shades of your feelings, you have to experience them intensely yourself." What Miss Chatterton and Stanislavsky both omitted in their quick statements was that the art of developing a fine sensitiveness to situation and fine shades of feeling are techniques of high order.

PLATFORM MOVEMENT

Movement on the platform is not essentially different from movement anywhere else. You should avoid two extremes, the extreme of standing stock-still throughout the speech and the other extreme of moving constantly like a caged animal. Entire lack of movement tends to lose audience interest and let their minds wander. Too much movement tends to distract attention.

In general, effective platform movement is made forward and backward, instead of from side to side. Side-to-side movement often signifies only nervous pacing. Forward and backward movement, on the other hand, is part of the half-million-year-old visible code. People step closer to others, or lean toward them, when they are deeply in earnest or want to be especially emphatic. Speakers do the same thing.

Backward movements, though not necessary, are useful at times to indicate divisions of the speech. They are like chapter headings or paragraph indentations in print. In effect they say to listeners, "I now come to a new part of the subject."

Remember especially that as a speaker you are the center of all eyes. Every movement catches the eyes of the audience. Therefore school yourself to firm self-control, make all movements purposeful, and avoid those that betray only restlessness and nervousness.

Now all this rather homely advice may seem unnecessary. It may seem like saying what everybody knows. But remember that speakers on the platform are under nervous tension. This tension tends to find outlet in aimless wandering, toying with objects, and other distracting movement, until finally it becomes a habit. Habit is a powerful force. You had best get it on your side from the first. What you do in practice you will more likely do later in performance. From the start, therefore, practice controlled posture and movement.

ASSIGNMENTS

ON STUDYING COVERT ACTION

Study the covert action of various types of speakers as listed below, using the following main lines of analysis:

a. Was the speaker free from restraint, extreme reserve, or self-consciousness? Was he phlegmatic? Was he awkward? Was he fidgety? Was he spontaneous, intense, dynamic?
b. What were the cues that told you of his mood and inner state of mind? Muscle tensions? Posture? Muscular tone of the whole body? of the head? face? shoulders? arms and hands? torso? legs?
c. What did these cues tell you about the speaker's momentary feelings? His personality? His character?
d. Did you at any time "feel in," with the speaker? If so, describe this in detail.

1. An especially intense scene in a moving picture, stage, or television play.
2. A salesman in a store; or better, one making a house-to-house canvass.
3. Your companions at the dinner table engaged in discussing a hot campus topic.
4. Someone trying to persuade you to quit studying and go to a show.

5. A student telling about last night's date.

6. A lively living-room conversation.

7. Your most interesting teacher.

8. Your least interesting teacher.

9. Live shots of nationally known speakers as seen in the News Reels or over television.

ON DEVELOPING PLATFORM MOVEMENT

10. In matters of the speaker's appearance, perhaps the mirror is the best and frankest critic. Use it freely. If you do not have access to a full-length glass, an ordinary dresser mirror will suffice. By tilting it at different angles, you may observe every part of the body.

11. Standing before the mirror, study your bodily and facial appearance for poise, alertness, self-control, and friendliness. Are all details such as to command respect and interest?

12. Still before the mirror, try out various movements and note the effect. Learn to recognize nervous and unhelpful movements and to eliminate them. Step backward and forward while repeating sentences. Come forward on the emphatic parts. Drop back as the thought changes. Make all movements purposeful and easy.

13. Work out a relationship between change of thought and change in movement or posture. Figure out how you can "paragraph" a speech while you are giving it.

14. Practice in your room and demonstrate in class suitable posture and movements to communicate the meaning of the following passages:

a. "But here, my friends, is the most important aspect of the matter." (Try stepping forward to emphasize its importance.)
b. "So much for this side of the question. Now let us consider it in another light." (Would you step backward to emphasize the change of thought?)
c. "Do you ask why we oppose the measure? Then consider these facts."
d. "So I appeal from the men in silken hose [i.e. from the old South] who danced to music made by slaves and called it freedom, from the men in bell-crowned hats [i.e. from old New England] who led Hester Prynne to her shame and called it religion, to that Americanism which reaches forth its arms to smite wrong with reason and truth." (Would you actually move? or turn? or punctuate the contrasts by the shifting of weight?)

15. Practice the following exercises in your room until you get the feeling of ease and control; then demonstrate them in class:

a. Walking to the platform as though you had something important to say.

b. Moving forward and backward on the platform so as to emphasize a point or to turn from one idea to another.
c. Standing behind a speaker's table, with your hands resting *lightly* on it, but your weight resting fully on the feet.
d. Shifting the weight from one foot to the other without walking.

BASIC HAND ACTION

Posture, covert action, and platform movement tell of the speaker's mood, state of mind, personality, and even character. Details of thought and feelings are also carried by overt action of the hands. The following six types of hand action are a universal sign language, older in the human race than words, and understood by people regardless of whatever word-language they use:

1. *Locating.* You point to an idea or a thing. "A hundred years ago," you say—as you point behind you to indicate that you are speaking of the past. "Tomorrow," you say—as you point forward to indicate the future. "This idea," "that principle," "yonder map," "at the right," "on the left," "before us"—all such things are pointed out for the eye of the listener. In a sense, they "see" what you are talking about.

2. *Dividing.* You have a series of facts or ideas, and you want them to be kept separate and distinct in the listeners' minds. Therefore, you use dividing action. "On the one hand, liberals say . . . ,"—while with the palm held vertically you put the liberals on your left. "On the other hand, conservatives say . . . ,"—while with the same action you put the conservatives on your right. In the same way, "this vs. that," or "first, second, third," are divided by the hand into their separate parts. In print, you can divide ideas with subtitles and paragraph indentations. In speech, you use dividing action.

3. *Describing or imitating.* This type of action suggests the shape, size, or movement of things. "It was this long," you say—and measure the distance with both hands. "It was so high," you say—as you measure the height from the floor up to your palm. "It was round"—and with both hands you round it out. In the same way you indicate movement. "It winds through the valley"—and you trace its winding with a finger. Or "It zoomed by"—and you suggest the zoom with a hand.

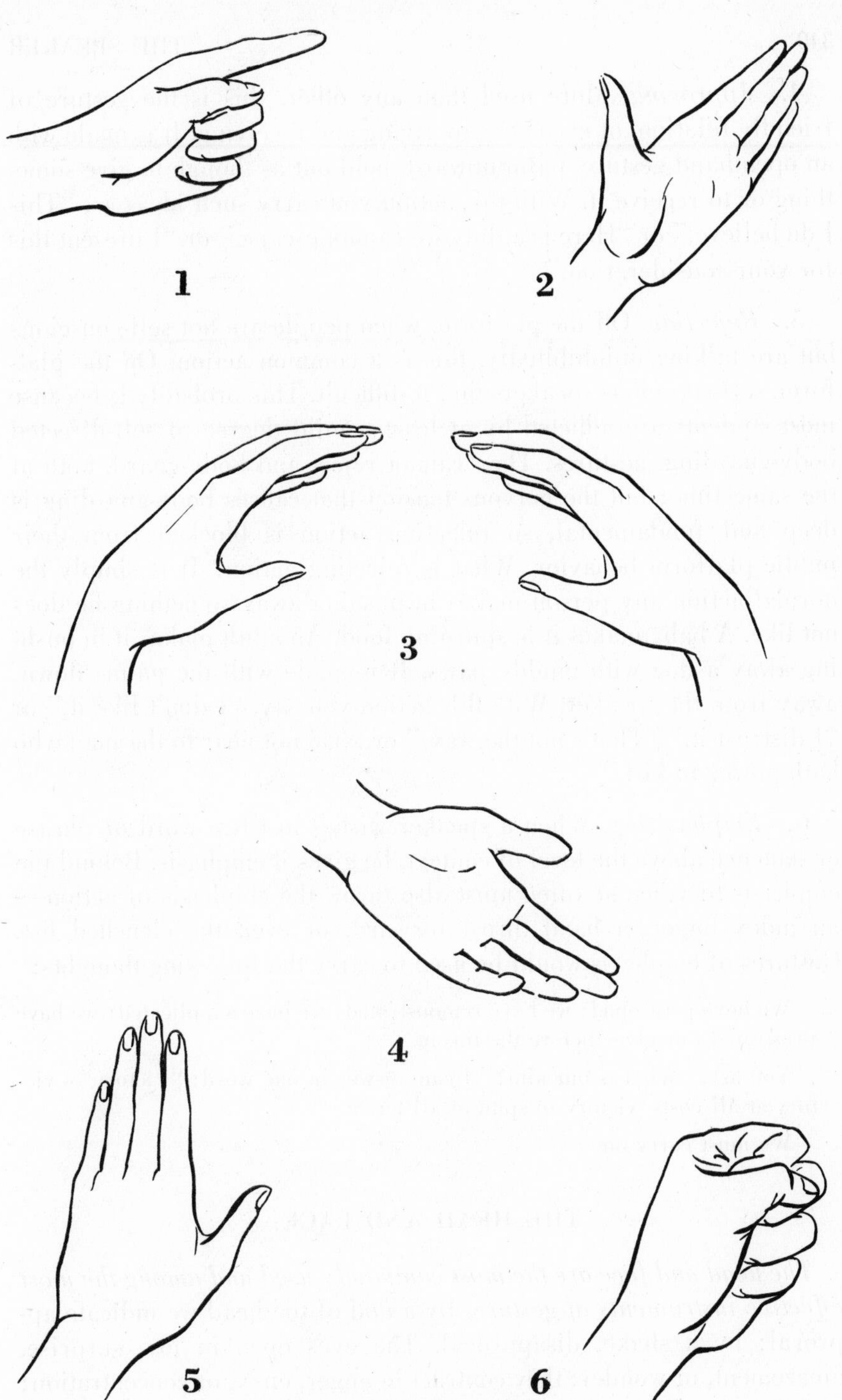

BASIC HAND ACTION

4. *Approving.* More used than any other, this is the gesture of friendly relation, of exchange, of giving and receiving. It is made with an open hand gesture, palm upward, held out as though to give something or to receive it. With this action you carry such ideas as, "This I do believe," or "Here is a duty we cannot escape," or "I present this for your consideration."

5. *Rejecting.* Off the platform, when people are not self-conscious but are talking uninhibitedly, this is a common action. On the platform, self-conscious speakers find it difficult. This probably is because most students are afflicted by at least a mild degree of self-directed body-guarding, gestures. They cannot reject and body-guard, both at the same time; but the nervous tension that causes body-guarding is deep and fundamental, so rejecting action is blocked from their public platform behavior. What is rejecting action? It is simply the normal action any person makes in pushing away something he does not like. A baby makes it in spurning food. An adult makes it in pushing away a dog with muddy paws. It is made with the palms down, away from the speaker. With this action you say, "I don't like it," or "I distrust it," "That's not the way," or, "Go not near to the man who hath power to kill."

6. *Emphasizing.* When a speaker wishes to lift a word or phrase or sentence above the level of context, he gives it emphasis. Behind the emphasis of voice he often must also throw the emphasis of action—an index finger, a hand thrust forward, or even the clenched fist. Gestures of emphasis would be used to carry the following thoughts:

> We have petitioned; we have remonstrated; we have supplicated; we have prostrated ourselves before the throne.
>
> You ask, "What is our aim?" I can answer in one word: "Victory"—victory at all costs, victory in spite of all terror.
>
> We must carry on.

THE HEAD AND FACE

The head and face are the most commonly used and among the most effective instruments of gesture. By a nod of the head we indicate approval; by a shake, disapproval. The eyes open in joy, surprise, amazement, or wonder; they contract in anger, envy, or concentration; and they sparkle with happiness or glitter in wrath. Lips may curve into a smile, or curl in contempt; they may be pulled down in a frown, or pursed into a straight line of determination. Good conversationalists use these symbols in private speech; good speakers use them in public speech.

ASSIGNMENTS

ON OBSERVING ACTION IN OTHERS

1. Study the photographs of speakers as found in speech textbooks, magazines, and newspapers. Study both overt and covert action.
   a. What does the covert action tell you of the speaker's true emotional state? His personality?
   b. What overt action is he using? Include body, head position, facial expression, and hand action.
   c. Is it spontaneous? Or posed? Or self-directed? Or phlegmatic?
   d. Does it seem to carry his ideas or feelings?

2. Hear some speaker. Using the main points of this chapter as your basis of judgment write an analysis of his audience contact, posture, and action.

3. Analyze some speaker's action. In one column write the statement he reinforces by gesture. In an opposite column note the kind of action used. Note whether he tended to use one type of gesture (as, for example, locating gestures) more effectively or more extensively than others. Note also whether he conspicuously lacks any of the six kinds of action described on pages 338-340.

ON DEVELOPING ACTION

4. In the privacy of your room examine your face in a mirror, and find out to what extent you use it in carrying thought: (1) Raise both eyebrows, then raise each one separately. (2) Wrinkle your forehead. (3) Spread your lips into a wide smile. (4) Lift each corner of your mouth, then try to lift both at the same time. (5) Draw down the corners of each side of your mouth, then try to draw down both at the same time. (6) Pucker your lips. (7) Purse your lips. (8) Set them in a straight line. (9) Take a selection in this book and read it; as you read try to *show in your face* the emotion of the words. (10) Compare yourself with actors you have seen on the screen. Where are you weakest? What do you want to do about it?

5. Before a mirror work on each of the six types of hand action described in this chapter. Be careful to get the action out toward your image in the mirror. Note whether your open palm is clean and neat. Or are your fingers cupped? Or are they awry, pointing in different directions? Note whether your index gesture is centered in the forefinger. Or is your thumb thrust up like a flagpole?

6. In your room practice the following until you get the feeling behind them; then demonstrate your mastery in class:

a. Getting the *whole* body into all action.
b. Using the *approach, stroke,* and *return* in hand action.
c. Freeing the wrist so that action will not seem wooden.
d. Getting the hand *open* instead of leaving the fingers curled and awry.
e. Turning the palm toward the audience.
f. Using *both* hands, instead of one only as beginners tend to do.

7. In your room practice the following passages and demonstrate before the class your ability to communicate them. Among the kinds of action that will be needed are: *the total body, stepping forward or backward, shifting of weight, head emphasis, facial expression:*

a. "Come over here, will you please? I have a problem I want you to look at. . . . It is here on page 12, the fourth problem."
b. "There they came! A thin column of soldiers advancing with the slow step of a funeral procession. Shells screamed overhead. Occasional bullets kicked the dust at their feet. But they went forward with dead, plodding steps—up and out of sight beyond the slope."
c. "Ladies and gentlemen: we ask you to believe in us and to have faith in us. We have not succeeded, not entirely succeeded, at least. But we have made progress. We have fought the good fight; we have kept the faith; and we have followed the course, not for ourselves but for you."
d. "Step forward, please. . . . No, that's too much! Back about two inches. . . . There, that's about right. Now to the left two feet or so. . . . Too much! To the right a little. . . . Hold it! That's exactly right."

8. Read the following short paragraph until you have it word-perfect; then practice communicating it with action:

> Nor must a young man compare himself with others or measure his success by theirs. It makes no difference how other men succeed. Their success is theirs; not yours. It matters nothing to me that Edison can invent the electric light and I can't; that Kipling can write a "Recessional" and I can't; that you can plead the law and I can't. You can do one thing; I try to do another. But success is for both of us just so far as we do well what we can do. Every man is himself, and it is in proportion as he gets out of himself the power there is within him that he succeeds—succeeds in doing the thing he is best fitted to do.
>
> EDWARD BOK

In actual public speaking, gestures should be made spontaneously. But, when you are learning to make them, practice drills are helpful just as with music—

or with football. Let us, therefore, devise specific gestures for the paragraph by Bok, gestures to be used in specific places for purposes of practice.

Give the first sentence without any hand gesture at all. On the second sentence, "It makes no difference how other men succeed," you want to express the idea of negation. Obviously you will use your head, shake it so as to say "no." At the same time use a rejecting gesture (palm down) carried well to the side as though you were putting the idea away from you. Now take the third sentence, "Their success is theirs; not yours." Suppose you use an emphasizing gesture with the index finger. Let the stroke fall on the word *their* and again on the word *theirs.* Accompany these two gestures with a vigorous nod of the head for additional emphasis. Now revert to the type of gesture in sentence two. Again use a *rejecting* gesture (palm down), and shake your head as you say *not yours.* In the sentence beginning "It matters nothing to me," suppose, for variety, that you try the hand opposite to that used in sentence two. Again we are expressing negation, with the palm down. Put the stroke on the word *nothing,* on *light,* and on *can't.* Now, in the next sentence, "You can do one thing; I try to do another," make an *approving* gesture (palm up) toward the audience with the stroke on *you;* then turn the gesture toward yourself with a stroke on *I.* In the sentence that follows, try a two-handed *approving* gesture (both palms up) with the strokes on *success, both,* and *well.* Continue the double palms-up, perhaps throwing the hands a little farther apart on *every man,* giving an additional stroke on *himself;* then change back to the emphasizing index gesture, and emphasize strongly the remainder of the sentence, giving the strokes of the gesture on the words you think are most important, continuing the use of the gesture to the very end of the paragraph.

Now try the practice again, using different types of gesture from those suggested, to see whether you can improve on the communication. Stand before a mirror as you do it, and observe the effect. We must always remember that all training in gesture leads ultimately to better and more nearly complete expression and that gestures are never ends in themselves.

9. The following selection is somewhat more conversational. Try reading this, utilizing your principles of gesture to make it most effective:

> But your wealth is too near. I was speaking in New Britain, Connecticut, on this very subject. There sat five or six rows from me a lady. I noticed the lady at the time, from the color of her bonnet. I said to them, what I say to you now, "Your wealth is too near to you! You are looking right over it!" She went home after the lecture and tried to take off her collar. The button stuck in the buttonhole. She twisted and tugged and pulled and finally broke it out of the buttonhole and threw it away. She said: "I wonder why they don't make decent collar buttons?"
>
> Her husband said to her: "After what Conwell said tonight, why don't you get up a collar button yourself? Did he not say that if you need anything other people need it; so if you need a collar button there are millions of people needing it. Get up a collar button and get rich. 'Wherever there is need there is a fortune.' "
>
> Then she made up her mind to do it; and when a woman makes up her

mind, and doesn't say anything about it, she does it! And she invented this "snap button," a kind of a button that snaps together from two pieces, through the buttonhole. That very woman can now go over the sea every summer in her own yacht and take her husband with her. And if he were dead she would have enough money left to buy a foreign count or duke, or some such thing.

RUSSELL H. CONWELL

"Anybody can talk," runs a thoughtless adage, hence arises a grave mischief. The "talk" of actors like Rex Harrison, here seen in *Venus Observed,* is the product of sustained training.

CHAPTER 17

Improving Voice Quality and Variety

CHAPTER 17

We now come to the role of voice, of *sound waves,* in communicating thought. "Anybody can talk," runs a thoughtless adage, hence arises a grave mischief. Some people have voices that are weak and thin, and some are shrill and rasping. Some have voices that seep through the nose. Some are victims of lingual inertia and immobile lips. Some do not open the mouth; they open it to eat but half open it to speak. Some do not actually carve the sounds of speech; they only approximate them. Some speak in a flat tone, without informing inflection or luster of any sort, that sounds to listeners like the dripping of a distant tap. To say that these people talk is a liberal extension of the meaning of that word. More exactly they mumble, drone, mutter, muffle, sputter, haw, and croak. Or to paraphrase Sinclair Lewis, they may attack you with a voice like the sound of a file being drawn across a saw. Such voices do not make communication impossible, but they do seriously impair the speaker's attempt to arouse in others the thought existing in his own mind.

"Only five persons out of a hundred are born with good voices. The rest of us have to work for one," said a supervisor of announcers for NBC. The statement is obviously broad and general, for it hinges on the definition level of a good voice, but scientifically conducted surveys show that only a minority of people do have good speaking voices.

Some voices are poor because of organic difficulties. They need diagnosis and treatment from experts in speech correction. This is beyond the scope of a course in basic speech, although, of course, your instructor can advise on what to do and where to go for help.

Other voices reflect problems of personality. A whining voice may come from a nagging disposition. A shrill voice may be testimony of a shrewish nature. A curt, blunt voice may arise from lack of regard for the feelings of others. A magpie chatter may betray shallow emotions that overflow easily. When voice difficulties are thus the index of temperament or character, treatment of the cause is needed, not of the voice which is merely effect.

Still other voices reflect shortcomings of speech preparation or speaking discipline. A weak voice may come from lack of confidence or lack of conviction. A dull voice may come from lack of sincerity, or inadequate preparation. A flat voice may arise from failure to see in the mind, at the moment of utterance, the hues and forms of thought; the speaker may be only reciting words. The cure for these deficiencies is not in training the voice. It is in the choice of a subject and its preparation.

But in addition to these outlying causes, there are other causes that arise from mismanaging the voice itself. These we shall consider here, and to that end shall look at how speech sounds are produced, what makes voices unpleasant, and what makes them effective. Along the way you will make an inventory of your voice.

How speech sounds are produced

You have no speech organs per se. Every organ used in speech was originally given man for an older biological use. The lungs are used for breathing to sustain life. The tongue, teeth, and lips are used for eating. Even the voice box itself is used as a valve to keep foreign bodies (especially food and water) out of the lungs, and to regulate the amount of air entering and leaving the lungs. In learning to speak man *appropriated* organs that were biologically intended for other purposes. In cases of extreme tension, or other disturbances, the older biological functions may assert themselves, whereupon there is trouble with the speech mechanism carrying out its newly-acquired speech function. When such trouble arises, your problem is to reassert the dominance of speech over these organs.

In producing speech four stages are involved: breathing, phonation, resonation and articulation. We shall consider each in detail.

BREATHING

The primary purpose of breathing is biological. You breathe to live. Breathing is automatic, and you cannot voluntarily stop it. You can only regulate it within obvious limits. Somewhere along the way man learned to use breathing for making speech sounds.

Lung capacity varies, but a fair average is perhaps 225 cubic inches for men and 175 cubic inches for women. This is the volume of air that can be inhaled and exhaled in a single respiration. It is known as the *vital capacity*. In normal breathing, however, we use less than 15 per cent of this vital capacity. The average is about 30 cubic inches. This is known as *tidal air*. Thus we have an enormous reserve that can be used for extreme exertion, but is not required for ordinary use.

Look at it another way. In *quiet* inhalation you ordinarily use four sets of muscle. In *deep* inhalation you may use twelve sets of muscles directly, plus the indirect use of five additional sets. In *passive* exhalation you use relatively few muscles, since gravity, plus the elastic recoil of lungs and bones and viscera, forces air out of the lungs. But in *controlled* exhalation, which is required for producing speech sounds, you must use from five to ten sets of muscles.

Thus breathing for speech calls for a modification of the respiratory cycle. In silent breathing you use relatively few muscles and the periods of inhaling and exhaling are about equal. In breathing for speech you inhale quickly, using more muscles, and you exhale much more slowly while calling on a relatively large group of muscles to direct the outgo into making speech sounds. Some people can modify the respiratory cycle effectively and unconsciously. Some cannot. You will want to take inventory on the following matters:

1. *For public address inhalation is deeper, or more rapid, or both, than in ordinary breathing*. The reason is obvious. You need an adequate air supply for greater volume of voice and sustained tones, not only more than in ordinary breathing but more than in private conversation. The actual amount of air used in speech is not large, but to project with sufficient strength of tone you need a reasonable amount of breath in the lungs at all times. This reserve is to maintain vigor of tone and also to prevent running out of breath and trailing away into nothingness at the end of a phrase. The habitual shallow breather finds voice projection difficult. The deep breather finds it easier.

2. *For public address exhalation must be more forceful and more controlled than for ordinary breathing*. Ordinary exhalation is passive. You relax, and the air flows out. In producing speech a different process is involved. You *hold* the air in the lungs, and you *regulate* its outgo so as to produce speech sounds. The expenditure is definitely related to the intensity of speech sounds. To attain greater intensity,

such as needed in public address, there must be a greater outflow of air through the speech organs. Furthermore, the amount of air needed varies with different speech sounds. Thus a voiceless fricative like *s* (as in mi*ss*) requires more air than an explosive like *d* (as in *d*o), and a wide-open vowel like *ah* requires more air than a slightly-open one like *ee*. Effective speech requires you to use the regulating muscles to supply the needed amount.

3. *This power must be supplied by muscles of the thorax and abdomen without undue tension of muscles in the throat and face.* The tendency of the nervous speaker is to tighten up all over. But effective use of the human body calls for tension only of the muscles needed, without the interference of other muscles that might get in the way. Applied to speaking, this means that undue tension of muscles in the throat and face produces a poor voice quality. The operating rule for good speech, there, is *power in the abdomen, relaxation in the throat, and flexibility in the face.*

ASSIGNMENTS

FOR DEVELOPING CONTROL OF BREATHING

1. Breathe as deeply as possible, making sure that you expand both the chest and abdomen as far as you can without straining any part of the body.

2. Learn to use the muscles that give you "frontal chest expansion" as follows:

   a. First, exhale completely (note that it is exhale, not inhale). Then hold your breath and try to expand your chest voluntarily. It may help you to learn if you simply lift the chest at first.
   b. Exhale and hold your breath while you both expand and contract the front chest walls.

3. Learn to use the muscles that give you "lateral chest expansion" as follows:

   a. Stand relaxed and pant lightly but rapidly for about five seconds. The intercoastal rib muscles and the muscles of the lower back should begin to respond by short fitful movements.
   b. Concentrate on movements of the intercostal rib muscles until you capture the sensation of their movement. If necessary continue the panting exercise daily for several weeks until you have developed a conscious use of the intercostal muscles.

4. Learn to use fully the abdominal muscles as follows: Force the abdominal muscles outward; while these muscles are still tense, inhale as deeply as possible; then exhale.

5. Take a slow deep breath, tapping a) the chest on either side of the sternum, b) the ribs at the side, c) the muscles at the small of the back, d) the upper part of the abdomen. Practice this until you sense the co-ordinated expansion of the whole breathing area.

6. Take a deep breath as described in Exercise 5, *relax the throat,* and count from 1 to 10 at the rate of two or three numbers per second.

7. Inhale and extend the count to 20, then 30, then as far as your breath supply will go. Do not force the last few counts, and always stop before your breath supply is exhausted. Are you willing to try this for a week, twice daily, and see how far such practice will extend the count?

8. Use the following poem as an exercise in breath control as follows: First, read each two lines on one breath, at a normal rate. Then continue practice until you can read four, six, and finally eight lines on a single breath, always with an ample air reserve at the end of the last line:

OUT IN THE FIELDS

The little cares that fretted me,
  I lost them yesterday
Among the fields above the seas,
  Among the winds at play,
Among the lowing of the herds,
  The rustling of the trees,
Among the singing of the birds,
  The humming of the bees.

The foolish fears of what might happen,—
  I cast them all away
Among the clover-scented grass,
  Among the new-mown hay;
Among the husking of the corn,
  Where drowsy poppies nod,
Where ill thoughts die and good are born
  Out in the fields with God.

Elizabeth Barrett Browning

PHONATION

On the way out air passes between the "vocal cords" of the larynx and produces sound. This process is known as phonation. Actually these vibrators are not cords at all, but are pearly white *voice lips,* roughly three-quarters of an inch long in men and one-half an inch in women, but with wide individual variations. In silent breathing they open wide and let air in and out without hindrance. In whispering they open partly, let out large amounts of air, and produce only frictional sounds. In speech they come together under tension and the controlled air pressure from the lungs vibrate them in about the same way a trumpet player vibrates his lips in the mouthpiece.

The tone thus produced is weak, poor in quality, and with little carrying power. It does not become strong and rich until it has been amplified and reinforced by the human resonators as described below under *resonation*.

ASSIGNMENTS

FOR ESTABLISHING THE CONCEPT OF PHONATION

1. Relax all muscles of the jaw and shake your head until the jaw flops.

2. Drop your head forward as if you were almost asleep. Then gradually begin to shake the head, using the muscles in the back of your neck. Increase the shaking until the jaw wobbles.

3. Yawn gently but thoroughly, and note at the finish how the muscles of the jaw and throat feel when relaxed. *This is the muscle tonus you want for speaking.*

4. Open your mouth as if to yawn, but instead leave the mouth open wide and say *high ho.*

5. With a relaxed throat repeat the letters of the alphabet.

6. Read the following selections quietly, with open and relaxed throat:

The Moving Finger writes; and, having writ,
Moves on; nor all your Piety nor Wit
  Shall lure it back to cancel half a Line,
Nor shall your tears wash out a Word of it.

OMAR KHAYYÁM

The curfew tolls the knell of parting day,
The lowing herd wind slowly o'er the lea,
The ploughman homeward plods his weary way,
And leaves the world to darkness and to me.

THOMAS GRAY

Give a man a pipe he can smoke,
  Give a man a book he can read:
And his home is bright with calm delight,
  Though the room be poor indeed.

JAMES THOMSON

RESONATION

If you strike a tuning fork and hold it in the air, the tone is thin and weak. But set the vibration fork on a table, and at once the volume swells. Or hold it over an open tube of proper length, and again the volume increases. This is resonance. A piano string without its sounding board gives out only a fraction of the sound produced when the string is provided with the sounding board. An organ reed not coupled to its pipe does not sound at all like the coupled instrument in a pipe organ.

So with the human voice. Without resonance it would be too feeble to be heard at any distance. Without adequate resonance it is still thin or enfeebled. Full and complete speech sounds requires (1) a generator, or vocal cords, plus (2) resonators to amplify, enrich, and give each speech sound its exact quality.

The human voice has a variety of resonators of various sizes and shapes, the chief ones with their approximate sizes in cubic centimeters (16 cc. equals roughly one cubic inch) being as follows:

bronchi and trachea	60 cc.
larynx	25 cc.
pharynx (connecting mouth and nasal passages)	80 cc.
mouth	100 cc.
nose	60 cc.
nasal sinuses (four pairs)	75 cc.
Total	400 cc.[1]

In addition to the above tubes of various sizes and shapes, the human voice also uses to more or less extent the following sounding boards as resonators:

the skull bones, particularly the facial bones
the sternum (chest bone) and ribs

Thus the human voice has a large variety of resonators, larger by far than man-made musical instruments. Furthermore, the voice uses two types of resonators, fixed and adjustable.

Fixed resonators give what is often called head resonance. They are those immovable and unchanging resonators: the skull bones, the nose, nasal sinuses, trachea.

Adjustable resonators are those resonators that can be changed in

[1] L. S. Judson and A. T. Weaver, *Voice Science* (New York: Appleton-Century-Crofts, Inc., 1942), p. 95.

size, shape, and tenseness: the mouth, pharynx, and larynx. These adjustable resonators change the pitch of your voice. They give it the rising and falling inflections. They impart the subtle variations of vocal quality. Especially they give it the vowel quality, for by changing the size, shape, and tension of these adjustable resonators you can turn one sound into *e*, another into *o*, still another into *i*. Altogether in

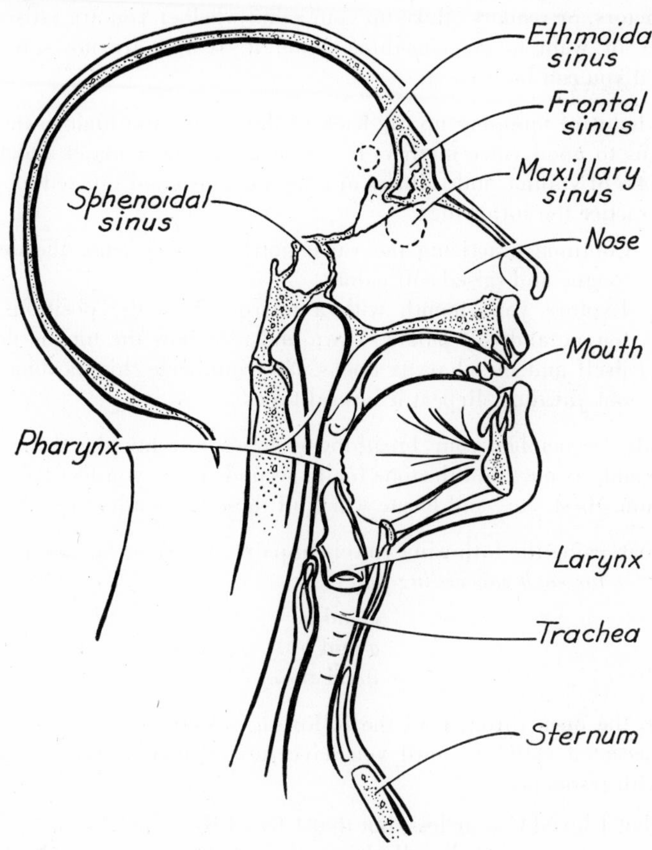

BODILY RESONATORS

the language some 15 vowel sounds are commonly used, each of which is produced by a different size, shape, and tenseness of the adjustable resonators.

Some people use these resonators efficiently; and we say they have "good voices." More do not use them efficiently; and they have various degrees and types of poor voices.

ASSIGNMENTS

FOR ESTABLISHING THE CONCEPT OF RESONANCE

1. Hear yourself as others hear you by making a recording of your voice and listening critically to the playback. Compare your playback to that of others in the class. Compare it also with available recordings of eminent speakers, actors, or readers. Make up your mind whether you are satisfied with your voice, or want to do something about it. If you are not satisfied, be assured that you can improve it.

2. The habit of humping up the back of the tongue too high in the mouth is disastrous to good voice quality. It obstructs the vocal outlet and leads to a serious loss of volume and fullness of tone. For open and relaxed mouth and pharynx practice the following:

   a. Continue practicing the yawn until you can sense the depressed tongue and raised soft palate.
   b. Explore your mouth with a mirror. Note the positions of the tongue and soft palate. Yawn and note how the tongue depresses itself and the pharynx opens. Now duplicate this movement without yawning. Repeat it several times.

3. Inhale (remember your breathing exercises), relax the throat, flatten the tongue and say *ah.* Hold the tone for 15 seconds while you feel the cranium, jaw, sternum, chest, etc., and locate which of these resonators are vibrating.

4. Repeat, using the following vowels in pairs. *Note that the mouth must be opened wider for each succeeding pair:*

e and *oo*
a and *o*
i and *ah*

5. With the open throat read the following selections. *Prolong* the vowel tones of accented syllables until you have *formed* them carefully and *built them up* with resonance:

> Not that I loved Caesar less, but that I loved Rome more. Had you rather Caesar were living and die all slaves, than that Caesar were dead, to live all free men? As Caesar loved me, I weep for him; as he was fortunate, I rejoice at it; as he was valiant, I honor him; but, as he was ambitious, I slew him. There is tears for his love; joy for his fortune; honor for his valor; and death for his ambition.
>
> Brutus in SHAKESPEARE'S *Julius Caesar*

> Life is a narrow vale between the cold and barren peaks of two eternities. We strive in vain to look beyond the heights. We cry aloud, and the only answer is the echo of our wailing cry. From the voiceless lips of the unreply-

ing dead, there comes no word; but in the night of death, hope sees a star, and listening love can hear the rustle of a wing.

ROBERT G. INGERSOLL

Once upon a midnight dreary, while I pondered, weak and weary,
Over many a quaint and curious volume of forgotten lore—
While I nodded, nearly napping, suddenly there came a tapping,
As of someone gently rapping, rapping at my chamber door.
" 'Tis some visitor," I muttered, "tapping at my chamber door—
Only this and nothing more."

EDGAR ALLAN POE

ARTICULATION

By articulation is meant the utterance of clear and distinct syllables. First, it is the skillful shaping, molding, and modeling of speech sounds. Next, it is combining the separate sounds to make up intelligible speech. In the language are approximately 40 different sounds, including vowels and consonants. The average person speaks at the rate of about 300 syllables to the minute, or five per second. Now the listener must catch these syllables on the wing and translate them into thought. This listeners must do instantly, without faltering and scarcely without pausing. If the sounds are slurred, muffled, or projected weakly, the listener is kept under tension. If he misses any essential part of the sounds, and stops to think back, "What was that?" he misses those words that come in that instant of thinking back, and so part of the meaning is lost.

Therefore, you will be permitted to take an inventory of your articulation. The test to be used is one of extreme accuracy, perfected by speech scientists after years of experiments on many types of tests for the purpose of testing intelligibility of communication in the Armed Forces of the United States.[2]

[2] The tests given below are the word multiple-choice tests found in OSRD Report No. 5567 of the Voice Communication Laboratory, Waco, Texas, John W. Black, director. They were prepared by C. Hess Haagen. Originally classified as containing information affecting national defense, they have now been declassified and made available for general use. These multiple-choice tests were found to be superior to the spondiac word lists, the phonetically balanced word lists, and the various types of write-down tests. They discriminate between untrained and trained speakers and measure reliably as indicated by split-half correlations, corrected for length, of about .80.

MULTIPLE-CHOICE INTELLIGIBILITY TEST

Directions to Instructors for Administering

1. The test is devised to be given to groups of 12 or less. Hence there are 12 tests and 12 answer sheets.

2. Before the test period starts supply each student with the 12 answer sheets, preferably mimeographed. (Students could mark answers directly on the answer sheets in the textbook, of course, but this would require the instructor either to do the grading in class or to collect the 12 textbooks for grading later.)

3. Since each student can read the articulation test from the textbook, there is no need of separate copies of the test itself.

4. For highest accuracy give the test under the following conditions:
   a. Set up at least the noise of an electric fan for masking. The hum of a loudspeaker, or relatively loud phonograph music, will serve *if the amount of noise is measured and is exactly duplicated in the second articulation test to be given later.*
   b. Seat listeners in desk-arm chairs at 30 feet distance from the speaker.
   c. Have listeners turn their faces at right angles to the speaker, and instruct them not to look at the speaker during the test.

5. Instruct the students as follows:

   When it is your turn to read, give your name and test number. Be *sure* that both are understood by every member of the class. For example, "My name is John Doe, d-o-e. I will read test 8."

   Then read from the Speaker Test List. The test consists of 8 sets of 3 words that are read in this fashion (instructor will point out the sample words given below and read them at an acceptable rate; pausing after each set of 3 words): "Number 1, mortar . . . shut . . . assist. Number 2, blimp . . . injure . . . knob," and so on until all 8 sets of 3 words have been read. Remember to pause after each group of 3 words to give your listeners time to mark their papers.

   While you are reading these words, this is what your listeners will be doing. For every word that you have read, they have, on their answer sheets, a choice of 4 similar-sounding words. When the word "mortar" was read, for example, they had the choice of "order, mortar, border, and water." Since "mortar" was the word read, they put an X on number 2. The second word was not "shook, shout, or shot," but "shut" so they put an X on it. The next choices are "enlist, resist, assist, and insist." Since "assist" was the word read, they place an X on it. Then they go to the second set of 3 words, and so on for all 8 sets.

   Listeners will look carefully and be certain to place an X on the number of the word you think was read. In some cases there is a difference of only a single letter, so make your selection carefully. Also remember that only one of the group of 4 words is correct. If 2 words within a single group are marked it is an error. If you have marked a word and then decide that the choice is wrong, either erase the mark or write *no* beside it. The first word that is read is always in column to the left. The second word is always in the center column. The third word is always in the column to the right. Be careful to place the X directly on the number of the word.

Fill in the names of the speakers as they are read to you. Are there any questions? Do you have a pencil? Do you have the answer sheets to all 12 tests?

One final word of caution. When you are the speaker, be certain to read from your assigned speaker test number, and remember to pause after each group of 3 words to give listeners time to mark their answer sheets.

All set, the test will begin immediately.

Sample Intelligibility Test

Number 1: mortar, shut, assist

Number 2: blimp, injure, knob

Sample Answer Sheet

1 order	1 shook	1 enlist
X 2 mortar	2 shout	2 resist
3 border	X 3 shut	X 3 assist
4 water	4 shot	4 insist
1 flip	X 1 injure	1 sob
2 limp	2 insure	X 2 knob
X 3 blimp	3 picture	3 cog
4 limb	4 contour	4 nod

INTELLIGIBILITY TEST, FORM A[3]

Speaker Test List

Speaker 1

1 swarm, canvas, quart
2 airport, bark, tassel
3 group, flicker, beef
4 legion, wonder, horn
5 threat, deer, garden
6 curtain, export, final
7 rage, city, all
8 knuckle, dress, screech

Speaker 2

1 skid, mood, twist
2 profane, thin, receive
3 hard, fasten, anger
4 joke, shaft, knitting
5 course, balance, rank
6 lanky, horror, unfold
7 pipe, beast, spray
8 drift, concern, first

Speaker 3

1 feed, conclude, train
2 virtue, hire, patch
3 dinner, envy, rumor
4 spear, goal, mettle
5 fault, birch, praise
6 slack, kernel, drab
7 go, lady, break
8 chain, ten, heart

Speaker 4

1 pardon, hall, double
2 top, cruel, storage
3 eight, dissolve, needle
4 fable, recline, volley
5 shade, infect, card
6 brain, squad, tramp
7 plan, lift, behold
8 glory, not, force

Speaker 5

1 crook, fair, amble
2 brick, dim, matching
3 shook, opal, trail
4 flame, were, relief
5 plot, kind, sleeping
6 eighty, swoop, quit
7 world, handy, dot
8 unfit, reverse, budget

Speaker 6

1 term, hate, commit
2 proud, waist, meaning
3 deflect, law, jobber
4 tell, invite, flat
5 faithful, suit, became
6 rural, noon, save
7 edge, binding, prince
8 desk, vote, young

Speaker 7

1 chisel, bond, dream
2 forge, seal, notion
3 verse, harvest, tight
4 guide, jungle, blunt
5 pun, speed, hail
6 eat, pad, depth
7 wife, rocket, keep
8 content, fork, ask

Speaker 8

1 gadget, why, belt
2 sandy, power, fit
3 attic, main, describe
4 cattle, heel, tare
5 ring, option, class
6 killer, span, thimble
7 dozen, guard, chapter
8 wealth, prevent, foremost

Speaker 9

1 endure, clam, absent
2 bacon, perfect, decide
3 fearful, start, gown
4 drove, thirty, roller
5 barge, select, pride
6 light, heading, jump
7 gift, catch, misfire
8 fuel, toe, odor

Speaker 10

1 recent, confront, lame
2 perfume, gamble, what
3 frame, scatter, harness
4 you, treason, disgust
5 talent, cook, musket
6 gone, plenty, rub
7 center, less, fox
8 defeat, some, beach

Speaker 11

1 play, bright, which
2 robe, dash, enrage
3 swear, ground, confess
4 fast, caution, shower
5 prefer, keel, hope
6 flare, endorse, locate
7 ballet, rod, abound
8 health, outline, thud

Speaker 12

1 brief, define, near
2 raid, sneeze, pension
3 corpse, mad, zero
4 tree, when, air
5 bean, afraid, crane
6 share, guess, fence
7 demote, pain, ladder
8 untold, hood, torment

[3] There are 24 tests of equivalent difficulty which are arbitrarily divided into two groups of 12 for use as initial and final tests. The intelligibility scores of these 24 tests do not deviate more than 0.5%. The first group of 12, known as Form A, is given here. The second group of 12, known as Form B, is given in the next chapter (page 422). By taking any one of the tests in Form A prior to training, and taking any one in Form B following the training, each student will be able to measure improvement in intelligibility with a very high degree of reliability.

ANSWER SHEET FOR MULTIPLE-CHOICE INTELLIGIBILITY TESTS, FORM A

*Speaker 1 is*________________ *Speaker 2 is*________________

1	1 form	1 campus	1 court	1 skid	1 move	1 swim
	2 warm	2 canvas	2 fort	2 skin	2 mood	2 twin
	3 swarm	3 pamphlet	3 port	3 hid	3 food	3 swift
	4 storm	4 panther	4 quart	4 hit	4 smooth	4 twist
2	1 air force	1 spark	1 tassel	1 proclaim	1 spin	1 repeat
	2 airport	2 park	2 tackle	2 domain	2 pin	2 receive
	3 air corps	3 dark	3 cattle	3 cocaine	3 thin	3 recede
	4 airborne	4 bark	4 pastel	4 profane	4 fin	4 reprieve
3	1 group	1 quicker	1 beef	1 heart	1 fasten	1 angle
	2 troop	2 flicker	2 beast	2 barge	2 passion	2 amber
	3 coupe	3 slicker	3 beat	3 lard	3 fashion	3 anger
	4 fruit	4 liquor	4 beam	4 hard	4 passing	4 anchor
4	1 reason	1 wonder	1 corn	1 yoke	1 chat	1 heading
	2 region	2 blunder	2 torn	2 joke	2 chap	2 sitting
	3 legion	3 thunder	3 horn	3 choke	3 shack	3 knitting
	4 legend	4 sponsor	4 born	4 dope	4 shaft	4 fitting
5	1 stretch	1 hear	1 guard	1 court	1 balance	1 drank
	2 threat	2 steer	2 hearten	2 cord	2 ballot	2 rank
	3 dread	3 near	3 garden	3 horse	3 gallons	3 ranch
	4 bread	4 deer	4 bargain	4 course	4 valid	4 drag
6	1 certain	1 export	1 file	1 banking	1 borrow	1 unfold
	2 pertain	2 extort	2 panel	2 flanking	2 horror	2 untold
	3 person	3 expert	3 funnel	3 lanky	3 father	3 controlled
	4 curtain	4 escort	4 final	4 blanket	4 power	4 uphold
7	1 raid	1 fitting	1 owl	1 pipe	1 beast	1 dray
	2 rate	2 pretty	2 call	2 pike	2 beat	2 grey
	3 range	3 city	3 hall	3 type	3 meat	3 spray
	4 rage	4 sitting	4 all	4 tight	4 least	4 pray
8	1 uncle	1 dread	1 screech	1 thrift	1 confirm	1 verse
	2 buckle	2 dress	2 preach	2 drip	2 confer	2 first
	3 knuckle	3 rest	3 reach	3 drift	3 conserve	3 burst
	4 stucco	4 red	4 street	4 grip	4 concern	4 hurt

ANSWER SHEET FOR MULTIPLE-CHOICE INTELLIGIBILITY TESTS, FORM A—*Cont.*

*Speaker 3 is*________________ *Speaker 4 is*________________ .

1	1 deed	1 protrude	1 train	1 stardom	1 call	1 bubble
	2 weed	2 conclude	2 crane	2 pardon	2 ball	2 stubble
	3 seed	3 construed	3 strain	3 garden	3 hall	3 trouble
	4 feed	4 include	4 terrain	4 autumn	4 small	4 double
2	1 virtual	1 hide	1 pack	1 top	1 tool	1 storage
	2 curfew	2 five	2 patch	2 hop	2 cruel	2 porridge
	3 virtue	3 hire	3 catch	3 pop	3 drool	3 shortage
	4 virgin	4 fire	4 cat	4 prop	4 cool	4 story
3	1 dimmer	1 envy	1 rumor	1 eight	1 revolve	1 needle
	2 dinner	2 empty	2 roamer	2 ache	2 involve	2 fetal
	3 thinner	3 entry	3 rubber	3 hate	3 resolve	3 eagle
	4 tinner	4 ending	4 rover	4 bake	4 dissolve	4 beetle
4	1 sphere	1 gull	1 petal	1 able	1 recline	1 folly
	2 fear	2 gall	2 mettle	2 stable	2 refine	2 volley
	3 spear	3 gold	3 meadow	3 fable	3 reclaim	3 polish
	4 beer	4 goal	4 settle	4 table	4 reply	4 trolley
5	1 fault	1 burst	1 trade	1 gave	1 effect	1 hard
	2 vault	2 hurt	2 trace	2 shade	2 expect	2 card
	3 dog	3 first	3 praise	3 fade	3 inspect	3 cord
	4 fog	4 birch	4 pray	4 shave	4 infect	4 harsh
6	1 black	1 kernel	1 graft	1 strange	1 wad	1 plant
	2 track	2 curdle	2 draft	2 bring	2 wash	2 clamp
	3 slack	3 turtle	3 drab	3 rain	3 squad	3 cramp
	4 flak	4 hurdle	4 grab	4 brain	4 squash	4 tramp
7	1 glow	1 late	1 break	1 clad	1 lift	1 behave
	2 go	2 laden	2 rake	2 clan	2 rift	2 withhold
	3 grow	3 lazy	3 great	3 plan	3 drift	3 revolt
	4 goat	4 lady	4 grape	4 plant	4 list	4 behold
8	1 change	1 pen	1 hard	1 quarry	1 such	1 force
	2 chain	2 pin	2 part	2 glory	2 touch	2 fourth
	3 stain	3 tent	3 harsh	3 gory	3 nut	3 course
	4 shame	4 ten	4 heart	4 sorry	4 butt	4 horse

ANSWER SHEET FOR MULTIPLE-CHOICE INTELLIGIBILITY TESTS, FORM A—*Cont.*

*Speaker 5 is*________________ *Speaker 6 is*________________

	Speaker 5			Speaker 6		
1	1 cook	1 fair	1 annual	1 squirm	1 hate	1 commit
	2 crook	2 bare	2 ample	2 firm	2 haste	2 submit
	3 brook	3 care	3 amble	3 term	3 eight	3 permit
	4 book	4 pair	4 apple	4 turn	4 take	4 commence
2	1 brink	1 skim	1 action	1 cloud	1 waist	1 feeling
	2 bridge	2 hymn	2 matching	2 crowd	2 wake	2 meeting
	3 brisk	3 vim	3 magic	3 proud	3 wade	3 feeding
	4 brick	4 dim	4 smashing	4 prod	4 wait	4 meaning
3	1 took	1 open	1 trial	1 neglect	1 lost	1 robber
	2 shook	2 oboe	2 file	2 deflect	2 long	2 jobber
	3 shock	3 opal	3 frail	3 reflect	3 log	3 harbor
	4 cock	4 oval	4 trail	4 reflex	4 law	4 shopper
4	1 flame	1 worm	1 relieve	1 held	1 invite	1 blast
	2 blame	2 work	2 receive	2 bell	2 insight	2 flat
	3 claim	3 word	3 relief	3 fell	3 inside	3 flak
	4 plane	4 were	4 release	4 tell	4 advice	4 black
5	1 clock	1 kind	1 leaping	1 playful	1 suit	1 depend
	2 block	2 pine	2 sleeping	2 faithful	2 shoot	2 detain
	3 plot	3 fine	3 creeping	3 fateful	3 boot	3 became
	4 blot	4 time	4 reaping	4 baseball	4 fruit	4 retain
6	1 eighty	1 proof	1 whip	1 plural	1 noun	1 brave
	2 aching	2 hoop	2 quit	2 neutral	2 new	2 stave
	3 dainty	3 group	3 quick	3 rural	3 nude	3 bathe
	4 baby	4 swoop	4 twist	4 ruler	4 noon	4 save
7	1 world	1 happy	1 dodge	1 egg	1 finding	1 tint
	2 whirl	2 handy	2 dark	2 edge	2 binding	2 print
	3 wool	3 candy	3 dot	3 hedge	3 blinding	3 prince
	4 would	4 envy	4 dock	4 head	4 landing	4 tense
8	1 conscript	1 refer	1 budget	1 desk	1 both	1 yawn
	2 conflict	2 rehearse	2 bucket	2 deck	2 boat	2 jump
	3 assist	3 reverse	3 bunion	3 death	3 vote	3 junk
	4 unfit	4 revert	4 budge	4 debt	4 quote	4 young

ANSWER SHEET FOR MULTIPLE-CHOICE INTELLIGIBILITY TESTS, FORM A—*Cont.*

*Speaker 7 is*________________ *Speaker 8 is*________________

1	1 cheerful	1 barn	1 ream	1 dagger	1 why	1 milk
	2 drizzle	2 bond	2 green	2 gadget	2 wine	2 built
	3 chisel	3 born	3 dream	3 jacket	3 wire	3 felt
	4 fiddle	4 bomb	4 scream	4 jagged	4 wise	4 belt
2	1 gorge	1 seal	1 lotion	1 fancy	1 collar	1 fit
	2 forge	2 steel	2 motion	2 brandy	2 pilot	2 sit
	3 ford	3 feel	3 ocean	3 sandy	3 tower	3 spit
	4 board	4 field	4 notion	4 candy	4 power	4 fifth
3	1 bird	1 harbor	1 height	1 adding	1 main	1 destroyed
	2 birth	2 Harvard	2 pipe	2 addict	2 fame	2 prescribe
	3 first	3 harvest	3 kite	3 acting	3 fade	3 deprive
	4 verse	4 horrid	4 tight	4 attic	4 maid	4 describe
4	1 dive	1 jungle	1 blunt	1 tattle	1 field	1 fair
	2 side	2 tinkle	2 blood	2 tackle	2 feel	2 tare
	3 died	3 shingle	3 flood	3 paddle	3 heel	3 hair
	4 guide	4 single	4 stunt	4 cattle	4 eel	4 pair
5	1 pun	1 seed	1 sail	1 bring	1 option	1 clash
	2 punch	2 speed	2 hail	2 ring	2 auction	2 class
	3 pond	3 bead	3 rail	3 rink	3 object	3 clap
	4 punt	4 greed	4 stale	4 drink	4 action	4 clad
6	1 eat	1 past	1 death	1 teller	1 band	1 thimble
	2 heat	2 pass	2 debt	2 pillar	2 span	2 symbol
	3 heap	3 path	3 depth	3 killer	3 spend	3 temple
	4 deep	4 pad	4 deaf	4 color	4 bend	4 simple
7	1 wipe	1 rocking	1 keep	1 dungeon	1 barge	1 capture
	2 wife	2 locker	2 feet	2 cousin	2 dark	2 captor
	3 wide	3 rocket	3 peep	3 dozen	3 barred	3 chapter
	4 white	4 locket	4 heat	4 doesn't	4 guard	4 captain
8	1 contest	1 fort	1 add	1 weld	1 prevent	1 formal
	2 contend	2 fore	2 have	2 wealth	2 present	2 forebode
	3 content	3 force	3 ax	3 whelp	3 resent	3 foremost
	4 contempt	4 fork	4 ask	4 well	4 revenge	4 promote

ANSWER SHEET FOR MULTIPLE-CHOICE INTELLIGIBILITY TESTS, FORM A—*Cont.*

*Speaker 9 is*______________ *Speaker 10 is*______________

1	1 insure	1 calm	1 abscess	1 region	1 confront	1 lame
	2 endure	2 come	2 absent	2 recent	2 comfort	2 flame
	3 obscure	3 comb	3 accent	3 regent	3 convert	3 plane
	4 injure	4 cob	4 absurd	4 rescind	4 confirm	4 blame
2	1 taken	1 turret	1 divide	1 consume	1 camel	1 watch
	2 bacon	2 turkey	2 bedside	2 presume	2 gamble	2 swat
	3 vacant	3 perfect	3 deride	3 perfume	3 sample	3 squat
	4 beacon	4 purpose	4 decide	4 curfew	4 shamble	4 what
3	1 carful	1 start	1 found	1 crane	1 scatter	1 hornet
	2 cheerful	2 dart	2 down	2 rain	2 chatter	2 harness
	3 fearful	3 starch	3 gown	3 train	3 shatter	3 harvest
	4 careful	4 dark	4 brown	4 frame	4 gather	4 hardly
4	1 throw	1 dirty	1 roller	1 shoe	1 freedom	1 distrust
	2 grow	2 thirty	2 polar	2 cue	2 reason	2 discuss
	3 grove	3 sturdy	3 molar	3 hue	3 treason	3 disgust
	4 drove	4 pretty	4 colder	4 you	4 freezing	4 distress
5	1 barge	1 deluxe	1 pride	1 talent	1 nook	1 messkit
	2 carve	2 collect	2 hide	2 palace	2 book	2 basket
	3 large	3 select	3 cried	3 challenge	3 hook	3 cross cut
	4 barb	4 elect	4 bride	4 pilot	4 cook	4 musket
6	1 like	1 hitting	1 jump	1 gone	1 planting	1 rub
	2 mike	2 headache	2 dump	2 dawn	2 plenty	2 rob
	3 might	3 heavy	3 junk	3 guard	3 twenty	3 rug
	4 light	4 heading	4 drunk	4 darn	4 pretty	4 rough
7	1 ship	1 cash	1 inspire	1 censor	1 left	1 fox
	2 skip	2 catch	2 spitfire	2 sender	2 let	2 docks
	3 gift	3 patch	3 expire	3 center	3 led	3 blocks
	4 shift	4 pitch	4 misfire	4 slender	4 less	4 box
8	1 duel	1 coal	1 motor	1 deceit	1 come	1 beat
	2 fuel	2 tone	2 mortar	2 defeat	2 numb	2 beach
	3 pool	3 toe	3 order	3 receipt	3 some	3 speech
	4 jewel	4 cold	4 odor	4 repeat	4 thumb	4 meat

ANSWER SHEET FOR MULTIPLE-CHOICE INTELLIGIBILITY TESTS, FORM A—*Cont.*

*Speaker 11 is*________________ *Speaker 12 is*________________

1	1 sway 2 slay 3 play 4 pay	1 bribe 2 bride 3 bite 4 bright	1 twist 2 which 3 switch 4 twitch	1 screech 2 grief 3 brief 4 breach	1 refine 2 define 3 behind 4 decline	1 near 2 dear 3 fear 4 mere
2	1 road 2 robe 3 row 4 roam	1 dash 2 bash 3 gash 4 flash	1 defrayed 2 enrage 3 engage 4 mislaid	1 rage 2 raid 3 raise 4 rate	1 plead 2 please 3 sneeze 4 siege	1 pension 2 mention 3 engine 4 tension
3	1 prayer 2 swear 3 where 4 square	1 brown 2 drowned 3 ground 4 round	1 concept 2 contest 3 compress 4 confess	1 corpse 2 cord 3 court 4 caught	1 mad 2 bad 3 bag 4 man	1 bureau 2 arrow 3 here 4 zero
4	1 bat 2 bask 3 fast 4 fat	1 cautious 2 conscious 3 cousin 4 caution	1 sour 2 scour 3 shower 4 tower	1 three 2 sea 3 free 4 tree	1 went 2 when 3 wind 4 win	1 car 2 here 3 error 4 air
5	1 prefer 2 refer 3 recur 4 preserve	1 peel 2 keel 3 heal 4 feel	1 halt 2 oak 3 hope 4 oath	1 bean 2 beam 3 bead 4 bee	1 parade 2 obeyed 3 afraid 4 appraise	1 crave 2 terrain 3 train 4 crane
6	1 flare 2 blare 3 clear 4 glare	1 endure 2 adore 3 indoors 4 endorse	1 locate 2 rotate 3 okayed 4 bouquet	1 chair 2 share 3 scare 4 beer	1 gassed 2 guest 3 get 4 guess	1 bent 2 fence 3 spent 4 sent
7	1 ballad 2 ballot 3 balance 4 valid	1 rod 2 prod 3 ride 4 fraud	1 about 2 aboard 3 around 4 abound	1 steamboat 2 devote 3 demote 4 remote	1 tame 2 pain 3 paid 4 gain	1 ladder 2 lather 3 matter 4 leader
8	1 help 2 felt 3 health 4 self	1 outside 2 combine 3 alpine 4 outline	1 thud 2 bud 3 blood 4 mud	1 unsold 2 unfold 3 untold 4 uphold	1 put 2 could 3 good 4 hood	1 foreman 2 ferment 3 torment 4 comment

SCORING SHEET FOR INTELLIGIBILITY TEST, FORM A

The sequence of three numbers indicate the correct words in each group for each reader. If reasonable precaution is taken for accuracy the scoring may be done in class.

	Speaker 1	*Speaker 2*	*Speaker 3*
Group 1	3—2—4	1—2—4	4—2—1
Group 2	2—4—1	4—3—2	3—3—2
Group 3	1—2—1	4—1—3	2—1—1
Group 4	3—1—3	2—4—3	3—4—2
Group 5	2—4—3	4—1—2	1—4—3
Group 6	4—1—4	3—2—1	3—1—3
Group 7	4—3—4	1—1—3	2—4—1
Group 8	3—2—1	3—4—2	2—4—4

	Speaker 4	*Speaker 5*	*Speaker 6*
Group 1	2—3—4	2—1—3	3—1—1
Group 2	1—2—1	4—4—2	3—1—4
Group 3	1—4—1	2—3—4	2—4—2
Group 4	3—1—2	1—4—3	4—1—2
Group 5	2—4—2	3—1—2	2—1—3
Group 6	4—3—4	1—4—2	3—4—4
Group 7	3—1—4	1—2—3	2—2—3
Group 8	2—3—1	4—3—1	1—3—4

	Speaker 7	*Speaker 8*	*Speaker 9*
Group 1	3—2—3	2—1—4	2—1—2
Group 2	2—1—4	3—4—1	2—3—4
Group 3	4—3—4	4—1—4	3—1—3
Group 4	4—1—1	4—3—2	4—2—1
Group 5	1—2—2	2—1—2	1—3—1
Group 6	1—4—3	3—2—1	4—4—1
Group 7	2—3—1	3—4—3	3—2—4
Group 8	3—4—4	2—1—3	2—3—4

	Speaker 10	*Speaker 11*	*Speaker 12*
Group 1	2—1—1	3—4—2	3—2—1
Group 2	3—2—4	2—1—2	2—3—1
Group 3	4—1—2	2—3—4	1—1—4
Group 4	4—3—3	3—4—3	4—2—4
Group 5	1—4—4	1—2—3	1—3—4
Group 6	1—2—1	1—4—1	2—4—2
Group 7	3—4—1	2—1—4	3—2—1
Group 8	2—3—2	3—4—1	3—4—3

COMPUTING THE MULTIPLE-CHOICE INTELLIGIBILITY SCORE

Add the number of errors made against each speaker. Locate this number in the "No. of Errors" column. Read across the table to the column labeled with the appropriate number of listeners. This figure is the Intelligibility Score. For example, if a speaker had 107 errors against him by 9 listeners, the Intelligibility Score would be 50.

To compute scores not included in this table: (1) Add the number of words understood correctly by each listener. (2) Divide the total by the number of listeners times 24 (number of words spoken). Carry the product to two decimal figures. The result will be the Intelligibility Score.

No. of Errors	*No. of Listeners*				
	7	*8*	*9*	*10*	*11*
21	87	89	90	91	92
22	87	89	90	91	92
23	86	88	89	90	91
24	86	87	89	90	91
25	85	87	88	90	91
26	85	86	88	89	90
27	84	86	87	89	90
28	83	85	87	88	89
29	83	85	87	88	89
30	82	84	86	87	89
31	82	84	86	87	88
32	81	83	85	87	88
33	80	83	85	86	87
34	80	82	84	86	87
35	79	82	84	85	87
36	78	81	83	85	86
37	78	81	83	85	86
38	77	80	82	84	86
39	77	80	82	84	85
40	76	79	81	83	85
41	76	79	81	83	84
42	75	78	81	82	84
43	74	78	80	82	84
44	74	77	80	82	83
45	73	77	79	81	83
46	73	76	79	81	83
47	72	76	78	80	82
48	71	75	78	80	82
49	71	74	77	80	81
50	70	74	77	79	81
51	70	73	76	79	81
52	69	73	76	78	80
53	68	72	75	78	80
54	68	72	75	77	80
55	67	71	75	77	79
56	67	71	74	77	79
57	66	70	74	76	78
58	65	70	73	76	78
59	65	69	73	75	78
60	64	69	72	75	77
61	64	68	72	75	77
62	63	68	71	74	77
63	62	67	71	74	76
64	62	67	70	73	76
65	61	66	70	73	75
66	61	66	69	72	75
67	60	65	69	72	75
68	60	65	69	72	74
69	59	64	68	71	74
70	58	64	68	71	73
71	58	63	67	70	73
72	57	62	67	70	73
73	56	62	66	70	72
74	56	61	66	69	72
75	55	61	65	69	72
76	55	60	65	68	71
77	54	60	64	68	71
78	54	59	64	67	70
79	53	59	63	67	70
80	52	58	63	67	70
81	52	58	62	66	69
82	51	57	62	66	69
83	51	57	62	65	69
84	50	56	61	65	68
85	49	56	61	65	68
86	49	55	60	64	67
87	48	55	60	64	67
88	48	54	59	63	67
89	47	54	59	63	66
90	46	53	58	62	66
91	46	53	58	62	66
92	45	52	57	62	65
93	45	52	57	61	65
94	44	51	56	61	64
95	43	51	56	60	64
96	43	50	56	60	64
97	42	49	55	60	63
98	42	49	55	59	63
99	41	48	54	59	62
100	40	48	54	58	62
101	40	47	53	58	62
102	39	47	53	57	61
103	39	46	52	57	61
104	38	46	52	57	61
105	37	45	51	56	60
106	37	45	51	56	60
107	36	44	50	55	59
108	36	44	50	55	59
109	35	43	50	55	59
110	35	43	49	54	58
111	34	42	49	54	58
112	33	42	48	53	58
113	33	41	48	53	57
114	32	41	47	52	57
115	32	40	47	52	56
116	31	40	46	52	56
117	30	39	46	51	56
118	30	39	45	51	55
119	29	38	45	50	55
120	29	37	44	50	55

WRITE-DOWN INTELLIGIBILITY TEST [4]

You will also have the option of taking a simpler and shorter write-down intelligibility test. Although it is not so accurate as the preceding multiple-choice test, it does have a high degree of reliability if given under controlled conditions. It may be preferred where it is not convenient to supply mimeographed answer sheets.

Directions to Instructors for Administering

1. The test is devised to be given to groups of 12 or less. Hence there are 12 tests having an equal spread of intelligibility values.
2. For highest accuracy, give the test under the following conditions:
   a. Set up at least the noise of an electric fan for masking, preferably more. The hum of a loudspeaker, or relatively loud phonograph music, will serve *if the amount of noise is measured and is exactly duplicated in the second articulation test to be given later*.
   b. Seat listeners in desk-arm chairs at 30 feet distance from the speaker.
   c. Have listeners turn their faces at right angles to the speaker, and instruct them not to look at the speaker during the test.
3. Instruct the students as follows:

   During this hour each of you will be given an intelligibility test that consists of a list of 12 words. When it is your turn you will give your name and the test number: "My name is John Doe, d-o-e. I will read test number 5." Then read the test exactly as it is printed. "Number 1 is shoeblack. Number 2 is harpoon," and so for all 12 words. Be certain to pause after each test word to give listeners time to write the word you have spoken. If you read too fast your score will be lowered simply because listeners did not have time to record what they heard. An easy way to control your rate is to count 2 silently after each test word.

   Remember to speak each test word only *once*. Do not repeat.

   When you are not the speaker, you will record what the other students read. Use a *separate* sheet for each speaker. At the top center write the speaker's name and the test number. Then as he speaks each word, you will write its number and the word as you heard it. If you are not sure what was said, guess. There is no penalty for guessing. If you cannot make a guess, draw a line in that space and go on to the next word.

[4] The tests below are the 12-word write-down tests developed by the Voice Communication Laboratory, Waco, Texas, John W. Black, director. They are found in OSRD Report No. 5414, prepared by C. Hess Haagen. Under laboratory conditions they discriminate between trained and untrained speakers and measure reliably as indicated by split-half correlations, corrected for length, of about .75. But these laboratory conditions, among other things, included a masking noise level of about 105 decibels (i.e., much louder than a very loud radio), and when lower masking noises were used the test was less reliable.

Are there any questions? Remember not to read too rapidly. Do not compare papers at any time during the test. Does everyone have a pencil? Does everyone have 11 sheets of paper? Write your name at the upper right corner of each sheet. We will begin immediately.

Write-Down Intelligibility Test, Form A [5]

Test 1	*Test 2*	*Test 3*	*Test 4*	*Test 5*	*Test 6*
ramp	charge	impulse	practice	forecast	farther
select	defeat	cleared	southeast	hit	cancel
break	slow	bail	flare	ground	gliding
moment	eastward	gun	top	dainty	find
escape	describe	flounder	decrease	pancake	door
throb	scatter	reckon	ask	injure	blimp
cotton	volley	slam	start	missile	sweep
jump	bomb	headwind	pressure	cloudy	take-off
center	circuit	flag	balance	tank	reduce
tree	late	end	misfire	raid	ditch
folder	release	pierce	front	flight	office
guard	fog	battle	cripple	nothing	calm

Test 7	*Test 8*	*Test 9*	*Test 10*	*Test 11*	*Test 12*
ampere	cartridge	ignite	roll	regain	barge
high	speed	blow	forest	cold	tent
pivot	mortar	edge	wash	burning	vision
salute	full	suburb	single	passage	ceiling
caution	dugout	neutral	cushion	dashboard	unit
fort	piston	binding	missing	spiral	fair
beach	measure	canvass	socket	wrench	hood
rocket	gunfire	section	fuel	gangway	shower
course	defend	deadly	headphone	corpse	govern
bandit	compass	try	pain	forenoon	cockpit
darken	tight	flame	blast	spray	distance
plenty	blind	gearshift	discard	narrow	target

[5] There are 24 tests of essentially equal difficulty levels. The first group of 12, known as Form A, is given here. The second group of 12, known as Form B, is given in the next chapter (page 430). By taking any one of the tests in Form A prior to training, and taking any one in Form B following the training, each student will be able to measure improvement in intelligibility with a fairly high degree of reliability.

Computing the Write-Down Intelligibility Score

Add the total number of errors made against each speaker. Locate this number in the "No. of Errors" column below. Read across the table to the column labelled with the appropriate number of listeners. This figure is the Intelligibility Score. For example, if the speaker had 93 errors made against him by 11 listeners, the Intelligibility Score would be 30.

To compute scores not included in this table: (1) Add the number of words understood correctly by each listener. (2) Divide this total by the number of listeners times 12 (number of words spoken). (3) Carry the product to two decimal figures. The result will be the Intelligibility Score.

No. of Errors	*No. of Listeners*					*No. of Errors*	*No. of Listeners*					*No. of Errors*	*No. of Listeners*				
	7	*8*	*9*	*10*	*11*		*7*	*8*	*9*	*10*	*11*		*7*	*8*	*9*	*10*	*11*
11	87	89	90	91	92	51	39	47	53	58	61	91	0	5	16	24	31
12	86	87	89	90	91	52	38	46	52	57	61	92	0	4	15	23	30
13	85	86	88	89	90	53	37	45	51	56	60	93	0	3	14	23	30
14	83	85	87	88	89	54	36	44	50	55	59	94	0	2	13	22	29
15	82	84	86	88	89	55	35	43	49	54	58	95	0	1	12	21	28
16	81	83	85	87	88	56	33	42	48	53	58	96	0	0	11	20	27
17	80	82	84	86	87	57	32	41	47	53	57	97	0	0	10	19	27
18	79	81	83	85	86	58	31	40	46	52	56	98	0	0	9	18	26
19	77	80	82	84	86	59	30	39	45	51	55	99	0	0	8	18	25
20	76	79	81	83	85	60	29	37	44	50	55	100	0	0	7	17	24
21	75	78	81	83	84	61	27	36	44	49	54	101	0	0	6	16	23
22	74	77	80	82	83	62	26	35	43	48	53	102	0	0	6	15	23
23	73	76	79	81	83	63	25	34	42	48	52	103	0	0	5	14	22
24	71	75	78	80	82	64	24	33	41	47	52	104	0	0	4	13	21
25	70	74	77	79	81	65	23	32	40	46	51	105	0	0	3	13	20
26	69	73	76	78	80	66	21	31	39	45	50						
27	68	72	75	78	80	67	20	30	38	44	49						
28	67	71	74	77	79	68	19	29	37	43	48						
29	65	70	73	76	78	69	18	28	36	43	48						
30	64	69	72	75	77	70	17	27	35	42	47						
31	63	68	71	74	77	71	15	26	34	41	46						
32	62	67	70	73	76	72	14	25	33	40	45						
33	61	66	69	73	75	73	13	24	32	39	45						
34	60	65	69	72	74	74	12	23	31	38	44						
35	58	64	68	71	73	75	11	22	31	38	43						
36	57	62	67	70	73	76	10	21	30	37	43						
37	56	61	66	69	72	77	8	20	29	36	42						
38	55	60	65	68	71	78	7	19	28	35	41						
39	54	59	64	68	70	79	6	18	27	34	40						
40	52	58	63	67	70	80	5	17	26	33	39						
41	51	57	62	66	69	81	4	16	25	33	39						
42	50	56	61	65	68	82	3	15	24	32	38						
43	49	55	60	64	67	83	1	14	23	31	37						
44	48	54	59	63	67	84	0	12	22	30	36						
45	46	53	58	63	66	85	0	11	21	29	36						
46	45	52	57	62	65	86	0	10	20	28	35						
47	44	51	56	61	64	87	0	9	19	28	34						
48	43	50	56	60	64	88	0	8	19	27	33						
49	42	49	55	59	63	89	0	7	18	26	33						
50	40	48	54	58	62	90	0	6	17	25	32						

What makes voices unpleasant

Your Intelligibility Score is an inventory of one aspect of your voice, an important aspect, but not the only one. A voice may be intelligible, yet unable to communicate attitudes. It may be unpleasant, even irritating, to listeners. Therefore, let us consider some common types of poor voice quality, their causes, and treatment.

NASALITY

Nasality comes from allowing too much of the tone to escape through the nose. Only three sounds of the language are nasal: *m, n,* and *ng*. These are properly made by closing off the mouth with the lips, tongue, or soft palate, and allowing the air stream to go through the nose. Theoretically, all other sounds are made by closing off the nasal passage and sending the breath stream through the mouth. What we call nasality, therefore, is the nasalizing of non-nasal sounds. Usually it is caused by an over-all sluggishness of the speech organs: (1) inadequate breathing, (2) constricted throat, tongue, and jaw, (3) mouth not open wide enough for all vowel sounds, (4) tongue raised too high in the mouth, and (5) a sluggish soft palate. Indeed there is a direct relationship between nasality and the size of mouth-opening during speech. The wider the mouth-opening, the less the nasality. It is also generally true that the wider the mouth-opening the less over-all sluggishness of the speech organs.

To correct nasality, first make a disc recording as a permanent record from which you can measure improvement. Then start with the exercises given in the first part of this chapter on breathing, phonation, and resonation. These general exercises are more fundamental to overcoming nasality than any specific exercises on mere soft palate control.

If specific exercises are required, work first on the sounds that are made through the nose: *m, n,* and *ng*. Hum these sounds and prolong them until you can *feel* the vibration in the nose. Then, still humming the nasal sound, slowly lower the jaw, then finally open the mouth and let the tone turn into an *ah:* m-m-m-m-a-a-h, n-n-n-n-a-a-h, ng-ng-ng-ng-a-a-h.

Next, drill on paired words like those given below. The first word in each pair contains a nasal sound. The second should have no nasality.

bean	bead	damper	dapper	strumming	strutting
bin	bid	fain	fade	tame	tape
bang	bag	fang	fag	time	tide
bone	bode	home	hope	tongue	tug
came	cape	languor	lacquer	tiny	tidy
come	cup	rhyme	ripe	wing	wig
crank	crag	seem	seep	whine	white
dandy	daddy	seen	seed	wander	water
downy	dowdy	sang	sack	whenever	whatever

HARSHNESS

Harshness is generally due to throat constriction. The constrictor muscles are too tense. Free vibration is thus interfered with and the voice is harsh, hard, or strident.

The causes are several: (1) Often it is found in high-strung and restless people, an index of a general emotional condition. (2) Sometimes it is found in people who are cold and unsympathetic. These are causes outside the scope of this chapter, but they are causes that you ought to face honestly. (3) But the most common cause is the old public speaker's "pinched throat," which comes from trying to speak louder by constricting the throat.

The remedy for a pinched throat you know already. Go back to the first part of this chapter on breathing (everything starts with breathing), phonation, and resonation. Work on the exercises to relax the throat, and to keep the power in the abdomen. Apply the axiom given earlier: *Power in the abdomen, relaxation in the throat, and flexibility in the face.*

HOARSENESS AND HUSKINESS

Hoarseness, sometimes called huskiness, is a rough aspirate quality like that in acute laryngitis.

Its cause may be physical—infected sinuses, growths on the vocal cords, etc.—and for that reason a physician should be consulted. Most hoarseness, however, comes from misusing the voice. The speaker perhaps is attempting to talk at an extremely low pitch, far below the normal range. Sometimes it comes from the childhood carry-over of attempting to talk like an adult. Sometimes it comes from the attempt to imitate the deep bass or contralto voice of some actor or speaker, and sometimes from someone's bad advice "to lower the voice." Often it is caused by the deliberate effort to enrich the voice by lowering the pitch. Now what happens when the pitch is artificially lowered beyond the range of human resonators? The volume is decreased to a small fraction of its original power, simply because the resonance chambers cannot amplify an artificially low pitch (this is elementary physics). *Thereupon the speaker tenses the throat and tries to gain volume by forcing more air through the vocal cords.* The result is a hoarse voice with an internal vocal rumbling which the speaker mistakes for resonance. With constant use it also produces "the preacher's sore throat," which is a natural result of prolonged voice abuse.

The treatment, of course, is to relax the throat and raise the pitch. But it is not so simple as the saying. You should start at the beginning with exercises on breathing (everything starts with breathing!), on phonation, and finally on resonation. With these exercises your purpose is to eliminate the strain and tension, relax the throat, get the pitch where it belongs, and get power from the abdomen and chest. As a guide for improvement, you might first make a disc recording. This will give you a permanent record of the original hoarseness from which you can measure improvement.

THINNESS

Thinness is lack of carrying power. A thin voice has no body or fullness. Usually it seems to be pitched too high, although this often is not true.

For treating a thin voice, first make a disc recording so as to have a record for measuring improvement. Then start a program of daily exercises in breathing, phonation, and resonation. Focus especially on establishing the *concept* of resonance (see exercises for this under Resonation earlier in this chapter). Listen to the recordings of professional actors and good speakers. Compare them with your own. Bear in mind two conditioning factors. First, do not expect to develop good resonance within a day or two, or from casual intermittent effort. Second, be assured that you can distinctly improve your voice by proper systematic exercise.

BREATHINESS

Breathiness is a fuzzy, feather-edged voice, a part whisper in which you hear about as much breath as voice.

It is caused by failure to bring the edges of the vocal cords closely enough together, which allows the escape of unvocalized air. This may come from weakness of the vocal muscles or from irregularities on the edges of the vocal cords, but these are not the usual reasons. The more common reason is improper breathing and inefficient use of the larynx.

The treatment is re-education in producing voice. Start with a disc recording so as to have a record for measuring improvement. Then return to the exercises given earlier in this chapter on breathing, phonation, and resonation. For specific exercises, after practice on these basic general exercises, you must remember that the vocal cords are not under direct voluntary control, like the tongue; therefore you must resort to indirect methods. Start with the "glottal catch." This is accomplished by starting a stream of unvocalized air through the larynx (simply breathing out), then suddenly stopping the breath in the throat. Actually you do this by bringing the vocal cords sharply together. If this is properly done a sharp click will be heard, and the breath will stop instantly. Be sure that the shut-off is in the larynx and not in the back of the mouth. If you cannot identify the glottal catch in this exercise, try coughing. We usually start a cough with the glottal catch. After you identify it with a cough, get set for starting to cough, hold the position for a moment, then open glottal catch and say *a-a-a-h*. Now reverse the process by starting with *a-a-a-h*, then cutting off the sound with the glottal catch.

For further specific exercises, practice the following word pairs. For words in the first column, start by bringing the vocal cords together as though you were going to cough, then vocalize carefully without breathiness: *e-e-a-t*. Then take its opposite pair starting with the sound of *h*, being careful not to use an excess of air on the *h*, nor to delay too long in voicing the vowel:

eel	heel	ooze	whose
ill	hill	old	hold
ate	hate	all	haul
at	hat	oil	Hoyle
eye	high	art	heart

ASSIGNMENTS

FOR TESTING AND IMPROVING VOICE QUALITY

The basic exercises are found earlier in this chapter under breathing, phonation, and resonation. After you have made progress with them, work on the exercises below.

Remember that "practice makes *permanent*" (not perfect), and that practice of your old faults will only fix them more firmly. Therefore, practice these exercises with proper breathing habits, relaxed throat, open mouth, and a conscious concept of resonance.

A little learning is a dangerous thing;
Drink deep, or taste not the Pierian spring;
There shallow draughts intoxicate the brain,
And drinking largely sobers us again.

ALEXANDER POPE

Once more; speak clearly if you speak at all;
Carve every word before you let it fall:
Don't like a lecturer or dramatic star,
Try overhard to roll the British R.

OLIVER WENDELL HOLMES

Afoot and light-hearted I take to the open road,
Healthy, free, the world before me,
The long brown path before me leading wherever I choose.

Henceforth I ask not good-fortune, I myself am good fortune,
Henceforth I whimper no more, postpone no more, need nothing,
Done with indoor complaints, libraries, querulous criticisms,
Strong and content I travel the open road.

WALT WHITMAN

Maris is simple and chaste—
She's pretty and tender and modest—
But on one or two matters of taste
Her views are distinctly the oddest.
Her virtue is something sublime—
No kissing—on that there's a stopper—
When I try, she says, "All in good time—
At present it's highly improper."

GILBERT and SULLIVAN

We hold these truths to be self-evident, that all men are created equal, that they are endowed by their Creator with certain unalienable Rights, that among these are Life, Liberty and the pursuit of Happiness.—That to secure these rights, Governments are instituted among Men, deriving their just powers from the consent of the governed,—That whenever any Form of Government becomes destructive of these ends, it is the Right of the People to alter or to abolish it.

Declaration of Independence

With malice toward none; with charity for all; with firmness in the right, as God gives us to see the right, let us strive on to finish the work we are in; to bind up the nation's wounds; to care for him who shall borne the battle, and for his widow and orphans—to do all which may achieve and cherish a just and lasting peace among ourselves, and with all nations.

ABRAHAM LINCOLN, *Second Inaugural Address*

The destiny of America was proclaimed in prophecy spoken by our first president in his first inaugural address in 1789—words almost directed, it would seem to this year of 1941: "The preservation of the sacred fire of liberty and the destiny of the republican model of government are justly considered . . . deeply . . . finally, staked on the experiment intrusted to the hands of the American people."

If we lose that fire—if we let it be smothered with doubt and fear—then we shall reject the destiny which Washington strove so valiantly and so triumphantly to establish. The preservation of the spirit and faith of the nation does, and will, furnish the highest justification for every sacrifice that we may make in the cause of national defense.

In the face of great perils never before encountered, our strong purpose is to protect and perpetuate that integrity of democracy. For this we must muster the spirit of America, and the faith of America. We do not retreat. We are not content to stand still. As Americans, we go forward, in the service of our country, by the will of God.

FRANKLIN D. ROOSEVELT, *Third Inaugural Address*

You ask, "What is our policy?" I will say: "It is to wage war, by sea, land, and air, with all our might and with all the strength that God can give us; to wage war against a monstrous tyranny, never surpassed in the dark, lamentable catalogue of human crime. That is our policy." You ask, "What is our aim?" I can answer in one word: "Victory—victory at all costs, victory in spite of all terror, victory however long and hard the road may be; for without victory there is no survival." . . . But I take up my task with buoyancy and hope. I feel sure that our cause will be suffered to fail among men. At this time I feel entitled to claim the aid of all, and I say, "Come, then, let us go forward together with our united strength."

WINSTON CHURCHILL, On Becoming Prime Minister

What makes a good speaking voice

By this time you know what basically makes a good speaking voice, and how to work toward improving yours. Let us now apply these principles in the following steps:

SUPPLY VOCAL POWER FROM BELOW THE LARYNX

A public speaker needs ample vocal energy, energy enough to be heard easily, and energy enough to carry tone color and informing inflections. Here you face two difficulties. First, some people try to get power by constricting the muscles in the throat and neck; the result is the harshness and hoarseness described above. Second, some try to speak without adequate vocal energy; and the result is lifeless tones without salt and spirit.

Vocal power, as we know, comes from pressure behind the breath stream. This pressure, in turn, comes from muscles in the abdomen and between the ribs. In the words of actors in the old Victorian days, you "*pack your tones against your belt.*" This is a good way to think of it. Lift the front wall of the chest. Harden the abdomen. Pull down the diaphragm until it draws air into the lungs like a suction pump. Now you are in position to "pack your tones against your belt." Further steps for using vocal energy are these:

Maintain a steady pressure of air as you talk. In good voices the action of exhaling muscles is steady. In poor voices it tends to be jerky. Steadiness, of course, does not mean uniform pressure. You change the pressure for emphasis and accent. You vary the gradations according to the thought. By steady pressure is meant that you are not wavering or jerky, not booming forth the first part of a sentence and then fading into inaudibility as you come to the end.

Maintain an adequate breath reserve. You do not keep your lungs filled to the last cubic inch, or else you soon will have a chest full of air with burned out oxygen. Instead, you take a reasonably deep breath and fill the chest comfortably. In the same way, you do not keep on talking until you run out of air, but smoothly along the way you refill with short catches of breath. Thus the lungs are never entirely inflated, nor ever too empty. This ample breath reserve enables you to maintain vigor of voice to the end of each thought.

You have previously had exercises on vocal energy, but a few more are here given for review and reinforcement:

ASSIGNMENTS

VOCAL ENERGY

1. Practice breathing again. Stand erect. Pull down the diaphragm and draw air into the lungs. As you thus inhale, do also the following: (1) Lift the upper chest. (2) Push out the ribs. (3) Harden the abdomen. (4) See if you can feel the pull of muscles in the small of the back. When you have done this your bellows will be expanded to its maximum. The pressure should now be entirely below the larynx, and the throat should be *open and relaxed*. After a few seconds exhale without a sound by letting the air flow silently through the lips.

2. Stand erect and inhale as above, but this time fill the chest comfortably and speak one of the following lines. Speak with a relaxed and open throat, and prolong the stressed tones with maximum vocal energy for three counts:

All aboard!
As you *were!*
For*ward! March!*
Roll back the *tide* of eigh*teen hun*dred *years.*

3. Stand erect and inhale until the chest is comfortably filled. Then speak the following selections with maximum vocal power. Keep the throat relaxed and open. Supply power from below. Sustain the stressed sounds:

Breathes there a man with soul so dead,
Who never to himself hath said
This is my own, my native land?

SIR WALTER SCOTT

Hear the mellow wedding bells,
Golden bells!
What a world of happiness their harmony foretells!

EDGAR ALLAN POE

The bell invites me.
Hear it not, Duncan; for it is a knell
That summons thee to heaven or to hell.

SHAKESPEARE, *Macbeth*

USE AMPLE RESONANCE

The vibrating vocal cords produce only a thin and feeble tone. You must amplify and enrich this tone with the resonators. Remember that you have two types of resonators, fixed and adjustable. The fixed resonators are unchangeable in size: the skull bones, nose, nasal sinuses, trachea, sternum, and ribs. When you use any group of them you get the *feeling* of resonance in that part of your body. Close the lips and hum *m-m-m-m-m* until you get this feeling. Then put your hand on top of your head and you will know whence comes that "feeling." It is the real thing, for your skull bones are vibrating! Also feel the chest. If you are using enough energy down in your bellows, the chest bones are also vibrating.

Next, are the adjustable resonators: mouth, pharynx, and larynx, You change the size and shape of these resonators when you change voice pitch. You also change the size and shape for each of the fifteen or so different vowel sounds. Hence it is that good voice production requires "*flexibility in the face.*" These are the operating principles for flexibility:

1. Each vowel sound needs a special size and shape of the adjustable resonators.
2. Certain so-called vowels are really diphthongs, or double vowels, especially the sounds in *ice, how* and *oil.* For full utterance these require two sizes and shapes.
3. Two sounds are really triphthongs, or triple vowels. They are the sounds in *fire* and *our*. They require three sizes and shapes.
4. Changes in pitch need changes in size and shape.
5. Changes in inflection need changes in size and shape.

You have had basic exercises in resonation. For additional special exercises practice the following:

ASSIGNMENTS

RESONANCE

Stand erect and inhale until the chest is filled comfortably. Practice these exercises with exaggerated movements of the mouth and pharynx. Watch yourself in a mirror to be sure the movements are as exaggerated as they feel. Be sure the throat is relaxed and open, and that the power comes from the bellows down below.

> I have but one lamp by which my feet are guided, and that is the lamp of experience.
>
> PATRICK HENRY

> There are maidens in Scotland more lovely by far,
> That would gladly be bride to Young Lochinvar.
>
> SIR WALTER SCOTT

I know not whether Laws be right,
  Or whether Laws be wrong;
All that we know who lie in gaol
  Is that the wall is strong;
And that each day is like a year,
  A year whose days are long.

OSCAR WILDE

When the night wind howls in the chimney cowls, and the bat
  in the moonlight flies,
And inky clouds, like funeral shrouds, sail over the midnight
  skies.

GILBERT and SULLIVAN

And I have loved, thee, Ocean—and my joy
  Of youthful sports was on thy breast to be
Borne, like thy bubbles, onward; from a boy
  I have wantoned with the breakers.

LORD BYRON

Ship me somewhere east of Suez, where the best is like the worst,
Where there aren't no Ten Commandments an' a man can raise a thirst;
For the temple-bells are callin', an' it's there that I would be—
By the old Moulmein Pagoda, looking lazy at the sea;
On the road to Mandalay,
Where the old Flotilla lay,
With our sick beneath the awnings when we went to Mandalay!
On the road to Mandalay,
Where the flyin'-fishes play,
An' the dawn comes up like thunder outer China 'cross the Bay!

RUDYARD KIPLING [6]

USE YOUR NORMAL KEY

Your voice has a normal key. This is the general pitch level best coupled to your particular resonators. Your voice will rise and fall above and below this median, but it tends always to return to it.

The normal key varies with different persons, and it varies greatly between men and women. In this respect voices are like musical instruments. Each will produce sound within a given range, some high, some medium, some low. Outside this range it does not perform so well.

[6] Rudyard Kipling, *Barrack-Room Ballads* (New York, The Macmillan Company, 1892). For the first magazine publication of this famous poem, see *Fortnightly Review*, LX (November 1, 1893), 602-603.

Thus some women's voices are contralto, and others are soprano. Some men's voices are bass, and others are tenor. For example, Franklin D. Roosevelt's voice was a tenor; he spoke with a wide inflection variation, but at a normal key of about 196 vibrations per second—or G below middle C. The speaking voice of the Metropolitan bass-baritone Friedrich Schorr had a normal key of about F, or 175 vibrations per second. That of Rabbi Stephen S. Wise was about E, or 165 vibrations per second.[7]

If you do not use your normal key, you cannot attain best potential voice quality. If you speak below it, you will tend to speak at a deep hollow tone without flexibility. If you speak above it, you will tend to have a thin, high, squeaky voice, with the same lack of flexibility.

There are several methods for finding your normal key. One is to close the mouth, press down the tragus (flap in front of the opening) of the ear, and hum from the highest possible tone to the lowest, using an *even* breath pressure. Somewhere along the way you will find a tone that is louder than the others. This is the median tone best fitted to your resonations. It is your normal key.

Probably the most accurate method, however, is to sing from your lowest key to your highest, including your falsetto. Your normal key is about *one-fourth* the way up from your lowest tone.

ASSIGNMENTS

ESTABLISHING THE NORMAL KEY

Using the methods described above, find your normal key. By going frequently to a piano and sounding the proper key, you can keep this pitch continually in mind and help to make its use habitual.

Using your normal key, read the following, but do not read in a monopitch. Instead, communicate the meaning by as much variety of pitch as you need, but use your normal key as the median.:

> There was an old preacher once who told some boys of the Bible lesson he was going to read in the morning. The boys, finding the place, glued together the connecting pages. The next morning he read on the bottom of on page: "When Noah was one hundred and twenty years old he took unto himself a wife, who was"—then turning the page—"one hundred and forty cubits long, forty cubits wide, built of gopher-wood, and covered with

[7] For a report on the normal key of these speakers and others, see Arleigh B. Williamson, "Diagnosis and Treatment of 72 Cases of Hoarse Voices," *Quarterly Journal of Speech*, XXXI (April, 1945), 192.

pitch inside and out." He was naturally puzzled at this. He read it again, verified it, and then said: "My friends, this is the first time I ever met this in the Bible, but I accept it as an evidence of the assertion that we are fearfully and wonderfully made."

HENRY W. GRADY

We are spinning our own fates, good or evil, never to be undone. Every smallest stroke of virtue or vice leaves its never-so-little scar. The drunken Rip Van Winkle, in Jefferson's play, excuses himself for every fresh dereliction by saying, "I won't count this time!" Well, he may not count it, and a kind Heaven may not count it; but it is being counted none the less. Down among his nerve-cells and fibers the molecules are counting it, registering and storing it up to be used against him when the next temptation comes. Nothing we ever do is, in strict scientific literalness, wiped out.

WILLIAM JAMES

SPEAK WITH A FLEXIBLE AND RESPONSIVE VOICE

To communicate full meanings you need a flexible voice. First, a good voice has variety of *rate.* Just as an automobile slows down for curves and villages, so the sensitive speaker changes his rate to best carry the meaning. E. H. Sothern, a discriminating Shakespearean actor, read Hamlet's soliloquy, "To be or not to be," at a meditative 80 words a minute, whereas Hamlet's advice to the players, "Speak the speech I pray you," was spoken trippingly on the tongue at 170 words a minute. Indeed, we might paraphrase the author of *Hamlet* and say, "Suit the rate to the word, and the word to the rate."

Next, a communicative voice has variety of *emphasis.* Behind the weight of thought comes the thrust of vocal energy. By emphasis we reveal meanings, indicate degrees of importance, and tell how we feel about them. Hence a speaker says "*Now* is the time," or "*This* is the way," or "We shall *fight* in the *fields* and in the *streets,* we shall *fight* in the *hills;* we shall *never surrender.*"

Finally, a communicative voice has a wide range of pitch and inflection. Try saying, "Y-e-e-s, I supp-o-o-ose that's so-o-o," and make it mean, "Yes, I suppose that's so, but I'm doubtful, very doubtful." Do this to carry the full extended meaning, and you will find that it calls for long, extended inflections. As a matter of fact, an investigation of leading actors on Broadway shows that they averaged two full octaves from the highest to the lowest pitch. One measurement of Franklin D. Roosevelt's voice showed a range from 96 to 256 vibrations per second, or almost 18 semitones. In a short reading, Julia Marlowe's voice ranged from 192 to 438 vibrations per second—one and one-third octaves. A study of college students' voices showed that those which other students rated as "better" voices had a greater number of rising inflections, greater number of falling inflections, longer range of inflection, greater number of shifts in pitch, and a greater extent of shifts in pitch. The poorer voices fell short on each of these forms of flexibility. The voice, then, that communicates best thought is a flexible voice. The deadly drone of an unchanging voice communicates poorly. As Gilbert Highet said of Prime Minister Stanley Baldwin's pompous chant, "Half an hour of this put everybody to sleep. Several years of it put Britain to sleep."

ASSIGNMENTS

DEVELOPING A FLEXIBLE AND RESPONSIVE VOICE

1. Vary the rate of speaking the following sentences so as to communicate the indicated meanings:

    a. "I told her I couldn't come."

    Slowly, expressing regret
    Faster, argumentatively defending your answer
    Still faster, meaning "I didn't want to go, and I got out of it."

    b. "What do you think we ought to do?"

    Very slowly, as though asked by a tired and confused person
    Normal rate, asking a simple question
    Fast, to mean, "I'm in a hurry."

2. Vary the emphasis of the following so as to communicate the indicated meanings:

    a. "There is no other answer. You have asked me that question a thousand times, and my reply has always been the same. It always will be the same."

    Mild emphasis, as though explaining it the thousandth time
    Sustained emphasis, meaning "Don't ask me again!"
    Short sharp emphasis, to communicate fear

    b. "Yes, I know about it. I've known it all the time."

    Mild emphasis, merely to offer information
    Prolonged emphasis, to mean, "I'm tired of hearing about it."
    Explosive emphasis, meaning, "Don't tell me I don't know!"

3. Vary the pitch of the following so as to communicate the indicated meanings:

a. "I wouldn't do that if I were you."
Slight inflections, giving mild advice
Wide inflections, pleading
Narrow sustained inflections, threatening, "You just dare!"

b. "Who is she?"
Medium inflections, merely asking
Wider inflections, meaning, "What a frump!"
Extreme inflections, meaning, "She's a glamor girl!"

4. If possible record part or all of the following exercises, listen to the playback, and assess the flexibility of your voice. Do you speak with a pitch range of two notes, or four, or six, or eight, or more? Do you have a "repeated pitch pattern," in which the voice changes are all alike? In reading poetry does your voice rise at the same point in each line, and fall at identical points in each line? If so, you are not communicating meaning, but are only singing a kind of song. Do you read everything at the same rate, regardless of its mood and meaning? Do you have real emphasis, or do your words come back to you like the ticking of a grandfather's clock? Hear yourself as others hear you, and let not your judgment be too much tempered by charity.

No! Not *really!*

You don't *say* so!

Hold it, brother! That's *my* coat!

The publisher said the *author* was a *fool.*

The *publisher* said the author was a *fool.*

They *tell* us, sir, that we are *weak* . . . *Sir,* we are *not* weak.

Wherefore rejoice? What conquest brings *he* home?

What *tributaries* follow *him* to Rome

To *grace* in *captive bonds* his *chariot-wheels?*

Never in the field of *human conflict* was so *much* owed by so *many* to so *few.*

There is a *tide* in the *affairs* of *men*
Which, taken at its *flood,* leads on to *fortune;*
Omitted, all the *voyage* of their *life*
Is *bound* in *shallows* and in *miseries.*

SHAKESPEARE

A little *work,* a little *play*
To *keep* us *going*—and *so, good-day!*
A little *warmth,* a little *light*
Of *love's* be*stowing*—and *so, goodnight!*

A little *fun*, to *match* the *sorrow*
Of *each day's growing*—and *so, good morrow!*
A little *trust* that *when* we *die*
We *reap* our *sowing*! And *so—good-bye!*

GEORGE DU MAURIER

MAKE YOUR VOICE THE VEHICLE OF THOUGHT AND FEELING

This is the be-all and end-all of voice training. Everything else in this chapter has been ways and means to prepare for it. The ultimate goal is a voice that is the vehicle of your thought and feeling. You cannot "deliver" a speech, remember. You can only use light waves and sound waves to make listeners think what you think and to feel about it as you feel. A good voice, then, carries to listeners your finest degrees of thought, and slightest shade of values, every color and hue. Unhappily the percentage of such voices is small.

Perhaps foremost of all things your voice should tell is *sincerity*. To all who hear, it should say, "You may disagree with what I say, but you cannot question my sincerity." In an investigation of what listeners thought to be essential in good speaking, *87 per cent listed sincerity.*[8] This reaffirms the position of George Pierce Baker that, "One has only to examine the great speeches from Demosthenes to Webster to see how earnestly the orators in all parts of their work impressed their sincerity on their audiences; one has but to consider the wrecked careers among orators to realize that sincerity is the chief essential of persuasion. Without it all else, in the long run, goes for naught."

Yet no listener, of course, really knows whether a speaker is sincere. He can know only whether a speaker *seems* sincere, and he must determine this most of all from the speaker's voice. "Say what you think," William Jennings Bryan used to say to his daughter, "but *feel* what you say." Now sincerity is not easily feigned. The surest way, the only safe way, to sound sincere is to *be* sincere. We are concerned here with your freeing the voice so as to communicate that sincerity to the audience.

Once you have established sincerity, then comes the meaning of the words themselves. Remember that when you speak or read you communicate *two* simultaneous meanings. First, you say, "This is what I

[8] William K. Clark, "A Survey of Certain Audience Attitudes. . . . ," *Speech Monographs*, XVIII, No. 1 (March, 1951), 67.

am talking about." Second, you say, "Here is how I feel about it." Like the two legs of the human body, both are essential.

There is no absolute meaning any word must have. The dictionary establishes only a frame of reference by recording many meanings for almost every word. At the moment of utterance you must give each word its exact meaning in context. You must spot the important words, let listeners know they are important and why, and communicate their meanings—as you use them—with precision. You must penetrate beneath the surface of language, make clear your basic thoughts, show why they are basic, and what follows from them. This is not done by the mere utterance of words, for the mere flow of words—even the right words—may confuse the listener if their exact meaning and their relation to the whole is not made clear.

Finally, you must tell listeners, "This is how I feel about these things." This is done by what we call *emotional color*. You have been using emotional color and hearing it in others all your life without probably knowing the term. Listen to a good speaker, and you know unhesitatingly whether he feels determination, anger, contempt, friendship, or indifference. Each attitude carries its own particular tone-color. The tone-color of each attitude is distinct from others, arrogance from assurance, friendship from flattery, and mirth from melancholy.

How do you make voice the vehicle of thought and feeling? Shall you say, "I shall emphasize this word," or "Here I want to show determination; therefore, I shall use the emotional color of a determined person"? Not if you want to be a real speaker. If you do this, the result will be like that described (in this case a bit unjustly) by a critic of Olivia de Havilland: "She never seems to feel the part—only the importance of it. She never seems in love with Romeo—only with *Romeo and Juliet.* She recites poetry where she should radiate it; and goes through the role as though following a score marked presto or lento, *ff*. or *pp*." Listeners know when a speaker is really friendly, and when he is only feigning friendship; when his basic attitude is anxiety or suspense, and when he is merely reciting words. This is old knowledge in the human race, learned early in every life.

If you soliloquize, your voice will be a soliloquy. If you only half-grasp the thought, your voice will be perfunctory. If you look on speaking as an external exhibition, your voice will be a mechanical imitation, painstaking perhaps but only a gallant try and a double miss. To communicate thought you must be thinking on your feet, creating or recreating the full thought at the moment of utterance. To communicate attitudes you must *experience* the attitude as you speak. "Expression," said Cicero, "is always perfect." Within the limits of your own particular voice this is true. To make voice the vehicle of thought and feeling, then, you must think in terms of ideas, feelings, and concepts instead of mere words.

ASSIGNMENTS

MAKING VOICE THE VEHICLE OF THOUGHT AND FEELING

1. The word *yes* can be spoken to carry at least twenty different meanings. Try speaking it to carry each of the following meanings. Remember to *think* the meanings.

Plain affirmation	"O Yeah?"
"Certainly"	"Are you serious?"
"Maybe"	"I don't like it"
"I doubt it"	"No!"

2. Give *oh* each of the following meanings:

Indifference	"I see now!"
Disappointment	Mild surprise
Pity	Great surprise
Disgust	"How terrible!"

3. Study the following selection, get its central theme and supporting details, then read it so the full meaning will be communicated:

> One comfort is that great men taken up in any way are profitable company. We can not look, however imperfectly, upon a great man without gaining something by it. He is the living fountain of life, which it is pleasant to be near. On any terms whatsoever you will not grudge to wander in his neighborhood for a while.
>
> THOMAS CARLYLE

4. What is the dominant mood in the following selection? Is it reverence, loyalty, admiration, entreaty, command, coaxing, anxiety, remorse, or gratitude? Decide which you think it is, and read it to communicate that mood:

> And Ruth said, Intreat me not to leave thee, or to return from following after thee: for whither thou goest, I will go; and where thou lodgest, I will lodge: thy people shall be my people and thy God my God: Where thou diest, I will die, and there will I be buried: the Lord do so to me, and more also, if ought but death part thee and me.
>
> Book of Ruth, I:16-17

5. Is the underlying mood of Adelaide Anne Procter's "The Lost Chord" awe, excitement, explanation, gayety, irony, sadness, tranquility, or wonder? Decide which it means to you, and read it to communicate that mood. Notice especially its "vocal climax," the feeling that rises steadily with increasing intensity. Can you communicate it as you read?

Seated one day at the organ,
  I was weary and ill at ease,
And my fingers wandered idly
  Over the noisy keys.

I do not know what I was playing,
  Or what I was dreaming then:
But I struck one chord of music,
  Like the sound of a great Amen.

It flooded the crimson twilight
  Like the close of an angel's psalm,
And it lay on my fevered spirit
  With a touch of Infinite calm.

It quieted pain and sorrow,
  Like love overcoming strife:
It seemed the harmonious echo
  From our discordant life.

ADELAIDE ANNE PROCTER

LONGER SELECTIONS FOR COMMUNICATING THOUGHT AND FEELING

Study the following selections to get the thought and feeling. Practice reading them aloud, using the principles studied in this chapter to communicate vividly the full meaning. Some selections require unusual volume, some require a slower-than-normal rate, some require a narrow pitch range, and some an extreme range. All of them require breath control, resonance, pure tones, and good articulation.

1. JUDGE MEDINA'S *Charge to the Jury During the Communist Trial*

. . . These defendants had the right to advocate by peaceful and lawful means any and all changes in the laws and in the Constitution; they had the right to criticize the President of the United States and the Congress; they had the right to assert that World War II, prior to the invasion of Russia by Germany, was an unjust war, an imperialist war and that upon such invasion it became a just war worthy of all material and moral support; and they had the right publicly to express these views orally and in writing. They had the right thus to assert that the Government was at all times exploiting the poor and worthy workers for the benefit of the trusts and monopolies.

They had a right thus to assert that what they call the democracy of Russia is superior in all respects to American democracy. They had a right thus to assert that the Marshall Plan was a mistake, that billions of dollars should be loaned to Russia and that legislation adversely affecting Communists should not be passed. Whether you or I or anyone else likes or dislikes such or similar and analogous views . . . is . . . not entitled to the slightest consideration in deciding this case. Unless a minority had a right to express and to advocate its views, the democratic process as we understand it here in America would cease to exist and those in power might remain there indefinitely and make impossible any substantial changes in our social and economic system. . . .

I charge you that if the defendants did no more than pursue peaceful studies and discussions or teaching and advocacy in the realm of ideas you must acquit them. . . . Do not be led astray by talk about thought control, or putting books on trial. No such issues are before you here.

But no one could suppose nor is it the law that any person has an absolute and unbridled right to say or to write and to publish whatever he chooses under any and all circumstances.

Words may be the instruments by which crimes are committed, as in many familiar situations; and it has always been recognized that the protection of other interests of society may justify reasonable restrictions upon speech in furtherance of the general welfare. . . .

You must be satisfied from the evidence, beyond a reasonable doubt, that the defendants had an intent to cause the overthrow or destruction of the Government of the United States by force and violence . . . as speedily as circumstances would permit it to be achieved.

. . . I charge you that it is not the abstract doctrine of overthrowing or destroying organized government by unlawful means which is denounced by this law, but the teaching and advocacy of action for the accomplishment of that purpose, by language reasonably and ordinarily calculated to incite persons to such action. . . .

No such intent could be inferred from the open and aboveboard teaching of a course on the principles and implications of Communism in an American college or university, where everything is open to the scrutiny of parents and trustees and anyone who may be interested. . . . That is why it is so important for you to weigh with scrupulous care the testimony concerning secret schools, false names, devious ways, general falsification and so on, all alleged to be in the setting of a huge and well-disciplined organization, spreading to practically every state of the union and all the principal cities and industries.

Harold R. Medina

2. *The Crisis: "These Are the Times That Try Men's Souls"*

These are the times that try men's souls. The summer soldier and the sunshine patriot will, in this crisis, shrink from the service of their country; but he that stands it *now,* deserves the love and thanks of man and woman. Tyranny, like hell, is not easily conquered; yet we have this consolation with us, that the harder the conflict, the more glorious the triumph. What we obtain too cheap, we esteem too lightly; it is dearness only that gives every thing its value. Heaven knows how to put a proper price upon its goods; and it would be strange indeed if so celestial an article as FREEDOM should not be rated highly. . . .

A noted tory, who kept tavern at Amboy, was standing at his door, with as pretty a child in his hand, about eight or nine years old, as I ever saw, and after speaking his mind as freely as he thought was prudent, finished with this unfatherly expression, "*Well! give me peace in my day.*" . . . A generous parent should have said, "*If there must be trouble, let it be in my day, that my child may have peace*"; and this single reflection, well applied, is sufficient to awaken every man to duty.

THOMAS PAINE

3. *History as Literature*

The true historian will bring the past before our eyes, as if it were the present. He will make us see as living men the hardfaced archers of Agincourt, and the war-worn spearmen who followed Alexander down beyond the rim of the known world. We shall hear grate on the coast of Britain, the keels of the Low-Dutch sea-thieves whose children's children were to inherit unknown continents. We shall thrill to the triumph of Hannibal. Gorgeous in our sight will rise the splendor of dead cities, and the might of the elder empires of which the very ruins crumbled to dust ages ago. Along ancient trade routes, across the world's waste spaces, the caravans shall move; and the admirals of unchartered seas shall furrow the oceans with their lonely prows. Beyond the dim centuries we shall see the banners float above armed hosts. We shall see the conquerors riding forward to victories that have changed the course of time. We shall listen to the prophecies of forgotten seers. Ours shall be the dreams of dreamers who dreamed greatly, who saw in their vision peaks so lofty that never yet have they been reached by the sons and daughters of men.

THEODORE ROOSEVELT

4. *Against Meat Rationing Among the Navajos*

The Navajo are a nomad people. They must follow their sheep from one grazing range to another. To live, they must kill and eat their sheep. They have no refrigeration to store meat.

Nowhere in the Treaty of Guadalupe is there mention of the Office of Price Administration. Nowhere does it say the white man has the right to investigate the Indian's eating habits.

The Navajo Reservation is vast. Its canyons are steep and rocky, treacherous to the feet of the unlearned. The OPA investigators would push damn easy.

CHEE DODGE, Navajo Tribal Chief

5. *The Big Man and the Little One*

William James was one of the great men of this country. People crowded to hear him talk. Students patterned their writing and their thinking after him. Books about him, or dedicated to him, or showing the admiration of their writers for him or his influence upon them, appear every day and probably will for many years. He really was a great man.

Now one way you can tell a great man is by the way he acts toward a little one. When Mr. James was a professor at Harvard, a freshman was standing one day in front of a book store. There were some books in the window, and among them a volume of O. Henry's stories. Another man came up whom the freshman did not know. "Have you read the new one?" asked the other man. "No," answered the freshman. "Neither have I," said the other man, "but I have read all the others." "He's great, though—don't you think so?" asked the freshman. "Grand," replied the other man. "Let's go in and buy this one." So they did.

Coming out of the store the other man said to the freshman, "You'd better come home to dinner with me; my folks are away and I'm all alone tonight." He did not ask the freshman's name, and the young man took him for some instructor.

They went to the other man's house, a big house on a quiet street with plenty of easy chairs and lots of books. After dinner they sat around and talked—about football, about the big men among the students, about the things the students liked and didn't like, about fraternities, college clubs, comic operas, and why one man was popular and another man was not. The freshman got the impression that the other man was about his own age.

Finally, at eleven o'clock, the freshman started to go home. As he stood in the doorway telling the other man what a good time he had had, the other man said to him, "You must come again, and we'll have another talk." Then he added, "I don't think I know your name." The freshman told him, and said, "And now may I ask yours?" "William James," replied the other man.

There are plenty of men who will make you afraid of them because they think they are big, or because they try to make you think so. But when you meet a really big man, you need never be afraid of him.

CARL S. PATTON [9]

6. *He Was Scared*

When Philip Gibbs came to this country from England he was very much scared. He had been all through the war as a newspaper correspondent. He had been in the trenches, and under fire, and out in no-man's-land. But in America he was scared. He was scared first, he says, by the traffic in New York, and he thought he surely would be killed.

But he was most scared when he had to make speeches. "As we drove up to Carnegie Hall," he tells us, "I was cold with fright. My fear increased until I was chilled with it when my brother shook hands with me, patted me on the back as if I were about to go over the top, and pushed me through a little door. I found myself facing a great audience. I was conscious of innumerable faces, white shirt fronts, and eyes—eyes—eyes, staring at me from the great arena of stalls and from the galleries up to the roof. My tongue stuck to the roof of my mouth, my knees weakened."

[9] Carl S. Patton, *Two-Minute Stories* (New York: Harper and Brothers, 1930). Used by permission.

Then came another terror. "There was a sudden movement," he says, "like a tidal wave, among all those people. It was as if they were all advancing upon me, possibly with intent to kill." Then suddenly it came over him. They were paying him a great honor! They were standing up, not to move down on him and kill him, but just to greet him, and show him how glad they were to see him.

The chairman made an introduction. Sir Philip didn't hear a word of it. He knew now that they weren't going to hurt him, but he was still scared. He got going. Six times he looked at his wrist watch to see if it was time to stop. Then another terror seized him. Probably the watch had stopped, maybe he had spoken an hour too long! He put it to his ear; the great crowd burst into laughter, and then—according to Gibbs—"Some spirit of friendship and good will reached up to me and gave me courage."

This is a sort of parable of what happens to us all in life. We are scared, often. Scared of the things we have to do, scared of what may happen to us, scared generally and mostly of people. By and by it comes to us that people do not mean us any harm. They are not moving down on us to kill us, but only standing up to be nice to us. The longer I live the more I feel that there isn't much to be afraid of. So take from me this one little piece of advice—don't be scared.

Carl S. Patton [10]

7. *The Lord Is My Shepherd*

The Lord is my shepherd; I shall not want.

He maketh me to lie down in green pastures; he leadeth me beside the still waters.

He restoreth my soul: he leadeth me in the paths of righteousness for his name's sake.

Yea, though I walk through the valley of the shadow of death, I will fear no evil: for thou art with me; thy rod and thy staff they comfort me.

Thou preparest a table before me in the presence of mine enemies: thou anointest my head with oil; my cup runneth over.

Surely goodness and mercy shall follow me all the days of my life: and I will dwell in the house of the Lord for ever.

Twenty-third Psalm

8. *For Whom the Bell Tolls*

No man is an *Iland,* intire of it selfe; every man is a peece of the *Continent,* a part of the *maine;* if a *Clod* bee washed away by the *Sea, Europe* is the lesse, as well as if a *Promontorie* were, as well as if a *Mannor* of thy *friends* or of *thine owne* were; any mans *death* diminishes me, because I am involved in *Mankinde;* And therefore never send to know for whom the *bell* tolls; It tolls for *thee.*

John Donne

[10] *Ibid.* Used by permission.

9. *I Have Not Loved the World*

I have not loved the world, nor the world me;
I have not flattered its rank breath, nor bowed
To its idolatries a patient knee,
Nor coined my cheek to smiles—nor cried aloud
In worship of an echo: in the crowd
They would not deem me one of such—I stood
Among them, but not of them—in a shroud
Of thoughts which were not their thoughts, and still could,
Had I not filed [defiled] my mind, which thus itself subdued.

LORD BYRON

10. *Elegy Written in a Country Churchyard*

The curfew tolls the knell of parting day,
The lowing herd wind slowly o'er the lea,
The ploughman homeward plods his weary way,
And leaves the world to darkness and to me.

Now fades the glimmering landscape on the sight,
And all the air a solemn stillness holds,
Save where the beetle wheels his droning flight,
And drowsy tinklings lull the distant folds:

Save that from yonder ivy-mantled tower
The moping owl does to the moon complain
Of such as, wandering near her secret bower,
Molest her ancient solitary reign.

Beneath those rugged elms, that yew-tree's shade
Where heaves the turf in many a mouldering heap,
Each in his narrow cell for ever laid,
The rude forefathers of the hamlet sleep.

The breezy call of incense-breathing morn,
The swallow twittering from the straw-built shed,
The cock's shrill clarion, or the echoing horn,
No more shall rouse them from their lowly bed.

THOMAS GRAY

11. *A Musical Instrument*

What was he doing, the great god Pan,
  Down in the reeds by the river?
Spreading ruin and scattering ban,
Splashing and paddling with hoofs of a goat,
And breaking the golden lilies afloat
  With the dragon-fly on the river?

He tore out a reed, the great god Pan,
  From the deep cool bed of the river,
The limpid water turbidly ran,
And the broken lilies a-dying lay,
And the dragon-fly had fled away,
  Ere he brought it out of the river.

High on the shore sat the great god Pan,
  While turbidly flowed the river;
And hacked and hewed as a great god can,
With his hard bleak steel at the patient reed,
Till there was not a sign of the leaf indeed
  To prove it fresh from the river.

He cut it short, did the great god Pan,
  (How tall it stood in the river!),
Then drew the pith, like the heart of a man,
Steadily from the outside ring,
And notched the poor dry empty thing
  In holes, as he sat by the river.

"This is the way," laughed the great god Pan,
  (Laughed while he sat by the river),
"The only way, since gods began
To make sweet music, they could succeed."
Then dropping his mouth to the hole in the reed,
  He blew in power by the river.

Sweet, sweet, sweet, O Pan!
  Piercing sweet by the river!
Blinding sweet, O great god Pan!
The sun on the hill forgot to die,
And the lilies revived and the dragon-fly
  Came back to dream on the river.

Yet half a beast is the great god Pan,
  To laugh, as he sits by the river,
Making a poet out of a man:
The true gods sigh for the cost and pain —
For the reed which grows nevermore again
  As a reed with the reeds in the river.

ELIZABETH BARRETT BROWNING

12. *Marc Antony's Speech at Caesar's Funeral*

Friends, Romans, countrymen, lend me your ears;
I come to bury Caesar, not to praise him.
The evil that men do lives after them;
The good is oft interred with their bones;

So let it be with Caesar. The noble Brutus
Hath told you Caesar was ambitious:
If it were so, it was a grievous fault;
And grievously hath Caesar answer'd it.
Here, under leave of Brutus, and the rest,
(For Brutus is an honourable man;
So are they all, all honourable men;)
Come I speak in Caesar's funeral.
He was my friend, faithful and just to me:
But Brutus says, he was ambitious;
And Brutus is an honourable man.
He hath brought many captives home to Rome,
Whose ransoms did the general coffers fill:
Did this in Caesar seem ambitious?
When that the poor have cried, Caesar hath wept:
Ambition should be made of sterner stuff:
Yet Brutus says, he was ambitious;
And, sure, he is an honourable man.
I speak not to disprove what Brutus spoke,
But here I am to speak what I do know.
You all did love him once, not without cause;
What cause withholds you then to mourn for him?
O judgment, thou art fled to bruitish beasts,
And men have lost their reason!—Bear with me;
My heart is in the coffin there with Caesar,
And I must pause till it come back to me. . . .

But yesterday, the word of Caesar might
Have stood against the world: now lies he there,
And none so poor to do him reverence.
O masters! if I were dispos'd to stir
Your hearts and minds to mutiny and rage,
I should do Brutus wrong, and Cassius wrong,
Who, you all know, are honourable men:
I will not do them wrong; I rather choose
To wrong the dead, to wrong myself, and you,
Than I will wrong such honourable men. . . .

Good friends, sweet friends, let me not stir you up
To such a sudden flood of mutiny.
They that have done this deed are honourable;
What private griefs they have, alas! I know not,
That made them do it; they are wise and honourable,
And will, no doubt, with reasons answer you.
I come not, friends to steal away your hearts;
I am no orator, as Brutus is;
But as you know me all, a plain blunt man,

That love my friend; and that they know full well
That gave me public leave to speak of him.
For I have neither wit, nor words, nor worth,
Action, nor utterance, nor the power of speech,
To stir men's blood: I only speak right on;
I tell you that which you yourselves do know;
Show you sweet Caesar's wounds, poor, poor dumb mouths,
And bid them speak for me: But were I Brutus,
And Brutus Antony, there were an Antony
Would ruffle up your spirits, and put a tongue
In every wound of Caesar, that should move
The stones of Rome to rise and mutiny.

SHAKESPEARE, *Julius Caesar*, Act III, Scene ii

A voice communication class in the Whiting Naval Air Station. By scientific research highly reliable tests have been developed for determining speech intelligibility, and scientific procedures have been perfected for improving it.

CHAPTER 18

Being Heard and Understood

CHAPTER 18

In the introductory chapter of a refreshing book, *The Pews Talk Back,*[1] Luke Missett observes "how unfortunate it is that the people in the pews never get a chance to talk. Why not let them do it?" His first witness was a kindly old lady with honest courage. "Mrs. Callaghan, what do you expect of the preacher?" Her answer was the collective indictment of speakers by long-suffering listeners everywhere ". . . I would be satisfied if I could hear him."

After the centuries, inaudibility or semi-audibility is still the curse of mine-run speakers. Sometimes it is the lack of earnestness, animation, passion, or fire to carry full meaning. Sometimes it is lack even of energy enough, mental or physical, to be understood at all except in splotches. Public address is *enlarged* conversation, but the enlarging gives trouble, for in speaking—as in photography—enlarging is an exacting process that requires experience and attention. It starts with the nature of hearing itself.

The nature of hearing

Hearing in public address is done at greater distance and under more adverse conditions than in private conversation. Therefore, the nature of hearing enters acutely into the picture. This we can understand by examining the operation of the ear.

When the sound waves arrive at the ear they must, first, be translated into a pattern of nerve impulses; then these nerve impulses in turn must be translated into thought in the listener's mind. Now what we call sound waves are really a series of *pressure* waves. The pressure waves of the faintest audible tone at the most favorable pitch move the ear drum in and out by less than a hundred-millionth of an inch. When this movement reaches the inner ear it contacts an auditory nerve which has some 30,000 fibers. These fibers are the pathway through

[1] Luke Missett, C. P., *The Pews Talk Back* (Westminster, Md., Newman Book Store, 1946).

which the dot-dot-dot code of nerve impulses reach the brain and are translated into thought. This inner ear is the sound analyzer. Among its chief means of analysis are these:

1. *By energy of sound.* The louder the tone, the greater is the number of nerve fibers stimulated. Also the louder the tone, the more impulses pass along each fiber every second. Thus the speaker who uses greater energy of sound increases the total number of nerve impulses delivered to the listener's brain in two ways: (1) More fibers are active, and (2) more impulses are sent per fiber. Here we begin to see why speaking that is just barely loud enough to be heard is not enough, and why the speaker who uses more energy carries more meaning.

2. *By rhythm.* Each language has a characteristic flow determined partly by its grammar and partly by its pronunciation. We have thus learned to expect certain rhythms as natural, and the ear is conditioned to translate them. Hence an artificial rhythm hinders understanding.

3. *By stress and accent.* Certain melody patterns are standardized, and the ear is conditioned to receive and translate them. So it is that by timing of syllables, and by pauses between them, the ear translates additional meanings. So it is that the monotonous voice lacking stress and accent, gives the ear fewer impulses to translate.

4. *By pitch.* The inner ear sorts out the various frequencies in each complex sound. Each frequency stimulates a corresponding group of the 30,000 nerve fibers. Stimulation of certain fibers causes us to hear a high-pitched tone, and stimulation of others cause us to hear a low-pitched tone. To use analogy, "hearing a high-pitched tone corresponds to feeling a touch on the face, and a low-pitched tone to a touch on the foot." [2]

So it is that what we think of as "hearing others talk" is far indeed from simple. We can understand it better if we recognize that even under ideal conditions, in a quiet living room, we do not hear as much as we think. Continually we are filling-in, guessing at sounds, and even words, we do not hear. If a friend speaks with lingual inertia, we may learn to understand him without too much difficulty after we are

[2] Hallowell Davis, *Hearing and Deafness* (New York: Murray Hill Books, Inc., 1947), p. 47.

accustomed to his peculiarities. But a stranger is less understandable until we are conditioned to his shortcomings.

Listening at greater distance and in greater noise compels us at best to guess more and fill-in more, and of course there is an obvious limit to guessing and filling-in. Therefore, "increasingly higher levels of intelligibility are required in the friendly conversation, the classroom with a small class, the classroom with a large group, and the public platform and stage." [3] As communications thus become more difficult special skills and techniques are required of the speaker.

Compulsions of the public platform

DISTANCE-TO-LOUDNESS RATIO

The first compulsion of the public platform arises from distance of speaker to audience. Sound travels spherically from its source, and loses energy as it goes. To be exact, *the intensity of sound varies inversely as the square of the distance from the source.* Were it not for reflection from walls, floor, and ceiling, a sound of given intensity at 5 feet would have only *one-fourth* that at 10 feet, *one-ninth* that intensity at 15 feet, and *one-hundredth* that intensity at 50 feet.[4]

In a room or auditorium the loss of energy, though not falling off with the square of the distance, is none the less far greater than you realize. *From a given source of sound, loudness, as received by the listener, varies inversely with the square root of the volume of the room.* Observe how this works in practice. Suppose you are talking in a small room, 12 x 15 x 9 feet. The volume of the room would be 1620 cubic feet, and the square root of 1620 is about 40. (Keep this 40 in your mind; it is your base.) Now suppose you are speaking in a room of the same acoustical material but 40 x 40 x 60 in size. Its volume would be 96,000 cubic feet, and the square root of 96,000 is about 309. Since loudness, as received by the listener, varies inversely with the square root of the volume of the room, and since 40 is only slightly more than one-eighth of 309, loudness as received by the listener in the large room would be only about *one-eighth* of that in

[3] William B. McCoard, "Contribution from the Military Programs in Voice Communications," *Quarterly Journal of Speech,* XXXIII (October, 1947), 370. In this useful article McCoard discusses the significance to public speakers of techniques developed in the Armed Services.

[4] Intensity and loudness, though not the same, are related. Within the pitch range of the human voice they can, for practical purposes, be considered identical.

the small room. If the room were 50 x 100 x 200 feet, loudness as received by the listener would be only *one-twenty-fifth* as great as in the small room.

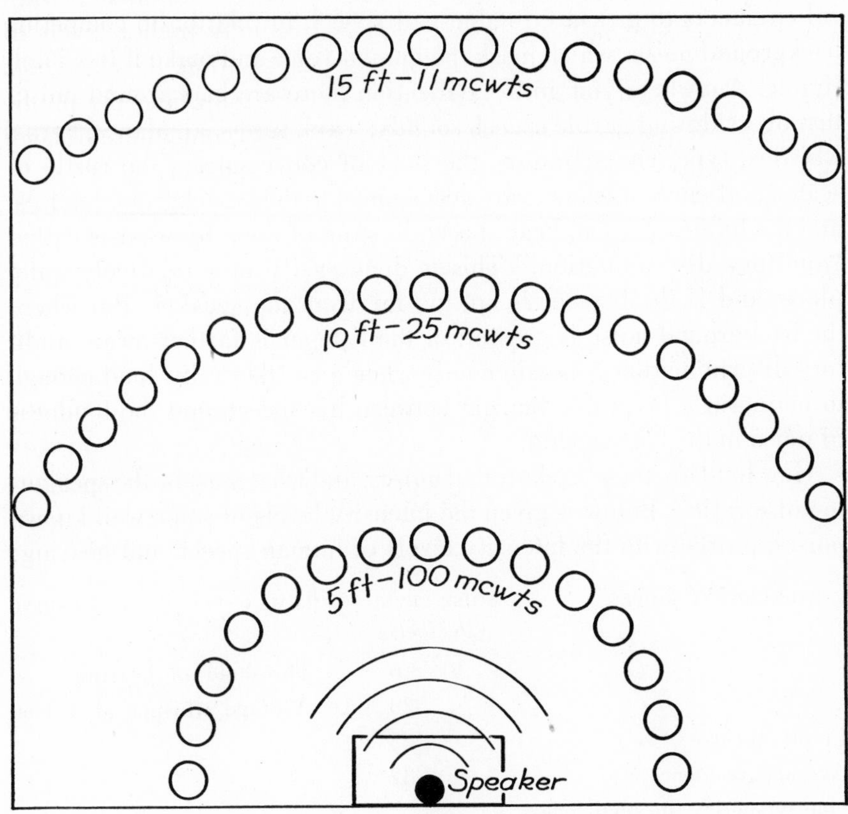

LOSS OF INTENSITY OF SOUND

A speaker may fail to meet the distance-to-loudness situation in three ways: (1) He may simply not use enough vocal energy, and the listener is forced to guess and fill-in. (2) He may use enough energy to be heard, but not enough for effective stress, accent, emphasis, inflection, and tone-color. The listener can "hear" but the ear does not receive enough impulses to translate the sound into full meaning. (3) He may not articulate with sufficient precision. This is another way of saying that *consonant* sounds are not projected with enough energy. They fade out along the way, and reach the listener's ear below the minimum threshold of audibility.

SPEAKER-TO-NOISE RATIO

Distance is not the only factor reducing to a speaker's audibility. Also there is the speaker-to-noise ratio. This is a term used by acoustical engineers to measure loudness of speech in relation to competing background noises which mask the human voice and make it less intelligible. Anywhere you go in civilization there are background noises that override and garble speech sounds: cars, trains, airplanes, horns, whistles, typewriters, radios, the buzz of conversation, the rustle of seated audiences. Listeners are accustomed to these background noises, and the human ear can hear speech in spite of them by what is called "auditory discrimination." This is done easily in a relatively quiet place, and if the listener is not too far from the speaker. But where the background noise is greater, or the listener is farther away, auditory discrimination is possible only when a speaker talks loud enough to maintain a favorable margin between his speech and the loudness of noise in the background.

How loud are these background noises, and what must be the speaker-to-noise ratio? Below is given the intensity levels of some well-known noises, paired with the intensity levels of human speech and hearing:

BACKGROUND NOISES	NOISE LEVEL (*Decibels*)	HUMAN SPEECH AND HEARING
	0	Threshold of hearing
	20	Average whisper at 4 feet.
Empty theatre	25	
Average residence	32	
One typewriter in small office Very quiet radio in home	} 40	Faint speech
Theatre with audience	42	
Noisy residence	45	
Average office	47	
	55-65	Ordinary conversation at 3 feet
Noisy restaurant Busy street traffic	} 70	
Very loud radio in room	80	Loud speech
Inside subway train	100	
Nearby airplane engine	120	Average threshold of discomfort
Largest air raid siren at 100 ft.	140	Threshold of pain

From this table you will see that the outside noises entering an empty theatre are louder than the average whisper at 4 feet, that faint speech is exactly equal to a very quiet radio in the home and less than the rustling of people sitting quietly in a theatre, and that even loud speech barely rises above the noise of busy street traffic. To be heard, of course, your speech cannot merely *equal* the intensity of background noises. You must exceed it far enough for listeners to understand you in spite of all other competing noise.

Mere loudness of speech, therefore, is not a measure of intelligibility. The true criterion is the *relative* loudness in comparison with background noises.[5]

How loud, then, must you talk? The obvious answer is "loud enough to maintain a favorable margin between your speech and the background noise." This at first is not very helpful, yet it does give you a starting point. It is the place where you want to go, if you can know when you get there. So, first, face up to the situation. Recognize that few students know how their voice should sound in a large room. Be willing to give up ineffective levels of loudness, no matter how habitual or how comfortable they are to you. Here you need to depend on the judgment of others. Get the advice of others in the class on how loud you seem to them and how loud you are by comparison with others. Get the verdict of your instructor. After taking this inventory, start working on ample loudness-to-distance and loudness-to-background noise ratios. *Listen* to your voice as you talk. Work for the *feeling* of ample loudness. Develop an ear for it. Finally and above all, *watch listeners at the back of the room.* They will tell you without asking. You can read it in their faces and attitude. Are they listening with interest? Are they turning their head sideways to hear better? Or have they given up trying to guess and fill-in, and stopped listening altogether?

Communicating the full meaning

You will remember that the inner ear is the sound analyzer. It takes in the sound waves, translates them into nerve impulses, and sends

[5] See OSRD Report No. 3802, page 52, Psycho-Acoustical Laboratory, Harvard University. Also OSRD Report No. 5414, page 6, Voice Communication Laboratory, Waco, Texas. These reports, formerly classified as affecting national defence, are now available for public use. See also "Studies in Speech Intelligibility," issue of *Speech Monographs* XIII (1946), No. 2, especially Harry M. Mason's article (p. 22) showing that the mean intelligibility was nearly *twice* as high with a 2/1 speech-to-noise ratio as with a 3/2 ratio.

them to the brain along selected groups of the 30,000 fibers of the auditory nerve. But it cannot analyze what is not there. You must supply the material. The more you supply, the more the analysis there is and the more meaning. The human race, in fact, has evolved a code of meaning from changes in pitch, time, and emphasis—a code that is independent of the words themselves. Its use is as involuntary as the twinkle of the eye:

COMMUNICATING MEANINGS BY CHANGES IN PITCH

We communicate meanings by two kinds of pitch changes: *steps* and *slides*. The step is used in the following sentence:

he
do?
What
did

You will notice that after each word there is a step-up in pitch or a step-down, a total of nearly an octave if well spoken. Step, then, is the abrupt changes *between* words and syllables, either up or down. It is a distinct jump, and communicates a sharp shift of thought or feeling.

The slide is even more common, and is constantly used for communicating subtle shades of thought. (In everyday language we call the slide an *inflection.* Here it is convenient, however, to use the word *slide* in order to show its relation to the step.) These are changes by gliding from one pitch to another *during* the syllable, as in saying sarcastically:

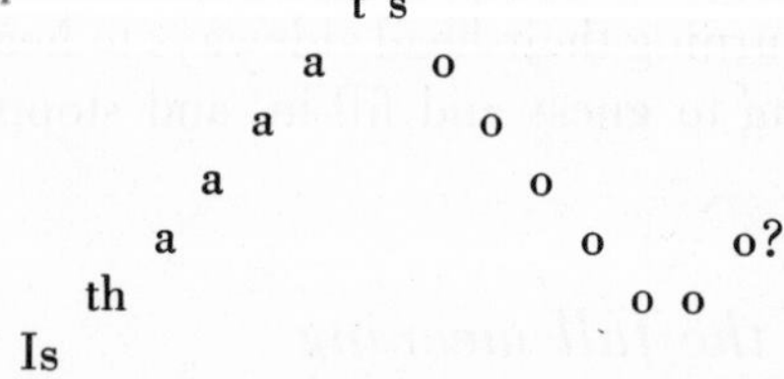

For thousands of years these pitch changes have been used to communicate meanings. Each human being will have his own personalized variations, but the standard meanings are far older than any words of the English language and quite as definite:

1. *A rising inflection communicates incompleteness of thought, uncertainty, or inconclusiveness.* Thus when you ask a question, hesitate,

are in doubt, or cannot make up your mind—your voice says so with a rising inflection.

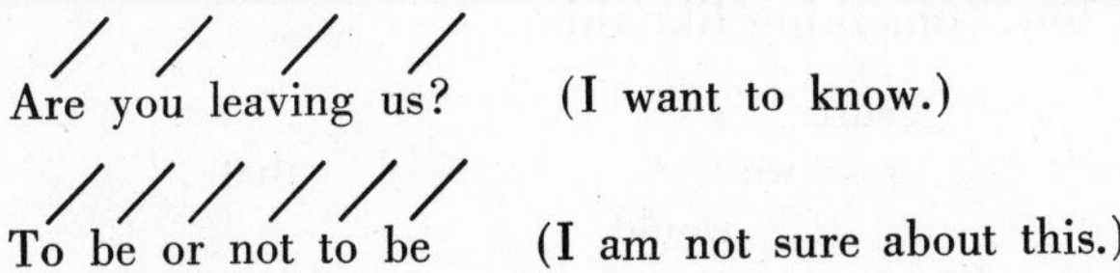

Are you leaving us? (I want to know.)

To be or not to be (I am not sure about this.)

2. *A falling inflection communicates completeness of thought, assurance, conviction, or determination.* This is the inflection of decision and assurance. Though used less often than rising inflections, they carry more definite and important meanings.

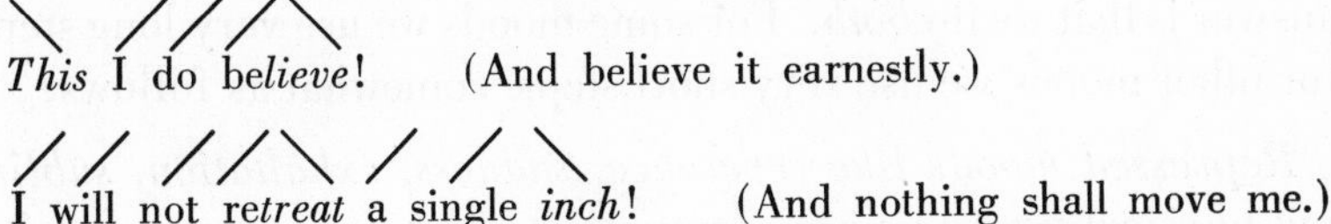

This I do be*lieve*! (And believe it earnestly.)

I will not re*treat* a single *inch*! (And nothing shall move me.)

3. *A wave, or double inflection, communicates the rich double meanings of humor, sarcasm, and subtle thought.* Not all thought is plain and straight. Much of it involves compound discrimination. We really say two things at once. Such meanings are carried by a voice wave, or double inflection. In other words, when there is a double thought in the mind, there is a double inflection in the voice.

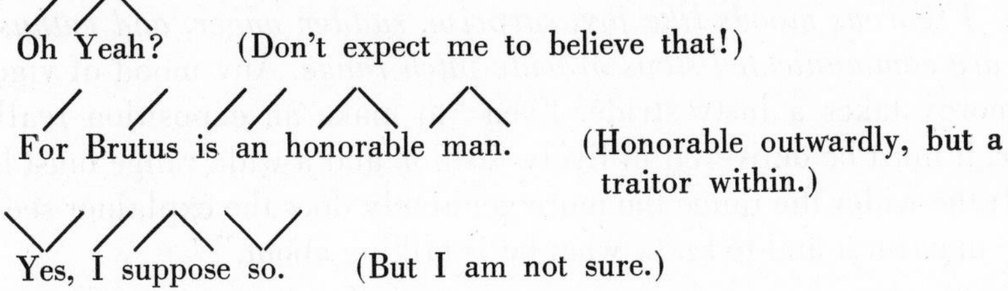

Oh Yeah? (Don't expect me to believe that!)

For Brutus is an honorable man. (Honorable outwardly, but a traitor within.)

Yes, I suppose so. (But I am not sure.)

Bare words, in short, mean little. They are given fullness of meaning by subtle shadings of voice. The word "no," said Charles H. Woolbert, can be spoken to carry at least twenty different meanings, one of them being "yes."

In public speaking the special problem is to enlarge the inflection to fit the enlarged occasion. The short inflection, suitable enough for ordinary conversation, is not enough for the enlarged conversation of public address.

4. *Normal moods are communicated by steps of normal pitch range.* Interesting people do not talk in one key. They range up and

down, with almost no two words at the same pitch. But for normal moods such people use the middle range of steps, not ranging very high or very low, something like this:

sure
we that
would
I'm
to
agree
all

For more intense feelings do we use longer steps, or shorter ones? The answer is that we do *both.* For some moods we use very long steps, and for other moods we use very short steps, somewhat as follows:

5. *Repressed moods like reverence, sadness, exhaltation, sublimity, and physical weakness are communicated by steps of narrow pitch range.* The very repression of the mood is indicated by the constant subtle steps, always narrow:

blue ocean,
on, dark
Roll deep and roll.
thou

6. *Vigorous moods like joy, surprise, sudden anger, and enthusiasm are communicated steps of wide pitch range.* Any mood of vigor or energy takes a lusty stride. Even "to make an exposition really clear, it must be delivered in lively fashion and a wide range must be used; the wider the range the more genuinely does the explainer seem to be in earnest and to know what he is talking about." [6]

himself
with
Nor young compare
must a man
others

---

[6] Charles Henry Woolbert and Joseph F. Smith, *Fundamentals of Speech, Third Edition* (New York; Harper and Brothers, 1934), page 246.

Not that I loved Caesar less, but that I loved Rome more

ASSIGNMENTS

COMMUNICATING MEANINGS BY SLIDES, OR INFLECTIONS

1. Read the following so as to communicate the indicated meanings:

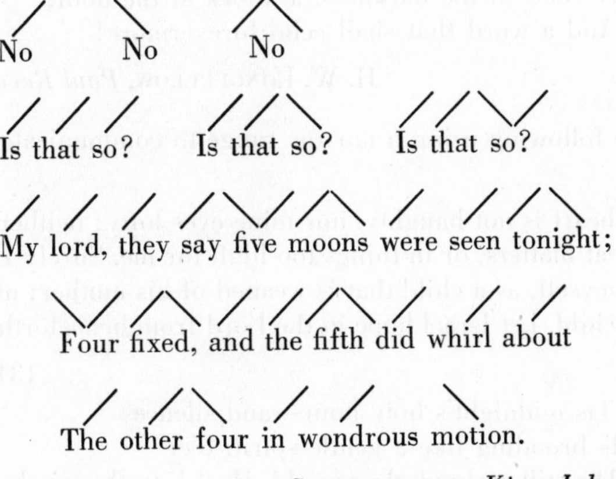

No No No
Is that so? Is that so? Is that so?
My lord, they say five moons were seen tonight;
Four fixed, and the fifth did whirl about
The other four in wondrous motion.

SHAKESPEARE, *King John*

2. Read the following so as to communicate the question-and-answer current of ideas:

Does the road wind up-hill all the way?
  Yes, to the very end.
Will the day's journey take the whole day long?
  From morn to night, my friend.
But is there for the night a resting-place?
  A roof for when the slow dark hours begin.
May not the darkness hide it from my face:
  You cannot miss that inn.
Shall I meet other wayfarers at night?
  Those who have gone before.

CHRISTINA ROSSETTI, Up-Hill

COMMUNICATING MEANING BY STEPS

3. Read the following using steps of normal pitch range in communicating the meaning:

I'm but a soldier. Could I fight my way
Into a maiden's heart, why well and good;
I'd get there, somehow. But to talk and sigh,
And whisper pretty things—I can't do that!
I tried it, but I stammered, blushed, and failed.
Myrine laughed at me—but, bless her heart,
She knew my meaning, and she pulled me through!

GILBERT and SULLIVAN, *Pygmalion and Galatea*

And so through the night rode Paul Revere;
And so through the night went his cry of alarm
To every Middlesex village and farm,—
A cry of defiance and not of fear,
A voice in the darkness, a knock at the door,
And a word that shall echo forevermore!

H. W. LONGFELLOW, *Paul Revere's Ride*

4. Read the following using a narrow range to communicate the repressed moods:

Lord, my heart is not haughty, nor mine eyes lofty: neither do I exercise myself in great matters, or in things too high for me. Surely I have behaved and quieted myself, as a child that is weaned of his mother: my soul is even as a weaned child. Let Israel hope in the Lord from henceforth and for ever.

131st Psalm

'Tis midnight's holy hour—and silence
Is brooding like a gentle spirit, o'er
The still and pulseless world. Hark! on the winds
The bell's deep tones are swelling—'tis the knell
Of the departed year.

GEORGE D. PRENTICE, *The Closing Year*

5. Read the following using wide steps to communicate the vigorous mood:

Remember March, the ides of March remember:
. . . Shall one of us,
That struck the foremost man of all this world
But for supporting robbers, shall we now
Contaminate our fingers with base bribes,
And sell the mighty space of our large honors
For so much trash as may be grasped thus?
I had rather be a dog, and bay at the moon,
Than such a Roman.

SHAKESPEARE, *Julius Caesar*

COMMUNICATING MEANINGS BY VARIATIONS IN TIME

The flow of time is the flow of life itself. In speaking we capture and use an infinitesimal part of the flow by techniques of rate, word grouping and pause, syllable duration, and rhythm.

1. *Rate.* People differ in tempo, mental and motor. Some think fast and talk fast. Some think and talk at a deliberate tempo. Webster, for example, is estimated to have spoken at 80-100 words a minute, Lincoln at 100 words a minute, Henry Clay at 130-160, John C. Calhoun at 180, and Rufus Choate at 200. By accurate timing, Franklin D. Roosevelt spoke at 117 words a minute, Phillips Brooks at 215, and Floyd Gibbons at 217. Each of these speakers talked according to his own personality and his capacity for clear articulation. If you try to talk too fast, the sounds become obscure and the meaning is lost. If you talk too slow, the *ahs* and *ers* and blank pauses tend to increase. In general a rate of more than 150 words a minute is too fast, and if you slow to 100 words a minute, there is danger of the audience's losing interest—unless you speak with exceptional syllable duration and with especially effective pauses. In general, also, your rate in public speaking will be slower than in private conversation. Distance-to-audience and background noises are the chief factors in this necessity. Your task is to find a rate at which you can maintain interest and still be perfectly clear. In this you will need the criticism of others in the class and the judgment of your instructor.

So far we have been considering the *average* rate. Actually, we do not speak long at an even rate. When dealing with narrative, suspense, or excitement, we speed up the rate to fit the mood. When explaining or moving through a difficult thought, we slow the rate markedly. To sum it up: *Talk fast enough to be interesting. Take time to be distinct.*

2. *Word Grouping.* People do not talk in single words, but in groups of words. We throw our words together, into separate bursts, grouped according to meaning. One word group, for example, may carry the central meaning of a thought and the others merely fill in the details. If we change the grouping, the identical words may have the exactly opposite meaning, as seen in the following example:

> The teacher said the student is a fool.
> "The teacher," / said the student, / "is a fool."

To make thoughts clear we must know which words belong together and which are to be separated from others, but this is only part of the process. Words must be *firmly* grouped, so firmly that listeners can have no doubt whatsoever of the meaning. Weak grouping is the bane of beginning students. It indicates mental uncertainty in some form or other—lack of positive conviction, or lack even of thought itself. To listeners, weak grouping is like air with too little oxygen; the volume is there, but the life-giving stuff is not in it. The essence of grouping for clear meaning is this: *Group together those words which stand for ideas that belong together, and separate that group from others by emphasis and pauses.*

The essential means of effective word grouping is the *pause.* You do not have commas, semicolons, and periods in speech. You have the pause. It is the punctuation mark of speech—the comma, semicolon, and period all rolled into one. During the pause listeners concentrate on what has just been said and get set for what is to come. An effective pause is the "thunder of white silence" that stills the audience, causes restless listeners to look at the speaker, and to listen sharply. But beginners seldom know how to pause. They are afraid of the silence, like a child of the dark, and hurry on to fill it up with talk, take a fresh breath on the fly, and pause only at that blessèd final word. This is not real speaking. It is a race with time. Consider, therefore, your habits of pausing and grouping words, and your mental attitude in doing so. Do you group words firmly enough? Do you pause positively enough? Can you listen to the silence of your pauses, allowing listeners this moment of golden silence to digest what you have said and to get set for what is to come?

One final word of advice. Beware of pausing at every place you find a punctuation mark on the printed page. For the most part pausing and punctuation fall at the same place, but emphatically not always. Punctuation is for the eye. Pausing is for the ear. For the eye punctuation is like this:

> Let us, therefore, brace ourselves to our duties, and so bear ourselves that, if the British Empire and its Commonwealth last for a thousand years, men will still say, "This was their finest hour."

But for the ear the pauses come at five places where there is punctuation, and at three additional places where there is no punctuation. Furthermore, there are no pauses at two places where there is punctuation:

Let us, therefore, / brace ourselves to our duties, / and so bear ourselves / that, if the British Empire and its Commonwealth / last for a thousand years, / men will still say, / "This / was their finest hour." /

3. *Syllable duration.* Some sounds of English are longer than others, as will be seen in the following columns:

SHORT	LONG
it	ate
met	meet
mull	mile

Some sounds are longer in certain combinations than in others:

LONG	LONGER	LONGEST
lace	lays	lay
goat	goad	go
rice	rise	rye

Such is the basic nature of English sounds. When we start putting words into thoughts, these differences in syllable duration are enormously magnified, for the moment a sound is stressed it becomes much longer than when it is unstressed. The more it is stressed the longer it becomes.

Skillful writers, especially poets, deliberately select words of wanted duration and put them together for special effect. That is one reason why reading poetry is not easy and often not well done. Students as a rule seem to have at first no sense of changing syllable duration to fit the mood or thought. If they habitually have staccato speech, they will read Byron's "*Roll on,* thou *deep* and *dark blue ocean, roll,*" in staccato tones that miss entirely the undercurrent of long deep ocean swells that mark this poem. Or if they habitually drawl they will also drawl a Gilbert and Sullivan quatrain. The first thing, then, is to develop an awareness of syllable duration to carry meaning and mood.

Applied to public speaking, syllable duration is significant for two reasons. First, the audience is larger and is farther away. You must prolong stressed syllables longer—much longer—in order for them to reach the audience with any reasonable meaning at all.

Furthermore, syllable duration in public speaking is longer in order for you to be understood at a greater distance. In a large room fast staccato speech is the least understood. (We are assuming that other factors, like articulation, are equal.) A moderate rate is more understandable. But the most understandable speech of all comes from the one who *prolongs the stressed sounds,* no matter whether the rate be reasonably fast or slow.

Now prolonging does not mean drawling. The last thing in the world any speaker wants to develop is a drawl. Syllable duration is something else. It keeps the original rhythm, and only slows its tempo. The speaker is simply concerned that the most distant listeners understand —not merely understand the bare word, but also its mood and color and exact degree of thought. Therefore, he sustains the word, builds it up, gives it the hue and color, then sends it forth to the farthest listeners.

ASSIGNMENTS

VARYING RATE TO COMMUNICATE MEANING

1. Which of the following would you read at a faster rate, and which slower? In succession read the two at rates that seem best for you.

Out of the North the wild news came,
Far flashing on its wings of flame,
Swift as the boreal light which flies,
At midnight through the startled skies.
And there was tumult in the air,
    The fife's shrill note, the drum's loud beat,
And through the wide land everywhere
    The answering tread of hurrying feet.

And there the startling drum and fife
Fired the living with fiercer life;
While overhead with wild increase,
    The great bell swung as ne'er before.
It seemed as it would never cease;
And every word its order flung
From off its jubilant iron tongue
Was, "War! *War*! WAR!"

T. B. Read, *The Revolutionary Uprising*

Fourscore and seven years ago our fathers brought forth on this continent a new nation, conceived in liberty, and dedicated to the proposition that all men are created equal.

Now we are engaged in a great civil war, testing whether that nation, or any nation so conceived and so dedicated, can long endure. We are met on a great battlefield of that war. We have come to dedicate a portion of that field as the final resting place for those who here gave their lives that the nation might live. It is altogether fitting and proper that we should do this.

Abraham Lincoln, *Gettysburg Address*

2. Try your hand at grouping thoughts correctly in the following sentence:

Woman without her man would be a savage
What do you think I will let you use my new car
That that is is that that is not is not

3. Pause forcibly with packed meaning to communicate full meaning on the following:

Books are the best of things well used; abused; among the worst.

He batted his eyes, and the lightnings flashed;
He clapped his hands, and the thunders rolled.

I tell you earnestly and authoritatively you must get into the habit of looking intensely at words, and assuring yourself of their meaning, syllable by syllable—nay, letter by letter. . . . You might read all the books in the British Museum and remain an utterly "illiterate," uneducated person; but if you read ten pages of a good book, letter by letter,—that is to say with, with real accuracy,—you are for evermore in some measure an educated person.

JOHN RUSKIN, *Sesame and Lilies, I*

4. Read the following with adequate syllable duration for a small audience. Then read it with longer syllable duration suitable for an audience of 100 people.

I am an old-time school teacher. I have taught 40 years. I just want to tell you something categorically that most laymen, who don't know much about school teaching, just don't believe, but I'm going to tell you flat-out: You can teach a child to read, and he will go out in the world and read; you can teach him to add and subtract, and he can go out in the world and add and subtract; but you teach him the Gettysburg Address, and that doesn't mean he's going to be able to go out and live in a land conceived in liberty and dedicated to the proposition that all men are created equal. You can buy a book on golf, but that doesn't mean that the drive goes down the fairway. You can buy a book on swimming, but it doesn't mean that you won't drown. If you have a matter that requires action; if you're going to teach it, you have to tie knowledge and action together when you're doing the teaching.

WILLIAM F. RUSSELL, *Citizenship Education*

I remember Russell Lowell telling us that Daniel Webster came home from Washington at the time the Whig party thought of dissolution a year or two before his death, and went down to Faneuil Hall to protest. Drawing himself up to his loftiest proportions, his brow clothed with thunder, before the listening thousands, he said, "Well, gentlemen, I am a Whig, a Massachusetts Whig, a Faneuil-Hall Whig, revolutionary Whig, a constitutional Whig. If you break up the Whig party, sir, where am I to go? And says Lowell, "We held our breath, thinking where he *could* go."

WENDELL PHILLIPS, *Eulogy on Daniel O'Connell*

COMMUNICATING MEANINGS BY DEGREES OF EMPHASIS

We do not emphasize every word equally. If we did human speech would resemble the noise of a typewriter, with the sounds coming out *tap, tap, tap,* each one equally strong. But speech is not like that at all. It comes in bursts and swells.

In each word-group a single idea dominates, and this idea is conveyed often in a single word—with all the other words being mere undercover support. In speaking we highlight the important idea-carrying words by emphasis, and let the others fade into the background:

> Two centuries ago / the common man could live in *hunger* / and he *did* live in hunger / while college students were taught *Plato* and *Plutarch* / in a curriculum that *excluded* / the study of human *welfare* / in the age of *machines* /

Emphasis is given especially by six means:

1. by added force;
2. by lifting the word to a very high level of pitch;
3. by dropping it to a very low level of pitch;
4. by lengthening, drawling it, holding it;
5. by giving it a special inflection, as characterized by the typical American retort, "oh yeah?";
6. by giving it with a strange or unusual quality of voice.

In public speaking emphasis is far stronger than in private conversation. This, in part, is because the audience is composed of persons of varying degrees of intelligence and alertness, and it is necessary to reach all—including the dullest. Again, speaker-to-audience distance is a factor. The farther away a speaker is, the harder it becomes to read his facial expression and other minute signs of meaning, and the more the audience must depend on the speaker's distant voice and on action that cannot be seen close up. Finally, the thought is usually more matured in a public speech than in a conversation, and the added maturity calls for added emphasis. In sum, *enlarged conversation demands enlarged emphasis.*

ASSIGNMENTS

DEVELOPING AWARENESS OF EMPHASIS

1. Read the following so as to bring out the full force of the neat insult:

> Sir, I admit your genial rule,
> That every poet is a fool,
> But you yourself may serve to show it,
> That every fool is not a poet.
>
> Alexander Pope

2. In the following speech on "The American Scholar," Emerson attacks the traditional higher education of over a century ago. His style is condensed and it will require full emphasis to communicate the meaning. Read it as to an audience of one hundred people.

> Books are the best of things, well used; abused, among the worst. . . . The book, the college, the school of art, the institution of any kind, stop with some past utterance of genius. This is good, they say—let us hold by this. They pin me down. They look backward and not forward. But genius looks forward: the eyes of man are set in his forehead, not in his hindhead: man hopes: genius creates.
>
> Ralph Waldo Emerson

3. In a speech shortly after VJ Day, a Nebraska-born American citizen of Japanese ancestry, with thirty flying missions over Europe and twenty-eight more over Japan, spoke on intolerance. Can you communicate the subtle undercurrent of thought contained in his words?

> I'm no authority; I'm not an expert or a big wheel. I don't know anything that any boy from Nebraska couldn't tell you. But I know this: I fought with a lot of men in this war, all kinds—a Polish gunner, a Jewish engineer, a German bombardier, and even a full-blooded Dakota Indian. I saw men wounded, and whatever land their grandfathers came from, their blood was always the same color. And whatever church they went to, the screams of pain sounded just about the same.
>
> I've had fifty-eight bombing missions now, and I'm still tired enough so my hands shake, and plenty of nights I don't sleep so well. I'd like to go home to Nebraska and forget the war, and just lie under a tree somewhere and take it easy. It's hard to realize that the war is not over for me. Not for a lot of us, Jewish-Americans, Italian-Americans, Negro-Americans, Japanese-Americans. While there is still hatred and prejudice, our fight goes on. Back in Nebraska on our farm, when I planted seed, I knew that after a while I'd get a crop. That's the way it was with a lot of us in this war:

we went to plant the seeds to bring in a crop of decency and peace for our families and our children.

Back in high school in Nebraska, one of the things they taught me was that America is a land where it isn't race or religion that makes free men. That's why I went to Tokyo. I went to fight for my country, where freedom isn't color but a way of life, and all men are created equal until they prove it otherwise. That's an old idea we have in Hershey, Nebraska, just down the highway from Cozad, which is near North Platte.

SERGEANT BEN KUROKI [7]

COMMUNICATING MEANINGS BY DISTINCTNESS OF ARTICULATION

In the preceding chapter we discussed articulation as one of the four stages in producing speech, and offered a series of tests for measuring your speech intelligibility. This was done without giving instructions on how to improve articulation, for two reasons: First, to enable you to measure speech intelligibility *before* the instruction began. Second, to let you know well in advance whether your speech intelligibility needed improving. In this way you could be prepared, mentally, at least, to work on improvement. We now come to the problem of improving articulation.

Loudness of speech is mainly in the *vowels*, but intelligibility is mainly in the *consonants*. Hence the maxim, "the vowels give beauty, the consonants give clarity." Unfortunately consonants are not loud at close range; and, unfortunately also, they fade quickly with distance. This is particularly true of stopped, voiceless consonants such as *p*, *t*, and *k* which are hard to distinguish at best, but it is true in less degree of all consonants.

In general you must sharpen the articulation of consonants if you expect to be easily understood in public address. A consonant sound that is heard easily at five feet may be inaudible at fifty feet, and you must partly make up for this difference by added sharpness. The following tested procedures will be helpful:

1. *Pack plenty of breath pressure behind the consonants.* Explode the initial *p* as in *pull*, *t* as in *talk*, and *k*-sound as in *chemist*. Use ample breath pressure to sound the medial consonants like the *zh*-sound in *measure*, the *sh*-sound in *nation*, and the *s*-sound in *recent*.

[7] Herald Tribune Forum, 1945, by permission of Ben Kuroki and the *New York Herald-Tribune*.

Carry this breath pressure all the way through to the final consonants: explode the *t* in *don't,* hiss the *s* in *miss,* and prolong the *l* in *control.* It takes far more breath to project consonants than to vibrate resonant vowels. Shallow breathers take note.

2. *Articulate with alacrity, don't slur, mumble, or muffle.* People with good articulation use a wide mouth opening. They are active with jaw, lips, face, tongue and pharynx. Ironically, you not only can hear good articulation but you can look at the speaker and see it as well. There is the constant nimble movement as the visible speech organs move into position for the consonant, make the sound, and speed swiftly to the next one. Here are two broad and convenient self-made tests:

First, look at yourself in the mirror as you talk. Do you see the swift and nimble movements that come from the strength of contact and quickness of release of the visible articulating organs?

Second, listen to your voice, both as you speak and from recording playbacks. Do you say *What's that* or *Whassat? Let me* or *lemme? Don't know* or *dunno? Nothing* or *nuthin? Government* or *guverment? Recognize* or *reckernize? Particular* or *partikerler? Manufacture* or *manerfacture?*

3. *Sustain the friction-like consonants:* the *s* in *sit* and *hiss,* the *z*-sound in *his,* the *sh*-sound in *motion,* the *zh*-sound in *occasion,* the *f* in *half* and *four,* the *v* in *never* and *move.* These are sounds made by partially blocking the breath stream at some place in the mouth and by forcing out the breath at this place in a *continuous* stream. Make the stream continuous.

4. *Hold the long consonants until you get them rolling:* the *l* in *hill,* the *r* in *road,* the *n* in *now,* the *m* in *home,* and the *ng* in *going.* These are sounds that require a build-up. Therefore, build them up.

5. *Do not ignore medial consonants.* Which do you say: *twenty* or *twenny? Started* or *starded?* Do you have clear medial consonants in ro*str*um, hu*nd*red, e*xt*ra, di*spr*ove, ti*ngl*ed?

6. *Sound the final consonants in a word group.* When combinations of consonants occur within a word group, we blend them, as in "The fair bree*ze bl*ew, the whi*te f*oa*m fl*ew." But when a consonant sound falls at the end of a word group, it needs to be carried through and articulated with full breath pressure:

> Nights candles are burnt ou*t,* / and jocund day
> Stands tiptoe / on the misty mountain to*ps.*

7. *Master the difficult consonant combinations.* The English language is famous, or perhaps infamous, for its many difficult consonant combinations. There are 22 two-consonant groups that number far over a hundred individual combinations. Beyond that are 58 reasonably common three-consonant and four-consonant combinations. The following list is helpful, though far from being exhaustive. Practice it, being careful to pronounce all of the consonants without slurring or omitting any within the combinations:

TWO-CONSONANT COMBINATIONS [8]

su*bm*it	brace*l*et	ro*bbed*	so*ngs*	mu*st*	he*lm*
ou*ts*ide	noi*sel*ess	ri*bbed*	wa*ked*	pa*st*	he*lp*
pu*bl*ic	a*lm*ost	li*ved*	loo*ked*	a*sk*	cla*sp*
nu*mb*er	i*ll*ness	rai*sed*	pu*shed*	my*ths*	mo*nth*
i*ns*ect	rai*lr*oad	to*ld*	corru*pt*	bu*lb*	fee*ds*
di*sm*al	mi*lli*on	pu*lls*	*apt*	si*lk*	bri*ngs*

THREE-CONSONANT AND FOUR-CONSONANT COMBINATIONS [9]

di*spl*ease	*aptly*	fi*xed*	ne*xt*	fo*lds*	po*sts*
e*xpl*ain	abru*ptly*	a*sked*	corru*pts*	hi*nged*	gue*sts*
mi*spr*int	exa*ctly*	wa*tched*	a*cts*	arra*nged*	de*pths*
e*xtr*a	dire*ctly*	rea*ched*	dire*cts*	wa*sps*	ei*ghths*
mi*squ*ote	so*ftly*	cha*nced*	prote*cts*	li*sps*	le*ngths*
di*scr*eet	mo*stly*	comme*nced*	ju*dged*	a*sks*	mo*nths*
va*nqu*ish	gha*stly*	lu*nched*	e*dged*	de*sks*	wi*dths*
la*ngu*age	ki*ndly*	pi*nched*	ho*lds*	te*sts*	a*ngles*

ASSIGNMENTS

TAKING INVENTORY

1. Pronounce the above word lists to a friend. Have him sit at right angles to you or with his back turned, so he cannot see you but must depend wholly on sound. Ask him to write down the words that seemed to be slurred or weakly articulated. Here is your starting list. Remember that these are not mere words that give you trouble; they are *sound combinations.* Note the combinations. (You will find them italicized in the above word lists.) Make up a list of words containing these sounds for future practice.

[8] Remember that letters and sounds are not identical. Thus in the second column "brace*l*et" is pronounced with the sound of *sl*, "noiseless" is pronounced *zl*, and "mi*ll*ion" is pronounced *ly* (mi*ly*un). Especially observe that in the fourth column "wa*ked*" and "loo*ked*" are pronounced *kt*. Finally, do not be disturbed that words like "mo*nth*" and "bri*ngs*" are spelled with three final consonant letters. They have only two-consonant sounds since *th* and *ng* are single sounds.

[9] Note that the words in column 3, although spelled *ed*, are pronounced *t*.

2. If possible record these two word lists and listen to them yourself. The recording ought to be on high-fidelity equipment, reasonably accurate up to 10,000 cycles and preferably to 15,000, otherwise distortion will prevent your hearing the consonant as you actually spoke them.

3. If possible get your instructor or someone who knows the sound structure of English to mark the sound combinations that are slurred or weakly articulated. Use this list for future practice.

INCREASING DISTINCTNESS OF ARTICULATION

4. Open the mouth wide. Stretch the tongue out as far as it will go, first up toward the nose, then down toward the chin, and finally right, then left.

5. Open the mouth wide. Press the tongue firmly against the upper teeth, the gum ridge, and the roof of the mouth. Repeat until you can greatly increase the pressure.

6. Open the mouth wide. Press the under side of the tongue against the roof of the mouth. Repeat until you can greatly increase the pressure. Now curl the tongue until the tip touches the front portion of the soft palate. Repeat until you can increase the pressure.

7. With a firm pressure practice the following sounds: *p*, *b*, *t*, *d*, *k*, *g*, (as in *go*)

8. Practice sustaining the following sounds with a continuous breath stream: *f*, *v*, *th*, *s*, *z*, *sh*, *zh*. (Remember that it is the *sounds* you want to practice, as in "*f*ive," not the letters.)

9. Practice prolonging the following sounds for full power: *l* (as in pu*ll*), *r* (as in *r*ed), *y* (as in *y*es), *m* (as in co*m*e), *n* (as in o*n*), and *ng* (as in si*ng*).

10. Pronounce the following pairs of words so that listeners can easily distinguish one word from the other:

*p*ear	*b*ear
*t*oe	*d*ough
*f*ine	*v*ine
*wh*at	*w*att
ba*ck*	ba*g*
hi*ss*	hi*s*
ri*ch*	ri*dge*

11. Drill on the following words until you can pronounce them without slurring or omitting any of the sounds:

WRONG	RIGHT	WRONG	RIGHT
ke*p*	ke*pt*	brea*z*e	brea*th*es
sle*p*	sle*pt*	mon*ts*	mon*ths*
exac*k*ly	exac*tly*	*aw*-right	*all* right
corre*k*ly	correc*tly*	wa*d*er	wa*t*er
co*ss*	co*sts*	uni*d*ed	uni*t*ed
insi*ss*	insi*sts*	a*ss*	as*k*s

12. Read the following sentences with emphasis on absolutely clear (but not stilted) enunciation:

They asked only for a drink of water.
A ready wit is an asset to everyone.
No two sisters look exactly alike.
Baked apples are good for the health.
It doth appear you are a worthy judge.
Go thither and observe for yourself.
Christmas comes but once a year.
I live in a house by the side of the road.
I never knew the half of it.

13. Read the following selection and be careful not only of articulation, but also of communicating the meaning and mood.

A spray of bullets whipped the ground about him, and he nose-dived into the shell hole. He was out of sight, but the machine gun kept it up, in repeated bursts of half a dozen bullets, the bursts coming a scant second apart. They sounded like an elephant's cough—if elephants coughed. He had never heard one, but this sounded like it, anyway.

The elephant stopped coughing. "Hi, buddy," he called.

"Right here," replied a voice almost beside him.

"Toss me a pebble, so I can spot you," said Akron. "Easy, though. Don't excite that machine gunner again."

"Here she comes," and a pebble rose from the next shell hole and dropped beside him.

"I'll be over as soon as that son-of-a-Jerry gets his mind off my shell hole," promised Akron. He waited a minute. . . . Two minutes. . . . Then off to the right he heard the thump of bullets, and before the machine gunner could traverse back to him again he had backflopped from his shell hole into the next.

"Welcome," said the wounded man. "Cramped quarters, but they are big enough for two." Then he stared with amazement at his rescuer. "What are you doing here?" he wanted to know.

"Paying a debt," replied Akron. "Two of your men hauled me half a mile when I got crocked."

Diary of an Anonymous Soldier

14. Do you want to try tongue twisters? Pronounce them *slowly* and firmly:

Three gray geese in the green grass grazing; gray were
the geese and green was the grazing.

The sun shines on shop signs.

The sea ceaseth, and sufficeth us.

Truly rural.

Sixty-six sick chicks.

Strange strategic statistics.

Tie twine to three tree twigs.

Shy Sarah saw six Swiss wrist watches.

Amidst the mists and coldest frosts,
With stoutest wrists and loudest boasts,
He thrusts his fists against the posts
And still insists he sees the ghosts.

TESTING IMPROVEMENT IN INTELLIGIBILITY

In the preceding chapter were given two intelligibility tests. By taking either of them you would have a reliable measure of your Intelligibility Score before training. Below is given Form B of each of those tests. By taking the Form B test, and comparing the Intelligibility Score on it with that made on Form A of the same test taken earlier, you can measure your improvement with a high degree of reliability. For best results these tests ought to be taken at least three weeks apart.

MULTIPLE-CHOICE INTELLIGIBILITY TEST FORM B [10]

Speaker 1

1 piston, firm, banner
2 eve, attain, scream
3 rupture, tour, medal
4 ark, spotter, gain
5 cannon, detract, made
6 lumber, case, pierce
7 jail, glimmer, ward
8 nature, enact, old

Speaker 2

1 muzzle, carve, author
2 scorch, able, cloth
3 vision, fumble, grown
4 cape, lecture, high
5 possess, blow, single
6 divide, fiction, maker
7 leaf, section, rich
8 traitor, eastward, join

Speaker 3

1 traffic, woolen, swim
2 can, pulp, eldest
3 tank, promote, apt
4 bad, defend, slight
5 formal, unpack, license
6 socket, find, misuse
7 quarter, kit, rummage
8 lock, bold, grind

Speaker 4

1 tender, beg, swift
2 wise, nothing, shark
3 map, full, observe
4 pace, list, contrast
5 unheard, just, grow
6 range, hungry, fade
7 confine, boast, white
8 naval, race, discard

Speaker 5

1 year, prone, forest
2 stable, blast, visit
3 oval, shock, cost
4 tack, vital, mar
5 glimpse, bomb, untied
6 dike, salute, mock
7 fort, dance, pirate
8 nest, release, cold

Speaker 6

1 splash, clock, lag
2 attack, flavor, gloom
3 clap, weak, this
4 pause, yet, southeast
5 drop, arrest, leather
6 court, fall, navy
7 bandit, vast, shatter
8 word, blame, needy

Speaker 7

1 tree, pressure, own
2 cannon, surf, tonight
3 ramp, mold, choose
4 bench, cancel, arch
5 senate, got, plunge
6 harm, flight, drain
7 fact, throat, it
8 air, gate, outing

Speaker 8

1 trench, repay, stiff
2 rabbit, exempt, shield
3 coach, former, preside
4 blunder, quaint, worm
5 purr, dental, bed
6 keys, good, disturb
7 aspire, chute, help
8 germ, await, seaside

Speaker 9

1 call, handle, vacant
2 dust, wallet, leave
3 fruit, bail, pants
4 dish, sitting, jolly
5 replace, hunter, bath
6 journal, fluid, none
7 plate, cabin, acute
8 suffer, clown, grim

Speaker 10

1 rock, try, ceiling
2 drawer, creep, wool
3 funnel, nap, lure
4 shake, hanger, crop
5 zone, intend, throw
6 morning, duck, art
7 inn, kennel, false
8 belly, shell, bin

Speaker 11

1 salt, crash, furnace
2 moment, ride, broom
3 clipper, door, tie
4 sink, matter, half
5 carbon, end, tone
6 us, passage, front
7 rate, punch, hotel
8 dart, bill, at

Speaker 12

1 raider, view, fear
2 screen, man, beaver
3 tense, gun, achieve
4 captain, salad, drive
5 instance, brass, helpful
6 sweep, drill, meantime
7 grasping, file, wave
8 click, wrench, throb

[10] From OSRD Report No. 5567 of the Voice Communication Laboratory, John W. Black, Director. Prepared by C. Hess Haagen. The 12 tests of Form B are of equivalent difficulty with the 12 in Form A given in the preceding chapter. The intelligibility scores of the 24 tests do not deviate more than 0.5%.

Directions for administering are found on page 356. For highest accuracy give the test under the same conditions, in the same room, with students seated in the same seats, and with the same amount of masking noise, as in Form A.

ANSWER SHEET FOR MULTIPLE-CHOICE INTELLIGIBILITY TESTS, FORM B

*Speaker 1 is*______________ *Speaker 2 is*______________

1	1 system 2 pistol 3 distant 4 piston	1 firm 2 foam 3 burn 4 term	1 banner 2 manner 3 mother 4 batter	1 puddle 2 muddle 3 muzzle 4 puzzle	1 carve 2 car 3 tarred 4 tired	1 offer 2 author 3 often 4 office
2	1 heave 2 heed 3 ease 4 eve	1 detain 2 obtain 3 attain 4 maintain	1 scream 2 screen 3 green 4 stream	1 porch 2 torch 3 scorch 4 court	1 fable 2 stable 3 table 4 able	1 cross 2 cough 3 cloth 4 claw
3	1 Roger 2 rupture 3 rapture 4 obscure	1 pure 2 poor 3 tour 4 two	1 petal 2 battle 3 meadow 4 medal	1 vision 2 bishop 3 vicious 4 season	1 bubble 2 tumble 3 stumble 4 fumble	1 thrown 2 drone 3 prone 4 groan
4	1 art 2 heart 3 arch 4 ark	1 sponsor 2 spotter 3 ponder 4 plunder	1 game 2 gain 3 gage 4 gang	1 cape 2 hate 3 take 4 tape	1 texture 2 lecture 3 mixture 4 rupture	1 eye 2 high 3 tie 4 hide
5	1 comment 2 comic 3 cannon 4 carbon	1 exact 2 retract 3 detract 4 attack	1 made 2 fade 3 vague 4 may	1 process 2 protest 3 profess 4 possess	1 glow 2 blow 3 below 4 low	1 single 2 jingle 3 cycle 4 sprinkle
6	1 bumper 2 number 3 lumber 4 lover	1 cave 2 cake 3 cage 4 case	1 pier 2 pierce 3 fierce 4 spear	1 divide 2 devise 3 define 4 divine	1 kitchen 2 mission 3 friction 4 fiction	1 baker 2 major 3 maker 4 banker
7	1 gale 2 jail 3 dale 4 bail	1 glamour 2 slimmer 3 swimmer 4 glimmer	1 ward 2 wart 3 wash 4 war	1 leap 2 leaf 3 lease 4 leave	1 second 2 suction 3 section 4 sexton	1 rich 2 ridge 3 bridge 4 grip
8	1 danger 2 feature 3 nature 4 major	1 enact 2 impact 3 relax 4 intact	1 hold 2 old 3 ode 4 hoed	1 crater 2 traitor 3 trainer 4 treasure	1 seaport 2 keyboard 3 piecework 4 eastward	1 joy 2 going 3 join 4 dawn

ANSWER SHEET FOR MULTIPLE-CHOICE INTELLIGIBILITY TESTS, FORM B—*Cont.*

*Speaker 3 is*________________ *Speaker 4 is*________________

	Speaker 3			Speaker 4		
1	1 tropic	1 willing	1 trim	1 center	1 big	1 quit
	2 traffic	2 wallet	2 twin	2 tender	2 bag	2 twist
	3 trapping	3 women	3 swim	3 timber	3 bank	3 swift
	4 tramping	4 woolen	4 slim	4 fender	4 beg	4 whip
2	1 pan	1 pope	1 pelvis	1 why	1 nothing	1 sharp
	2 hand	2 pulse	2 eldest	2 wide	2 shopping	2 shock
	3 ten	3 pulp	3 elder	3 wise	3 message	3 short
	4 can	4 pump	4 welder	4 wives	4 jumping	4 shark
3	1 pain	1 remote	1 axe	1 vamp	1 full	1 occur
	2 paint	2 promote	2 aft	2 map	2 pull	2 absurd
	3 plank	3 provoke	3 apt	3 mat	3 fold	3 observe
	4 tank	4 revoke	4 at	4 vat	4 cold	4 conserve
4	1 bad	1 depend	1 alike	1 paste	1 left	1 compress
	2 bed	2 defend	2 all right	2 pace	2 list	2 contract
	3 mad	3 descend	3 delight	3 paid	3 lisp	3 contact
	4 fed	4 descent	4 slight	4 paint	4 lid	4 contrast
5	1 normal	1 unpack	1 license	1 unheard	1 dusk	1 grope
	2 formal	2 attack	2 light	2 concurred	2 dust	2 grove
	3 corporal	3 compact	3 lighten	3 converge	3 just	3 grow
	4 fumble	4 relax	4 liken	4 conserve	4 judge	4 glow
6	1 socket	1 fine	1 misuse	1 grain	1 ugly	1 fade
	2 pocket	2 mine	2 diffuse	2 grange	2 hungry	2 vague
	3 bucket	3 bind	3 dispute	3 range	3 country	3 made
	4 sprocket	4 find	4 confuse	4 train	4 concrete	4 spade
7	1 quarter	1 pit	1 rubbish	1 confine	1 boat	1 wife
	2 porter	2 kick	2 rummy	2 design	2 boast	2 twice
	3 water	3 kit	3 running	3 assign	3 booth	3 quite
	4 order	4 pitch	4 rummage	4 combine	4 both	4 white
8	1 clock	1 bone	1 blind	1 naval	1 rate	1 discord
	2 rock	2 bold	2 grind	2 Mable	2 grace	4 discard
	3 lock	3 bowed	3 shrine	3 table	3 rake	2 pasteboard
	4 flock	4 bald	4 rind	4 able	4 race	3 discharge

ANSWER SHEET FOR MULTIPLE-CHOICE INTELLIGIBILITY TESTS, FORM B—*Cont.*

*Speaker 5 is*________________ *Speaker 6 is*________________

	Speaker 5			Speaker 6		
1	1 hear	1 prone	1 foreign	1 fox	1 gnash	1 drag
	2 ear	2 cone	2 forest	2 block	2 splash	2 flag
	3 year	3 tone	3 forehead	3 clock	3 slash	3 lag
	4 gear	4 thrown	4 force	4 flock	4 flash	4 rag
2	1 table	1 glad	1 desert	1 waver	1 contact	1 gloom
	2 total	2 blast	2 vivid	2 flavor	2 unpack	2 broom
	3 stable	3 grass	3 physic	3 labor	3 attract	3 plume
	4 fable	4 black	4 visit	4 favor	4 attack	4 glue
3	1 over	1 shock	1 coast	1 week	1 collect	1 list
	2 oboe	2 shook	2 cost	2 wheat	2 flap	2 disc
	3 old	3 shot	3 cough	3 wink	3 collapse	3 bid
	4 oval	4 shop	4 caught	4 weep	4 clap	4 this
4	1 tack	1 bridal	1 bar	1 yes	1 claws	1 downbeat
	2 tact	2 final	2 far	2 jet	2 cause	2 stampede
	3 pact	3 vital	3 are	3 get	3 pause	3 false teeth
	4 pack	4 title	4 mar	4 yet	4 hoard	4 southeast
5	1 limp	1 bond	1 aside	1 harass	1 rock	1 leather
	2 shrimp	2 bob	2 confide	2 caress	2 strop	2 lever
	3 blimp	3 bomb	3 untied	3 arrest	3 throb	3 letter
	4 glimpse	4 dog	4 complied	4 erect	4 drop	4 lather
6	1 bite	1 salute	1 mock	1 hall	1 court	1 baby
	2 sight	2 saloon	2 mop	2 ball	2 course	2 navy
	3 night	3 balloon	3 box	3 fall	3 cord	3 maybe
	4 dike	4 dilute	4 balk	4 call	4 cork	4 hazy
7	1 fork	1 dance	1 tyrant	1 bath	1 bandit	1 cracker
	2 fort	2 badge	2 pirate	2 vast	2 banded	2 chatter
	3 porch	3 band	3 pilot	3 fast	3 banquet	3 shatter
	4 force	4 damp	4 tirade	4 grasp	4 bandage	4 shadow
8	1 test	1 relief	1 code	1 blame	1 blurred	1 feeding
	2 nest	2 retreat	2 hold	2 flame	2 were	2 needy
	3 pest	3 repeat	3 cold	3 lame	3 word	3 speedy
	4 best	4 release	4 hole	4 plane	4 bird	4 meaning

ANSWER SHEET FOR MULTIPLE-CHOICE INTELLIGIBILITY TESTS, FORM B—*Cont.*

*Speaker 7 is*____________ *Speaker 8 is*____________

1	1 plea 2 free 3 spree 4 tree	1 stretcher 2 pressure 3 treasure 4 precious	1 bone 2 phone 3 own 4 ode	1 french 2 drench 3 wrench 4 trench	1 prepay 2 repay 3 defray 4 repast	1 stiff 2 fifth 3 sniff 4 gift
2	1 cannon 2 famine 3 solemn 4 salmon	1 turf 2 surf 3 first 4 thirst	1 tonight 2 ignite 3 unite 4 goodnight	1 rabid 2 rapid 3 rabbit 4 ravage	1 preempt 2 exempt 3 except 4 attempt	1 sealed 2 yield 3 shield 4 field
3	1 wrap 2 rent 3 lamp 4 ramp	1 bold 2 hold 3 mold 4 fold	1 choose 2 fuse 3 shoes 4 huge	1 coat 2 coach 3 coke 4 coax	1 former 2 farmer 3 firmer 4 foreman	1 proceed 2 perceive 3 precise 4 preside
4	1 fence 2 dense 3 bench 4 bent	1 pencil 2 anvil 3 handle 4 cancel	1 harsh 2 arch 3 heart 4 art	1 plunder 2 thunder 3 blunder 4 lumber	1 paint 2 quaint 3 plain 4 quake	1 warm 2 warn 3 work 4 worm
5	1 tenant 2 senate 3 sentence 4 tennis	1 got 2 dot 3 dock 4 scotch	1 lunge 2 lunch 3 punch 4 plunge	1 purr 2 cur 3 purge 4 curve	1 dental 2 gentle 3 simple 4 dimple	1 head 2 bed 3 dead 4 fed
6	1 arm 2 farm 3 barn 4 harm	1 light 2 fight 3 flight 4 slight	1 brain 2 drain 3 braid 4 grade	1 tease 2 cheese 3 keys 4 ease	1 could 2 hood 3 good 4 stood	1 disturb 2 absurd 3 disperse 4 superb
7	1 fact 2 pact 3 back 4 sack	1 broke 2 throw 3 throat 4 boat	1 hit 2 it 3 hip 4 itch	1 aspire 2 acquire 3 attire 4 admire	1 cute 2 suit 3 shoe 4 chute	1 health 2 elk 3 felt 4 help
8	1 here 2 car 3 air 4 error	1 skate 2 stake 3 date 4 gate	1 outing 2 mounting 3 ousting 4 housing	1 firm 2 yearn 3 adjourn 4 germ	1 away 2 assay 3 await 4 awake	1 beside 2 seaside 3 beehive 4 decide

ANSWER SHEET FOR MULTIPLE-CHOICE INTELLIGIBILITY TESTS, FORM B—*Cont.*

*Speaker 9 is*________________ *Speaker 10 is*________________

1	1 crawl	1 candle	1 baker	1 lock	1 try	1 stealing
	2 cow	2 sandal	2 station	2 rock	2 cry	2 feeling
	3 call	3 handle	3 bacon	4 rot	3 pride	3 kneeling
	4 cough	4 scandal	4 vacant	3 spot	4 fry	4 ceiling
2	1 duck	1 warrant	1 leave	1 roar	1 cream	1 wall
	2 dust	2 Wallace	2 lead	2 chore	2 creep	2 wolf
	3 dud	3 wallet	3 feed	3 door	3 creak	3 wool
	4 dutch	4 wallop	4 please	4 drawer	4 crease	4 woe
3	1 fruit	1 pail	1 pan	1 funnel	1 snap	1 lurk
	2 root	2 mail	2 pants	2 tunnel	2 nap	2 lore
	3 brute	3 bell	3 past	3 bundle	3 man	3 lure
	4 boot	4 bail	4 pen	4 frontal	4 cap	4 lower
4	1 fish	1 fitting	1 trolley	1 chase	1 anchor	1 crop
	2 stitch	2 finish	2 jolly	2 cake	2 hanker	2 prop
	3 this	3 city	3 dolly	3 shake	3 anger	3 drop
	4 dish	4 sitting	4 galley	4 shape	4 hanger	4 stop
5	1 replace	1 utter	1 bat	1 known	1 intend	1 drove
	2 retrace	2 hunter	2 bad	2 zone	2 intense	2 go
	3 refrain	3 hunger	3 back	3 stone	3 intent	3 throw
	4 reclaim	4 under	4 bath	4 gone	4 incense	4 grow
6	1 gentle	1 fluid	1 gun	1 morning	1 buck	1 arc
	2 journal	2 shrewd	2 sun	2 warning	2 duck	2 arch
	3 general	3 would	3 done	3 boarding	3 stuck	3 aren't
	4 colonel	4 hood	4 none	4 hoarding	4 dug	4 art
7	1 plate	1 cabbage	1 astute	1 him	1 kettle	1 fault
	2 quake	2 cabin	2 excuse	2 hand	2 gentle	2 fog
	3 quaint	3 habit	3 acute	3 end	3 kennel	3 fall
	4 weight	4 heaven	4 accuse	4 inn	4 general	4 false
8	1 seven	1 clown	1 rim	1 belly	1 shall	1 bend
	2 sucker	2 cloud	2 trim	2 barely	2 shelve	2 bin
	3 suffer	3 proud	3 grim	3 bury	3 shell	3 bid
	4 supper	4 town	4 brim	4 bailing	4 shelf	4 bent

ANSWER SHEET FOR MULTIPLE-CHOICE INTELLIGIBILITY TESTS, FORM B—*Cont.*

*Speaker 11 is*_______________ *Speaker 12 is*_______________

1	1 salt 2 fault 3 soft 4 golf	1 rash 2 crash 3 thrash 4 smash	1 burning 2 furnish 3 furnace 4 burnish	1 razor 2 raider 3 greater 4 reader	1 knew 2 you 3 few 4 view	1 beer 2 fear 3 clear 4 here
2	1 open 2 omen 3 woman 4 moment	1 ride 2 right 3 ripe 4 fried	1 broom 2 groom 3 gloom 4 room	1 dream 2 clean 3 green 4 screen	1 band 2 fan 3 man 4 land	1 either 2 beaver 3 fever 4 neither
3	1 dipper 2 clipper 3 slipper 4 flipper	1 shore 2 door 3 store 4 gorge	1 pie 2 eye 3 high 4 tie	1 tent 2 tempt 3 tense 4 ten	1 son 2 gone 3 fun 4 gun	1 achieve 2 exceed 3 retrieve 4 reprieve
4	1 seek 2 thick 3 think 4 sink	1 pattern 2 better 3 batter 4 matter	1 hot 2 have 3 half 4 had	1 happen 2 hatpin 3 captive 4 captain	1 valid 2 solid 3 salad 4 volley	1 drive 2 strive 3 derive 4 dry
5	1 carpet 2 carbon 3 common 4 carve	1 in 2 aunt 3 end 4 and	1 tone 2 cone 3 comb 4 told	1 instance 2 infants 3 incense 4 instant	1 brass 2 grass 3 grab 4 brad	1 healthful 2 local 3 helpful 4 elbow
6	1 must 2 cost 3 us 4 hush	1 passing 2 package 3 packing 4 passage	1 front 2 fun 3 blunt 4 brunt	1 weak 2 sweet 3 wheat 4 sweep	1 drill 2 kill 3 thrill 4 girl	1 mealtime 2 decline 3 meantime 4 peacetime
7	1 rake 2 rate 3 break 4 great	1 perch 2 punt 3 punch 4 touch	1 propel 2 hotel 3 lapel 4 foretell	1 drafting 2 grafting 3 grasping 4 drastic	1 style 2 file 3 dial 4 vile	1 way 2 weighed 3 waste 4 wave
8	1 dart 2 dark 3 start 4 starch	1 fill 2 still 3 bill 4 built	1 ask 2 axe 3 act 4 at	1 quick 2 click 3 trick 4 cliff	1 rent 2 wrench 3 rest 4 reach	1 throb 2 rob 3 fog 4 drop

SCORING SHEET FOR MULTIPLE-CHOICE INTELLIGIBILITY TEST, FORM B

The sequence of three numbers indicate the words in each group for each reader. If reasonable precaution is taken for accuracy, the scoring may be done in class.[11]

	Speaker 1	*Speaker 2*	*Speaker 3*
Group 1	4—1—1	3—1—2	2—4—3
Group 2	4—3—1	3—4—3	4—3—2
Group 3	2—3—4	1—4—4	4—2—3
Group 4	4—2—2	1—2—2	1—2—4
Group 5	3—3—1	4—2—1	2—1—1
Group 6	3—4—2	1—4—3	1—4—1
Group 7	2—4—1	2—3—1	1—3—4
Group 8	3—1—2	2—4—3	3—2—2

	Speaker 4	*Speaker 5*	*Speaker 6*
Group 1	2—4—3	3—1—2	2—3—3
Group 2	3—1—4	3—2—4	4—2—1
Group 3	2—1—3	4—1—2	4—1—4
Group 4	2—2—4	1—3—4	3—4—4
Group 5	1—3—3	4—3—3	4—3—1
Group 6	3—2—1	4—1—1	1—3—2
Group 7	1—2—4	2—1—2	1—2—3
Group 8	1—4—4	2—4—3	3—1—2

	Speaker 7	*Speaker 8*	*Speaker 9*
Group 1	4—2—3	4—2—1	3—3—4
Group 2	1—2—1	3—2—3	2—3—1
Group 3	4—3—1	2—1—4	1—4—2
Group 4	3—4—2	3—2—4	4—4—2
Group 5	2—1—4	1—1—2	1—2—4
Group 6	4—3—2	3—3—1	2—1—4
Group 7	1—3—2	1—4—4	1—2—3
Group 8	3—4—1	4—3—2	3—1—3

	Speaker 10	*Speaker 11*	*Speaker 12*
Group 1	2—1—4	1—2—3	2—4—2
Group 2	4—2—3	4—1—1	4—3—2
Group 3	1—2—3	2—2—4	3—4—1
Group 4	3—4—1	4—4—3	4—3—1
Group 5	2—1—3	2—3—1	1—1—3
Group 6	1—2—4	3—4—1	4—1—3
Group 7	4—3—4	2—3—2	3—2—4
Group 8	1—3—2	1—3—4	2—2—1

[11] For computing the Intelligibility Score see conversion table following Form A, page 366.

WRITE-DOWN INTELLIGIBILITY TEST, FORM B[12]

Test 1	*Test 2*	*Test 3*	*Test 4*	*Test 5*	*Test 6*
burning	gangway	bandit	pancake	defend	gunfire
fuel	regain	vision	break	hood	eastward
deadly	farther	wash	headphone	cushion	center
circuit	cotton	single	tent	full	missing
try	battle	unit	injure	reduce	beach
bail	canvass	edge	decrease	cockpit	folder
ampere	sweep	jump	cleared	forecast	speed
plenty	forest	defeat	gliding	narrow	rocket
find	discard	front	slam	volley	distance
spray	tree	southeast	raid	start	bomb
gearshift	ignite	calm	flame	pressure	corpse
end	piston	moment	neutral	target	tight

Test 7	*Test 8*	*Test 9*	*Test 10*	*Test 11*	*Test 12*
fog	slow	dugout	flare	spiral	flag
dashboard	reckon	caution	take-off	misfire	suburb
cold	balance	mortar	door	flounder	cripple
flight	cartridge	govern	guard	ditch	office
headwind	high	barge	fort	pivot	blimp
roll	cloudy	tank	select	charge	dainty
missile	forenoon	shower	wrench	ground	top
course	throb	release	blind	blast	nothing
binding	late	ceiling	cancel	escape	ask
practice	darken	passage	pain	section	compass
socket	pierce	blow	measure	hit	gun
impulse	salute	fair	ramp	describe	scatter

[12] From OSRD Report No. 5414 of the Voice Communication Laboratory, Waco, Texas, John W. Black, director. Prepared by C. Hess Haagen. The 12 tests in Form B are of essentially equal difficulty levels as those in Form A given in the preceding chapter. By comparing the Intelligibility Score made on Form A before training with that made on Form B after training each student will be able to measure improvement with a fairly high degree of reliability.

Directions for administering the test are found on page 367. Conversion table for computing the Intelligibility Score is on page 369.

Ethical persuasion operates on a different level in a free society than in a totalitarian state. Warren R. Austin (*right*), American Delegate to the United Nations General Assembly, and Jacob Malik (*left*), Delegate of the USSR, are representatives of these two respective levels.

CHAPTER 19

Ethical Persuasion

CHAPTER 19

So far in this book we have talked about the techniques and disciplines of public address: the audience, subject matter, and what is conveniently called "delivery." Now the time has come to look at the Great First Cause—beyond the range of techniques and disciplines—that determines how effective any speaker can ever be. This is the kind of person the speaker is, or at least the kind of person the audience thinks he is and is led by the speaker to believe he is. It includes what the audience may know about the speaker in advance of the speech: his character, his general reputation for integrity and good will, and his specific reputation as an authority on his subject. It includes also what the speaker reveals during the speech: his sagacity, his friendly disposition, his trustworthiness, his freedom from intemperate statement and obvious prejudices, and the ethical level at which he discusses the subject. Ancient writers called this *ethical persuasion.* Literally translated, it is not exactly a good term, but we have never acquired another one as good.

Ethical persuasion, of course, operates on a different level in a free society than in a totalitarian state; and because twentieth-century free societies have faced the threat of two powerful totalitarian combinations—Naziism and Communism—we should examine the operation of ethical persuasion in each.

Both Naziism and Communism have used with success the techniques of the repeated "Big Lie," character assassination, name-calling, the hysterical approach, and the seductive slogan. In using these techniques totalitarian propagandists call slavery freedom, and call freedom slavery. Democracies become "imperialistic states," and dictatorships are sweetened into the "people's government." Those who attempt escape to freedom become guilty of "crimes against humanity," and those who remain and are coerced are blessed with "unity plans." Thought control is described as "the practice of learning," and toeing the party line is being "adjusted to the new way of thinking." These techniques for convenience we shall call the Big Lie Repetition. They are used relentlessly and effectively in totalitarian states.

Their use, of course, does not arise from the personal ethics of individual speakers, but from planned techniques of speakers who have been required to surrender their minds to their superiors "in the service of nationalization." (The phrase is Eugen Hadamovsky's, onetime leading theorist of Nazi propaganda and dictator of the German radio.) With the Communists the evidence, though wholly internal, is ample. Of the Nazis the evidence is also external. Their documents are now open to the world.[1] Under Nazi orders their propagandists were "not to search unto truth," but to put it over. They were warned against the "great danger" of falling "into bookish knowledge" or trying to speak "some wisdom gained from reading." Problems were to be discussed "less by positive knowledge than out of the infallible National Socialist [Nazi] instinct." A perturbed German remarked in 1932 that "Hitler always seems to be attacking someone." What he did not then know was that a Nazi manual that year had issued an order to speakers that "Your weapon is political assault."

On its face the Big Lie Repetition might seem to be successful, the triumph of falsehood over truth, and a set of techniques available to anyone who is willing to adopt them. That they are available is true. That they are effective over the long run is quite another thing, and needs to be examined further.

Parenthetically we might note that the successful Big Lie Repetition carries its own seeds of destruction. Naziism is a prime recent example; its Third Reich, constructed "to last for 1,000 years," destroyed itself within twenty years. Dionysius of Syracuse, 407-367, B.C., will serve as an older example. Neither is an exception. Both, rather, are typical. The destruction of Naziism from without should not lead us to overlook the other even stronger inherent destroying force, namely destruction from *within* by creating mass cynicism, distrust, and apathy toward rulers who year after year practice the Big Lie Repetition. But all this is only by way of passing.

Basically the Big Lie Repetition is not successful over the long run.

[1] See Adolf Hitler, *Mein Kampf* (Boston: Houghton Mifflin Company, 1939); *The Goebbels Diaries* (New York, Doubleday and Company, 1948); Ross Scanlan, "The Nazi Party Speaker System," *Speech Monographs* XVI, No. 1 (August, 1949), 82-97, and XVII, No. 2 (June, 1950), 134-148.

Always it must be reinforced by the concentration camp and the firing squad. To put it in Hitler's words, "the one means that wins the easiest victory over reason" is "terror and force." Totalitarian rulers, therefore, never trust the Big Lie Repetition to put them in power or to keep them in power. They have good reason, for significantly no Nazi or Communist regime has yet won a free election, which is another way of saying that no amount of Big Lie Repetitions has ever won a majority vote unless it were accompanied by terror and force. Always these regimes have come to power by violence, and once in power have never allowed a free election. People do not "try" communism any more than they "try" potassium cyanide. They are not trusted to vote it in by free elections, and later vote on whether they like it. Totalitarian rulers believe in the Big Lie Repetition as a weapon of political assault and character assassination. They do not trust it as an instrument of persuasion.

For this reason it fails in the long run in a free society, for here there is no censorship and no thought control, and always there will be refutation. In plain words, the Big Lie can be nailed to the flagpole—not instantly but ultimately.

As everyone knows, a free people always has demagogues. Usually they are skillful, for only "good" men are stupid enough to believe they don't need to speak well, and hence there is a tendency for the Big Lies to be presented more skillfully in a free society than are the voices of reply. Also, in contrast to the methods in a totalitarian state, they are less outrageous, being refined into techniques of innuendo and half-truths that deliberately confuse ends and means, or using the well-known scattershot technique of firing a broadside in the hope that part of it will hit something.

The truth is there is a large amount of this kind of speaking in every free society. The important point is that only a small amount is successful and its success can be described as both local and temporary. Take the United States Congress as an example. Of its 531 members at no time will 10 per cent be composed of men who, measured objectively, could be classified as demagogues, or practitioners of the half-truth, or habitual users of scattershot techniques. Indeed, an examination of the roster of Congress for half a century past will show that rarely will the Senate contain more than two such persons at any one time, and seldom will the House claim more than half a dozen—definitely a *small* minority. (Indeed such men in public life are unduly conspicuous because there are so few.) Considering the large proportion of such speakers functioning at large, those who come to temporary power have always been so small as to be proof that the techniques of the Big Lie Repetition are not in the long run successful in a free society. In summary, in a free society shysters are free to talk, honest men are free to refute them, and the people are free to distrust them.

Henceforth in this chapter we are concerned with ethical persuasion in a free society.

Character and personal integrity

Our society today not only has the demagogue, already discussed, but more than in the past we have organized groups engaged in manipulating others for their own private interests. The listening public, distrustful of being thus exploited, has a magnified "will-to-believe" any speaker who is thought to represent the virtues of sincerity, personal integrity, and good will. We believe men of good will more fully and more readily than others. We distrust a speaker if we do not look upon him as a man of probity, who does not himself believe what he attempts to make credible to us, or whom we suspect of exploiting us for personal gain. In the words of Ralph Waldo Emerson, "The reason why anyone refuses his assent to your opinion, or his aid to your benevolent design, is in you. He refuses to accept you as a bringer of truth, because . . . you have not given him the authentic sign." There you have it. *"You have not given him the authentic sign."*[2]

The authentic signs

We cannot assume integrity, as we put on clothes. It is not a technique, but a moral sense. More than ever perhaps, in our present manipulative society, confused listeners especially crave it. When they find it, they have not only the "will to believe," but the "need to believe," and the desire for a flight into faith. What are the "authentic signs" of such speakers?

[2] See Aristotle, *Rhetoric*, 1356a and 1378a, for the importance given ethical persuasion in classical rhetoric. See Lester Thonssen and A. Craig Baird, *Speech Criticism* (New York: Ronald Press, 1948), pages 383-391, for its importance in the history of speechmaking. See Franklyn S. Haiman, "An Experimental Study of the Effects of Ethos in Public Speaking," *Speech Monographs* XVI (September 1949), No. 2, 190-202, for a report on three significant statistical studies that measured the effect, by shift of opinion, of reputation, character, competence, fair mindedness, sincerity, etc.

We trust the speaker who shows intellectual integrity and sound judgment. To one of the most effective demagogues in American public life today, an acquaintance said, "You are master of the half-truth." (Unfortunately I cannot give his name, but the instance is authentic.) The reply was, "Of course! Did you ever notice how much better a half-brick is than a whole brick when you want to throw it? You can wrap your fingers around it, draw back, and let go. You can't do that with a whole brick. It's too cumbersome. The same is true of half-truths and whole truths." Now this is the moral sense of certain kinds of speakers, and as we have seen they have influence at certain levels and in certain areas. But their influence, though strong, is limited to special groups. Outside these groups they are known as masters of the half-truth. Broad and general trust goes to speakers who show intellectual integrity and sound judgment. [3]

We also trust the speaker who refrains from rash and exaggerated statement. "That terrible sanity of the average man" is always watching the speaker who deals in sweeping assertion and reckless overstatement. It demands that a speaker be *responsible* for what he says, responsible for speaking the truth, responsible for being fair-minded and intellectually honest, responsible for avoiding reckless assertion, responsible for avoiding evidence which—even though accurate—misleads by omission and exclusion, responsible for lifting the tone of discussion above the level of mere name-calling. These are the "authentic signs" in ethical persuasion.

Applied to students they lead to this homely advice: Don't pretend to be an authority on government, politics, crime, or what-have-you. If you need authority, get it, and tell when and where your authority testified; but be intellectually honest about what you know, and how you know it.

Don't give listeners a chance to call you an exaggerator, or to brand you as being casual with truth. Stay within the bounds of evidence, and far enough within so listeners will not wonder whether you are hovering on the boundary line. Don't pretend to prove more than you have proved; for what counts is not what you say you have proved, but what the listeners think you have proved. All in all, present your case in such a way that those who are doubtful or who disagree will say, however reluctantly, "He spoke honestly."

[3] Public opinion research that bears this out is found in Robert Merton, *Mass Persuasion* (New York: Harper and Brothers, 1946), and in Paul F. Lazarsfeld, Bernard Berelson, and Hazel Gaudet, *The People's Choice* (New York: Columbia University Press, 1944).

We trust the speaker who seems to know what he is talking about. We like to know that a speaker is well fitted to discuss a subject because of his experiences or because he has investigated it thoroughly. Such speakers are effective because their treatment of the subject says, "A part of this I saw," or "For all of this I am personally responsible." Therefore, brace yourself to the duty of testing and processing trustworthy information. Especially, be suspicious of making yourself the mouthpiece of propaganda articles and propaganda books. It is perfectly legitimate for a speaker to explain his authority, if he can do it without boasting or a vulgar display of egotism. There are simple ways of doing so: "When I was checking some material for this speech, I ran across an unusual book. . . ." Or, "I want to talk about 'How to Study,' because last year my grades told me I did not know too much about it; and this year I resolved to do better by inquiring into what psychologists had learned about it." Or, "Out in my home state of Wyoming. . . ." Or "I was working last summer on the graveyard shift. . . ."

We trust a speaker who shows moderation, restraint, and good will. Don't make listeners out as ignorant. Don't tell them by word or tone that they are stubborn. Don't put them hopelessly in the wrong. Don't tell them dogmatically that you are right, and everybody else is wrong. Don't tell them what they must believe, as if they had no minds of their own. In short, don't punch them in the nose.

Remember that listeners' beliefs and attitudes are important to them. They usually have been held a long time, they are deeply rooted, and they satisfy deep-felt wants. Therefore, don't attack them outright. Don't even try to make listeners suddenly give them up and take on a set of new ones. Instead, *water and cultivate ideas to produce growth and change,* just as you would water and cultivate crops to promote growth. You are a cultivator of ideas, and not a human bull who bellows defiance and gores the beliefs of others. "Make haste slowly," is a proverb to be followed literally.

Especially, don't use speaking as an excuse for airing thinly-veiled prejudices. Don't, therefore, praise or damn indiscriminately. Congress, the President, Russia, labor, capital, private enterprise, or anything or anyone. Instead, get your facts, present your case, and let the facts speak for themselves. No question is too controversial to discuss, if you will give listeners light and not heat, and if you do so with moderation, restraint, and good will.

We trust the speaker who identifies himself with our interests. We want to have a sense of belonging. We don't want to be manipulated, used as a cat's paw. Therefore, we especially trust the speaker who is identified with our welfare, our needs, our hopes, our aspirations. A lecture bureau manager wrote, out of his thirty years of experience, "I could go right down the line, naming excellent educators and other experts whom we have to stop using as speakers after their first year. They did not care a whit for the people in the audience; in fact, most of them despised the audience, often telling us so frankly, and they made no effort to understand them, to give them food that would nourish and build them. For all their other qualities, these speakers rate the mark of Failure."

A speaker may identify himself in many ways. Abraham Lincoln, whose later speeches are still read today, spoke first for a partisan faction, then later for a nation beset by disunion. In this crisis he identified himself as the Voice of the People, one who spoke less *to* them than *for* them. In his words, confused listeners recognized what they had been trying to think, but had not been able to put into form. In the later speeches, those that we read today, Lincoln became the Voice of Mankind, the spokesman for the hopes of mankind in all generations: "that government of the people, by the people, and for the people, shall not perish from the earth."

Among twentieth-century speakers, Winston Churchill was the Voice of Freedom. He warned of the dangers ahead, launched the lifeboats, and led the rescue parties. To those who faltered, he said, "I have nothing to offer but blood, toil, tears, and sweat," but added, "Follow me."

Franklin D. Roosevelt was the high-born aristocrat, as removed from the masses by social caste as he was by physical infirmity. He stood afar off, but reached them with the Voice of Assurance. To restless and troubled people, frightened by the calamities of depression, unemployment, bank failure, and war, came his voice from Olympian heights, "This is the way. You have nothing to fear but fear."

Of Eric Johnston, then speaking as president of the United States Chamber of Commerce before a group of labor leaders, Walter Lippmann explained his ethical persuasion in these words: "Speaking the whole truth, he was more than the advocate of management. He was a citizen, a man concerned with solving a problem and not solely with winning his case. *What he said was, therefore, persuasive;* it was capable of making men think and change their minds, because he himself showed that he had thought and had his own mind open. If only this could become the fashion in public speech, how different would be the coming campaign and how much more adult, how much saner, our public life! For we are cursed with the endless declamation of men who charge, accuse, berate, defend but never seek to persuade. Only too rarely to do we here citizens discussing the state of the nation, humbly looking for the truth and earnestly seeking the light. The air is loud with the shrill voices of men who see only the good in their own case and only the error in the other man's." [4]

Perhaps Emerson had the final word: "But I say, *provided your case is really honest.*" If it is not, "There is always the previous question: How came you on that side? Your argument is ingenious, your language copious, your illustrations brilliant, but your major proposition palpably absurb. Will you establish a lie? You can't write up what gravitates down."

ASSIGNMENTS

ANALYZING ETHICAL PERSUASION IN OTHER SPEAKERS

1. Make a list of two or three speeches you have heard recently outside of class that lacked adequate ethical persuasion. Write a brief criticism of each, explaining in the terms of this chapter where each of them failed, or was weak, in the "authentic signs."

2. Do the same with two or three speeches that were effective in ethical persuasion.

3. Draw up two lists of speeches heard in class, one that had effective ethical persuasion, and one that did not. For each speech analyze your reasons.

ANALYZING ETHICAL PERSUASION IN YOUR OWN SPEECHES

4. Go over the outlines of the major speeches you have previously given in class. Where were you weak or strong in the "authentic signs" of ethical persuasion? How might you have been more effective?

5. For your next speech ask other members of the class to write their frank judgments on your effectiveness in ethical persuasion. Platitudes and non-committal statements will not help you, and may even mislead. You want honest judgments, untempered by evasion. Perhaps your colleagues would be more frank if they handed their statements unsigned to the instructor instead of giving them directly to you. These judgments may not make pleasant reading, and what you do about them will also be an ethical question. No one likes adverse criticism and not all can receive it with the meekness of Moses (see *Numbers* 12:1-3), but those who can will grow in ethical stature.

[4] "Today and Tomorrow," March 18, 1944.

Part V OCCASIONS AND FORMS

"A significant 20th Century characteristic of U.S. life is the revival of public discussion. There is plenty to talk about." This panel at Ohio Wesleyan University is discussing farm subsidies.

CHAPTER 20

Discussion

CHAPTER 20

A free society is sustained by discussion and cannot be sustained without it. The connection was well stated by Walter Bagehot, penetrating English thinker, in 1873: "The change from the age of status [force] to the age of choice [democracy] was first made in states where the government was to a great and growing extent a government by discussion, and where the subjects of that discussion were in some degree . . . matters of principle. . . . A free state—a state with liberty—means a state . . . in which there is discussion. . . . The power of government by discussion as an instrument of elevation plainly depends—other things being equal—on the greatness or littleness of the things to be discussed. . . . It is on this account that the discussions of savage tribes have produced so little effect in emancipating those tribes from their despotic customs. The oratory of the North American Indian—the first savage whose peculiarities fixed themselves in the public imagination—has become celebrated, and yet the North American Indians were scarcely, if at all, better orators than many other savages. Almost all of the savages who have melted away before the Englishman were better speakers than he is. But the oratory of the savages has led to nothing, and was likely to lead to nothing. It is a discussion, not of principles but of undertakings; its topics are whether . . . village A is the best village to plunder, or whether village B is a better. Such discussions augment the vigour of language, encourage a debating facility, and develop those gifts of demeanour and gesture which excite the confidence of the hearers. But they do not excite the speculative intellect, do not lead men to argue speculative doctrines, or to question ancient principles." [1]

On the present status of discussion in American public life the editors of *Time* in their Mid-Century Appraisal, reported as follows: "A significant 20th Century characteristic of U. S. life is the revival

[1] Walter Bagehot, *Physics and Politics* (New York: Appleton-Century-Crofts, Inc., 1873), pp. 158-167.

of public discussion. There is plenty to talk about. All over the U. S. colleges, newspapers, businessmen's clubs, churches, and women's clubs arrange lectures, forums, panel discussions. Busy and learned men give their time to these gatherings in the American belief that an informed and alert citizenship is the basis of democracy."[2]

There is reason enough for this revival of what had been neglected half a century before. The free society of men is dangerously challenged from without by successive waves of Naziism and Communism, and from within by economic tides and tornadoes. Man's problem is how to order his life, and, though not a new problem, the waves and tides of the twentieth century have given it a dreadful urgency. In facing up to these problems discussion has a unique value. It gives premium to intelligence.

By "discussion," as you have now rightly sensed, is not meant aimless unorganized talk. Such talk, though it may be interesting and even profitable, is not "discussion" in its special and historical sense. Discussion in that sense, is the purposive talk of people who meet to consider a common problem: in committees, in conferences, in public groups. It is the activity of problem-solving by thinking together and purposefully talking it out.

Like any cultivated plant, discussion flourishes only under special care and proper conditions. First, it is necessary to know what the controversy arising out of the problem is about, or in other words "what the assertions assert." Second, there must be a desire to think it out, and this desire must be stronger than the desire to win an argument; until a civilization, and groups within it, have risen to this level, there can be no discussion but only dispute. Third, there must be an area of agreement from which to start, a common goal which all agree is the desirable state of things; if there is no area of agreement—if, for example, one group wants to preserve liberty, and another wants to destroy it—there can be no discussion, but only war with words, and any conclusion is at best an armed truce.

Types of discussion

Discussion is found in many places: in clubs, in churches, in dormitories, in the classroom, in committees and conferences, before public audiences, over radio and television. Discussion is found at many

[2] *Time*, LIII (April 11, 1949), 27.

levels. Sometimes the problems covered are of little concern to anyone except those present. At others the issues concern large groups of people, even the nation, or the world. Consequently there are many types of discussion—from the Film Forum to the Public Hearing—but here we shall consider only those types that are most useful to small groups:

INFORMAL GROUP DISCUSSION

Here not more than twenty people sit around a circle, or in some form of close group, and discuss a subject of mutual interest. There is no audience and there are no formal speeches. The group simply converses under the guidance of a chairman. This type of discussion is often difficult to keep within bounds and to keep moving profitably through the various steps of the problem. Members may spend too much time on some early interesting aspect, and so never get very far into the problem. Or they turn up a new subject entirely, drop the old one and follow the new one. If the chairman holds the reins too tightly, or interrupts too often, the spontaneity is lost and the spirit of discussion is killed. For all its shortcomings, however, the rudiments of discussion are there; and if the members understand the problem-solving nature of discussion and are grounded in the steps of logical thinking, Informal Group Discussion can be profitable as well as interesting.

COOPERATIVE INVESTIGATION

This is a splendid method for training in discussion. It involves eight steps:

1. The discussion group meets in advance and elects a leader. The subject is then divided into a number of subtopics, and each member undertakes to investigate at least one of these subtopics.

2. The leader may call and hold one or more meetings, so that members can know what others have done and can work out final plans.

3. When the discussion meeting is held, the leader *analyzes* and *defines* the problem.

4. Each investigator then presents his information in a brief report. *The report contains no argument,* but only information set forth in concise and orderly form.

5. When these reports have all been made, the leader calls for any other pertinent information that members may have.

6. The leader may, if he desires, succinctly summarize the information

thus pooled. Then he opens the meeting to a discussion of what ought to be done in the light of the facts thus presented. Possible solutions are not debated, but are talked over in a cooperative manner. Each member tries to help the group reach an informal judgment. Disadvantages in proposed solutions are carefully considered, and ways of overcoming them are taken up.

7. Finally, if the nature of the problem permits, the ways and means of putting the best solution into operation are considered.

8. At the end the leader once more may give a brief summary of the procedure which has been adopted.

This is approximately the method used (they simplify it but do not change it basically) by such groups as city councils, boards of education, church boards, adult education groups, women's clubs, Boy and Girl Scouts, 4-H Clubs, etc.

THE PANEL FORUM

The panel portion of a Panel Forum is composed of a chairman and a small group, usually from two to six, who discuss a problem before an audience. They sit at a table where the audience can see them easily.

Of course, the chairman, and the panel members have prepared themselves carefully for the discussion. They follow much the same procedure as that set forth above for the Cooperative Investigation, but one new feature is added. Panel members must talk loud enough for persons in the audience to hear. There are no formal speeches. No one talks for more than a minute or two at a time, and, on the average, the members talk much less than that. The members remain seated. Sometimes they talk to one another, sometimes they address the chairman, and at other times they talk directly to the audience —but always they will talk so that people in the audience can hear them easily.

When the panel has explored the problem, the chairman gives a brief summary of what has been said and then turns the meeting into a forum (hence the name Panel Forum) by *opening the discussion to members of the audience.* Approximately half of the available time should be reserved for audience participation.

THE SYMPOSIUM

The Symposium comes closer to formal public speaking than either the Cooperative Investigation or the Panel Forum. It consists of a chairman and several speakers, usually two, three, or four. The speakers stand and speak rather formally. Each presents his own personal viewpoint, but the speeches are not debates. They are not aimed at convincing the audience that the speakers' views should be adopted. Each speaker tries to add information and raise pertinent questions. When the speakers have finished, the chairman then invites the audience to participate in the question period. These questions are for the purpose of getting additional information from the speakers, or to weaken or strengthen the speakers' arguments. They may be submitted to the chairman in writing, or the questioner may stand and ask his question directly.

THE COMMITTEE MEETING OR CONFERENCE

These discussions ordinarily are not held in public. When an organization cannot discuss all the business that comes before it, some of the problems are referred to Committees which are composed of members who have special qualifications. A chairman is designated by the organization or elected by the committee members themselves. The Committee meets and discusses the problem, prepares a formal report, and presents it to the organization. Conferences sometimes are held publicly. Committee hearings like those of Congress are sometimes conducted publicly. But the audience simply listens. It does not participate.

Stating the discussion question

Not all questions can be discussed. We do not discuss questions that call for measurable facts, such as who ran the fastest mile or who is mayor of Detroit; we simply investigate and find out. Nor do we discuss nonsense questions such as that poser of the Middle Ages, "How many angels can dance on the point of a pin?" If you must know the answer to that one, you can find it by producing the pin and angels, and counting them. Discussion will not help.

We discuss problems that concern our welfare. By discussing them we attempt to find the causes of our difficulties and to arrive at suitable solutions for our disagreeable situations. When a question so concerns us, the first step is to state it precisely. Two suggestions on phrasing questions may be helpful:

1. *State the question so it is limited to one specific problem.* If you try to discuss such a multiple question as, "Should the powers of the

United States Federal Government be reduced and those of the United Nations be increased?" you will find that it involves at least four specific and separate questions, as follows:

a. Should the powers of the United Nations be increased?
b. Should the powers of the U. S. Federal Government be decreased?
c. If they are decreased, should all powers taken from it be transferred to the United Nations?
d. Or, if they are decreased, should some of the powers be transferred to the forty-eight states?

You cannot discuss four intermixed questions at one time, or two. Limit your question to *one* specific problem.

2. *State the question so the answers will not be "yes" on one side and "no" on the other.* If, for example, you state the question as, "Should the United States maintain a policy of reciprocal trade agreements with foreign nations?" the discussion will turn into a downright debate, with one side arguing "yes" and the other arguing "no." Each side will try to *prove* its case, and neither will be primarily concerned with constructive ideas on foreign trade.

On the other hand, if you state the question as, "How can the United States best develop its foreign trade?" neither side can argue "yes" or "no." In fact, *there will not be any sides,* and the discussion will more likely evoke constructive ideas about improving foreign trade, including the effect of tariff on trade.

Qualities of good discussion

To the inexperienced, good discussion may sound like good ordinary conversation, lively and informal, and, of course, interesting. But, underneath, it is fundamentally different. It is *planned* conversation. It starts at a given point and goes through the definite steps of defining and exploring and solving a problem. *It requires a knowledge of the processes of thinking.*

This process involves the following well-known Six Steps:

1. What is the *nature* of the problem confronting the group?
2. What *caused* the problem?
3. What are the *several possible solutions?*
4. What are the *advantages and disadvantages* of each?
5. What, finally, seems to be the *one best solution?*
6. How may this solution be *put into operation?*

Of course, intelligent discussion does not plod automatically through each of these Six Steps. Naturally, people who are talking over a problem take stock of the situation, consider where they stand, and how far they may safely or wisely go. Perhaps they already know the nature of the problem (Step 1). Perhaps they even know what caused it (Step 2). The discussion would then pass over these aspects of the question and go at once to the possible solutions (Step 3). At another time there might be only one possible solution; consequently, the focus of discussion would be on how to work this solution into tangible form and put it into effective operation (Step 6).

Still again, the problem may be so complex that it cannot be solved in the near future, and has not yet developed far enough to determine which one solution is best. At the moment, the only thing to be done is to consider the nature of the problem and its causes, and to develop the several possible solutions which might be adopted—then wait for time to reveal which of them is best (Steps 1, 2, and 3).

How to participate effectively

ACQUIRE AND ORGANIZE INFORMATION ON THE SUBJECT

People who know little or nothing about a subject cannot discuss it intelligently or with profit, nor can they form trustworthy opinions on it. They can only pool their ignorance. Before intelligent discussion is possible, the participants must have information. Before they can form judgments, they must have facts. When you are assigned to a discussion, then, your first task is to prepare.

First, think over what you know about the problem, and jot down the main points in a concisely organized outline.

Second, investigate the subject systematically and thoroughly. The *Reader's Guide* and other standard references in your library will supply material. Generally it is unwise not to consult enough of these references to find out what others have recently written on the subject. Nor are recent references the only valuable ones. The philosophy, foundations, and assumptions are important, and ought to be examined or re-examined.

Third, read systematically and take notes on what you read. By the aid of notes you can keep information at hand for constant reference. You can also be sure of exact facts, dates, quotations, or opinions.

Fourth, organize your information once more into a concise outline. You may write the outline on paper or arrange it on cards. If you put it on paper, it is quickly visible to the eye. If you put it on cards, the outline can be more complete and detailed than it ordinarily would be if it were written on paper.

TAKE PART IN A COOPERATIVE SPIRIT

Please remember that a discussion is not a contest. It is not a debate. You don't try to score a point, to prove that your "side" is right or that the other "side" is wrong. There really are no "sides" in a discussion. There are only different viewpoints among people who are concerned for the common good of all. You don't try to prove yourself clever or witty, or to stand out as a big shot. You are one of a group that is *thinking together*, and anything that disrupts the process of thinking together is out of place. When you take part, put aside intense individualism and the desire to excel, to dominate the group, or to insist that others accept your ideas.

Learn, instead, to think and feel and talk in terms of group welfare, and to cooperate with others in thinking on the problem. For example, don't sit with an impatient air of one who is waiting to interrupt and get the floor. *Learn to listen*, and to digest what you hear. Ask questions when you need further information, but don't talk too glibly or let go with half-formed ideas. Don't jump on an idea just because it is not yours. Rather consider what good there is in it, and whether it has drawbacks and weaknesses. If you think the idea is good, say so when it comes your turn to talk. If you think there are drawbacks and weaknesses, call attention to them, but always in the spirit of cooperation, of trying to make the idea better rather than to kill it.

Remind yourself reasonably often that your opinions are not sacred merely because they are yours. If you present an opinion, and weaknesses show up after others have worked it over, give your judgment a chance to overweigh your pride. It is a poor mind that can't fix up reasons for saving face, of course, but a face thus saved is not a thing of beauty nor a joy forever. It loses the dignity, if not the nobility, gained by one who invites others to pass judgment on his ideas, and rises above bias and emotional resistance when they do so. You are met to work out a problem, so commit yourself to an open-minded search for facts, to a mutual sharing of ideas, to proper sympathy for the attitudes of others, and to thinking *with* the group.

BE SENSITIVE TO TECHNIQUES THAT MAKE THE DISCUSSION PROFITABLE TO LISTENERS

A constant hazard of discussion is that it becomes profitless talk. Not only can it do this by ignoring the processes of thinking and straying from the point at issue. It can also do it by ignoring the listeners. Here are a few obvious things about listeners that participants should especially keep in mind:

First, be sure that all listeners can easily hear, even when you are overtly talking to other discussion members. To state this seems to repeat the obvious. Unfortunately, here is still the most common cause of failure, the failure to include the entire audience in the range of audible speech. The discussion members simply do not reach out and share their ideas with all the listeners.

Second, remember that when you enumerate points, "1, 2, 3," they are far more listenable than when you make three points one after another without such enumeration.

Third, address other participants directly, rather than toss an idea into thin air, or pick up another speaker's point without referring to him. For the listener this gives the discussion a personal touch, and gives it movement.

Fourth, remember that apt anecdotes and brief humorous stories heighten interest, and also reinforce serious points.

Fifth, always restate a question that is not clearly worded or audibly spoken, whether the question comes from another member or from the floor. It is irritating to listeners for a speaker to answer a question mumbled by someone down front. The answer is pointless, for listeners don't know the question.

Sixth, keep the ball rolling. Remember that sooner or later it will be tossed in your lap when you don't expect it, so be ready always to handle it. Keep noting mentally what you would say. If necessary jot down items on a card. Then when it comes your way you can keep it rolling like Old Man River.

How to be a good discussion leader

The person who leads a discussion performs a unique role. He is not simply a chairman. He is not a teacher or a lecturer. He is not a persuader. He is not a dictator who dominates the discussion. Instead he personifies the spirit of democracy by assisting the discussion group to work toward a solution of their problem, yet doing so without either directing or controlling their thinking.

GENERAL QUALIFICATIONS OF THE DISCUSSION LEADER

Leading a discussion is a difficult task, and frankly not everyone can handle it. But it might help to set down the general qualities needed by such a leader, if only to enable you to check them against your own abilities and know how to be on guard at those points where you may face personal difficulties.

1. *He should know the rules of the game,* should know, for example the Six Steps in Discussion, whether he is directing a Panel Forum or a Symposium, when the audience is to be called on to participate, how to keep on schedule, and how to draw the ends together at the close.

2. *He should be willing to remain in the background.* "A quarterback who always elects himself to carry the ball whenever there is a chance for a touchdown will seldom be popular." A good discussion leader may indeed grow impatient, because a discussion sometimes moves slowly, but the good leader must move patiently with it, and not cut in to tell the group what's what.

3. *He should respect the opinion of others.* He may not share those opinions, but he should not let this become known to the audience. Throughout the meeting the leader gives equal opportunity to all members to express ideas. He listens to them, believing that what others think is important. He summarizes the consensus of the meeting without regard to his own personal opinions.

4. *He should be courteous, fairminded, and impartial.* A lively discussion is at times turbulent, and some of the less-controlled participants may clinch in heated arguments and resort to angry words. But the good leader never, even for an instant, loses his courteous manner. He is the moderator who not only restrains the violence of others, but who sets an example of courteous conduct. When the argument gets hot, he breaks in with a smile and gentle hint, such as, "I think we all know how Brown and Johnson feel about this. Now who else would like to get in on it?" If a hint of this sort does not break it up, the leader can remind the group that the purpose of the discussion is

to reach some solution to the problem, that the argument between the two members is preventing calm discussion, then ask these two persons to cease the argument and to permit the group to continue its discussion. A gentle admonition, courteously given by the leader, will usually quiet even the most violent member.

The good leader, above all, is thoroughly fairminded and impartial. He never favors one viewpoint and restricts another. He not only permits all viewpoints to be brought out, but he tries diligently to have them brought out. To persons of every viewpoint, he conveys assurance that he is a leader who plays no favorites.

The leader's role in group discussion

When asked to become the leader of a discussion group, there are certain specific tasks for which you ought to prepare:

1. *Confer in advance with other formal participants.* This will enable the leader to learn their viewpoints and to know in advance what direction the discussion is likely to take. It will also enable the leader to find out whether the other participants fully understand what is expected of them, and to make sure that each one understands the time limits of his remarks.

2. *Prepare a discussion outline.* You do not want to straitjacket the discussion by holding it to an outline prepared in advance, yet you cannot allow it to start hit-and-miss and wander whither it will. You will need to have a brief but carefully-prepared outline for use in guiding the discussion. (See page 447 for the Six Steps giving the pattern for such an outline). Once the discussion is under way, it may suddenly turn in a wholly unexpected direction from that planned in your outline. If so, let it go the new way, so long as it is not irrelevant to the question. You may even have to make up a new outline as you go along. Very well, that is better than having no outline at the start.

3. *Open the meeting with remarks that are brief and to the point.* When a discussion group meets, it wants to get going. A leader can dull this zest and nearly kill it by long and rambling opening remarks. Know in advance what you are going to say. Rehearse it. Keep it short, and to the point.

4. *Keep the discussion moving.* Once the discussion is under way, it can often get stalled if the leader is not on the alert. The moment

the talk begins to repeat itself, the good leader cuts off that topic and moves to the next one. If the discussion wanders from the point, he brings it back by some such remark as, "This is very interesting, but let us get back to our subject, namely. . . ." If persons with little or no information and few if any ideas try to monopolize the time (and who ever heard of a large discussion group where this did not happen?), the leader tactfully cuts them off with an explanation such as, "We have heard this member's contribution; you know, of course, that the aim of this meeting is to get everyone to participate and not to impose this burden on a few. Therefore, I know that this member will now want to hear from others."

Or if the leader faces the talkative person who has strong opinions but no facts, he will ask courteously but definitely for evidence: "Now that you have stated your opinions, will you give us the evidence on which they are based?" Then if the member still insists on repeating his opinions without evidence, a tactful leader will cut in with, "Thank you very much. I think we now understand your views. Can any other member offer evidence that would give support to this opinion?" In short, the good leader keeps the ball rolling.

5. *Make occasional summaries.* After the discussion has run for awhile, or some phase of it has been completed, the leader should present a summary in order that participants can see where they now stand. Make the summaries brief and impartial. A good leader often asks the group to check him for accuracy, to make sure that he has not misstated a viewpoint, and to add points he has overlooked.

6. *Bring out all viewpoints on the subject.* Here is a test of the leader's highest genius. Again and again, all the discussion will be on one side of the subject. Seemingly nobody will have an opinion on the other side. Don't be deceived. This does not always mean that nobody holds an opposite opinion. More often it means that the minority, feeling that their views are unpopular, are simply keeping quiet. A good leader *studies the faces* of the group and notes whether they seem to be in disagreement. (This requires no mind reading or mental telepathy, for people in groups show rather well in their faces whether they are for or against an idea.) The leader then specifically invites opposing arguments, or even suggests one or two himself in order to encourage the other side to follow up. Or he may add, "I see by their faces that there are some people who hold opposing opinions. Would one of them care to state his views?"

7. *Close the meeting by a summary of the whole discussion.* Such a summary is not in the form of a set of resolutions, but is rather an attempt to state the consensus of the group. It is done with due allowance for differences of opinion, "Some believe that . . . others believe that. . . ." A good summary sends the members away with the feeling that they have got somewhere, that the discussion has helped to solve, or at least to understand, the problem involved.

ASSIGNMENTS

1. Listen to a radio or television discussion and report on the following: (a) Which of the Six Steps of discussion were covered. (b) Whether in your opinion any steps left out should have been covered, or any covered should have been left out. (c) How you would have discussed the problem differently if you had been a participant.

2. Listen to three discussion broadcasts during a one-week period. Report on the following: (a) The type of each discussion and the techniques used. (b) The kind of audience for which each seemed to be especially adapted. Among the discussions available to you are the following well-established ones, but they are far from being inclusive: (a) American Forum of the Air, (b) America's Town Meeting of the Air, (c) University of Chicago Round Table, (d) Northwestern University Reviewing Stand.

3. Analyze the discussion heard in one of your classes: (a) Which of the various kinds of discussion was it? (b) To what extent did it measure up to the qualities of good discussion set forth in this chapter, and where did it fail? (c) To what extent did the leader have those qualifications for discussion leadership described in this chapter. (d) To what extent did the other participants effectively take part, and how could they have been more effective.

4. Assume that you are to lead a campus discussion: (a) What subject would you select? (b) What kind of discussion would you hold (Panel Forum, Symposium, etc.)? (c) Whom would you invite to take part? (d) What outline of topics would you follow?

5. The class will select a topic for Cooperative Investigation, then elect a leader. The leader, of course, will lay careful plans: (a) Appoint a special committee to give the topic preliminary consideration and to divide it into subtopics (or the leader may do this himself, or in conference with others). (b) Appoint members of the class to investigate each of the subtopics. (c) Conduct the Cooperative Investigation with the entire class taking part.

6. There is probably not time for each member of the class to take part as a panel member in discussion, but, in order that members may know how a good Panel Forum is operated, one may be held. The instructor will appoint the chairman and other panel members. The class will decide on

the topic. Panel members will prepare carefully for their parts. Probably they should meet a few times and construct an outline of the points they want to cover, although each member will be left free to present his own viewpoint. Class members who are not on the panel should remember that they have parts also: both of listening carefully to the panel and of being ready to take part in the ensuing forum discussion.

7. Every member of the class can acquire experience in discussion by serving on a committee. A practical way is for the class to organize itself into a Legislative Assembly and set up a group of committees so that each person in the class is a member of one committee. Class members can then introduce bills into the Assembly, as many as they want. When all bills have been presented, the Assembly will vote on which bills it wants to consider, and the Speaker of the Assembly will refer these bills to the committees, taking care to see that every committee has a bill referred to it. The committees will then meet and discuss the bills. This discussion, of course, ought to follow the regular Discussion Steps and ought to represent cooperative group thinking. At the end of the discussion a report will be prepared, and, if the committee members cannot agree on a single report, two reports may be prepared—a majority and a minority report. The committee chairman will then present the report at the next class meeting, and, if there are both a majority and a minority report, another committee member can report the second one. After the bills have been reported, the Assembly can discuss them further and vote on them, but this is not necessary for the purpose of this project. The real purpose is to give committee members experience in working on a problem by thinking and talking together.

A century ago the range of the human voice was only a few hundred feet. Today by radio and television people thousands of miles apart can, at the same instant, hear the discussion of serious ideas. Ear-minded people, who outnumber the print-minded, can at last become well informed.

CHAPTER 21

Radio and Television Speaking

CHAPTER 21

In 1863 Abraham Lincoln spoke at Gettysburg to 15,000 people. In 1896 William Jennings Bryan travelled nearly 18,000 miles in a presidential campaign, gave 592 speeches, and he estimated that 5,000,000 people came within the sound of his voice. In 1925 Russell H. Conwell died, just as radio was emerging. During his long speaking career of 60 years, his biographer proudly wrote, he had spoken to 10,000,000 people. Ten years later radio had arrived full scale, and Franklin D. Roosevelt again and again spoke to 50,000,000 people in a single address. By 1951 television had a strong foothold, and Douglas MacArthur was seen or heard in his address to Congress by nearly 70,000,000 people.

Radio, Television, and Democracy

Radio and television are not mere scientific inventions. They are agents of revolution that are profoundly influencing the operating nature of democracy. Remember that in early civilizations large nations faced the perpetual problem of disintegration because of size. Space always has been a barrier to communication, and people separated by great distance grew out of touch, and in time simply fell apart. This was a limiting factor even in the size of authoritarian states, and it was acutely so in the early democracies. Aristotle, analyst of constitutional government as well as of the science of persuasion, observed that, "To the size of states there is a limit. . . . For who can be the general of such a vast multitude, or who the herald, unless he have the voice of a Stentor?" [1] The Roman Republic extended the potential size of a unified nation by its famous roads, but Roman roads and Roman couriers had definite limitations beyond which they could not develop or hold a cohesive free society. The next advance in communication was the printing press, invented at the end of the Middle Ages

[1] *Politics*, 1326a-b.

(and one reason for the end). This made it easier to "get words out of town," and again extended the potential size of a free society.

Such had been the development of communication before the United States was born and began to grow westward from the Atlantic seaboard. Printed communication traveled at first by river and road. Then came the railroad, telegraph, and telephone, which enabled news to be assembled, and magazines and newspapers to reach the homes of the people. Communication had made progress. Ideas and information could now travel swiftly. But printed communication, vital though it was and still is, had drawbacks. People could read only what others digested for them, what others thought the people wanted to know, or what others wanted the people to know. People could not by means of print hear or see the events themselves. Furthermore, most people (ten years ago it would have been said "many people," but research now has shown that it is "most people") did not read much, or read critically. Print lacked the human touch, the human voice, the man in action. Therefore, during the period that print was the primary means of communication, sectional interests and customs in the United States separated people into North and South, East and West, city and rural. Space and time were still barriers to fullest potential understanding.

Then came radio and television with the greatest advances in human communication since the invention of the printing press. They eliminated at last the barriers both of space and time. Heretofore, only a few persons had been able to see and hear a speaker in person, or to witness an event of national concern; and when such affairs were communicated by print to the mass of people, most would not *read* a speech, even a speech by a world leader, and most would read only casually about the significance of great events. But now by radio and television they could *hear* the speaker and *see* him in action. They could witness events—public hearings, conventions, discussions, inaugurations, and significant sessions of Congress. More people, far more people, became interested in seeing and hearing than were ever captured by the print of newspapers and magazines. At last the barriers of space and time were overcome.

Radio and television, therefore, have set in force two revolutionary influences that operate on the nature of democracy. First they have overcome the limitations of space and time that caused older nations to fall apart, and that intensified sectionalism in the early days of American life. They have given impetus to the communication of serious ideas. They have at last made possible an alert and informed citizenry regardless of the size of a nation, even in an area as vast as the United States.

Second, radio and television have increased the power of the mass of people. As everybody knows democracy is ruled in the long run by public opinion. Its laws, institutions, morals, customs, and standards of right and wrong derive their authority from public opinion. But who is the "public" whose opinion wields such power? At the founding of the United States government, this public was not the mass of people, for the mass of people were not allowed to vote. The Fathers of the Republic feared the masses as Cicero feared the proletariat of ancient Rome. Even Jefferson shrank from the implications of universal suffrage until long after he had penned the Declaration of Independence, and Webster as late as 1820 warned that equal suffrage always ended in revolution and bloodshed. The first "public" that ruled by public opinion was a supposedly all-wise elite, men of property, men of education. Universal suffrage came later, but even then the mass of people did not come to full power. They were not reached effectively by print, and did not make their numbers count. Now at last radio and television have supplied a mode of communication that reaches the masses. Today the people of the nation can listen to discussions of national questions and form opinions much as people of a single town could do in the days of town meetings. "It is the common people who compose the human race," said Rousseau. It is finally the common people who control the welfare of this country and of all its people.

This transfer of the balance of power from the elite minority to the masses sets up a profound change in the operating nature of our democracy. The voice of the people is not the voice of God. It is not infallible. But one of the principal contributions of research in public opinion has been the light thrown on the competence of the mass of people to pass on questions of public policy. This research gives statistical validity of the wisdom of the mass of people, and has vindicated the ethical foundations of democracy by scientific evidence. The mass may not be brilliant or intellectual, and most are not well read; but they show a remarkably high degree of common sense, and they are able to understand public questions when stripped of jargon and put in plain language. Furthermore, they are excellent judges of public policy. As Samuel Butler exclaimed, "The public may not know enough to *be* experts, but they know enough to judge between them." [2] Henceforth it is to the mass of people, not an elite minority only, that national leaders must speak. It is to the mass that leaders must explain public policy. It is the mass whose public opinion leaders must mobilize. Only those who learn to speak effectively to the masses, in terms of their understanding and needs, will become leaders.

Not only have radio and television expanded the old tools—public address and discussion—by which democracy was developed. Not only have they profoundly influenced public opinion. They have influenced the nature and concept of democracy itself. Like atomic energy, they are explosive, with enormous power for havoc as well as good.

Against this background we can better understand the significance of speaking commonly heard on radio and television. In addition to that of political groups are the commentators—Elmer Davis, H. V. Kaltenborn, Fulton Lewis, Jr., Edward R. Murrow, Drew Pearson, Raymond Swing, Lowell Thomas, to name a representative few—who interpret news to millions, most of whom rely primarily on radio and television rather than newspapers for information. In addition to the commentators there are discussion programs such as the American Forum of the Air, America's Town Meeting of the Air, the University of Chicago Round Table, and the Northwestern University Reviewing Stand. Finally and especially are the religious speeches represented by the sermons of Bishop Fulton Sheen and Dr. Ralph Sockman, who reach audiences of a size beyond the imagination of ministers of the last century like Henry Ward Beecher and DeWitt Talmage.

Adapting a speech to the radio

The lack of a visible audience in radio increases the necessity for observing the techniques of speaking, for you must now compensate for the lack of visual cues. This is true whether you speak without a studio audience or with one, for out beyond is your real audience, scattered and unseen. Consider this unseen audience for a moment. You may be talking to 50,000 people, but they are not a 50,000-size-audience. They are separated into groups of twos and threes sitting comfortably in their own homes. The women perhaps are wearing

[2] For discussions on what research has revealed on the competence of the mass of people for making judgments, see H. L. Childs, *An Introduction to Public Opinion* (New York: John Wiley & Sons, 1940), pp. 26-32; George Gallup, *Public Opinion in a Democracy* (Princeton: Princeton University Press, 1939), p. 13.

house dresses; the men are smoking, perhaps with their neckties loose and feet in house slippers. Usually they are giving only half attention to the radio, meanwhile also glancing at a newspaper, talking, eating, or tinkering. If anything that comes out of the radio seems especially good, they pause to decide whether it is worth the effort of careful listening, then either turn to the radio with close attention or relax as before. They are not in a social situation, not influenced by the mass presence of others, and not subject to the heightened responsiveness that characterizes the crowd.

In a public audience few people will leave the auditorium, no matter how poor the speaker. No such compulsion is on the radio listener. By a turn of the wrist he cuts off an uninteresting program and picks up another. He chooses what he wants to hear. He has many programs to choose from.

PLANNING THE SPEECH

Under the conditions of radio listening, few speakers can hold that unseen audience for more than 15 minutes. Those who can are so rare that you can count yourself out—definitely out. Your problem is how to hold the radio audience for 15 minutes or less. The first minute or two is critical. Out across the ether in those thousands of homes you are being sized up. If you do not arrest attention and arouse those distant listeners to a lively interest, out will go several thousand hands in several thousand homes—and off the air you will go. In a sense, a radio speech is a race between arousing interest and being cut off the air.

The following suggestions come from persons with long radio experience:

1. *Write your talk.* For most speakers talking face-to-face with an audience extemporaneous speaking (note that we said extemporaneous speaking, not impromptu speaking) is the most effective of all modes. But not for the radio speaker. The radio speaker often does not "face" an audience at all. He faces only a cold microphone. His unseen audience cannot observe his smile, lift of eyebrow, turn of body—actions that carry personal meanings to spectators. Even a long pause, which is common enough in face-to-face speaking, cannot be used because it gives the radio audience the uneasy feeling that the radio has gone dead. Finally, your radio program is timed with exactness that allows only a variation of three seconds from the time

allotted.[3] In sum, you have no alternative but to write the speech. Most radio stations indeed will not let you in the studio until you present a manuscript.

2. *Organize the speech by a simple thought pattern.* You might want to review the discussion of thought patterns found in Chapter 11, for you will now need to apply that knowledge as never before. Avoid a complex pattern. You cannot watch the listeners to tell whether they understand you, and if you could there is not a second time for you to pause and clear up confusion. Therefore, for the main structure use two or three clearly related ideas, so phrased that the relationship is instantly clear.

3. *Plan to get the listener's attention at once, and to hold it.* By "at once" is meant in the first sentence. Cut all wind-up. You know the ways of supporting an idea so as to hold attention, for you have previously studied them: Illustrations, Specific Instances, Comparison and Contrast, Description, Narration. Use them here. Make your talk vital with human interest stories, narrative illustrations, references to events and things that are familiar in everyday life.

4. *Use simple words and short sentences.* As the Columbia Broadcasting System puts it, "Inflation, as an economic term, means little to people. But expressed as pork chops at a dollar a pound, it means an awful lot." The word "domicile" is highbrow, but "home" carries meaning to all. People like plain simple words. Use them.

Avoid long twisting sentences; make them short and straight. It is a radio maxim that any sentence over twenty words is too long. Make yours, then, twenty words or less, and strip the elaborate phrases and winding clauses.

Finally, make your writing sound like *talk.* Especially, use the contractions that well-bred people use in every day speech. People simply don't say, "It is. . . ." but "*It's.*" They don't say, "We do not," but "*We don't.*"

5. *Give double care to transitions, summaries, and the statement of main heads.* The radio listener is deprived of those little transitions and punctuations that good speakers often unconsciously give with

[3] See John S. Carlile, *Production and Direction of Radio Programs* (New York: Prentice-Hall, Inc., 1939), Chapter IX, "Three Seconds Leeway," pp. 119-127; also Earle McGill *Radio Directing* (New York: McGraw-Hill Book Company, 1940), pp. 102-113, and Girard Chester and Garnet R. Garrison, *Radio and Television* (New York: Appleton-Century-Crofts, Inc., 1950).

the head, face, hands, and body. The radio speaker, therefore, must supply them with actual words. A safe precaution is to label each main topic in advance, and when finished to summarize it tersely. Throughout the speech give more than usual care to the essential connections—words like *but, and, also, furthermore, hence,* and *therefore.*

6. *Type your manuscript in readable form.* Studios recommend that speeches be double spaced on white or yellow paper (don't use crackly paper) roughly 8½ x 11 inches in size, and spaced with a 2-inch margin all around. This makes the copy easy to read and also allows space for marginal notations.

The following reproduction shows how a typical manuscript is marked for reading:

```
(In other words,) on any "important" educational program -- not
just reading, writing, and arithmetic, but on the great "goals" of
education -- you can't do it by "precept" alone. You must do it by
"practice." You can't practice enough inside the school room walls.
You have got to get out into "life," into the city halls, the factories,
the shops and offices. George Săn-tĭ-AN-ă might call that training for
the mere masses. I prefer to call it education for the "people."
```

THE KEY

(In other words)—parenthesized phrases indicate that the voice is dropped.

"important"—the underlining means special emphasis; the quotation marks mean even more emphasis.

"goals"—multiple underlinings mean terrific emphasis.

Săn-tĭ-AN-ă—indicates the pronunciation.

7. *Mark your manuscript so as to help you bring out the full meaning of each thought.* This is now a common usage among good speakers and announcers. Each develops his personal system of markings.

Some use red and green pencils, different colors for different directions. Some use single and double underlinings, and single and double pause-markings. However you mark it, do it so the marks will have meaning to you. Your particular markings may not be clear to anyone else, but they must have a definite meaning for you.

Marking the copy will help you read the speech so it sounds like talk. Reading so it sounds like talk is difficult, more difficult than speaking *extempore.* You see the words flat on the page, all written in the same size. You tend to read flat words in a flat tone, all with the same emphasis and timing, giving as much stress to tie-up words like *of, to, the,* and *a,* as to the important thought-carrying words. The result is a patter of words, not the melody and stress of talk. By marking the manuscript you will make it easier to concentrate on *ideas,* to use the pause to get set for the next thought, and to construct the thought in your mind.

8. *Rehearse your talk.* In that interesting little booklet published by Columbia Broadcasting System on *Making Friends with the Microphone,* the question is asked, "Don't we rehearse?" and the answer given is "We certainly do." In fact, many able radio speakers do more than merely rehearse; they make an advance recording of their speech, play it back and study it objectively. This helps you check the delivery—rate, emphasis, variety, and equality of tone—to find out whether you tend to "blast" the microphone with overemphasis on certain sounds, or fade out inaudibly at the end of sentences.

9. *Time your speech carefully in advance.* On the radio even three seconds count. For example, in a 15-minute program, 30 seconds is allowed for technical station and network operation. That leaves 14 minutes 30 seconds actual speaking time. Of this, the announcer ordinarily takes about 1 minute in the opening and closing. That leaves the speaker 13½ minutes. He must not run over and he must not run short. He must come out "on the nose."

With a manuscript in hand and the words in plain sight the tendency is to read too fast. How fast does a good radio speaker talk? That depends on the person. Franklin Roosevelt spoke at 117 words a minute. Some commentators go as high as 200 words a minute and over. The average radio speaker talks about 140 words a minute, with good speakers varying 10 to 25 words either way. Do not try to talk at a predetermined rate, but use the pace that seems most natural for you, that permits you to communicate ideas with best effect. Reading in this way, *time your speech, page by page, and mark the time at the bottom of each page.* Then when you broadcast the speech you can check this marked time against the studio clock (it is always big, and visible to the radio speaker), and make sure you are talking at the rate you have planned.

FACING THE MICROPHONE

At last you are ready to give the speech. You have a manuscript. You have rehearsed it, marked it, timed it. You are now standing or sitting before the microphone and the second hand on the big studio clock is ticking toward the zero second. You get the signal. You are on the air!

In preparation for that moment, there are a few things you ought to know about facing so sensitive and delicate an instrument as the microphone:

1. *Remember that you are talking to unseen groups of only two or three persons:* No matter how many thousands are listening, they are gathered in groups of two and threes. Do not talk to them as you would to a hundred people in an auditorium, but rather as you would talk to people sitting beside you—in your very best conversational tone.

2. *Don't raise your voice pitch.* Under the tension of speaking the tendency is to tighten the muscles of the throat, and thus raise the voice pitch. But on the radio a high-pitched voice sounds especially strained and affected. A quiet, easy voice is best; and the most pleasant registers are the normal middle and lower ones. So relax those throat muscles and let the pitch down to its normal level. Don't be alarmed if your voice sounds a bit flat, or if the pauses seem a shade long. These are the normal effects in a room with special studio acoustics.

3. *Don't blast and fade into the microphone.* The microphone is a sensitive instrument that goes to both extremes. If you explode a word the result will be a blast. On the other hand, if your voice falls away at the end of a sentence (this is called *dropsy* in some studios) your words will fade into inaudibility. Your voice will then come out of the loudspeaker something like this:

> Ladies and gentlemen: MMMMPHMMM [unintelligible because of blast] I want to talk about today is mmmmm of the prrmmmmmm [can't be heard because of fade].

Inequalities in volume that would pass unnoticed in an auditorium will simply ruin a radio speech. Therefore, avoid sudden sharp changes in volume. For emphasis changes in *intensity* are better than changes in volume.

4. *Don't weave back and forth, or turn away from the microphone.* If you change the distance from your mouth to the microphone your voice will fade, boom, and distort. Keep the same distance. How far back you should stand or sit in the first place, depends on the type of microphone and on your particular voice quality. The experts in the studio will take care of that for you. Your responsibility is to stay put so that an *even* tone goes into the microphone.

5. *Keep all other noises out of the microphone.* What other noises, you may wonder, can possibly get into a microphone that is in a soundproof studio. The answer is noises that you make.

First, don't clear your throat, smack your lips, cough into a microphone, tap a pencil, drum on the table, or snap your fingers. These are high-pitched sounds that often crack like a pistol shot in the ears of those far-off listeners. If you must cough, turn your face away and bury it deep in a handkerchief. If such a cough gets into a microphone anyhow apologize for it so the audience will know you are not a boor. A simple, "Sorry," or "I beg pardon," is enough to let the audience know you are not wantonly "coughing in their faces."

Second, avoid rustling the pages of your manuscript. To the listener crackling paper sounds like hail on a tin roof. A good procedure is to make a final check just before you go on the air to see that your pages are in proper order, then remove the clip (never speak with a manuscript clipped together!). As you finish with each page, simply let that sheet fall to the table or floor. You have thus got rid of it without the chance of a rustle.

Third, breathe silently. At this advice you might be tempted to protest, "What? Can't a person even breathe in peace before a microphone?" That depends on how you breathe. A sudden intake is magnified by the microphone into a whistle. So you had best keep relaxed and breathe silently and deep.

Fourth, keep your hands off the microphone. Avoid that temptation to "stroke it, tickle it, pat it, tap it, and climb it." These aimless little efforts produce sounds not unlike those of an artillery bombardment.

Finally, say absolutely nothing for at least fifteen seconds before and after you are on the air. That microphone might be open! You cannot tell by looking at it! There was once a man who thought he was off the air, and so he said to the announcer, . . . But maybe you heard about that one. Don't let it happen to you.

Adapting a speech to television

Planning and writing a television speech is the same as in a radio speech, except that in television you may want to add the use of visual aids. But facing a television camera is markedly different from facing a microphone. The speaker's face, clothes, the way he wears his necktie, and the manner of the man himself—or the women—assume accumulative significance. The speaker must conform both to the limitations of the microphone and to the television camera, in which the latter requires movement yet restricts the area of movement. Techniques are not yet fully explored but the following represent their present development.

1. *Consider the possibilities of visual aids.* A basic requirement of television is *variety*, for listeners will not look at an unchanging image on the screen for ten minutes, or even two or three. Therefore every available technique should be used for making seemingly natural changes of image on the screen. One of these available to you as a speaker is visual aids—maps, charts, diagrams, models, slides, and films. Sometimes, especially with maps and charts and diagrams, they are placed beside or just behind you, so you can point to them, or mark them as you talk with large visible crayon. Or they may be located a few feet away where you can step over to them while talking. Materials that you do not need to explain by pointing are set up some distance to be picked up by another camera. Slides and films, of course, are handled from the projection booth.

2. *Find out in advance where you will stand or sit, and how far you may move without getting outside the camera range or depth of focus.* The size of image on the screen is determined by the distance of the camera and by the focal length of the lens being used. By changing the distance and changing the lens the cameras can shift the image from face-only to waist-up, full-view, and distant-view including background scenery or visual aids. Also, photographs are made from different angles—front, side, above, below—and to give variety changes will be made in both angles and distance while you are speaking.

Almost always two cameras are used, but if only one is used it will be panned and dollied as you speak.

The studio will instruct you as a matter of procedure about staying within camera range and focus, but you will want to arrange for placing your manuscript so it will not be conspicuous; and if visual aids are used you will want to know in advance how they are to be located, and where is the best position for you to stand in explaining them.

You don't want to appear conscious of the camera while speaking, yet mentally you should keep track of which camera is picking you up, and should adapt your movements to its angle. (You can know this easily because at the bottom of the camera small red lights turn on when it goes in action.)

3. *Learn about clothes and make-up that give best effect.* The television camera has a high response to infra-red rays which changes the appearance of clothes and gives the effect of seeing beneath the skin. The older cameras, for example, made tuxedo lapels look gray, and some figured dresses look as though an egg had been smeared on them. The normal reddish color of the lips disappeared, freshly shaven men had that "five-o'clock shadow," clean faces appeared to be dirty, and the natural shadows of the face looked unnatural. They do better now; both cameras and lighting have been improved. Even so, be careful. Avoid black and white, including white shirts. Shirts of pale blue, tan, gray, and eggshell are all right, but not white. Be careful of contrasts. The television camera will not handle the contrasts some people wear in everyday life, and it makes a little contrast go a long way. A gray suit with pinstripe and a gray shirt, for example, may look almost the same color to the human eye, but not on television; there it will show up in pleasing contrast.

To avoid bizarre effects you had best inquire about what clothes to wear and whether you need make-up. Especially also, watch jewelry and shining objects. Assuredly on the television screen all that glitters is not gold. Beads, rings, pins, earrings, and even bald heads will also glitter dazzlingly.

4. *Don't let the manuscript come between you and the audience.* Handling notes or manuscript is the most difficult adjustment a speaker has to make for television speaking. As on the radio your speech needs to be timed close to that "three seconds leeway," hence you need a carefully prepared one. Unlike radio, you cannot read it.

It is obviously disastrous for a television audience to see only the top of your head, or to see it constantly bobbing up and down over a manuscript. You can't let that manuscript come between you and the audience.

There is no easy way around the problem; whichever way you go is rough. Memorizing is seldom the answer, for most memorized speeches *sound* memorized. Therefore, commentators and speakers are meeting the problem in three other ways: (1) Most public officials still use a manuscript, but have it so well in mind that they need merely *glance* at it at moderate intervals, and seem almost to be speaking without notes. Some, like Thomas E. Dewey, keep almost verbatim to the words of the copy. Others, like Harry S. Truman, follow a semi-*ad-lib* method. (2) News commentators generally use a half-notes-half-memorized system. If, let us say, there are six news stories going at the moment—on Italy, Argentina, U.S. price control, etc.—they *memorize* the development of each story. Then for the telecast they set up very large cards right near the camera, so they can be almost looking into it when they look at the cards. On these cards might be set up leads of four or five words, or a list of topics they are going to cover. They speak *extempore,* but follow the memorized development of each story. If there are technical details not easy to memorize, they arrange to show them on a map or other design, and while the camera is fixed on the map the commentator reads verbatim from a script. (3) A few speakers, including General Eisenhower in giving his first television speech, adopt a method developed by shows like *We the People* for handling fresh casts of inexperienced, and only slightly rehearsed, participants. It consists of putting the entire speech on huge cards, about 3 x 5 feet, with about eight lines to the card. These cards are placed beside one of the cameras so the speaker is almost looking into the camera as he reads from them.

5. *Converse directly and intimately as though to a small group.* A telecast speech is an intimate thing. The camera's electronic eye makes a picture that almost literally goes beneath the surface. Your audience, as in radio, is seated in small groups. The screen is small compared with the great silver screen of moving pictures. Everything lends itself to the illusion of closeness. Speak, therefore, as though you were talking earnestly to a small group face-to-face. Remember that television is no place for a high-pressure speaking tone or excited

manner. These give the effect of your trying to push the listeners around, and their automatic retort will be, "quit pushing."

Since the audience sees as well as hears, the rate of speaking will tend to be a little slower than in radio. Pauses, bodily action, and facial expression carry part of the meaning, and these will consume a slight additional time.

6. *Adapt your action to close-up speaking.* Television restores much of the communication by the eye so conspicuously missing in radio, but action on television is not identical with action in an auditorium. It moves in the direction of best action in private conversation. In an auditorium you need extended action—a sweep of the arm, large movements of the body—for people to see at a distance. On television such extended action is overdone and marks you as a "ham." On television more often than not you do not stand up and speak formally, but are seated at a desk, as in an office, or even in an easy chair, as at home. This is a new kind of posture. You don't want to sit stiff-backed, but rather to sit as in alert friendly conference or conversation. Thus far you can be merely "natural" if your natural manner in private conversation is good enough. But from this point on, you can't be "natural." You must adopt a technique that gives the *illusion* of naturalness. For example in private conversation you might sit for a minute or two without deliberately changing posture. Not in television. You must have variety on that screen, and to do this you need deliberately to change position with reasonable frequency and do so in a way that gives the illusion of doing it naturally. You may lean forward to emphasize an idea, turn your body or nod your head to mark a transition. You may explain, describe, locate, and differentiate ideas with your hands—not with extended action, but in reduced form as though talking to people sitting beside you. You will look at the camera, and look away. You will consciously seek for variety that seems natural, attempting an art that conceals art.

Furthermore, in doing this you must conform to the limitations of the television camera: keep within camera range, and keep action away from that foreground where it will be out of focus.

Finally, watch your mannerisms. Many of us are guilty of trick manners, facial contortions, wasted motions, and repetition of action, of which we are usually unaware. Our friends are accustomed to them, and are less distracted by them than are strangers. Such mannerisms do not go well on television. They are made prominent by the illusion of closeness on the screen; and to strangers they are distracting. Now this does not mean that you are to give up the hallmarks of your own personality and become a standardized robot. Effective television speaking, in fact, demands that you intensify your personality as much as you can. But it also demands that you get rid of annoying mannerisms. You can't check yourself on this. You will need the advice of others who are willing to watch you rehearse.

ASSIGNMENTS

1. Listen to a good radio speaker and report on what you think are the factors of his effectiveness. Include manner of speaking, articulation, speech content, manner of organization, and use of language.

2. Listen to a good television speaker. (a) Report on the things you *saw* that contributed to his effectiveness. (b) To focus your consciousness on the technique of action, count how often the speaker changed his position or posture during a 3-minute period. (c) Count the number of camera changes, of distance and angle, are made during a 3-minute period.

3. Visit a radio studio and study firsthand the conditions under which a speaker broadcasts.

4. If possible, visit a television studio and study the conditions under which a speaker telecasts.

5. Recast one of your previous speeches in this course so it will be adapted for radio broadcast.

6. Recast one of your previous speeches in this course for telecasting. With marginal notes indicate what visual aids you would use. Also indicate special adaptations of posture and movement that you would use.

7. Write out a one-minute newscast and make a recording of it. Remember that the announcer's problem of reading aloud is like that of the actor. He must *seem* natural but he cannot *be* natural. In everyday American speech, sounds are often slurred and final phrases lost. Should you talk in this "natural" way over the microphone, without the aid of gestures and sight, your voice simply will not make sense. An announcer, like an actor, must overdo to seem natural. The good announcer overdoes just enough to make it seem natural, whereas the "ham" overdoes in a way that makes him seem obviously unnatural.

8. Write out and record a three-minute radio speech:
   - **a.** Type the manuscript, double spaced, and mark for reading.
   - **b.** Time it carefully, and in order to make sure of not running over, put your limit at 2 minutes 50 seconds. (This will enable

the speech to be recorded on an 8-inch disc, if desired.) *Do not* write a 3-minute 30-second speech, then try to pack it into 2 minutes 50 seconds by fast reading, for the faster you read the less the listener comprehends. If you have a 3:30-minute speech, read it in 2:50 minutes of time, and the listener gets 1:30 minutes worth, that is poor economy.

c. Above all, be earnest; talk directly to your unseen listener.

President Vincent Auriol of France addressing the United Nations Assembly. UN meetings are made difficult because some members come from nations where parliamentary procedure is hardly known and not respected.

CHAPTER 22

Parliamentary Procedure

CHAPTER 22

Parliamentary procedure is relatively new in democratic society. The early democracies had hardly even the rudiments of it, nor did the republics of the Middle Ages. But when rural England began developing the system of representative government, some eight hundred years ago, it needed a technique for operating that system. When this technique was developed it became known as parliamentary procedure—i.e. the procedure for operating a parliament.

American parliamentary procedure inherited its spirit from England, but not all of its form. Transplanted in the New World, it evolved from town meeting to colonial assembly to Continental Congress. When the Constitution was adopted Thomas Jefferson used the customs of the British Parliament for drawing up rules of procedure for the House of Representatives, but tempered them distinctly out of his experiences in the Virginia House of Burgesses and the Continental Congress. In 1876 Henry M. Robert used the procedure of the House of Representatives in drawing up his rules of order for general public use. Since then over a hundred other writers have modified and streamlined Robert's rules of order.

There is no one fixed set of rules, therefore. There are differences in the procedures of the British Parliament, the United States Senate, the United States House of Representatives, and the various state legislatures; and clubs and societies use a procedure (to be set forth in this chapter) that varies slightly from that of any state or national legislative body. Each organization or group has relied on precedent and experience to develop a procedure best fitted to its own needs. The important thing is not that minor differences exist, but that the procedure has the same objectives and is based on the same principles. The objectives are to protect each member of the organization, yet make it possible for the assembled group to act effectively—adhering to the axiom that "when there is no law, but every man is right in his own eyes, there is the least real liberty." The principles on which it rests are these:

1. Rule of the majority, with full respect and full protection of minority rights.
2. Equality of membership.
3. Free and full discussion.
4. Consideration and disposition of one matter at a time.
5. Discussion of topics, not personalities.

Getting business conducted

When business is carried on by a group there is a danger that the operation will veer toward one of two extremes. First, the group may bog down and get nothing done; the members waste their time in aimless talk and pointless delays. Second, going to the other extreme, it may cease to be a deliberate body and become only a ratifying body that passes motions without discussion, but with unanimous "ayes." The world has witnessed a succession of such ratifying bodies in the twentieth-century resurgence of dictator states, in which the Leader speaks and their designated parliamentary puppets shout *ya* or *da.* In contrast, parliamentary procedure was evolved as a technique to enable groups to *deliberate* without stagnating.

ORDER OF BUSINESS

Every group will have an order of business, usually specified in its by-laws. If not otherwise specified the following is the common procedure:

1. Call to order
2. Minutes of the previous meeting, reading, correcting, approving
3. Reports of officers (especially secretary and treasurer)
4. Announcements
5. Reports of standing committees
6. Reports of special committees
7. Unfinished business
8. New business
9. Program
10. Adjournment

THE CHAIRMAN

The chairman holds a position of authority and responsibility. He must get business done, but he must get it done democratically. He must protect the assembly from dilatory and frivolous motions, must enforce the observance of order and propriety among members—yet he is the servant of the assembly. The duties of a chairman may be summarized thus: (1) *Keep the business moving as rapidly as may be done with real deliberation.* (2) *In the conduct of business be vigorous and positive, in the treatment of members be courteous and impersonal.* The following is a useful guide for all chairmen:

1. Keep with you a copy of the constitution and by-laws.

2. Commit your Order of Business to memory.

3. Master such basic parliamentary considerations as the nature, purpose, and order of precedence of commonly used motions.

4. Keep at hand a chart showing precedence of all the various motions.

5. Keep a committee roster, so you can quickly check the personnel of the different committees.

6. Recognize each speaker by name, or if you do not know the name ask, "Will the member state his (or her) name?"

7. If two or more members claim the floor at the same time, recognize the one you choose, but in principle alternate the discussion between those who favor and those who oppose the motion. Also do not allow a few persons to do most of the talking so long as others want to participate.

8. State each motion clearly and exactly, so the full membership will know what business is before the house.

9. Keep business moving by such means as will prompt deliberation and action: "Is there a second?" "Is there any discussion?" "Any further discussion?" "If there is no further discussion the chair proposes to put the question to a vote."

10. Especially use the Unanimous or General Consent vote where the group opinion seems to be unanimous: "It has been moved that the assembly do so-and-so. If there are no objections so-and-so will be done." After a pause for objection you will say "It is so ordered."

11. When members make "suggestions" ask them to put the suggestion in the form of a motion.

12. In voting viva voce, call for "Those in favor say '*aye*.' Those opposed say '*no*.'" Do not brand yourself as a parliamentary illiterate by calling for "Those opposed, same sign," thereby making the "*noes*" vote "*aye*."

13. Announce the results clearly.

14. Insist that the assembly recognize the parliamentary necessity of considering one matter of business at a time. Invariably some members will offer a main motion while another main motion is pending, and these must courteously be put aside.

15. If a member ignorantly makes an improper motion, courteously suggest the proper one whenever you can do so, instead of merely ruling him out of order.

16. Always refer to yourself as "the chair," and not by the first person pronoun.

17. Make full use of your secretary. Remember that the secretary keeps a running account of the proceedings.

VOTING

Nearly all motions must be voted upon. Most of them require only a simple majority, although those which would change established custom, such as amendments to the constitution or by-laws, or those which would limit or restrict the individual's normal rights, such as limitation on debate, require ⅔ majority. Following are the more common methods of voting:

Viva Voce (vī′va vō′se, or voice vote by ayes and noes). This is the most commonly used method. It should not be used in voting on motions requiring a ⅔ majority. In putting the question, the chairman simply says, "The question is on the adoption of the motion that . . . "All in favor say 'aye,'" and then, "All opposed say 'no.'"

Standing Vote. The chairman should call for a standing vote if he has reason to believe that the vote will be too close to be determined by viva voce. He may call for it following a viva voce vote if he is not able to determine whether there were more ayes or noes.

Show of Hands Vote. This form of voting may be used in place of the standing vote, except when division of the assembly has been called for, in which case the standing vote should be used.

Ballot. The ballot is used only when a secret vote is desired. Most organizations prefer the ballot for the election of officers, and for election to club membership. If someone desires a ballot on a question on which the constitution does not require it, it is in order for a member to rise and say, "Mr. Chairman, I move that the vote on this question be taken by ballot." This motion is undebatable, and requires a simple majority. A ballot vote which is not unanimous may not be made so by a motion to that effect.

Roll Call (recorded yeas and noes). If someone wants the organization to have a record of the vote on a particular question, he obtains the floor, and says, "Mr. Chairman, I call for the yeas and noes on the motion. . . ." Upon hearing a second, the chairman says, "The aye and no vote has been called for on the motion. . . . Those in favor say 'aye.' Those opposed say 'no.' The ayes have it, and the vote on this question will be taken by yeas and noes." Following debate, the secretary will call roll, recording an "aye" or a "no" after the name of each member present and voting. This record is incorporated into the minutes.

Unanimous or General Consent. This is the kind of vote actually used when the chairman states that if there is no objection, such and such will be done. It is an expedient that is highly desirable, and is in common use. Nearly all organizations, for example, use it in approving the minutes. A single objection forces a formal vote, and it is not applicable to any motion affecting the constitution and by-laws, or to any rule which protects absentees.

Voting by the Chairman. The chairman votes when:

1. The vote is by ballot.
2. The vote is by roll call (recorded yeas and noes).
3. In all other cases when his vote will change the result. For example, he might vote "yes" to break a tie that exists, or "no" to create a tie, and thus cause the defeat of a motion.

QUORUM

A quorum is the minimum number of members (usually a percentage of membership) necessary for the legal transaction of business. It refers to the number present, not to the number voting. The quorum is usually specified in the by-laws, but if none is specified, it is presumed to be a simple majority of the entire membership. If there is no quorum, members present may discuss any business whatsoever, but they can take no legal action. A quorum is not necessary for motions to *adjourn*, to *recess*, or to *fix the time and place to reassemble.*

ELECTIONS

The mode of election should be explicitly set forth in the constition and by-laws.

Nominations. Usually nominating committees are used, for committees are in position to select the nominees with considered care and they greatly expedite election procedure. A few small organizations nominate entirely by ballot, with no names placed before them; after the first round of balloting two or more names begin to emerge as the group choice, and the election can be accomplished within four to six ballots. The poorest method is to have desultory nominations from the floor without a prior committee report or consideration. Off-the-cuff nominations and elections may be done in a few minutes, and the society may suffer the penalties of poor officers for the whole duration of their term. If a nominating committee is used, other nominations for each office may be made from the floor *after* the nominating committee has submitted its selections. (This gives the assembly a check on any committee that might attempt to ignore the will of the majority.) Before proceeding to election the chair should inquire if there are additional nominations.

Seconding nominations. Nominations, of course, do *not* require a second, this in spite of the frequent parliamentary ignorance shown by glib members who are willing to chorus, "I second the nomination." Any person whose name is presented to assembly is a nominee, and the nomination needs no further sponsorship from any other member.

Closing nominations. When there are obviously no further nominations the chair may declare nominations closed, or a member may move to close nominations by vote. Such a motion requires ⅔ majority, since it deprives members of one of their rights.

Voting on the candidates should be by ballot.

The nature, purpose, and precedence of parliamentary motions

Motions are the media through which business is transacted. The secretary may read a communication, or a member may outline a proposal; but there is no business before the assembly until someone offers a motion. There are four classes of motions, each having its special set of purposes and all of them, from the first to the last, having a fixed order of precedence: (1) Principal Motions, (2) Subsidiary Motions, (3) Incidental Motions, and (4) Privileged Motions. We shall consider each group separately.

PRINCIPAL MOTIONS

1. Main Motion
2. Reconsider
3. Rescind
4. Expunge
5. Take from the Table

The various parliamentary manuals are in agreement on Subsidiary, Incidental, and Privileged Motions. Concerning the group here presented, however, there is some disagreement. We shall use the term "Principal" in describing them. Various parliamentarians group them under such heads as "unclassified," "miscellaneous," "incidental main," or "renewal"; but for the following reasons they are here grouped with the main motion under the heading of "Principal Motions":

1. They have the same order of precedence (rank) as the main motion.
2. Like the main motion, they introduce a new matter of business.
3. Generally, like the main motion, they may not be introduced when any other question is pending.

The object, form, and characteristics of each of these motions are given below.

MAIN MOTION:

Object: To introduce original business.

Form: "Mr. Chairman, I move that this club buy a new gavel," "Mr. Chairman, I move that this organization go on record as approving the immediate withdrawal of all American combat troops from Africa." "Mr. Chairman, I move the adoption of the following resolution: . . . ."

Characteristics:
1. Is out of order when any other business is pending.
2. Takes precedence over no other motions, and yields to all other motions except other principal motions.
3. Requires a second, is debatable, is amendable, and requires a simple majority vote.

RECONSIDER:

Object: To bring before the assembly a question already voted upon.

Form: "Mr. Chairman, I move to reconsider the action of this assembly in. . ."

Characteristics:
1. Must be proposed and seconded by members *who were on the prevailing side* in the original voting.
2. Must be made at the *same meeting or the next meeting following the original voting.*
3. Requires a second, is debatable only if the motion to which it applies is debatable, in which case the original question is again open to debate, is not amendable, and requires a simple majority.

RESCIND:

Object: To nullify a vote (practically, its object is same as that of to reconsider).

Form: "Mr. Chairman, I move to rescind the action of . . . taken at the . . . meeting."

Characteristics:
1. May be introduced at any time, in contrast to the motion to reconsider, which must be introduced not later than the meeting following that at which the original vote took place.
2. Requires only a simple majority provided previous notice has been given; otherwise either ⅔ majority of those present, or a simple majority of the entire membership.
3. Requires a second, is debatable, and is amendable.

EXPUNGE:

Object: *To eradicate a former action completely* by striking its record from the minutes.

Form: "Mr. Chairman, I move to expunge from the records (here state the order, the resolution, or the objectional words) as found in the journal of (give date and place in the record)."

Characteristics:
1. Requires a majority vote of the entire membership.
2. If adopted, it requires the secretary to draw a line around that part of the record to which it applies, and to write across the face of it, "Expunged by order of the assembly this ____________ day of ________, A.D. 19____."
3. Requires a second, is debatable, and is amendable.

TAKE FROM THE TABLE.

Object: To bring up for consideration a motion previously laid on the table.

Form: "Mr. Chairman, I move to take from the table the motion. . . ."

Characteristics:
1. If adopted, it makes the motion taken from the table the next order of business.
2. If it is rejected, it may be proposed later in the same meeting after other business has been considered.
3. Requires a second, is not debatable, is not amendable, and requires a simple majority.

SUBSIDIARY (SECONDARY) MOTIONS

1. Postpone Indefinitely
2. Amend
3. Refer or Commit
4. Postpone to a Definite Time
5. Limit Debate
6. Previous Question
7. Lay on the Table

Subsidiary motions, as the term indicates, modify or dispose of certain other motions to which they may be applied, particularly principal motions, and even more particularly the main motion. Naturally, they must be disposed of before the motion to which they apply can be given further consideration. For example, action must be taken on an amendment before further consideration can be given the motion which it would amend. Incidental motions and privileged motions take precedence over them, and as a group they must be learned in the order of their precedence. They are listed above in order of rank from lowest to highest. To lay on the table, therefore, takes precedence over all other subsidiary motions. Commit them to memory in the order listed.

POSTPONE INDEFINITELY:

Object: To dispose of a question (a motion) without voting on the question itself. It is often used to test voting strength on a question without having to vote on the question itself.

Form: "Mr. Chairman, I move to postpone the question indefinitely."

Characteristics:
1. If adopted, *it kills the motion to which it applies.* The question would have to be re-introduced at some future meeting.
2. It has the same rank as the motion to amend, neither being in order when the other is pending.

3. It requires a second, is debatable, and reopens debate on the motion to which it applies, is not amendable, and requires a simple majority vote.

AMEND:

Object: To modify a question before the assembly.

Form: "Mr. Chairman, I move to amend the motion by *deleting* the words. . . ."
"Mr. Chairman, I move to amend the motion by *adding*. . . ."
"Mr. Chairman, I move to amend the motion by *inserting* the words . . . between . . . and. . . ."
"Mr. Chairman, I move to amend the motion by *striking out* the words . . . and *inserting* the words. . . ."
"Mr. Chairman, I move to amend the motion by *substituting* for it the following. . . ."

Characteristics:

1. In phrasing your amendment, guard against ambiguity. State what your amendment proposes; that is, whether it will delete, add, insert, strike out and insert, or substitute. Be direct; say "I move to amend . . .," not "I think we ought to. . . ."
2. A "primary" amendment or amendment "of the first order" amends a question. A "secondary" amendment or amendment "of the second order" amends an amendment. An amendment "of the third order," that is, an amendment to an amendment to an amendment, is out of order.
3. An amendment must not negate; that is, to propose the insertion of "not" is out of order. It must not be antagonistic in any other way.
4. An amendment must be germane to the motion or the amendment it proposes to change.
5. The chairman has the authority to demand that an amendment be submitted in writing, and he should do so if it is ambiguous or long and involved.
6. An amendment has the same rank as the motion to postpone indefinitely, neither being in order when the other is pending.
7. It requires a second, is debatable if the motion being amended is debatable, is amendable, and requires a simple majority vote.

REFER OR COMMIT:

Object: To assign a question to a committee for the purpose of (1) obtaining more information on the subject, (2) re-writing in the interest of clarity, or (3) smoothing out troublesome differences.

Form: "Mr. Chairman, I move to refer this question to the Executive Committee (or some other standing committee)." "Mr. Chairman,

I move to refer the question of selecting a playground site to a committee comprising Mr. Xray, Mr. Yolk, and Mr. Zebra, to submit their recommendations to the next meeting."

Characteristics: 1. A motion to commit or refer should specify the number to be on the committee, how they are to be appointed or elected, what their power is to be, and, if apropos, when they are to report.
2. It requires a second, is debatable, is amendable, and requires a simple majority vote.

POSTPONE TO A DEFINITE TIME:

Object: To defer action upon a pending question.

Form: "Mr. Chairman, I move to postpone the consideration of the question until the next meeting (or until the arrival of Mr. Roger) (or until 2:30)."

Characteristics: 1. If it is adopted, the secretary will note that the question to which it applies becomes the order of business (order of the day) at the time fixed.
2. It requires a second, may be debated as to the propriety of postponement, may be amended as to the time proposed, and requires a simple majority vote.

LIMIT DEBATE:

Purpose: To restrict time available for debate in order to expedite business.

Form: "Mr. Chairman, I move that debate on the pending question be limited to two speeches of two minutes each per member." "Mr. Chairman, I move that debate on the pending question end at 2:30." (Note: The same form may be used to extend debate. "Mr. Chairman, I move that Mr. Wilco's time be extended three minutes.")

Characteristics: It requires a second, is not debatable, is amendable, and requires *a ⅔ majority vote.*

PREVIOUS QUESTION:

Purpose: To stop debate, and bring the assembly to a vote.

Qualified Form: "Mr. Chairman, I move (or call for) the previous question on the amendment to the amendment."

Unqualified Form: "Mr. Chairman, I move (or call for) the previous question."

Characteristics: 1. To move the previous question is tantamount to saying, "I move we stop debate, and vote."
2. Note that if a series of debatable motions is pending (for example, a main motion, an amendment, and an amendment to the amendment, the previous question may be proposed either for the whole series (unquali-

fied form), or for only the immediately pending motions, in this case, the amendment to the amendment (qualified form).

3. It requires a second, is not debatable, is not amendable, and requires *a ⅔ majority vote.*

LAY ON THE TABLE:

Purpose: Temporarily to lay aside the pending question with the privilege of discussing it at a later date.

Form: "Mr. Chairman, I move that the question be laid on the table."

Characteristics:

1. Notice that this motion takes precedence over all other subsidiary motions.
2. With few exceptions, when a question is ordered laid on the table, it takes with it all pending motions pertaining to it in the exact form in which they were when the motions to lay on the table was made.
3. To lay on the table expeditiously disposes of a motion without killing that motion, as indefinite postponement does.
4. A question laid on the table is brought up again by voting to take it from the table (see page 484).
5. It requires a second, is not debatable, is not amendable, and requires a simple majority vote.

INCIDENTAL MOTIONS

1. Point (Question) of Order
2. Appeal
3. Division of the Assembly
4. Division of the Question
5. Leave to Withdraw a Motion
6. Parliamentary Inquiry
7. Suspension of Rules

Whereas subsidiary motions *modify* or dispose of certain other motions, incidental motions *rise out of* some discussion or other matter of business. A point of order, for example, rises out of some action; a division of the assembly, out of a vote. Since they are purely incidental matters, they are proposed and dealt with as the need arises, and, like principal motions, have no order of precedence among themselves. Incidental motions yield to privileged motions, and most of them are undebatable, and may not be amended. We shall consider only the very common ones.

POINT (QUESTION) OF ORDER:

Object: To direct the attention of the chairman to a violation of parliamentary law.

Form: "Mr. Chairman, I rise to a point of order." The chairman says, "State your point." You then say, "The amendment proposed by Mr. Oboe is not germane to the main motion and is therefore out of order," or "the motion has not been seconded, and is therefore not before the assembly."

Characteristics:

1. You may raise a point of order whenever you feel that a member is guilty of indecorum (misbehavior), that remarks are irrelevant, that debate is out of order, or that a mistake of any kind has been made.
2. The chairman ordinarily rules on a point of order, although he may put it to the vote of the assembly.
3. It does not require a second, is not debatable, is not amendable, is in order when another has the floor, and requires no vote unless the chairman puts it to the assembly, in which case it requires a simple majority.

APPEAL:

Object: To compel the chairman to submit a disputed decision to the assembly.

Form: "Mr. Chairman, I appeal from the decision of the chair." The chairman then asks, "On what ground is the appeal made?"

Characteristics:

1. The appeal is used by a member who believes that the chairman has ruled incorrectly on a point of order. It requires the chairman to submit his ruling to a vote of the assembly.
2. If the matter cannot be settled simply by referring to a rule, that is, if it is a matter involving judgment, the chairman puts the appeal by stating, "The decision of the chair has been appealed from. Those in favor of sustaining the chair say 'Aye'... Those opposed say 'No'."
3. If there is a tie vote the chair is sustained and the chair (if a member of the assembly) may vote to cause a tie.
4. Whether the appeal is debatable or not, the chairman may state the basis of his original decision. If it is debatable, each member may speak once during the debate.
5. It requires a second, is not amendable, is debatable except (1) when it arises out of an undebatable question, (2) when it relates to indecorum in behavior or debate, and (3) when it relates to priority of business, and is in order when another has the floor.

Division of the Assembly:

Object: To force a standing vote.

Form: "Mr. Chairman, I call for a division of the assembly," or simply, "Division!"

Characteristics:
1. This motion is used *when you think the chairman has erred in his announcement of an aye and no vote.*
2. It does not require a second, is not debatable, is not amendable, and requires no vote.

Division of the Question:

Object: To divide a question in two or more parts in order to consider each part separately.

Form: (As applied to the motion that Mr. Wilco and Mr. Roger be invited to address the club.) "Mr. Chairman, I move to divide the question into two parts and consider invitations to Mr. Wilco and Mr. Roger separately."

Characteristics:
1. Division of the question is often handled by general consent so that a formal vote is not necessary.
2. Questions should be divided when first introduced.
3. Division of the question does not require a second if it relates to different subjects which are independent of each other, is not debatable, is amendable, requires a simple majority vote, and is in order when another has the floor if it relates to different subjects which are independent of each other.

Leave to Withdraw a Motion:

Object: To withdraw a motion.

Form: "Mr. Chairman, I move that the consent of the assembly be granted for the withdrawal (or modification) of the motion. . . ."

Characteristics:
1. Up until the time a motion is stated by the chair, its mover may withdraw (or modify) it merely with the consent of the member who seconded it.
2. After the motion is stated by the chair, it may be withdrawn by common consent. ("Mr. Queen wishes to withdraw his motion. If there is no objection, the motion that . . . will be withdrawn.)
3. If there is a single objection to withdrawal, the method indicated under "Form" above must be used.
4. It requires no second, is not debatable, is not amendable, and requires a simple majority vote.

Parliamentary Inquiry:

Object: To obtain information.

Form: "Mr. Chairman, I rise to a parliamentary inquiry." The chairman says, "State your parliamentary inquiry." You then ask, "May I move indefinite postponement of the main motion at this time?"

Characteristics: It does not require a second, is not debatable, is not amendable, ordinarily does not require a vote, and is in order when another has the floor.

Suspension of Rules:

Object: To set aside temporarily certain standing rules.

Form: "Mr. Chairman, I move to suspend the rules which interfere with the consideration of. . . ."

Characteristics:
1. Suspension of the rules is not applicable to the constitution. By-laws, except those relating to business procedure, cannot be suspended unless the by-laws themselves specifically provide for their suspension.
2. It is commonly applied to the order of business.
3. It requires a second, is not debatable, is not amendable, and requires a ⅔ *majority vote.*

PRIVILEGED MOTIONS

1. Call for the Order of the Day
2. Question of Privilege
3. Take Recess
4. Adjourn
5. Fix Time and Place

Privileged motions are those concerned with the welfare of the group as a whole, and, as such, require immediate consideration. They, therefore, take precedence over all other motions. As in the case of subsidiary motions, you must learn them in their order of precedence. Commit them to memory as listed, from lowest rank to highest.

Call for the Order of the Day:

Object: To direct the attention of the chairman to a scheduled event which has apparently been overlooked.

Form: "Mr. Chairman, I call for the order of the day." The chairman says, "The order of the day has been called for. If there is no objection, we shall proceed to the business scheduled for this time." If there is an objection, the chairman says, "What is the will of the assembly? Those in favor of proceeding to the order of the day say aye," etc.

Characteristics:
1. To call for the order of the day is simply to insist that a matter of business scheduled for the particular

time be considered. For example, it might now be the time at which the assembly had agreed to recess, or at which a motion postponed to a definite time is scheduled to come up.

2. There are two kinds of Orders of the Day:
   a. *General orders* are questions assigned to a particular time without interfering with any established rule of the assembly. For example, main motions to which definite postponement has been applied become general orders. It requires a ⅔ majority vote to consider such a question before its assigned time, but it may be considered later than its assigned time by a simple majority.
   b. *Special Orders* are so called because they do interfere with some business already scheduled. They might, for example, interfere with some matter that had been made a general order for that time, or they might require the suspension of a rule. They originate in a definite motion to make a particular matter a special order at a particular time. They require a ⅔ *majority vote.*
3. Call for the order of the day requires no second, is not debatable, is not amendable, and is in order when another has the floor.

QUESTION OF PRIVILEGE:

Object: To provide for immediate action by the assembly on matters affecting the comfort and convenience of the members (heating, lighting, ventilation, conduct of other members, etc.).

Form: "Mr. Chairman, I rise to a question of privilege." The chairman says, "State your question of privilege." You then say, "will the chair instruct the reader to read more loudly?" etc.

Characteristics:
1. Be careful to differentiate between questions of privilege and privileged motions.
2. Questions of privilege are often handled by general consent, the chairman ordinarily granting the request.
3. When handled formally, they require a second, are debatable, are amendable, require a simple majority vote, and are in order when another has the floor.

TAKE RECESS:

Object: To give the assembly a rest without interfering with the continuity of the meeting.

Form: "Mr. Chairman, I move that we recess for ten minutes (or until 2 P.M.)"

Characteristics: 1. Recess is moved in order to give the assembly a brief intermission for rest, for luncheon, for awaiting the report of a committee, etc.

2. It requires a second, is not debatable, is amendable, requires a simple majority vote, *is not in order when another has the floor,* and *may be made when no quorum is present.*

ADJOURN:

Object: To close a meeting.

Unqualified Form: "Mr. Chairman, I move that this meeting be adjourned."

Qualified Form: "Mr. Chairman, I move that we adjourn *sine die.*" "Mr. Chairman, I move that we adjourn and meet again tomorrow."

Characteristics: 1. The unqualified form suffices for organizations that meet regularly. On the other hand, organizations like Congress must use the qualified form in adjourning particular meetings. To adjourn *sine die* (without setting a day for reassembling), for example, dissolves the assembly, and closes the session.

2. It is the chairman's prerogative to declare a meeting adjourned when there is not a quorum present or when disorder interferes with the transaction of business.
3. The motion is in order *when no quorum is present.*
4. When it closes an ordinary meeting (a meeting as differentiated from a session) the business interrupted is the first to be considered after the reading and approval of the minutes at the next meeting.
5. A meeting is not adjourned until the chairman announces it adjourned.
6. If defeated, adjournment may be moved again after transaction of the business then before the assembly.
7. It requires a second, is not debatable, is not amendable, requires a simple majority vote, and is not in order when another has the floor.

FIX TIME AND PLACE:

Object: To fix the time or place, or both, for the next meeting (not the time of adjournment for the present one).

Form: "Mr. Chairman, I move that *when* we adjourn, we adjourn to meet at (specify time or place for reassembling)."

Characteristics: 1. It is the highest ranking of all motions.

2. It is in order even after a vote on adjournment has been taken if that vote has not been announced.
3. If some other motion is pending at the time it is made,

it is not debatable. *If no other business is pending, it is debatable.*

4. After it is voted upon, the business interrupted proceeds.
5. It is in order *when no quorum is present.* It requires a second, is amendable as to time or place, requires a simple majority vote, and is not in order when another has the floor.

TABLE OF PARLIAMENTARY MOTIONS

Arrangement is in order of precedence, from lowest to high rank. Each motion on a line below takes precedence over all motions listed on lines above.

Where two motions have the same rank, as with the subsidiary motions "to postpone indefinitely" and "to amend," they are listed on the same line. If one is before the house the other cannot be introduced.

I. *Principal Motions*		Deb ½
II. *Subsidiary Motions*		
1. Postpone Indefinitely	2. Amend	Deb ½
3. Refer to Committee		Deb ½
4. Postpone to Definite Time		Deb ½
5. Limit Debate		Undeb ⅔
6. Previous Question		Undeb ⅔
7. Lay on the Table		Undeb ½
III. *Incidental Motions*		
1. Point of Order		NS AoF Undeb NV *
2. Appeal		AoF Deb * ½ **
3. Division of the Assembly		NS AoF Undeb NV
4. Division of the Question		NS AoF Undeb ½
5. Leave to Withdraw a Motion		NS Undeb ½
6. Parliamentary Inquiry		NS AoF NV
7. Suspension of Rules		Undeb ⅔
IV. *Privileged Motions*		
1. Call for the Order of the Day		NS AoF Undeb ½
2. Question of Privilege		AoF Deb ½
3. Take a Recess		Undeb ½
4. Adjourn (unqualified)		Undeb ½
5. Fix Time and Place at which to Reassemble		Undeb * ½

KEY TO SYMBOLS

Deb—debatable
Undeb—undebatable
½—simple majority
⅔—⅔ majority
NS—no second required
NV—no vote required
AoF—in order when another has the floor
*—exceptions exist; consult full explanation of motion
**—(Appeal) tie vote sustains the decision of the chair

Organizing a permanent society

You will not always be a member or officer of an established deliberative group. Sooner or later you are likely to help organize one, an occasional meeting, convention, or permanent society. Therefore, let us consider how a group is organized and set in motion. We shall examine the organization of a permanent society, with the understanding that occasional meetings and conventions follow the same direction with a simplified procedure.

THE PRELIMINARY MEETING

Step 1: *Laying the groundwork.* Upon deciding to organize a permanent group those interested should consult together and lay the groundwork. At this conference the following should be determined:

1. Whether a sufficient number of others will be interested.
2. Time and place for the first meeting.
3. How to advertise the meeting.
4. Who will (1) call the first meeting to order, (2) be proposed as temporary chairman, (3) be proposed as temporary secretary, (4) explain the purpose of the organization, (5) introduces the resolution, and (6) move the appointment of a constitutional committee.

THE FIRST MEETING

Step 2: *Electing a temporary chairman.* When the meeting starts there is, of course, no chairman; so Miss A comes forward, calls the meeting to order, and says, "I move that Mr. B serve as temporary chairman." Mr. C (who has been previously designated for the purpose) seconds the motion. This is not a nomination, but a motion, so other nominations are not called for, and Miss A puts the motion to a vote: "It has been moved and seconded that Mr. B serve as temporary chairman. All in favor say aye." The affirmative vote is counted, then Miss A says: "The ayes have it; the motion is carried, and Mr. B will take the chair. If the motion loses, she says: "The noes have it; the motion is lost; and another nomination for temporary chairman is now in order." The process is then repeated.

Step 3: *Electing a temporary secretary.* Immediately on taking his place, the temporary chairman calls for the election of a temporary secretary. The process is identical to that of electing the temporary chairman. (Your attention is again directed to the fact that with these temporary officers nominations are presented in the form of main motions, and the method is different from the election of permanent officers later on.) After the secretary is elected the chairman may pause a minute to allow him to bring the minutes up to date.

Step 4: *Stating the purpose of the meeting.* The temporary chairman then resumes business by calling on Mr. D to state the object of the meeting. (Mr. D, like all others who have participated so far, has been pre-designated.) Mr. D rises, addresses the chair, and when recognized proceeds to state the object of the meeting. A discussion will usually follow, for others will want to make additional remarks and some will want to ask questions.

Step 5: *Introducing the resolution.* When it is apparent that most of the group understand the object of the meeting, Miss E (who also has been pre-designated) rises, addresses the chair, and on being recognized, moves the adoption of a suitable resolution: "Resolved, That a College Forum be established by this group in order to make possible a more profitable discussion of current controversial issues." This resolution probably should be written out, and after being read should be presented to the chairman, who, in turn, will hand it to the secretary for accurate entry into the minutes. The motion to adopt the resolution is a main motion, and must be seconded. After it is seconded, the chairman says: "The motion to adopt the resolution (here he might have the secretary re-read it) has been made and seconded. Is there any discussion?" After the discussion and possible amendment, the motion is put to an aye-and-no vote. If it carries, the chairman proceeds to the next step.

Step 6: *Appointing a constitutional committee.* After the group has adopted the resolution, Mr. F rises (he, too, has been pre-designated), addresses the chair, obtains the floor, and says: "Mr. Chairman, I move that the chair appoint a committee of three to draft the constitution and by-laws, and that the committee report one week from today in this same room." This is likewise a main motion, requires a second, and is open to discussion, and may be amended. Assuming the motion passes, the chairman says: "I appoint Miss A, Mr. D, and Mr. Y as the constitutional committee to report one week from today."

Note the nature of the motion to create the constitutional committee. It was specific; that is, it left no question as to the number, how or by whom appointed, and when they were to render a report. Under other conditions it might be desirable to name the members in the motion, or to have them elected by the assembly. Whatever is done, the motion should be explicit.

When this business of the first meeting is finished, an hour is agreed on for the next meeting, and the meeting is adjourned.

Drafting the constitution and by-laws. During the interim between the first and second meetings the constitutional committee does its work. Since the constitution and by-laws are basic, their provisions should be carefully deliberated and the wording of each article and each section tested and weighed. The constitution will need five basic provisions:

1. Name and purpose of the organization
2. Membership: kinds and qualifications for each one
3. Officers: election, duties
4. Meetings: time of
5. Amendments: method of

The following is a sample of how such a constitution might read:

Article I. NAME AND PURPOSE

Section 1. This organization shall be known as the College Forum.

Section 2. The purpose of this organization shall be to provide opportunities for its members to discuss current controversial questions.

Article II. MEMBERSHIP

Section 1. Active membership shall be limited to those who pay dues, participate as a member of at least one discussion group each year, and who attend at least six meetings annually.

Section 2. Faculty members of the College are eligible for membership ex-officio.

Article III. OFFICERS

Section 1. The officers of the Forum shall consist of a President, a Vice President, and a Secretary-Treasurer.

Section 2. Officers shall be elected at the last regular meeting of each academic year.

Section 3. The duties of the officers shall be as prescribed in Robert's *Rules of Order.*

Article IV. MEETINGS

Section 1. The organization shall have monthly meetings during the academic year.

Section 2. Special meetings may be called by a majority vote of those present at any regular meeting, or by the President of the organization.

Article V. AMENDMENTS

Section 1. This Constitution may be amended at any regular meeting of the Forum by a two-thirds vote of the members present provided the amendment has been presented at a previous meeting.

Section 2. This Constitution may also be amended at any special meeting called for that purpose provided the amendment has been presented at a previous meeting, and provided also that the special meeting is held at least one week after the meeting at which the amendment has been presented.

The by-laws contain the details of putting the constitution into operation: (1) Dues and other obligations of membership not stated in the constitution, (2) Method of electing officers, (3) Duties of officers, (4) List of standing committees and their duties, (5) Definition of a quorum, (6) Provision for parliamentary authority, (7) Order of business, and (9) Method of amendment.

THE SECOND MEETING

At the appointed time, the second meeting is called to order by the temporary chairman. He orders the minutes of the first meeting read, and after they are approved, calls for the report of the constitutional committee.

ADOPTION OF THE CONSTITUTION AND BY-LAWS

First Reading. When the temporary chairman calls for the report of the constitutional committee the chairman of that committee reads the constitution and by-laws, moves their adoption, and hands the original and one duplicate copy to the chairman. (Both the secretary and chairman will need copies.)

The Second Reading. The motion to adopt having been seconded, the chairman states, "The motion before the house is the adoption of the constitution and by-laws as reported by the constitutional committee. We shall consider it, discuss and possibly amend it, article by article, and section by section. The secretary will read Article I, Section 1." After this section has been read, discussed and possibly amended, the chairman applies the same procedure to each subsequent section and article, until the entire document has been considered.

The Third Reading. The constitution as thus amended is now read in its entirety, and an opportunity is given to amend it as a whole.

The Fourth Reading. When all amendments which may have been offered during their reading have been acted upon, the constitution is again read in its entirety. At this reading the group should particularly watch for any conflicting amendments which might inadvertently have crept in. After the fourth reading the constitution is then put to a vote, and if it is adopted, a recess is declared in order that the members may sign the document.

Following this the by-laws are given four readings, amended if necessary, and adopted in the same manner.

ELECTION OF OFFICERS

When the constitution and by-laws have been adopted, steps should be taken to elect permanent officers as prescribed therein. If, for example, the by-laws provide for nominations to be made by a nominating committee, this committee should be appointed, or elected, and the election of officers held at a third meeting.

ASSIGNMENTS

1. Write out and hand in a report on what method of voting you would use in the following instances, assuming that your by-laws did not specify:

   a. An election of officers
   b. On adopting the main motion
   c. On a motion to limit debate
   d. On a main motion following a call for the division of the assembly
   e. On a question on which vote by "yeas and noes" has been ordered
   f. On a motion which obviously was favored by all present

2. Write out and hand in a report on the following:
   a. During the interim of what two meetings does the constitutional committee do its work?
   b. By what other term is the viva voce vote sometime referred to?
   c. What is the quorum if it is not specified in the constitution and by-laws?
   d. What motion has the effect of killing the motion to which it is applied?
   e. What items should the articles of the constitution and by-laws cover?
   f. What kind of vote should be taken in election of officers?
   g. What motion "nullifies a vote"?
   h. What motion may be proposed only by someone who "originally voted on the prevailing side"?
   i. Who is the first person to read the constitution and by-laws to the assembly?
   j. What two subsidiary motions are of the same rank?
   k. What does an amendment of the second order amend?
   l. What would you propose to do with a motion on which the assembly needs to have more information?
   m. You believe that the chairman had ruled incorrectly on a point of order. What motion do you make?
   n. To what may suspension of rules not be applied?
   o. What two subsidiary motions require a $2/3$ majority vote?
   p. What principal motion must be made not later than "the next meeting following the original motion"?
   q. You want to stop debate on a proposed amendment, but not on the main motion. Would you use the qualified or unqualified form of the previous question?
   r. You believe that the chairman has made a mistake in announcing a vote. For what do you call (what do you move)?
   s. You do not want to discuss a main motion now, but you do want to discuss it at a later date. What motion do you make?
   t. When does a meeting stand adjourned?
   u. What three motions are in order when no quorum is present?
   v. What motion removes an action from the record?
   w. Under what condition is fix time and place debatable?
   x. What privileged motion is ordinarily handled by "general or unanimous consent"?
   y. When is an amendment not debatable?

Commencements are a common occasion for ceremonial speaking. Here shown are the graduation exercises of a United States Naval Reserve Midshipmen's School on board the U.S.S. *Prairie State*.

CHAPTER **23**

Speeches on Special Occasions

CHAPTER **23**

So far in this book the center of attention has been on speeches to water and cultivate thought, to influence attitude, to modify opinion, to promote action. In every civilized society—at least in every free society—such speaking is an instrument for public enlightenment, rousing public opinion, explaining measures in the halls of legislature, maintaining justice in the courts, and renewing the faith of man in the temples of worship. These are the basic types.

But man as a social being has also developed an etiquette, if not a ritual, for ceremonial speaking. The Greeks called it frankly "the ceremonial oratory of display." They were not ashamed to say outright that it was ceremonial and that its purpose was display. Twentieth-century minds wince at such brashness. Having a larger vocabulary than these early fathers of civilization, we prefer to put such concepts in words of less acuity. Hence it seems more fitting to our ears to call this ceremonial speaking the "speeches on special occasions."

In twentieth-century usage such speeches include the introducing of other speakers, presenting or receiving gifts or awards, welcoming official guests, and responding to welcomes, formal farewells, commemorating anniversaries and events like graduation, eulogies, nominating candidates, inaugurating terms of office, and speaking appropriate words at social occasions like banquets.

This is not a new genus of speaking, but only a new variety developed from old cultures. The basic speech techniques and methods are still basic. Some, indeed, have heightened value—especially clear thought patterns, vivid supporting material, vigor and grace of style, humor, and lively utterance. Over and above these, however, is the dominant influence of each special occasion that prescribes an etiquette of its own.

The form and content of these speeches have no particular similarity to one another, but they do have a common *plane*. The plane of those basic speeches we have previously been considering is *utility*. The test is whether they cultivate thought, influence attitude, modify opinion, promote action. If they be pleasing to the ear and delightful to the mind, so much the better; the plane, nevertheless, is utility. But the plane of special-occasion speeches is *art. Do they please? Do they say the fitting thing? Do they have grace and beauty?* They may have utility, to be sure. They often must have utility. But they are expected also to have art. The Greeks were literally right in calling them "the ceremonial oratory of display."

Beginners, of course, face the usual hazard of amateur artists. They mistake the garish for art, not knowing that art is simple in outline and chaste in detail. In these speeches, therefore, beware of adjectives and verbose forms of all types. Restrain the impulse to say "On this *illustrious* occasion," ". . . *happy* privilege," ". . . *high* honor." Instead circling around an idea, or backing in it, with "It gives me great pleasure and delight," go into it straight with "I have the pleasure." Use words with color and feeling as well as meaning, but use them with an artist's restraint. And remember that exhibitionism is not art and not good taste.

Speeches of courtesy

You will often have to perform appropriate acts of courtesy on public occasions—introduce a speaker, welcome a guest, present a gift or an award, etc. Custom requires you to say something. The occasion limits what you can say, and how long you can talk. You haven't much elbow room, yet you are supposed to perform with grace and charm. For these speeches, etiquette and the limits of the occasion establish the following four requirements:

They are brief. Brevity is, in fact, a complication; for brevity demands terseness, and terseness demands preparation. Most of us are like Lord Lyons, who, writing hastily to a friend, began, "I trust you will pardon the length of this letter. I have not the time to be brief." Without equal excuse, many speakers have the same failing; and because of length their speeches of courtesy become speeches of discourtesy. Be brief. Pack the speech full, but make it short.

They have a streamlined structure. This is because of brevity. Usually there is no formal division into introduction, discussion, conclusion; and no formal series of main heads. If you have heard or read of speeches that are exceptions, well and good; we are here looking at the typical. These are speeches with a simple unit, possibly a one-cell unit (see page 210), that goes straight to the point.

They give the necessary information. Usually there is a core of information that listeners need. Who is this speaker you are introducing, and how came he an authority? What has this person done that you are welcoming? Why was this award established, and exactly what did the winner do to gain it?

Their dominant mood is gracious and pleasant. The purpose of these speeches is to cultivate appreciation and promote good will. They should not, therefore, be entirely solemn or sober. Good speeches of courtesy may carry a large dose of humor. They may be refreshing and stimulating, like a breeze on a hot day. But whatever else they contain, they will also be marked by friendship, good cheer, and good fellowship.

Common Speeches of Courtesy include the following:

The Introduction	The Presentation
The Address of Welcome	The Acceptance
The Response	The Farewell

THE INTRODUCTION

The speech of introduction is the most common of all. Indeed it can be said with approximate mathematical accuracy that speeches of introduction comprise one-half the grand total of speeches, since practically every main speech is launched by its speech of introduction. Almost everybody is called on for this public act of courtesy—butcher, baker, spark-plug maker. The mine run of such speeches are poor, unbelievably poor, unnecessarily poor. They are poor in substance, poor in presentation. In substance, the typical speaker gives the appearance of gasping for ideas, as seen in these verbatim specimens:

"*It is* with pleasure *that* I introduce this speaker. . . ."

[Two fouls in the first sentence: (1) Who cares about the chairman's pleasure? Listeners want to learn about the speaker. (2) The grammatical form, "It is . . . that," backs into a thought, crab-like, instead of walking forward into it human-like. Note that the word bunglers use it habitually, and skilled artists seldom.]

"Our speaker is *very* well qualified. . . ."

[Two more fouls: (1) The statement does not give the audience any information, "but is as broad and general as the casing air." A brief speech should come to the facts without windup. (2) "Very" is a cluttering modifier; it has no meaning.]

"This speaker needs no introduction."

[Every speaker needs an introduction as a matter of courtesy, even though it be only one sentence. This is a mere gasp for thought.]

". . . I present Mr. Jones who will speak to us *at this time* on 'Illusions of History.' "

["At this time" is an obvious absurdity, in slightly better taste but as palpably absurd as saying "With his clothes on." No one ever introduced a speaker who was going to talk tomorrow or next week.]

These typical speeches of introduction are also poor in presentation, too often half audible, except for the *ers* and *ahs,* which somehow by the grace of Allah never seem to be inaudible. Conan Doyle once satirized the behavior of a typical chairman as follows:

> Professor Murray will, I am sure, excuse me if I say that he has the common fault of most Englishmen of being inaudible. . . . [He] made several profound remarks to his white tie and to the water-carafe upon the table, with a humorous, twinkling aside to the silver candlestick upon his right.

Such is the typical speech of introduction. In contrast, a minority of presiding officers give them with a sure hand and deft touch. They bring together speaker and audience so each will know the other better and both are eager to continue the acquaintance for the duration of the speech. How do they do it? First, they are sensitive to the occasion. They know what the audience wants to know about the speaker. They find out what the speaker feels would be helpful for the audience to know about him and his subject. These things they do not leave to chance, intuition, or blind luck, but confer in advance with the speaker or otherwise definitely inform themselves. Thus prepared, they can say in effect "Here is a speaker you will enjoy, and this is why."

Second, these speakers do not whisper or mumble to the lectern or water glass, but standing erect like creatures of God, they talk aloud to the fellow creatures who compose the audience.

Etiquette, custom, and the occasion prescribe the following main lines of content:

1. *Tell the audience about the speaker.* Without adulation give the speaker's record, what he has done, where he has been, why he is especially fitted to talk on this subject. Be accurate, and be exact. Instead of reciting that insipid bromide, "The speaker was for a number of years. . . ." better say "for three years," or "from 1949 to 1952." Some of the best speeches of introduction ever given to speakers little known to the audience have been taken, with credit given, almost verbatim from *Who's Who in America.* They were not imaginative, but they gave the information precisely and helpfully.

2. *Announce the subject, but don't discuss it.* You may tell why the subject is important for the audience, but don't put the speaker on a limb by discussing it per se. Otherwise you might anticipate his opening remarks and force him to recast his treatment on the moment, or may pronounce a novice's judgment on it that forces him painfully to correct you. Present the speaker and the subject, but let him discuss the subject.

3. *You may also on occasion present the audience to the speaker.* At times there are pertinent facts about the audience that can be told the speaker in the introduction. Thus a speaker may say, "Mr. Speaker, most of this group have read your latest book." Or "This group has been holding a series of discussions for the past year on the subject of South American trade, and repeatedly in these discussions your name was quoted, until the members finally concluded that they would not be content until they heard you in person."

4. *If the occasion is significant, explain it.* An anniversary, annual meeting, or unusual occasion of any sort can be touched on briefly: "Each year we meet to commemorate the founders of this organization. On this thirty-first anniversary, it seemed fitting to have one of those founders address us."

These lines of content, remember, are to be applied with imagination and intelligence, not treated as laws of the Medes and Persians. One of the most effective introductions ever given consists of five words. The last time we heard it was at an alumni banquet. The program had been long, and the last speaker—known to all—was the college president. The presiding officer arose and said, "Ladies and gentlemen: The president."

We shall not give models of each of these speeches. They are available in speech collections. But an exception will be made with the speech of introduction. The following, given by United States Senator

James Hamilton Lewis of Chicago, has neatness of structure, vivid example, humor, grace of style, and a steady movement toward the speaker's name as a climax:

> The *Christian Advocate* publishes that a little boy in Tennessee, answering his examination in anatomy, defined the spinal column as "a long wriggly bone running down a man's back, with the man's head and brains settin' on one end, and the man hisse'f settin' on the other." [*Laughter.*] Tennessee claims to be the backbone of the South. We grant her that unction. And while she sits upon that end of the consolation, we remind her that the head and brains of the other end have been transferred to the shoulders of Chicago. [*Applause.*] And while we accept the hostage with the acclaim of a proud conquerer, nevertheless we hear the moan of his first mother and she wails out, in the words of his favorite *Odyssey*, "Ulysses is gone, and there's none left in Ithaca to bend his bow." I have the honor to present to the toast that national statesman, international lawyer and orator, former distinguished Tennessean, now illustrious Illinoisan, Honorable J. M. Dickenson. [*Applause.*]

THE ADDRESS OF WELCOME

The formal reception of an important person or group calls for an appropriate speech. The object, of course, is to say with tact and taste, "We are glad you are here." The content of such a speech usually is derived from pertinent facts about the guests and the hosts, but they are not recited as mere facts. They are tempered judiciously with praise and cordial welcome.

The main lines of thought include the following:

1. *Pay fitting tribute to the achievements of the person or group you are welcoming.* Explain the achievements. Tell of their importance.

2. *Review the purpose and spirit of the organization that extends the welcome.* Especially review matters interesting to the guests, things they might profit from knowing, or things that would increase the cordiality of the welcome.

3. *Point up the purpose and spirit of the occasion.* Tell why it is fitting and proper for hosts and guests to meet together on this particular day, at this place, or under these present circumstances.

4. *If guests have come on a special mission, as for a conference or convention, wish them success in their deliberations and progress in the future years.*

Remember also that a true speech of welcome is brief. A wordy welcome cannot be redeemed by having other good qualities. It offends good taste.

THE RESPONSE

A speech of welcome calls for a response which says, likewise with tact and taste, "I appreciate your welcome." Yet in this outwardly simple response the speaker faces a hazard. He cannot minimize the praise of his hosts without seeming to impair their judgment or taste. Nor can he applaud their praise without giving the effect of inflating himself. "Before destruction the heart of man is haughty, and before honor is humility." He must accept their praise and be grateful, and must wear the humility that goes with honor.

Furthermore, the response cannot be independent either in thought or tone from the address of welcome. The speaker of welcome has set the pace, and the response must follow it—at least at the beginning. Whether the responding speaker likes it or not, he simply must pick up the line of thought, the dignity level, the tone of humor and graciousness, of the address of welcome.

Its main lines will include the appropriate items along the following:

1. *Express appreciation for the welcome and pay tribute to the group extending it.* In other words, you ask: Why do I esteem this welcome? What will be its effect on me or my organization? Who are these people that have gone to such trouble? How much effort did it cost them? The answers to such questions you put into appropriate form.

2. *Explain the purpose and method of doing the things for which you are welcomed.* What was the need? Why were you led to work on it? How was the work done? Don't be tedious. Do it in a few pointed sentences, or a single brief illustration.

3. *If you represent a group, do not fail to emphasize the contribution of others.* An oversight of this amenity would reflect on your reputation for generosity. Hence you will say, "In behalf of my organization I express appreciation." Or "I am one of many who have done this work. I speak on their behalf." Or "My associates share in this occasion. We have worked as one."

4. *Point up the significance of the occasion.* Why have you come? What will be the significance of your visit, or conference, or deliberations? Of what interest or value will it be to your hosts?

Not all of these lines of thought will be stressed, or even mentioned. But they represent the topics from which you make a judicious choice.

THE PRESENTATION

When a gift, award, or memorial is presented on a public occasion it is not enough to say, "Here it is." The occasion calls for an acknowledgment of the recipient's attainment, for praise and congratulations. Often there are also important secondary purposes attached to the occasion which must not be overlooked, such as creating or strengthening good will between donors and recipient, stimulating others to appreciate the achievement, and impelling them to greater effort or higher conduct. A speech of presentation, therefore, is often not a mere act of presenting a gift or award. It is also the occasion for stimulating others.

The main lines of thought are these:

1. *Review the exploits of the recipient.* What were the accomplishments? What skills, abilities, or qualities of character made them possible? What significance does the achievement have for others present?

2. *Appraise the gift.* The gift is subordinate to the act of giving, but it should not be overlooked. Why was it chosen? From what was it made, or how? Who shared in sponsoring it or producing it? What is its symbolic significance? Of what is it a token?

3. *If there are losers present, don't overlook them.* Where the prize or award is won in competition, reserve brief high praise for others who played the game, who made the effort, but did not win. They too share in the honor, for they furnished the standard which the winner exceeded. Without losers there would be no winners.

THE ACCEPTANCE

The theme of an acceptance speech is gratitude. Whatever else the audience may think, don't let it be, "Well! He wasn't grateful!" The temptation is to mumble, "Thank you," and sit down. A recipient can do this without too much impropriety if everyone knows he cannot talk in public, or if he has the presence of mind to say, "I never learned to make a speech, but I can say with deepest feeling, thank you!" Yet in a society where public talk is expected of all who achieve even mild success, this is weak testimony from an educated person, and people will wonder whether the award is deserved. Etiquette calls for an acceptance in words of good taste along these general lines of thought:

1. *Praise the spirit of those who presented the gift.* The donors have expended time and effort and expense. Make it clear that you understand and are grateful.

2. *If it is of interest, explain the purpose or method by which the attainment was won.* Do this with care not to magnify yourself, but only to confirm the donors' satisfaction in what they have done.

3. *Discuss the merit of the gift or the uses to which it will be put.* If it is a symbol or token, show that you recognize its symbolic significance. If it has a material use, appraise it.

4. *Share the honor if possible with others.* Few achievements are made alone. Others have gone before, laid the groundwork, or set up the goal. Others have given encouragement. Others may have worked with you. Recognize the debt. Say that you are one of many. Tell who the others were, and what they did.

THE FAREWELL

A time of parting may call for ceremony, a public testimony of friendships, courtesies, and services received. Thus an officer retires after long services with an institution, a person retires from office, leaves a community in which he has lived and worked, or undertakes a mission at some distant place. They do not go unwept, unhonored, and unsung. And however glad they are to go, there are regrets at what is left behind. To these they give expression and pay tribute. Some of the topics to be covered are these:

1. *Explain the reasons for leaving, if they are not known.* This was the first topic discussed in the most famous farewell address of the twentieth century, that of the former King Edward VIII of England when he retired to become the Duke of Windsor: "At long last I am able to say a few words of my own. I have never wanted to withhold anything, but until now it has not been constitutionally possible

for me to speak. . . . I have found it impossible to carry the heavy burden of responsibility and to discharge my duties as King as I would wish to do without the help and support of the woman I love."

2. *Testify to the relations with the institution or group you are leaving.* If they have been satisfactory, say so, and pay tribute to those who have rendered service and given friendship. Abraham Lincoln, in the most famous farewell address of the nineteenth century, could say to the people of Springfield with full truthfulness: "To this place, and the kindness of these people, I owe everything. Here I have lived a quarter of a century, and have passed from a young to an old man. Here my children have been born, and one is buried." If the relations do not merit such testimony, don't pretend an untruth. Without rancor, either pass them by as being known, or touch on them with tact and discretion. Your purpose is to express the regret of parting, and to create a regret in those who are left behind.

3. *Look at the future.* Henceforth there are to be two futures, yours and those you are leaving. You may properly say a word about where you are going and what you are going to do. You may also, if retiring from office, bespeak good will for your successor. Certainly you will bespeak good will for the organization. As Vice President Thomas R. Marshall said to the United States Senate on his retirement: "I leave with the same inarticulate cry in my soul with which I came to you: 'My country.' "

Speeches of commemoration

Public custom calls for memorial speeches of persons, events, and institutions. "A Town, or City, or State is very human," observed George Frisbie Hoar. "In sorrow it must utter its cry of pain, in victory its note of triumph. As events pass, it must pronounce its judgment. Its constant purpose must be fixed and made more steadfast by expression. It must give voice to its love and its approbation and its condemnation. It must register the high and low water mark of its tide, its rising and its sinking in heat and in cold." [1]

The purpose of these speeches is to pay tribute. Some person, action, or institution is to be praised. The speaker is not charged with the task of changing the listeners' attitude or promoting action. His is the duty of testifying to the achievement and honor, of giving them

[1] *Autobiography of Seventy Years* (New York: Charles Scribner's Sons, 1903), II, 356.

weight and reality, of renewing faith, of uplifting sentiments. "He is working for the most part with intangibles, and his success depends upon the truth and force of his imagination. He will draw word pictures; he will dramatize; he will elevate, enlarge, and dignify. Above all he will stir and create emotions, knowing that imaginations are released by emotional disturbances and then act to heighten the very emotion that has set them free." [2]

The six usual types of commemorative speeches are these:

The Eulogy	The Inauguration
The Anniversary Speech	The Nomination
The Dedication	The Commencement Address

THE EULOGY

Tribute is paid in a eulogy to the services and character of a person, usually deceased. The speaker necessarily draws his material from eulogized person's life, along one or more of these lines: (1) The person's attainments—the handicaps under which he started, the obstacles he faced, the final achievements. (2) His life purposes—why he was led to make effort. (3) His qualities of character, (4) His influence during his lifetime and on later times. The eulogist's general proposition is, "Here is a person deserving to be remembered, and these are the reasons why." There are two traditional ways to handle these lines of thought:

The first is biographical. John Quincy Adams, a professor of rhetoric and oratory before he was a foreign diplomat and President, described the biographical eulogy in words that are still classic: "Its divisions are uniform, and are precisely the same in every subject, to which they are applied. It traces the hero of the story through his genealogy to the moment of his birth; accompanies him through life; follows him to the grave, and gathers all the flowers ever scattered on his tomb." [3]

The second is selective. For its principal divisions it takes the prominent qualities of the person celebrated, and seeks to answer questions like these: (1) What was the guiding purpose of this person's life? (2) What were the sources of his power? (3) What were

[2] Wilbur Samuel Howell and Hoyt Hopewell Hudson, "Daniel Webster," in *A History and Criticism of American Public Address* (William Norwood Brigance, ed., New York: McGraw-Hill Book Company, 1943), II, 678.

[3] *Lectures on Rhetoric and Oratory* (Cambridge: Hilliard and Metcalfe, 1810), I, 246.

the qualities that made him great? (4) What debt do we owe him? (5) What inspiration or lesson do we gain from his life?

The eulogist operates under limitations of etiquette and custom. He is bound to strict adherence to truth. He is denied the dangerous indulgence of ancient eulogists known as "moral approximation," which allowed them to transpose virtues with their corresponding vices—substituting courage for rashness, generosity for extravagance, sagacity for cunning, simplicity for dullness, and an honest heart for ignorance. Yet the eulogist is not, like a biographer, bound to treat errors and failings along with virtues and achievements. His purpose not history, but praise. He may not praise the errors, follies, and vices of the person eulogized, but unless too major to be ignored he can cover them with a veil of silence; and if they cannot be ignored, he can counterbalance them by transcendent virtues. He speaks in praise of one whose life, as a whole, deserves praise. Within the limits of morality and truth, he can permit charity to cover its multitude of sins.

THE ANNIVERSARY SPEECH

This type commemorates an event or action of the past: Fourth of July, Thanksgiving, Memorial Day, centennials, and founders days. Its purpose was expressed in the famous resolution passed by the town of Boston in 1783, authorizing an annual Fourth of July address "in which the Orator shall consider the feelings, manner, and principles which led to this great National Event as well as the important and happy effects whether general or domestick, which already have, and will forever continue to flow from this Auspicious Epoch." [4]

Such a speech is both a review and an inventory, a memorial of the past and an incentive for the future. Its theme is derived from the following lines of thought: (1) A review of the event, action, or beginnings of the institution being commemorated. (2) The character of the men and women who took part. (3) The influence of the event, action, or beginnings on the past and present. (4) Lessons to be drawn from it for present and future conduct.

The speaker, of course, is dealing with intangibles. He cannot rely on mere recital of history. He pictures, describes, presents examples, comparisons, and testimony. He weaves them into an artistic whole that elevates, dignifies, and stimulates.

[4] From the Boston Town Records, March 25, 1783, quoted in George V. Bohman "The Colonial Period," *A History and Criticism of American Public Address* (supra fn. 2) I, 52.

THE DEDICATION

Opening new buildings and public centers, laying cornerstones, and unveiling monuments and memorials—all from long tradition are occasions for ceremony and for speeches of dedication. (It took at least three speeches of dedication for the Bunker Hill Monument, two of them by Daniel Webster; two speeches for the national Capitol, one of them by Daniel Webster; and two speeches for the Gettysburg cemetery, one being by Abraham Lincoln. In the twentieth century, two ceremonies—one at the ground-breaking and one at the completion—are customary for major dedications like the Jefferson Memorial, the Grand Coulee Dam, and the United Nations building. Constructions of local importance usually are limited to one ceremony.)

The theme stresses the importance of the day or event. The purpose is to pay tribute to the achievement and the achievers, and by means of the tribute to rouse loyalty, pride, and patriotism. The main lines of thought include these four: (1) The purpose for which this edifice was constructed—the material need, symbolic importance. (2) The people who produced it, and at what cost, against what obstacles. (3) Its tangible use, or intangible value. (4) The tasks ahead to which we should be here dedicated.

THE INAUGURATION

The public ceremony on entering office requires some type of address, formal or informal. It may be a stately ceremonial occasion like the inauguration of a president or governor, an informal occasion like the installation of new club officers, or an important policy-making occasion like the coming to office of a new corporation president.

The theme flows from the occasion. There is a change of administration. The old one departs with dignity, and usually with honor. The new one takes up its task with bouyancy and hope. The occasion imposes one or more of four major duties upon the speaker: (1) To express appreciation to those who put him in office. (2) To unite the group, heal the wounds of the campaign if any, and to make it clear the new administration represents not only a faction, but the whole group. (3) To affirm the officer's determination to discharge his duties and to abide by the letter and spirit of the organization. (4) To present the broad outline of a program for the coming term.

THE NOMINATION

To present a candidate for office requires only the announcement of his name: "Mr. Chairman, I nominate George Smith." Or "Mr. Chairman, the nominating committee presents the name of Dave Gerard." For some occasions like political conventions, however, public ceremony and campaign compulsions require also a declaration of reasons. So it is that the literature of speechmaking contains examples of famous nominating speeches like Robert G. Ingersoll's "Blaine, the Plumed Knight," and Franklin D. Roosevelt's "Alfred E. Smith, the Happy Warrior."

The theme of a nominating speech is, "These are the qualifications, this is the man." Custom prescribes limitations in treating this theme. First, you cannot say outright that your nominee is better than any other particular ones; such bluntness is reserved for the closed caucus and for workers behind the scene; it is not for public utterance. (The caucus argument at the Republican convention of 1860 was, "The nomination of Seward will defeat the Republicans in Illinois, Ohio, and Pennsylvania; the nomination of Lincoln will carry all three." This was not stated in the speech nominating Lincoln.)

Next, examples, comparisons, and references of all kinds should have a specific meaning for listeners, but in ceremonial nominations like those at political conventions they are not couched in terms of absolute specificity. To say, "He will get the votes of AFL and CIO," would be out of tune. If you want to remind listeners that your nominee would get these votes, put it more obliquely, such as, "He is trusted by the wage earners, who will assist in electing him to office." Being specific is one of the most important principles of speechmaking, but in ceremonial nominations it is done in moderation.

The main lines of thought in a ceremonial nominating speech are:

1. Analysis of qualifications for office, its duties and responsibilities, the manner of person required to fulfill them: courage, wisdom, sense of justice, special skills, leadership, experience.

2. Statement of the nominee's qualifications: his special virtues ("*. . . honesty that lets a man sleep of nights, fearing no Senatorial investigation.*"); his experience ("*. . . who represented us abroad for a critical decade, preserving friendship in time of crisis.*"); his accomplishments ("*. . . a man who has preserved in Congress what our soldiers won upon the field.*")

3. Perhaps a prophecy of victory under the leadership of this candidate. ("*. . . has the will to win, who not only deserve victory, but commands it. Victory is his habit.*")

In political conventions the nominee's name is usually withheld until the very end, which permits even a mediocre speaker to close with a magnificent climax. ("*Illinois nominates . . . that leader of leaders, James G. Blaine.*" "*. . . the happy warrior—Alfred E. Smith.*") The main reason for this procedure, however, is to prevent premature demonstrations, which are planned in advance, and scheduled to be touched off by mention of the candidate's name. The custom in Congress, state legislatures, and city councils—whose members are trained in the school of political conventions—is also to withhold the name until the end. Precisely for this reason it is not good practice elsewhere. If the organization is favorable toward the nominee, the speaker usually gives his name at the very beginning. If it is doubtful or hesitant, it is commonly given as soon as the way is prepared by the discussion of his qualifications.

THE COMMENCEMENT ADDRESS

Few classes escape from high school or college without a commencement address. The custom is old, very old. It was centuries old in 1782 when Ezra Stiles recorded that illuminating time schedule of commencements as then conducted: eight speeches—half of them in Latin—consuming 3 hours and 15 minutes, and dealing with political, literary, religious, and philosophical subjects that covered almost the whole field of human knowledege.[5] Less endurance is now required of graduates, but the ceremony remains fixed as firmly as in centuries past.

A day of graduation is a day of achievement, a day of dignified celebration, and a day of commencement or entrance into a new life outside of academic halls. Traditionally the speaker's responsibility is twofold: (1) First, he congratulates the graduates on their achievement and pays fitting tribute to its importance. He employs the theme, but varies the words, of George William Curtis' opening remarks to a graduating class of the nineteenth century:

> The theme of to-day seems to me to be prescribed by the occasion. It is the festival of the departure of a body of young educated men into the world.

[5] Bohman, *op. cit.*, p. 44.

This company of picked recruits marches out with beating drums and flying colors to join the army. We who feel that our fate is gracious which allowed a liberal training, are here to welcome and to advise.[6]

In the mid-twentieth century this ceremonial part of the address is given less emphasis, at least in higher education, than it was given in earlier periods. An examination of recent college and university commencement addresses shows that over three-fourths omit it entirely, or give it a mere sentence in passing. Perhaps this is because college education is more taken for granted, perhaps because by commencement day the graduates already have been congratulated too often and too casually, and especially perhaps because continuing crises fix attention more actively on critical problems of the day. Nevertheless, at high-school graduations it is still given modest attention.

(2) The main theme of the address is upon the state of affairs that face the graduates—problems such as the intellectual and emotional adjustment to the world as it is, opportunities for young people of this day, carrying on with education out of school, making use of education, the duty of educated people in public life. Always there are plenty of problems, some continuing and constant that face graduates in every generation, and some emerging from special issues of the day. A commencement speaker asks himself: What are the compelling problems that face these graduates? Which one of them can I discuss most profitably for them? The occasion itself is ceremonial, but the speech definitely is not. It is a deliberate speech to cultivate thought, influence attitude, modify opinion, or promote action.

After-dinner speeches and speeches after dinner

The development of easy transportation, combined with the concentration of population in cities, has vastly increased the speaking at luncheons and dinners. In Colonial America this type of speaking was rare. By the mid-nineteenth century it was fairly common, as illustrated by a dinner in the Astor House, New York, in 1837. The meal was served at 7:30 P.M., and was followed by toasts and speeches until 2:00 A.M. whereupon the chairman proposed a toast to "Massa-

6 *Orations and Addresses of George William Curtis* (New York: Harper and Brothers, 1894), I, 264-265.

chusetts and Daniel Webster—the Champion of the Constitution." The eloquent Daniel, according to the newspapers, thereupon arose and spoke until 3:20 A.M. in a speech that "enchained the attention of his audience." [7] If twentieth-century dinner speeches are less long and less eloquent, they are at least a hundredfold more numerous—made so by the growth of dinner clubs, luncheon clubs, and even breakfast clubs, as well as conferences, conventions, and special meetings. Speaking from behind tableware is now commonplace.

What is an "after-dinner speech," and how does it differ from other speeches? It cannot be defined as one defines a speech of introduction or dedication. It is not a type of speech at all, but merely a situation where speeches follow food. One is tempted to say facetiously that it is a situation where there is first food for the body, then food for the mind. But this neat alliteration is not true to fact, for not all after-dinner speaking is food for the mind. It ranges from raillery and nonsense to important discourse. As a working definition, however, we can set up two major kinds of speeches given at dinners: the *mere speech after dinner*, and the *true, traditional after-dinner speech.*

THE MERE SPEECH AFTER DINNER

This is identical with that given at any other time and place. The dinner, or luncheon, simply furnishes a convenient time and means of assembling the audience. Many professional lecturers today make no adjustment for the occasion, but when on tour give the same speech at a dinner that they give at an evening meeting. Usually there is only a short preliminary program, if any, and the speaker is allowed thirty, or forty, or fifty minutes for a full-length address. Nevertheless you should take certain precautions: First, find out in advance whether there is a preliminary program, and how much time has been allowed for your speech. Remember that not all chairmen are experienced. Some will allow unscheduled matters to consume time. Therefore you had best be prepared to cut a section of the speech if necessary, and especially so if it is a luncheon meeting where members of the audience must return to work on schedule. Second, remember that the audience listens on a full stomach. You must now do what every speaker ought to do always, get quick attention and keep the listeners awake.

[7] Howell and Hudson, *op. cit.*, p. 715.

THE TRADITIONAL AFTER-DINNER SPEECH

This is a special ceremonial species. Its occasion is not a luncheon, and usually not a professional convention or conference dinner. Usually it is a banquet for the special purpose of relaxation and enjoyment, and after-dinner speeches are one of the features of entertainment. Outwardly the purpose of such a speech is entertainment (see Speeches of Interest, page 179), beneath which lies almost invariably a vein of serious thought. The good after-dinner speech has humor, vivid example, and lively treatment, but these are not to be confused with reciting a string of outworn anecdotes and pointless stories. There is grace, wit, good humor—and also good sense. Instead of a compact line of reasoning, the thought is carried forward by a line-of-thought or series-of-parables, sustained by illustrations, comparisons, contrasts, description, narration, and fresh turns of phrases. The audience listens with pleasure, and leaves remembering that beneath the surface of enjoyment was a core of thought worth remembering.

All this is a large order. From the experience of those who have gone before comes the following helpful advice:

1. *Observe the time limit.* The program for a mere speech after dinner usually calls for one speech only. It permits a longer time, and the speaker who knows the closing hour may plan in advance how to meet it. The traditional after-dinner speech is not so simple, in that on the program is not one speech but a group—frequently four to eight, and sometimes, alas, even more. Each speech needs to fit the program time schedule, and obviously the speaker ought to know in advance the expected time limit. A good chairman, of course, works out a time schedule; he knows how much after the scheduled hour the banquet will get under way, how long the dinner will take, how long each speech is supposed to be. Not all chairman are good. Some make no plans for limits of time, and if a speaker asks outright how long he should talk, they will even say, "As long as you like," or worse, suggest a length beyond limits like, "Forty minutes," or "About an hour." You had better find out what kind of chairman you have, and find out what is on the program. If in doubt, plan a speech of five minutes, or ten.

2. *Remember that the treatment is more important than the subject.* Many speakers spend their time groping for an inherently amusing

topic. Yet no subject is amusing unless you make it so, and any subject can be amusing if you make it so—public speaking, literature, psychology, economics, baseball, glass, salesmen, college education, summer vacations, getting a job, even the atom bomb. It is the treatment, not the subject. Yeager lists five causes of laughter that are available in the treatment of almost any subject: [8]

First, is making the audience laugh at the speaker. Any audience will laugh with the speaker who pokes fun at himself, and will admire his willingness to do so. Meredith Nicholson illustrates this technique in a speech to fellow Hoosiers:

> At one time I had some slight political aspirations. I thought the people had risen. [*Applause.*] . . . But the Civic League endorsed me [*laughter and applause*]; they called attention to my moral character. . . . I was defeated. [*Laughter and applause.*]

Second, familiar to everyone, is telling an amusing story. In an after-dinner speech it should be brief, pointed, and apt, as seen in this one by Henry van Dyke:

> There are some who rejoice in this professed change [in American ideals] and congratulate themselves upon it. Their congratulation reminds me of what a New England farmer said, who borrowed from Emerson a copy of his Plato, and when the farmer brought it back again, he said: "I kind of like that Greek fellow; he has got some of my ideas."

Third, is to belittle in a good-natured way important persons, ideas, or things. Among the topics available are the most important things in life: education, patriotism, love, marriage. Especially high on the after-dinner speaker's list are the hosts and guests of the occasion. Joseph H. Choate demonstrated the method in speaking to a Chamber of Commerce banquet in New York:

> I had prepared a serious and sober essay, . . . but I have laid all that aside; I do not intend to have a single sober word tonight. [*Laughter.*] I do not know that I could. [*Renewed laughter.*] There is a reason, however, why nothing more of a sober sort should be uttered at this table; there is a danger that it would increase by however small a measure the specific gravity of the Chamber of Commerce of New York. Certainly nothing could be a greater calamity than that. [*Laughter.*]

Fourth, is to magnify little persons, things, and ideas. The humor arises from obvious exaggeration in which the little, the trivial, or

[8] Willard Hayes Yeager, *Effective Speaking for Every Occasion* (New York: Prentice-Hall, Inc., 1951), pp. 314-316.

the unimportant, is inflated beyond bounds. Private John Allen, the famous humorist in Congress, habitually used it in speaking of his home town of Tupelo:

> [When the South seceded from the Union] I am reliably informed that . . . Horace Greeley and others sought Mr. Lincoln and asked him to "let the wayward sisters depart in peace," [but] he shook his head and said, "No; this secession takes from the United States Tupelo [*laughter*] and we will not submit to it." And it was to rescue for the Union this town that brought on the war. [*Renewed laughter.*]

Fifth, is joining together of two obviously unrelated things. Cause and effect are assumed where none exist. Phenomena are associated which have no relation. Joseph A. Stevenson illustrates the method:

> The Democrats put on a torch-light parade. The gloating Democratic paper next day boasted of how big the parade was. It was so long, the paper said, that it took three hours for it to pass a given point. The day following, the Republican newspaper hit the streets. It said, "Yes, the Democrats did hold a torch-light parade, and it did take three hours for it to pass a given point—but the given point was Mulhollen's Saloon!"

Laughter is the lubricant of the after-dinner speech. It is the oil in the crank case. You know how far an engine can run without oil.

3. *Plan the opening remarks with special care.* The beginning is the critical part of the speech. If it falls flat you are in trouble. Sometimes you start with the tide against you. The audience may not yet be in a mood for humor. The chairman has failed to kindle their interest, or the preceding speaker has wearied them. These are conditions you must meet with carefully planned opening remarks. To be sure, during the dinner or at the moment of introduction you may reshape these opening remarks, change them, or add to them. But a speaker with experience will not trust to inspiration. He is ready with something already planned, like George Ade, who, knowing there would be at least mild applause when he was presented, produced laughter with the opening sentence, "It may be that your ovation arises from the fact that I am going abroad shortly to remain a long time."

4. *Adapt your materials to the audience.* Usually the after-dinner audience is a unified group: New Yorkers, Californians, lawyers, teachers, bankers, candy manufacturers. They have a common inter-

est and a common background. They have often met together before and know one another. These are your most available source of materials. Said Chauncey M. Depew at a meeting of a Dutch society in New York, "Good evening, Van," and three hundred listeners whose names began with "Van," burst into laughter and applause. St. Clair McKelway, speaking before a society of china importers, began, "The china I buy abroad is marked 'Fragile' in shipment. That which I buy at home is marked: 'Glass—This Side Up With Care.'. . . [Yet] there is a great deal of smashed crockery in the world." And he discussed the smashed crockery in theology, medicine, society, politics, and law. F. Charles Hume, a lawyer speaking to the American Bar Association, took his materials from the law: "From the lawyers of Texas I come—unarmed—bringing to you the message of civilization. Without hope of reward, and without fear of recognition, I have come to lend the charm of high professional character, and impart tone to this meeting. . . . I am a modest man." His theme was the young lawyer, his pretences, and problems.

REFERENCES

Models of speeches on special occasions are not so available as those of basic deliberative types. They seldom appear in the two standard publications given to contemporary speeches: A. Craig Baird, *Representative American Speeches* (annual volume since 1938; New York: H. W. Wilson Publishing Company), and *Vital Speeches of the Day* (published twice a month by the City News Publishing Company, 33 West 42nd Street, New York 18, N. Y.) Chief available sources are as follows:

1. SPEECH COLLECTIONS:

George P. Baker, *The Forms of Public Address* (New York: Henry Holt Company, 1904)

David J. Brewer, *World's Best Orations,* 10 vols. (Chicago: Ferd P. Kaiser, 1899)

W. N. Brigance, *Classified Speech Models* (New York, Appleton-Century-Crofts, 1928)

Ella A. Knapp and John C. French, *The Speech for Special Occasions* (New York: Macmillan Company, 1911)

J. M. O'Neill, *Classified Models of Speech Composition* (New York: Appleton-Century-Crofts, 1921)

J. M. O'Neill, *Modern Short Speeches* (New York: Appleton-Century-Crofts, 1923)

J. M. O'Neill and Floyd K. Riley, *Contemporary Speeches* (New York: Appleton-Century-Crofts, 1930)

Thomas E. Reed, *Modern Eloquence,* 10 vols. (Philadelphia: John D. Morris & Company, 1900)

W. A. Wood, *After-Dinner Speeches* (Chicago: T. H. Flood and Company, 1914)

2. Published papers and addresses of individual persons. Though not easily available these run into the hundreds, from earlier British and American public men like Edmund Burke and Alexander Hamilton to later ones like Franklin D. Roosevelt and Winston Churchill. Among this array, the following are representative:

Wendell Phillips, *Speeches, Lectures, and Letters,* second series, 2 vols. (Boston: Lee & Shepard, 1891)

The Works of Robert G. Ingersoll, Dresden Edition, 12 vols. (New York: The Ingersoll Publishers, Inc. 1929)

Orations and Speeches of Henry W. Grady, E. D. Shurter, ed. (New York: Hinds, Noble & Eldredge, 1910)

Arguments and Addresses of Joseph Hodges Choate, Frederick C. Hicks, ed. (St. Paul: West Publishing Company, 1926)

Chauncey M. Depew, *Orations and After-Dinner Speeches* (New York: Cassell Publishing Company, 1896)

The Public Papers of Woodrow Wilson, 6 vols., Ray Stannard Baker and William E. Dodd, ed. (New York: Harper and Brothers, 1925-1927)

The Public Papers and Addresses of Franklin D. Roosevelt, 13 vols., Samuel I. Rosenman, ed. (New York: Random House, 1938; Macmillan Company, 1941; Harper and Brothers, 1950)

Winston S. Churchill, *Blood, Sweat, and Tears* (New York: G. P. Putnam's Sons, 1941)

3. Year Books and Proceedings of organizations. Among those distinguished for containing excellent speeches are the following:

Year Books of the Holland Society of New York, the New York Southern Society, the New England Society in the City of New York, the Ohio Society of New York, the Indiana Society of Chicago.

Annual Proceedings of the National Education Association, American Bar Association, American Chamber of Commerce, etc.

ASSIGNMENTS

1. Prepare a speech of Introduction for some speaker who recently appeared on your campus, or is soon to appear.

2. Group the class into pairs, and have each pair present the following series of speeches:

   a. Welcome and Response
   b. Presentation and Acceptance

3. Prepare a speech of Welcome for one of the following:

   a. A football, basketball, track, or baseball team from a rival institution
   b. A visiting delegation of some national club, fraternity, or sorority of which you are a member
   c. A new president, dean, or professor, whom you welcome in behalf of the student body
   d. A distinguished visitor like the governor, a scientist, or author
   e. A new minister to your church
   f. Any similar occasion of your choice

4. Prepare a speech of Presentation for one of the following occasions:

   a. Presenting athletic awards to members of a team
   b. Awarding a prize to the winner of a speech contest
   c. Presenting a gift to the college or university from an organization of which you are a member
   d. Presenting a gift to a minister, professor, or other person who is leaving the city
   e. Any similar occasion of your own choice

5. Prepare a Eulogy on some person who was eminent in the field of your major subject: an author if you are majoring in literature, a scientist if in science, a musician or composer if in music, etc.

6. Prepare a Founders Day address that would be appropriate for a club of which you are a member.

7. Assume that a new building has just been completed on your campus and that you have been invited to represent the student body at its dedication. Prepare a suitable speech.

8. Prepare a speech nominating someone for office in a club of which you are a member.

9. Attend a banquet, time its running schedule, and make a report that includes the following:

   a. How late was it in getting started?
   b. How long did the meal itself take?

c. How long was the program, how was it apportioned, and in what way would you have changed it if you had been chairman?
d. By what means did the chairman set the tone of the meeting and get the program off to a good start?
e. Study the seating order at the head table. Do you find a pattern of arrangement, such as placing the most distinguished guest on the chairman's right, the next on his left, etc.? How were the wives or husbands (if any) of the guests fitted into this pattern?
f. Write your judgment on the program as a whole.

10. Plan a banquet program in which you give special consideration to the aspects listed below.

a. Selecting the date, hour, and place, including room or building.
b. Planning the theme of the program.
c. Choosing the speakers and other performers, if any. Tell why you chose them; and tell what other persons were considered and discarded, and why.
d. Consider whether there are persons who must be on the program because of their prestige or position in the organization, but who will make a poor appearance (poor speakers, long-winded, etc.). If so, can you use them, yet keep them in a minor role?
e. Remember to have someone available for the invocation.
f. Consider whether there should be music, and if so have a definite agreement with the director as to its length.
g. Consider how you will arrange for publicity.
h. Estimate how much later than the designated hour the banquet will start, and arrange with the dining room manager for serving promptly at this later-than-designated hour.
i. Plan a time schedule, but allow for run-overs. Tactfully, but specifically designate the maximum time reserved for each speaker.

11. Prepare a three-minute after-dinner speech applying the principles set forth in this chapter.

Part VI THE INFLUENCE OF SPEECH-MAKING ON INDUSTRIALISM AND DEMOCRACY

Walter P. Reuther addressing a labor union meeting. The United States, once an Agrarian Republic, is now an Industrial Democracy. The change has brought pressing problems that can be met only by peaceful persuasion or forceful domination. Which we adopt will determine how successfully we survive.

CHAPTER 24

Dynamic Persuasion in an Industrial Democracy

CHAPTER 24

Two dominant social forces—Industrialism and Democracy—are changing the structure of our society; and there are only two ways of effecting change: forceful domination, or peaceful persuasion of men's minds. What, then, is the role of public address in peaceful persuasion?

The principles of public address have been discussed per se, of course, in earlier chapters. What we shall here do is to bring forward selected ones and discuss their application to the urgent industrial problems which now beset us. In order to do this, let us look first at how these problems arose.

Industrialism and democracy

The accumulating crises of the twentieth century do not arise from Naziism, Communism, collectivism, or so-called radicalism. These are only surf riders on the crest. *The real revolution is the rise of the little man all over the world;* 2,000 years ago he was a slave; 500 years ago he was a serf; 200 years ago he was a political eunuch, not allowed to vote; 100 years ago he was unorganized and inarticulate; half a century ago, of him Edward Markham asked the question:

> How will it be with kingdoms and with kings—
> With those who shaped him to the thing he is—
> When this dumb terror shall rise to judge the world,
> After the silence of the centuries?

The twentieth century is now required to answer this question. It is not a new question. Rather it is a question that governments, and educated people, have never *had* to answer—and therefore have never answered. Now the hour of answer is at hand. Two centuries ago, this little man could live in hunger—and did live in hunger—while governments ignored him, and college students concerned themselves with Plato and Plutarch. Today if he lives in hunger he can destroy nations, and he will destroy them. Two centuries ago this little man could suffer from the economic ignorance and indifference of governments and leaders—and he did suffer—while governments exploited colonial empires, college students were taught Cicero and Virgil, and educators ignored in the curriculum the effects of Iron, Coal and Machines on human welfare. Now governments and leaders can ignore the little man no longer, for he has power to destroy the nation, or tax it to death, or merely socialize it.

Karl Marx's remedy of communism was terribly wrong. But educators, who were supposed to supply ideas for the world, had clung to medieval scholasticism in their thinking and in their curriculum. Political leaders had clung to the outworn concepts of colonialism in foreign policy and exploitation of labor in domestic policy. Thinking people everywhere had not learned the obvious lesson of history, that principles which make a nation great in one period, can lead to decay if people cling to them after they are outworn. So we let the fast-moving twentieth century pile up on us, until millions of people all over the world have turned to one form of totalitarianism after another, and free societies everywhere stand in anxiety.

That is the world situation. Look at it specifically in America. The American government established by the Constitution in 1787 was a republic, but not a democracy. Not more than one adult in five was then eligible to vote or hold public office. Most of the Founding Fathers did not believe in democracy, and they had valid reason for disbelief. Madison and Hamilton were agreed that "real liberty" was never found in such "extremes." Roger Sherman, as democratic a man as sat in the Constitutional Convention, said, "The people should have as little as may be to do with the government, for they are constantly liable to be misled." Daniel Webster, as late as 1820, argued that "equal suffrage was incompatible with inequality in property." The learned Chancellor Kent of New York, in the same year, warned the landed class that "one master capitalist with one hundred apprentices, and journeymen, and agents, and dependents, will bear down at the polls an equal number of farmers of small estates in his vicinity, who cannot safely unite for their common defense." These warnings were of no avail against the determined mass of citizens who demanded the right to vote, and got it. From that day, the welfare of the nation was no longer in the hands of an all-wise elite, but in the hands of the mass of people. Thus was Democracy superimposed on the representative republic established by the Constitution.

Next came Industrialism. Discovery and invention had given us the Machine, and in swift succession came the ages of Coal, Oil, Electricity, and Atomic Energy. Industrialism has changed the physical world of man and it has strained the old structure of society. The traditional economic and political theories, formulated by early thinkers before the coming of perpetual invention, obviously needed readjustment and realignment. But how, and in what direction? The answer is not yet clear. So it is that admiration over "progress" is tempered with doubt, and even alarm, over where we are going. As Arnold J. Toynbee pointed out,[1] the antique road traveled by man before the age of Machines was thronged with primitive vehicles: wheel-barrows, ox-carts, stage coaches, and covered wagons. The road was crowded and there were frequent collisions, yet few were hurt because traffic was slow and the force propelling it was feeble. There were no traffic regulations and no traffic lights. The highway of today is far different. On it high-speed power-driven vehicles travel at ominous velocity: trucks with the momentum of landslides, sport cars faster than the speed of wind. Collisions are both frequent and disastrous. We have annihilated space, but are in danger of annihilating one another.

The problem is not technological, but one of human relations. What kind of traffic regulations do we need? How can a people, whose grandfathers handled nothing more powerful than a two-horse team, be equipped for the moral responsibility of handling a 100-horsepower engine? The machine age also compels us to face two other persistent and recurring questions:

1. How can we salvage the individual in an economy dominated by vast, impersonal, and largely incomprehensible forces?
2. How can we adjust the eighteenth-century concept of liberty *or* government—of government being a necessary evil—to the felt necessity by many people today for a welfare state?

THE FRAMEWORK OF PERSUASION

The direction of growth and change in any civilization comes from its creative minority, not the mass of people. This creative minority

[1] *A Study of History*, abridgement by D. C. Sommervell (New York: Oxford University Press, 1947), pp. 205-206.

supplies the ideas and puts them into operation. A civilization breaks down when one of two conditions arise. First, the creative minority goes soft with luxury, or is made impotent by sterile education. It fails to supply the ideas that drive a civilization onward. It fails to recognize new realities and to adjust itself. It assumes that old customs and concepts, familiar and dear to it, must last forever. It steeps itself in the culture of the past at the cost of losing its sensitivity to the problems of the century in which it lives. When these conditions come to pass, a civilization starts down.

Next, a civilization gets in trouble when its dominant minority tries to rely on force instead of persuasion. Even in totalitarian states the masses endure only so much force before they rise up and destroy the leaders. In totalitarian states they are destroyed by the violence of guns. In democracies they are destroyed by violence at the ballot box. The creative minority is always outnumbered. Always it must "persuade or perish." In the American twentieth-century industrial free society, when the masses have the power of the ballot, this necessity operates more quickly and more inexorably than a century ago.

Can the masses be persuaded? This question harasses certain leaders in America today. Some are convinced that the mass of people are unreasonable, and incapable of making decisions. But the awful truth is that when such a state is reached, it is the leaders, not the masses, who have failed. *They have failed to learn how to persuade.*

Modern research confirms the proposition that masses *are* capable of sound judgment. We may properly repeat here what was said in Chapter 21 on "Radio and Television Speaking," that this research gives statistical validity of the wisdom of the mass of people. Like the judgment of leaders, it is not infallible, but it is in the main sound. The masses are not brilliant or intellectual. They are not well informed. They are not capable of *supplying* the ideas. But the mass of people have a high degree of common sense, and are excellent judges of public policy, *if the leaders are equal to the task of persuasion that is implicit in leadership.*

Any attempt to set down the postulates of persuasion in this twentieth-century industrial democracy is obviously hazardous. It leaves the author vulnerable to attack from all quarters. Inept leaders who want the benefits of Industrialism without having to face its problems, will cry "radicalism." Timid educators who are afraid of the twentieth century, and who would escape it emotionally by pleading with Mortimer Adler that "not one single new idea has appeared in any book published during the twentieth century," will charge that persuasion is unethical, and that man should be left to do his own "thinking." Educators who recognize realities can, with reason, say that any set of postulates is an oversimplification and is not adequately tested. Nevertheless, we are living in this twentieth-century Industrial Democracy in which creative controversy has been born out of industrial conflict. We must accept the fact, even as Margaret Fuller finally "accepted the universe." Aware of the risks, we shall none the less set down exploratory postulates on dynamic persuasion in this twentieth-century industrial democracy.

YOU MUST TALK IN TERMS OF MASS UNDERSTANDING

People's modes of thinking develop out of their way of life. Therefore, they are not equipped to understand words that represent a different way of life. Leaders sometimes assume that limitations of intelligence prevent workers or farmers from understanding complex national and world affairs. Not so. It is not lack of intelligence in these groups, but lack of thought-skill and word-skill on the part of those who would be leaders. They have not learned to talk with the steel worker, coal miner, or dirt farmer about political and economic factors that operate in their immediate environment. They ignore the fact that such workers have a limited frame of reference. Within that limit, they can talk sense and listen intelligently to others who talk sense. They are capable of reacting intelligently to propositions if presented in terms of their own experience. But they are not familiar with the language of the professional economist or specialist in management.

Too often these professional experts and specialists are simply not interested in talking to the mass of people in understandable language. Too often it is only the political demagogue, and labor demagogue, who is so interested. Can we say the fault lies only with the demagogues? Does it not lie also with the so-called experts and specialists, who forget that in this industrial democracy even they are servants of the people, and that it is imperative duty of experts to be able to communicate effectively with those in ultimate power?

For example, research by the Opinion Research Corporation and the Psychological Corporation reveals that workers think net profits in industry average about 25 per cent, and some workers believe profits run as high as 60 per cent. Actually, at the time the research was done, industrial profits averaged about 5 per cent, but nobody had explained this in terms that workers could understand. Again, workers believed that out of every wage dollar, the salaried man got 75 cents and the worker 25 cents. Actually the managers and owners got 13 cents and the workers got 87 cents, but this had not been told them in words they could understand. In fact, only one worker out of five remembered ever having been told anything whatsoever about wages and profits of the company where he was employed.

In contrast to this widespread breakdown in communication and failure of persuasion, are those management experts who have really learned how to talk in terms of their workers' understanding. Typical of these is one who reported on his method of talking to workers at the annual meetings at which the bonus was paid and workers were told about their wage dollar. Said he: We stack up a hundred dollars in coins where everybody can see them. We say that we are now going to show where the company money goes, every dollar and every penny out of each hundred dollars. We also say that we had this worked out by a firm of expert accountants, that it is the set of figures on which we pay taxes, and we certainly hope they are right; for if they are not, we will be in jail when the next annual meeting comes. Then we say, "Last year we paid $35.78 out of every $100.00 for the raw material used in making our goods. Will the raw-materials agent please come forward and get his money?" A man designated to represent this group comes forward, and we pay him $35.78 out of that pile of $100.00. Then we say that the freight haulers get so much; up comes a man representing the railroads and truckers, and we pay him off. After that we pay off the office force, including the managers and the president; this is only, say, $5.00 out of that $100.00. Next we call out the workers' share and it is a whopping big figure, $45.00 or $50.00; and a man representing all the workers comes forward and gets his big slice. Finally we come to the owners, "those stockholders," we call them; and on the table is now left only a couple of dimes and maybe a penny. Up comes a man for the stockholders and gets his pair of dimes. After this, our workers can go home with a clear picture in their minds of where the money goes and how much of it they get.

In the early days of Industrialism, when there were only a few workers, national welfare was not affected by what these people thought, knew, or did not know. In those days before the final appearance of Democracy, when the mass of people did not vote, national leaders had less concern with what they thought, knew, or did not know. Certainly leaders had no problem of winning assent from the masses, or of speaking in language that they could understand. The audience that counted in that day was an elite audience. Such was the audience of Edmund Burke and Daniel Webster. That day is gone. In the Industrial Democracy of today, the world is turned upside down and the masses have voting control. Modern instruments of mass communication have enabled information to be spread at an increasing rate, but technology and social changes have increased at an even more rapid rate the amount of information that needs to be known. Every leader, every educated person, thereby incurs the obligation of learning how to put this information in words that the mass of people can understand.

It does no good to protest against these facts of life, and to lament that we are now ruled by people unfit to rule. Such protests and laments ignore realities. They also ignore that salient discovery of this century, that the mass of people *are* capable of judging values when leaders measure up to their responsibility of being able to communicate. We repeat what has been said earlier in this book: "The public may not know enough to *be* experts, but they know enough to judge between them," said Samuel Butler. "Never overestimate the people's knowledge, nor underestimate their intelligence," insisted Raymond Clapper. If there is a breakdown in the twentieth-century rule by the masses, it will come because the leaders have failed to supply the ideas that move a civilization forward, or because they have failed to learn to talk to the mass of people in terms of their understanding.

YOU MUST SPEAK IN TERMS OF PEOPLE'S WANTS

This, of course, is an old principle of persuasion. It was centuries old when Aristotle wrote his *Rhetoric*. It was recognized by the Great Teacher when He included wants things among essential to a spiritual life: "give us this day our daily bread." It was given expression in the charter of American independence: ". . . that among these are Life, Liberty and the pursuit of Happiness." It was written in the preamble to the American Constitution: "We the People of the United States, in Order to form a more perfect Union, establish Justice, insure domestic Tranquility, provide for the common defense, promote the general Welfare, and secure the Blessings of Liberty to ourselves and our Posterity do ordain and establish this *Constitution* for the United States of America."

Various names have been given this operating force by thinkers in different fields: motives, springs of action, felt needs, "rights," and even "higher law." They are merely different terms to designate, and translate into action, the eternal groping of man for what the ancients called "happiness," and "the good life." Behind them all is the tacit recognition that people believe, think, live, and act in terms of human wants. All of this has previously been discussed in Chapters 6 and 7. We are here concerned only with its particular application to persuasion on political, economic, and social problems in this twentieth-century industrial democracy.

There is a general misunderstanding of the place of wants in persuasion. A loose notion exists that when you "appeal to wants" (or as some even more loosely say, "appeal to emotions"), you must thereby violate reason and logic. As an "economic expert" protested recently to a teacher of speech, "You should teach students to appeal to reason instead of appealing to emotions." Three fallacies roost in that statement. First, effective persuasion does not "appeal" to emotion. Second, effective persuasion does "appeal" to reason. Third, "wants" (to use the proper term) are not the antithesis of "reason." We can see this more clearly by analogy. Suppose the man had said, "People should either wear good clothes or use good sense." The fallacy would be obvious, for there is no antithesis between good clothes and good sense. There is not "either-or" choice. You can have both, either, or neither.

So with wants and reason. If a man "wants" his daily bread, he can irrationally go forth and steal it, or he can use reason and judgment in learning how to earn it. If a people "want" life, liberty, and the pursuit of happiness, they can blindly and emotionally try to gain them by destroying other people who have them, or they can use reason and judgment to develop a way of life to secure them for themselves and their posterity.

When we say, therefore, that you must speak in terms of people's wants, we do not mean you should reject "appeal to reason," and descend to "appeal to wants." Effective persuasion does not "appeal" to anything, and whosoever gives tongue to the notion that it does "appeal" to this, or "appeal" to that, speaks at random and is not to be relied on. Effective persuasion *bases* argument *on* human wants, on the desire for bread, life, liberty, and the pursuit of happiness. That is at the opposite pole from "appealing to." It recognizes, in the words of Justice Oliver Wendell Holmes, that you "cannot argue a man into a desire," that "you must begin by wanting to." It recognizes that wants are not attained for the mere wanting, that if people want life, liberty, and the pursuit of happiness, someone must supply the reason and intelligence for enabling them to attain them.

Now we are ready to apply this principle to the problems of this modern Industrial Democracy. Its single most important problem—on which its very life depends—is that conflicting groups learn to live together. Specifically, unless management and workers learn to live together we are doomed, no matter how high our skyscrapers or how big our industrial plants. This is not a problem of economics or politics, but of persuasion, and it is at this point that many industrial leaders have failed or fallen short. They have given their genius to the machine, not to the men who run them. They have failed to understand or give weight to the deep-felt wants of the workers. In America these workers do not, as in most parts of the world, live close to the border line of hunger. The genius of American business leaders has relieved them of that. But they do live close to the border line of frustration and fear. Most of them no longer own their own tools, as their forebears did a century ago. They tend machines owned by the "company." They perform one act in the process of manufacturing—staple a wire, tighten a nut, or insert the spark plugs—and only with persuasive skill can they be given a pride of production in the commodity they have so small a part in producing. They do not know the "owners." They seldom know or see the "manager." They are separated by barriers of distance and numbers. Yet in each dwells the basic want of all human beings, the wish for worth, the desire to be important, the satisfaction of doing something worth while. To satisfy this want for self-respect calls for techniques of persuasion on the part of management that were unheard of in the day when America was an agricultural nation.

The mass of people live, too, not exactly in fear, but rather in fear of fear: fear of loss of employment, fear of layoffs, fear of sickness—all of which mean loss of income, nonpayment of rent and gas bills. They tend to believe that management and the owners, on the other hand, have no such fears. It is not easy for them to understand that another set of problems like the falling of market demand, increase in taxes, and government restrictions, keep management and owners in the same state of uneasiness that workers themselves feel. It is not easy for them to realize that the life of the average manager is shorter than that of the average worker, and that worry is one of the chief causes of the difference. Here, too, is a demand for techniques of persuasion that were not called for before the age of Industrialism.

The sum of the whole is that management is concerned with wants like markets, lower production costs, and higher profits. The worker is concerned with wants like sense of achievement and guarantee of security, not knowing that "security is an illusion," and that only death and taxes can be totally guaranteed. The specific wants of the two are so different that it has become difficult for one group to understand those of the other. Management thus faces the perennial task of persuading workers to recognize that management's wants are essential to the workers' welfare.

Can this be done? Certainly. It is being done by skilled managers. Consider one of the lines of persuasion used in showing that corporation profits are essential to workers' wants:

> Gentlemen of Labor: You need something we of management have. Without it you die. You need jobs. Therefore, let's look at how jobs are created.
>
> In 1890 there were 18,000,000 jobs in this country. In 1950 there were 62,000,000 jobs. In 60 years 44,000,000 new jobs had been created. How was it done? Accidentally? No. England did not more than double the workers' jobs in that period. Nor did France, or Germany, or Russia, or any other country.
>
> How did we do it in America? By taking risks with our spare capital. By taking these risks we created 20,000,000 jobs in industries that did not even exist in 1890—automobile, electric, airplane, and radio and television. Consider how we did in one industry alone, automobiles. Do you remember the names of such cars as Haynes, Chandler, Marmon, Stutz, Winton, Pierce-Arrow, Graham, Paige, Reo, Stephens-Duryea, Auburn, and Cord? Some of them are names you never heard, but all of them are automobiles that were once manufactured in this country that went out of business. Most of them in plain language went broke, and their owners lost millions of dollars. But in the process of losing millions, we created an automobile industry that today gives jobs to 7,000,000 workers. The development of air lines tells much the same story. These lines have never yet paid dividends equal to the losses sustained by the owners, yet they have created jobs for hundreds of thousands of workers.
>
> Gentlemen of Labor, in the next 25 years we must create 25,000,000 new jobs for you. If we don't, you won't get $1.90 an hour, or 75 cents an hour. Some of you—or your children—won't have jobs.
>
> Therefore, gentlemen, help us earn profits today that can be used for investing to create jobs tomorrow. Remember that if we don't earn profits today, we don't use them to create jobs tomorrow. Remember that if we don't create jobs tomorrow, some workers are going to be without jobs all the time, or all workers are going to be without jobs part of the time.

These are the lines of persuasion needed by public leaders, and especially leaders of labor and industry. It is persuasion in terms not only of the workers' understanding but especially also in terms of their wants.

YOU CANNOT OPPOSE SOMETHING WITH NOTHING

When deep-felt wants arise from the inarticulate masses, demagogues, crackpots, and sincere spokesmen with clouded perception come forth with panaceas. So long as Industrial Democracy exists we must expect Townsend Plans, Share-the-Wealth programs, and Soft Money projects. The issue is how shall real leaders deal with them? The postulate here laid down is that when panaceas are proposed for meeting real wants, you cannot in the long run successfully oppose them with nothing.

Now many leaders do not believe this. As one of them said, "When you try to prevent a man or a nation from jumping off a high cliff you have quite a program, although it may appear to be negative to the man or nation about to jump." Another put in substance as follows: "You tell us that our policies are *negative*. We are always *against* this or that; we seldom come forward with original and constructive legislation. But if we campaign in behalf of what we feel to be the best interests of the American people, our program *will* appear to be negative. It will call for the abolition of undesirable programs, and much more that is 'negative.' If we are guilty of 'negativism,' then at least we have high authority in the example of the Founding Fathers of the Constitution."

Many leaders believe this sincerely, and they propose to follow it as a line of persuasion. The postulate here laid down is that such a procedure violates the principles of persuasion as they have been developed through twenty-five centuries, and that it is doomed to failure in the long run. It brings us again to the classic statement of Aristotle, validated by twenty-three centuries of experience: that truth and justice are stronger than falsehood and injustice; and hence when the latter win, it is not the fault of depraved voters, but of inept speakers who neglected the science of persuasion.

Examine the details of those two quoted statements in defense of opposing something with nothing: "When you try to prevent a man or a nation from jumping off a high cliff you have quite a program, although it may appear to be negative." Does a man or a nation try to jump off a high cliff unless driven by some desperate want or fear, real or imagined? Will it relieve the desperate want or fear if either is prevented from jumping off, and nothing is done to reduce the state of mind that led to desperation? Again, "If we campaign in behalf of what we feel to be the best interests of the American people, our program *will* appear to be negative." Is it to the best interests of the American people merely to be negative, and at the same time permit the vast impersonal forces of Industrialism to terrorize the mass of voting citizens who cannot understand them? Still again: "If we are guilty of 'negativism,' then at least we have high authority in the example of the Founding Fathers of the Constitution." Do they? A little reading of history would clear the point. The Founding Fathers knew the tenets of persuasion. When Shays Rebellion threatened property (which is a basis of any civilization), and wildcat money had brought trade and commerce low, the Founding Fathers produced a *positive* program. They set up a Constitution that established order and protected both liberty and property. One of the first acts of that brilliant Father, Alexander Hamilton, was to fund the debt and to set up a sound monetary system. Both were positive measures. Neither opposed something with nothing.

Dynamic persuasion in an Industrial Democracy cannot oppose something with nothing. If its leaders attempt negative persuasion, the result will be like that described by Arnold J. Toynbee: a disintegration from internal stresses, and the cause of death will not be murder, but suicide. As Senator Irving Ives of New York sharply reminded his colleagues, "We can't just say 'no, no, no.' We've got to have answers to some of the gigantic problems . . . we are facing." As Eric Johnston put it, if industrial leaders do not want government planning, they must themselves plan as never before.

Yet in the face of this testimony of history and the verified experience of persuasion through the centuries, a segment of would-be leaders persist stubbornly in resorting to negative persuasion. Like the Bourbons, they never learn, they never forget. Why? Through their behavior runs one compelling reason. It takes no constructive thinking to oppose something with nothing. It takes only a blind willfulness to say "no." As every student soon learns, a hatchet speech is easy. You only chop down, and never build up. You only denounce sin, and call the sinners an assortment of names. But to have answers for the gigantic problems requires the hard labor of thought. In the class room, as in national affairs, hatchet speeches are the telltale signs of minds that lack the power to produce ideas.

Other leaders, when they are told that you cannot oppose something with nothing, say that it is the wrong principle "to project programs that would compete with hand-outs of those who are most generous with other people's money." Of course that is right, but it shows a misunderstanding of the science of persuasion. Dynamic persuasion does not imply that you oppose one hand-out by substituting another. It simply affirms that you cannot solve gigantic problems by saying, "no, no, no," that you must solve the problem and explain its solution in terms of the people's understanding.

Take any proposal for spending public money to meet a public need, real or alleged. That perennial one will serve: socialized medicine, or if you prefer the term, national health insurance. (But remember that we are concerned with the science of persuasion, not with the merits of this, or any, question.) One method is to attempt persuasion by charging that, "nobody wants it but the bureaucrats," that it is "more collectivism," and is "another vicious piece of socialistic legislation." That is the "no, no, no" approach. It opposes something with nothing. Another line of approach would use the science of persuasion, roughly as follows:

I. Of course we need adequate medical care. Modern medicine has increased the span of human life in the last 50 years by approximately 16 years, and the end is not in sight. All the people have a right to share in greater health and longevity. The issue is which is the best way, and which is the cheapest.

II. You cannot get something for nothing. You cannot get medical care for nothing any more than food or clothes. The real question is in what form you pay for it.

   A. You cannot soak the rich to pay for it, for a report based on Treasury figures show that, "Even if the Government took the drastic and destructive step of taxing away all income over $25,000 a year the yield would be less than $1 billion a year above present taxes." This would be less than 2 per cent of the total tax budget. Hence any further increase in taxes must come from small incomes.

   B. Socialized medicine will cost such-and-such amount. [To date no acceptable nonpolitical figure seems to be available, even though one could be computed. So let's assume a figure of $12 billions annually, remembering that in a real instance an accurate and trustworthy figure would be indispensable.]

III. Therefore the real question is whether you want to pay this medical cost by increased tax or by some other method.
   A. The "brokerage charge" of Federal grants is inevitably high. Some say it runs to 15 per cent, some say it is 44 per cent. Whichever figure it is, you must pay it. You cannot avoid this charge because it costs money to route taxes from your pocket to Washington and back again.
   B. You can figure out for yourself what it will cost you. If your income is $3,000 and you have two dependents, the minimum increase of your income tax will be $50 a year. If you have an income of $4,000 a year and three dependents, the minimum extra taxes you will pay will be $90 a year.
   C. Therefore, the issue you must decide is: Do you want to increase your taxes $50 a year, or $90, or do you want to use a voluntary medical insurance plan like the Blue Cross or Blue Shield?

Omitted from this brief digest are other effective lines of persuasion, such as political interference with medical service, the effect of regulation on its quality, etc. But it gives the broad outline of how the science of persuasion can be applied to one of the perennial issues of our Industrial Democracy. It does not oppose something with nothing. It gives the people concerned the right to choose between one plan or another, and gives them the information on which they can formulate a choice.

Industrial Democracy has brought not only luxury and progress. It has brought acute problems in human relations. Man was invented before machines. Man is not a gadget. He cannot be treated as a gadget, with a push-button. He can be dealt with only by the powers of persuasion that adjust his "want-to," and recognize his eternal groping for a sense of destiny. Here is the challenge to the leaders, the creative minority, the educated people. Can they fulfill their obligation of leadership which must forever include the ability to treat men as men, not as machines, and to lead—not pull—their thinking?

Appendix

SPECIMEN SPEECHES

REVERSE MR. JUSTICE HOLMES

By *Henry R. Luce*

THIS SPEECH undertakes an extremely difficult purpose, to criticize venerated ideas that had been promulgated by a man who was revered both for his ideas and himself. Broadly, there are two methods of doing this. One is the hatchet method that is heard continually, including political campaign speeches and not excluding speeches in Congress. This is the method of denouncing the persons or ideas as being sinful, and of calling an assortment of names: "experts in guile," "political gangsters," "propaganda booby trap," (these are copied from a single page in a current issue of the *Congressional Record*). The epithets are usually interchangeable; they can be used on either side, and on almost any question. The method inflames prejudices, but does not persuade the doubtful or give light to the uninformed.

The other method, demonstrated in this speech, is based on the science of persuasion as discussed in this book. It involves "ethical persuasion" (see Chapter 19), a courteous sensitivity to the listeners' attitudes, and a penetrating discussion of the idea. It rises above Name-Calling, avoids provoking dispute, and abstains from exaggerated statement. Skillfully it cultivates thought.

The speech was given to the Southwestern Regional Convention of the American Bar Association held at Southern Methodist University, Dallas, Texas, April 19, 1951. The speaker, Henry R. Luce, is publisher of the magazines *Time, Life*, and *Fortune*.

WE HEARD this morning able speeches on The Law and Business, The Law and Labor, and The Law and Education. I propose to speak on The Law and Everything. This may seem to be an unwarranted extension of my assignment The Press, but actually it is not, for the business of The Press is Everything—more or less. The original motto of *Time* was: "de omni re scibili et quisbusdam aliis"—"of all things known and whatever else." A less elegant version of the same matter is that a good journalist is one who knows a little about everything and not much about anything. That still seems to leave us in a rather happier position than the modern specialist who is said to be learning more and more about less and less.

The claim of right of the journalist to talk about Everything is one which, I think, you are inclined to grant—with somewhat the same indulgence that kings of old granted it to the court jester. Indeed the modern journalist might be likened to the King's fool. If the fool be both conscientious and prudent, he will contrive to tell the truth and to get paid for it. That is perhaps why we call it the newspaper game. But I shall not be fool enough to betray to you—at least not intentionally—the tricks of our trade. Indeed the solemn profession of our guild is that we have no tricks at all—that we are soberly dedicated to "objective truth." In another age, such a claim might have been regarded as the basis of a deliberate fraud, but since in this age we have been so well taught by the learned doctors of Harvard, Yale, and Southern Methodist University that there is no such thing as "objective truth"—outside of a physicist's laboratory or an atom bomb—no substantial fraud is committed by this humorous claim.

The claim of your profession to be concerned with capital J—Justice—may be taken similarly, I suppose, as a harmless fantasy.

But even though journalism may have the right to talk about the Law along with everything else, you will have noted that the Press in fact says very little about the Law as Law. To be sure, we are not laggard in exploiting the field of criminal justice—lower case "j." But the Law itself enjoys an extraordinary immunity from public interest. And so do lawyers as lawyers. That's one way in which they are smarter than anybody else.

The American people are governed by lawyers—and they always have been. Thus in our gush of talk about politics and government we are speaking of lawyers—or ex-lawyers. But in modern times, there are very few lawyers whom even educated laymen know of *as lawyers.*

Fortunately for me there is currently one lawyer who is known even to movie fans—the late Mr. Justice Oliver Wendell Holmes.

As soon as I thought of him I knew that whatever I might have to say today could be said in terms of the towering figure of the Magnificent Yankee.

But just what was it that I wanted to say—out of my heart, and, to use a criterion which has Holmes' stamp on it, "out of my experience"?

As a young man, I knew of Holmes as an immensely attractive figure and it seemed unthinkable not to concur in the liberal adoration of the old gentleman.

But then some while later, as our world was shaken by catastrophic events one after another, I began, like most people, like all of you, I'm sure, to try to look a little more deeply into the nature of things. And—along with many other matters—this involved taking another look at Holmes, especially as after his death the glorious myth grew, and his name was placed on the high altars of our culture and enshrined in books, both popular and learned, in essays, biographies, plays and motion pictures. And the more I looked at Oliver Wendell Holmes, the more troubled I became.

And so, looking forward to being with you today, I thought I would try to define this trouble and to present it to you.

I discovered, of course, that the task of identifying the Holmes trouble has already been done, and far better than any layman could hope to do it. It has been done especially well by Mr. Harold McKinnon in the April 1950 issue of the American Bar Association Journal.

Mr. McKinnon, as many of you will recall, opens his article as follows:

> "Two things about Justice Oliver Wendell Holmes need reconciliation. He had a very bad philosophy. Yet he ranks among the greatest men of our time.
>
> "His philosophy was agnostic, materialistic, hopeless of the attainment of any ultimate truth, meaning or standard of value."

And my question to you is this—an honest question asking an honest answer: Does it really matter that Holmes had a very bad philosophy?

The characteristic American answer would, I suppose, be: "No—if Holmes was a good man and did good, his philosophy doesn't matter—and anyway it couldn't have been too bad." That would be the characteristic American answer—and the American having made that answer would feel unhappy about it, uneasy, worried, puzzled, wondering.

And this uneasy answer, I submit, indicates, as unmistakably as the finger of a clock, the point at which America has arrived: we have arrived at the point historically where we can no longer proceed with any health or happiness on the blithe assumption that it doesn't matter what any of us believe—or whether there is really anything to believe.

I submit to you today that we ought to believe what is true, and that the truth is that we live in a moral universe, that the laws of this country and of any country *are* invalid and will be in fact inoperative except as they conform to a moral order which is universal in time and space. Holmes held that what I have just said is untrue, irrelevant and even dangerous.

I submit to you further that you as lawyers have one urgent task more important than all others—to reverse Mr. Justice Holmes—and to do so for the sake of The Law itself, for the sake of the American people, and for the sake of our own individual peace of mind.

There is one great thing—among others—to be said for Mr. Holmes. He knew what he believed. Most of his disciples today don't. Do you?

What did Holmes believe? He believed, most importantly, that there is no ultimate truth anywhere to be believed in.

Since that was his clearly stated belief, some of his more melodramatic dicta which I shall quote are *not* of the context of his general thought.

Holmes said: "there is no reason for attributing to man a significance different in kind from that which belongs to a baboon or a grain of sand."

Holmes said that men have no natural rights; and if a man will fight for what he calls his rights, so will a dog fight for a bone.

Holmes said: "Truth is the majority vote of that nation that can lick all others."

Holmes said: "I believe that force . . . is the ultima ratio."

The "clear and present" labels of this philosophy are materialism, militarism, relativism, agnosticism and, in the most charming and civilized sense of the word, cynicism.

Such was the fully disclosed belief of this American hero. And note well, Holmes was essentially a *spiritual* hero—one who disclosed and revealed truth. Mr. Justice Frankfurter says that Holmes is Plato's "philosopher become King" and the late Mr. Justice Cardozo speaks of Holmes as "the great overlord of the Law *and its philosophy*."

And note well, again, that the fame and glory of Mr. Justice Holmes did not arise from his popularity with the common man. It was the elite who successfully promoted his canonization. It was not only the rising elite of the Law; he appealed also to writers, artists, and nearly the whole of the academic world. Though he was skeptical about reform, he appealed to social reformers. The victorious liberals and their fellow travelers of the '30's put his name—along with Jefferson's—on their banner, while neglecting or rejecting the names of Washington, Adams, Madison, Hamilton and Marshall. This fact cannot be dismissed as a mere aberration of children following a Pied Piper, nor the sudden insanity of Gadarene swine. The worship of Holmes was connected with much, perhaps most, of what was good in the recent past of our nation.

But what had this veneration of Holmes to do with his philosophy? Was he canonized because of or in spite of his philosophy? Partly both. And here I should like to make full acknowledgment of the sympathetic view that can be taken of Holmes' philosophy. Certainly it has corollaries, especially as he drew them, that were attractive in the ancient Stoics and always will be. Courage, style, the love of learning and of excellence—we shall never have enough of these Holmesian qualities. Moreover, he used these qualities, along with his enormous vitality, to undertake a work in the world that needed doing in his time.

When I say his work needed doing, I venture into a field you knew better than I. Holmes, I take it, was the elder prophet (Roscoe Pound being the younger) of that school of American legal realism which brought our 19th century jurisprudence back into touch with the facts of life. He and his friends forced your profession to admit that other disciplines, such as Mr. Brandeis' sociology, had something to contribute to the perennial quest for justice; that the distribution of property, especially in a democracy, has some bearing on the right to it; and that even judges may be subject to bias and indigestion. Since these propositions were an open secret among all who sued in our courts or voted in our elections, it was well that they be brought to the attention of our "aristocrats of the robe." The Holmesians undertook this corrective work. They fought a long battle, which ended in 1937, but from which the Law has not recuperated yet, for in correcting one evil they created a worse—the undermining of the Law itself.

Holmes' philosophy foreshadowed this disaster. Yet the only charge to be leveled at that philosophy is that it denies the immutability and unity of Truth. Does it matter? Do we care?

It seems to me that it does and we do. I give you this observation as a journal trying to discern the signs of the times—it seems to me that we as a nation have come to the point where the most immediately urgent questions are precisely those questions which are perennial and profound. Can we believe anything? What, then, do we believe? That, I think, is already the No. 1 question in America, outranking in historical priority even our fight against Soviet Russia.

I could not hope to persuade you that this assertion is true unless I could make an appeal to the pragmatism that lies close to the heart of every American. Why is it so urgent to settle *now* philosophic questions which will never finally be settled until Kingdom Come? Let me illustrate the pragmatic necessity by reminding you how Americans look—how *you* look—to people in Europe, in Asia, to people everywhere overseas. You do not look good. We do not look good. I think you know that. The picture they paint of us, you resent—and so do I. They say we are materialists—the spawn of a materialism preferable to that of Communism, but materialists nevertheless. They say that we are only interested in gadgets—in motor cars, bathtubs, ice boxes, and T.V. We rebut that description, and in part the rebuttal is accepted. Yes, we have many good qualities—"human" qualities—we are generous, open-hearted, kindly, in a sort of tactless way, etc. But when all is said, America and the Americans still do not present an attractive picture to the world. Why? Because the people of the world do not feel that we stand for anything—nor for anything deeply and fundamentally relevant to the mighty drama of human destiny—with its eternal dialect of tragedy and redemption.

And *do* we stand for something? How about the Law? Do we stand for the Law? What Law? Coming from where and going where? And with what relation to universal truth beyond the pragmatic boundaries of Texas politics! Now if you could give answers to these questions (with all humility in the face of an infinite universe and yet clear answers)—then the world would hear.

When I say you—I mean of course you, on behalf of all of us.

But who can give this answer? Could the Supreme Court? I tell you that the Supreme Court of the United States could win the world-wide battle for the minds of man by one humble affirmation of faith that we and all men live in a moral universe. The Supreme Court could win this battle but not without reversing Mr. Justice Holmes. Oh, they might not have to reverse a single one of his legal opinions. They would have to reverse simply his philosophy—his clear and beautiful and brave and mistaken notion of Truth.

But you are still not convinced. If a nation lacks the understanding that comes from reason and faith; if a nation lacks faith, it cannot overnight achieve faith as an expedient means of avoiding disaster.

So, I say to you this nation still has the faith. The faith is there beneath all the dreadful clutter and confusion of our noise, The faith is there; it needs only to be evoked.

As a test case, let me present to you a statement of The American Proposition —in two brief paragraphs. For this statement I am indebted to my colleagues of FORTUNE, Mr. Russell Davenport and Mr. John K. Jessup. These two paragraphs give the philosophic basis of the founding of the United States of America. They are *historically* sound. I do not think any historian could seriously challenge them.

But what is historically true is not necessarily true for today and for our future destiny. That is what you have to decide. Here is the test case—in only two paragraphs—as follows:

> "The essence of the American Proposition can be understood only against the long religious history of mankind.... Freedom is real because man is created by God in the 'image' of God. Man carries within him something that the merely animal does not have, the divine spark, the 'image'. The human individual thus has a special status with regard to all other things and beings on earth: he must live, and must be entitled to live, by the laws of God, not just by the laws and directives of men.
>
> "According to the American Proposition, this special status of the individual is couched in certain Rights.... These Rights are 'unalienable,' grounded in the universe itself, reflecting universal laws of nature: that is to say, they are natural, not merely political, Rights."

Between the general philosophy stated there and the general philosophy of Holmes there is no middle ground. As an inescapable consequence, there is no middle ground between the *political* philosophy stated there and the *political* philosophy by Holmes. A choice must be made.

In suggesting that the Supreme Court make solemn pronouncement of its choice, I am not being entirely whimsical. I realize I intrude upon your lawyers' instinct. You will say that philosophical utterances from the court are at best mere obiter dicta. Look deeper. Look deeper.

To borrow for a moment, the notion of social contract: this nation was founded unarguably, upon a social contract expressed in those two paragraphs. That social contract has been breached and violated—its moral basis undermined by humanistic explanations. That social contract must be restored and made whole. Either that or you will have a totally different social contract, to which, Gentlemen, many of you will *not* in conscience give your allegiance. I am suggesting today that it is above all the challenge to the legal profession to find means to spread across the American sky the news that the Law by which we seek to live, however imperfect a copy it may be, is nevertheless grounded in the Law of the Universe.

Unless the true social contract is most explicitly reestablished, confusion will spread. Confusion, which is already the word by which this mighty nation most commonly describes itself, will spread and spread and spread. Heroic measures are required: heroic measures of mind and spirit.

It is beyond your skill and ingenuity to bring into all the great Courts in our land, the clear issue as to what we do deeply believe about the Law? Somehow in our time this case will be tried. It may be your supreme service to bring the issue to trial before it is too late.

You may say that you cannot talk in the 20th century the language of the 18th or 13th. Very well—then "restate" the American Proposition. You have only to believe that Truth itself is great—so great that not all the physical laboratories and not all the books in the libraries can obscure the radiance of what is forever true.

The secular order is conformable to the spiritual order when it accepts, in reason if not in faith, the moral basis of all things. This was the basis of the American social contract. It can be so again.

In this social contract there is full liberty of conscience. Anyone can doubt anything. The believer is indebted to the doubter for constant reminder that Truth is always greater than we think and the doubter is indebted to the believer for his very life and existence and partial sanity.

And now, gentlemen, if I have spoken extravagantly, I ask your indulgence and plead that if your profession is in want of anything, it is not in want of sobriety, caution, discretion, prudence; if it is in want of anything, it is in want of extravagance, enthusiasm, heroism, and these qualities I would willingly incite.

One word more, I have challenged your profession while being myself a member of another profession—or at least, vocation. Then let me say that the sins and shortcomings of my vocation are serious; and they are also very apparent for all to see. The problems of The Law are less visible to the casual citizen. Surely we agree that all of us—all professions—all Americans, are deep into the greatest crisis of our history and therefore all of us should strive to do all that we can to meet the profound challenge to all that is good. But your profession is many centuries senior to mine—and, in fact, mine isn't a profession at all. Thus I accord to you the prior position in the great struggle for Liberty and Order—Liberty *under* Law. In my view, it is not the primary duty or competence of The Press to discover and declare the standards of faith and excellence by which men and nations must live. But it is the duty of The Press—and should be its most joyful duty—to be an honest broker between the great thinkers and the great prophets of truth and the mass of men. If in your so great and honored profession, there shall arise deeds of heroism—heroism of the mind and spirit—I pray that we of The Press will not be far behind to note and to give thanks. To give thanks that man's humanity is restored to him in the sign of faith.

PREDICTIONS FOR THE UNPREDICTABLE FUTURE

By *Mildred McAfee Horton*

THE SPEAKER, audience, occasion, and theme are perfectly matched in this speech. Dr. Horton had been born in Missouri. Before her marriage she had been Dean of Women in Oberlin College and President of Wellesley College. During World War II she had been national director of the WAVES with the rank of captain in the United States Naval Reserve. Because of her eminence as an educator she had been awarded honorary degrees by 16 colleges and universities.

The address was given to the graduating class of Christian College—a women's college—Columbia, Missouri, at the 100th Commencement in 1951.

MEMBERS of this graduating class have been asked to do all kinds of strange things in order to qualify for the diplomas they are about to receive. Let me ask for one final test of your imagination. *Suppose this were 1851* instead of 1951. Of course you would not be graduating from Christian College which would not open until next fall. Suppose, however, that you were girls of your age, living in that age.

It would be an age in which people live—and happily too—without electric lights, radio, television, modern plumbing, automobiles, airplanes, telephones—imagine getting through high school without a telephone! A little more than a month ago I flew from New York to Amsterdam leaving at ten o'clock one morning, arriving in Holland twelve hours later. Four weeks ago today I left Beirut, Lebanon, stopped for a few minutes in Stamboul, three hours in Munich, a brief stay in Brussels and after a nine hour stop-over in London I reached New York Thursday morning—. . . . Tuesday night in Lebanon, Thursday morning in New York. Within the last hundred years the inventions which made that trip possible have become almost matters of fact to be taken for granted.

Think for a moment what a difference these inventions of communication and transportation have made in our relations with people living in different parts of the world. Men, driven by fear or adventure, braved the oceans to settle new continents, an occasional explorer returned from a daring trip into the great unknown, but surely it would seem strange to the young ladies of 1851 to find their neighbors and friends personally acquainted with Arabs or Guamanians or Japanese or Filipinos or Chinese or Australians. I admit that it has taken me a half century and more to achieve a trip to the Near East. It is still an unusual experience but, having been there, I marvel at the number of other people who match my tales with ones growing out of far more extended and frequent visits than mine.

Surely it is not necessary to labor the point that if this were 1851 instead of 1951 you and I would be living lives very different from the ones we actually know: However, not being a social historian, I am not going to venture further into a description of the differences. You can look that up for yourselves which is advice teachers like to give!

I have high regard for the vision of the founders of your college. It was interesting to discover that one of them came from Harrodsburg, Kentucky. That is where my ancestors settled just before they moved to Missouri in time for my immediate family to be native Missourians. We even have a McAfee memorial at Harrodsburg at the site of the Old Fort established, I think, by Daniel Boone himself. Our memorial is in the form of a stile, steps going over a fence leading from a parking lot to a cemetery. I've never quite developed the meaning of that, but I'm sure there must be one.

I have high regard for your founders because they were the kind of people who acted in the present in regard to a truly unpredictable future—our present. How could they imagine a world in which all the normal tools of our trade, the most familiar instruments of our culture—as yet uninvented—would be available to such a large proportion of our population? Perhaps they thought the future would be fundamentally like their present. Perhaps they acted as though the future would be static. Whatever their understanding of the situation they acted for a future which proved to be unpredictable and what they did made a difference in the kind of future which developed long after they were gone.

Let me mention three facts about your founding fathers in this college, facts which explain our presence here this morning.

1. These founding fathers believed that minds are important tools for everybody. They believed this so strongly that they created the opportunity for even underprivileged people—women—to develop their intellectual skills. They knew it was important to have citizens who are provided with trained minds. Not that women were full political citizens. Maybe some of your founders dreamed of the day when women would vote but my guess is that *voting* women were almost inconceivable even to people so progressive that they believed in educating women. But the founders of Christian College believed in educating even second-class citizens in order to help them become first-class citizens.

2. Your founding fathers saw the importance of accomplishing their purpose by working through the great institution of the Church. Don't you think it interesting that it was the Church, proclaiming a faith, which established hundreds of colleges, insisting in effect that faith needs reason. Protestant Colleges like this are not institutions in which students are indoctrinated in the articles of their faith but they are colleges in which it is good to remember that the Church had a major part in their establishment.

I sometimes think that colleges are so fearful of indoctrination that they do too little to expose students to the facts of their religious heritage. They act a bit like those parents who seem to me so inconsistent. They do all they can to cultivate children's taste in art, offer them every possible opportunity to cultivate the social graces, train them in sports, insist on regular visits to the dentist, the oculist, the eye-ear-nose and throat specialist, the x-ray clinic, guide and guard their children at every point except one. So far as religion is concerned children "must decide for themselves" with no previous experience.

That was a parenthesis—an inappropriate one so far as this particular college is concerned—but one I like to insert whenever I can make the opportunity. It was a kind of side remark which I do not intend as too much of a distraction from my main observation that when your founding fathers had an idea of a new venture to improve the world, they established a new college but did it in cooperation with the great established institution of the Church, rooted in history with sanctions which far supersede the sanction of any one historic era.

3. My third observation is that it was a very small number of people who accomplished the establishment of the institution. They were a like-minded minority with imagination and determination.

Now come back if you will to the year 1951. We are living happily—I hope —with our lives organized in the familiar patterns. The most familiar thing about them is the fact that nobody knows what may happen next. I defy anyone to describe the world of 2051. (Even the television shows don't go into much detail, though I presume that Video Rangers expect to drink postum a hundred years from now!)

Nobody knows whether we will progress or regress. As you well know there are those who think we will blow ourselves up. Others foresee a great era of increasing world unity. What the gadgets of ordinary life will be is as far beyond our imagining as television would have been to the planners of this college. So how can a college educate you or anybody else to live in a world which is so thoroughly unpredictable? Well, I predict that whatever the unpredictable future it will be important to have people in it who have the traits I have been associating with the founders of Christian College.

The future will need as many well-trained, usable minds as possible. Minds are instruments to be used for understanding our world. They are instruments for solving problems. Uncritical, undisciplined minds are usable by people other than their rightful owners. It is a great achievement in this era of mass communication, mass production, standardization of taste—it is a great thing to have a mind of one's own. Anybody can have a temper of his own, an emotional orgy all his own, but minds belong to the people who use them and some people—even in a country like ours which boasts of its educational opportunities—some people really don't bother to use their minds. They drift along with mass prejudices, jumping to standardized, socially correct conclusions with very little concern about thinking for themselves.

Our democracy functions on the daring assumption that everyone over 21 is entitled to a share in the making of important decisions. This can be disastrous if the minds of individuals are worked upon by people who choose to manipulate them for their own ends. Truth is achieved when free minds meet and sift error from truth. Minds which are blunted, inept in operation, are inadequate instruments for that search for truth. People with minds trained to think for themselves will be potential assets in adjustment to whatever new situation lies ahead.

But intelligence all by itself is not an assured asset. Minds trained as expertly as possible could easily be misused without a wholesome standard of values. That is the importance of acting in cooperation with the established institutions which embody the values which endure.

Institutions are fascinating things. The church, the school, the state, the family, the economic order . . . people spend lifetimes in an effort to describe them and their function. Most of us accept them as facts of experience and we relate ourselves to them consciously or unconsciously at different stages of our development.

We often hesitate to identify ourselves with established institutions because our experience with some representative of them has been unfortunate. We can never know more than a fraction of the whole institution. If we have had an adverse impression of that fraction, we sometimes repudiate the whole institution.

Suppose your family attends a church whose minister bores you. Under such circumstances too many people jump to the conclusion that all preachers are bores and the church is a stuffy, boring institution. Or you dislike some particular Congressman and jump to the conclusion that all Congressmen are stupid . . . and service to the state is scratched off your list of possible vocations or avocations.

People sometimes hesitate to throw in their lot with established institutions because they see these institutions moving so slowly toward desirable ends. The very fact that the institutions embody the heritage of the ages conduces to their ponderous, slow-moving nature. Remember, though, that the weight that slows them down also exerts tremendous influence when it is wielded effectively. Changes come within institutions by leadership of people who see that changes are desirable. Make the change within the framework of the institution which has the power of established recognition and it is apt to survive. Sometimes the institutional innovation develops into a new institution, becoming an independent creation . . . witness the United Nations . . . but remember that the creation of that new institution is accomplished with the cooperation of many established groups, the very institutions we include to criticize for being so slow-moving.

One hundred years ago your founding fathers set another example. They saw something that needed to be done. They undertook to do it, a few of them. Whatever the future, it will have room in it for people who will do something about the meeting of needs.

You probably have in this class—most classes do—girls who have already learned the art of doing something that needs to be done. You probably have others who are sure things are wrong but have done very little to set them straight. These latter are professional "viewers with alarm." You know them—even if they don't know themselves. They haven't liked the college regulations but were never willing to take the trouble to do anything constructive about them . . . except to object. Probably some of you really believe that somebody else is always to blame for your difficulties. You got a poor grade because you had a poor teacher. Your good work was your credit; your bad work was your teacher's fault . . . or maybe your parents didn't give you the right kind of brain. You were bored in that class because the material was dull—not because you never bothered to read any of the extra readings. Unless you snap out of that point of view you will not be among the minority which gets things done and thus begins to build a more interesting future.

A more common handicap to modern college women seems to be the inclination to do nothing because there is so much to do. In sincere humility you don't feel qualified to undertake big jobs and little ones seem futile in the face of the gigantic needs of the world.

Your founders were willing to start small, not sure what the future would hold for their college venture, but eager to do something.

The old graveyard in a New Hampshire town I know has a tombstone with the inscription, "She done what she could." What more could be asked of anyone? Every big accomplishment involves many small ones.

One odd thing about life is that anybody can predict right now what you will be doing thirty years from now but we can be reasonably sure that all you have been doing and what you do next will take their place in preparing you for whatever your future holds. If you have a great ambition, take as big a step as possible in the direction of fulfilling it, but if the step is only a tiny one, don't worry if it is the largest one now possible.

Trained minds, identification with established values tested through years of the development of our great social institutions, personal initiative—the founders of your college had these traits. May you who profited from them hand them on to yet unborn generations.

By so doing, you will supply your world with the kind of person who will be useful in the immediate present and the unpredictable future—and if the experience of the years means anything, it indicates that you will be supplying yourself with a life of perennial interest. A life devoted to being safe must be a dull and ever-dissatisfied one. How can anybody be safe? I noticed in a recent Sunday N. Y. *Times* that Secretary Tobin said twice as many people had been killed by accidents at home as had been killed in the Korean fighting. A friend of mine once said she wanted me to have lunch with her fiance. When I suggested taking another friend with me, she said, "Oh, no, don't let Mary meet him. That wouldn't be safe!" What a dull thing to be considered "safe" or to make one's own safety and security the ultimate ambition.

Working for the security of otherwise endangered people is, on the other hand, an exhilarating and challenging occupation. Enlarging one's interests by identifying one's self with other peoples' needs keep life from narrowness and monotony. A WAVE gave me a hard-worked text during the war when she said one time that she liked Navy discipline. She said, "there is a lot of it but it hits everybody alike and *none of it is for my own good.*"

May the Christian College graduates of 1951 like their predecessors through the century before them so live that their academic descendants in 2051 will know that they have done their share to make the unpredictable future one worthy of our great American and Christian ideal. If they will so live it will surely be that they and their age share the congratulations we all offer on this your Commencement Day.

COMMON CONFUSIONS

By *Carter Davidson*

THERE IS obvious skill in the use of speech principles in the following address, by which thought is given full force through easily recognized structure and use of superior supporting materials. Dr. Davidson, now president of Union College, was active in forensics while an undergraduate in Harvard, and taught speech in the University of Idaho, University of Chicago, Carleton College, Knox College, and Union College.

The address was given at the University of Buffalo, June 4, 1947.

WHEN OUR friend, Alice, took her famous trip into Wonderland, she was more than commonly confused by the similarities joined with differences in the Tweedledums and Tweedledees of that looking-glass country. Lewis Carroll was no fool, but a learned professor of mathematics, attempting to show his readers what a vast amount of discrimination is needed to distinguish sense from nonsense. In this connection as an educator I always enjoy reading Alice's discussion with the Mock Turtle on the curriculum. He remarked that he had taken "the usual course," consisting of "Reeling, and Writhing, and Rhythmetic, in all four branches, Ambition, Distraction, Uglification, and Derison." These sounded so much like the real thing to Alice, that she was confused—and well she might be, for this was her first experience with the puzzling science of semantics, or the origins and meanings of words. Stuart Chase has written a book about "The Tyranny of Words," which convinces its readers that words are dangerous swayers of human opinion and destinies.

Americans seem particularly susceptible to these confusions of words and meanings, perhaps because they are distinctly an impatient people, endowed with what the mediaeval scientist would have called the "good humor" of red-blooded sanguinity, instead of the "bad humors" of melancholy, phlegm, and anger. Perhaps, therefore, Americans need to be warned about these words and ideas which look alike but have such difference effects.

For example, *Americans often confuse Size and Importance.* We have seen it happen in our judgment of human beings, and it is similarly true of colleges, business corporations, cities, and nations. Yet, if we think twice about it, we must agree that excessive size often destroys the very purposes of life and society, and that Ben Jonson was right when he wrote "it is not growing like a tree in bulk, doth make man better be."

Again, the twentieth century has *tended to identify Speed with Progress,* and looks upon the automobile zooming over our paved highways, the streamlined trains tearing across country at a hundred miles per hour, the aeroplanes bridging the Atlantic in seven hours, and the radio or television bringing speakers from Hollywood to Buffalo in nothing flat, as the finest flower of our civilization. Factories are judged by the speed with which they turn out vast quantities of their product, not by the quality and lasting power of the product itself. Yet, what do we do with all the time saved by these processes? We either waste it, or speed up our whole rate of living until we become neurotic, exhausted, casualties of our war for speed.

In our economic thinking, we *Americans tend to confuse Money with Wealth,* putting our millionaires at the top of our social and political scale, and forgetting that often true wealth is not convertible into cash, but resides in the love and respect of our friends, the satisfaction which we derive from our work, or our store of experiences from which we can draw pleasant memories. Benjamin Franklin, one of our wisest Americans and also wealthiest in the satisfactions of life, advised that it is simpler to reduce our financial wants to a point below our income, than to increase our income to the point where we will have no unsatified cravings. Think over the list of men and women you like most, and ask whether their wealth is spiritual, intellectual, social, or merely financial.

Similarly, *we tend to confuse Authority with Wisdom,* perhaps because they should be combined. Generals and Admirals, presidents of banks or universities, and other "brass hats" are often given credit for knowledge and wisdom, when all they possess is authority. Unfortunately authorities in one field often speak as if they had wisdom in all fields, and eminent automobile manufacturers are quoted on problems of religion or international politics, religious leaders on scientific investigations and industrial economics. "To each his own" would be a good theme-song for men and women to whom responsibilities have been assigned.

Since the war it has been particularly noticeable that *we are confusing Excitement with Pleasure or Enjoyment.* It is well known that alcohol and marihuana tend to excite the nerve endings and the physical sensations but joy and genuine pleasure are deeper and more lasting. In this craving for excitement, the American public has run wildly after gambling, dangerous driving, and even lynching—none of them pleasant or enjoyable through beauty or accomplishment. The remark of a fifteen-year-old boy the other day, that he had killed a man "just because I wanted to see a man die" is too typical of our generation; it is the psychology of the Roman arena where the crowds came to see the gladiators kill one another or the lions tear to pieces the Christians or other undesirables. Music, drama, and the other arts should be natural means of enjoyment, but even they have been invaded by sensationalism. Human friendship and love between men and women, sources of real happiness since the world began, have been perverted, partly by the influence of the movies, the radio, and the newspapers, into mere physical excitement. Are we, as a people, headed for a debauch of excitement which will result in the sickness of disillusionment and the headache of regret? Why not come to our right mind before, rather than after?

The confusion between Religion and Theology has caused more quarreling, dissension, war among men than any of the other confusions I have mentioned. Yet the line is clear: religion deals with the standards by which a man lives and relates himself to his universe and society, whereas theology is the study of the theory of the universe and its creation. Theology is practically impossible of logical or scientific proof, religion is proved in practice every day.

Theology with its variant theories tends to separate men into sects; religion by its very nature must bind men together. The hope of peace on earth and good will among men lies in a universal religion, but theologians in general are doing all they can to prevent it; perhaps the true religion of the future will come from the hearts of the common men, instead of from the theological seminaries.

The trouble makers in our political world are also busy *confusing our minds about Democracy and our Republicanism.* They are not the same: democracy refers to the spirit which pervades a society, which insists upon the rights of individuals, our freedom personal and intellectual, religious, economic, political, and educations; our republic, on the other hand, refers to our form of government, which allocates responsibilities to executives, legislature, and judiciary, sets up checks and balances between the federal government, the states, the townships, and the citizens, and provides the machinery for effective social organization. The world has been full of tragic examples, during recent years, of countries which had republican forms of government without a democracy; on the other hand, England and the Scandinavian countries have achieved a democratic society under the forms of monarchy. Some critics of America have been arguing of late that the founders of our nation were interested in establishing a republic, but had no faith in democracy. I insist that the same men who wrote the Constitution also wrote the first ten amendments, the Bill of Rights for democratic freedoms; the genius of the United States of America is that it has successfully combined a republican form of government with a democratic free, society almost unique in the annals of man.

But I am particularly concerned today about common confusions in the area of education, where you have been spending the last sixteen years. These confusions have caused considerable damage to our schools and colleges, and therefore to our students, and commencement may seem to you a rather late date for me to try to clear them up. But I am assuming that your educational growth is merely well begun, that all of you are planning to educate yourselves from this point on, now that you have learned the secrets of the profession. Therefore, let us draw some distinction, based upon your experience, but looking toward the Scyllas and Charybdises ahead.

First, we have been confused about Education and Training. Training, however, is clearly a process by which the pupil is taught to perform an act by imitating the manipulations of the teacher, doing it over and over until the act approaches perfection. That is the way we learn to operate a typewriter, a lathe, or a plasterer's trowel. Education, on the other hand, should acquaint the student with the ways of analyzing problems of all sorts and descriptions, so that his mind is keen to understand the basic meanings and implications, and when he is faced one day by problems he has never solved or even seen before, he will be able to analyze the problem into its elements, and proceed toward its solution. Education may use training extensively; the pianist will need to be trained in finger exercises and piano techniques, but he should also be educated in interpretation and expression. Don't fall into confusion of believing you are educated in a field when you are merely well trained; seek for the plus sign of education. Animals of the lower orders can be trained to work, to talk, to do tricks; only human beings can be educated. Why not take advantage of your human inheritance?

Closely connected is another persistent confusion, between Preparation for Life and Participation in Life. An old physics teacher of mine, in high school, used to ask us "When the first quarter-mile of a mile race has been run, would we say that the runners are merely preparing to run the race?" Most of you in this graduating class have already lived from a third to a fourth of your alloted span; if you haven't begun to live by now, perhaps you never will. If you haven't made decisions for yourself while you've been in college, what makes you think that you ever can make such decisions? If you haven't lived democratically to date, what magic potion will make you democratic now? Students must live fully while they are in school or college; that is really the only way by which we can learn to live richly later. But, you say, our economic society is constructed to allow a long period of preparation for producing citizenship; we can't vote, or marry, or get a job until we reach a certain age. Granted. As human beings living in a benevolent America in 1947, you have been privileged to spend sixteen years filling the bins upon which you must draw during the sixty years ahead. Jesus, we remember, was thirty before he began to teach; by then, his mind and heart and spirit were filled to overflowing, and he poured himself out without stint.

Don't stop filling the bin just because you are drawing out the grain. Minds like bank accounts, can be exhausted, and problems returned stamped "Not Sufficient Funds." Miniver Cheevy, you will recall, cursed the day that he was born, because he wished he had been born in the middle ages, when knights were bold; disgusted with his own day, "he kept on drinking." We have thousands of Minivers among us, who refuse to participate because they wish they were somewhere else. The disease is represented today on Broadway in two popular current productions, "Finian's Rainbow," and "Brigadoon." The old Irishman who has brought the pot of gold to Missitucky has very little to suggest for the problems of his neighborhood, but is always asking "How are things in Glocca Morra?" an imaginary land beyond the seas. The people of Brigadoon, desiring to protect themselves from the changes of life, have placed a magic spell upon their village so that it reappears for only one day in each century. Educated men can't live in a dream world or escape from time; they must participate in life to the full.

While they participate, they must prepare for the next step; reflection and action must go hand in hand. In the distant past we have seen the Emperor Marcus Aurelius meditating over philosophy in the midst of his military campaigns; we recall that Leonardo da Vinci found time for painting the Mona Lisa and writing sonnets while he was serving as city engineer; Johann Wolfgang von Goethe wrote the great philosophical drama, "Faust," while serving as prime minister of the busy duchy of Weimar; and my most famous predecessor as president of Union, Eliphalet Nott, found time to invent forty types of stoves while he was occupied ostensibly in establishing the modern pattern of college education. Even in more recent times we have found a Sir William Osler distinguished in the practice of medicine but turning from the sickroom to write philosophical essays; a T. E. Lawrence profoundly scholarly but able to manipulate and lead a revolt in the desert; a John Buchan, writing romances with the flair of a Dumas or a Stevenson, but serving as a distinguished Governor General of Canada; a Justice Oliver Wendell Holmes, member of the Supreme Court of the United States, but retaining a wise interest in every field of knowledge and culture; and a Thomas Vernor Smith, a college professor of Philosophy who served with distinction in the congress of the United States. These men give concrete proof to my thesis: we must combine participation with preparation, action with reflection.

Finally, I would like to attempt to clear up another educational confusion, that between Reading Knowledge and Reading for Knowledge. The study of foreign languages had been very badly handled in America; we try to teach students to read Latin or French or Spanish, and then give them nothing to read, or nothing which will add to their knowledge. The language requirement which is never implemented in the rest of the curriculum is a bitter waste of time. We teachers are prone to assume that in college we have established habits from which the graduate will not depart; and among these, we hope, is the habit of reading worthwhile books. Of this I have grave doubts; the average college graduate is more than likely to limit his reading to the newspaper, the comic books, a picture magazine, a magazine of condensations, and the book elections of a commercial literary club. If college men and women haven't learned to read the originals, to seek out the significant, they are literate but ignorant. Which is better, a nation of illiterate wise men, or of literate ignoramuses? Must we be either?

A perusal of a recent publication of the Grolier Club, entitled "One Hundred Influential American Books Printed before 1900," reveals that our wisdom as a people has come to us through devious channels. Among the hundred, as you would expect, are some great novels by Mark Twain and Nathaniel Hawthorne and Herman Melville, some great poems by Poe and Whitman, some great essays by Emerson and Thoreau. But I jotted down a dozen or so titles which may surprise you because they are not what you ordinarily think of as "great books." They are:

1640 "The Bay Psalm Book," our first American hymnal; the hymns we sing in our churches, despite the fact that we rarely note their meaning, have molded our attitudes.

1758 "Poor Richard's Almanack," Benjamin Franklin's interspersing of bits of wisdom among the statistics of phases of the moon, weather prophesies, and the like.

1776 The Declaration of Independence, and, eleven years later, the *Constitution of the United States.* How many of us have read them carefully, as we would a contract for a new job or for building a house? Yet they affect us more.

1783 Noah Webster's Speller, the standardizer of our American language, the inspiration of the Spelling Bee, and the curse of the schoolboy's life.

1830 Joseph Smith's "Book of Mormon," the inspiration for a religious sect who carved a great new state of the wilderness.

1836 "McGuffey's First Reader," one of a series which taught morals along with reading. Even I can remember how "Rosamond and the Purple Jar" taught me that attractive exteriors may conceal hollow interiors.

1852 Harriet Beecher Stowe's "Uncle Tom's Cabin," a novel which helped to start the Civil War.

1863 Abraham Lincoln's Gettysburg Address, a brief dedication speech which has served as a new charter for a reunited America.

1868 Horatio Alger, Jr.'s "Ragged Dick," the first of a series of success stories for boys, which set an ideal of honesty and hard work. Compare this with the ideals now being established by Captain Marvel and Superman, who have merely to say "Shazam" in order to possess supernatural powers.

1872 The Montgomery Ward Catalog, which made available to every home via the mail order, the appurtenances of civilizations; this probably did as much as any one thing to standardize the American way of living, especially in rural areas.

1884 Mrs. Lincoln's "Boston Cook Book," which helped to provide the same standardization for American meals, and to introduce some variety into our steak and cornmeal diet.

1888 Edward Bellamy's "Looking Backward," a stimulating social prophecy which foresaw the radio and other scientific inventions improving the lot of the lower classes in the America of the twentieth century.

1890 William James' "Principles of Psychology," the first readable book about the new science which is now dominant in education, medicine, and industry.

1894 Dr. Holt's "Care and Feeding of Children," a medical handbook for the home which undoubtedly cut down the death rate among children.

How, then, can we learn to avoid these common confusions, these mistakings of the show for the reality? How can we acquire the power of discrimination? I suggest that we must try to develop for ourselves two more senses, in addition to the five old or the nineteen new senses of physiology.

First of these new senses is the aesthetic sense, or the sense of good taste, which will reveal to us, after constant practice, the difference between the good and the bad, in art and conduct. There are men who make a good living as "tea tasters," sensitizing the taste buds on their tongues until they can tell by the flavor the kind, the locale, and the grade of tea leaves. If the individual can improve his physical apperceptions to this point, he can do the same for his mental and moral taste. To say of college graduate, "He shows bad taste" in his manners, his dress, his talk, his companions, his recreation, or his reading is a serious reflection upon the education provided by his college.

The other new sense, which is even harder to acquire, is the sense of humor. Some people insist this cannot be taught or even acquired, but is innate. I am not so pessimistic. I believe all of us have it, but in many it is undeveloped; we say of such that they have "lost their sense of humor." Essentially it consists of an ability to perceive incongruities—the fat man slipping on the banana peel, the Falstaff in love, the self-important boaster revealed as a fool. Of course, it exists on many levels, from the lowest pie throwing to the highest wit, and the state of our education is revealed by the thing at which we laugh.

The individual can, however, improve his own sense of humor by trying to see himself as others see him, by viewing himself objectively. As Robert Burns remarked, "It would from many an error free us, and foolish notion." If we can see ourselves clearly, perhaps we can avoid another common confusion, that of our outward reputation with our true character.

This should bring me to the conclusion . . . When we, like Alice in Wonderland, are confused and befuddled by the similarities of phrase which conceal a vast difference of meaning, or by the clever misinterpretations of propaganda, let us call a halt to sift the true from the false, to discriminate fairly, to apply our new senses of good taste and good humor.

STORY BEHIND THE ATOMIC BOMB

By *Reuben G. Gustavson*

ONE MONTH after the first atomic bomb ever used in war had been dropped on the Japanese city of Hiroshima (August 6, 1945)—while people were confusedly wondering what an atomic bomb really was, and what the release of atomic energy meant in terms of the survival of human life on this planet—one of the outstanding scientists in America discussed this topic before an audience of non-scientists.

The speech is an excellent specimen of the presenting of complex information, given by a speaker who says that "attempting to communicate the findings of science to laymen has been a hobby of mine for many years." It was delivered before the Executives Club of Chicago on September 7, 1945.

Dr. Gustavson, a chemist, was vice president and dean of faculties of the University of Chicago. He is now chancellor of the University of Nebraska.

AS THE Chairman has just stated, probably no event in the history of mankind has so challenged the imagination of men as the development of the atomic bomb. Mankind probably faced no more serious problem than the problem of what we are to do about it now that we have it.

It has been my privilege to know the men who have worked on this bomb rather intimately. I know that they have given a great deal of attention to the problem which every one of us faces—what are we to do about it. It is their very definite feeling that in a country like ours which is a democracy, and where the people in the last analysis, based on whatever information they may have, make decisions, it is most important that the citizens of our country should be informed about this new development because it is only as the citizens of a democracy are given accurate information by way of the press, by way of the radio, by way of the individuals who can speak to them, that we can hope that their decisions will be wise.

I want to trace for you in the moments that are available to me the general development of the atomic bomb, and then after we have discussed that, I should like to say something about the great problems that face us as a result of the series of events which led to the manufacture of the bomb.

I

The notion that matter is made up of atoms is a very old one. It goes away back into Greek philosophic thought. Rather definite notions of the atom began to develop about the time of Sir Isaac Newton, and at that time our general notions were that the different elements were made up of atoms, and we conceived of these atoms as being something of a billiard ball character, hard masses which could be subjected to the greatest of mechanical and chemical forces without in any way destroying them.

We had to have this notion of indestructibility of the atom in order to explain what we then thought of as one of the most fundamental properties of matter: namely, that matter could not be destroyed. So we start then with that *billiard ball conception of the atom.*

We thought that the atoms of the different elements had different weights, but that the atoms of any given element all had the same weight. We took for awhile as our unit a very light element, hydrogen, which we called (1). The atom of another element was 16 times as heavy as the hydrogen atom, and we called it (16), so we built up a series of weights which we called atomic weights, which represented the weights of individual atoms relative to the hydrogen atom.

That concept served us very well until after 1896 when, as a result of a series of epoch-making discoveries, we began to get acquainted with radio-activity, and here, thanks to the work of Becquerel, of Madame and Pierre Curie, and others that we could mention, we discovered elements which were not stable. We may take radium as an example. It had all the properties of an element, but it differed from the elements that we had previously known in that it was spontaneously going to pieces. It was throwing off from itself some particles of matter which were positively charged, which we called alpha particles; some particles which were negatively charged, which we now call electrons or beta particles; and then a type of radiation of the general nature of light, which we called gamma rays, and which were closely related to X-rays.

Now this discovery gave us our first jar with respect to our notions of the constitution of matter. In the first place, it was evident that the elements were not indestructible because here were elements that were spontaneously going to pieces. At the same time it became evident that the amount of energy that in some way was locked up in matter was enormous.

Steam does the work of the world. The work that steam does is due to the fact that the small particles of steam which we call molecules are in rapid motion, and the piston in the steam engine moves because literally billions of these particles pound on it. Now, how fast do they move? Well, they move with a velocity of about a quarter of a mile per second, which is pretty fast.

How much energy do they contain? Well, the energy of a moving particle, as you will remember from your physics—perhaps I should say, as you will have forgotten from your physics—is equal to one-half of its mass multiplied by the square of its velocity.

Well, let's figure that out for steam. The mass of the water particle is 18. One-half of it is 9. It moves with a velocity of a quarter of a mile per second. We square that, and we get one-sixteenth. The answer then becomes one-half of 18, which is nine, divided by 16. Let's call it roughly one-half. How much energy is there in this so-called alpha particle positively charged thrown off from radium? Well, it is thrown off with a velocity of approximately 10,000 miles per second. Let's calculate its energy.

It has a mass of 4, relative to 18 for water. One-half of 4 is 2. Two times 10,000 times 10,000. If my mathematics is any good, that is of the general order of 200,000,000. How does the ratio then of the energy of the particle thrown off from radium compare with that of steam? Well, it is the ratio of 200,000,000 to ½, which if my arithmetic is again right, is 400,000,000.

In other words, the particle thrown off from radium when it spontaneously goes to pieces is roughly 400,000,000 times the energy contained in the steam particle which does the work of the world. That jarred our imaginations. Radium is continually giving off heat. One ounce of radium, for example, will give off roughly about, let us say, 28,000 British thermal units per year. I am trying to stay with units that you are somewhat familiar with. Well, you say, that isn't so much. A ton of coal would contain about 9,000 British thermal units.

Well, let's look at it. Radium goes to pieces, but it loses half of its mass in about something like two thousand years, to stay with round numbers. It loses another half in another two thousand years. You can see then if you multiply the amount of energy given off by an ounce of radium, roughly 28,000 British thermal units per ounce per year, by the length of time which it lasts, again you run into this tremendous quantity of energy.

Scientists discovered then or realized at this time that in the particle that was shot off from radium they had the greatest concentration of energy known to man, a particle which contained roughly, as I have stated, 400,000,000 times the energy of the steam particle which does the work of the world.

As a result of that discovery, men began to wonder—since we have here a bullet, as it were, a particle which moves with this tremendous velocity—let's see if we could pound matter to pieces with it, and so we find Rutherford, for example, the great Canadian physicist, taking an element such as nitrogen and pounding it with the particle shot off from the sun, which was radium, with a velocity of 10,000 miles per second. Out of that grew a very interesting discovery; namely, that the nitrogen which we had theretofore thought of as an element would go to pieces and give off another element which we knew as hydrogen.

Our concepts began to get into difficulties. Then a very ingenious physicist by the name of C. T. R. Wilson conceived the notion of shooting these particles with this tremendous velocity through water vapor, under which conditions the water vapor would condense as a cloud and he could therefore follow its path. When he shot this alpha particle from radium through water vapor and photographed its pathway, he found that it would literally go through millions of particles of water as though nothing were present, and then it would suddenly be deviated as though it had struck something very hard and something very dense.

In other words, the path of the particle became something like the path of a high-speed automobile. It is going down the straightaway, and as long as every thing is clear, all is well, and then suddenly if you find that happening [indicating] you know that something was hit where the angle of the pathway changes.

That led to the question—what does this mean? Well, you can see it can't mean that the particles are like billiard balls. It can't mean that because we are shooting through millions of them without apparently being affected by them, so that gave rise to the motion that *the atom must not be of billiard-ball-like structure, but perhaps it is something like the solar system with a central sun* where most of the mass of the atom is located and which we called the nucleus, surrounded by planets similar to the planets which surround the sun.

That became the new kind of atom then that we began to deal with, and some chemists immediately became interested in these planetary particles. These electrons that occurred outside of the nucleus or the central sun. There were questions of arithmetic involved. How many planets did the different atoms have? There were questions of geometry involved. What kind of pathways do these particles follow? Do they go around in circles? Do they go around in ellipses? Finally there was the question of the mechanics of these particles. Do they all stay in the same pathway, or do they jump from one path to another?

II

That became the kind of thing that chemists and physicists became interested in. Then we gradually turned our attention from the planetary structure of this miniature solar system back to that central sun or the nucleus. We began to make discoveries about its contents. We discovered, for example, that it contained in it a positively charged particle about the same weight as the hydrogen atom. We called that the *proton,* and then Chadwick in England, by bombarding an element called beryllium—which you will hear a lot about as time goes on—with this alpha particle, again from radium which is the shotgun of the physicist to knock things to pieces, discovered a particle which had no electrical charge and was therefore called the *neutron.*

The neutron then became a particle that began to be used by the physicist and the chemist. This particle had properties that were unique. Primarily the one we were interested in was that it had no charge. And why were we interested in that? Well, if you have the center of an atom which is positively charged, and you are shooting another positively charged particle at it, you can see what happens. You will again have forgotten from your elementary physics that positive charges repel each other with a force that varies directly as their charges, and inversely as the square of the distance.

In other words, the closer two positively charged particles come to each other, the greater is the repulsion between them. Therefore, if you attempt to shoot at this central sun or the nucleus of an atom which is positively charged, another positive particle, as it approaches the other, the repulsion becomes great, and probably it shoots off to one side.

This neutral particle, the neutron, had the advantage that we might shoot it at various atoms to see what would happen, and we would not have this repulsive force between the nucleus of the atom and this neutral particle which we call the neutron.

A number of workers began to use neutrons in their studies. Madame and Monsieur Joliot, the daughter and son-in-law of the great Madame and Pierre Curie, tried it on a number of elements and found that some elements which had heretofore been regarded as stable became unstable, became artificially, as it were, radioactive. Then a new kind of nuclear chemistry began to be born. It was an interesting kind of chemistry, but it was basically this: If you hit this nucleus, this central sun with a small particle, it becomes unstable, and it gives small particles back. The energy involved in the liberated particle isn't any greater, if it is as great, as the energy that it took to drive the particle in.

Professor Fermi, then at work in Italy, asked himself what would happen if you took this neutron, this neutral particle, and allowed it to hit one of the heaviest of our atoms; namely, uranium, which was already unstable, going to pieces spontaneously like radium. He tried the experiment. He found that there was a very definite increase in its radio-activity, in its instability, and for that discovery Fermi was given the Nobel Prize in physics.

Some German workers, one outstanding woman, Dr. Meitner, Hahn and Straussmann, examining this experiment of Fermi's, discovered that it involved something that was different from anything that had been heretofore discovered; namely, that when the neutron strikes the uranium atom, instead of giving off some small particle like the hydrogen particle or the helium particle, the uranium particle actually falls apart, goes to pieces, breaks up roughly in half, and the interesting thing was that when you added the weights of these fragments together, you didn't come out with the weight of the original uranium atom.

It is as though we have a sixteen-ounce loaf of bread, and we cut it in half. We weigh the two fragments, and instead of weighing sixteen ounces, they weigh thirteen ounces. Now, barring the possibility that some youngster stole a slice of bread, there is something wrong about that, isn't there? It ought to weigh sixteen ounces, but instead of that, it weighs, we will say, fifteen ounces.

What happened to that mass, that matter which was lost? Einstein years before, growing out of some work that had been done on the electron in vacuum tubes, had come to the conclusion that if matter were destroyed, converted into energy, the energy which would be liberated when the matter would be destroyed would be given to you by this equation: that E—the energy—would be equal to M—the mass destroyed—multiplied by—and here is the amazing thing—the square of the velocity of light.

The velocity of light is roughly 186,000 miles per second. When you square it, you see you get an enormous number. Therefore, even though the amount of matter destroyed might be small, when you multiply a small mass by the square of 186,000 miles per second, to keep it in these big units, the figure is enormous.

When these German workers, Meitner particularly, saw that apparently in this experiment of Fermi's we had seen the actual destruction of matter, they realized, on the basis of the Einstein equation, the tremendous quantity of energy which must be liberated when that destruction takes place. Therefore, if you could make the mass destroy anything appreciable, the energy liberated would be tremendous.

You will remember, at that time Hitler was ruling the world or making a very brave attempt to. He made a number of mistakes. Among the great mistakes that he made was to persecute certain members of its population. Meitner went to Stockholm. She sent a telegram to Niels Bohr, who at that time was in this country, giving him the interpretation of the Fermi experiment.

That telegram probably caused more discussion than any telegram that has ever come across the sea because in that these scientists saw the possibilities of liberating the tremendous quantities of energy wrapped up in the atom, and immediately men began to speculate about this: What happens when the neutron strikes the uranium atom?

Well, as I told you, it falls apart, but something more than that happens. It liberates more neutrons. You can see that this is easily possible. *One neutron strikes the uranium atom. It goes to pieces and liberates more neutrons which might strike more uranium atoms which would fall apart, liberating tremendous quantities of energy, liberating more neutrons, and so the thing would go until you would have something of explosive violence.*

When it looked, therefore, as though war were inevitable, a group of scientists in this country—two of whom were refugees from Hungary—went to President Roosevelt with an introduction from Dr. Einstein, saying that these men had something of the greatest importance to talk over with him. What they talked over with him was the possibility of the creation of an atomic bomb which had to have the attention of the President for two reasons: First, if that discovery should be made by Germany, if Germany, the home of science and industry, were able to organize her forces so as to create an atomic bomb, then indeed it would be difficult to visualize how anybody could meet the German onslaught; and second, if such a bomb should be developed by our own scientists, we would possess one of the most powerful tools in modern warfare.

Permission was given to these men to go ahead and to investigate its possibilities. Now, the thing that I want to point out to you up to this stage in our discussion is that all that I have said up to this point is common knowledge to the whole world. As I have indicated to you, Germans first saw the significance of the Fermi experiment. Fermi was an Italian. Niels Bohr, with whom they communicated, is a Dane.

These notions are all written up, chain reaction so to speak, in the Russian journals, in the journals of the Swiss people, of the French, of the English, of the American, of the Japanese. It is common knowledge everywhere. As far as fundamental principles are concerned—and this is most important—as far as fundamental principles are concerned, they are now known to the entire scientific world. There is no secret as far as the fundamental principles of the atomic bomb are concerned.

III

What became of our problem then at this point? It became a problem of getting quantitative data. It became a problem of finding out under what conditions uranium would react with neutrons with such violence that this tremendous amount of energy is liberated. That became the problem then for these scientists. As you can readily see, it involved a number of things.

In the first place, at this stage in the game we recognized that one of the assumptions that we had made very early, namely, that all of the atoms of a given element have the same weight, was wrong, that the atoms differ slightly among themselves.

For example, it is as though you were to take 100,000 people in Chicago and weigh them and get their average weight and come out with—shall we say, to flatter us—150 pounds. Then you go out to Colorado, and pick 100,000 people, and you determine their average weight, and you get 150 pounds. Since you do that all over the world, you say, "Well, all men weigh 150 pounds. That isn't true." All men just average 150 pounds.

It turns out these weights we have been determining were average weights. *Uranium was made up of three kinds of atoms, 234, 235, 238.* The question came up, what is the effect of this neutron on these three different kinds of uranium atoms? The 234 exists in such small quantities that we can neglect it. The 235 is less than one per cent of the uranium. This turns out to be the one that goes to pieces when it is struck by the neutron. Obviously one method of making a bomb then is to separate out this less than one per cent of uranium 235, set up a series of conditions so that you will have a high concentration of neutrons striking a certain critical mass of uranium 235 so that the chain reaction takes place in a short time, which will give you the explosion.

How are you going to separate two things that way so close to one another as 235 and 238? You can't do it chemically because the chemistry of these atoms is identical. Whatever method of separation you use, it has to be based upon physical properties. You can immediately see some possibilities. We separate cream from skimmed milk by the centrifuge. Well, that was tried; the supercentrifuge. Don't ever think that they used a dairyman's apparatus, but in principle it is the same. It didn't work very well.

Then we know that gases that are made up of heavy particles move more slowly than gases made up of light particles. For example, the air particles in this room move with a velocity of roughly a quarter of a mile per second. Hydrogen moves with a velocity of a mile per second. It is easy to separate hydrogen from oxygen if you have them mixed as gases, just depending upon that fact.

What you do is set up a sort of a race track. I am sure that you would say that if School A has a bunch of kids that can run a mile a second, and School B has a bunch of kids that only run a quarter of a mile a second, it is easy to separate them. Let them run a race, and after awhile School A will be away out here [indicating], and School B away back here.

That is the way in principle they tried to do it. Only it turns out that the velocity varies inversely as the square root of the mass, and when you determine the difference in the rate at which a gas containing uranium 235 will move and that having 238 will move, it is very small.

In the first place, you have to find a gaseous compound of uranium. Well, that was known; it was well known. It is uranium hexafluoride. When you determine the difference in which the rate of the gaseous particle of U-235 moves compared to 238, it turns out to be of the order of something like a few feet per second. You see then if you want to separate these particles from one another, you have to have a long race track. That was a part of the job.

By the so-called barrier methods, putting up a barrier, something like porous porcelain, let us say, in which the lighter particles would get through a little bit faster than the heavier particles—by having miles and miles and miles of that thing, you could gain something of a separation.

Another method that was tried was by the so-called electro-magnetic, and we will pass with that. That was developed by Lawrence, largely, out in California, and turned out to be a most successful method. The only trouble with it is that it yields only very, very small quantities of material.

This method of separating particles was well known before the war. In fact, it was this method that Dempster used when he discovered uranium 235, Dempster being the Professor of Physics at the University of Chicago, and I cannot help but stop for just a moment to say how little the world sometimes notices discoveries of tremendous importance. I am sure that when Dempster reported that he had found the uranium atom having a weight of 235 compared with the average one which was usually present, of 238, scientists were interested; but I am sure that if someone had appeared at The Executives' Club of Chicago and said, "Gentlemen, I just came to report to you that Dr. Dempster of the University of Chicago, using electromagnetic methods, has found that there is a particle of uranium which weighs 235 instead of 238," you would have said, "So what the hell!"

Well, the "what the hell" fell on Hiroshima and Nagasaki.

Having worked out methods of separating these two kinds of atoms, in the construction of a bomb, the first one which was used, was the question of getting enough 235 of high purity with the concentrated source of neutrons, details of which we are not privileged to give.

Then the question became, what about 238? Well, it was found that when element 238 is struck by a neutron, it is converted into another element which is called neptunium, named after the planet Neptune because the planet Neptune was discovered in connection with the planet Uranus. It was found that this element goes to pieces in a few days and forms another element which is called *plutonium.* The element plutonium turns out to be an element which is relatively stable. It goes to pieces in about 30,000 years, about half of it goes to pieces in that time, so for all practical purposes you can consider it stable.

This element plutonium, however, is interesting because it has the same properties as 235; that is, if it is struck by a neutron, it also goes to pieces, losing mass and liberating tremendous quantities of energy.

What became the problem then? *The problem became one of setting up piles of uranium in such a way that neutrons would strike them and build the element plutonium.* Now that turned out to be not as simple as one might think. It turned out that the neutron is going too fast and won't be captured, so you have to slow it down. It was slowed down by graphite and by heavy weights. The other interesting thing that turned up—and this apparently the Germans never knew—is that impureness has a tremendous effect on those neutrons, capturing them and not allowing the uranium to capture them. Boron turns out to be one of the most vicious elements.

It was necessary to prepare graphite—graphite being used to slow down the neutron—that contained less than one part of boron in 500,000 parts of graphite in order to be successful in this project.

I think that all of you can realize that important as the basic work was, carried out at the University of Chicago and other places in the development of this bomb, that no one can give too much credit to industry which solved the gigantic problem of preparing chemicals in a state of purity heretofore known only in the laboratory in very small quantities, and yet industry was asked to deliver this high purity uranium and high purity graphite, not in dram lots, not in pound lots, but in ton lots, and American industry delivered it.

The problem then became one of setting up uranium in graphite sticks, the neutrons wandering around in the graphite sticks until their velocity was slowed to a critical velocity, captured by the uranium 238, converted into the element plutonium, and then the big problem of separating plutonium from the uranium. The amount of plutonium which is formed is practically infinitesimal in any given quantity of it, and yet that material was made—a man-made element—in pound lots. Again it took industry, working on a gigantic scale, to accomplish this result.

You must remember that here we had a race going on. Nobody knew what the Germans were doing. How far along were they? You couldn't leisurely work out in the laboratory a fundamental principle and then say, "Well, there are about four ways we can separate these isotropes. Let's try one, and if that doesn't work, let's try the other." We had to try all four of them at once. You couldn't take a chance on the Germans getting ahead of us. You couldn't wait until you had enough material accumulated so you could carry out a decent pilot plant experiment.

You first worked with infinitesimal quantities of material. You learned the properties of plutonium with quantities of material so small they defy description, and we built a pilot plant out near Stagg Field where this was tried out on a sort of semi-pilot scale. Then it was moved out to the outskirts of Chicago, and here again the Forest Preserve Commissioners made available some thousands acres of land and gave it the protection in order that this pilot plant might be utilized. Here again let me say that it was this team work, it was this cooperation between the citizens, people who made up the Commission of the Forest Preserve, recognizing what was involved here, that made this job possible.

There were tremendous health hazards concerned in this project. Fluorine is one of the most poisonous elements known to man; plutonium is exceedingly poisonous. All of these radio-active substances are highly destructive of living tissue. We went to the Rockefeller Foundation and said, "We have to have a grant for a very secret project which we can't tell you anything about, but we have to have a lot of money in order to organize the health service." Here again this imagination of the American came into play. The Rockefeller Foundation said, "Here is your money. Tell us after a while what you did with it," and a health service was organized, and so efficiently was that carried out that as far as we know, not a single bit of damage has been done to any worker who worked on this project.

IV

Then, of course, finally the great day came. I was down in Santa Fe the day after the bomb was tried out in that vicinity. I never want to play poker with Sam Allison or Enrico Fermi because, believe me, there wasn't a single thing on their faces that betrayed to me that they had the day before witnessed the destruction of matter in an explosion of such gigantic size that it defies description to measure it.

I was down there as a traveling salesman and I was trying to sign these boys up for the Institute of Nuclear Studies, and they are coming to Chicago. It might interest you to know that in the new Institute of Nuclear Studies and related institutes at the University of Chicago, you are going to have, without any question, the greatest concentration of scientific ability that is known any place in the world.

I have talked to the men who witnessed that explosion; you have read about it in papers. It is difficult to imagine. Dr. Allison was six and a half miles away from the bomb. He had something to do with giving the time at which it was to explode. He was in a heavy cement dugout facing away from the bomb at six and a half miles distant. Dr. Allison told me that the light, the reflected light, which came into that cement dugout was the most intense light that he had ever witnessed—six and a half miles away.

The brilliance of this light, in Fermi's own words, was so great that Fermi, who was something like thirteen miles away, doesn't even remember the explosion, which gives you some idea of the intensity of the thing. Of course you have all read about that. The rest of the story we know.

V

Well, what are we going to do about it? It seems to me there are about three attitudes we can take. One is that now that we possess the atomic bomb, we can take over the world. We can say to Russia, "Surrender, or we'll bomb you." We know we are not going to do that.

The second is that we can say, "We have this secret; we shall keep it." But remember, all the fundamental principles of this bomb are well known, and even the most conservative of the scientists who have worked on the project have said that Russia can do this in two to seven years with ease. She doesn't have to work as intensely as we worked. She doesn't have to try out four different things at once. She has the benefit of knowing that the thing will go, which we never had until it was tried.

That results in an armament race. That means that from here on out science devotes itself to greater and greater methods of destruction. Certainly we can't have that. It seems to me there is only one thing left; that is, some sort of international control of this weapon whose secrets must be known to all, and that our safety lies in our pledge to each other that we will learn to live in peace because surely the handwriting is on the wall. Unless we learn to live in peace, we shall surely die.

There is no security in secrecy. You cannot get scientists to work under conditions of secrecy indefinitely. Why? For the simple reason that science does not prosper under those conditions. If you set a group of scientists off by themselves to work and not even allow them to confer very much with one another and let the rest of the world have a free interplay of ideas, the progress made by the rest of the world will be so great, will outstrip the group of isolationists by such distances, that the imagination will never be able to describe it.

You can't have secrecy. It isn't in the very nature of the problem, and then it seems to me there is something else here. Having succeeded in developing this weapon, what can we do with it? What can we do with this energy that we have learned to release in such a short period of time? Well, can it be used for power in general? There is no question about that.

And if any one of you people will give the University of Chicago from $50,000 to $100,000, we will have a place running for you by next April. Will it be economically possible, or will it be an economic adventure to do it? That is something that we cannot at the moment say. I would guess that the probabilities are that it will be, but that is a phase of the work which has yet to be done.

These various substances, elements that have been rendered radio-active, may have great peacetime uses. Perhaps in these radiations we shall have the cure of cancer. Let's look at the cancer problem for just a minute. The cancer problem is an old one. A group of cells in some organism go on a rampage and divide without following any law. What is the cause of it? We know it isn't an organism that is blocked out. The probabilities are that it isn't food.

In 1914 Yamagiwa and Ichikawa, two Japanese workers, showed us that if you paint coal tar on the skins of animals, they would develop tumors, and that gave us the notion that chemicals might be the cause of cancer. Then World War I came along, and all of that work stopped.

Then in about 1925 Kennaway in England took up the problem and began to work on coal tar. He isolated a compound called benzpyrene. When this compound is applied to the tissues of a living animal, it causes cancer. We now know some two hundred different chemical compounds which will produce cancer. We have every reason to believe it is a chemical disease.

Who is working on the problem? Wieland in Germany; Lacassagne in France; Kennaway in England, a number of workers in the United States, and World War II came along—where are these workers? Wieland we don't hear from; Lacassagne we don't hear from; Kennaway in war work; workers in this country in war work. Again the cancer problem is forgotten. Isn't the lesson of this tremendous success that we have had that if we will attack this problem with the same tenacity of purpose as we attacked the atomic bomb that there is no question but what we will be successful?

People have asked, should the atomic bomb have been dropped. Let's remember the atomic bomb did not cause the war. It ended the war. We spent $2,000,000,000 on it, a lot of money; it cost that much money to run the war just nine days. If you shortened the war by just nine days, you are money ahead.

What is the difference whether you have a thousand planes carrying ten-ton bombs with all the personnel necessary to manage a thousand planes dropping destruction on Hiroshima, or whether you risk the lives of one group of young men in one plane? When you are in war, you are in a dirty business. It doesn't make much difference how you do the killing, since victory depends on doing it effectively.

We have arrived at a stage in our discoveries where we have a weapon so terrible now that we cannot think of destruction any more without thinking of destroying ourselves. Let us here highly resolve that we shall learn to live in peace because if we don't make that resolve, and we don't live up to it, the echo will surely be, "Ye shall die."

Somebody who is a wisecracker said the other day, "Perhaps from here on we ought to say, 'I believe in one uranium atom, divisible, with oblivion for all.' "

INDEX